Canadian Issues

A Contemporary Perspective

Daniel Francis
Jennifer Hobson
Gordon Smith
Stan Garrod
Jeff Smith

Oxford University Press

OXFORD
UNIVERSITY PRESS

Oxford University Press Canada
70 Wynford Drive Don Mills Ontario M3C 1J9
http://www.oupcan.com

Oxford New York
Athens Auckland Bangkok Bogotá Buenos Aires Calcutta
Cape Town Chennai Dar es Salaam Delhi Florence Hong Kong
Istanbul Karachi Kuala Lumpur Madrid Melbourne Mexico City
Mumbai Nairobi Paris São Paulo Singapore Taipei Tokyo
Toronto Warsaw

and associated companies in Berlin Ibadan

Oxford is a registered trade mark of Oxford University Press

Canadian Cataloguing in Publication Data

Main entry under title:
Canadian issues: a contemporary perspective

Includes index.
ISBN 0-19-541134-X

1. Canada - History - 20th century.
2. Canada - Civilization - 20th century.
I. Francis, Daniel.

FC600.C3 1998   971.06   C97-932543-9
F1034.2.C3 1998

Design: Brett Miller
Cover illustration: Rocco Baviera
Cover credits:
Front left: North American West Coast Totem Pole (© Weldon Owen
Pty Ltd)
Front upper right: Chinatown, Vancouver (National Archives of Canada)
Front lower right: Aerial of Vancouver (Forst Enterprises Foto Flight)
Back: Selkirk Mountains (Glenbow Library and Archives)

Printed in Canada by Friesens

This book is printed on permanent (acid-free) paper ∞.

5   02 01 00

Acknowledgements

The publisher wishes to thank the following people for
their contribution in reviewing the manuscript.

Bliss Dodd
Wellington Secondary School
Nanaimo, BC

Phil Foster
Amy Woodland School
Cranbrook, BC

David Morden
Holy Cross Regional Secondary School
Surrey, BC

Don Phillips
Magee Secondary School
Vancouver, BC

Ralph Switch
Pittmeadows Secondary School
Pittmeadows, BC

Peter Thrift
Duchess Park Secondary School
Prince George, BC

CONTENTS

Photo Credits

Abbreviations   t = top; b = bottom; c = centre; l = left; r = right

AGO = Art Gallery of Ontario, Toronto; BCA = British Columbia Archives; CTA = City of Toronto Archives; CVA = City of Vancouver Archives; CWM = Canadian War Museum; Glenbow = Glenbow Archive, Calgary, Alberta; NAC = National Archives of Canada; NGC = National Gallery of Canada, Ottawa; VPL = Vancouver Public Library

2: Photographie Musée du Québec/Jean-Guy Kérouac; 4: The Granger Collection, New York; 5: CVA/BU.P.498, N589; 6: Giraudon/Art Resource, New York; 8: (t) Notman Collection No. 8884/Provincial Archives of Nova Scotia/N-4268, (b) CTA/DPW 32-191; 9: (t) Provincial Archives of Manitoba/Thomas Burns Coll. 581, (c) Provincial Archives of New Brunswick/George Taylor Studio, (b) Provincial Archives of Alberta/B5584; 10: (t) Glenbow/NC-43-13, (b) CTA/DPW 11-87; 11: NAC/C15037; 12: General Motors of Canada; 14: BCA/A00375; 15: BCA/F08377; 17: Royal British Columbia Museum/PN10083; 18: NAC/C12272; 22: Wilson Studio Collection; 25: University of British Columbia Special Collections/BCXXXVI-17; 26: (l) National Archives of Quebec at Quebec/J.E. Lawrence, (r) CTA/SC 244-8027; 27: Glenbow/NA-2676-6; 28: NAC/C56164; 29: Courtesy Canada Post Corporation; 30: Courtesy of Betty Anderson/Donated to the Centre for Women's Studies/OISE; 31: Toronto Reference Library; 32: NGC; 34: (l) VPL/5266, (r) VPL/1874; 36: BCA/A04531; 38: CWM/8911; 40: Imperial War Museum/Q211B2; 45: Imperial War Museum/Q13336; 46: NL/1054; 47: NAC/C932; 48: CVA/STR.D.422, N.404; 49: (t) Provincial Archives of Manitoba/Foote Coll./83/N1783, (b) CTA/DPW 32-632; 50: Glenbow/NA-3452.2; 52: Al Harvey; 54: VPL/6228; 56: CTA/James 824; 58: CWM/8058; 60: McCord Museum; 61: CWM/8940; 62: Glenbow/NC-6-3311; 63: NAC; 65: (t) CTA, (b) CTA; 66: NAC/PA2468; 67: Dalhousie Archives; 69: City of Edmonton Archives/EA-10-2016; 74: Provincial Archives of Manitoba//N12296; 76: (l, r) Saskatchewan Archives Board/R-A8223-1 and R-A8223-2; 78: Archive Photo/Popperfoto; 80: NGC; 83: Frank Driggs/Corbis-Bettman; 85: Brian Milne/First Light; 86: Courtesy Canadian National/27557; 87: Topham Picturepoint; 88: Archives of Ontario/F1066-S12842; 89: NGC; 90: (t) NGC, (b) BCA/D-06009; 91: NGC; 92: University of Toronto Archives/B87-0082/943/Album 6, p. 25 (98.08)/With permission of the Master and Fellows of Massey College; 93: NAC/PA127556; 94: (l) NAC/C5799, (r) NAC/C47342; 95: NAC/C39555; 98: NAC/C21247; 100: CTA/James 2530; 102: National Aviation Museum/1219; 103: Glenbow/NA-1258-22; 104: Archives of Ontario/Eaton's Catalogue/F229-1-0-76; 106: Courtesy Canada Post Corporation; 107: NAC/PA138909; 108: NAC/C3187; 110: NAC/PA127295; 112: UPI/Corbis-Bettmann; 113: UPI/Corbis-Bettmann; 114: AGO/Gift of J.S. McLean Fund, 1954; 120: BCA/D-05656; 122: BCA/A-03256; 123: (l) CTA/SC 244-1683, (r) NAC/PA35133; 124: Provincial Archives of Manitoba/Settlement 98/N1087; 125: CNE Archives; 128: NAC/PA39647; 130: NGC; 131: Hart House Permanent Collection; 132: Glenbow/ND-3-6742; 133: NAC/C80134; 134: Trail City Archives/6248A; 136: Canapress; 137: NAC/PA129184; 138: With permission, Anita Chambers, Halifax; 140: NAC/C80917; 141: Imperial Oil Limited/366; 143: UPI/Corbis-Bettmann; 144: NAC/PA116882; 145:NAC/PA114788; 146: NAC/PA119013; 147: NAC/C38723; 148: CWM/14231; 152: *Dieppe Raid* by Charles Comfort/CWM/12276; 157: NAC/PA116510; 158: (t) NAC/PA51512, (b) UPI/Corbis-Bettmann; 161: NAC/PA129126; 162: Japanese Canadian National Museum and Archives Society/Alec Eastwood Coll.; 164: CWM/95-00710; 165: NAC/PA179108; 167: NAC/C20129; 174: Saskatchewan Archive Board/R-A7917-1; 176: Hanson/Canapress; 178: NAC/PA130065; 179: Provincial Archives of Manitoba/Canadian Army Photo Coll./3561/N13202; 181: 20th Century Fox (Courtesy Kobal Collection); 182: Provincial Archives of Manitoba/Canadian Army Photo Coll./151/N12666; 183: Canadian Mortgage and Housing; 184: NGC; 188: NAC/PA128280; 189: NAC/C79009; 192: York University Archives/ASC1123/Toronto Telegram Collection; 193: BCA/I-21886; 194: Saskatchewan Archives Board/R-B4707-4; 195: Courtesy Canadian Wheat Board; 199: Courtesy St. Lawrence Seaway Authority; 200: UPI/Corbis-Bettmann; 201: MGM (Courtesy Kobal Collection); 202: NAC/PA111390; 203: Courtesy Canadian Hockey/Abalene; 206: (l) McCord Museum/M1443, (r) With permission, Adrian Raeside; 207: With permission, Winnipeg Free Press; 208: Canapress; 210: National Aviation Museum/17756; 214: NAC/PA123915; 216: NAC/C94168; 218: AGO/Gift from the McLean Foundation, 1966; 221: Canapress; 222: Canapress; 223: Canapress; 224: Dick Hemingway; 226: J.M. Petit/Publiphoto; 227: La Presse; 232: Ford of Canada Archives; 237: Reprinted with permission — The Toronto Star Syndicate; 238: Canapress; 240: Jim Young/Canapress; 242: Courtesy Shauna Taylor/Statistics Canada; 244: Rothschild/Amalie/Corbis-Bettmann; 245: The Toronto Sun; 246: Courtesy Stephen Peck/Canadian Coast Guard; 247: Reuters/Corbis-Bettmann; 248: Greenpeace/Weyler; 250: NAC/PA113485; 253: NAC/PA129838; 254: The Toronto Sun; 255: The Toronto Sun; 256: Courtesy Masters Gallery and Janet Mitchell; 258: UPI/Corbis-Bettmann; 260: City of Calgary Archives/PID Box 2, File 13; 262: With permission, Adrian Raeside; 264: Al Harvey; 265: (tl) Mug Shots/First Light, (tr) Courtesy British Columbia Building Corporation, (b) Chris Harris/First Light; 267: Glenbow/NA-2864-23502; 268: Canapress/News of the North; 270: Courtesy Dr. Sun Yat Sen Gardens; 274: Winnipeg Free Press; 276: Uniphoto/Canapress; 279: Hamilton Public Library Special Collections/David Groggen Photography; 280: Courtesy Ontario Hydro; 282: Canapress; 283: Canapress; 284: Ball/Canapress; 288: (l, r) Canapress; 290: Reproduced with the permission of the West Baffin Eskimo Co-operative Ltd., Cape Dorset, NWT; 292: Reuters/Corbis-Bettmann; 296: NAC/C104125; 308: (t) NASA/Courtesy Spar Aerospace, (b) NASA/Canadian Astronaut Space Program; 310: Al Harvey; 312: Thornhill/ The Toronto Sun; 314: Hanson/Canapress; 316: Komulainen/Canapress; 318: Courtesy Media Relations/Vancouver Airport; 319: *Summer Camp Scene,* 1969, stonecut/Reproduced with the permission of the West Baffin Eskimo Co-operative Ltd,. Cape Dorset, NWT; 320: Canapress; 322: AGO/Anonymous Gift (acrylic and metallic paint on galvanized steel and gouged plywood, 236.3 x 244.0 cm); 324: © Liba Taylor/Panos Pictures; 325: Reuters/Corbis-Bettmann; 327: Stoody/Canapress; 328: Courtesy Ministry of the Solicitor General and Correctional Services Community Initiatives; 334: CP Railway; 336: Hanson/Canapress; 338: Courtesy Sheridan College; 340: (t) The Toronto Sun, (b) Remiorz/Canapress; 341 (t) Dick Hemingway, (b) Brash/Canapress; 342: (t) Phillips/Canapress, (b) Hanson/Canapress; 343 (t) Dick Hemingway, (c) Phillip/Canapress, (b) Médecins Sans Frontières; 348: Ian Smith/Vancouver Sun; 350: Dick Hemingway; 352: Ron Watts/First Light; 354: Remiorz/Canapress; 356: Vancouver Art Gallery/Trevor Mills; 358: Hanson/Canapress; 363: (t) UPI/Corbis-Bettman; (b) Roger LeMoyne/CIDA; 364: Dick Hemingway; 365: UN/DPI Photo/M. Grant; 373: RADARSAT data © Canadian Space Agency 1996/Received by the Canada Centre for Remote Sensing/Processed and distributed by RADARSAT International; 380: David Nunuk/First Light; 384: M. Tcherevxoff/Image Bank.

Introduction

Issues are ideas, values, events, or problems that give rise to different points of view or interpretation. An issue may be social, cultural, political, legal, economic, or environmental, or it may be a combination of several of these elements. An issue may occur between countries, within a country as a whole, or within a local community. It may affect people around the world, or only those people in one small part of the world.

How we analyse and interpret an issue is shaped by our experiences, values, beliefs, and traditions. Often, deep-rooted emotions can lead to passionately held points of view. The result may be heated debate among those who hold strongly opposed opinions. Those seeking a solution to an issue must search for common ground on which to lay the foundation for compromise.

Even when an issue seems to have been resolved, its effects may last for a long time. Human memory and cultural traditions can serve to keep a past issue alive. In addition, a solution to a current issue may be the basis for other issues in the future. Many of the issues in Canada today, such as Quebec's place in Confederation and the rights of Aboriginal peoples, have their roots in a much earlier era when Canada had yet to become a nation.

Issues, however, do not always create divisions or cause conflicts. An issue can also bring people together, open up the lines of communication, lead to new ideas and institutions, and lay the foundations for change. Without issues, human societies would not evolve. How we resolve differences of opinion on major issues is the key to a nation's stability. Many people believe that the true measure of a nation's progress is the way in which its people deal with the issues that divide them without resorting to intolerance, coercion, or force.

Fast-paced change, growing populations, new means of producing and transporting goods, the rapid communication of ideas across great distances, and terrifying new weapons of mass destruction all helped to shape the twentieth-century world. At the same time, the mass migration of people, changes in the distribution of wealth, the expansion of educational opportunities, the rising importance of science and technology, and the emergence of new political ideas resulted in changes to Canada's social, economic, and political structures. These in turn led to debates, disputes, and conflicts as new ideas clashed with old. Issues also arose as wealth, power, and influence passed from one group to another, or, as frequently happened, failed to change hands at all.

Among the major issues that affected Canadians in the twentieth century were key relationships between:

- Aboriginal peoples and the non-Aboriginal population
- Quebec and the rest of Canada
- Canada and Britain, and
- Canada and the United States.

In addition, there were a variety of social, cultural, political, legal, economic, and environmental issues that challenged and transformed Canadians, including:

- the role and status of women
- immigration
- cultural identity
- recessions, depressions, and inflation
- crime and public safety
- international peace and security
- the Constitution and government
- industrialization, and
- the preservation and conservation of the environment.

Some of these issues have deeply divided Canadians; others have led to co-operation and combined efforts to fight common enemies or deal with common problems. All have played significant roles in shaping Canada's history during the twentieth century.

Canadian Issues: A Contemporary Perspective focusses on the key issues that have affected Canada in the twentieth century. The units examine the social, cultural, political, legal, economic, and environmental issues that shaped each decade. The final unit focusses on Canada's role in the global community and looks towards the century that lies ahead. In studying the key issues that have shaped Canada and Canadians throughout the twentieth century, we can make connections between the past and the present and gain greater insights into the future.

UNIT 1:

Clarence Gagnon, *Brise d'été à Dinard (Summer Breezes at Dinard)* (1907)

Clarence Gagnon (1881-1942) was one of the forerunners of Impressionism. Gagnon's early paintings frequently captured the intense light of midday, with dominant tones of blue. He was closely associated with his colleague J.W. Morrice.

A NEW CENTURY DAWNS

1901-1910

*Skills and Processes

A NEW ERA
The World in 1901

The century that began on New Year's Day, 1901 began a new era. What changes took place in the industrial world that marked the emergence of mass society?

New Year's Day, 1901

In the great cities of the world, New Year's Day, 1901, was greeted with grand celebration. Fireworks displays filled the skies in places like London, New York, and Tokyo. In the streets, revellers made their way past electric streetcars, their paths brightened by electric streetlights. Some drove through the streets in their automobiles. People telephoned their friends to wish them a "Happy New Century." Passengers on the great ocean liners sent telegrams from mid-sea to family around the world.

The death of Queen Victoria in 1901 marked the end of an era.

Yet in the small villages and isolated farming communities where 70 per cent of the world's 1.6 billion people lived, the dawn of a new century passed largely unnoticed. For these people, the twentieth century differed little from the nineteenth century. The pace of life was slow and predictable. Most people lived and died without ever having travelled more than a few kilometres from their homes.

Yet the world was changing rapidly. While these changes were more obvious in the cities than in the countryside, the effects were being felt everywhere. Some of the changes, such as the networks of industrial towns linked together by railway lines crisscrossing Europe, Japan, and eastern North America, were obvious. Other changes, such as improvements in medicine and sanitation, were more subtle, but would have an equally dramatic impact on the quality of life.

Death rates began to fall sharply by 1901, while birth rates remained high. The result was a population explosion that would severely strain the resources of much of Europe and Asia.

Mass Society

One of the most striking characteristics of industrialization was the city. Increasingly, people were drawn to the urban centres from rural areas. There they found them-selves living in a crowded and complex environment. Most aspects of their lives were regimented, much like the factories in which they worked. In the industrial cities of Europe, North America, and Japan, a new society was being created—**mass society**.

Industrial development and technological change had resulted in the **mass production** of goods. The factory system, the assembly line, a skilled labour force, and specialized machinery meant that large quantities of goods could be produced quickly at low unit cost. This created economic benefits for both producers and consumers. Producers were able to increase profits, while consumers were able to buy goods at lower prices. In some cases, the economic benefits were passed on to workers in the form of higher wages and other benefits.

The large-scale mechanization of the printing industry created the beginnings of **mass media**. Newspapers, magazines, and books were published in large numbers to inform, educate, entertain, or influence their readers. But mass media were not confined to the printed word. Industrial technology had created a new medium, the motion picture. Movies were mass produced and widely distributed as both entertainment and political **propaganda**.

A New Industrial Order

The new mass society was evident in both the factories and the cities. Factories often employed thousands of workers. New categories of employment emerged, ones which distinguished between those workers who ran the machines and loaded the trains and those who kept the accounts and managed the business.

In the new industrial order, many factory workers felt they had little control over their working conditions and wages. To protect their interests, workers began to organize into unions. Their employers often responded by firing union activists. Consequently, workers staged demonstrations or went on strike. Police were frequently summoned to force an end to the labour unrest. In industrialized countries, the labour movement gave rise to its own political parties.

CASE STUDY

THE BELL TELEPHONE OPERATORS' STRIKE OF 1907

In February 1907, 400 female operators in Toronto walked off their jobs as Bell's "hello girls." The company was demanding that operators increase their work day from five to eight hours, without offering any pay raise.

"Operating" was a totally female occupation. Each operator looked after 80 to 100 switchboard lines with more than 6000 possible connections. They placed an average of 300 calls per hour, switching lines while seated on backless stools. Supervisors were encouraged to "nag and hurry the girls" to increase their productivity. Long distance operators reported receiving severe electrical shocks.

Bell switchboard operators in Vancouver, 1907

As the strike continued, Bell brought in strike-breakers, but public sympathy was with the operators. The dispute finally ended when the minister of labour, Mackenzie King, investigated the workers' complaints. The exchange manager claimed that the women were happy to work for "pin money." "They come to us to earn a fur coat or something like that and leave to get married after two or three years." Actually, nearly 40 per cent of the women were self-supporting. Physicians testified that the work resulted in exhaustion "more mental and nervous than physical."

A compromise was reached: seven hours work spread over a nine-hour day, with wages equivalent to eight hours of work per day. The operators had made minor gains, but without union protection, they could not fight the telephone giant effectively.

Jan Coomber and Rosemary Evans, Women Changing Canada. Copyright © Oxford University Press Canada 1997. p.12. Reprinted by permission.

MAKING CONNECTIONS

1. At the turn of the century, newspapers were often associated with political parties. How might the fact that newspapers reflected the views of political parties affect their use as **primary sources**?

2. The role of women began to change at the beginning of the twentieth century. Find out more about the "new woman" of the early 1900s and outline how women's roles had been changing since the **Victorian era.**

KEYWORDS

mass society

mass production

mass media

propaganda

primary sources

Victorian era

THE MODERN WORLD
Cultural and Political Change

As the new century began, significant changes in culture and politics were taking place. What were these changes, and what impact did they have on the world?

A Cultural Revolution

If you visited one of the bars or cafés where artists gathered in Paris in 1901, you might have encountered a young Spanish painter named Pablo Ruiz. Ruiz would soon change his name to Picasso, and his work would soon change the visual arts forever. Yet Picasso was only one of hundreds of young artists who were drawn to Paris, the centre of European culture. At the start of the century, the French capital was vibrant with new ideas about art and its place in a changing world. Picasso and colleagues like Henri Matisse and Georges Braque mingled with poets, playwrights, and composers. Many of the poets had been influenced by nineteenth-century symbolist writers like Charles Baudelaire, Paul Verlaine, and Stéphane Mallarmé, who sought to create evocative impressions through their poetry. Claude Debussy, Maurice Ravel, and Erik Satie were but a few of the composers whose radical new approaches to sound and musical

Georges Braque, Musical Instruments, *1908. Together with Picasso, Braque (1882-1963) is considered the creator of Cubism.*

structure shocked a public used to the symphonic melodies of Beethoven, Brahms, and Schubert.

The music, poetry, dance, and paintings of this period were filled with energy and feeling. The ideas of these artists shattered all traditional concepts of "respectable" art. Instead, these innovators created strange new shapes, sounds, and movements. Their inspirations came from many sources: Greek mythology, Japanese woodblock prints, Afro-American jazz, and Aboriginal art from Africa, the South Pacific, and the Americas. Artists and writers from around the world came to Paris to take part in this cultural revolution. In so doing, they internationalized it.

Not everyone approved of these revolutionary changes in artistic expression, however. Critics considered much of this work to be childish and primitive. Braque, Matisse, and their contemporaries were labelled *les fauves*—"the savages." Church leaders condemned the new art as immoral. Audiences jeered in protest when they heard the unfamiliar sounds of the new music performed. Yet the new technologies, such as the camera and the wax recorder, made realistic representation of images and sounds redundant for creative individuals. As a result, artists continued to experiment with new and unique forms. They ignited a debate over modern art that would last throughout the century.

Universal Suffrage

Change was also at the heart of the most hotly debated political issue at the turn of the century—power. By 1901, **universal male suffrage** had been achieved in almost all of the industrial countries of Western Europe and in Canada, the United States, Australia, and New Zealand. In these countries, all males over the age of majority (usually 21) could vote. Women, however, regardless of their education or social status, had the right to vote only in New Zealand (1893) and Australia (1902).

Elsewhere, women in Europe, the United States, Canada, and Britain organized movements demanding the right to vote. These advocates of women's suffrage were known as **suffragettes**. In 1903 in Britain, Emmeline Pankhurst established the Women's Social and Political Union. Pankhurst and her followers earned a reputation for boldness and militant action in their fight for political rights. They used every means possible, including boycotts, bombings, pickets, and the harassment of politicians, to get their message across. They held public rallies, scuffled with police, and chained themselves to fences in order to draw attention to the exclusion of women from the political process. Many of the suffragettes were arrested and jailed. Behind bars, they resorted to hunger strikes as a means of protest. Yet it would be nearly two decades before women in Canada, Britain, and the United States would gain the right to vote.

Anarchism and Socialism

In **autocratic** countries like tsarist Russia, there was no democracy. No one had the right to vote. At the turn of the century, however, intellectuals as well as some nobles began to demand democratic reforms. Their calls went unheeded, forcing even moderate advocates of democracy to join secret political societies. Authoritarian regimes in Russia and other parts of Europe became targets for **anarchist** and **socialist** revolutionaries who were influenced by the ideas of anarchist Mikhail Bakunin and revolutionary theorist Karl Marx. They called for the destruction of the autocratic state and the transfer of political power to workers. In 1905, after Russia's defeat by Japan in the Russo-Japanese War, revolutionaries attempted to overthrow the tsarist government. The uprising was suppressed when demonstrators were fired upon. Tsar Nicholas II responded by introducing political reforms but opposition continued. In time, the revolutionary forces would prevail.

◄█— MAKING CONNECTIONS —█►

1. In what ways did the cultural revolution and the suffrage movement reflect the development of mass society?

2. Select one prominent artist from the first decade of the twentieth century and write a one-page essay describing how this person influenced and contributed to the cultural revolution.

KEYWORDS

universal male suffrage

suffragette

autocratic

anarchist

socialist

PICTURE GALLERY

Life at the Turn of the Century

FOCUSSING ON THE ISSUE

They say that "a picture is worth a thousand words." What do these photographs reveal about Canada at the beginning of the twentieth century? What don't they tell you?

The guests at this Halifax garden party represent the "refined" culture that existed in Canada at the turn of the century. Judging from this photograph, who were the members of this culture?

What are the conditions exhibited in this Toronto yard around 1910? In what part of town do you think this building might be located? Why?

What "modern" consumer symbol is evident in this photograph taken in Winnipeg?

This photograph shows child labourers at a cotton mill in Marysville, NB. The photo was commissioned by the owner of the cotton mill. Do you think this makes a difference to what you see in the photo? Explain.

Do you think these immigrants, shown at a **Galician haymarket** in Edmonton in 1903, have been in Canada long? How might you tell? Why are there no women in the picture?

This immigrant woman is mowing oats in Benyon, Alberta, in 1909. What was the role of women in the early 1900s in Canada? In what ways might the lives of immigrant women have differed from those of English- or French-Canadian women? In what ways might their lives have been similar?

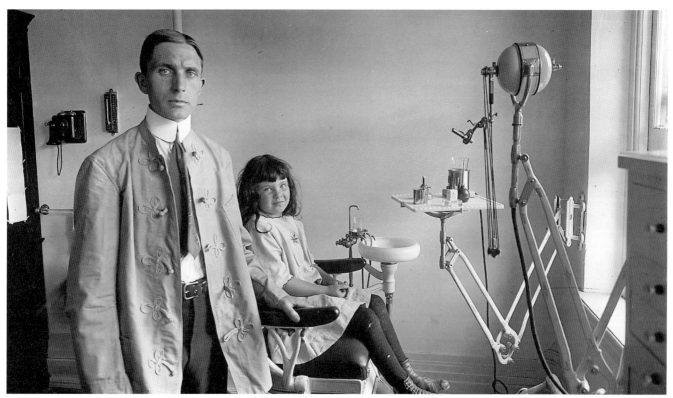

What evidence is there of improved living standards for Canadians at the turn of the century? Do you think education and health care were available to all Canadians? Why or why not?

These Aboriginal youth attended a residential school in Methakahtla, BC. The schools were funded by the federal government and operated by missionaries. What do you notice about the boys in this photograph? What does this suggest to you?

◄▢▬ MAKING CONNECTIONS ▬▢►

1. a) What are the social, political, cultural, and economic values that you perceive in this photo gallery?
    b) From the photographs, find examples of the following contrasts. Use one sentence to summarize each:
    i) rural/urban; ii) child/adult; iii) rich/poor; iv) male/female; v) agricultural/industrial; vi) Aboriginal/non-Aboriginal.

2. a) As you work through this book, create a photo gallery of your own. Start your collection now by looking through other resources for pictures that illustrate life in Canada at the turn of the century.
    b) When you have completed the course, prepare a photo display in your classroom to illustrate how life in Canada has evolved in the twentieth century.

KEYWORDS

Galician

haymarket

THE GLOBAL ECONOMY
An Interconnected World
FOCUSSING ON THE ISSUE

The world economy was increasingly interconnected by 1901, and Canada's economy was expanding rapidly. What factors led to a global economy? How did Canada's economy develop during this time?

Interdependence

As the twentieth century began, the world was becoming increasingly interconnected and interdependent. New industrial technologies required raw materials from every continent. No invention better illustrated this new economic interdependence than the automobile. Mines in Canada and the United States provided the iron ore needed to manufacture steel. Plantations in Malaysia and Brazil provided the rubber for tires. Ranches in Australia and Argentina supplied the leather for upholstery. These and other resources crisscrossed the globe en route to the automobile manufacturing plants of the industrial world. The automobile, which would eventually come to symbolize the twentieth century, demonstrated the links in the new **global economy**.

Three forces, closely connected and made possible by new industrial technologies, helped create the global economy. The first was the fast-growing urban populations of the industrialized countries, which required trade to provide them with raw materials for production, construction, and food. The second factor was increased trade between nations, made possible by larger and faster steamships that cut shipping costs and travel times. By 1901, producers and consumers in Europe and North America could shop the world to get the best prices for grain, meat, textiles, and other products. The third factor was **economic imperialism**—the quest by European, American, and Japanese industries to find cheap sources of raw materials using low-cost labour.

Canada's Economy

In 1901, Canada was a land of great opportunity. Immigrants were being drawn to the West in record numbers, lured by the promise of free land and the abundance of natural resources. Canada's population grew from 5.4 million people in 1901 to 7.2 million people in 1911—a growth rate of 34 per cent. This growth provided a source of labour as well as a ready market for the products of Canadian mills, farms, and factories. Thus rapid economic growth paralleled the growth in population.

Canada was one of the first non-European countries to benefit from the trend towards a global economy. Industrialization in

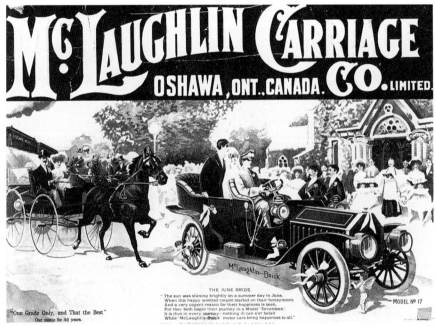

The automobile industry began in Canada in the early 1900s. Carriage makers, such as the McLaughlin Company, now began to produce automobiles. In 1904, Henry Ford set up his first Canadian car plant in Ontario.

WHEN WHEAT WAS KING

The growing population of Europe provided a hungry market for Canadian wheat. During the first decade of the century, Canada's main source of export revenue shifted from forestry to agriculture. Prairie cities such as Winnipeg, Edmonton, and Regina became important regional centres for grain exports. The value of wheat and flour exports increased from $14 million in 1900 to $279 million in 1920.

Wheat production in most of the prairies was a risky business. Variations in rainfall patterns created inconsistent annual yields. Early frosts were a constant threat to harvests, while diseases and grasshopper infestations added to the risks. As a result of such unpredictable conditions, farmers could experience a bumper crop one year, followed by disaster the next.

In addition to unpredictable yields, farmers faced price fluctuations on world grain markets, high transportation costs, and protective **tariffs** imposed by some countries. All these factors caused farmers' costs to increase and raised prices for consumers. In order to expand the wheat-growing area, scientists set out to create new varieties of wheat that would reach maturity during the short growing season of the Canadian Northwest. Red Fife, a variety of wheat that originated in eastern Poland and Ukraine, proved to be hardy enough for most prairie conditions except for the early frosts. Scientists William Saunders and his sons, Charles and Percy, worked at the Department of Agriculture's Central Experimental Farm in Ottawa to invent a frost-resistant wheat. Crossing Red Fife wheat with Red Calcutta, they created the world-famous Marquis wheat. First introduced to prairie farms around 1907, by the 1920s Marquis wheat greatly expanded the wheat-producing region of the Prairies and accounted for 90 per cent of all spring wheat in Canada.

Canada was largely funded by British, American, and other foreign investors looking for promising opportunities. This investment increased from about $1 billion in 1901 to nearly $3 billion by the decade's end. Almost 80 per cent of foreign investment in manufacturing and hydroelectric power production prior to the First World War was concentrated in Ontario and Quebec where large populations provided a ready market for the new industrial economy. Railway construction further stimulated the growth of manufacturing. Railway lines across Canada increased from a total of 29 000 km in 1900 to more than 63 000 km in 1920. This resulted in a sharp increase in the demand for iron and steel products. Railway yards and shops in Calgary, Winnipeg, Toronto, and Montreal turned out hundreds of locomotives and thousands of railway cars. This, in turn, stimulated the mining industry as more and more coal and iron ore were needed to feed the steel mills of Canada's **industrial heartland**.

MAKING CONNECTIONS

1. The boom in Canada's economy coincided with technological advancements and declining ocean freight rates. Explain how each of these factors contributed to Canada's economic growth.

2. Draw a **web diagram** with a railway train in the centre. Illustrate how this economic activity was connected to a wide range of other economic activities. Be sure to include the people who work for the railway and the part they play in the economy as both producers and consumers.

KEYWORDS

global economy

economic imperialism

tariffs

industrial heartland

web diagram

"SPANS THE WORLD"
The Canadian Pacific Railway

The Canadian Pacific Railway came to symbolize Canada's participation in the global economy in the early 1900s. In what way did the CPR contribute to the Canadian identity?

A Canadian Symbol

"Spans the World"—that was the motto of the Canadian Pacific Railway at the start of the twentieth century. The logo was seen across the country as it flashed by on box cars from Halifax to Vancouver. In the early 1900s, the CPR transported thousands of passengers to destinations across the country each day. Regions that only a few decades earlier had been remote and almost inaccessible were now within reach as a result of the CPR. The web of CPR tracks spanned east and west from Canada's **industrial heartland**, then south to the US. By 1910, manufactured goods, including farm machinery and automobile parts, were being shipped to the US via the CPR and its American branch lines, along with the more traditional exports of raw materials.

Nothing symbolized Canada's place in the new industrialized world better than the CPR. With the introduction of the company's famed *Empress* ocean liner service across the Pacific from Vancouver in 1891, the CPR truly spanned the world. The products of Canada's farms, forests, fisheries, and mines travelled by CPR's railcars to the country's seaports. From there, they were shipped to markets in Europe and Asia. In return, silk, tea, rubber, and other products from Asia and the Pacific region were carried in Canadian Pacific steamship vessels to Vancouver, then shipped by rail to markets across Canada and the United States.

The CPR was also part of the communications revolution that was sweeping the world. Its telegraph service, introduced in 1887, linked Canada from the Atlantic to the Pacific. On the east coast, the CPR's telegraph lines were linked by trans-Atlantic cable to Britain and Europe. In 1902, the completion of a trans-Pacific ocean cable to Australia and New Zealand from Vancouver Island linked the CPR's telegraph lines to most of the world. In fact, it was now possible to send a message around the world in just 15 minutes!

Though prominent in the country's seaports and on its railways, the Canadian Pacific Railway was not Canadian-owned. Like many other "Canadian" businesses, the majority of its shares were held by foreign, mainly British, investors. Not until the early 1970s were a majority of CPR shares held by Canadian investors.

Who Should Operate the Railways?

In the early 1900s, there was a heated debate over who should own and operate railway lines in Canada. When the railway had been completed in 1885, the CPR had been granted a **monopoly** over rail lines in western Canada for 25 years. Now many prairie farmers and business people called for new lines and competition to reduce the costs of shipping grain and freight to and from western Canada. Prime Minister Wilfrid Laurier and the Liberals supported the idea of competition. In 1903, they introduced a new policy offering government support to companies building new lines into the west. Two companies, the Grand Trunk Pacific and the Canadian Northern, received funding to build their own transcontinental lines. But three railways proved to be too many for the population of the country. It soon became evident that the government would have to continue its sponsorship if the railways were to keep running. The Opposition Conservative party, led

The Canadian Pacific played a big part in opening up Canada to tourism. Along its tracks through the Rocky Mountains, the company built grand hotels and lodges. The most famous was the Banff Springs Hotel in Canada's first national park, the Rocky Mountain Parks Reserve (now Banff National Park). Wealthy visitors from Europe, Asia, the United States, and eastern Canada came to marvel at the spectacular scenery, hike the mountain trails, and bathe in the hot springs. How might such visits contribute to Canada's image abroad?

by Robert Borden, proposed that the government buy the part of the CPR running through the Canadian Shield from Winnipeg to Georgian Bay. They wanted the government to double track the line and operate it for the benefit of all three railways. They believed the plan would benefit producers, consumers, and the railways. But Laurier insisted that there would be no government ownership of the railways. As a result, Canada ended up with three

transcontinental rail lines, two of which quickly sank into a sea of red ink. By 1917, the Canadian Northern and the Grand Trunk Pacific lines were on the verge of **bankruptcy**. In 1918, a new Conservative government in Ottawa passed legislation enabling the government to nationalize the bankrupt lines. In 1923, they were reorganized into the Canadian National Railways, a federally owned **Crown corporation**.

MAKING CONNECTIONS

1. What impact might the globalization of the CPR's transportation system have had on Canada's identity as a nation? On its image abroad?

2. Discuss how the speed of communications at the beginning of the twentieth century would have affected business, politics, and the spread of ideas.

KEYWORDS

industrial heartland

monopoly

bankruptcy

Crown corporation

BECOMING A MINORITY
Aboriginal Peoples in Canada
FOCUSSING ON THE ISSUE

After European contact, Aboriginal peoples found themselves in the minority in the land they had inhabited for thousands of years. How did the pressures created by European settlement threaten the survival of Aboriginal culture?

European Settlement

The first permanent inhabitants of North America were Aboriginal peoples. They had occupied the continent for over 10 000 years prior to the arrival of Europeans in the sixteenth century. Aboriginal peoples had developed their own distinct cultures. They had adapted to their environment and provided for their own needs. They had their own governments and their own social structures. They educated their children and observed their own spiritual practices and traditions. The arrival of Europeans, however, imposed values and a way of life that were foreign to Aboriginal peoples. Disease, land encroachment, and **assimilation** policies changed Aboriginal culture forever.

Disease

Diseases such as smallpox, diphtheria, and tuberculosis were common in Europe, but they did not exist in North America prior to European settlement. Because Aboriginal peoples had no immunity, they were particularly susceptible to these illnesses. As a result, by the beginning of the twentieth century as much as 60 to 70 per cent of the populations of many Aboriginal communities had fallen victim to these diseases. This unprecedented loss of life had a devastating effect on Aboriginal society, and especially on Aboriginal leadership. Communities were left vulnerable to pressures from government and missionaries to assimilate into English-Canadian society.

Loss of Land

While disease took its toll on the population, European settlement destroyed traditional Aboriginal lifestyles. Under the Dominion Lands Act of 1872, European settlers could claim legal title to a plot of land in the West simply by living on it. This system of land encroachment displaced Aboriginal peoples and dealt a critical blow to their **subsistence economy**. Aboriginal peoples were no longer free to follow a traditional **nomadic** lifestyle in which they provided for their own needs by hunting, gathering, trapping, and fishing. Instead, they were forced to settle on **reserves**, where they were encouraged to become farmers. Yet the government offered little practical assistance in shifting from a nomadic lifestyle to a settled agricultural one. Financial **subsidies** were usually short-lived; in many cases, they were replaced with coercive tactics. Not surprisingly, the government failed in its attempt to impose agriculture on Aboriginal peoples on reserves.

Assimilation

The government set out to regulate Aboriginal peoples' lives in unprecedented ways. The Indian Act of 1876 was designed to eliminate Aboriginal culture and assimilate the people into English-Canadian society. The act defined who was an Indian and regulated legal Indian status. An Indian woman who married a white man, for example, lost her Indian status. The act also ruled that an Indian could not be a lawyer, doctor, or minister, or even earn a university degree, and still remain an Indian. The hope was that Aboriginal peoples would choose education over their own culture and identity, thereby accelerating the process of assimilation. As Duncan Campbell Scott, deputy superintendent of the Department of Indian Affairs, stated: *The happiest future for the Indian race is absorption into the general population, and this is the object of the policy of our government. The great forces of intermarriage and education will finally overcome the lingering traces of native custom and tradition.*

The Indian Act also banned the **potlatch** and other ceremonial and spiritual practices that government authorities considered "backward." They saw these traditions as barriers that prevented Aboriginal peoples from "progressing" and becoming "civilized." In 1895, the act was revised to prohibit even more ceremonies. This forced Aboriginal spiritual practices to move "underground," creating the misconception that the ceremonies were **pagan** or primitive. Those who practised their sacred traditions were denounced by authorities. This facilitated the efforts of the missionaries trying to convert Aboriginal peoples to Christianity.

In response to these pressures, Aboriginal peoples began to lose their sense of identity. Alcoholism and other social problems became more prevalent. Ultimately, the laws created barriers between individuals and their families, between families and other families, and between Aboriginal leadership and the people as a whole.

CASE STUDY

THE POTLATCH

The potlatch is a traditional ceremony practised by many Aboriginal peoples of the Pacific Northwest Coast. *Potlatch* is a Chinook term meaning "give." The gifts of the potlatch are payments to those who witness a family ceremony, such as a marriage. The ceremony legitimizes social rankings in a community, particularly the political ranks of chiefs and the prestige that is associated with them. In the ceremony, much of a chief's property is given away. This serves to redistribute wealth. One cannot become a chief without observing this important ceremony.

The potlatch also plays a critical role in retaining and developing Aboriginal culture. It teaches young people about spiritual values and personal growth. Children discover their own identity and learn who they are as individuals and as members of a family, clan, or house (one's family lineage).

The ban against the potlatch was revoked in 1951. Since then, Aboriginal peoples have returned to celebrating the potlatch in large numbers.

When the potlatch was banned, many Aboriginal cultural articles, such as masks, rattles, and baskets, were seized and sold to museums around the world. Since the rebirth of Aboriginal cultural practices, many of these items have been returned to Aboriginal communities.

MAKING CONNECTIONS

1. How would you react if you were forbidden to speak your language and practise your cultural traditions?

2. Policymakers at the turn of the century debated the question of assimilation of Aboriginal peoples. Why might some people have favoured assimilation? Why might others have opposed it?

KEYWORDS

assimilation

subsistence economy

nomadic

reserves

subsidy

potlatch

pagan

COLONIAL TIES
Canada and Britain
FOCUSSING ON THE ISSUE

*In 1901, Canada was still a colony, a member of the British Empire.
Why was this a source of political tension within Canada?*

British Colonialism

The British Empire was an association of dependent colonies that spanned the world and were controlled by Great Britain. Some of the colonies were governed directly by the British. Others—Canada, for example—were self-governing dominions, running their own domestic affairs with little outside interference. Even Canada, however, lacked true independence when it came to its relations with other countries. Britain still negotiated treaties on Canada's behalf and controlled its foreign policy.

The majority of Canadians did not object to this situation. On the contrary, most were happy to be part of the British Empire. They believed that membership in the Empire brought great economic benefits to Canada. They took pride in the fact that Canada was part of the movement to spread British justice and democracy around the world.

Not all Canadians were **imperialists**. French-speaking Canadians did not feel the same sympathy for the Empire. They thought it was an excuse to entangle Canadians in foreign disputes that had nothing to do with Canada's interests.

These differences came to the surface in 1899 when Britain went to war against the Boers in South Africa. The war unleashed an outpouring of enthusiasm in English Canada for the British cause, and a demand that Canadian troops go immediately to fight alongside the British. Not so fast, said Henri Bourassa, a leading Quebec politician. Canadians have no quarrel with the Boers, Bourassa argued, let the British fight their own wars.

Prime Minister Wilfrid Laurier was caught in the middle. On the one hand, his government depended for its survival on support from Quebec. On the other hand, English Canada cried out for troops to be sent. Seeking a compromise, Laurier arranged to send a force of Canadian volunteers who would become the responsibility of the British when they arrived in South Africa. The compromise satisfied neither side. It only served to show how the issue of Empire divided Canadians.

More Independence

Even though support for the Empire remained strong, Canada asked for, and received, a more independent role in the conduct of its relations with other countries. This was partly a result of the Alaska Boundary Dispute. For many years the border between Alaska and British Columbia was in dispute. Finally, in 1903, an international **tribunal** ruled that the border would be drawn to give the United States, which owned Alaska, control of territory Canada had claimed. The British judge on the six-person tribunal voted with the three Americans against the two Canadians. The decision infuriated many Canadians, who concluded that Canada needed more control over its own relations with other countries. Thereafter, Canada began negotiating its own treaties. In 1909, the government created a department of external affairs, and

Canadian soldiers prepare to leave Manitoba for South Africa to fight in the Boer War.

in 1910, Canada established its own navy. All these were steps to full independence.

Once again, this trend was not to everyone's liking. The naval issue in particular sparked a loud debate. The British, engaged in a struggle with Germany for supremacy on the world's oceans, wanted Canada to contribute money to buy imperial warships. Bourassa, speaking again for many anti-imperialists, denounced the idea. He founded a daily newspaper, *Le Devoir*, to battle against the imperialist view.

In the end, Laurier's government decided to create a Canadian navy, but one that could be handed over to the British in times of war. Once again, the solution pleased few people. Imperialists dismissed the so-called Tin-Pot Navy as an embarrassment, while Bourassa argued that it could be used to fight in far-off wars that were of no significance to Canadians.

The issue of Canada's role in the British Empire continued to bedevil Canadian politics and relations between French and English Canadians. It also divided those who believed that Canada should maintain strong ties with Britain and those who believed that Canada should become an independent nation. This was called the "Canadian Question," and it continued to stimulate debate for many years.

VIEWPOINTS

THE IMPERIAL TIE

Ontario premier George Ross gave a speech in 1900 that summed up the view that the future of the Empire and the future of Canada were identical.

There is no antagonism in my opinion between Canadianism and imperialism. The one is but the expansion of the other. To be a true Canadian...is to place yourself in harmony with the spirit of the empire, with its love of liberty, with its resolute defence of its rights, with its enterprise, with its disposition to deal even-handed justice to its subjects, irrespective of race and creed, with its interest in all that refines and ennobles the human race and with its unfailing trust in the principles of our common Christianity. That is imperialism as I understand it. That is Canadianism as I would like it to be....
London Advertiser, *28 September 1900*

Henri Bourassa was a Quebec politician and journalist. He was a member of the Liberal party until he broke with Laurier over the decision to send Canadian troops to fight in the Boer War. He became an outspoken opponent of Canada's involvement in the Empire.

I say to sincere Imperialists: 'Come back to earth, see men as they are, you cannot make an Englishman out of a Canadian...' Gentlemen, I respect and I honour the sincere Imperialists; but neither they nor I nor Mr. Laurier nor Mr. Borden nor any government nor any party can change the course of history and prevent the gap between two peoples separated by an ocean, from always widening, and each of these people from going along the road along which Providence and the development of new instincts lead them.

1. a) Describe the difference in opinion between Ross and Bourassa.
   b) What were Bourassa's objections to imperialism?

MAKING CONNECTIONS

1. "You cannot make an Englishman out of a Canadian," Bourassa argued. With reference to Ross's remarks, explain if you think that this is what imperialists wanted to do.

KEYWORDS

imperialist

tribunal

TWO NEW PROVINCES
Alberta and Saskatchewan
FOCUSSING ON THE ISSUE

In 1905, two new provinces—Alberta and Saskatchewan—joined Confederation.
What were the issues surrounding the creation of the new provinces?

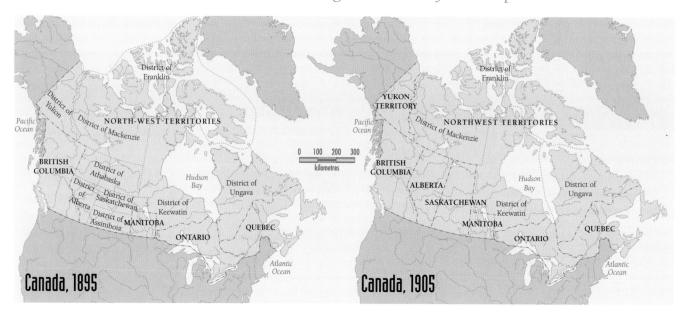

Canada, 1895

Canada, 1905

Western Expansion

As the twentieth century began, the territory between Manitoba and British Columbia was still not organized as a province. It was called the North-West Territories, and while it had a government of its own, it did not have the same powers as the other provinces.

With the arrival in the West of so many immigrants, and the success of the grain-growing economy, people in the North-West Territories felt they were ready to join Confederation as a province, or as provinces. The rapid expansion of the population was creating a need for new schools and other government services, but the Territories did not have the money

to pay for them. Western leaders wanted to become a province so they would qualify for the same grants the federal government gave to the other provinces.

At first, Prime Minister Wilfrid Laurier refused to act. He preferred that the federal government maintain control of developments in the West and not have to share power with any new province. Pressure from the West forced him to change his mind, however. In 1904, he promised that if his government was re-elected in that year's election, he would settle the issue of provincehood. Laurier and the Liberal party were re-elected, and in 1905 the House of Commons prepared to deal with the matter.

The Issues

The reorganization of government in the North-West Territories raised three difficult questions.

1. *How many provinces should be created?* Most westerners, led by the premier of the Territories, Frederick Haultain, wanted one large province stretching from the Rocky Mountains east to Manitoba, and from the US border north to the 60th parallel of latitude. On the other hand, Laurier and his government worried that a single province would be too large to administer and too powerful politically.
2. *Who should control public lands in the West and the resources they*

contained? The original provinces in Confederation controlled their own resources and the money these created, but in the West the federal government wanted to keep control. It argued that settlement was not complete and that responsibility for development could not be handed over to the provinces.

3. *Would there be French-language and Catholic schools in the new provinces?* This was the thorniest question. As English-speaking settlers flooded into the West, they far outnumbered French speakers and began to lobby for a single-language school system. They wanted the schools to be a vehicle for "Canadianizing" new immigrants who arrived speaking a variety of languages. Westerners thought that it was essential to national unity that newcomers be encouraged to join the English-speaking, Protestant mainstream. On the other hand, French and Catholic settlers fought to retain the rights promised them by the federal government.

Provincial Status

In 1905, Laurier introduced his Autonomy Bills in the House of Commons. The bills created two new provinces—Alberta and Saskatchewan. The boundary line between them was the 110th meridian of longitude, chosen because it divided the area roughly in half. The new provinces did not gain control of their own resources, but they did receive an annual cash payment from Ottawa instead. The size of this payment was a constant source of tension between the two provinces and Ottawa.

On the issue of schools, the Autonomy Bills guaranteed a place for Catholic schools and for French-language teaching in the new provinces. Laurier was committed to a **bicultural** Canada in which the rights of the minority (in this case, the French in the West) were preserved. However, this went against the wishes of the English-speaking majority in the West, and against the wishes of powerful cabinet minister Clifford Sifton. The parts of the bills dealing with education had been slipped in while Sifton was out of town. When he returned and found out what his government had done, he was so furious that he resigned from the Cabinet. Sifton believed in single-language schools. He also believed the wishes of the majority in the West had to be honoured.

In response to the controversy, Laurier asked Sifton to rewrite the parts of the Autonomy Bills dealing with education. A compromise was reached. The new law stated that there had to be an English-language public school in every school district in the new provinces. Beyond that, minorities were free to establish a separate school if they wished. Sifton was not asked back into the Cabinet, however, and he later broke with the Liberal party completely.

On 1 September 1905, Alberta and Saskatchewan became provinces of Canada.

◄━◘═ MAKING CONNECTIONS ═◘━►

1. a) What were the advantages of becoming a province?
   b) Why did the federal government prefer the **status quo**?
   c) On the main issues dividing the Territories and the federal government, which side was most successful in getting its way?

2. Write a newspaper editorial defending Clifford Sifton's position in the schools controversy. Alternatively, write an editorial defending the position of the federal government.

KEYWORDS

bicultural

status quo

IMMIGRATION
Melting Pot or Mosaic?

*Thousands of immigrants arrived in Canada in the early 1900s.
Was Canada destined to become a melting pot or a cultural mosaic?*

The Growth of Immigration

Following Confederation, the number of immigrants to Canada was relatively low. By the 1890s, however, the rate of immigration began to increase. The Canadian Pacific Railway had been completed. World wheat prices were high, holding the promise of profitable grain farming on the prairies. Now all the government needed were settlers to farm the rich prairie soil.

Beginning in 1896, Clifford Sifton, minister of the interior in Laurier's government, launched an aggressive campaign to attract immigrant farmers to the West. Each family was offered 160 acres (400 ha) of free land, with the opportunity to buy more land along railway lines at low prices. The introduction of modern farm machinery made the prospect of farming more efficient and therefore more appealing to immigrants.

Using elaborate advertising campaigns and recruitment networks, Sifton sought immigrants from across the United States, Britain, and Europe. Sifton liked American immigrants because they were accustomed to the demands of prairie farming. He promoted emigration from Britain in order to retain Canada's British character. Sifton's greatest challenge, however, was promoting the Canadian West in Europe. Most European governments either resisted or prohibited emigration; in countries where direct soliciting of potential immigrants was forbidden, Sifton's approach was in the form of secret agreements with shipping agents under the guise of the North Atlantic Trading Company. His efforts attracted large numbers of European farmers, among them Ukrainians, Scandinavians, Poles, Germans, and Dutch. But Sifton's immigration policy was selective; it excluded Africans, Jews, Asians, East Indians, and southern Europeans because these groups were considered to be neither good farmers nor able to **assimilate**.

During his years as minister of the interior, Sifton succeeded in attracting thousands of immigrants to the Canadian West. Between 1891 and 1911, more than 2 million immigrants came to Canada. Almost half of these were of non-British origin. The growing populations in Manitoba and the North-West Territories had led to the creation of two new provinces, Saskatchewan and Alberta, in 1905. (See page 20.) By 1911, over 80 per cent of the people in the western provinces had been born outside Canada.

Eastern European immigrants arrive in Saint John, NB, 1909. They are being greeted by a man from the Canadian Bible Society, who is handing out inspirational pamphlets. As an immigrant, how do you think you would react to such an experience?

The question of immigration and how immigrants should adapt to their new country was a topic of debate in early twentieth-century Canada. Many people of British heritage supported the concept of *Anglo-conformity* in which immigrants abandoned their cultural traditions for the behaviour and values of English-Canadian society. Others saw Canada as a *melting pot* in which cultural ties to the homeland would be severed and immigrant cultures would blend to form a new and uniquely Canadian identity. The third viewpoint favoured a *cultural mosaic* in which immigrants preserved their culture as an integral piece of the country's overall social fabric. The following quotes express some opinions of the day.

Foreigners in large numbers are in our midst....How are we to make them into good Canadian citizens?...They must in some way be unified. Proper distribution may do much. There is a very natural tendency for people of the same nationality to settle in large colonies...dominated by alien ideas. It would seem a wise policy to scatter the foreign communities among the Canadians, in this way facilitating the process of assimilation.

J.S. Woodsworth, 1909, in Stranger Within Our Gates
(Toronto: University of Toronto Press, 1972), p. 234.

In Western Canada there is to be seen today that most fascinating of all human phenomena, the making of a nation. Out of breeds diverse in traditions, in ideals, in speech, and in manner of life...one people is being made. The blood strains of great races will mingle in the blood of a race greater than the greatest of them all.

Ralph Connor, The Foreigner: A Tale of Saskatchewan (1909).

The Canadian people today presents itself as a decorated surface, bright with inlays of separate coloured pieces, not painted in colours blended with brush on palette. The original background in which the inlays are set is still visible, but these inlays cover more space than that background, and so the ensemble may truly be called a mosaic.

John Murray Gibbon, Canadian Mosaic: The Making of a Northern Nation (Toronto: McClelland & Stewart, 1938) p. viii.

1. Which of these three viewpoints do you think is the most **egalitarian**? Explain your answer.

Source of Immigrants, 1871

Other 0.2%
Europe 4.9%
United States 10.9%
Great Britain 84.0%

Source of Immigrants, 1901-1911

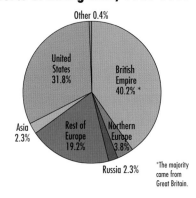

Other 0.4%
United States 31.8%
British Empire 40.2% *
Asia 2.3%
Rest of Europe 19.2%
Northern Europe 3.8%
Russia 2.3%

*The majority came from Great Britain.

Before 1900, most immigrants came from Britain. But in the first decade of the twentieth century, Canada opened its doors to immigrants from a variety of countries. What are the changes in immigration shown in these two graphs?

MAKING CONNECTIONS

1. As an immigrant to Canada in the early 1900s, what challenges would you face in assimilating into Canadian society? How would your experiences influence your attitude towards the Canadian identity?

KEYWORDS

assimilate

Anglo-conformity

melting pot

cultural mosaic

egalitarian

OPPOSING IMMIGRATION
The Vancouver Riot

Opposition to immigration from Asia was widespread in British Columbia at the beginning of the twentieth century. What was the source of this prejudice? How was it exhibited?

Hostile Relations

On the evening of 7 September 1907, a large crowd gathered outside city hall in Vancouver. The meeting was called to protest immigration from China, Japan, and India. Several speakers gave inflammatory speeches arguing that the newcomers were taking jobs from local residents.

While the speeches continued, a mob of several hundred people marched to the Chinese and Japanese sections of the city. They began throwing stones through the windows of shops and businesses. People on the street were beaten. The violence lasted for four hours, until Japanese-Canadian residents drove the rioters away.

The Vancouver riot showed just how bad relations were between the majority of residents in BC, who were British and American in background, and the Asian newcomers. In response to this tension, governments passed a series of laws aimed at restricting the number of Asian immigrants to British Columbia.

What Caused the Riot?

Like most events, the Vancouver riots had more than one cause. Historians describe several factors that led to the events in 1907.

1. The number of immigrants from Japan and India increased suddenly early in the year.

2. Rumours spread that there was a scheme to flood BC with cheap Asian workers. Labour unions worried that their members would lose jobs to the newcomers.

3. It was feared that Asian newcomers were so successful at business that they would soon control the economy.

4. British Columbians resented the fact that Asian immigrants worked for lower wages and they believed this limited their own job opportunities.

5. British Columbians did not believe that the federal government was sympathetic to their concerns about immigration.

6. Speakers at the gathering outside city hall ignited their audiences with their strong demands for an end to Asian immigration.

Timeline: Chinese Immigration to Canada

1858 The first Chinese immigrants to Canada arrive in BC to seek gold on the Fraser River.

1875 Chinese lose the vote in provincial and federal elections; they do not regain it until 1947.

1880-85 Thousands of Chinese labourers arrive to work on railway construction.

1885 The first **head tax** is imposed on Chinese immigrants. The tax has to be paid before a Chinese person is allowed into the country. It begins at $50, but eventually rises as high as $500.

1911 The Chinese population in British Columbia is 20 000.

1923 July 1st the head tax is abolished, but it is replaced by restrictions that stop virtually all Chinese immigration to Canada. This day is known to Chinese Canadians as "Humiliation Day."

1939-45 500 Chinese-Canadian soldiers fight for the Allies in the Second World War.

1947 Chinese Canadians regain the vote, and some of the restrictions on immigration are lifted.

1967 Restrictions on Chinese immigration are removed entirely.

1991 There are 586 645 Canadians of Chinese background, amounting to 2.17 per cent of the population.

A Vancouver police officer guards a vandalized store in Chinatown in the aftermath of the riot. Total damages were estimated at $9000. Five rioters received jail terms, and one was fined $50.

VIEWPOINTS

CHINESE IMMIGRATION

There were a variety of opinions about Chinese immigration to British Columbia in the early 1900s.

...it is necessary that legislation should be introduced to protect our own people from the competition of cheap Oriental labour.

Francis Carter-Cotton, journalist, 1900

We are not yet strong enough to assimilate races so alien from us in their habits. We are afraid that they would swamp our civilization such as it is.

Nanaimo Free Press, 29 May 1914

I have been here 12 years. My wife and two children are in China....I would like to bring my wife and children here....The people in this country talk so much against the Chinese I don't care to bring them here.

Chinese market gardener, 1901

We must not allow our shores to be overrun by Asiatics, and become dominated by an alien race. British Columbia must remain a white man's country.

R.B. Bennett, future prime minister of Canada, 1907

We must recognize the fact that all history has so far demonstrated the fact that the Oriental and white races do not assimilate. This is fundamental and vital. It is not to say that these races are inferior to us. In some ways they show a decided superiority, but it is that they are different—different not only in colour and physical build, but in habits, in traditions, in ideals and customs.

Rev. A.C. Cooke, 1921

1. List the reasons why many British Columbians opposed Chinese immigration.
2. At the time of the Vancouver riot, people often complained that the Chinese lived apart and did not establish their families in the province. What explanation for this behaviour does the gardener give?

MAKING CONNECTIONS

1. Events have causes that are underlying and other causes that are immediate. How would you categorize each of the causes of the riot? List the causes in order of importance. Explain your reasoning.

KEYWORDS

head tax

CANADIAN YOUTH
Life in the Early 20ᵗʰ Century

Canadian youth in the early twentieth century grew up in a much different environment than they do today. What was life like for young people at the turn of the century? What social reforms improved the quality of life?

Two Worlds

In the early 1900s, there were two worlds of childhood in Canada. One was a world in which children were sheltered and protected in comfortable homes and schools. These children could look forward to an education and a social life of sports and entertainment. The other was a world in which children worked on farms and in factories. These children were frequently forced to leave school (if they went to school at all) so they could get jobs and contribute to the family income.

The prevailing attitudes at the turn of the century paid little attention to a child's individuality and emotional well-being. As a result, many children were left unprotected from life's hardships. In rural areas, working on the family farm took precedence over attending school. In the cities, children were often exploited as cheap labour in the new industrial factories. Child labour laws had been introduced following an investigation by the Royal Commission on the Relations of Labour and Capital in the 1880s. They reduced the hours children could work, raised the minimum age for child labour, and introduced compulsory primary education. Still, by the early 1900s the problem of child labour persisted.

Social Reform

In response to the continuing problem, social reformers launched a campaign to improve life for working children. The importance of nurturing a child's physical, spiritual, and educational well-being gradually replaced old attitudes. Reformers viewed the family as the primary social force through which Canada could overcome the negative effects of industrialization—poverty, disease, crime, and poor working conditions. They believed that if they could improve the quality of family life, they would improve the quality of childhood.

The children in these photographs come from two contrasting worlds of childhood. From what you see in these photographs, how would their lives differ? Consider health, education, family, and overall quality of life.

To achieve this, they demanded better housing and more day nurseries and supervised playgrounds. They worked to improve health through greater public education and awareness. Compulsory **immunization** was introduced, while "fresh air" camps were set up for urban children. New legislation regulated the working hours and conditions for children. New family laws protected the rights of women and their children in the event of separation or divorce. Compulsory education was required for all children between the ages of seven and twelve in all provinces except Quebec. These reforms applied to all children, and they gradually helped to reduce the gap between the two worlds of childhood.

CASE STUDY

RURAL VERSUS URBAN SCHOOLS

Most rural schools were one-room schoolhouses. Students from grades 1 to 8 were taught the basics of reading, writing, and arithmetic. The school year was closely linked to the seasons and the harvest so that children were free to help their parents on the farm.

The main scholastic event of the year was the grade 8 high-school entrance exam. For most students, this was the highlight of their educational careers, as prior to the 1920s only 15 to 20 per cent of rural children went on to high school. The teacher in a one-room schoolhouse was usually either a young unmarried woman or an older man. Teachers knew the children well, not only as students but as neighbours. This created a close relationship between teacher and student and fostered a strong sense of community.

In small towns and in cities, the foundation of the modern school system was established with the introduction of the **consolidated school**. These schools connected adjacent school districts and provided common services such as transportation. Their facilities included gyms, laboratories, and auditoriums. Students were classified according to age, gender, and achievement. The teachers were well trained and the schools offered a variety of courses beyond reading, writing, and arithmetic. These included manual training, domestic science, stenography, and physical education. The courses students took, however, were largely determined by gender. Boys enrolled in classes that prepared them for work or higher education. Girls took classes that prepared them for family life. Still, all students now had the opportunity to receive a better education than had ever been possible before.

1. Imagine you attend a one-room schoolhouse in early twentieth-century Canada. Your school district is to become part of a new consolidated school system. In a diary entry, reflect on how your education will change.

A typical one-room schoolhouse had a wood-burning stove, rows of wooden desks, a raised platform for the teacher's desk, and windows placed to the left of the students. Why would the windows have been installed in this way?

⊶ MAKING CONNECTIONS ⊷

1. The first textbook on domestic science stated: "Educate a boy and you educate a man; educate a woman and you educate a family." Explain what this statement meant in early twentieth-century Canadian society.

KEYWORDS

immunization

consolidated school

PROHIBITION
Social Reform and the WCTU
FOCUSSING ON THE ISSUE

Women were at the forefront of social reform, and in particular the prohibition movement, in the early 1900s. One of the most prominent groups was the Women's Christian Temperance Union. What did the WCTU hope to achieve? Was it successful?

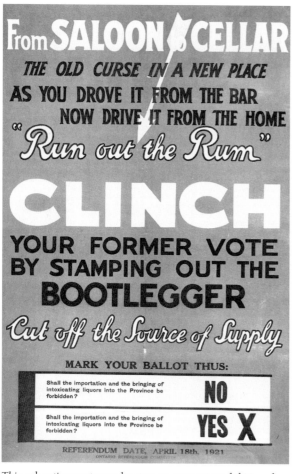

This advertisement urged voters to support prohibition during a referendum in 1921.

Social Reform

In many respects, the Women's Christian Temperance Union (WCTU) was typical of most social reform movements in Canada at the turn of the century. Its members were predominantly English, Protestant, and middle-class, and it considered women to be the moral guardians of society. However, not all social reform movements had as ambitious a goal as the Women's Christian Temperance Union: the **prohibition** of alcohol.

The Women's Christian Temperance Union originated in the United States. The Canadian branch of the WCTU was founded in Owen Sound, Ontario, in 1874 by Letitia Youmans. The WCTU viewed the consumption of alcohol as one of society's most serious problems. The union blamed alcohol for poverty, disease, unemployment, crime, spousal and child abuse, and the general immorality that they believed was characteristic of the new urban, industrial society. In particular, alcohol was seen as a male vice, with women as its main victims. The WCTU believed that prohibiting alcohol would solve these social problems and would establish women's moral authority.

Prohibition at Last

To end the liquor traffic, the WCTU had to convince the federal and provincial governments to adopt prohibition. This was no easy task. Most governments exhibited little enthusiasm for the cause. Tax revenues obtained from the sale of alcohol were substantial, and governments were reluctant to abandon this lucrative source of income. Moreover, prohibition was not popular with many Canadians, and politicians did not want to alienate the voting public. While the WCTU and other prohibitionist groups eagerly campaigned for the cause, governments responded with delaying tactics and compromises. At the turn of the century, only Prince Edward Island prohibited the sale of alcohol.

Like so many other reform movements of the time, prohibition could only succeed if the provincial and federal governments actively intervened. The First World War provided the necessary impetus for governments across Canada to adopt prohibition. With the pressures of war, alcohol was suddenly seen—even by Canadians who had scoffed at **abstinence**—as a waste of both human and material resources; to abstain from alcohol was to be patriotic. Beginning in 1915, provincial governments across the country banned alcohol. In 1917 and 1918, using the War Measures Act, the federal government issued **orders-in-council** that prohibited the sale, importation, interprovincial transportation, and manufacture of any beverage containing more than 2.5 per cent alcohol. It appeared that the WCTU and the prohibition movement had won their battle.

The victory, however, was short-lived. In 1919, a year after the First World War ended, the extraordinary provisions of the War Measures Act that had been used to adopt prohibition expired. Provincial governments could not resist the revenues generated by liquor sales. By the late 1920s, prohibition had been repealed in all provinces except Prince Edward Island. Still, there was some compromise. There would not be a return to the free-wheeling days of the liquor trade that existed prior to prohibition. Instead, government-run liquor stores were established. Governments could now regulate liquor traffic while continuing to collect tax revenues.

What caused the shift in government attitudes towards alcohol and prohibition? Canadian society had changed in the first decades of the twentieth century. Social ills could no longer be blamed on a single factor such as alcohol. Many social reformers came to realize that the problems the new industrial society faced were much more complex and therefore required more complex solutions. Nevertheless, the WCTU played a revolutionary role in early-twentieth-century Canadian society. It gave middle-class women the opportunity to become politically active and helped set the stage for the **enfranchisement** of women. It also provided a forum for women to advocate a variety of social reforms and gave women a greater voice in a traditionally male-dominated society.

BIOGRAPHY: NELLIE McCLUNG

Born in 1873, Nellie McClung began her career as a schoolteacher and went on to become a writer/journalist, public speaker, **suffragist**, legislator, and one of Canada's great social reformers. She was influential in gaining the provincial vote for women in Manitoba and Alberta, and she fought for prohibition and other reforms, such as **dower rights** and factory safety for women. She was the only Canadian woman appointed to the Canadian War Conference in 1918, the only female voice at the Methodist Ecumenical Congress of 1921, and a Canadian representative to the League of Nations in 1938. Always outspoken but with a touch of humour, McClung had as her motto "Never retract, never explain, never apologize—get the thing done and let them howl." Nellie McClung continued to work for equality and human rights until her death in 1951.

MAKING CONNECTIONS

1. With a partner, write a dialogue between a prohibitionist and a liquor trader in which you identify the main arguments for and against prohibition. Role-play your conversation before the class.

2. Compare and contrast modern attitudes towards alcohol with attitudes during prohibition. What forces might cause Canadian attitudes to change?

KEYWORDS

prohibition

abstinence

order-in-council

enfranchisement

suffragist

dower rights

SKILL BUILDER
Making Oral Presentations
FOCUSSING ON THE ISSUE

Making oral presentations is an important skill. What steps are needed to plan and deliver an effective oral presentation?

Planning

As students, you are sometimes asked to make oral presentations. Later, in your chosen occupation, you may also be required to speak in front of other people. Some people enjoy being in front of an audience; others are less enthusiastic about the prospect. There are basic steps everyone can follow, however, to make their oral presentations informative and effective.

The first step is to be sure that you understand the topic and the purpose of your presentation. Establish your objective—that is, what you hope to achieve and the message you want to convey to your audience. If you are uncertain, ask questions.

Once you have defined the purpose, prepare a written outline of your topic. List the main ideas, then fill in the subpoints. For example, the topic of your presentation might be the role of women in Canada at the turn of the century. Your outline could look like this:

**Women in Canada
at the Turn of the Century**
- Introduction
- The Victorian Tradition
- Legal Realities
  - Equality
  - Marital rights
- Political Realities
  - Women's organizations
  - Suffragist movements

- Economic Realities
  - Domestic service
  - Office work
  - Professional occupations
- Social Realities
  - Family life
  - Education
- Cultural Realities
  - Immigration
  - Artists
- Summary

The introduction should state the main theme or purpose of your presentation. Capture your audience's attention at the start using a powerful quotation, a startling statistic, a thought-provoking question, or a dramatic visual. For example, the poster advertising for wives to settle in western Canada speaks volumes about how women were viewed in Canadian society at the turn of the century.

The main body of your presentation should include your ideas and the facts that support them. Be sure you have researched your topic carefully. Present your points in a clear and logical way and include evidence to back up your arguments. Props will help to clarify your ideas and prove your points. Charts, photographs, slides, videotapes, and tape recordings all enhance an oral presentation and help your audience focus on your topic. A magazine cover like the one on page 31, for example, says a lot about the role of women in

URGENT !

Thousands of nice girls are wanted in THE CANADIAN WEST.

Over 20,000 *Men* are sighing for what they cannot get—**WIVES !** *Shame !*

Don't hesitate—COME AT ONCE. If you cannot come, send your sisters.

So great is the demand that anything in skirts stands a chance.

No reasonable offer refused They are all shy but willing. All Prizes ! No Blanks.

Hustle up now Girls and don't miss this chance. Some of you will never get another.

Special Application Card

Why do you think this advertisement might spark your audience's interest?

Canadian society during this period. Statistical comparisons like the ones showing women as a percentage of the labour force in the 1900s and the 1990s provide sharply contrasting pictures of women in society then and now.

Finally, your presentation should have a strong summary that reinforces the theme. A thought-provoking question or powerful quotation may be an effective finale. To end a presentation on the role of women at the turn of the century, a quote from a prominent **suffragist** like Nellie McClung would clearly

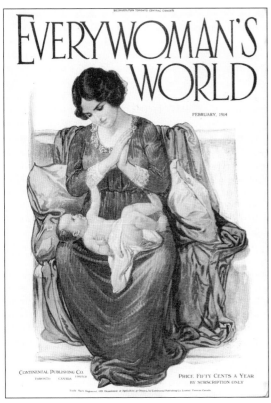

EVERYWOMAN'S WORLD

FEBRUARY, 1914

CONTINENTAL PUBLISHING CO.
LIMITED
TORONTO   CANADA

PRICE FIFTY CENTS A YEAR
BY SUBSCRIPTION ONLY

What message would this magazine cover from 1914 convey to your audience about the role of women at the turn of the century?

Women as a Percentage of the Labour Force, by Occupation, 1901 and 1993		
Occupation	1901	1993
Managerial	3.6	41.5
Professional	42.45	55.7
Clerical	22.1	81.2
Sales	10.4	43.4
Service	68.7	57.3
Skilled Labour	12.6	44.8
All Occupations	13.4	44.8

(Figures for 1901 are for females age 10 and over; figures for 1993 are for females age 25 and over.)

What information would this data convey to your audience?

make the point that women were demanding change:

The world has never been partial to the thinking woman....Long years ago, when women asked for an educa-tion, the world cried out that it would never do. If women learned to read there seemed to be a possibility that some day some good man might come home and find his wife reading and the dinner not ready—and nothing could be imagined more horrible than that! That seems to be the haunting fear of mankind—that the advancement of women will sometime, someway, someplace, interfere with some man's comfort!

Nellie McClung, In Times Like These, 1915

Delivering

Once you have prepared your presentation, read it so that you know it thoroughly. Using a tape recorder or videotape, or standing in front of a mirror, practise delivering your presentation several times until you are comfortable with the material and no longer require your notes. You might want do to a practice run in front of family or friends. Time your presentation to make sure it is the appropriate length.

Before your presentation, make sure you have an outline to keep you on track and that all of your visual props are organized. When you deliver your presentation, speak clearly and evenly. Maintain eye contact with the audience so that they feel you are speaking to them personally. Be enthusiastic about your topic. If you show that you are interested in what you have to say, your audience will be too!

The key to successful public speaking is practice. As with all skills, the more we perform them, the more comfortable and confident we become.

KEYWORDS

suffragist

MAKING CONNECTIONS

1. Prepare a checklist of the key points to consider in planning and delivering an oral presentation. Use it when you make presentations in class.

2. Research and prepare an oral presentation on one of the following topics:
   a) the legal, political, social, economic, and cultural status of Canadian women at the turn of the century
   b) the legal, political, social, economic, and cultural status of Canadian women today
   c) child labour in Canada at the turn of the century
   d) issues facing young people in Canada today
   e) a legal, political, social, economic, or cultural issue of your choice from the turn of the century or today.

EXPATRIATES
Canadian Artists in France

Many Canadian artists at the beginning of the century left the country to practise their art abroad. Why was Canada so inhospitable to the arts?

Exodus to Paris

At the beginning of the century, Canada was not a friendly place for artists. The president of the Canadian Arts Club listed the challenges for an artist: *The lack of sympathy with his aims and objects, the lack of artistic facilities of any kind, the lack of intelligent critics, the lack of suitable buildings where works of art can be properly shown, and, above all, the lack of any apparent desire to see things change for the better.*

In 1900, Canada was only 33 years old. Much of the country was an unsettled frontier. Even in the large cities, people were preoccupied with earning a living and providing for their families. The arts would have to wait. There were few schools for young painters, only a small number of galleries existed, and few people could afford to buy art for their homes. In other words, there was almost no audience, and without an audience the arts cannot flourish.

*The Ferry, Quebec, was painted by James William Morrice 1909. Morrice (1865-1924) was the first Canadian artist to gain international recognition. He was part of the **bohemian** world of painters and writers living in Paris at the beginning of the twentieth century. He was deeply influenced by the French **impressionist** painters—Claude Monet, Auguste Renoir, Edgar Degas—who were the pioneers of modern art. The impressionists used bright colours and spontaneous brush strokes to record light, movement, and change. Morrice returned to Canada regularly and painted Canadian subjects, like this one.*

In this climate, aspiring artists looked to Europe for their inspiration. They copied European styles and went to Europe to study, seeking a place where art was considered important and the artist was respected. Almost every painter who later gained success in Canada studied overseas. While most eventually returned to Canada, others remained permanently in exile from their homeland.

In the years before the First World War, Canada was starting to become a more hospitable place for artists. In 1907, a group of painters formed the Canadian Art Club to encourage the latest modern techniques among local artists. At the same time, an Arts and Letters Club was formed in Toronto, bringing together writers, musicians, designers, and painters in support of the arts. In 1910, the National Gallery in Ottawa named its first director and soon began showing its collection of paintings in its first permanent building.

All these developments showed that Canadians, and Canadian artists, were beginning to feel confident enough to seek their own forms of expression. At the same time, the Canadian public was beginning to appreciate that art was about themselves, not some other place. The stage was set for a blossoming of the arts in the years following the First World War.

VIEWPOINTS

CANADIANS IN PARIS

Emily Carr went to Paris from Victoria in 1910 with her sister Alice to study painting.

My sister studied the history of Paris, kept notes and diaries. I did not care a hoot about Paris history. I wanted now to find out what this "New Art" was about. I heard it ridiculed, praised, liked, hated. Something in it stirred me, but I could not at first make head or tail of what it was all about. I saw at once that it made recent conservative painting look flavourless, little, unconvincing.

I had brought with me a letter of introduction to a very modern artist named Harry Gibb....Some of his pictures rejoiced, some shocked me. There was rich, delicious juiciness in his colour, interplay between warm and cool tones. He intensified vividness by the use of contemporary colour....After one look, my sister dropped her eyes to the floor. Modern Art appalled her.

From Growing Pains: *The Autobiography of Emily Carr, 1946*

A.Y. Jackson, later a member of the Group of Seven (see page 88), was another Canadian artist who left the country to study.

In 1907 I went to Paris. All right-minded Montreal artists aspired to go to Paris and most of them wanted to study at the Academie Julian. It was not the instruction, which amounted to about ten minutes a week, that attracted them to Julian's, it was the association with students from all over the world. They were a riotous but enthusiastic and hardworking crowd....

After six months at Julian's, I went with a group on an Easter excursion to Italy, where we visited Rome, Florence and Venice, spending most of the time in galleries....One of our fellow travellers was a Scotsman who had lived for years in Rome, working as a chemist. We could not have had a better guide in a city where the creative arts have flourished for hundreds of years. He took us about Rome to see the work of the great masters on the very walls where they had been painted.

From A.Y. Jackson, A Painter's Country: The Autobiography of A.Y. Jackson *(Toronto: Clarke Irwin & Company, 1958). Reprinted by permission of Stoddart Publishing Co. Limited.*

1. a) What attracted Canadian artists to Europe?
   b) Why do you think Canada was unsympathetic to what Carr called "New Art"?

MAKING CONNECTIONS

1. Study the painting *The Ferry, Quebec*, by J.W. Morrice. What elements of the painting identify this as a Canadian scene?

KEYWORDS

bohemian

impressionist

URBANIZATION
The Growth of Cities
FOCUSSING ON THE ISSUE

Cities have always been divided into different neighbourhoods. Some neighbourhoods are more desirable than others. What factors created these divisions in Canadian cities?

Economic Factors

At the beginning of the twentieth century, Canada's cities were expanding as more people arrived to work in the new industrial factories. In 1900, there was little public transportation. Most workers lived within walking distance of their workplace, which was usually in the city's industrial areas. Tiny houses were built close together on small lots. Most of the occupants were renters. Many landlords were reluctant to spend money on maintenance, so many of the homes fell into disrepair. In contrast, wealthy families built large homes well away from the factories and businesses. They sought neighbourhoods where they could purchase large lots, often with picturesque views.

Neighbourhoods were sometimes divided by the railway lines that serviced the urban industrial areas. The factory and office workers lived on one side of the tracks while the wealthy families lived on the other. The division created by the rail lines produced the concept of "the wrong side of the tracks." To come from the "wrong side of the tracks" was to come from the poorer side of town.

Geographic Factors

It was not always the railway lines that created a divide between rich and poor. Sometimes it was geography. The slope of the land and the **prevailing winds** played a major role in creating urban divisions. Because sloping land provided a view, it was considered more desirable. If the prevailing winds were from the west, they carried the smoke and pollution from the factories to the east. The result was that land that was flat or on the east side of the city was less desirable, and therefore cheaper, than land that sloped or was on the west side. And so wealth continued to define the "wrong side of the tracks," even when there were no railway tracks in the city.

Planned Development

By the beginning of the twentieth century, city governments had begun to designate land for specific purposes, such as industrial, commercial, or residential. Planned development was considered "modern" and progressive. Transportation companies built electric streetcar lines to serve local areas and tram lines to provide **interurban** transportation. This gave people the opportunity to move to residential neighbourhoods in the new **suburbs**. These were usually well away from the industrial and business districts. In the suburbs, families could buy houses on larger lots at affordable prices.

The photo on the left is Vancouver's West End near Stanley Park. The one on the right is east of Granville Street in downtown Vancouver. Both pictures were taken around 1905. Which is the "wrong side of the tracks"? How can you tell?

THE GROWTH OF VANCOUVER

The impact of the factors that influence **urban development** can be seen in the growth of Vancouver in the early twentieth century. On the west side, towards Stanley Park and English Bay and upwind of the mills and factories, stood the stately homes of Vancouver's wealthy families. The neighbourhoods of working families lay sandwiched between the industrial areas surrounding Burrard Inlet and False Creek.

As the land between False Creek and Burrard Inlet became more desirable for business and commercial development, land prices in the area rose. The construction of streetcar and tram lines to the east and across False Creek to the south and west allowed working families to move to the cheaper land found in these areas. They could now buy small lots at relatively low prices and build their own houses. They could still get to work quickly and easily via public transportation. As the downtown core expanded westward onto the CPR lands around Granville Street, the luxury housing moved from the West End to Shaughnessy Heights on the south side of False Creek. With its views of the city and the mountains to the north, Shaughnessy Heights quickly became the most prestigious place for wealthy families to build their homes. The patterns established in the early years of Vancouver's development are still evident today.

Downtown Vancouver

MAKING CONNECTIONS

1. Consider the area in which you live. What geographic factors have determined the location of residential areas in your community?

2. Create a land-use map of your local area. Include industrial lands, commercial tracts, residential areas, and parks and recreational lands. Refer to page 371 for the appropriate colour codes for your map.

KEYWORDS

prevailing winds

interurban

suburbs

urban development

KING COAL
Mining on Vancouver Island
FOCUSSING ON THE ISSUE

Coal mining, which was a dominant feature of the early economic development of Vancouver Island, was one of the first natural resource industries in BC. Why did the Vancouver Island coal industry collapse?

Fuel for the Empire

At the beginning of the twentieth century, many of the ships protecting the British Empire and carrying its Pacific trade were fuelled by coal from Vancouver Island. The Esquimalt and Nanaimo Railway delivered British Columbia coal to the ships at the British naval base at Esquimalt and the coal ports of Union Bay, Nanaimo, and Ladysmith. These ports supplied the fuel for ships trading along the coast and across the Pacific, as well as for the rapidly expanding Canadian and American railways. Regular coal shipments also went to Vancouver, Seattle, and San Francisco to provide heat for the homes and buildings of growing West Coast cities.

Working in the Mines

Many of the miners who worked the coal mines of Vancouver Island were recruited from Britain. When they arrived, they were in debt to the mine owners for their travel costs. The miners and their families lived in company towns where they rented company-owned houses.

They were expected to buy their food, clothing, mining tools, and other supplies at company-owned stores at company-dictated prices. This **truck system** meant that most of the miners were continuously in debt to the company.

Vancouver Island coal mines were dangerous places to work. Explosions and cave-ins were frequent. But the most feared dangers were the mine gases—the "damps," as the miners called them. Black-damp was a mixture of coal gases that was highly explosive. After-damp, the silent killer, was air with

This company townsite is at Cumberland. Why are there so many stumps? What did the people do for water, sewers, and garbage? What purpose did the railway line serve?

THE CHINESE MINERS

Like most Chinese workers in British Columbia at the turn of the century, Chinese mine workers were immigrants who left their homeland to earn money in North America. Because of the **head tax** that was imposed on Chinese immigrants, these men had no choice but to leave their families behind. Ultimately, their goal was to return to China with enough money to buy a small plot of land. When Chinese workers arrived on Vancouver Island they were in debt, either for their transportation fare or their head tax, or both. Therefore they had little control over their working conditions or wages. It was common practice to assign Chinese workers to the most dangerous and dirty jobs and to pay them half the rate of other mine workers. Frequently, however, the Chinese miners stood up to the mine companies and refused to work unless their wages or working conditions improved.

Chinese workers also faced restrictive housing policies. They were forced to live in separate areas in the mining camps. Because they intended to eventually return to China, Chinese workers had no real incentive to **assimilate**. As a result, an atmosphere of misunderstanding, suspicion, and hostility was fostered between the Chinese workers and the other miners.

---

a high enough concentration of carbon monoxide that it could kill almost instantly. Yet little attention was paid to ensuring safety in the mines. Inspections were rare. Most miners believed that the coal companies were more concerned about profits than about their safety.

Wages were also poor. Since miners were paid according to the amount of coal they produced, the quality of the seam they worked affected their earnings. Time spent digging rock to make a tunnel large enough—and therefore safe enough—to work in meant less time mining coal and therefore less money at the end of the shift.

Together, the truck system, the lack of safety precautions, and the poor wages caused many miners to support attempts to organize mine workers' unions. The mine owners, however, had other ideas and often took extreme measures to prevent unions from gaining a foothold. During a miners strike in 1903, for example, mine owner James Dunsmuir refused to meet with the miners' union representatives. Instead, he fired all the union leaders and evicted the striking miners from their company houses. The miners had no choice but to live in tents on the beach until they abandoned their strike and their attempts to unionize and returned to work.

A Rapid Decline

By 1910, coal mining on Vancouver Island faced a gloomy future. Workers were less willing to accept dangerous working conditions. The mining companies' unwillingness to deal with miners' concerns, coupled with their power to fire any worker suspected of being a union member or supporter, led to prolonged labour disputes. The result was a drop in production and, consequently, sales. The decline of the industry was hastened by the fact that the nature of the coal trade itself was changing rapidly. Ships and railways were increasingly turning to oil as a source of fuel, which meant a loss of customers for the island coal mines. As coal shipments steadily declined, one by one the mines began to close.

MAKING CONNECTIONS

1. How did geographic and economic factors lead to the development of the Vancouver Island coal mining industry?

2. Using an atlas, locate and identify the coal mining regions of British Columbia today. Mark these sites on an outline map of BC. Add statistics citing coal production and coal exports in the province.

KEYWORDS

truck system

head tax

assimilate

UNIT 2:

Frederick Varley, *For What?* (1918)

Frederick Varley (1881-1969) came to Canada from Britain in 1912. He was quickly drawn into the artistic community of the Group of Seven. As an artist for the Canadian War Records Office, Varley created some of the most dramatic work of any of the war artists.

FACING THE WORLD

1911 - 1920

	Social	Cultural	Political	Legal	Economic	Environmental
THE BALANCE OF POWER The World in 1911.........40			✔		✔	✔
THE EASTERN QUESTION Confrontation in the Balkans.........42			✔			✔
THE BRITISH EMPIRE Canada and the Dominions 44			✔			✔
THE ELECTION OF 1911 Reciprocity.........46		✔	✔		✔	
PUBLIC HEALTH Crisis in Canadian Cities.........48	✔		✔		✔	✔
ROCK SLIDE Endangering the Salmon Run.........52					✔	✔
COMING TO CANADA The *Komagata Maru* Affair.........54	✔	✔				
CANADA ENLISTS Reactions to the War 56			✔			
AT WAR IN EUROPE The Western Front 58			✔			
WAR ARTISTS The War Memorials Fund 60		✔	✔			
CANADA AT WAR The Home Front 62	✔		✔	✔	✔	
THE WAR HITS HOME The Halifax Explosion 64						✔
A COUNTRY DIVIDED The Conscription Crisis 66	✔		✔	✔		
THE SUFFRAGE MOVEMENT Women Get the Vote 68	✔		✔	✔		
CANADIANS IN RUSSIA The Bolshevik Revolution 70			✔			
SKILL BUILDER Recognizing Bias* 72	✔					
LABOUR UNREST The Winnipeg General Strike 74	✔				✔	
CULTURAL ASSIMILATION Residential Schools.........76	✔	✔	✔			
PEACE AND SECURITY Versailles and the League of Nations..78			✔			

*Skills and Processes

THE BALANCE OF POWER
The World in 1911
FOCUSSING ON THE ISSUE

The developed world was poised on the brink of war in 1911, with Britain and Germany in an arms race and all the great powers locked in precarious alliances. What economic, military, and political factors set the stage for war?

Economic Growth

The world in 1911 was emerging from a decade of unprecedented economic growth. Industrialization was rapidly expanding in many parts of the globe. Factory smoke-stacks rose in every major city in countries, such as Russia, where few industries had existed a decade earlier. In cities around the world, electric streetcars, automobiles, and gasoline-powered trucks and buses were replacing horse-drawn vehicles.

The population of the world was about 2 billion. More than 25 per cent of these people lived in Europe, where they severely strained the **carrying capacity** of the land and the economies of many countries. In many parts of eastern Europe, poverty was widespread. Under these conditions, **infant mortality rates** were high and **life expectancy** was low. The average eastern European in 1911 could expect to live 30 years, much less than someone living in Canada or the United States, who could expect to live 50 years.

The fastest economic growth was in the United States, Germany, and Japan. By 1911, the United States had passed Germany as the world's leading developed nation; Britain was a distant third. The US accounted for more than 33 per cent of all the goods produced in the world, more than twice the amount of either Germany or Britain.

Eventually, the rate of economic growth began to subside. Although the world economy was experiencing a downturn by 1913, the great powers were expanding their militarism with an arms race. Their factories continued to turn out warships and weapons at a record pace.

The Dreadnought Race

In 1906, Britain launched the first of a new class of battleships, the HMS *Dreadnought*. Germany's kaiser, Wilhelm II, who sought to rival Britain on the high seas in order to support his new imperialist *weltpolitik*, ordered similar ships to be built. By 1914, Britain had built 29 of the huge **dreadnoughts**, while Germany had completed 18 of the super battleships. The Germans planned to build a total of 40 battleships and 60 cruisers by the end of the decade. These two European great powers were now locked in an arms race. Their heavy industries and advanced technologies were creating a vast array of modern weapons. Throughout Europe, people were beginning to talk of the possibility of war.

Alliances

In 1911, Germany, Austria-Hungary, and Italy were linked together in the Triple Alliance. Its foundation had been established in 1879 with the signing of the Dual Alliance, linking Austria-Hungary

The dreadnought launched the battle between Britain and Germany for supremacy on the high seas.

and Germany. The **alliance** had been forged by Bismarck in order to gain control over Austrian foreign policy and, at the same time, to warn off Russia, should the latter seek to expand its influence in Europe. This treaty bound Germany to come to Austria-Hungary's aid should it be attacked by Russia.

In 1882, the German chancellor, Otto von Bismarck, negotiated a similar treaty with Italy after it called upon Germany to defend the Italians should they be attacked by France. This effectively turned the Dual Alliance into the Triple Alliance. The purpose of the Triple Alliance was to isolate both France and Russia and to prevent any ties between the two powers that might lead to Germany being involved in a two-front war.

By 1911, Russia, France, and Great Britain were allied in their opposition to the Triple Alliance. In the 1890s, the French and Russians had established diplomatic ties of military and economic importance. Russia needed loans and modern weapons; France needed Russian support should it go to war against Germany to recover its "lost" provinces of Alsace and Lorraine. In 1894, Russia and France entered into a formal military alliance, binding the two nations to aid each other if either were attacked by Germany. It was to stay in force as long as the Triple Alliance endured.

At first, the British viewed the Franco-Russian Alliance with suspicion and alarm. Relations between Paris and London were strained until the end of the century. By 1900, however, Britain realized that Germany posed a far greater threat than did France, Britain's traditional European enemy. Britain abandoned its established policy of isolation from European affairs and great power alliances and entered into the Entente Cordiale with France in 1904. A similar **entente**, linking Britain and Russia, was signed in 1907.

No formal treaty bound Britain, France, and Russia to mutual defence in the case of war. However, by 1914, on the eve of war, their growing spirit of co-operation in the face of a mutual German threat had created a common interest often referred to as the Triple Entente.

The Triple Entente and the Triple Alliance in 1911

- Member of the Triple Entente
- Member of the Triple Alliance

The Outbreak of War

The arms race, **nationalism**, **imperialism**, and the system of alliances would all contribute to the outbreak of the Great War of 1914–1918. The First World War would dominate the decade and would have an impact on almost every part of the globe.

KEYWORDS

carrying capacity

infant mortality rate

life expectancy

weltpolitik

dreadnought

alliance

entente

nationalism

imperialism

⊪ MAKING CONNECTIONS ⊪

1. Why did Britain consider Germany to be a far greater threat than its established enemy, France?

2. Do you think that alliances contribute to or hasten the outbreak of war? Explain your reasons.

THE EASTERN QUESTION
Confrontation in the Balkans
FOCUSSING ON THE ISSUE

Events in the Balkans between 1911 and 1914 would set the stage for the First World War. How did issues in the strategically important region of the Balkans bring the world to the brink of war?

A Vacuum of Power

At the start of the twentieth century the Ottoman Empire was in decline. By 1911 the great powers were eager to get their hands on key Ottoman territories. The strategic location of these lands, which included parts of the Balkan Peninsula and the area that is now Turkey, made them attractive to Russia, Austria, and Great Britain. The system of alliances, however, meant that all the European great powers would be affected by events in this region.

The decline of the Ottoman Empire could potentially create a **vacuum of power**. The problem of how to deal with this vacuum came to be known as the "Eastern Question." Russia wanted access to the Mediterranean via the Dardanelles, the waterway dividing Europe from Asia. Austria-Hungary wanted to expand its empire into the Balkans but did not want Russia to increase its influence in the region. Great Britain, fearful of Russian ambitions in the Middle East and Afghanistan, supported the Ottoman Empire, hoping to keep the Russians bottled up in the Black Sea. Germany was in the process of building a railway from Berlin to Baghdad to bypass the Suez Canal. Since the tracks would run through the Balkans, Germany wanted to maintain stability in the region.

The Balkans, 1914

The Balance of Power

Both Austria-Hungary and Russia took advantage of **nationalist** feelings among the various peoples of the Balkans. There was great resentment towards the Ottomans, who had ruled the region since the fifteenth century. The Russians encouraged and supported the **Slavic** peoples—the Serbians and Bulgarians—with whom they shared a common religion and similar language. Austria-Hungary promoted the conflicts between the Slavic and non-Slavic peoples, especially the Greeks and Romanians. With Russian support, the Serbians and the Bulgarians were able to gain independence from the Ottoman Empire in the late nineteenth century. By 1901, Ottoman territory in the Balkans had been reduced to Macedonia and Albania in the south, and the provinces of Bosnia-Hercegovina in the north, administered for the Ottomans by Austria-Hungary.

The "Young Turk" Revolution of 1908 gave new life to the dying Ottoman Empire, threatening Austria's interests in the Balkans.

When Austria decided to add Bosnia-Hercegovina to its empire, Russia agreed provided that Austria-Hungary supported opening the Dardanelles to Russian ships. Austria, however, jumped the gun by formally **annexing** Bosnia-Hercegovina in October 1908. This left Russia deeply humiliated and without international support for its plans to gain access to the Mediterranean. Even more upset were the Serbians, who threatened to invade Bosnia to "liberate" the region from Austrian oppression. Austria-Hungary vowed to destroy Serbia, and sought the support of Germany on this issue.

When Italy and Turkey went to war in 1911, the independent Balkan states saw this as an opportunity to drive the Ottomans out of Europe completely. In 1912, war broke out in the Balkans. Montenegro, Serbia, Bulgaria, and Greece quickly defeated the Ottoman forces, capturing all of Turkey's European territory except Constantinople. Landlocked Serbia annexed Albania but was forced to give it up in 1913

under the terms of the Treaty of London, which ended the war. Serbian nationalists were outraged and demanded Russian assistance for the southern Slavs. Russia, seeking to avoid another humiliating blow to its prestige in the region, promised to back Serbia in any future conflict with Austria-Hungary.

A second Balkan war broke out in 1913, this time between Serbia and Bulgaria over disputed territory. Serbia and Greece declared war on the Bulgarians. They were soon joined by Romania and the Ottoman Empire. Bulgaria was swiftly defeated by this odd coalition, losing large amounts of its territory to the victors.

The Balkan Wars greatly affected the course of world history over the next two years. The wars had left the key Balkan region deeply divided and unstable. Serbia had emerged strong and ambitious, but with deep resentments. The peace settlements engendered fear and anti-Serbian sentiment in neighbouring Austria-Hungary. The dismantling of the Ottoman Empire and the weakening of Bulgaria had created dangerous tensions in southeastern Europe.

Interest in the region by the great powers remained focussed. Austria-Hungary had obtained from Germany assurances that it would support Austria-Hungary in any future conflicts with Serbia. Russia, pledged to support Serbia, reminded Great Britain and France of their alliance. The stage was now set for a much larger war should hostilities resume in the Balkans.

MAKING CONNECTIONS

1. Look at the map of the Balkans. Identify the countries that do not have access to the sea. Why would this be a problem?

2. Research the history of one of the Balkan countries during the twentieth century and present your findings to the rest of the class. Your presentation should include the following information:

   • the point(s) at which your chosen country shifted from one political sphere of influence to another

   • the event surrounding each shift, as well as its historical significance

   • the issues related to the event

   • the implications of the event for your chosen country and for other areas of the world.

KEYWORDS

vacuum of power

nationalist

Slavic

annex

THE BRITISH EMPIRE
Canada and the Dominions

FOCUSSING ON THE ISSUE

Britain's vast empire in 1911 included four self-governing dominions. What relationship did the dominions have with Britain? To what extent were the dominions able to establish their own identities as independent nations?

The Dominions

In 1867, Canada was the first British colony to be granted self-government. Australia was next in 1901, followed by New Zealand in 1907, and South Africa in 1910. The dominions shared many social, cultural, and political characteristics drawn from their common British origins. Each was in the process of shaping a distinctive identity as a nation in the years before the First World War. And each would be profoundly affected by that war.

Systems of Government

The four dominions shared many features of the system of government they inherited from Britain. Each had an elected form of **parliamentary representation**; each had as its head of state the British monarch who was represented by a governor general. Under the governor general, the executive branch consisted of a prime minister and a Cabinet. Australia, Canada, and South Africa were federal unions, with constitutions that divided powers between two levels of government. New Zealand chose not to join the Australian colonies in their Commonwealth Federation in 1901.

Like Canada, Australia's federal constitution was based on both British and American practices. Australia was created as a **parliamentary democracy**, with a prime minister and Cabinet responsible to a **bicameral** legislature. The Australian House of Representatives, like the House of Commons in Canada and in Britain, is based on popular representation. The Senate, similar to its American counterpart, represents the former colonies, which are now states. Unlike Canada, the Australians adopted a constitution that limits the powers of the federal government; the Australian states enjoy more powers and greater autonomy than Canada's provinces.

New Zealand had achieved considerable independence and self-government from Britain by the mid-1800s. Unlike Canada or Australia, New Zealand has a **unicameral** parliament, also known as the House of Representatives. In the early 1900s, New Zealand was one of the most progressive nations in the world. In 1893, New Zealand became the first country to give women the vote. By 1912, legislation established a minimum wage and provided for the compulsory arbitration of labour disputes.

Under the terms of the treaty that ended the Boer War in Southern Africa in 1902, Transvaal and the Orange Free State became British colonies. In 1906 and 1907, they were given their own constitutions as self-governing colonies. With the South Africa Act of 1910, the British Parliament created a fourth dominion, the Union of South Africa. This, too, was a federal union with the four colonies—Transvaal, the Orange Free State, Cape Province, and Natal—becoming provinces. The system of government was modelled on the British system. The legal system was the common law of the Netherlands, supplemented by modern English law. Black South Africans played virtually no part in the political founding of South Africa. This was to be the start of a long resistance to minority white rule.

Like Canada, Australia and South Africa were federations created from several separate colonies. Each faced problems of national unity and identity as a result of competing interests and influences among their varied communities. In Australia, the differences were largely regional, while South Africa was divided by deep national, cultural, and racial differences.

The Impact of War

The dominions joined the British effort in the First World War. As with Canada, Australia and New Zealand's participation helped define their national identities. The

At Gallipoli in 1915, the Australian and New Zealand Army Corps (ANZAC) was ordered to attack Turkish forces in the Dardanelles. It suffered heavy losses in a losing effort. The date of that landing, 25 April 1915, marked Australia's coming of age. Known as Anzac Day, it remains the country's most significant day of remembrance.

war had a very different effect on South Africa, however. It divided the Dutch-descended Afrikaners and the British-born South Africans. The split was similar to that between French and English Canadians. But it would have very different results.

Australians twice rejected **conscription** during the First World War. Yet they volunteered to fight in great numbers, sending more than 330 000 volunteers to join the Allied war effort. In many ways, the war transformed Australia from a loose union of six former colonies into a united country, keenly aware of its new identity. New Zealand also actively participated in the war effort, sending 124 000 troops to fight with the British forces in Egypt and in the Gallipoli campaign of 1915. In 1916, New Zealanders fought in France as a separate division in the first Battle of the Somme.

When the First World War broke out, South African prime minister Louis Botha offered Britain full support. In 1915, his government crushed an uprising by an extremist group of Afrikaners, many of whom had fought in the Boer War against Britain and opposed joining the Allied forces. South African forces under the command of Botha himself captured German South West Africa (today known as Namibia). In 1920, this territory became a League of Nations mandate under South African supervision.

◄▣ MAKING CONNECTIONS ▣►

1. What were the similarities and differences in the systems of government in Canada, Australia, New Zealand, and South Africa?

2. What was the impact of the First World War on the four dominions? How did it shape their identities?

KEYWORDS

parliamentary representation

parliamentary democracy

bicameral

unicameral

conscription

THE ELECTION OF 1911

Reciprocity

FOCUSSING ON THE ISSUE

In 1911, a clear Canadian identity had yet to emerge. The election that year was in many ways a test of where Canadian loyalties lay. What issues of identity and loyalty faced the country in 1911? How did they affect the outcome of the election?

Building a Nation

As the second decade of Canada's twentieth century dawned, Prime Minister Wilfrid Laurier was leader of a country that was growing stronger and more prosperous every day. Canada's economy was booming in the summer of 1911. Grain from the prairies, minerals and manufactured goods from Ontario, pulp wood from Quebec, and lumber from the forests of British Columbia were being shipped in ever-increasing amounts to markets at home and abroad. Nova Scotia was enjoying a coal and steel boom. Two new railways were being built across Canada. Thousands of immigrants were coming to Canada every week.

In this season of prosperity, Laurier found himself and the Liberal party under attack from nearly every quarter of the country. Much of the criticism arose from Laurier's handling of the issue of whether or not, and to what extent, Canada should support Britain in its naval arms race with Germany.

Laurier's policy of trying to create a more independent and sovereign nation had led to the erosion of support for his Liberal party. A major cause was Laurier's decision in 1910 to create a Canadian navy rather than contribute to Britain's Royal Navy. Laurier's Naval Service Bill was quickly denounced in both Quebec and Ontario.

Reciprocity

Faced with growing opposition in both English and French Canada, the Liberal government's popular support dropped sharply in 1910. However, Laurier's sagging political fortunes received a boost from an unlikely source—the United States. The American economy was expanding rapidly. In 1911, President William Howard Taft offered Canada a reciprocal trade agreement in raw materials and natural products. Laurier saw **reciprocity** as a chance to boost the Canadian economy, as well as a way to win votes, especially among prairie farmers.

Caught off guard, the Conservative leader, Robert Borden, was at first unprepared to mount any organized opposition. However, aided by prominent Conservative politicians in the provinces, he soon used the reciprocity agreement as further proof of Laurier's lack of loyalty to Britain. Borden and the Conservatives, using procedural arguments, stalled passage of the reciprocity agreement in the House of Commons. The debate dragged on. Laurier decided to take the issue to the people.

An election was called for 21 September 1911. It would be fought on one major issue—reciprocity—but the real question was one of loyalties and identity. Supported by Ontario manufacturers, the Conservatives campaigned using such pro-British, anti-American slogans as "No navy made in London, no reciprocity made in Washington" and "No truck nor trade with the Yankees!" Canadians awoke on 22 September to learn that the slogans had been effective. Laurier and the Liberals had been defeated by the Conservatives. Robert Borden would be Canada's new prime minister.

A NEW FIELD FOR CONQUEST.

What does this cartoon suggest about some Canadians' attitudes to reciprocity with the United States?

Laurier fought hard to bridge the gaps that deeply divided French and English Canadians after the Boer War and the execution of Louis Riel. He worked equally hard to make all Canadians feel part of a common undertaking to build a great nation. Within the British Empire, Laurier had gained much respect as the leading advocate of greater independence for the dominions. Yet at home he was criticized by both French and English Canadians.

*I am branded in Quebec as a traitor to the French, and in Ontario as a traitor to the English. In Quebec I am branded as a **Jingoist**, and in Ontario as a Separatist. In Quebec, I am attacked as an Imperialist, and in Ontario as an anti-Imperialist. I am neither. I am a Canadian. Canada has been the inspiration of my life. I have had before me as a pillar of fire by night and a pillar of cloud by day a policy of true Canadianism, of moderation, of **conciliation**. I have followed it consistently since 1896, and I now appeal with confidence to the whole Canadian people to uphold me in this policy of sound Canadianism, which makes for the greatness of our country and the Empire.*

From a campaign speech given in St. Jean, Quebec, by Sir Wilfrid Laurier during the 1911 election.

1. a) How could Laurier be perceived in such contradictory ways by English and French Canadians?

   b) How did Laurier define the characteristics of a true Canadian? Do you agree that this is a characteristic that distinguishes Canadians from other peoples?

◄▬ MAKING CONNECTIONS ▬►

1. a) Why would many western Canadians support reciprocity?

   b) What differences in economic development influenced attitudes towards reciprocity in eastern and western Canada?

2. Henri Bourassa, Laurier's chief opponent in Quebec, has been described as being both a Quebec patriot and a Canadian nationalist. Is such an identity possible in Canada today?

KEYWORDS

reciprocity

jingoist

conciliation

PUBLIC HEALTH
Crisis in Canadian Cities

*Canada's urban population experienced rapid growth in the early 1900s.
What factors led to urbanization and what health problems resulted from it?
What forces contributed to public health reform?*

Urbanization

At the beginning of the twentieth century Canadian cities were growing at an unprecedented rate. **Urbanization** was being experienced in all parts of the country. The census of 1901 revealed that one out of every four Canadians was living in a town or city with 5000 people or more. Between 1901 and 1911 the urban population of the country increased by 62 per cent. By 1911 four cities—Montreal, Toronto, Winnipeg, and Vancouver—had populations over 100 000. People were moving to the cities to find jobs in factories. Immigrants were arriving by the thousands. The **rate of natural increase** was soaring.

Pull-Push Factors

The lure of urban life lay in the per-

ceived opportunities for upward social and economic mobility. These **pull factors** encouraged rural residents to leave farms and villages for the cities to seek higher education or better working conditions and incomes. Others were drawn to the cities simply by the promise of adventure and excitement. At the same time, there were a variety of factors that forced many residents

from rural communities to urban ones. These **push factors** included the exhaustion of free land for **homesteading**, which drove up the cost of farmland. This affected both farm labourers and the younger sons of farm owners. Labourers could no longer earn enough money to establish farms of their own, or even to support themselves. Likewise, because of the tra-

Vancouver was Canada's fourth-largest city by 1911.

ditional pattern of inheritance by the eldest son, younger sons who might once have homesteaded elsewhere could not afford to start up their own farms. As a result, many young men went to the cities in search of work. The fact that daughters did not usually inherit meant that many young women also left farms for the city, seeking greater economic and social opportunities. Many of these young women trained as nurses or teachers and later returned to work in smaller urban centres close to their family farms. Others, however, stayed on in the larger cities where growing populations resulted in the construction of new hospitals and schools.

However, the growth of Canada's urban centres was fuelled largely by immigration. Though Canada's immigration policy focussed on the settlement of the vast western plains, most immigrants came from European cities. Their experiences and skills made Canada's new and growing cities natural places for them to settle. Immigrant families were drawn to communities where others who shared their cultural, linguistic, and religious background had already made their homes. There, they could find help starting a new life in Canada.

As urban areas grew, they experienced significant growing pains. For working-class people, living and working conditions were difficult. They generally lived in city centres where factories were located. Many lived in dimly

In the early 1900s children were not sheltered from the grim realities of city life. What effect do you think the experience shown in this picture would have on these children?

Mothers who did not breast-feed their infants fed them milk or formula, which, if not refrigerated or sterilized, could cause severe illness or death. Well-baby clinics distributed pure milk and prescribed feeding formulas, and taught mothers how to care for their infants.

lit, overcrowded housing with little or no sanitation. Serious health problems resulted from these conditions. There was inadequate and inequitable access to health care, and ignorance about the causes of disease.

Urban Social Problems

While all of urban Canada experienced social problems as a result of rapid growth, these problems were most evident in the larger centres. The greatest problem was poverty. The more people who moved to the cities, the greater the number of urban poor. People below the **poverty line** lived in the worst housing conditions, experienced **malnutrition**, and suffered from a host of illnesses. By 1920, almost half of all urban working-class Canadians lived in such poverty.

Housing for those living under the poverty line was overcrowded, with poor sanitation and no yards or open spaces. There was no such thing as government-subsidized housing, and local politicians were unwilling to raise taxes to provide running water, sewers, and electricity for poor inner-city neighbourhoods. Yet the demand for housing, created by a growing urban population, caused rents on even deplorable housing to increase. Unable to afford a place of their own, it was common for two, three, four, or even five families to crowd together in a small house of only a few rooms.

Poverty also affected education. In poor and working-class districts, children left school as early as grade 5 to find work to contribute to the family income. Children were frequently abused in the workplace as they endured long work hours

under harsh conditions. Demands for compulsory education were resisted by the poor out of economic necessity.

Inferior housing and inadequate nutrition in Canadian cities contributed to high overall death rates and high **infant mortality rates**. In Toronto, for example, 11 out of every 1000 infants under the age of one died of communicable diseases in 1911, while 44 of every 1000 died of severe **gastrointestinal** disease. In 1912, almost 20 per cent of new-born children in Winnipeg died before they were one year old. Why were so many babies dying? These deaths usually resulted from contaminated food and drink and an overall ignorance about health, sanitation, and nutrition. There was little refrigeration; milk, baby bottles, and nipples were not sterilized, and drinking water was impure.

CASE STUDY

THE INFLUENZA EPIDEMIC

The influenza **epidemic**, or "Spanish flu," of 1918–19 struck the world with a vengeance. Canada did not escape its terror. Soldiers returning from the war overseas carried the influenza virus with them. The virus entered the body of its victim through the respiratory tract, then spread to cause symptoms such as fever, chills, headache, sore throat, cough, gastrointestinal discomfort, and muscle pain. Weakened by the virus, influenza sufferers often contracted pneumonia, which, rather than the influenza itself, was the major cause of death in the days before sulpha drugs and penicillin. The death rate in Canadian cities was high, particularly among adults aged 20 to 40. Across the country, cities and towns responded to the epidemic by closing schools, theatres, and churches. In some communities there were even attempts to impose a total **quarantine**. In all, about 50 000 Canadians died of influenza.

Face masks were worn by the public during the influenza epidemic of 1918–1919.

Urban Public Health

Although poverty, overcrowded cities, and impure milk and water supplies were certainly factors in infant mortality, so too was inadequate medical care at birth. Dr. Helen MacMurchy, a Toronto physician who studied the causes of infant mortality, noted: *The Canadian city is still essentially uncivilized—it is neither properly paved nor drained, nor supplied with water fit to drink, nor equipped with any adequate public health organization.*

Public awareness of health problems gradually increased. In the 1880s and 1890s, there had been attempts to alleviate the misery of poor and working-class people in Canadian cities by private organizations, such as the Humane Society and the Children's Aid Society, and through reform legislation at the municipal and provincial levels of government. Reformers soon learned, however, that private services and social legislation were not enough to meet the needs of an increasingly complex urban population. It was essential that the federal government take action.

In the early years of the twentieth century statistics on live births were generally not available, especially on new-borns in poor families. The children were usually born at home and therefore their births were not registered. Public health departments instructed their visiting nurses and well-baby clinics to search out these infants. This situation, combined with the growing need for birth data brought on by the First World War, led provincial and federal governments to start collecting vital statistics on a national basis. Gradually, public health departments and private clinics began to tackle the problems of infant mortality and public health. They launched campaigns to clean up housing and streets, create clean water and milk supplies, and immunize people against infectious diseases such as smallpox and diphtheria. The result of these efforts was a gradual improvement in public health in Canada. As knowledge of the fundamental causes of illness, disease, and mortality increased, there was greater impetus to find solutions.

The Creation of the Department of Health

Under the constitution, jurisdiction over public health was divided among the three levels of government. The federal government controlled border quarantines, while the provinces were responsible for hospitals. The role of municipalities in public health varied from province to province, and even from city to city. But at every level of government, decisions were frequently made at the whim of the officials in charge. Thus public health policy was haphazard at best, and at times almost destructive.

As a result of the influenza epidemic and in the interests of rebuilding the Canadian population after the First World War, the federal Department of Health was established in 1919. The new department took charge of all the old federal health functions (quarantine, for example) and co-operated with the provinces and voluntary organizations in campaigns such as child welfare. Although the impact of the department was limited in the first years of its existence, it did signify that Canadians were increasingly interested in combating the health effects of urbanization.

KEYWORDS

urbanization

rate of natural increase

pull factor

push factor

homestead

poverty line

malnutrition

infant mortality rate

gastrointestinal

epidemic

quarantine

MAKING CONNECTIONS

1. In the early 1900s, how did public attitudes towards health care begin to change?

2. a) Using newspapers and magazines, identify problems and issues of urban life in Canada today. What are the similarities with those in the early 1900s? What are the differences?

   b) In your opinion, what is the most important issue in urban Canada today? Explain.

ROCK SLIDE
Endangering the Salmon Run

In 1913, a rock fall at Hell's Gate in the Fraser River Canyon provided dramatic proof of the impact of human activities on natural systems. How did the rock slide affect salmon runs on the river?

Hell's Gate

The workers who were building the Grand Trunk Railway line to the Pacific clung to ropes and wooden ladders as they set their dynamite charges. It was dangerous work. There was always the risk that they might be killed in a dynamite blast or by rocks falling from the cliffs above. Hundreds of metres below, they could see the raging waters of the Fraser River as it plunged through the narrow gorge known as

Hell's Gate. People and mules had plunged to their deaths in that appropriately named place.

From late July to October, the workers on the rock face high above the canyon could watch the sockeye salmon coming up river to **spawn**. The churning waters flashed red and silver in the sun. Millions of fish made their way up the Fraser and into its tributaries each year. There were so many fish that the workers joked that they could walk across the river on their backs.

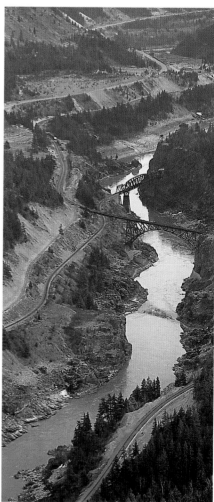

*The Fraser River Canyon was formed about 20 million years ago. The river has cut a deep canyon because **tectonic** forces uplifted the southern part of British Columbia's Interior Plateau, causing the river to flow more rapidly towards the sea. What problems might this landscape have posed to workers trying to build a railway through here in the first decades of the twentieth century?*

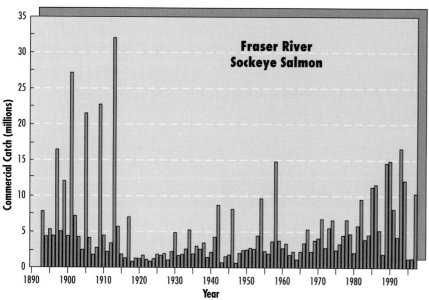

*Write a **hypothesis** for each of the following changes shown in the graph:*
a) the change in the number of sockeye salmon caught before and after 1913.
b) the change in the number of sockeye salmon caught before and after 1940.
Your hypotheses must offer an explanation for each of these changes. Record your hypotheses, then discuss how you might test them. Identify sources of information you might use to test your hypotheses.

In 1913, and again in 1914, blasting for the construction of the railway line caused serious rock falls at Hell's Gate. The giant boulders that plunged into the Fraser River blocked the route for the spawning sockeye salmon. Five years after these rock falls, the number of sockeye returning to spawn had dropped to less than one-third of their earlier levels. The rocks had disrupted a long-established natural system. This environmental mishap also had significant economic effects. Sockeye salmon caught on the Fraser were canned at Steveston, near the mouth of the river. The sharp drop in the number of salmon resulted in less money for the fishing crews and fewer jobs in the canneries.

The rocks were too huge for people or machines to move. For nearly 30 years, engineers and biologists considered what to do to restore the sockeye salmon run on the Fraser. In the early 1940s, a concrete fish "ladder" was built around the fallen rock. This artificial fish-way was completed in 1944. The numbers of salmon making their way up the Fraser to spawn gradually increased. But they never returned to the levels observed by the railway builders before 1914.

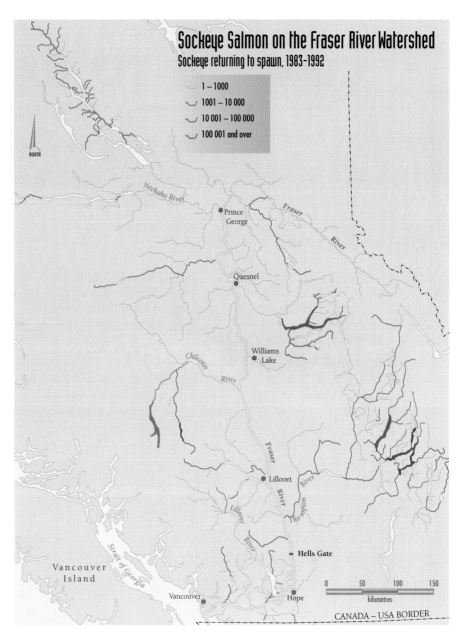

The Fraser River and its tributaries showing major sockeye salmon spawning areas.

MAKING CONNECTIONS

1. a) Refer to the map of the Fraser River. How far do spawning salmon travel along the river before they reach the nearest spawning grounds? the farthest spawning grounds?
   b) Locate Hell's Gate on the map. How far is it from the mouth of the Fraser River?

2. What problems might returning sockeye salmon have encountered in 1913 as they swam up the river from its mouth to Hell's Gate? How might those problems have changed since then?

KEYWORDS

spawn

hypothesis

tectonic

COMING TO CANADA
The *Komagata Maru* Affair
FOCUSSING ON THE ISSUE

Newcomers from South Asia began arriving in British Columbia in 1903. Why did government policy discriminate against them?

Battle in the Inlet

As the world prepared for war, conflict of another kind broke out in Vancouver. Racial tensions had been evident in the city for many years. (See page 24.) In 1914, the *Komagata Maru*, a tramp steamer crowded with 376 people, lay at anchor in Vancouver harbour. The passengers, mainly Sikhs from India, wanted to live in Canada. But city authorities would not allow them to land. Government policy at the time forbade immigration from India except under special circum-stances. The *Komagata Maru* arrived at Vancouver on 23 May 1914. It was immediately **quarantined** at anchor and no one was allowed to disembark. Immigration officials ruled that the passengers were inadmissible to Canada.

Meanwhile, there was a growing fear that Sikhs already living in Vancouver might try to smuggle some of the passengers ashore. Officials ordered the captain to depart, but the passengers would not let him. As food and water on the ship ran low, demonstrations broke out in the city. Tensions between white and South Asian residents neared the breaking point.

On 18 July, in the middle of the night, a tug carrying 160 armed police made its way out to the *Komagata Maru*. The plan was to take control of the ship and force it to leave. The resulting "Battle of Burrard Inlet" was a fiasco! As the tug approached, passengers showered it with coal, bricks, and scrap metal. After almost capsizing, the boarding party had to beat a hasty retreat back to shore. Finally the government called in the naval vessel HMCS *Rainbow*. The appearance of the navy convinced the people onboard the *Komagata Maru* that they had no hope of changing the government's mind. They agreed to leave, and on 23 July, the ship departed Vancouver.

But the affair was not over. Sikhs in Vancouver deeply resented the treatment of the people on the *Komagata Maru*. They responded by attacking police spies. Several people were shot, including an immigration official, William Hopkinson, who was murdered while attending a trial at the Vancouver courthouse. His killer, Mewa Singh, was executed for the crime.

From India to Canada

The first immigrants from India to settle in British Columbia came in 1904. Within a few years there

Passengers aboard the Komagata Maru *waited to be allowed permission to disembark at Vancouver. What does this photograph tell you about the passengers?*

were 5000, almost all Sikhs from the Punjab in northern India. Many were single men who hoped to earn a good wage in Canada, then return to their homes in India.

The newcomers were met with hostility by resident British Columbians who wanted to keep the province "white." The majority, who were British or American in background, were prejudiced against people with different skin colours, religions, and cultures. They did not believe that people from Asia could adapt to the Canadian way of life. Prejudice was worsened by the issue of jobs.

Immigrants found jobs working in lumber mills, clearing land, and building railways. Some employers were happy to hire Asians, who worked for lower wages. British Columbians accused "foreigners" of taking their jobs.

The BC government put pressure on the federal government to do something to reduce the flow of immigration from Asia. In 1908, the law of continuous passage was enacted, which required all immigrants from India to travel directly to Canada without stopping anywhere else. Since there was no direct travel connection between

the two countries, the law effectively stopped all immigration from India. This situation led to the *Komagata Maru* incident.

After the war, immigrant men already in Canada were allowed to send for their wives and children. Otherwise, the same restrictions were in force and the community remained small. South Asians in Canada did not receive the vote until 1947, and they were barred from many jobs and organizations. It was not until changes were made to the immigration laws in 1967 that the South Asian population began to increase in Canada.

CASE STUDY

WHO ARE THE SIKHS?

Sikhism is one of the world's major religions. It was founded in northern India hundreds of years ago. The Sikhs suffered persecution at the hands of their enemies, so one of their leaders, Guru Gobind Singh, organized a fighting force known as the *Khalsa*, or brotherhood.

Members of the Khalsa are extremely devout. They take a vow never to cut their hair or beards; long hair is associated with spiritual strength. Members tie their hair in a knot on top of the head and cover it—with a turban for men or with a scarf for women. The turban is worn in public at all times; it is a sign of deep disrespect to remove it. Another traditional custom is carrying a

ceremonial dagger, called a *kirpan*. All Khalsa men take the name Singh, meaning "lion." Women take the name Kaur, meaning "princess."

The centre of Sikh religious and community life is the temple, or *gurdwara*. Here Sikhs worship and socialize. The first *gurdwara* opened in Vancouver in 1908. Today there is a *gurdwara* wherever there is a community of Sikhs.

1. a) Do you think there was a connection between Sikh customs and the antagonism met by early immigrants?
   b) Do you know of any instances of prejudice against South Asian Canadians today?

MAKING CONNECTIONS

1. Research your family history. How long has your family been in Canada? What has been your family's experiences in Canada? Write a journal entry in which you reflect on these experiences.

2. Discuss whether or not an incident such as the *Komagata Maru* affair could happen today. Give reasons for your answer.

KEYWORDS

quarantine

CANADA ENLISTS
Reactions to the War

During the summer of 1914 the storm brewing in Europe erupted, plunging much of the world into war. How did Canadians greet the news?

In the early days, the prospect of war seemed exciting to many people. Which groups in Canada would have been most likely to support the war? Which groups might have been less enthusiastic, and why?

The Eve of War

The writer Charles Gordon, better known by his pen-name Ralph Connor, describes the summer of 1914, on the eve of war:

On the morning of June 29, 1914, a headline in the Winnipeg Free Press *announced the murder of Archduke Francis Ferdinand in Austria by a half-crazed Serbian pressman at Sarajevo in Bosnia. I glanced at the headline. I had never heard of Sarajevo....We were packing up for our annual trek to our island home. Next day headlines of varied interest were in the paper and we forgot Sarajevo.*

Four weeks later we were camping on our island in the Lake of the Woods, near the little town of Kenora. It was glorious weather. With our canoes and boats, with our swimming and tennis, with our campfires and singsongs our life was full of rest and happy peace. It was a good world....On Sunday morning, August 2, we motorboated in to church. A little group of men were standing on the wharf listening to one of their number reading from a morning paper, in which red headlines announced that Germany had declared war on Russia.

Germany, Russia, Austria, Serbia were at war....

On August 4, after several days of furious diplomatic activity...the British ambassador at Berlin informed Sir Edward Grey that he had received his passports. Half an hour later Britain declared war on Germany and the old world had passed away.

Ralph Connor, Postscript to Adventure *(Toronto: McClelland & Stewart, 1937; reprint, 1975), pp. 202–3.*

Reacting to the News

When the announcement of war came on 4 August, almost every Canadian was as shocked and surprised as Charles Gordon. But almost immediately, surprise was replaced by intense excitement. Historian Maggie Siggins described the scene in Moose Jaw, Saskatchewan:

Moose Jaw reacted to the news like every other prairie town—with ecstatic excitement. The band of the 60th Rifles gathered at the post office at about 10:30 the night the dispatch was received. Belting out "Rule Britannia," they started off down Main Street and were soon followed by a thousand cheering citizens, many of whom had gotten out of their beds to participate. The makeshift parade paused in front of the Maple Leaf Hotel. It was here that the young men were already lined up, hoping to enlist before the night was out. Members of the Legion of Frontiersmen, who were overseeing the **recruitment***, stepped out onto the*

hotel's balcony, waved grandly as though they were foreign princes, and were greeted with a joyous roar. Someone yelled "Boots to the Kaiser" and "Let 'em have it!" Then a French-speaking Canadian...began reciting the words of the "Entente Cordiale." Somebody carrying a Union Jack stood to attention beside him. The band struck up "The Marseillaise," and two beefy British immigrants lifted the astonished man onto their shoulders and proceeded on their way down Main Street.

From Maggie Siggins, Revenge of the Land *(Toronto: McClelland & Stewart, 1991), p. 281. Used by permission, McClelland & Stewart, Inc. The Canadian Publishers.*

A wave of **patriotism** swept across the country. Canadians believed that if Britain was in peril, it was their duty to come to its aid. In Dawson City, Yukon, the news arrived as an audience was settling in to enjoy a movie at the local theatre. Martha Black, the wife of the Yukon commissioner, described what happened:

As though answering an overwhelming urge, they stood in unison and commenced to sing "God Save the King." The effect was electrical. With one move, the audience was on its feet, and never in the world, I dare say, was our national anthem sung with greater fervour or more depth of feeling than in that moving picture house in that little town on the rim of the Arctic.

My Ninety Years *(Anchorage: Alaska Northwest Publishing Company, 1976), pp. 104-5.*

Even Henri Bourassa, the enemy of **imperialism**, agreed that Canada must fight. He wrote in his newspaper, *Le Devoir*:

Canada, an Anglo-French nation, tied to England and France by a thousand ethnic, social, intellectual and economic threads, has a vital interest in the maintenance of the prestige, power and world action of France and England. It is therefore its national duty to contribute...to the triumph and above all the endurance of the combined efforts of France and England.

From Le Devoir, *8 September 1914.*

Occasionally a voice was raised warning that the war might take a terrible toll:

The people are blinded, absolutely blinded, as to what war means. Those of the great majority think that it is brass bands, braid and feathers, and the throwing out of the chest, but if you have ever seen the regiments of militia on parade you will notice that the stretcher-bearer section is there.

From The Voice, *a Winnipeg labour paper.*

In the beginning, at least, views such as this one were in a minority. Divisions and controversy would appear soon enough, but for the time being almost everyone agreed with Prime Minister Borden:

The Canadian people will be united in a common resolve to put forth every effort and make every sacrifice necessary to ensure the integrity and maintain the honour of our Empire.

◄◘ MAKING CONNECTIONS ◘►

1. According to Borden, why was Canada going to war? Why did Bourassa also think that Canada had to join the fight?

2. According to the writer in *The Voice*, what was war going to mean?

KEYWORDS

recruitment

patriotism

imperialism

AT WAR IN EUROPE
The Western Front
FOCUSSING ON THE ISSUE

*Canada followed Great Britain into the First World War with enthusiasm.
What role did the Canadian armed forces play in the war?*

Over the Top by Alfred Bastien. Once they left their trenches, soldiers were exposed to enemy fire with nothing to protect them. This painting shows the 22nd French Canadian Battalion in action, August 1918. By the end of the battle, every one of the battalion's officers was dead or wounded. What do you think the phrase "over the top" means with reference to this painting?

The Western Front

When Britain declared war on Germany at midnight, 4 August 1914, Canadians responded with enthusiasm. It was taken for granted by most people that when Britain went to war, Canada followed. "Canada, a daughter of Old England, intends to stand by her in this great conflict," declared Wilfrid Laurier. "When the call to duty comes, our answer goes at once: 'Ready, aye, ready.'"

Thousands rushed to enlist in the army, fearing that the fighting would be over before they saw action. They need not have worried. The war slogged on for four long years. It demanded a greater sacrifice than Canadians had ever known. By the time it was over, 60 661 Canadians were dead and another 173 000 were wounded, some of them permanently disabled.

When the war began, there were only 3000 soldiers in the

Canadian army. Thousands more volunteers had to be trained quickly. In April 1915, at the second battle of Ypres in Belgium, Canadian troops went into battle for the first time. In this battle the enemy used poisonous chlorine gas. It drifted across the line in yellowish-green clouds, leaving soldiers blind and gasping for breath. Survivors had their skin and lungs scarred for life. The battle at Ypres lasted three weeks. In the end it settled nothing, and the war continued as it had before. But for Canadian soldiers, it was their initiation, and they proved themselves as effective a fighting force as any of the other armies.

The First World War was a war of **attrition**. The strategy was to wear down the enemy by repeated attacks until it ran out of soldiers, or until it lost the will to continue fighting. Each side settled into trenches on their own side of the front line. They bombarded each other with heavy shells, and occasionally came out of the trenches to fight over small patches of muddy ground. Day after day, year after year, the casualties mounted, but nothing changed.

Life in the Trenches

In their trenches, the soldiers lived as best they could while waiting for orders to attack. The trenches were about 2 m deep and filled with rainwater and rats. The men were constantly dirty, wet, and, in the winter, frozen. They slept in holes dug out of the side of the trench. During bombardments, shells exploded all around. Enemy snipers shot at anyone who accidentally lifted his head above the trench. Rotting corpses lay strewn about. Under these conditions of constant tension, noise, and lack of sleep, many soldiers became disoriented and irrational. This was known as shell-shock, and some of its victims never recovered.

The most famous battle for Canadian soldiers was at Vimy Ridge in April 1917. German soldiers occupied a key point of high land that had to be taken. British and French forces had failed to capture the ridge earlier in the war. Now it was the Canadians' turn to try. For a week, **artillery** bombarded the German positions. Then, early one morning the Canadians were sent in. Struggling across the buffer zone under heavy fire, they reached the German trenches, only to find them abandoned. The enemy had retreated. The attackers pressed on to overwhelm the second line of trenches. It was a complete victory, and a moment of great pride for all Canadians when they learned about it. But the cost was great: 3598 Canadian soldiers died in the battle.

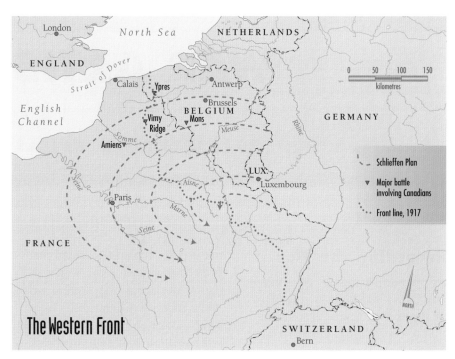

The Western Front

When the war began, German leaders based their military strategy on the Schlieffen Plan. This called for a swift victory using a concentrated assault from the north on Belgium and then France. But the Germans encountered Allied troops in northern France. The war then settled into a four-year stalemate as both sides dug trenches facing one another across an open buffer zone. This was the Western Front, where most of the major battles took place and where Canadians did most of their fighting.

Peace at Last

In the spring of 1918, the Germans made one final attempt to break through the Western Front, and almost succeeded. But the Allies fought back and began an advance of their own. In August, at the Battle of Amiens, the German army collapsed. Finally, on 11 November 1918, the shooting stopped.

The **armistice** was set to take effect at 11:00 a.m. Just before then, a Canadian battalion marched into a village near Mons, Belgium. "As we approached it, German machine-guns opened up and we got into a ditch," one of the soldiers later recalled. "I think it was Corporal Price who didn't get down..."

Corporal George Price was the last Canadian killed in action in the First World War. In total, more than 13 million people lost their lives in the war, more than the entire population of Canada at that time.

MAKING CONNECTIONS

1. It has been said that Canada "came of age" at the Battle of Vimy Ridge. Why?

2. Do you think that Remembrance Day should still be observed today? Discuss in a class forum.

KEYWORDS

attrition

artillery

armistice

WAR ARTISTS
The War Memorials Fund
FOCUSSING ON THE ISSUE

*During the First World War, many painters were enlisted to make a visual record
of the fighting overseas and the activities on the home front.
What did artists contribute to the war effort?*

Recording the War

As the war progressed, government leaders wanted to make a permanent record of Canada's contribution to the fighting. It occurred to Max Aitken, Lord Beaverbrook, a Canadian who was a member of the British government, that the best way of doing so was to hire a group of artists to paint scenes of the war. The result was the Canadian War Memorials Fund.

The fund began its work partway through the war. Before it was over, more than 100 artists from Britain, Canada, and Belgium had taken part. The artists visited the front lines to sketch the scenes of battle. Sometimes they had to work while enemy **artillery** shells rained down on them. "I work in cold and wind and rain, eat anything, and sleep on any bed without grumbling," one of them wrote. "I do believe I can do this work decently and that it is work which cries to be done."

The First World War, with its senseless slaughter and endless fighting from muddy trenches, destroyed any notions that war was romantic and heroic. The artists had to find new ways of painting what they saw. "What to paint was a problem for the war artist," explained A. Y. Jackson, one of the Canadians. "There was nothing to serve as a guide. War had gone underground, and there was little to see. The old heroics, the death and glory stuff, were gone forever."

On the Home Front

Some of the painters remained in Canada, where they recorded war activity on the home front. Arthur Lismer, for example, painted naval scenes in Halifax harbour. Other

BIOGRAPHY: LORD BEAVERBROOK, INDUSTRIALIST AND ART PATRON

The man behind the Canadian War Memorials Fund was Max Aitken, better known as Lord Beaverbrook. Aitken (1879–1964) grew up in Newcastle, New Brunswick. By the time he was 28 years old he had built a huge fortune in business. He moved to England, where he became owner of an important newspaper and a Member of Parliament. When war broke out, he saw himself as the voice of Canada in Britain. He wrote a book about the fighting, and created the War Memorials Fund. It was during the war that he was made a lord, tak-

ing the name Beaverbrook after a stream near his New Brunswick home.

After the war, Beaverbrook remained in England, where his newspaper chain gave him a great deal of influence. He was a friend of British prime minister Winston Churchill, and during the Second World War he played a key role as a member of Churchill's Cabinet. Beaverbrook never returned to live in Canada, but he lavished many gifts on his home country, including the Beaverbrook Art Gallery in Fredericton, New Brunswick.

artists did paintings of workers in shipyards and munitions factories, and of fighter pilots in training.

By war's end, the art collection numbered about 850 pieces. It went on exhibit for the first time in London, not long after the **armistice** that ended the war. It was exhibited in Toronto a few months later. The collection is a permanent reminder of the contribution Canadians made to the war effort. The Canadian War Museum in Ottawa now houses these historic pieces.

The work of the War Memorials Fund had an important impact on Canadian art. Canadians took pride in the fact that their artists were considered the equals of painters from Europe. Many went on to make names for themselves and became the leading painters of their generation.

CASE STUDY

ART AS PROPAGANDA

The most controversial work in the War Memorials collection was a bronze sculpture by the British artist Derwent Wood. Titled *Canada's Golgotha*, it depicts the corpse of a Canadian soldier nailed to a barn door as if being **crucified**. A group of enemy soldiers are mocking the body. In the Christian faith, Golgotha is the place where Jesus Christ was crucified.

Wood based his gruesome sculpture on an incident that was supposed to have actually happened. According to rumour, the body of a Canadian soldier was strung up during the second battle of Ypres in April 1915. But later, when authorities investigated, they could find no one who actually saw the incident. After the war, the Germans protested that it was untrue. The Canadian government did not want to embarrass a country with which it was no longer at war, so it stopped exhibiting the sculpture in public.

Canada's Golgotha is an example of the **propaganda** that was used by both sides during the war. Propaganda exaggerates (or invents) the evil deeds of the enemy in order to rally popular support for the war and to convince people to volunteer for the army.

1. What is the role of propaganda in war? Why is *Canada's Golgotha* considered propaganda?

2. Why is the sculptor comparing the Canadian soldier to Jesus Christ?

3. Is all war art propaganda? Stage a debate on this question.

◄▄▄ MAKING CONNECTIONS ▄▄▶

1. Compared to other media, such as newspaper reports, how would paintings have presented a different perspective on Canada's role in the First World War?

KEYWORDS

artillery

armistice

crucify

propaganda

CANADA AT WAR

The Home Front

The First World War brought significant changes to the home front. What involvement did Canadian women have in the war effort? What impact did the War Measures Act have on Canadian society?

Women in the War

Canadian women made an invaluable contribution to the war effort. While some women served overseas as nurses and ambulance drivers, most women helped out on the home front. Canadian women worked tirelessly to support the soldiers. Members of the Red Cross volunteered to knit socks, roll bandages, and wrap food parcels for the troops. Women staged variety shows and used the profits to buy candy, soap, writing paper, and other supplies to send overseas.

In these voluntary efforts women's traditional roles were largely maintained. In the economic sphere, however, women's participation expanded like never before. The shortage of men made it necessary for women to work outside the home. Often they took jobs that were traditionally considered "men's work." Not only did women work in banks, insurance firms, and the civil service, they also became gas jockeys, streetcar conductors, and fish cannery workers. Yet while they performed the same jobs as men, women were usually paid less.

When Prime Minister Robert Borden ordered compulsory military service in May 1917, women were called upon to run farms, build aircraft and ships, and work in **munitions** factories. In fact, women were largely responsible for sustaining the country's agricultural and industrial needs. As a result, by 1918 Canada was no longer the debtor nation it had been since Confederation. The economy was booming, and women could claim much of the credit. By the end of the war, they had earned the right to vote and were beginning to play a more prominent role in Canadian society.

The War Measures Act

Early in the twentieth century, the Canadian constitution had established limits on political power and divided power between the federal and provincial governments. War, however, changed all the rules. How could the Canadian government preserve democracy while at the same time respond to the emergencies of war? This was the overriding question Parliament asked itself in August 1914. Its response was quick: a War Measures Act.

In order to preserve "the security, defence, peace, order, and welfare of Canada," the War Measures Act empowered the federal Cabinet

Women worked in a lumber mill in Edmonton in 1918 as part of their contribution to the war effort.

to act swiftly and resolutely in an emergency. Instead of submitting its proposals to Parliament for approval, as it normally would do during peacetime, the federal Cabinet made decisions without parliamentary debate. In effect, this meant the suspension of democracy in Canada.

The War Measures Act had a significant impact on Canadian society. Before 1914, Canada had a **laissez-faire economy**. Once war began, however, it became increasingly important to regulate commerce. Trading with the enemy was prohibited. Industrial efforts were focussed on fuelling the war effort. With the growing demand for food, the government used its powers to establish a Board of Grain Supervisors, which tightly controlled wheat marketing. In order to conserve energy supplies, the Cabinet also appointed fuel controllers to promote "heatless days." During these days, people were encouraged to restrict their use of coal and to substitute it with hydroelectricity. To raise revenues, the Cabinet used its authority to introduce emergency financial measures: a war tax on business profits and an income tax. (Although these taxes were to be in effect only as long as the war lasted, one of them lingers to this day!)

Civil liberties were also affected by the War Measures Act. In 1914, over 500 000 people in Canada were classified as **enemy aliens**. While the government promised people of German and Austro-Hungarian heritage that they could keep their property and businesses, it became increasingly difficult for them to find jobs. Ultimately, they were encouraged to leave the country or face **internment**. Those who were interned were treated as **prisoners of war**. Other civil liberties restricted under the War Measures Act included the right to strike and the freedom of expression.

When the war ended, the powers of the emergency government were quickly dissolved. While the legislation served its purpose, the **paradox** is that in preserving democracy it limited the freedoms of all Canadians.

According to this poster, what were the penalties for hoarding food? How does this poster show the combination of voluntary and compulsory measures used under the War Measures Act to respond to emergencies during the First World War?

KEYWORDS

munitions

laissez-faire economy

civil liberties

enemy alien

internment

prisoner of war

paradox

MAKING CONNECTIONS

1. Imagine you are a young Canadian woman during the First World War. Compare the status you have as a Canadian woman in 1918 with the status you had at the outbreak of war. What changes might affect you once the war is over and the soldiers return?

2. Write a Viewpoints box in which you summarize the arguments for and against the War Measures Act.

THE WAR HITS HOME
The Halifax Explosion
FOCUSSING ON THE ISSUE

*While no battles were fought on Canadian soil, Canada sustained one war-related disaster.
In December 1917, two ships collided in Halifax harbour, resulting in the death
and injury of thousands. What risks does a war effort pose for civilian populations?
How does a community respond to a massive disaster?*

Halifax, 1917

As a major ice-free port, Halifax, Nova Scotia, played a major role in supplying the Allied war effort in Europe. It was from this port that most North American **convoys** carrying troops, food, and war materials began their dangerous journeys across the North Atlantic.

Thursday, 6 December 1917, was a crisp, clear morning. By sunrise, Halifax harbour was already bustling as a convoy was being formed. A French munitions ship,

the *Mont Blanc*, sat waiting to join the convoy. A Belgian relief ship, the *Imo*, was heading out of Halifax harbour. It had been scheduled to sail on 5 December, but a coal shortage had delayed its departure.

At 7:30 a.m., the *Mont Blanc* slowly made its way into the inner harbour. To the onlookers on shore, it was a small, barely seaworthy, tramp steamer, one of many pressed into wartime service. Only those on board knew that the *Mont Blanc* was loaded to the limit with 6400 t of explosives and ammunition.

Around 8:00 a.m. the *Imo* set out from the harbour. Already a day late, it was moving quickly through the harbour traffic when a slower tramp steamer forced it off course.

The *Mont Blanc*, not flying the red flag that would have warned other vessels it was carrying explosives, signalled the *Imo* to change course. But the *Imo* replied that it was going to continue moving into the channel where the *Mont Blanc* was travelling. This put the two vessels on a collision course. The *Imo*'s bow swung sharply to the right, causing it to hit the *Mont Blanc* and leaving a 3 m hole where the explosives were stored. The impact of metal on metal caused sparks to fly, igniting a fire. Almost 3000 t of explosives were set off. Black smoke and flames shot skywards from the munitions ship. The crew of the *Mont Blanc* quickly lowered lifeboats and escaped the burning vessel. The *Mont Blanc*, pushed by the impact of the collision, drifted out of control towards Halifax.

From Historical Atlas of Canada, Vol. III: Addressing the Twentieth Century, 1891-1961, Donald Kerr and Deryck Holdsworth, eds., Geoffrey J. Matthews, maps (Toronto: University of Toronto Press, 1990). Reprinted by permission of University of Toronto Press Inc.

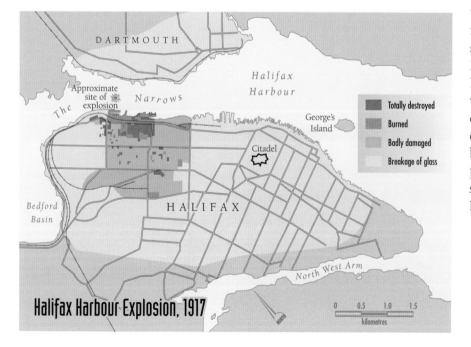

Halifax Harbour Explosion, 1917

■	Totally destroyed
■	Burned
■	Badly damaged
■	Breakage of glass

Few people on shore were aware of the danger. As the burning ship approached the docks, a shop-owner telephoned the fire department. It came quickly, unaware of the *Mont Blanc*'s deadly cargo. So did crowds of curious Haligonians. On the hillsides, thousands more pressed their faces to the windows to watch the spectacular events. One man on shore—the dispatcher at the railway station— was advised of the danger by a sailor. He sent a telegraph to an approaching passenger train, ordering it to stop. His message read, "Munition ship on fire, heading for Pier 6. Goodbye." It was just after 9:00 a.m. At 9:05, the *Mont Blanc* disintegrated in a blinding white flash.

The explosion could be felt 350 km away and was heard all over the province. It killed 1900 people immediately. Thousands more were blinded or injured. A gigantic wave created by the blast swept through the harbour, adding to the destruction. The death toll eventually swelled to over 2000. The exact number of deaths was never known.

The blast was one of the worst disasters in Canadian history. It was the most powerful artificial explosion the world had yet known. All that was ever found of the *Mont Blanc* were a cannon and part of an anchor that landed over 3 km away.

Rescue and relief efforts began immediately. Money poured into

The aftermath of the Halifax explosion was made worse by harsh winter conditions.

Halifax from around the world. The Canadian government provided $18 million towards the reconstruction of the city; Britain donated another $5 million. In total, nearly $35 million in relief money reached Halifax to help rebuild the shattered city.

MAKING CONNECTIONS

1. In what ways would the massive military presence in Halifax be a risk to the civilian population in 1917? In what ways would their presence have been beneficial after the explosion?

2. Draw up a relief plan for your community in case of a major disaster, such as an explosion or hurricane.

KEYWORDS

convoy

A COUNTRY DIVIDED
The Conscription Crisis
FOCUSSING ON THE ISSUE

*When the Canadian army began to run short of men in 1916,
the government turned to conscription to find the necessary replacements.
Why did the conscription issue cause such deep divisions in Canada?*

The Recruitment Crisis

By late 1916, the Canadian Expeditionary Force had participated in several bloody battles, and **casualty** rates were high. Most Canadian families had a relative or friend who had been killed or wounded. Since Canadian newspapers regularly printed the casualty lists, there were few Canadians who did not know of the losses. Although wounded soldiers were frequently returned to the front lines after treatment, those who were badly hurt were sent home.

The sight of these injured men deeply disturbed Canadians. The returning veterans also brought tales about the reality of war—the horrors of the trenches, the gas attacks, and the shortages of ammunition and supplies. Thus many young Canadians lost their enthusiasm and began to reconsider their ideas about the nobility of war.

Early in the war, Sam Hughes, the minister of militia, had convinced the Borden government that Canada should become a major producer of war materials. Many of the very profitable contracts for these materials went to Hughes's

friends. While most Canadians could accept that contractors should make a profit, many Canadians believed that if men were risking their lives in the war, businesses should forgo their profits. These Canadians were outraged by what they called **profiteering** on war supplies, and demanded that the government put a stop to it. When word reached Canada that Hughes and his friends were supplying rifles that jammed under heavy use, ammunition that did not fire, boots and uniforms that fell apart in the mud, and horses that were diseased and unfit, there was a public outcry. Many Canadians wondered why they should risk their lives so that Hughes and his cronies could get rich.

In Quebec, the government was having serious difficulty with its recruitment campaign. Hughes had refused to allow French Canadians to form their own units with French-speaking officers. In fact, he had publicly stated that the highest-ranking French-Canadian military officer was not fit to command troops in the field. In addition, both the Manitoba and Ontario governments had recently banned the use of French as a language of instruction in schools, even where the students were French-speaking. As a result, there was much anger in Quebec and few volunteers.

Gradually, stories about the horrors of the war began to spread throughout the country. By 1917, volunteers were not coming forward. Why not?

The 1917 Election

By late 1916, the shortage of volunteers led the Borden government to propose the introduction of **conscription**. Conservatives and Liberals who supported conscription formed a Union government. For the election, only one Union candidate was nominated in each riding. Those who opposed the Union candidates were accused of a traitorous betrayal of the men at the front.

Before the election, the government passed the Military Voters Act, which denied the vote to **conscientious objectors** and allowed all men and women in the armed forces, regardless of age or citizenship, to cast their votes in any riding they chose. This act was followed by the Wartime Elections Act, which gave the vote to the widows, wives, mothers, and adult daughters and sisters of Canadian men serving overseas. When the votes were counted, these two laws gave the Union government an overwhelming victory in every province except Prince Edward Island, where the vote was evenly divided, and Quebec, where all but three of the province's 65 seats went to the Liberals.

Conscription

The Military Service Act of 1917 granted exemptions from military service to those who were already engaged in important war work or who could provide a good reason

Slander!

That man is a slanderer who says that
The Farmers of Ontario
will vote with
Bourassa,   Pro-Germans,
Suppressors of Free Speech and Slackers

Never!

They Will Support Union Government

Citizens' Union Committee

What is the message in this election poster for the Union Party?

for not reporting. The act was not administered uniformly across Canada, which meant that some boards granted no exemptions while others gave exemptions to nearly everyone who asked. Those who lived in certain areas or who had the right connections were able to avoid military service. Many other men did not answer the summons when it came because they had already left their homes to work in the mines and forests. Since labour was scarce in these industries, the identities of the workers were not checked. Although nearly 100 000 Canadians were conscripted, no conscripts actually reached the battlefield before the war ended.

◄═ MAKING CONNECTIONS ═►

1. Why did the government pass the Military Voters Act and the Wartime Elections Act?

2. What was the purpose of allowing the votes of military personnel to be counted in any riding in Canada?

KEYWORDS

casualty

profiteering

conscription

conscientious objector

THE SUFFRAGE MOVEMENT
Women Get the Vote
FOCUSSING ON THE ISSUE

At the beginning of the twentieth century, women in many countries, including Canada, had begun to organize themselves to gain the right to vote. What were the accomplishments of the women's suffrage movement in Canada? Who were the key players in this impressive drama?

Too Delicate to Vote?

The struggle to achieve the female franchise in Canada was fought on different grounds than the **feminist movement** that would emerge many decades later. In the late-nineteenth and early-twentieth centuries, Canadian women fought for the vote while staying within their traditional roles as society's nurturers. Despite the fact that they had no legal or political status, women were seen, and indeed saw themselves, as the morally superior sex. There were powerful incentives for women, and some male supporters, to fight for **suffrage**. They believed that the right to vote would increase the effect of women's moral purity on society. In addition, it would correct injustice, bring about social change, and end women's political powerlessness.

The suffrage movement in Canada began in the 1870s with the emergence of several women's organizations. The movement was largely influenced by suffrage movements in Britain and the United States. The organizations included the Young Women's Christian Association (YWCA), the Women's Christian Temperance Union (WCTU), and the National Council of Women (NCW). These organizations recognized a distressing paradox for Canadian women: because they did not have the vote, they could not change their legal status; and until their legal status changed, they could not affect legislation.

By the turn of the century, the social issues created by rapid population growth and industrialization were beginning to take their toll on Canadian society. Consequently, the need for social reform to overcome the effects of poverty, prejudice, disease, and crime often took precedence over the desire for equal rights for women. At this time, the suffrage movement took on the character it would assume until its ultimate victory. It was a predominantly urban, upper- and middle-class struggle led by well-educated British- and Canadian-born Protestants who could afford to volunteer their time and energy to the causes of social reform.

Canadian women were granted voting rights in stages and not without significant opposition. Initially, women earned the right to vote for school trustees. This was followed by the municipal franchise, and finally the provincial and federal franchises. Along the way **suffragists** encountered resistance and criticism. Women were too delicate to vote, it was said; politics would take women away from their duties at home. Men were generally reluctant to welcome women into the traditionally male bastion of politics.

Suffrage at Last

The First World War emphasized the need to overcome political resistance to female suffrage in Canada. It also provided the conditions under which women finally obtained the vote. Women eagerly supported the war effort, which for some provided a more compelling argument for female suffrage than the democratic right of women to vote. In an increasingly industrialized society in which women's relationship to the home was changing, women needed to be able to influence the decisions of government. Women who were homemakers required the vote in order to regulate the sanitary conditions under which they and their families lived. Women who worked outside the home needed the vote in order to regulate their working conditions.

Gradually, the provinces began to concede to the persuasive arguments of the suffragists. From 1912 to 1916, the struggle for the vote raged across the western provinces, led by such prominent women as Nellie McClung and Emily Murphy.

In 1916, Manitoba gave women the right to vote in provincial elections, followed in turn by Saskatchewan, Alberta, British Columbia, and Ontario. By 1918, all Canadian women had obtained the right to vote in federal elections.

While suffragists in Canada sought equal rights for all women, their main purpose was to reform society. The suffrage movement in Canada differed from the movements in other countries in that it was generally peaceful. Canadian suffragists used a combination of humour, reason, and quiet persistence in their struggle to obtain the vote. Ultimately, the vote was won by the efforts of some of Canada's most intriguing and tenacious women.

BIOGRAPHY: EMILY MURPHY

Born in 1868 in Ontario, Emily Murphy became one of the most important suffragists and social reformers in Canada. In 1903, she moved west with her husband and daughters, where she wrote book reviews and magazine and newspaper articles. Murphy also published four books under the pen-name Janey Canuck. She became involved in many reform activities for women and children. As a result of public pressure organized by Murphy, the Alberta government passed the Dower Act in 1911, giving women rights to one-third of their husband's property. In 1916 in Edmonton, Murphy became the first woman magistrate in the British Empire. Soon after, she began a long and ultimately successful campaign to have women declared legal "persons," making them eligible for appointed positions, including the Senate. (See page 106.) Unfortunately, Murphy herself never achieved Senate appointment. She died in Edmonton in 1933.

MAKING CONNECTIONS

1. Nellie McClung, Emily Murphy, and many other Canadian suffragists were both teachers and writers. Why do you suppose these occupations were so common among women of their time?

2. In the Canadian suffrage movement, women were considered the morally superior sex, yet they sought equality with men. Explain this contradiction, and suggest why it did not bother the suffragists. Do contradictions still exist in Canada today? Explain.

KEYWORDS

feminist movement

suffrage/suffragist

CANADIANS IN RUSSIA
The Bolshevik Revolution
FOCUSSING ON THE ISSUE

During the First World War, Russia was an ally of Canada, Britain, and France until 1917. Then, a new government took power in Russia and withdrew from the war. Why were Canadian soldiers sent to Russia in 1918–1919?

Political Unrest

During the First World War, Russia went through a cataclysmic upheaval. The war devastated the country. Hundreds of thousands of soldiers were killed and injured in battles with Germany. Millions of civilians were left homeless and starving. More people died in Russia during the war than in any other country. Made desperate by the suffering, Russians turned on their political leaders.

The Russian government was a corrupt **dictatorship**, headed by the **tsar** and his family. But it was an important partner of the Allies during the war. By keeping the Germans occupied on their eastern flank, the Russian army prevented the Germans from massing all their forces to overwhelm the Allies in western Europe.

Finally, the misery caused by the war became too much for the Russian people to bear. Early in

The Russian Civil War

▼ Area where Canadian troops were sent

Territory controlled by Bolsheviks ("Red" army), Aug 1918

Advance of "White" forces

Advance of Western powers

Soviet territory, 1921

1917, a group of reformers seized control of the government, forcing Tsar Nicholas II from his throne in what became known as the February Revolution. The new government, led by Alexander Kerensky, introduced many reforms, but it made the fatal decision to continue the war. When the slaughter of Russian soldiers persisted, there was a second uprising known as the October Revolution. This time a group of **radical socialists**, the **Bolsheviks**, took power. Their leader, Vladimir Lenin, promised the people "peace, land, and bread" and made a separate treaty with Germany, withdrawing Russia from the war.

Intervention

The Bolsheviks hoped to bring peace to Russia so that they could carry out their plans for full-scale political and economic change. It was not to be. Their opponents rallied together, formed an army of their own, and attempted to overthrow the new government. The result was a civil war that lasted four years, pitting the so-called "White" army against the Bolshevik "Red" army.

While these events convulsed Russia, the First World War continued. The Allied powers felt betrayed by Russia's withdrawal from the conflict. They hoped that the White army would win the civil war and bring Russia back into the war against Germany. More than that, the Allies hated the Bolshevik regime and its radical socialist policies. The Bolsheviks were calling for revolution by working people all over the world. Allied governments, including Canada, feared the influence of Bolshevik ideas in their own countries, where many labour leaders spoke out in support of the "Red" regime in Russia, as well as the disappearance of the monarchy.

In mid-1918, with the world war still raging, the Allies sent a force of soldiers, including a handful of Canadians, to Murmansk in northern Russia. Supposedly, the objective of these troops was simply to take possession of supplies the Allies had been stockpiling there before Russia pulled out of the war. However, the troops remained in northern Russia long after the war with Germany ended in November 1918. It appeared as though the Allies were there to support the White army.

At the other end of Russia, in Vladivostock, another force of Canadian soldiers arrived on a similar mission: to protect supplies that had been sent when Russia was an ally. Once again this force stayed on after the war ended, although it did not engage in any serious fighting.

In Canada, public opinion turned against the **intervention** in Russia. There seemed to be no pressing reason for Canadian soldiers to be there. The war was over. Most Canadians felt that Canada had no business in Russia's internal conflict. Labour leaders accused the government of waging war against the Bolshevik regime. In the end, Prime Minister Robert Borden gave in to public pressure and brought the Canadian soldiers home.

Canada intervened in Russia in 1918–1919 in response to a request from Britain. The intervention began as part of the strategy of the war. It continued because some Allied leaders wanted to help the White army overthrow the Bolsheviks. In itself, it was a minor incident, but it had important long-term consequences. The Bolsheviks viewed the intervention as a conspiracy by the Allies to drive them from power. When the Bolsheviks won the civil war and secured control of the Russian government, they never forgot this interference. It played an important role in creating the tensions that existed between Russia and the West for most of the century.

MAKING CONNECTIONS

1. Look at the map showing Canadian troops in Russia in 1918. Why do you think Canadian troops went where they did?
2. a) What was the official reason for Canadian involvement in Russia? What did many people suspect was the real reason?
   b) What was the long-term impact of the intervention by Western nations in Russia?

KEYWORDS

dictatorship

tsar

radical

socialists

Bolsheviks

intervention

SKILL BUILDER
Recognizing Bias
FOCUSSING ON THE ISSUE

People have always attempted to leave records of the events of their lives. The job of the researcher is to produce an organized and factual account of these lives. What skills or techniques do researchers use to get as accurate a picture as possible of history?

Sources of Information

The sources historians use fall into three basic categories. Physical sources include geographic features: monuments and buildings, artwork, tools and utensils, and other **artifacts**. **Primary sources** consist of eyewitness accounts or commentaries by people who were present when events occurred. The third category—**secondary sources**—includes contemporary accounts by people who were not present and accounts based on primary sources. The simplest way to evaluate a source is to look at other sources to determine if they contain similar information. While there may not be complete agreement, if a number of sources can be found documenting the same event, we can be reasonably sure the event occurred. By carefully examining the information, we can sort out fact from fabrication.

The invention of the printing press led to a significant increase in the number of primary and secondary sources available to historians. The invention of photography, and later, sound recording, film, and video, produced an even greater quantity of material for researchers. Unfortunately, as technology improved, **forgeries** became

harder to detect. Therefore, it has become increasingly important to carefully analyse sources when doing historical research.

Assessing Accuracy

The first issue in source analysis is determining whether or not the statements or images are true. Depending on the type of source, the information can be examined and identified under several headings:

a) *Facts* are dates, times, locations, and people that can be proven by referring to other sources. Remember that "facts" may not be true; subsequent investigation may prove them false.
b) *Guesses* or *estimates* are sometimes mistaken for facts, but like facts they can be evaluated by referring to other sources.
c) *Opinions* are statements that are offered without supporting evidence, or statements that are **value judgements** made by the author.
d) *Inferences* are logical conclusions that have been drawn from the available information. It is possible, however, to draw logical conclusions from false statements.

e) *"Can't tell" statements* could be fact or opinion but require more information, which may or may not be available.

Assessing Credibility

The second issue in source analysis is evaluating the **credibility** of the author of the source. Frequently, the perceived involvement, expertise, occupation, personal interest, or status of an individual will add to or subtract from that person's credibility. An author's biases and point of view will affect her/his description and interpretation of events. Bias occurs when the author chooses to include certain details or words and to leave out others. Bias does not necessarily make a source inaccurate but it does affect our perception of the information. An author's point of view depends on her/his position on an issue. For example, we are less likely to believe a tobacco company executive who says smoking does not cause cancer than a cancer researcher who says it does. Because we all bring a wealth of knowledge, experiences, preconceptions, and beliefs to any situation, we all have a point of view and are biased to some degree.

Assessing Language

Evaluating the language that an author uses is the third issue in source analysis. Most words have a denotation, or simple dictionary definition, and a connotation, or implied meaning. The connotation of a word often arouses strong feelings in the reader. For example, most people recognize the difference between the terms *political leader* and *dictator,* or *crowd* and *mob*. This kind of terminology—dictator or mob—is called loaded language. Sometimes the language used by authors is simply a reflection of the passion and zeal they bring to the topic. At other times the language is deliberately chosen to appeal to emotions rather than to reasoned thought. When analysing source language you should always question why the author chose certain words or images instead of others.

VIEWPOINTS

A CREDIBLE SOURCE?

Read the following two reports of the same incident.

On Saturday, about 2:30 p.m., just the time when the parade was scheduled to start, some fifty mounted men swinging baseball bats rode down Main Street. Half were red-coated Royal North-West Mounted Police, the others wore khaki.... The crowd opened, let them through and closed behind them. They turned and charged through the crowd again, greeted by hisses and boos, and some stones....

Then, with revolvers drawn, they galloped down Main Street, and charged into the crowd on William Avenue, firing as they charged. One man, standing on the sidewalk, thought the Mounties were firing blank cartridges until a spectator standing beside him dropped with a bullet through his breast. Another, standing nearby, was shot through the head....

The Western Labour News in J.H. Stewart Reid, Kenneth W. McNaught, Harry S. Crow, A Source Book of Canadian History *rev. edn.* (Toronto: Longman, 1964), p. 401.

'The first shots were fired by the paraders, or those associated with them, and the Mounted Police fired only in self-defence. The information that we have is that the police acted with great coolness, great courage, and great patience, as is characteristic of the men of the Royal North-West Mounted Police....

The Hon. N.W. Rowell to the House of Commons (Canada, House of Commons Debates, 1919, p. 3843 et seq.)

1. Evaluate the accuracy of the sources. Identify each sentence as fact, guess, opinion, inference, or "can't tell" statements. Where a sentence contains a combination, for example, part fact, part opinion, divide the sentence and label the parts.
2. Identify examples of loaded language in each report. What effect does this language have on the reader?

MAKING CONNECTIONS

1. Make a list of some of the details you might want to know about the author(s) of a secondary source. Explain why each of these details could be important to the reader.

KEYWORDS

artifacts

primary source

secondary source

forgery

value judgement

credibility

LABOUR UNREST
The Winnipeg General Strike
FOCUSSING ON THE ISSUE

The most infamous labour conflict in Canadian history took place in Winnipeg in the spring of 1919. What factors led to the Winnipeg General Strike?

Background Causes

Events in history rarely happen for one reason alone. There are usually several explanations for why and how certain events happen. Some explanations may be traced back to factors that first developed years before the event occurred. A case in point is the labour unrest that convulsed Winnipeg in May and June of 1919.

During the First World War, the cost of living in Canada rose steadily. This rise in living expenses was not matched by increased wages. As a result, many Canadians actually grew poorer during the war years. In addition, the end of the war created a serious unemployment problem. War industries geared down, while a flood of returning soldiers entered the job market.

Many workers responded to the difficult economic situation by going on strike to try to obtain better wages and working conditions. In 1918 and 1919, a wave of labour unrest swept across Canada. Workers believed that the war had been fought to create a better world, one in which they might expect to gain a greater share of the country's wealth and more control over their own lives. **Radical** ideas about social change, influenced by the revolutionary events in Russia, appealed to a growing number of working people.

Employers and the government reacted to this discontent with alarm. They suspected that behind it all was the desire to spark a Canadian revolution. They saw what had happened in Russia in 1917, when a small group of dedicated activists had overthrown a centuries-old regime. Many people feared that the same situation might occur in Canada.

If widespread labour unrest was going to boil over into a **general strike**, it was no surprise that it happened in Winnipeg. The city was growing dramatically. As the eco-

*Mass demonstrations took place at Winnipeg's City Hall during the general strike. Judging by the banners, which side of the strike was this demonstration supporting? One banner refers to "the undesirable alien." Who were these "aliens?" Another says "Down with Bolshevism." What was **Bolshevism** and how did it relate to the strike?*

nomic centre of the Prairies, it attracted a large influx of new immigrants. Newcomers congregated in the city's North End. It was a poor but vibrant neighbourhood where people of many backgrounds came together, sharing ideas and building up a determination to make changes for the better.

But Winnipeg was a divided city. Wealthier people tended to live across the Assiniboine River in the south where the homes were large and comfortable and the streets were wide and lined with trees. These people also shared common ideas about the kind of society they wanted. They saw themselves as the defenders of British-Canadian values of justice and fairness against the demands of radical "foreigners" who imported dangerous ideas and spread them like a virus through the labour movement. Given the sharp divisions in Winnipeg—geographic, social, and political—the stage was set for a confrontation.

Immediate Causes

On 1 May 1919, workers in the building trades in Winnipeg went on strike. The various unions in the construction industry wanted a pay raise, and they wanted to negotiate together as a group. Employers refused. Two days later metal workers also walked off the job. Once again the unions wanted recognition of industry-wide bargaining. Once again the employers refused.

In support of the striking workers, the Winnipeg Trades and Labour Council (TLC), which represented members of many different unions, held a vote on a general strike. The outcome of the vote was an overwhelming "yes." At 11:00 a.m. on 15 May, about 30 000 people walked off their jobs. Canada's first general strike was on.

The strike paralysed the city. Streetcars stopped running; the telephone system shut down; mail and milk went undelivered; most businesses closed their doors. Early in June the entire police force was dismissed because members were sympathetic to the strike. They were replaced by a force of volunteers. As the strike progressed, authorities became convinced that this was the revolution they had been fearing. They decided to take steps to end the strike. Troops moved into the city. Before dawn on 17 June, eight strike leaders were arrested in their homes and charged with conspiracy to overthrow the government. Then, on 21 June—"Bloody Saturday"—a force of North-West Mounted Police attacked a pro-strike demonstration. One man was killed by police gunfire; many others were injured.

Five days later the strike ended. The provincial government agreed to hold a **Royal Commission** to investigate labour conditions. In return, strikers agreed to go back to work.

Outcome of the Strike

Just as events have immediate and background causes, they also have immediate- and long-term results. In the short term, the Winnipeg General Strike seemed to be a defeat for the strikers. Many of the arrested leaders were jailed for up to two years. Some strikers lost their jobs; others failed to make important gains in the workplace.

The long-term results of the strike were more positive. The strike drew attention to the social and economic conditions that working people had to endure. The Royal Commission concluded that the strike was caused by low wages, inferior working conditions, and the high cost of living. Several labour leaders went on to have successful political careers during which they voiced the concerns of working people. J.S. Woodsworth, who was arrested and later acquitted of conspiracy, became a respected Member of Parliament. Most historians agree that the strike was not an attempt at revolution but an attempt to gain better working conditions, just as most strikers claimed at the time. In the long term, workers may have "won" the strike after all.

ᐃᐧᐃ MAKING CONNECTIONS ᐃᐧᐃ

1. What is a revolution? Did the Winnipeg General Strike share any of the characteristics of a revolution?

2. Identify several factors that contributed to the general strike, and list them under two headings: Background Factors and Immediate Factors.

KEYWORDS

radical

general strike

Bolshevism

Royal Commission

CULTURAL ASSIMILATION
Residential Schools
FOCUSSING ON THE ISSUE

One of the ways government provided education for Aboriginal peoples was through a system of residential schools. What was the purpose of these schools, and what was their long-term impact on those who attended them?

Creating the System

Residential schools were boarding schools for Aboriginal children, funded by the federal government and operated by the churches. The first ones opened in Ontario in the 1840s. The federal government extended them across the country beginning in the 1880s. By 1910, there were 74 residential schools, most of them in western Canada.

Residential schools removed Aboriginal children from their families and placed them in a setting where everything they did was supervised and regulated by the missionary teachers. The residential school was a total system, designed not just to teach the ABCs but to transform individual character. The

Thomas Moore was an Aboriginal child who attended a residential school in Regina. He is shown here before he entered the school (left) and after he had been in attendance for a while (right). "Before-and-after" photographs like these were commonly used to illustrate the supposed benefits of the residential school experience. How do these photographs summarize the purpose of the residential school system?

government and the churches wanted students to abandon their ties to their Aboriginal culture and to become "civilized." To this end, youngsters learned table manners, deportment, personal grooming, and punctuality, along with the usual school subjects.

In most schools, all evidence of Aboriginal culture was suppressed. Students were forbidden to speak their own languages; often they were beaten for doing so. Uniforms and short haircuts replaced traditional dress. Students celebrated Christian holidays, such as Christmas and Easter, and learned to play sports such as cricket and soccer. Any contact with their families was discouraged.

Until 1920, attendance at the schools was voluntary, though government agents and missionaries applied pressure on Aboriginal families to send their children to the schools. By 1920, when it became clear that many Aboriginal parents were hostile to the schools, attendance was made compulsory for children aged 7 to 15 years.

Who Wanted the Schools?

The residential school system involved three interest groups, each with its own expectations for the schools. The federal government hoped they would promote economic self-sufficiency for Aboriginal peoples and **assimilate** them into mainstream society. Government officials believed that Aboriginal peoples had to abandon their **nomadic** hunting lifestyle and become farmers. The purpose of the residential schools was to force this change on the younger generation. The missionaries who taught at the schools wanted Aboriginal children to abandon their own spiritual practices and convert to Christianity. Aboriginal peoples themselves wanted their children to receive an education so they would be able to participate in the new economy. They knew that a new world was emerging. They wanted to be a part of it, but they did not see why this meant they had to abandon their Aboriginal culture.

Some residential schools had difficulty living up to these expectations. Many children died of fatal illnesses, or caught lingering diseases such as tuberculosis, which destroyed their health. One official admitted in 1914 that "fifty per cent of the children who passed through these schools did not live to benefit from the education they had received therein." Others were harshly disciplined and abused, both physically and psychologically. Ill-treated and lonely, children did not learn. Aboriginal parents began to withdraw their children from the schools and refused to participate in the system. For its part, the government did not want to spend the money needed to make the schools successful, so they remained underfunded and poorly run.

It was not until the 1960s that the government began to phase out the schools. They were either closed or turned over to Aboriginal bands to operate themselves. In the 1980s, horrible stories began to emerge about abuse at some of the schools. In 1992, a report by the Royal Commission on Aboriginal Peoples blamed residential schools for contributing to the high rates of substance abuse, suicide, and family problems among Aboriginal peoples. Police investigations led to charges being laid against some former teachers.

Several church organizations have formally apologized for the part they played in the residential school system. In January 1998, the federal government issued an apology to Aboriginal peoples and expressed regret over residential schools. They offered compensation of $350 million for victims of the schools, to be used for community projects. While some Aboriginal groups welcomed the apology, others felt it was too little, too late. As more is learned about the long-term effects of the schools on the lives of the people who attended them, it is clear that the legacy of the residential school system remains an unsolved dilemma for both the government and for Aboriginal peoples themselves.

MAKING CONNECTIONS

1. In what ways did the residential schools attempt to assimilate Aboriginal students? Explain how effective you think they were in accomplishing this goal.

2. Do some research to find out whether there was a residential school in or near your community. Find out the details of its history. Ask one or two Aboriginal people who attended the school to visit your class and share their experiences.

KEYWORDS

assimilate

nomadic

PEACE AND SECURITY
Versailles and the League of Nations

The armistice of 11 November 1918 stopped the fighting but did not end the war. What were the major issues facing the victorious Allied powers in 1919? What effect would the exclusion of Russia and Germany from the League of Nations have on the search for collective security? How did isolationism affect the League's success?

The Paris Conference

"A real and lasting peace." There were few people who did not share this sentiment when the war came to an end on 11 November 1918. Canada's prime minister, Robert Borden, carried with him similar hopes as he sailed for France in January 1919, bound for the Paris Peace Conference. Borden insisted that Canada have a seat, indepen-dent of Britain, as recognition that the country had taken its rightful place as a nation among the world's powers. It would be Borden, not

the British prime minister David Lloyd George, who would represent Canada at the Palace of Versailles.

It was obvious from the start, however, that three nations would dominate the negotiations. The United States, Britain, and France—each with a different agenda—would have the greatest influence. Belgium and Italy would also each have a voice, but the other 25 Allied nations would mainly act as observers. Russia did not attend the conference because the victorious Allies refused to recognize the **Bolshevik** government that had

seized power in 1917. While the Germans were there, they had no voice in the peace process. They would have to accept the terms imposed upon them by the victors.

The Treaty

On paper, the United States, France, and Britain appeared to get what they wanted. US president Woodrow Wilson had called for efforts "to make the world safe for democracy." The League of Nations was created to resolve international disputes through discussion, not war. Britain achieved its goal of see-ing Germany's navy and overseas empire dismantled. France and Belgium managed to impose the War Guilt Clause on Germany and to obtain massive **reparations** for war damages. In reality, however, the Treaty of Versailles was seriously flawed. It was a complex mixture of self-interest and idealism that served only to create an atmosphere of seething hostility throughout Europe.

The League of Nations

The League of Nations was founded on Wilson's belief that the war had been, in large part, the result of secret treaties and alliances that caused countries around the world to plot against one another. The

Borden had argued at the Imperial War Conference in 1917 that Canada and the other dominions should be recognized as "autonomous nations of an Imperial Commonwealth."

League of Nations was based on the idea of **collective security**. All members would be required to come to the aid of any other member that was under attack. But collective security depended on the participation of all powers. The three Great Powers—the United States, Germany, and Russia—were not members of the League. The US withdrew from the world stage when the Senate refused to ratify the Treaty of Versailles. The Americans now embarked on a policy of **isolationism**. Germany had been excluded from the League as punishment for its **war guilt.** Russia, with its new communist government, had not been invited to join the League. With three of the most important players on the world stage watching from the sidelines, it seemed that the League of Nations was doomed to fail.

While Canada was a member of the League, this did not mean that it was committed to all that the League stood for. Indeed, Canada's attitude was motivated by two contradictory objectives. One was the determination to assert its independence from Britain. Canada demanded a separate seat in the League's general assembly as a symbol of its **autonomy**. On the other hand, the government opposed the

▓	Territory lost by Austria-Hungary
▓	Territory lost by Bulgaria
▓	Territory lost by Germany
▓	Territory lost by Russia

Europe After the First World War

idea of collective security. Like the American isolationists, Canada did not want to be drawn into distant conflicts that could eventually lure the world back into war. This opposition to collective security played an important role in stifling the

work of the League of Nations. As one supporter of the League put it: "Of all the members of the League, Canada was the first to have robbed it of any teeth that it had."

MAKING CONNECTIONS

1. Germany and Russia were both excluded from the peace process and the League of Nations. What possible issues or problems do you think might have arisen from their isolation?

2. a) Define the concept of collective security. Explain why the absence of the United States, Germany, and Russia ultimately meant the League was doomed to fail.
   b) How would you evaluate the Canadian attitude to the League? Was Canada right to fear collective security?

KEYWORDS

Bolshevik

reparations

collective security

isolationism

war guilt

autonomy

UNIT 3:

Prudence Heward, *Rollande* (1929)

Prudence Heward (1896-1947) was a member of the Montreal artists known as the Beaver Hall Hill Group, a group known at the time for the substantial number of women artists it included. Heward painted both landscapes and figures, often combining the two genres to make a statement about the subject and her or his environment.

FROM BOOM TO BUST

1921-1930

	Social	Cultural	Political	Legal	Economic	Environmental
THE ROARING TWENTIES The World in 1921 82	✔	✔			✔	
SKILL BUILDER Cause-and-Effect Relationships. .84			✔			✔
MASS MEDIA Maintaining a Canadian Identity..... 86		✔	✔			
THE GROUP OF SEVEN New Expressions in Art 88		✔				✔
COMING OF AGE Canada Gains Independence 92			✔			
KING VERSUS BYNG The Role of the Governor General .. 94			✔			
GOVERNMENT IN CANADA The Canadian Constitution 96			✔	✔		
SOCIAL PROGRAMS The Canada Pension Plan 98	✔		✔		✔	
TAKING TO THE ROAD Canadians and the Automobile 100	✔				✔	✔
INTO THE BUSH Aviation in Canada 102					✔	✔
STOCK MARKET MANIA The Crash of 1929 104	✔				✔	
WOMEN AND POLITICS The Persons Case 106	✔		✔	✔		
THE ALLIED TRIBES Aboriginal Activism 108		✔	✔	✔		
THE NATIONAL PROGRESSIVES Creating a Multiparty System........ 110	✔		✔			
TOTALITARIANISM Setting the Stage for War 112	✔		✔		✔	

*Skills and Processes

THE ROARING TWENTIES
The World in 1921

The 1920s marked an era of prosperity and carefreeness, especially in North America. How did changes in technology affect the production and consumption of goods and services in the 1920s? How did the emergence of mass media affect popular culture around the world?

Recovery

The 1920s were a time of economic recovery in much of the industrialized world. Following a brief depression in 1919, Canada, the United States, and much of Europe went on a shopping spree. Part of this burst of economic activity was the result of pent-up demand. War had sharply curtailed spending by both consumers and producers as much of the Western world's industrial base had been devoted to wartime production from 1914 to 1918. By 1920, these factories were once again turning out capital and consumer goods for peacetime consumption. Now, however, technological changes and new means of organizing production meant that a greater number and variety of goods could be produced.

The world had entered a new era of **mass production**. Just prior to the outbreak of the First World War, American industrialist Henry Ford had pioneered the use of the **assembly line** to create the Model T. It was the first automobile produced in large enough numbers and at low enough cost to be affordable by others besides the wealthy elite. Less than a decade later, assembly lines could be found in factories around the world, turning out an ever-increasing range of goods.

At the same time, extensive advertising through the **mass media** and a greater availability of credit created consumer demand for these products. In the 1920s, household appliances, radios, automobiles, cameras, and many other products were advertised on billboards, in newspapers and glossy magazines, on movie screens, and in radio broadcasts. Often, these new products could be bought on credit for a small down payment, with the balance to be paid in monthly installments. **Mass consumption** of goods and services was now commonplace throughout the industrialized world and was increasingly characteristic of city dwellers in much of the rest of the world.

The Pace Quickens

The pace of life in the postwar world quickened greatly. By the 1920s, electric streetcars, subways, and **interurban** railways moved large numbers of commuters to and from their workplaces quickly and cheaply. Automobiles, trucks, and buses had replaced horse-drawn carriages and wagons in most of the world's great cities. Airplanes now carried mail and passengers. Messages could be beamed around the world in seconds by radio. Many of these messages, and the materialist cultural values they con-

tained, originated in the United States.

The Great War had left many scars—some physical, others less obvious—on the countries involved. One consequence of the war and its horrendous number of casualties was a loss of faith, by many people, in traditional institutions and values. Most families in Europe and the British Empire had lost sons, husbands, fathers, or uncles. In communities around the world, war memorials honoured the fallen and reminded the living of the horrors of global war. Mass media brought images of the war's brutality and suffering to the United States and other areas relatively unaffected by its violence. Many, particularly young adults, turned their attention to their material well-being, to personal pleasures, and to entertainment, all in an effort to dim the tragic memories of war.

Nowhere was this more true than in the United States. Americans now turned their energies to material ends, producing and consuming goods in record numbers. They worked hard and partied just as vigorously. The introduction of **prohibition** in 1920 created a flourishing subculture of illegal bars and nightclubs. Many women were now asserting their independence, not only in the workforce, but by smoking in public, wearing trousers or

Speakeasies (nightclubs where alcohol was illegally sold) vibrated to the sounds of African-American jazz bands like this one in Harlem, New York.

skirts that came to their knees, and cutting their hair short. Racial and cultural barriers were challenged, particularly in musical tastes. The sounds and images of the "roaring twenties" were widely distributed through phonograph records and motion pictures. Around the globe, American popular culture quickly became the standard for mass entertainment.

Canada and the US

By 1921, Britain's influence on Canada was declining rapidly.

While Canada grew more politically independent, the United States quickly became the major influence on its economic and cultural life. In the early 1920s, Americans were replacing the British as the dominant foreign investors in Canada. British investors had mainly granted loans to help Canadian firms establish railways or manufacturing plants. American investors, many made rich by the war, now invested directly in Canada's resource sector. They bought existing Canadian companies or launched their own

operations in mining and smelting, pulp and paper mills, and the new petroleum industry. By the mid-1920s, it was evident that Canadians were becoming increasingly integrated into a common economy with their American neighbours.

KEYWORDS

mass production

assembly line

mass media

mass consumption

interurban

prohibition

MAKING CONNECTIONS

1. Explain why advertising and the availability of credit were so important in a period of high mass production.

2. To what extent would the events in the United States have influenced Canadian attitudes towards the roaring twenties? Explain.

SKILL BUILDER
Cause-and-Effect Relationships
FOCUSSING ON THE ISSUE

One of the unique and distinguishing characteristics of human beings is our ability to reason. We use this ability to try to find out why things happen. What problems may arise when we use our reasoning skills to identify cause-and-effect relationships?

Causal Relationships

Most events have a **cause** and an **effect**. The cause is what makes an incident happen. The effect is the consequence of the incident. In examining events, we need to apply our reasoning skills to understand the relationships between cause and effect.

Some kinds of cause-and-effect reasoning are simple and straightforward. For example, if you take your shoes off, hold this book high above your head, then drop it on your bare foot, you will feel pain in your foot! If there is clearly no other cause, it is reasonable to conclude that dropping the book on your foot caused the pain.

There are many situations, however, in which cause and effect are not so clear. For example, you and a friend get caught in a winter rainstorm and get soaking wet. Two days later, you both develop colds. You think of the common event of getting caught in the rain and conclude that getting soaked caused you both to catch colds. But in this case you have overlooked an important fact: colds are caused by germs, not by getting wet in the rain. So what other cause could there be for you both catching colds? You both spent time with another friend who was carrying cold germs, so perhaps contact with

this person is the cause of your illness. It could also be that there is no connection whatsoever between you and your friend getting sick at the same time. It could simply be **coincidence**.

Direct and Indirect Causes

Many events are the result of several factors. These may be a combination of direct and indirect causes. For example, we may want to explain why a tornado happened, or why a war started, or why unemployment is so high. The first step in determining cause-and-effect relationships is to organize the relevant information into chronological sequence. This enables us to see how one event can lead to another. For example, we have identified the following facts about the First World War and its aftermath:

- In the aftermath of the war, many people experienced disillusionment and a loss of faith.
- When it ended, the First World War was the most destructive war in history.
- Many people focussed on the pursuit of personal pleasures in order to put memories of the war behind them.
- Over 60 600 Canadians lost their lives in the war.

But we would understand the cause-and-effect relationship more clearly if we organized this information sequentially:

- When it ended, the First World War was the most destructive war in history.
- Over 60 600 Canadians lost their lives in the war.
- In the aftermath of the war, many people experienced disillusionment and a loss of faith.
- Many people focussed on the pursuit of personal pleasures in order to put memories of the war behind them.

Faulty Reasoning

When we try to find out why things happen, we sometimes fall victim to one or more of a series of common reasoning **fallacies**. One of these is the fallacy of assumed causal relationship. For example, suppose you change the oil in the family car and then discover that the car won't start. You automatically assume that you must have done something wrong while changing the oil. A more careful inspection of the car reveals that the real cause is that the car's battery is low and there is not enough power to start the car.

A second fallacy is created by our unconscious preconceptions. We all bring preconceived ideas to many things we do. If new informa-

Many people attribute unusually wet winters in British Columbia and elsewhere to El Niño.

MAKING CONNECTIONS

1. A man jogs around the park near his home every day for three years. One day he changes his route and jogs around a nearby cemetery. Halfway around the cemetery he has a heart attack and dies.
   a) Describe any cause-and-effect relationship that seems to be present.
   b) Identify any reasoning fallacies.
   c) Describe what you would need to do to provide an accurate interpretation of this event.

2. For several years, the winters on Canada's Pacific coast were unusually wet. Wet winters are often preceded by an unusual warming of the equatorial current called **El Niño**. This information has led many people to conclude that El Niño caused all of the wet winters.
   a) Describe this cause-and-effect reasoning.
   b) Research the connections between ocean currents and wind belts. Is there any agreement on which causes which? What kind of research would be necessary to determine the relationship between El Niño and the wet winters?

tion we receive conflicts with these ideas or with our beliefs about what is true, we can fall into the trap of rejecting evidence without carefully examining it. For example, your friend is caught cheating on an exam at school. You believe your friend is honest and would never cheat. Despite compelling evidence to indicate that your friend cheated, you reject the idea based on your long-held beliefs about your friend.

A third fallacy has a fancy Latin name, which suggests it has been around for a long time! It is known as *post hoc ergo propter hoc*. This means "it happened after this (*post hoc*), therefore (*ergo*) it happened because of this (*propter hoc*)." A simple example is the idea that a rooster wakes up in the dark, crows loudly, and then the sun comes up. The suggestion is that the rooster's crowing causes the sun to rise. If this were true, it would be a very dark world if the rooster ever over-slept! Similarly, we must be careful not to apply such an erroneous cause-and-effect relationship to more important events. For example, some people might argue that the assassination of an Austrian prince was the only cause of the First World War. However, a closer examination of prewar events would reveal a great many factors that could be considered as causes of the war. It is important to remember that many events, whether social, historical, political, or geographic, rarely have a single and independent cause.

KEYWORDS

cause

effect

coincidence

fallacy

El Niño

MASS MEDIA
Maintaining a Canadian Identity
FOCUSSING ON THE ISSUE

As far back as the 1920s, some Canadians feared that American movies and radio were threatening their culture. How do mass media and mass culture shape our identities? What measures were taken to protect Canadian identity and culture? Were they successful?

The Canadian Identity

As Canadians, we often identify ourselves not so much by who we are as by who we are not. We are not American. We are not a **melting pot**. We do not live on an icecap. At the same time, we often seem tentative about defining who we really are. What are our values and ideas? What influences have shaped the way we think, the way we behave, and the way we communicate? These questions are relevant at the turn of the twenty-first century. They were equally relevant in the 1920s in Canada.

By the 1920s, Canada was becoming a modern, urban nation with a large, trained workforce and increasingly sophisticated technology. The Great War had given the country new maturity by raising the issues of national unity and national identity. At the same time, the United States had achieved world-power status, and American economic and cultural influences were increasingly being felt in Canada. Movies and radio had fundamentally changed **mass communication** and the lives of Canadians. Before the 1920s, urban daily newspapers and magazines were the only forms of **mass media**. They served the information needs of the country, but they did not have the same mass appeal that movies and radio

had. As many English-Canadian **nationalists** struggled to develop a sense of Canadian identity, they began to question who should own and control the mass media and whether Canada should allow mass media to be dominated by foreign influences.

Canadian Radio

Radio technology had existed since the late nineteenth century. When the First World War ended, electrical companies with surplus equipment decided radio could be used to transmit information and entertainment to large numbers of individuals simultaneously. In 1920, an

experimental station in Montreal, operated by the Marconi Company, aired the first radio broadcast in Canada. By 1923, there were over 30 broadcasting stations across Canada; this figure had doubled to 60 by 1930. In the early 1920s, few households had a radio. Ten years later, over 30 per cent of all Canadians owned a radio.

From the beginning, Canadians listened to American stations and were influenced by American tastes, trends, and stars. Nevertheless, radio broadcasting in Canada was different from other mass media in that government regulated it. When American radio broadcasting organized into two powerful networks

The parlour cars of the CNR were equipped with radios for the entertainment of the passengers.

(NBC and CBS) in 1927, Canadians became acutely aware of the threat this posed to private radio stations and to Canadian culture itself. To guard against Americanization, a Royal Commission on Radio Broadcasting (the Aird Commission) was established in 1928. In its 1929 report, the commission recommended that Canadian broadcasting be completely taken over by the government and that a Canadian Radio Broadcasting Commission be established. Three years later it was, and Canadian independence over its radio airwaves was established.

The Motion Picture Industry

The development of the Canadian motion picture industry was a dramatically different story. By 1920, there were 830 privately owned cinemas across Canada. Before the 1920s, movie-going had been a form of entertainment for poorer and less literate Canadians because it was cheap and available. When movies became more sophisticated and the Hollywood stars gained influence in the 1920s, however, the middle and upper classes began attending. When the era of silent movies ended and "talkies" were introduced in 1927, everyone became a movie-goer.

Despite the popularity of movies, the growth of the Canadian movie industry was slow. Between 1914 and 1922, a number of Canadian movies were made, including *Back to God's Country* and *The Man from Glengarry*. By 1923, however, Hollywood was already the centre of the world's movie industry, and the movie business was dominated by a few large companies that controlled everything, from production to distribution to exhibition. Independent movie producers in Canada could not compete with this kind of domination. While other countries, including Britain and Australia, took steps to protect their motion picture industries from American dominance, the Canadian government did not. No **quota** systems were established to help promote Canadian movies, and no tax incentives were offered

Canadian-born actress Mary Pickford, with film star Douglas Fairbanks, wears the style so popular in the 1920s: a slouch hat covering page-boy "bob" and a flapper dress. What influences does Hollywood have today in affecting fashion, dance, and social behaviour?

to private movie companies. Many talented Canadian film-makers, writers, and actors disappeared into the American marketplace.

MAKING CONNECTIONS

1. a) Compare and contrast the role of government in regulating the movie industry and radio broadcasting in Canada in the 1920s.
    b) Find out how government regulates and supports the Canadian film industry today.

2. In the 1920s, American ideas and values were considered "aggressively material" by some Canadians. Do Canadians on the whole still regard them this way? Discuss this in a class debate.

KEYWORDS

melting pot

mass communication

mass media

nationalist

quota

THE GROUP OF SEVEN
New Expressions in Art
FOCUSSING ON THE ISSUE

The Group of Seven, one critic said, was Canada's national school of painters.
How do artists contribute to national identity?

A "Big Idea"

During the 1920s, the most controversial artists in Canada were a group of painters in Toronto who called themselves the Group of Seven. The Seven were friends who shared a desire to paint the Canadian landscape. They travelled together into the north woods of Ontario to gather material for their art. They held joint exhibitions of their paintings, exhibitions that turned the art world on its head.

The Group did not paint tidy pictures of farms and gardens. Their paintings show a rugged landscape of gnarled trees, barren rock, and stormy lakes, painted with bright colours and rough edges. This was what made the Group different, and it was not to everyone's taste. "It's bad enough to have to live in this country without having pictures of it in your home," a woman complained to A.Y. Jackson, a member of the Group.

Members of the Group of Seven were trying to express what they found beautiful and significant in the Canadian landscape. They believed that the land expressed the unique character of the people who lived on it. "We believe wholeheartedly in the land," they wrote in the

Six members of the Group gather for lunch at the Arts and Letters Club, a hangout for artists and writers in Toronto, ca. 1920. They are (l. to r.) Fred Varley, A.Y. Jackson, Lawren Harris, Barker Fairley (an artist but not a member of the Group), Frank Johnston, Arthur Lismer, and J.E.H. MacDonald. The missing member is Frank Carmichael. What advantage did members of the Group of Seven see in joining together as a group? What were they trying to achieve?

catalogue for one of their shows. This was their "big idea," as they called it.

At first the Group painted mainly scenes from northern Ontario and Quebec. Later they spread out to paint the Rockies, Atlantic Canada, the Arctic, and the West Coast. Looking at their paintings, one critic wrote: "A definite school of Canadian landscape has emerged, as individual and as Canadian as the North-West Mounted Police or an amateur hockey team."

The Group of Seven stopped exhibiting together in 1931, but their influence was profound. They are probably the most famous painters in Canadian history. They did more to make Canadians aware of their native landscape than any other artists.

Terre Sauvage *by A.Y. Jackson. The work of Alexander Young Jackson (1869-1952) focussed on the Quebec landscape later in his career.*

VIEWPOINTS

THE CRITICS DEBATE

Exhibitions of paintings by the Group of Seven during the 1920s sparked heated debates between admirers of their work and critics who hated it. Many people believed that the Group had found a new, Canadian way to paint the landscape.

No one will deny, if he be fair-minded, that the artists have at least attempted to depict something new in a new manner, and that they have managed to work into their canvases a feeling of largeness, of optimism, of new horizons, that makes the old art seem quiet and tame.

Toronto Mail & Empire, *1922*

But other critics found the Group's paintings ugly and primitive. One called the Group "the hot mush school."

If the walls of the exhibition are to be covered with crude cartoons of the Canadian Wilds, devoid of perspective, atmospheric feeling and sense of texture, it is going to be a bad advertisement for this country.

Saturday Night, *1923*

1. "There never was a great country that did not have a great art," remarked one critic. What do you think he meant? Explain with reference to the work of the Group of Seven.

2. Over the years, paintings by the Group have appeared in many books, as posters, and on T-shirts and coffee mugs. They have became so familiar that critic Robert Fulford has called them "our national wallpaper." What do you think this phrase means? Is it positive or negative? Explain.

3. The Group of Seven painted the northern landscape because for them it was uniquely Canadian. If you were a painter, what subjects would you choose that are uniquely Canadian? Create a poster illustrating your idea.

A September Gale: Georgian Bay by Arthur Lismer. Lismer (1885-1969) actively promoted the **nationalism** *and* **modernism** *of the Group.*

BIOGRAPHY: EMILY CARR

As a young woman in Victoria, Emily Carr (1871-1945) struggled to make her way as an artist. She chose as her subject the villages and art of the first Aboriginal peoples who inhabited the West Coast. In search of material, she made many visits to their isolated communities.

But Carr gained little support for her work. In 1913, she was forced to give up painting altogether to earn a living as a boarding-house keeper. Then, in 1927, a visitor from the National Gallery in Ottawa saw Carr's paintings and asked to show some of them in an important exhibition. Carr travelled to Ontario where she met Lawren Harris and other members of the Group of Seven. With their encouragement, she began painting again. For the rest of her life she sought to express on canvas her deep feelings about the landscape of the West Coast rainforest. She is now recognized as one of Canada's greatest painters.

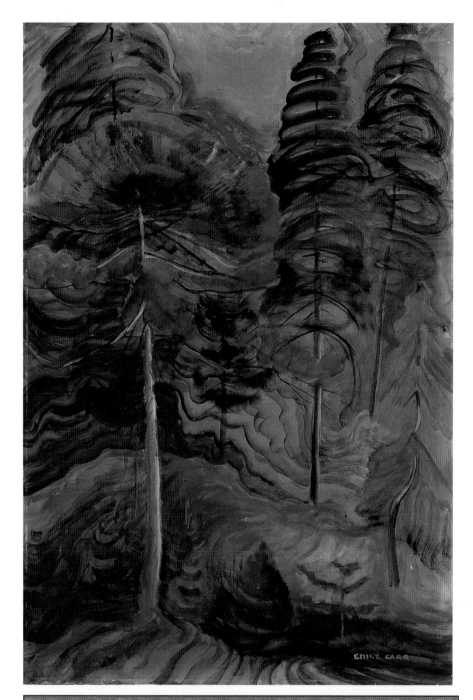

Forest Landscape II, *by Emily Carr. Carr (1871-1945) grew up in Victoria, where she rebelled against the expectations of traditional female roles.*

◄█► MAKING CONNECTIONS █►

1. In the painting titled *Forest Landscape II*, Emily Carr was expressing what she called a "British Columbia way of seeing." Do you agree that there is such a thing? How would you describe it? The paintings by Lismer and Jackson show Ontario scenes. Do they depict an "Ontario way of seeing"? Is there such a thing as a "Canadian way of seeing?" If so, how would you describe it?

KEYWORDS

nationalism

modernism

COMING OF AGE
Canada Gains Independence
FOCUSSING ON THE ISSUE

*After the First World War, Canada was ready to exchange its colonial status
for full independence. How did Canada emerge as a truly independent nation?*

A Turning Point

The First World War was a turning point for Canada's development as an independent nation. Canadians went into the war as a dependent colony of Britain with little foreign policy of their own. After the war, they expected that the great contribution they had made to the Allied victory had earned them a new role in world affairs. Prime Minister Robert Borden asked for, and received, his own place at the 1919 Paris peace talks to settle the war. When American president Woodrow Wilson complained, Canadian delegates pointed out that Canada had paid a far higher price in terms of lives lost during the war than had the United States.

The Paris conference was the first milestone on the road to a fully independent foreign policy for Canada. There were two impulses pushing the country towards independence. On the one hand, Canadians were feeling a new sense of national maturity. On the other hand, they did not want to get entangled in conflicts that might result in another tragedy on the scale of the First World War. When that war began, Canadians were automatically a part of it. If they were free to make their own decisions, then perhaps they could avoid foreign wars in the future. In a word, the mood in Canada during the 1920s was **isolationist**.

The Chanak Crisis

The Chanak Crisis of 1922 was exactly the kind of situation the newly elected Liberal government of William Lyon Mackenzie King wanted to avoid. The crisis involved a garrison of British troops stationed in a town in Turkey. A Turkish faction wanted the troops withdrawn, and threatened to attack the garrison. As usual, Britain called on its colonies—Canada among them—to show solidarity by sending soldiers. Times had changed, however. It was no longer the heyday of Empire. King was in no mood to comply, and he guessed that most Canadians agreed. He told the British that only the Canadian Parliament could decide to send troops, and then he employed the politics of delay by putting off calling Parliament together. The crisis in Turkey quickly passed before a decision had to be made. The importance of Chanak was that it demonstrated Canada's desire to make its own foreign policy rather than be dragged along on Britain's coattails.

Soon after Chanak, in March 1923, Canada signed a treaty with the United States regulating the halibut fishery on the Pacific Northwest coast. In the past, Britain had signed all foreign treaties involving one of its dominions. The Halibut Treaty was the first time Canada signed an international agreement on its own. This set a precedent that was later followed by all the other British dominions.

Vincent Massey (closest to soldiers) was Canada's first foreign diplomat. Here he inspects the 22nd Regiment on the White House lawns with US president Calvin Coolidge in 1927.

Leaving the Nest

Britain continued to hold Imperial Conferences with its former colonies. As these countries struggled to assert their independence, it became clear that a new relationship needed to be worked out with Britain. To clarify the issue, a committee at the Imperial Conference of 1926 issued the Balfour Report, named for British politician Arthur Balfour. The report declared that Canada, Ireland, South Africa, Australia, and New Zealand "are autonomous communities within the British Empire, equal in status, in no way subordinate to one another in any aspect of their domestic or external affairs, though united by a common allegiance to the Crown, and freely associated as members of the British Commonwealth of Nations."

Now that Canada seemed to be completely free of British control over its foreign relations, it began opening its own embassies in other countries. First came the United States, where a Canadian embassy opened in Washington in 1927. The US responded by sending an ambassador to Ottawa. The follow-

The first Canadian embassy in Paris opened in 1928.

ing year, Canadian embassies opened in France and Japan.

These developments culminated in 1931 with the Statute of Westminster. This law, passed by the British Parliament, gave formal recognition to the independence of the dominions. It declared that all the dominions were completely self-governing, bound by no laws other than their own. Britain could no longer make laws for Canada. In two areas Canada did not claim full independence, however. The highest court of appeal in the Canadian legal system remained the Judicial Committee of the Privy Council in Britain until 1949. (See page 176.) And because the federal and provincial governments could not agree on a method for amending the **British North America Act**, Canada's constitution, that power remained a British responsibility until 1982.

MAKING CONNECTIONS

1. The Statute of Westminster has been called Canada's Declaration of Independence. Do you think this is an accurate comparison with the American Declaration of Independence of 1776? Explain your answer.

2. Why did many Canadians want greater independence from Britain? What might have been the difference between French-Canadian and English-Canadian opinion on this issue?

KEYWORDS

isolationist

BNA Act

KING VERSUS BYNG

The Role of the Governor General

FOCUSSING ON THE ISSUE

The role of the governor general was the focus of controversy in 1926.
What is the role of the governor general in the government of Canada?

An Inconclusive Election

The federal election of October 1925, produced an inconclusive result. The Conservatives, led by Arthur Meighen, won more seats in Parliament than the Liberals (116 to 101), but 28 seats belonged to three smaller parties. No party controlled a clear majority of seats. In the parliamentary system, the party with the most seats usually forms the government. In this case, however, the Liberals, who had been in power prior to the election, decided to try to stay in office by winning the support of most of the MPs who were not Conservatives.

At first the Liberals were successful. Led by William Lyon Mackenzie King, they managed to

Arthur Meighen was prime minister in 1920-1921 and again, briefly, in 1926.

convince the minor parties to vote with the government. This allowed the Liberals to remain in power, and King to remain prime minister, but not for long. In the spring of 1926, a scandal erupted in the department of customs when it was revealed that public officials had been involved in illegal activities. King promised to take steps to clean up the situation, but he began to lose support in Parliament. The Conservatives wanted to hold a vote censuring the government for mishandling the scandal. If the vote passed, King and his Liberals would fall from office.

Knowing that he was about to lose the vote, King paid a visit to the governor general, Lord Byng. He asked Byng to dissolve Parliament so that an election could be called, as was the normal procedure. It was highly unusual for a governor general to refuse the advice of his prime minister. However, it was also unusual for a government to avoid a **motion of censure** by calling an election. Byng refused to do as King requested. He would not dissolve Parliament.

King immediately resigned as prime minister and the governor general asked Arthur Meighen, the Conservative leader, to form a government. He did so, and for a few days it survived a series of challenges in the House of Commons.

William Lyon Mackenzie King served longer than any other prime minister in Canada.

In the end, however, it too was defeated. Now Byng had no choice. Both of the leading parties had been unable to govern. He agreed to dissolve Parliament and let the voters decide.

During the election that followed, King claimed that the governor general had violated the constitution and had threatened Canada's independence. Many legal experts debated Byng's actions, but the voters agreed with King. The Liberals won a solid victory and he became prime minister again.

The Queen's Representative

Canada is a constitutional monarchy. In theory, this means that Canada is ruled by the British king or queen using powers limited by the Constitution. The prime minis-

The three key players in the political controversy in 1926 were Lord Byng, William Lyon Mackenzie King, and Arthur Meighen. In the following excerpts, each man explains his point of view.

Nine times out of ten a Governor General should take the Prime Minister's advice. But if the advice offered is considered by the Governor General to be wrong and unfair, and not for the welfare of the people, it behooves him to act in what he considers the best interests of the country.

From a dispatch from Lord Byng to L.S.Amery, British Secretary of State for the Dominions

Mr. King tried to run away from the just condemnation of himself and his Government by Parliament, but he was *not permitted to do so; he thereupon hatched a constitutional issue to act as a smoke screen.*

Arthur Meighen in Maclean's, *September 1, 1926*

I was not seeking to be continued in office...I was simply asking that the people be given an opportunity of themselves deciding by whom they desired their Government to be carried on.

William Lyon Mackenzie King in Maclean's, *September 1, 1926*

1. Explain and defend the position taken by each man.

2. What did this controversy indicate about relations between Canada and Great Britain?

Lord Byng was governor general from 1921-1926.

ter leads the government but the actual head of state, the ultimate authority, is the representative of the British monarch in Canada, the governor general. This goes back to colonial times when Canada was a colony first of France and then of Britain.

Over the years, as Canada became fully independent, the role of the governor general became more symbolic than real. Today the powers of the governor general are quite limited, and no governor general would think of acting against the wishes of the elected government. Nonetheless, the governor general still plays an important role (a role that is filled at the provincial level by the lieutenant governor). He or she approves all laws and important Cabinet decisions. The governor general reads the Speech from the Throne, which sets out government policy at the beginning of each session of Parliament, and acts as the official host for foreign heads of state visiting Canada. He or she also dissolves Parliament on the advice of the prime minister. It is this last authority that led to the disagreement between Prime Minister King and Governor General Byng in 1926.

The governor general is appointed by the British monarch on the advice of the Canadian prime minister. The appointment usually lasts five years. The governor general is considered to stand above politics and to represent the whole country, unlike the prime minister who can claim to represent only the people who voted for the party in power. As such, the governor general is considered a symbol of national unity.

MAKING CONNECTIONS

1. What qualities do you think a good governor general needs?

2. Who is Canada's governor general today? Research this person's background to find out why he or she might have been selected to be governor general.

KEYWORDS

motion of censure

GOVERNMENT IN CANADA
The Canadian Constitution
FOCUSSING ON THE ISSUE

*Canada is a federation with a constitutional monarchy
and a democratically elected parliament. How does the Constitution
determine legislative authority in Canada?*

The Rule of Law

Traditionally, rulers had arbitrary power to create laws at their own discretion. This power was often resented by the people and was frequently the cause of political revolutions. Over time, the governed demanded that those who governed them be bound by a set of rules. This was the case with the English barons who, in 1215, forced their king to sign the Magna Carta, the great charter of English liberties. Opposition to arbitrary power led to the development of the rule of law—that is, the principle that everyone is subject to the law, and that no one, no matter how powerful or important, is above the law.

In a democracy, the rule of law is safeguarded in a **constitution.** A constitution may be a written document or an unwritten agreement based on a set of principles and procedures. Although constitutions may vary widely from one country to another, they are an important characteristic of all democratic governments.

Canada's Constitution

Canada's constitution has been shaped by the countries that have most directly influenced its history. The Canadian constitution is similar to the formal constitution of the

United States in that the political philosophy, the structure of government, and the rights of citizens are written down. Yet it is also similar to the informal constitution of Britain because much of Canada's political system is based on British tradition and is unwritten. For example, there is no mention, in the written constitution, of the prime minister or the role of that office, nor of any Cabinet ministers or Members of Parliament. Other than the requirement that an election be held every five years, there is no mention of how a government is changed, nor is there any reference to the effect of a **nonconfidence vote** on the status of a government. These are all conventions of an unwritten constitution based on British principles and traditions.

The main written elements of Canada's constitution are the Constitution Act, 1982 and the Constitution Act, 1867 (originally called the British North America (BNA) Act). In addition, a number of other statutes, such as the provincial constitutions, the Dominion Act of 1875 that established the Supreme Court of Canada, and the Statute of Westminster of 1931 that confirmed Canada's independence, all form part of the written constitution. A key element of the Constitution Act, 1982 is the

Canadian Charter of Rights and Freedoms. (See page 300.) The Charter and an amending formula were added to Canada's constitution when it was **patriated** in 1982. (See page 296.)

Canada's original constitution reflected the new country's history and cultural heritage. The Constitution Act, 1867 established a parliamentary structure based on the British model, within a federal state like the United States. Within Quebec, French **civil law** was maintained.

The Constitution established three main branches of government; the executive branch, the legislative branch, and the judicial branch. The executive branch established Canada as a **constitutional monarchy**, with a governor general representing the monarch. (See page 95.) Parliament was granted all legislative powers, divided between an elected House of Commons and an appointed Senate. The judicial branch established the Supreme Court of Canada and the federal and provincial court systems.

Distribution of Powers

The most complex aspect of the Constitution was the distribution of powers between the federal and provincial governments. The founders of Confederation wanted

THE CANADIAN GOVERNMENT

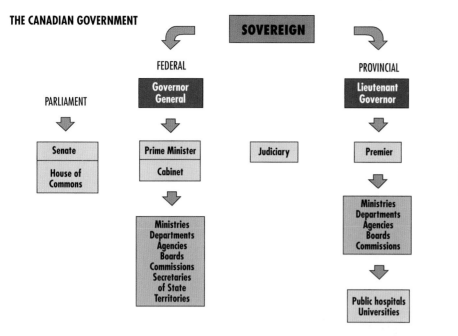

Since 1867, there have been many legal challenges over residual powers by both the federal and provincial governments based on the principle of *ultra vires*—that is, that a law is outside the enacting legislature's powers as defined in the Constitution. While the Constitution granted residual powers to the federal government, over the years the Justices of the **Privy Council** applied a narrow definition to the broad phrase "peace, order, and good government," limiting its use to emergencies only. On the other hand, they granted a broad definition of the provinces' powers over property and civil rights. Over time, this has effectively transferred residual powers from the federal government to the provinces. As a result, it has been impossible for the federal government alone to create programs such as the pension plan (see page 98) without having the courts declare them *ultra vires*.

to create a strong central government. Although the provinces received a great deal of power, there were also important restrictions. **Residual powers**—that is, authority over matters not expressly addressed in the Constitution—belonged to the federal government. A lieutenant-governor representing the monarch was established as the formal head of each provincial government.

Sections 91, 92, and 93 of the Constitution deal with the specific division of powers. Section 91 lists federal powers, including the maintenance of peace, order, and good government. Section 92 lists provincial powers, including property and civil rights, while Section 93 gives control of education to the provincial legislatures. Some powers, such as public health and justice, overlap. Shared powers have been a source of tension and conflict between the federal and provincial governments since Confederation.

MAKING CONNECTIONS

1. a) The residual power to deal with unforeseen circumstances must be assigned to some level of government. Who do you think should have residual powers, the federal government or the provinces? Explain your answer.
    b) Research another constitution, such as the US constitution, to see how it deals with the question of residual power. How does it compare with the Canadian constitution?

2. Air travel, telephones, and television were not foreseen by the founders of Confederation. Find out which level of government is responsible for these. What is the legal basis for that power?

KEYWORDS

constitution

nonconfidence vote

patriate

civil law

constitutional monarchy

residual powers

Privy Council

SOCIAL PROGRAMS
The Canada Pension Plan
FOCUSSING ON THE ISSUE

By the 1920s, many Canadians were living longer, but because they were unable to work, older Canadians were generally poor. What measures did the Canadian government take to improve the economic situation of these older Canadians?

A Lengthy Debate

In 1921, Canadian voters elected 117 Liberal, 50 Conservative, 64 Progressive, 2 Labour, and 2 independent Members of Parliament. The Liberal leader, William Lyon Mackenzie King, became prime minister. The leaders of the Progressive and Labour parties refused to join in a **coalition** with King, but agreed to support his government's legislation when it was compatible with their own policies. A priority for all three parties was the creation of an old-age pension plan. Early in the session, the government set up a parliamentary committee to investigate such a scheme.

In 1924, the committee produced a draft bill for the pension legislation. At the same time, however, it delivered a legal opinion that the federal government did not have the constitutional power to enact a pension plan. Pensions came under the property and civil rights section of the Constitution, and these powers were the exclusive domain of the provinces. As a result, the pension scheme was put on hold.

Late in 1925, King called an election seeking a **majority government**. But his government's lack of action on several programs, including the pension plan, caused many voters to reject the Liberals. When the votes were counted, Arthur Meighen's Conservatives had won 116 seats and the Liberals had only won 101. King had even lost his own seat. The Progressives won 24 seats, while Labour and independents each had 2. A **by-election** was held, King was re-elected, and, with the support of the Progressive and Labour parties, he remained prime minister. (See page 94.)

On 7 January 1926, King received the following letter from two MPs: J.S. Woodsworth and A.A. Heaps.

Dear Mr. King:
As representatives of Labour in the House of Commons, may we ask whether it is your intention to introduce at this session (a) provision for

The first pension cheque is presented to William Derby of Port Alberni, BC, in 1927.

the Unemployed; (b) Old-Age Pensions.

We are venturing to send a similar enquiry to the leader of the Opposition.

In reply, King invited representatives from both Labour and the Progressives to draw up a pension bill to be introduced in the House of Commons. The Conservatives opposed the pension plan, but because the voters favoured it, they were unwilling to attack it for political reasons. With no party openly opposing the legislation, the Pension Bill was quickly passed.

Approval of the Pension Bill in the Senate did not come as easily, however. The Senate, whose members were appointed for life at an income of $4000 a year, rejected the bill. In the election campaign of 1926, a major issue was the charge that the Senate, dominated by rich Conservatives, had denied older Canadians a pension. The Liberals were re-elected with a majority, and they quickly passed the Pension Bill again. This time, the Senate supported the measure, although not without dissent from some senators.

Qualifications

The Pension Act provided for a pension of $240 a year to applicants who were British subjects over the age of 70. They had to have lived in Canada for at least 20 years and to have lived in the province where they made their application for the last five years. A **means test** was established. Any person whose annual income was over $365 was ineligible to receive the pension. If the pensioner owned a home, **title** to it was to be transferred to the Pension Authority so that the pension payments (with interest at 5 per cent) could be recovered when the house was sold. An applicant who did not transfer the title received a reduced pension or no pension at all, depending on the value of the property. Anyone who transferred property to someone else in order to avoid transferring the title was disqualified from receiving a pension. Women were eligible for a pension only if they were widows. Aboriginal peoples were not eligible.

VIEWPOINTS

OPPOSITION TO THE PENSION PLAN

Some members of the Senate opposed the Pension Bill.

I feel that there are in the country many people who think they have the assurance that when they reach the age of seventy the Government will provide for them, and who...will not make very much effort to provide for their old age. I think...the bill places a premium upon extravagance and imposes a tax on thrift.

Hon. J.J. Donnelley, Senate Debates, 8 June 1926

This, in my opinion, is an iniquitous measure. First of all, it is unhealthy in its basic moral principle. It is going to stunt the growth if it does not altogether blight and wither an incentive for thrift and providence in the land.

Hon. C.P. Beaubien, Senate Debates, 8 June 1926

1. What do these comments imply about the senators' attitudes towards Canadian workers?

MAKING CONNECTIONS

1. The Constitution gave the federal government **residual powers** over those issues it did not directly address. Since the Constitution did not mention pensions, why was it so difficult to create a pension plan?

2. Find out what the terms of the Canada Pension Plan are today. Do you think the pension is enough to enable retired Canadians to live comfortably? What responsibility do you think individuals have to ensure that they have enough money for their retirement?

KEYWORDS

coalition

majority government

by-election

means test

title

residual powers

TAKING TO THE ROAD
Canadians and the Automobile
FOCUSSING ON THE ISSUE

In the 1920s, Canadians began a love affair with the automobile that has lasted to this day. What impact did the automobile have on Canada in the 1920s? What issues arose from the rapid growth in the number of automobiles?

The Auto Age

Cars first appeared in Canadian cities in significant numbers around 1910, but the truly explosive growth in the number of automobiles did not take place until after the First World War. In 1911, Canadians owned some 20 000 registered automobiles. In 1921, the number was more than 400 000! By the end of the decade, more than 1 million automobiles would be travelling Canada's roads and highways.

In the early 1920s, Canada was the second largest manufacturer of automobiles in the world. Much of the country's car production was being exported to the United States and to the other dominions. By the end of the decade, only the people of the United States owned more cars per capita than did Canadians. In total road distance per capita, Canada was also second in the world; only Australia had more kilometres of road per person.

The Impact of the Automobile

The most important aspect of the automobile was that it offered personal **mobility**. A product of mass production, the car seemed to free its driver from **mass society**. It allowed travellers to avoid the social contact of the railway car-

Cars lined the streets in a 1920s traffic jam in Toronto.

CASE STUDY

CHANGING ROAD PATTERNS

On 1 January 1922, Vancouver drivers switched from driving on the left to driving on the right. The following newspaper account reports that the change took place with relatively little confusion.

The City of Vancouver kept to the right at 6 a.m. just as it had been doing it for centuries. It was prophesied by croakers that there would be a scene of wild confusion at all the great nerve centres of the traffic system, that there would be innumerable accidents, that people would be killed every ten minutes, and the gods of all old customs would rise up and demand a continu-

ous stream of sacrifices. But there were no sacrifices and no confusion....

An air of uncertainty seems to pervade the minds of pedestrians while they are still safe on the sidewalk. You will see a man going quietly about his business till a streetcar approaches him on the new side of the road and then just for a moment there passes over his face a look of indecision....

From the Vancouver Daily Province, 1 January 1922.

1. Do you think it would be possible for Canadian drivers to make such a dramatic switch today? Explain.

riage, streetcar, or bus. Drivers could escape the crowded city for the peace and quiet of the countryside, limited in their freedom only by the road network. Farm families found the automobile invaluable as it allowed them to travel easily to cities where they could buy things at lower prices than through mail-order catalogues. The car also decreased the isolation and loneliness of farm life, making access to medical care, education, and other services easier. For young people, the automobile represented speed, freedom from parental restrictions, and a place to be alone with friends or lovers. By the 1920s, the car had become a symbol of independence and **individualism**; it had also become a combined sex and **status symbol**. The automobiles shown in the films of the 1920s reinforced this image and contributed to the growing demand for cars.

The increasing importance of the automobile gave rise to new service industries. Gasoline stations and repair shops became important elements of the motoring network. So, too, were the restaurants, campgrounds, motels, and other tourist facilities and attractions that sprang up to serve the motoring public. Tourism had emerged in Canada in the 1890s, the railways carrying the wealthy elite to exclusive wilderness resorts such as Banff and Jasper. The automobile made tourism much more accessible to ordinary Canadians.

VIEWPOINTS

REGULATING THE AUTOMOBILE

A major issue during the 1920s was to what extent governments should regulate automobile use. Most provinces required drivers and vehicles to be licensed and introduced speed limits and other traffic regulations. In Ontario, drivers' licences were introduced in the mid-1920s. During the debate over this issue, *Saturday Night* magazine ran the following editorial:

No Drivers' Licences for those Morally Unfit
It is the intention of the Ontario government to license all motor drivers. This law, we understand, will go into effect the coming year. If properly drawn and vigorously enforced, it should do a great deal to clear up a most

undesirable condition....There are people at present driving motor cars who are not fit physically for such an undertaking, and an examination, previous to the granting of a license, would uncover their deficiencies. There are still others driving motor vehicles who are morally unfit, that is to say they would not be passed by an efficient police official, being criminals or near criminals, and who sooner or later, aided by their motor cars, take part in robberies or crimes of violence.

Saturday Night *editorial, 1925*

1. Is a driver's licence a right or a privilege? What restrictions should apply?

MAKING CONNECTIONS

1. Assess the extent to which the things the automobile came to symbolize for Canadians are still true today. Suggest reasons why the car has been such an enduring feature in Canadian life.

2. The lowest priced new car in Canada in 1921 was $750; in that year, an average auto worker earned about $1500. Determine the lowest priced North American-built car today, then find out the average auto worker's income. Compare the ratio of the price of a car to an auto worker's income in 1921 to that ratio today. What can you conclude?

KEYWORDS

mobility

mass society

individualism

status symbol

INTO THE BUSH
Aviation in Canada
FOCUSSING ON THE ISSUE

*All kinds of people in many different professions contribute
to the growth of a country. What contribution did bush pilots make
to the development of Canada?*

A New Profession

The First World War created a new profession, the pilot. Hundreds of Canadians had learned to fly during the war and they returned home eager to continue flying for a living. Some went barnstorming, travelling from place to place putting on flying exhibitions and taking passengers up for short spins. Others got jobs as bush pilots, flying to remote locations to deliver people and supplies. There were no passenger airlines at the time. In the peacetime economy, the airplane found a role as the workhorse of the woods. Planes were used to spot forest fires, to haul the mail, to take aerial photographs, and to conduct **geological surveys**.

There were no airports in remote places. Planes were equipped with **pontoons** for landing on lakes and rivers; in the mid-1920s they were equipped with skis to set down on the snow. In 1926, James Richardson, a Winnipeg grain merchant, created Western Canada Airways, which pioneered flying into the North. Its planes carried prospectors into the rugged Canadian Shield country of northern Quebec and Ontario, across the West and eventually into the Arctic. By 1929, WCA added regular air service to the Arctic from its base in northern Alberta.

Bush pilots played a crucial role in the burgeoning resource industries of the Canadian North. The airplane made it possible to locate the resources and then to supply the mines and camps that sprang up to exploit them. Airplanes also allowed residents of isolated parts of Canada to communicate with each other. In a way, they completed the unification of the country by establishing links with the farthest reaches of the North.

Mercy Flights

Wilfrid Reid May, known as "Wop" May, was a First World War flying hero from Manitoba. He had been engaged in a **dogfight** with the German flying ace Manfred von Richthofen, the Red Baron, when the Baron was shot from the skies over France. After the war he started his own airline in Edmonton, performing stunts at

Aluminum float planes hauled freight to remote regions. By 1930, it was possible to get anywhere in the country by bush plane. List some of the uses for bush planes during the decade.

country fairs and pioneering mail flights into the Arctic.

In the winter of 1929, word reached Edmonton that diphtheria had broken out in the Peace River country of northern Alberta. One person was already dead and many more would die unless medicine could be flown into the area. Wop May, along with co-pilot Vic Horner, took off in his tiny, open-cockpit Avro Avian. The plane offered no protection from the freezing temperatures. The only heat came from small charcoal burners at the pilots' feet.

Part-way into the flight the wings iced up, forcing the plane to land at the tiny community of McLennan. There was no airport. Townspeople who were told the plane was coming had managed to tramp out a landing strip in the snow, marked by two rows of spruce trees. May landed safely and de-iced the plane. He took off again and arrived at his destination without mishap. With the medicine safely delivered, the two pilots had to make the flight all over again in the opposite direction. On their return to Edmonton they received a hero's welcome. Thousands of people turned out to meet their plane. It was one of the first **mercy flights** and illustrated another crucial use for airplanes in the North.

Fred McCall was a barnstorming pilot in western Canada after the war. Here he stands, complete with aviator's scarf and goggles, in front of a Curtiss Jenny JN-4D aircraft at the Calgary exhibition in 1919. McCall once crash-landed his plane on top of the merry-go-round at the exhibition. No one was hurt.

Mining the North

Clennell Haggerston Dickins, known as "Punch" Dickins, from Edmonton, was another wartime flying ace who turned to commercial flying in peacetime. As a pilot with Western Canada Airways, he carried the first airmail to the Prairies. In 1928, he flew 6500 km along the shores of Hudson Bay carrying prospectors looking for minerals.

The next year Dickins flew into Great Bear Lake in the Northwest Territories to pick up Gilbert Labine, who had been at the lake looking for copper deposits. As the plane took off, Labine noticed some discoloured rock from the air. He returned in 1930 and discovered radium deposits, which later formed the basis of Canada's valuable uranium industry.

KEYWORDS

geological surveys

pontoons

dogfight

mercy flight

STOCK MARKET MANIA
The Crash of 1929
FOCUSSING ON THE ISSUE

The 1920s was an era of rising expectations. People everywhere wanted to get rich quickly by investing in the stock market. But the bubble burst on 29 October 1929. To what extent was the prosperity an illusion? What caused stock prices to rise sharply and then fall even more dramatically?

Rising Expectations

During the 1920s, memories of the Great War faded and the risk of new wars breaking out in Europe or Asia seemed remote. **Mass media** conveyed cheerful, upbeat messages suggesting the world was indeed a happy place again. Never before had there been so much to buy— new houses, new cars, new appliances, all the wonders of modern living. Nowhere was this more true than in North America, the birthplace of **mass consumption**.

Hard work alone did not guarantee consumers would have enough money to buy everything they saw advertised. Real wages were not rising as quickly as prices. In fact, much of the seeming prosperity was based on buying on margin, or credit. Another source of apparent economic growth was **stock market speculation** — buying shares in the expectation that their prices would rise, allowing the purchaser to sell at a profit. Fast-rising stocks and real estate prices, easy credit, and assurances from politicians left many people with a false sense of security.

Once the exclusive world of wealthy financiers, the stock market now attracted ordinary people. In Canada, as in the United States and Britain, vast numbers of people

Advertisements for luxury items were common during the prosperity of the 1920s.

began to invest in the "market," either individually or in investment "clubs." Talk in streetcars, elevators, and coffee shops across the country focussed on the market as would-be millionaires exchanged hot tips and rumours. One firm of **stockbrokers**, Solloway, Mills, and Company, specialized in penny stocks—low-priced, high-risk investments—in Canada's expanding resource industries. Between 1926 and 1929, the company grew from one small office in Toronto to 40 offices across Canada with more than 1500 employees. Most of its business was with working men and women who were held in the grip of the world-wide stock-buying frenzy.

Stocks, too, could be bought on credit. This practice, known as buying on margin, allowed people to buy shares by paying only a small amount, usually 10 per cent of the selling price. The buyer planned to pay off the balance using the future profits reaped from the anticipated growth in the stock's value. Few buyers realized that share prices could also fall, leaving them liable for the full amount of the original purchase price. Voices of caution were drowned out by confident proclamations like the following editorial that appeared in *Saturday Night*, an influential Canadian magazine, in December 1928:

Never in our history has our country been in better shape, nor have our people faced the future with greater confidence....No country has made a greater recovery from postwar depression as has Canada, and today there is every reason to believe that the Dominion has embarked on a prolonged era of development and prosperity...

Such comments fuelled **consumer confidence** in Canada in 1929. The stock-buying craze continued through the spring and summer of that year. Then came the fall and news that an overproduction of goods and the accumulation of large amounts of unsold commodities were driving prices down.

On 29 October 1929, the economic euphoria came to an abrupt end as the stock market crashed. On that day, the average value of shares traded on the New York Stock Exchange fell more than 50 per cent. The news triggered a wave of panic selling. In Canada, the response on the markets was swift. The value of shares plummeted. Investors saw their paper fortunes wiped out in the mad rush to sell shares. Those who had bought on credit found themselves deeply in debt for their shares, many of which were now worthless.

Corporate leaders and the federal government tried to calm investors' fears and restore confidence in the Canadian economy. Edward Beatty, president of CPR, assured Canadians that:

It is probably a fact that, when the temporary adverse effects of [the market crash] shall have run its [sic] course, Canadian economic conditions will be that more soundly based, and it will be found that the way has been cleared for a more vigorous and better balanced forward movement than has been experienced in the past...

Prime Minister King proposed minor **tariff** adjustments to restore the economy while the Conservative Opposition, led by R.B. Bennett, called for **tariff barriers** to protect Canadian industries. Confident that the voters would support the government on the tariff issue, King called an election in 1930. To the surprise of most observers, Bennett's Conservatives won a clear majority. The voters, their mood made pessimistic by the market crash, had decided it was time for a change.

MAKING CONNECTIONS

1. Suggest some reasons why some business and government leaders might have expressed little concern about the stock market crash of October 1929.

2. In the late 1980s, and again in the late 1990s, stock markets rose as spectacularly as in the second half of the 1920s. Using financial magazines or electronic databases, compare and contrast both the causes and the consequences of these periods of rapidly rising stock values. Explain why the consequences of the later stock booms differed from those of the first.

KEYWORDS

mass media

mass consumption

stock market speculation

stockbroker

consumer confidence

tariff

tariff barrier

WOMEN AND POLITICS
The Persons Case
FOCUSSING ON THE ISSUE

Until 1929, Canadian women could not be appointed to the Senate because they were not considered "persons" under the BNA Act. How did women gain legal recognition as persons in Canada?

Emily Murphy

Women gained the right to vote in Canada in 1918 as well as the right to run for election in the House of Commons. But in many other areas, women still did not have political equality with men. This inequality was highlighted in the famous Persons Case.

One of Canada's prominent **suffragists**, Emily Murphy, was at the centre of this political controversy. Murphy was a successful author under the pen-name of Janey Canuck. In 1916, she was appointed magistrate of the police court in Edmonton, making her the first female judge in the British Empire. In court, Murphy was challenged by a defence lawyer, Eardley Jackson, who claimed that she could not stand in judgment of his, or any, client because, under the terms of the Canadian constitution, Murphy was not legally a person. Jackson argued that: *under British common law...the status of women is this: '...Women are persons in matters of pains and penalties, but are not persons in matters of rights and privileges.'* Since the office of Magistrate is a privilege, the present incumbent is here illegally. No decision of her court can be binding. Legally, Jackson was right. In 1920, however, the Supreme Court of Alberta ruled that every women had the right to be a judge.

Spurred by the Alberta ruling, a group of women petitioned Prime Minister Robert Borden for a woman to be appointed to the Senate. But they were refused on the grounds that women were not considered persons under the **BNA Act** and were therefore not eligible for the Senate.

Murphy then decided to challenge Canada's constitution. By law, any five people could petition the Supreme Court of Canada for interpretation of any point in the BNA Act. So in 1927, Emily Murphy and four other suffragists—Nellie McClung, Louise McKinney, Henrietta Edwards, and Irene Parlby—petitioned Ottawa to order a Supreme Court ruling on the controversial phrase "qualified persons." Their petition asked for an answer to the question: "Does the word persons in Section 24 of the British North America Act, 1867, include female persons?" In March 1928, the Supreme Court of Canada began hearing the Persons Case.

After weeks of deliberation, the Supreme Court delivered a unanimous ruling. The meaning of the BNA Act must be interpreted in light of conditions that existed in 1867. Since women did not have the vote in 1867, they were not eligible to become senators. So women were not considered "qualified persons" under the law.

EMILY MURPHY
WOMEN ARE PERSONS
LES FEMMES SONT DES PERSONNES

32 CANADA

*Emily Murphy and other suffragists fought tirelessly for women's rights in Canada, often without due recognition during their lifetimes. Why do you think so many suffragists were from western Canada? What do you think is the **legacy** of these women?*

An Appeal

Discouraged but not defeated, Murphy and her supporters, known as the "Alberta Five," decided to appeal the decision to the Privy Council in London, which was the final court of appeal in Canadian legal matters. In October 1929, the Privy Council reversed the decision of Canada's Supreme Court by declaring that, "the word persons includes members of the male and female sex...and that women are eligible to be summoned and become members of the Senate of Canada." The ruling noted that excluding women from the term *person* was a "relic of days more barbarous than ours."

So in 1929, Canadian women were recognized as persons under the law. Many people believed that Emily Murphy, a Conservative party reformer, should receive the honour of becoming Canada's first female senator. But Murphy was never appointed to the Senate. Instead, in 1931, two years after Murphy's victory, Liberal Prime Minister William Lyon Mackenzie King appointed Liberal social reformer Cairine Wilson as the first woman senator in Canadian history. Yet once the Persons Case was finally resolved, the women's movement lost its momentum. It would be more than three decades before women's rights regained national attention.

Timeline: The Road to Political Rights for Women in Canada

1916 Women win the right to vote and hold political office in Manitoba, Saskatchewan, and Alberta.

1917 Nurses serving in WWI and wives, widows, mothers, sisters, and daughters of soldiers extended the right to vote. Women win the right to vote in British Columbia and Ontario.

1918 Women who are over 21 and are British subjects win the right to vote in Nova Scotia and federal elections.

1920 Dominion Elections Act allows women to run for election to parliament.

1921 Agnes Macphail elected first female MP.

1922 Women get the right to vote in PEI.

1925 Women get the right to vote in Newfoundland.

1928 Supreme Court of Canada rules unanimously that women are not persons under the BNA Act.

1929 British Privy Council overturns Supreme Court ruling and recognizes women to be persons under the law.

1930 Cairine Wilson first woman appointed to the Senate.

1940 Women over 21 get the right to vote in Quebec.

Cairine Wilson was the first woman senator in Canada. What might explain why Wilson was appointed to the Senate rather than Emily Murphy?

MAKING CONNECTIONS

1. What reasons did the Supreme Court of Canada give when it ruled that women were not persons in 1928? Do you think the Court could have ruled any differently at that time? Explain.

2. In 1996, 22 per cent of Canada's Senate seats were held by women. Do you think more women should be appointed to the Senate? Give reasons for your answer.

KEYWORDS

suffragist

legacy

BNA Act

THE ALLIED TRIBES
Aboriginal Activism

Following the First World War, Aboriginal political movements were gaining strength at the grass-roots level in British Columbia. On what basis did the Allied Tribes pursue their land claims against the federal government? How did the government respond?

Staking a Claim

The federal government always expected that the Aboriginal "question" would eventually disappear as Aboriginal peoples became **assimilated** into white society. Indeed, in the House of Commons in the early part of the twentieth century, debate centred more on the division of Aboriginal lands once the people were finally assimilated than on the fate of the people themselves.

After the First World War, however, it became clear that Aboriginal peoples were not about to accommodate the federal government's expectations. The Allied Tribes of British Columbia was founded in June 1916. Its main objective was to settle Aboriginal land claims. In most provinces, colonial authorities had eliminated the possibility of Aboriginal land claims by signing treaties. But there were no such formal agreements in British Columbia. When the McKenna-McBride Commission on Indian Affairs recommended a reduction in the size of many **reserves** in BC, the Allied Tribes responded with a comprehensive land claim. It was rejected by the federal government, however, which proceeded to pass legislation based on the commission's recommendations. Among the new laws was Bill 14, which called for the automatic **enfranchisement** of Aboriginal war veterans. Duncan Campbell Scott, the deputy superintendent of the Department of Indian Affairs, made the bill's objective clear:

> *I want to get rid of the Indian problem....That is my whole point. Our objective is to continue until there is not a single Indian in Canada that has not been absorbed into the body politic, and there is no Indian question and no Indian Department and that is the whole object of this bill.*
>
> Brian Tilley, A Narrow Vision: Duncan Campbell Scott and the Administration of Indian Affairs in Canada, *Vancouver: UBC Press, 1986, p. 50.*

A London Delegation

Seeing little hope of reaching a settlement with the federal government, the Allied Tribes decided to present its case to the Privy Council in London. A decision the council had rendered in 1921 ruled that an Aboriginal group in Nigeria retained title to its land because colonial authorities there had never signed a treaty with them. In 1926, a delegation of the Allied Tribes went to London with a petition

As a poet, Duncan Campbell Scott wrote numerous poems on the plight of Aboriginal peoples, but as an administrator in the Department of Indian Affairs, he vigorously pursued a policy of assimilation.

Andrew Paull was a Squamish leader and one of the key organizers of the Allied Tribes. He was a flamboyant leader who captured the imagination of people at the grass-roots level. A gifted speaker fluent in both Chinook and English, Paull engaged in verbal battles with the government. His ability to poke fun at authorities for their pretentious claims to a higher moral ground and their refusal to obey their own laws of land ownership when it came to Aboriginal lands won him the support of Aboriginal peoples across the province and the country.

Following the collapse of the Allied Tribes, Paull continued to be an outspoken political activist. He spearheaded a new organization, the Progressive Native Tribes of British Columbia. He travelled regularly to Ottawa speaking on behalf of British Columbia's Aboriginal peoples on such topics as civil rights and the widespread hunger in Aboriginal communities caused by the Depression. In the late 1930s, Paull forged an alliance with the Native Brotherhood of BC, which united interior and coastal peoples. The union with the more conservative Brotherhood was short-lived, however. Nonetheless, Paull continued to encourage new political movements. He was the founder of two other groups, the Confederacy of Interior Tribes of British Columbia and the North American Indian Brotherhood, which included representatives from Quebec, Ontario, and Saskatchewan, as well as BC. Paull continued to be a prominent spokesperson for Aboriginal rights and issues until his death in 1959.

demanding a similar resolution to their land claims and challenging the Canadian government's right to enfranchise Aboriginal peoples. The final paragraph of the petition stated that "We do not want enfranchisement, we want to be Indian to the end of the world."

The delegation was intercepted by the head of the Canadian High Commission in London, who promised to deliver the petition to the proper authorities. That was where the mission to London ended. The delegates returned home. There they found the federal government willing to talk with them. At a meeting in Ottawa in the spring of 1927, however, Scott quickly dismissed the group's claim of land ownership, saying it would "smash Confederation." Ottawa then moved quickly to derail any further activism on the part of Aboriginal peoples. A law was passed making it illegal for anyone to solicit funds for the purpose of pursuing land claims. Other restrictions were placed on the right of Aboriginal peoples to assemble. This was the death knell for the Allied Tribes, which collapsed the same year. By 1930, the Aboriginal movements that had flourished in the postwar world had been stifled, at least temporarily, by the federal government.

MAKING CONNECTIONS

1. Prepare a timeline of key events in the Aboriginal movement from the end of the First World War until 1930.

2. Research one of the current Aboriginal political organizations in Canada. Present a profile of the organization's objectives and leadership.

KEYWORDS

assimilate

reserve

enfranchisement

THE NATIONAL PROGRESSIVES
Creating a Multiparty System

The National Progressive party, formed in the 1920s, was Canada's first "third party." What is the role of political parties in Canada?

Political Parties

The Canadian system of government depends on the existence of political parties. A party consists of a group of people who share similar ideas about what is best for the country. These ideas are formulated into specific policies, which the party then puts forward as its platform. Each party nominates candidates to run in elections, whether at the local, provincial, or federal level. It is expected that these candidates, if elected, will work to implement the party **platform**.

A party's policies must be broad enough to attract the support of enough people to get party members elected. The party that succeeds in electing the most candidates forms the government. All parties, however, must make a trade-off between principle and popularity. They must stand for policies they believe in, but at the same time they have to win support for their ideas at election time.

Canadian society is divided along many lines. The language we speak, the region we come from, the ethnic group we belong to—all these things differentiate us from each other. Political parties attempt to bring together all these groups to support ideas and values we all have in common. They are also an important way in which citizens influence government. Anyone may join a party, and members can get involved in party activities, whether as fund raisers or electioneers, or at party conventions where policies are formed. In these ways, parties are a force for national unity.

On the other hand, sometimes a political party represents a particular group in society. It becomes a vehicle for that group to express its dissatisfaction with the way the country is being run. In the 1920s, the National Progressive party was formed to speak for the interests of farmers.

The Farmers' Party

For many years following Confederation, Canada had just two political parties: the Liberals and the Conservatives. They competed in elections and alternated in power. Between 1867 and 1921, the Conservatives formed the government for 34 years, the Liberals for 20.

This two-party system ended in the 1920s with the emergence of Canada's first "third" party, the National Progressives. It spoke mainly for farmers, who believed they were being poorly represented by the old-line parties. Progressives wanted an end to the protective **tariffs** that made consumer goods coming into Canada more expensive. They rejected the National Policy that had been the backbone of government policy ever since Sir John A. Macdonald had introduced it 50 years earlier.

Progressives also believed that politics was dominated by business interests that had excessive influence because of their ability to finance election campaigns. The new party's answer was to make

Among the new MPs entering Parliament after the election of 1921 was Agnes Macphail, the first woman elected to the House of Commons. She found her new role difficult. "I couldn't open my mouth to say the simplest thing without it appearing in the papers," she complained. "I was a curiosity, a freak. And you know the way the world treats a freak."

politics more democratic. Progressives thought that voters should have a chance to propose their own laws, and to **recall** their MP if they did not agree with what he or she was doing.

In the federal election of 1921, the Progressives stunned everyone, including themselves, by winning 65 seats in the House of Commons. (One of the new members was Agnes Macphail, the first woman elected to the House of Commons.) That was 15 seats more than the Unionists, and second only to the Liberals, who won the election.

Despite their surprising success, the Progressives did not last long. They passed up the chance to be the official Opposition. Many members refused to accept the disciplinary style of the old-line parties and vote the party line on every issue. Before long, some Progressives were absorbed by the Liberals, while others dropped out of politics altogether. In the next election, the Progressive party was down to 24 seats. By 1932, when the next third party, the Co-operative Commonwealth Federation (CCF), was formed, the Progressives had disappeared altogether.

Despite their limited success, however, the Progressives mark the end of the two-party political system in Canada and the beginning of a multiparty system. They showed that two parties were not enough to represent the diverse points of view in Canadian society.

CASE STUDY

REGIONAL PROTEST: THE UNITED FARMERS OF ALBERTA

While there was social and political discontent on a national scale, most of the unrest of the 1920s was expressed in regional protest movements. The collapse of the international wheat market, combined with the beginnings of drought in western Canada, meant that prairie farmers did not share in the general prosperity of the 1920s.

The discontent was focussed in the established political parties of central Canada. In 1921, the United Farmers of Alberta swept aside the provincial Liberal government, winning 39 of 61 seats. The priority in the UFA's platform was to promote the concerns of farmers and agriculture, as well as to improve education and health care. Similar movements developed in Manitoba, where the Farmers party won control of the government, and in Saskatchewan, where farmers dominated the Liberal government.

MAKING CONNECTIONS

1. Brainstorm a list of the characteristics of a political party. What is the difference between a political party and other organizations that take an interest in politics, such as the Small Business Council of Canada or Greenpeace?

2. Sometimes individuals run in elections without the support of any political party. They are called **independents**. Why would people choose to vote for an independent candidate?

3. Why did the Progressive movement originate in western Canada?

KEYWORDS

platform

tariff

recall

independent

TOTALITARIANISM
Setting the Stage for War

In the 1920s, a new ideology, totalitarianism, emerged in Europe. Its followers would soon plunge the world into global war. What are the characteristics of totalitarianism? What factors led to the rise of these dictatorships?

A Unique Phenomenon

Totalitarianism was in many ways a uniquely twentieth-century phenomenon. Mighty empires and powerful rulers had existed in the past, but none had wielded as much power or control over countries and their citizens as the rulers of the new totalitarian regimes. Italian dictator Benito Mussolini coined the term *totalitario* in the early 1920s to describe his new **fascist** state in which "all is within

the state, none outside the state, none against the state." Under totalitarianism, such traditional methods of coercion and control as secret police, paid informants, and physical torture combined with the new mass media of radio and film to mould people's thoughts and attitudes through **propaganda**. Technology was used to monitor telephone calls, eavesdrop on conversations, and listen in on classrooms to ensure that everyone conformed to the "correct" behaviour

and thought. Those who opposed totalitarian regimes were branded as "enemies of the state" and were dealt with harshly, and often publicly, as a means of discouraging other voices of dissent.

Factors Leading to Totalitarianism

Why would citizens embrace such regimes? In Europe, politics in the aftermath of the First World War was becoming increasingly polarized between fascism on the right and **communism** on the left. A depressed economy and high unemployment focussed people's attention on the need for change. Fascism established its first stronghold in Italy, where Benito Mussolini brushed aside all democratic institutions and established a dictatorship in just a few short years. He capitalized on the industrialists' and wealthy landowners' fear of communism to win their support. He also appealed to working people by promising to restore prosperity to Italy. Mussolini became Italy's prime minister in 1922. By 1925, *Il Duce*, as he was known, had used intimidation and violence to eliminate all opposition to his Fascist party. The Depression gave Mussolini the justification to take complete control of the state economy. His popularity was

Mussolini, who was forced to resign in 1943, was captured and executed after trying to flee Italy in 1945.

Hitler wrote his political manifesto *Mein Kampf* (*My Struggle*) in 1925. What do his words reveal about his political ideology?

The Marxists taught—if you will not be my brother, I will bash your skull in. Our motto shall be—if you will not be a true German, I will bash your skull in.

The importance of physical terror against the individual and the masses...became clear to me.

One truth which must always be borne in mind is that the majority can never replace the man.

The great masses of the people...will more easily fall victims to a big lie than to a small one.

enhanced by the support he received from another fascist dictator, Adolf Hitler.

In Germany, fascism gained a foothold under Hitler and the National Socialist party (Nazis) in the late 1920s. Hitler's doctrine incorporated many of Mussolini's fascist principles, denouncing capitalism, communism, democracy, and liberalism. Hitler ignited the people's enthusiasm by calling for a strong and united Germany ready to reclaim a powerful place on the world stage. He relied on propaganda and terror to control the state and its people. Eventually all political opposition was banned. In 1933, Hitler was appointed chancellor. He combined the roles of chancellor and president to become *Der Führer*, the ultimate dictator of Germany. The stage was set for the world conflict to come.

In the Soviet Union, the Bolshevik Revolution of 1917 had called for a "dictatorship of the **proletariat**" based on the communist philosophy of Karl Marx. Marxist theory called for the elimination of the state and the creation of a socialist workers' democracy. In the 1920s, however, power in the Soviet Union was increasingly concentrated within the Communist party and particularly with its leader, beginning with Vladimir Lenin. Under Lenin's successor, Josef Stalin, the Soviet Union emerged a regime as totalitarian as either the Fascists in Italy or the Nazis in Germany, employing the same tactics of terror, coercion, and propaganda to maintain control and stifle all opposition. While the dictatorships in Italy and Germany would eventually be destroyed by the Second World War, that of the Soviet Union would rule for most of the twentieth century.

MAKING CONNECTIONS

1. Under what circumstances do you think a totalitarian regime might appeal to the citizens of a country?

2. Compare and contrast the use of totalitarianism in Italy, Germany, and Russia.

KEYWORDS

fascist

propaganda

communism

proletariat

UNIT 4:

Carl Schaefer, *Storm Over the Fields* (1937)

Born in Hanover, Ontario, Carl Schaefer (1903-1995) experimented with landscape painting under the guidance of members of the Group of Seven. During the Depression, he was forced to return to his rural home, which he painted in brilliant oils. Schaefer is the subject of Charles Comfort's famous portrait from the Depression, *Young Canadian*. (See page 131.)

THE DEPRESSION YEARS
1931-1940

*Skills and Processes

THE DEPRESSION
The World in 1931
FOCUSSING ON THE ISSUE

The economic downturn that began in 1929 had become a depression by 1931. What impact did the Depression have on the world? Why did it lead to a rise in right-wing politics?

Economic Intervention

By 1931, the effects of the 1929 stock market crash were being felt around the world. In developed countries, governments and businesses faced rising unemployment as consumer demand dropped and factories reduced their output. Developing nations were also affected as demand for their raw materials dropped in developed countries.

Responses to the downturn varied greatly. Many politicians and business leaders argued that government should not intervene in the economy. They believed the downturn was temporary. They thought the rise in unemployment would cause wages to drop, thereby allowing companies to start rehiring laid-off workers. This would lead to an economic recovery. Other leaders worried that prolonged unemployment and poverty would lead to social unrest or even revolution. By 1931, they saw the growing number of protests as proof that greater unrest could follow. They called for immediate government action to resolve the crisis. The debate over the role of government in the economy dominated editorial pages and parliaments around the world.

The United States

The Depression affected the United States far more than most countries.

Canada, because of its increasing integration with the American economy, shared that suffering. US president Herbert Hoover was opposed to handouts. He did try, however, to resuscitate the shrinking US economy. But his attempts to help American farmers and to encourage consumer spending by reducing interest rates were unsuccessful. By 1930, 8.7 per cent of Americans were out of work. In 1932, the unemployment rate skyrocketed to 23.6 per cent. Between 1929 and 1932, the US economy shrank by more than 30 per cent as factory output decreased and workers' incomes fell. Millions of people lost their life savings as American banks collapsed under the economic strain.

Against this backdrop, a presidential election was held in 1932. Hoover's opponent, Franklin D. Roosevelt, was a liberal Democrat who pledged to use the power of government spending to end the Depression. He won the election in a landslide victory. Roosevelt's **New Deal** strategy to combat the Depression would become a model for the Canadian government.

Europe and Asia

By 1932, trade between the United States and the rest of the world had dropped by 67 per cent from 1929 levels. In 1930, Hoover had

imposed heavy **tariffs** on imported goods. This had a devastating effect on its trading partners as they were cut off from the huge American market. In addition, American banks, desperate for cash, called in loans made to European governments during the First World War and the reconstruction period that followed. This move seriously affected the economies of Britain, France, and Germany.

Britain, heavily dependent on trade and burdened with an ageing factory system, was harshly affected by the Depression. In response, the Conservative government decided to end the **gold standard**, which fixed the value of the British pound. The government hoped that the **devaluation** of the pound would increase British exports by making them cheaper for foreign buyers. The government also offered low-interest loans to industries to encourage them to employ more workers. For the most part though, the British government left the task of reviving the economy to industry. Only when Britain began rearming in the late 1930s in anticipation of a war with Germany did unemployment significantly drop.

In France, both **left- and right-wing** parties gained support as the economy faltered. For much of the 1930s, France was governed by a socialist **coalition**. The government responded to workers' protests by introducing pro-labour legislation, including a 40-hour work week, paid holidays, and the right to strike. To help farmers, the government bought wheat and raised food prices. Armament and aircraft industries were nationalized. The reforms, however, were ineffective because they were not supported by adequate economic measures.

In many countries, political response to the Depression often meant a sharp ideological turn to the right. As democratically elected governments failed to solve the economic problems, **fascists**, **militarists**, and **ultra-nationalists** gained popular support. Italy had become a fascist state in 1925, but until 1930, Mussolini's ideas found only limited acceptance in other parts of Europe.

In the German election of 1928—the last year of economic prosperity—the National Socialists, led by Adolf Hitler, collected only 810 000 votes. By late 1932, with more than 6 million unemployed in Germany, Hitler gained 13.6 million votes, more than 40 per cent of the total. Hitler became chancellor of Germany in 1933 and he quickly set about creating a **totalitarian** state. (See page 113.) He ended unemployment through a massive government works program combined with military expansion and rearmament. The stage was being set for the Second World War.

In Japan, many people were adopting right-wing political views.

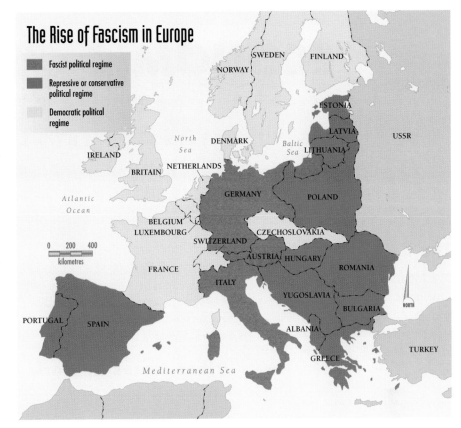

The Rise of Fascism in Europe

- Fascist political regime
- Repressive or conservative political regime
- Democratic political regime

Militarists and nationalists opposed three major world forces: China, the Western **imperialist** powers, and Soviet communism.

The Soviet Union was the only great power largely unaffected by the Depression. The USSR had few trading ties with other nations. As well, it was a **command economy** completely controlled by the state. There was no unemployment, although workers had little choice in where they worked or what kinds of jobs they held.

KEYWORDS

New Deal

tariff

gold standard

devaluation

left/right wing

coalition

fascist

militarist

ultra-nationalist

totalitarian

imperialist

command economy

◄▉ MAKING CONNECTIONS ▉►

1. How did the Depression force the Canadian and American governments to become more involved in the economy?

2. Suggest some reasons why unemployed people might be attracted to fascism.

ECONOMIC CYCLES
Was the Crash Inevitable?
FOCUSSING ON THE ISSUE

Free-market economies tend to follow a cyclical pattern known as the business cycle. Why do these economies experience periods of prosperity followed by economic decline? What issues are created by the business cycle?

The Business Cycle

The **business cycle** is marked by three stages. The first is a period of relative prosperity in which the economy approaches full employment. This stage is often accompanied by **inflation** as full employment and high income levels drive the price of labour and goods up. In the second stage the economy slows down, bringing about a **recession**. Few new jobs are created; some jobs are even lost as companies reduce their production of goods and services. This is known as cyclical unemployment. The final stage is a period of economic recovery during which production increases in response to increased consumer demand. New jobs are created as companies begin to recall laid-off workers and order new equipment. Some of this equipment, however, replaces labour. As a result, the economy may expand faster than the rate of increase in employment.

A **depression** occurs when the period of economic decline is prolonged and severe. During a depression prices of goods and ser-

vices fall dramatically. This is known as **deflation**. Wages also fall because there is a surplus of labour available to employers. Generally, wages tend to drop faster than prices during a depression.

Other Forces at Work

We will never know if the Great Depression of the 1930s could have been avoided. We know that the business cycle is a naturally occurring feature of free-market economies. But the Depression may have been intensified by forces that distorted the business cycle. Buying on credit and the stock-market mania of the late 1920s led businesses to expand production at a

much faster rate than normal market forces would have dictated. At the same time, anti-labour legislation kept wages low, thereby reducing the purchasing power of consumers. **Protectionist** legislation in the United States and other major trading countries ignored the fact that the world had become a highly integrated and interconnected economic system.

Economic Systems

Prior to the 1930s, the theory of **laissez-faire** economics left market forces free from government intervention. But inequalities in the system—such as child labour and unfair wages and working condi-

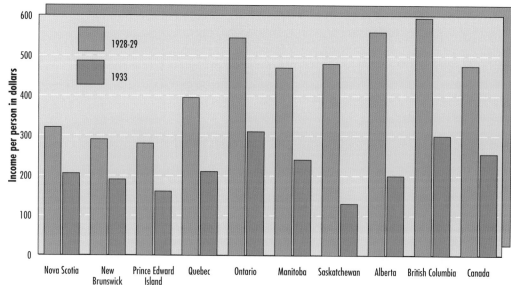

Decline in Incomes (per person) by Province, 1928-29 and 1933 (average)

Income per person in dollars

■ 1928-29
■ 1933

Nova Scotia | New Brunswick | Prince Edward Island | Quebec | Ontario | Manitoba | Saskatchewan | Alberta | British Columbia | Canada

WHO WINS AND LOSES IN A DEPRESSION?

A recession or depression can have a devastating effect on an economy, like Canada's, that exports large amounts of raw materials. Workers in manufacturing and service industries lose their jobs as a result of reduced production. Workers in resource-based industries are laid off because fewer raw materials are needed as factory production declines.

Small businesses also suffer in a depression. Shopkeepers, especially those selling non-essential goods, find that consumer demand evaporates quickly. During a recession, they cannot reduce their prices and still remain profitable. Small businesses often lack the financial resources to outlast a depression, and so are forced into bankruptcy.

Individuals and companies that have borrowed heavily or have large mortgages are also hurt by a depression. Declining incomes reduce a debtor's ability to repay money. Failure to repay the interest on a loan leads to foreclosure by the lender. As a result of these circumstances, many people in Canada during the Depression lost their businesses, homes, farms, and automobiles.

Some businesses and individuals actually profit from a depression. Deflation benefits anyone who has money in hand. As the prices of farms, houses, and land drop, those who have cash can buy these properties at bargain prices. When the economy recovers, they are able to make significant profits by selling them at much higher prices.

Large corporations also can survive a depression. In Canada, most major corporations remained profitable in all but one year of the Depression. Corporations are able to lay off workers, cut wages, and reduce production in order to operate profitably. In fact, as competition declined during the Depression, many Canadian companies were able to raise prices at a time when their production costs were dropping, thereby increasing their profits.

---

tions—prompted some people to argue that governments should plan and control the economy to produce the greatest good for the greatest number of people. This led to the establishment of **communist** systems, like that in Russia after the revolution. (See page 70.)

Other people believed governments could intervene in the economy without exercising total control over it. They argued governments could cut spending and raise taxes during prosperous periods, then increase spending and cut taxes during recessions. These measures would stimulate production and consumption.

During the Depression, leaders began experimenting with these ideas. As US president Franklin Roosevelt's **New Deal** appeared to stimulate the US economy, other leaders, such as Canada's prime minister, R.B. Bennett, began developing similar strategies.

Today, governments use their spending power, along with their ability to influence interest rates and the supply of money, to moderate the effects of the business cycle. In this way, they hope to be able to prevent another Depression.

KEYWORDS

business cycle

inflation

recession

depression

deflation

protectionist

laissez-faire

communist

New Deal

MAKING CONNECTIONS

1. Suggest some reasons why wages fall faster than prices during a depression. In your view, is this justifiable?

2. Should government play any role in the operation of the economy? Explain your views.

Analysing an issue or event requires a variety of sources of evidence. What are some sources of evidence, and how should we interpret them?

Historical Fiction

Fictional works, such as novels, short stories, and plays, sometimes provide valuable insights into the ideas and customs of another era or a different culture. (See page 128.) Sometimes works of fiction are based on real works. This historical fiction often preserves a fairly accurate picture of the society in which the events took place. However, it may also present a limited or even distorted view of the events. Therefore fictional work has to be examined carefully before using it as historical evidence.

The first step in analysing historical fiction is to identify the nature of the work. Consider who wrote the document and when, and try to determine whether there is any connection between the author and the events she or he describes. The second step is to examine the content of the work. How does the author describe events? Can you detect any bias in his or her presentation? (See page 72.) Finally, list what you have learned from this source and determine whether it provides sufficient information to be a valuable source of evidence.

Visual Evidence

Visual evidence, such as paintings, drawings, statues, and photographs, can reveal many clues about past events and other cultures. (See pages 128-129.) Visual evidence shows you the manner of dress, the forms of entertainment, and the things of importance in a given time and place. This type of evidence has its limitations, however, because as a viewer, you see only what the artist or photographer wants you to see.

In analysing visual evidence, you need to study the work carefully. First identify the subject and the action that is taking place. You might need to look at the work two or three times to make sure you observe all the details. Next, think about what the work is telling you about the subject. Remember, a single picture seldom reveals all there is to know about an event. Like

writers of historical fiction, artists and photographers bring bias to their work, perhaps simply by leaving out certain details. You have to evaluate the validity of the visual based on what you already know about the subject.

Statistics

Statistics are a concise method of presenting useful facts about a subject. They provide information in numerical form, but it is up to you to determine what these numbers mean. The key to interpreting statistics is to understand what information is being presented, and how.

To start, read the title of the table, then read the various head-

This photograph is of Vancouver in the 1930s. What can you determine about the city from the evidence in the photo?

A bibliography lists all the relevant sources of evidence used when investigating an issue or event. In setting up a bibliography, there are some general guidelines to follow. The bibliography should be placed at the end of the document on a separate piece of paper. Arrange the bibliography in alphabetical order by surname of the authors. For example, if you were to list this textbook in a bibliography, the entry would look like this:

Francis, Daniel, Jennifer Hobson, Gordon Smith, Stan Garrod, Jeff Smith, *Canadian Issues: A Contemporary Perspective*. (Toronto: Oxford University Press, 1998).

Unless the bibliography is short, it should be divided into sections according to the type of source. Books, for example, should be listed in one section, government documents in another, videotapes in yet another. Your bibliography could contain several sections.

1. a) Prepare a bibliography for a written presentation you are preparing in this or any other course. Consult style manuals to ensure that your sources of evidence are identified in proper bibliographic style.

    b) How does the style for a footnote differ from that for a bibliography? Give an example of the two methods of acknowledging sources of evidence.

ings and/or subject headings within the table. These tell you the topic, the timeframe, and the regions being studied. Next, scan the table as a whole to get the full scope of the data. Once you understand what information is being presented, interpret the data by finding relationships among the numbers. Finally, to draw conclusions about statistical data, you need to use your knowledge from other sources. As with all sources of evidence, be sure that the data comes from a reliable and unbiased source.

Graphs

Graphs are often used to present visual pictures of statistical data. (See pages 120 and 127.) They summarize key information in a clear and readable format. The most frequently used graphs are line graphs, bar graphs, and pie graphs. Line graphs and bar graphs illustrate changes that take place over time or under certain measurable conditions. Pie graphs divide information into parts and reveal how each part relates to the whole.

To analyse a graph, identify the information it is presenting using the title and the various labels that are used in the graph, such as those on the vertical and horizontal axes. This will tell you the subject and what makes the numbers show. If there is a legend, check this to find out what the different lines, colours, and symbols mean. Next, study the graph. What does it tell you? Using this information, draw conclusions about the event or issue. As with statistics, you will need to rely on your knowledge from other sources to reach your conclusions.

MAKING CONNECTIONS

1. On pages 122 to 132, you will have the opportunity to analyse each type of evidence as it applies to the Great Depression. Once you have done this, **synthesize** these sources of evidence by finding relationships among them. How does the information in one source support the information in the others? What conclusions can you draw about the effects of the Depression on average Canadians? Explain.

KEYWORDS

synthesize

STATISTICAL ANALYSIS
The Depression in Canada
FOCUSSING ON THE ISSUE

Economists use statistics to analyse and explain economic systems.
What do statistics reveal about the Canadian economy during the Depression?

Economic Data

Much of the information reported in the media about the state of the Canadian or world economy is in the form of **statistics**. The results of economic performance can be measured in terms of production and income. Chief among the gauges of the economy's overall performance is **Gross National Product** (GNP). This is the total value of goods produced and services provided within a country in one year (the **Gross Domestic Product**) plus the total of net income from abroad.

The unemployment rate indicates the number of people who want to work but are unable to find jobs. These figures are calculated monthly and then averaged for the year.

Direct **relief** is financial aid provided to families and individuals

What connections can you make between the photographs shown here and the statistical data?

by the federal and provincial governments. It was introduced during the Depression to help those hardest hit by the economic collapse.

Gross National Product in Canada, 1928-1939

Year	Total Production (billions of dollars)
1928	6.1
1929	6.1
1930	5.7
1931	4.7
1932	3.8
1933	3.5
1934	4.0
1935	4.3
1936	4.6
1937	5.2
1938	5.3
1939	5.6

Unemployment in Canada, 1928-1942

Unemployment rate (%) plotted against June of year, from 1928 to 1942.

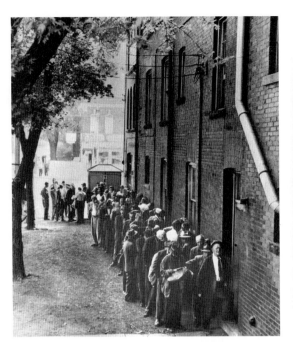

Number of People on Direct Relief in Canada, 1932-1939

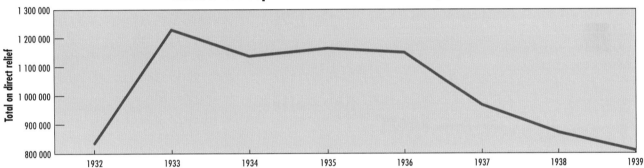

The Unemployment and Agricultural Assistance Act, 1940: Report of Dominion Commissioner of Unemployment Relief for the Fiscal Year Ending March 31, 1941 (*Ottawa, 1941*).

MAKING CONNECTIONS

1. What happened to the unemployment rate after the stock market crashed? When was unemployment at its highest level? When did the unemployment crisis end? Can you explain why?

2. Compare the graph of unemployment with the graph showing the number of people on direct relief. What relationship is there between the two sets of data?

3. a) Create a line graph showing the Gross National Product in Canada between 1928 and 1939.
   b) What pattern does the graph show? Which year had the lowest total production? What was the unemployment rate for that year? What can you conclude from this comparison?

KEYWORDS

statistics

Gross National Product

Gross Domestic Product

relief

TOUGH TIMES
The Impact on Families
FOCUSSING ON THE ISSUE

There were perhaps as many unique experiences during the Depression as there were Canadians. What was the impact of the Depression on Canadian families?

The Women Were Strong

I won't tell you my name but I'll tell you this. My husband walked out, just left like so many did in those days because they just couldn't take the shame of not being able to support their family. It was the women who were strong in those days.

I was left with two tiny children, one a baby, and the best I could get was a small room across from Vancouver General Hospital. My **relief** *was less than $10 a month.... The hot water heater had rusted through and the landlord wouldn't replace it, so there was no hot water. So every morning I'd put on a white dress that could pass for a nurse*

helper's uniform and I'd take my two babies across to the hospital and go into the big room there and I'd wash them. Nobody ever asked me what or how or why. Everybody thought I was on staff.

Barry Broadfoot, Ten Lost Years 1929-1939: Memories of Canadians Who Survived the Depression (New York: Doubleday, 1973), pp. 286-87. Copyright © 1973 by Barry Broadfoot. Used by permission of Doubleday, a division of Bantam Doubleday Dell Publishing Group, Inc.

Jamie's Got Relief Boots

Ever seen red boots before? I never did before and I never did since. I hated

them but I had no choice. Nine years old, what choice does a nine-year-old have? We got home and I put on the boots...I remember they were stiff....

I went out...and one kid spotted those Li'l Abners and yelled, "Relief boots. Jamie's got relief boots" and everybody laughed. A couple of others made smart remarks, and the first time we were scrimmaging with the ball I gave the first guy a swift kick in the shins. The other two guys got it shortly after....No one laughed at my boots again.

Barry Broadfoot, Ten Lost Years, pp. 76-77.

Every Last Cent

I knew where every last cent of my money went, feeding a husband and three boys. My grocery bill for the month, if it was over ten dollars I was just sick....Didn't know how I was going to pay it....If my grocery bill was more, then I'd go over my book, over and over again, and I'd find out what went wrong. Ten dollars, that was the tops, and my husband, my kids, they never starved.

Barry Broadfoot, Ten Lost Years, pp. 274-75.

We Live for Today

I am perfectly aware that being a girl out of work has its advantages: there are no girls in the bread line. We can

Many people were forced to abandon their homes and farms during the Depression.

busy ourselves in the house. But what girl with a business training wants to sew or cook, unless it be in her own home, building for the future? We are trained for business. We like it. We need the money, most of all in our youth. We are missing what our elders have had. My ambition was to save enough money to travel, after paying for a nice fat insurance for the future. I wanted to go through the Rockies, a dream which made work a pleasure. Today the height of my ambition is to keep off the rocks....We can only live for today. Tomorrow and tomorrow's plans we are obliged to ignore. Our sense of values is slipping. We read about a youth committing a robbery and being caught. We feel sorry for the poor devil—probably needed the money as badly as we do! We condone today what we condemned yesterday.

Mary Howlett, "Wanted—A New Tune," from Maclean's, 1 January 1934. Reprinted by permission.

In what ways do you think social gatherings helped people to cope with the hardships of the Depression?

A Dismal Future

I can remember several years ago my grandfather would begin: "When I was a boy..." and I would listen as he told me of his hardships in those early days—log cabins, miserable weather and so on. The old gentleman has passed on, and his grandson is faced today with the same hardships, magnified a hundred, yes, a thousand times. What progress has civilization made if after fifty or sixty years we find ourselves back where we started?

Despite radio, electricity, and advanced living conditions, we of the younger generation are facing a bleak, dismal future....I am not a prophet but an ordinary bewildered boy. The only thing I can see for me to do is to try as hard as I can to make good in my present situation, and to hope that in the near future there will be a change for the better.

Clarence E. Ford, "Pioneering—1934," Maclean's, 15 January 1934.

We Never Went Back

We tried to sell our ranch, and it was a good one, but nobody would buy it. Who would in those days when cows were selling for about six dollars each?...Finally the time came when those children just had to get to a school, so we just loaded up the wagon and drove away from it. We just left the ranch. Nobody wanted it, and we never went back.

Barry Broadfoot, Ten Lost Years, p. 52.

Life Went On

Life went on for farmers on relief in Saskatchewan as it did for the unemployed on relief in Regina, Winnipeg, and Edmonton. There was a dance someplace every week...and even the poorest couple seemed able to dig up the fifty cents admission price.

James H. Gray, The Winter Years: The Depression on the Prairies (Toronto: Macmillan, 1966), p. 178.

MAKING CONNECTIONS

1. What can you conclude about the impact of the Depression on families and family life in Canada?

2. Imagine you are a teenager living in Vancouver in the 1930s. Write a letter to the prime minister in which you describe how the Depression is affecting your family.

KEYWORDS

relief

REGULATING THE ECONOMY
The Government's Response
FOCUSSING ON THE ISSUE

During the Depression, farmers' prices and workers' incomes fell, while consumer prices and corporation profits remained high. Should the federal government have become more involved in regulating the economy?

Demanding Reform

The economic collapse of the Depression caused many people to re-examine their attitudes towards the role government should play in the economy. During the prosperity of the mid-1920s, urban life had improved considerably and most people looked forward to a continuation of the good times. As a result, few Canadians were concerned about the role of government in the economy—until the Depression. Then many people blamed the economic collapse on the failure of the **capitalist** system. Faced with widespread poverty and growing social unrest, Canadians began to demand both political and economic reforms.

Price Spreads

During the Depression, producers received lower prices for their products, but the prices they paid for their supplies did not experience a similar decline. Wages and salaries also fell rapidly, while prices for food and clothing dropped slowly, if at all. Many Canadians believed that these price

spreads were the result of greedy capitalists taking advantage of a powerless and impoverished public. They demanded that the federal government take decisive action to eliminate the problem. Yet no one was quite sure what action the government should take.

The response of Prime Minister R.B. Bennett was to appoint a **Royal Commission** to investigate price spreads. Vancouver MP and minister of trade and commerce Harry H.

Stevens was appointed to head the commission. The evidence presented at hearings held across the country painted a shocking picture of Canadian businesses. Workers reported widespread **sweatshop** conditions, with many workers being paid for **piecework**, which enabled manufacturers to pay less than minimum wage to employees working as much as 70 hours a week. But while the companies were saving costs, prices charged to con-

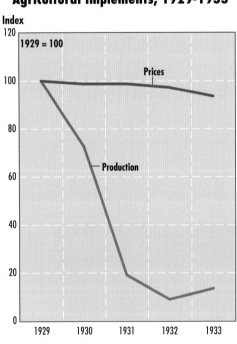

Prices and Production for Agricultural Implements, 1929-1933

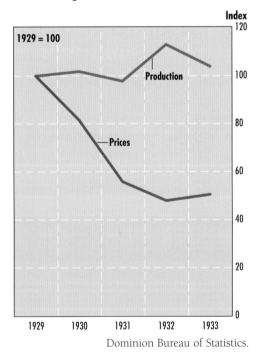

Prices and Production for Agriculture, 1929-1933

Dominion Bureau of Statistics.

Prices for agricultural implements remained high while production plummeted. Yet the prices for the products of agriculture declined while production increased.

sumers hovered at pre-Depression levels.

Stevens was convinced that the government should take tough action against these business practices. But his campaign for reform was not supported by Bennett or many of his Cabinet colleagues, who preferred that government involvement in the economy be limited. Faced with such strong opposition within his own party, Stevens was forced to resign in October 1934.

By 1935, however, there was still no end in sight to the Depression, and the Canadian public was increasingly dissatisfied with the government's inaction. With an election looming, Bennett decided to heed the public's demand for assertive action. Persuaded by the popular success of US president Franklin Roosevelt's **New Deal**, Bennett developed his own version of the New Deal. In January 1935, he announced his new policy to the nation in a live radio broadcast: *I am for reform. I nail the flag of progress to the mast. I summon the power of the state to its support.*

Bennett promised to establish unemployment insurance, set a minimum wage, limit the hours of work, guarantee fair treatment of workers, and control prices to ensure that businesses did not make unfair profits. His political opponents maintained that Bennett's conversion was nothing more than a scheme to gain votes in the election. They suggested that his proposals came too late to benefit most Canadians. The public agreed, and Bennett and his government were defeated by Mackenzie King and the Liberal party in the election of 1935.

VIEWPOINTS

THE REPORT OF THE ROYAL COMMISSION

When the report of the Commission was submitted to Parliament in 1935, its condemnation of Canadian business practices caused a sensation.

On closer study...it became clear that many of the grievances complained of, and the problems disclosed, were manifestations of one fundamental and far-reaching social change, the concentration of economic power....The corporate form of business not only often gives freedom from legal liability, but also facilitates the evasion of moral responsibility for inequitable and uneconomic practices. Therefore, it is essential that any investigation into business practices should concern itself with the growth and significance to the national economy of a

form of business activity which has harboured...so much that needs cleansing.
"Report of the Royal Commission on Price Spreads," *Sessional Papers*, 1935, p. 3ff

The Commission also recommended a constitutional amendment so that the federal government would be able to establish national standards for working conditions, wages, unionization, corporate operations, and pricing practices. Many Canadians supported this recommendation.

1. Should Canada have the kinds of national standards recommended in the Commission report? Explain.

MAKING CONNECTIONS

1. Do you think businesses have a moral responsibility to treat their employees fairly? Explain.

2. What do you think the role of government should be in the economy? Explain your position in the form of a newspaper editorial.

KEYWORDS

capitalist

Royal Commission

sweatshop

piecework

THE DUST BOWL
Economics and Climate Join Forces

During the Depression, human economic activities and climate cycles joined forces with the economy to create extremely difficult conditions for prairie farmers. How did climate change affect agriculture during this period? How did economic activities affect natural systems?

The Prairies

The Canadian prairies lie in the **rainshadow** of the western mountain ranges. As the **prevailing winds** from the Pacific are forced upwards over the mountains, they cool and release their moisture on the western slopes. As a result, east of the mountains the winds that sweep across the plains are often dry. The amount of precipitation in any season varies from year to year. Most precipitation falls in the summer, often in the form of thunderstorms. There may be several years in a row in which the climate is wetter or drier than usual.

The thick prairie grasses that once covered the plains were perfectly adapted to these climate con-ditions. The grasses served as a protective shield, retaining the soil's moisture and preventing the winds from eroding the soil. For thousands of years, herds of bison grazed here without disturbing the grassy cover. Aboriginal peoples developed a sophisticated economy based on the bison; they, too, left the natural vegetation as they had found it.

The arrival of European settlers early in the twentieth century brought great changes to the prairie landscape. These farmers brought with them steel ploughs with sharp blades that sliced easily through the thick sod. They began to plough up the natural grass cover to plant winter wheat. By the 1920s, grain farmers had stripped away almost all of the original prairie grass. In the 1930s, the prairies experienced a series of severe droughts. Without the complex root system of the grasses to anchor it, much of the soil was picked up by the winds. The resulting dust storms and sandstorms buried roads and houses.

The Dust Bowl

In Canada, the Depression is often referred to as the "Dirty Thirties." This label describes not only the difficult conditions experienced by many urban Canadians, but also the dry **Dust Bowl** that gripped the prairies in the 1930s.

The **dryland farm** areas of southern Alberta and Saskatchewan were hit by droughts in the summers of 1929, 1931, and 1933 to 1937. The crops failed because of inadequate rainfall. Typically, 8 to 10 cm of topsoil were blown away in the wind; in extreme cases, as much as 50 cm of soil particles were swept away in a single windstorm. At times, the windswept dust darkened the skies as far as the Atlantic coast. Further devastating the meagre crops were plagues of grasshoppers and an epidemic of a disease known as **wheat rust**. With their

Describe how you might have felt during a hot summer day in the Dust Bowl.

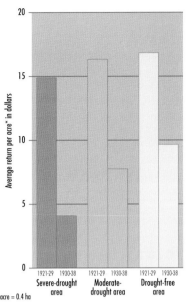

Wheat Returns by Area, 1921-1929 and 1930-1938

* 1 acre = 0.4 ha

Adapted from Historical Atlas of Canada, Vol. III: Addressing the Twentieth Century, 1891-1961, *Donald Kerr and Deryck Holdsworth, eds., Geoffrey J. Matthews, maps (Toronto: University of Toronto Press, 1990). Reprinted by permission of University of Toronto Press Inc.*

incomes drastically reduced, farmers could not purchase machinery or supplies. Many could not afford to pay the mortgages on their farms. By 1935, many prairie farms had been abandoned.

Together, drought and poor agricultural practices created the devastation of the Dust Bowl. There was little researchers could do about the vagaries of climate, but they could prevent further soil erosion. In 1935, the Prairie Farm Rehabilitation Administration (PFRA) was formed to introduce anti-erosion measures and water-storage facilities.

CASE STUDY

DEALING WITH THE PROBLEMS OF SOIL EROSION

One of the most notable anti-erosion techniques introduced in the prairies by the PFRA was trash farming, or stubble mulching. In this process the stubble is left on the fields after harvest to reduce wind erosion. Subsurface cultivators control weed growth on fallow land. Blades or rods on these machines are dragged through the soil to cut off the weeds at root level. The stubble gets chopped up, leaving the fields with an untidy appearance; hence the term *trash farming*.

In strip farming, another anti-erosion technique, crops are grown in strips along the line of the prevailing winds. Only narrow strips of soil are exposed to the wind at any one time. Shelter belts, or windbreaks, reduce wind speed and help to limit erosion and keep moisture in the soil.

In North America, wind erosion has resulted mostly from the cultivation of crops on land that would have been better left for grazing. After the Dust Bowl of the 1930s, municipalities took over much of the land affected by erosion and turned it into pasture.

MAKING CONNECTIONS

1. Do you think the Dust Bowl could have been prevented? Explain your answer.

2. Brainstorm other ways in which human economic activities adversely affect natural systems. What behavioural changes do we need to make to reduce these adverse effects?

KEYWORDS

rainshadow

prevailing winds

Dust Bowl

dryland farm

wheat rust

ART AND LITERATURE
Depicting the Depression
FOCUSSING ON THE ISSUE

The Depression was portrayed in fictional writing as well as in paintings. Why are these literary and artistic images valuable tools in capturing the experiences and attitudes of Canadians during the Depression?

Literary Images

Sinclair Ross was born on a homestead near Shelbrooke, Saskatchewan, in 1908. Until his retirement in 1968, Ross worked as a banker, but in his spare time he wrote short stories and novels. Perhaps his best-known work is *As For Me and My House*, published in 1941. Set in the fictional prairie town of Horizon, Saskatchewan, during the Depression, the novel tells the story of Mr. and Mrs. Bentley and their struggle to overcome the isolation and barrenness of small-town Saskatchewan. Philip Bentley is a frustrated member of the clergy. The story is a psychological study of prairie life during the Depression, told by Mrs. Bentley through her diaries.

Sunday Evening, April 16
Philip preached well this morning, responding despite himself to the crowded, expectant little schoolhouse. They were a sober, work-roughened congregation. There was strength in their voices when they sang, like the strength and darkness of the soil....Five years in succession now they've been blown out, dried out, hailed out; and it was as if in the face of so blind and uncaring a universe they were trying to assert themselves, to insist upon their own meaning and importance.
(page 26)

Sunday Evening, April 30
It's the most nerve-wracking wind I've ever listened to. Sometimes it sinks a little, as if spent and out of breath, then comes high, shrill and importunate again. Sometimes it's blustering and rough, sometimes silent and sustained. Sometimes it's wind, sometimes frightened hands that shake the doors and windows.... I sit thinking about the dust, the farmers and the crops, wondering what another dried-out year will mean for us.
(page 52)

Thursday Evening, May 25
It's been nearly dark today with dust. Everything's gritty, making you shiver and setting your teeth on edge. There's a crunch on the floor like sugar when you walk. We keep the doors and windows closed, and still it works in everywhere.
(page 81)

Wednesday Evening, August 9
It's raining again, and chilly like the fall....A gray, leaden light like early dawn is the best we have all day. The town from the window has a look of sodden disillusionment. The paintless little buildings, the draggled clumps of dried-up grass and weeds, the muddy streets with pools of cold gray

rain—it all merges into a November dreariness.
(page 159)

Sunday Evening, October 22
Tonight Philip made a sketch of Joe Lawson....The hands are mostly what you notice. Such big, disillusioned, steadfast hands, so faithful to the earth and seasons that betray them. I didn't know before what drought was really

Petroushka by Paraskeva Clark, 1937. Clark combined her art with politics. This work was a protest against the slaying of striking steel workers in Chicago by the city's police.

*like, watching a crop dry
up, going on again.*

(*page 183*)

*Sunday Evening, May 12
This is our last Sunday in
Horizon....It's blowing
tonight, and there's dust
again, and the room sways
slowly in a yellow smoky
haze. The bare, rain-
stained walls remind me of
our first Sunday here, just a
little over a year ago, and
in a sentimental mood I
keep thinking what an
eventful year it's been, what
a wide wheel it's run.*

(*page 215*)

Sinclair Ross, As For Me and My
House (*Toronto: McClelland and
Stewart, 1989*). *Used by permis-
sion, McClelland & Stewart, Inc.
The Canadian Publishers.*

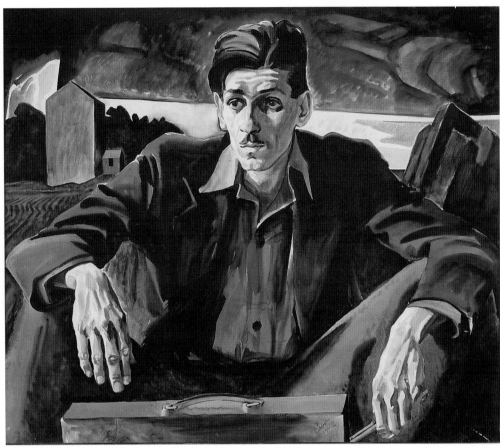

Young Canadian *by Charles Comfort, 1932. Comfort (1900) painted landscapes as well as memorable human images. This is a portrait of the artist's friend and painter, Carl Schaefer.*

Artistic Images

The dominance of **realism** in art during the 1930s was a response to the economic depression and social turmoil that gripped Canada. Often, in an attempt to reassert traditional values, some artists chose to focus on **agrarian** themes. Others concentrated on social themes, capturing the despondency and disorder of the Depression in order to underscore the need for social reforms. The images here and on page 114 are representative of the artistic mood of the era.

KEYWORDS

realism

agrarian

personal narrative

MAKING CONNECTIONS

1. Why do you think Sinclair Ross wrote his novel *As For Me and My House* as a **personal narrative** of prairie life during the Depression? In your opinion, is this an effective approach? Explain your answer.

2. Compare these literary and artistic images with other images of the Depression in this chapter. What similarities do you see? What differences? In a brief paragraph, draw your own conclusions about the extent to which art reflected life during the Depression.

NEW POLITICAL MOVEMENTS
Third Parties in Canada
FOCUSSING ON THE ISSUE

A number of new political movements emerged out of the Depression.
What is the role of so-called "third parties" in the Canadian political system?

A Time for Change

During the Depression, many Canadians looked at the political system and decided it was not working. The policies of the mainstream political parties—Liberals and Conservatives—were having no effect on the economic crisis. It was time for a change.

The Social Credit

Social Credit was a theory of economic reform developed by a British engineer named Major C. H.

Douglas in 1919. According to Major Douglas, the basic problem with the economic system was that people never had enough money to spend on the goods that were being produced. He proposed that government remedy this situation by making a regular payment (a **social dividend**) to every citizen. With extra cash in hand, consumers would spend more and the economy would prosper once again.

For many years no one took Douglas's theory seriously. Then came the Depression, and suddenly

it seemed to make a lot of sense, at least to a Calgary school principal named William Aberhart. Aberhart was a deeply religious man who moonlighted as a Bible teacher and a popular radio preacher. In 1932, he began to preach the ideas of Social Credit. Central to his theory was the idea that the government should pay $25 a month to every citizen.

Aberhart tried to convince one of the established political parties to support his proposals. When they did not, he formed his own party and entered the 1935 provincial election. Social Credit swept the province, winning 56 out of 63 seats in the legislature. Over the next few years, Aberhart tried to introduce many reforms to the banking system, but the courts declared them all **unconstitutional**. The prosperity certificates of $25 a month were often referred to as "funny money" because they were declared illegal and never paid out. Still, Social Credit remained the governing party in Alberta for 35 years. The party also came to power in British Columbia in 1952. Although it never had much success as a national party, there was also a prominent Social Credit presence in

A Depression family—with all their possessions—take to the road looking for work. What was the connection between the plight of families like this one and the rise of new political parties during the 1930s?

Quebec from 1961 through the 1970s known as the Ralliement des Créditistes.

The CCF

Social Credit had much in common with another political party that emerged during the Depression, the Co-operative Commonwealth Federation, or CCF. Both parties wanted to use government to defend ordinary workers and farmers against the banks and large corporations. Both wanted to extend health care, education, and **income security** to all Canadians. They differed, however, on a fundamental point. Social Credit argued that the economic system was inefficient and needed to be reformed. The CCF argued that the system was unjust and needed to be replaced.

The CCF emerged in 1932 in Saskatchewan with the formation of the League for Social Reconstruction, a group of university intellectuals who drew up a plan for restructuring the economy. Later that year, members of the League met with trade-union delegates, farmers, and a small group of independent Members of Parliament and decided to create a new party, the CCF. It held its founding convention in 1933 in Regina, where it adopted its platform of policies, known as the Regina **Manifesto**.

The CCF called for public ownership of banks and major services, improved health and social services, and higher taxes for the wealthy. The CCF's program was **socialist**, in the sense that it blamed the **free-market** system for the misery of the Depression and advocated more government control of the economy. At the same time it was a form of **democratic socialism**, committed to elections, free votes, and the parliamentary system. Members of the CCF were often accused by their opponents of being communists. However, they differed from communists in countries such as Russia and China in that they were committed to bringing about change through the free choice of all Canadians, not through **coercion** or armed revolution.

The CCF never had much success in Quebec or Atlantic Canada. In the West, however, and in Ontario, they became a major party. At one time they formed the opposition in British Columbia and Ontario, and in 1944 they surged to power in Saskatchewan. (See page 174.) Whether or not it was successful in elections, the party always stood for the interests of poor and disadvantaged people. Many CCF ideas were adopted and put into practice by other parties. In 1961, the party reorganized itself under a new name, the New Democratic Party, which is still active in Canadian political life today.

J. S. Woodsworth (shown here with his daughter Grace, who was also a Member of Parliament for many years) was the first leader of the CCF. He was a Methodist minister who was first elected to Parliament for the Labour party in 1921. A highly respected MP, Woodsworth was known for his dedication to the needs of ordinary people.

KEYWORDS

social dividend

unconstitutional

income security

manifesto

socialist

free-market

democratic socialism

coercion

MAKING CONNECTIONS

1. What does the phrase "third party" mean? Explain with reference to the CCF and the Social Credit.

2. How does a third party become a first party?

INTERNATIONAL POLLUTION
The Smelter at Trail

The addition of mineral smelting to BC's mining industry brought with it the problems of industrial pollution. By the 1920s, pollution from the smelter at Trail had become an international issue. How was the problem resolved?

The Trail Smelter

Smelting operations began at Trail in 1896 under American owner- ship. In 1906, Consolidated Mining and Smelter (Cominco), owned by the Canadian Pacific Railway, bought the Trail smelter. Cominco quickly took advantage of low-cost hydroelectric power from the Kootenay River to expand its opera- tion. In the 1920s, two tall smoke- stacks of 125 m were added, mak-

ing Trail the largest non-ferrous mineral smelter in the British **Commonwealth**. The thick yellow smoke rising from the operation became the symbol of prosperity for the town.

The expansion increased **sul- phur dioxide** emissions at the smelter from 4700 t a month in 1916 to more than 8000 t a month in 1927. In spite of Cominco's efforts to control emissions, the people of Trail and the surrounding

area complained that when the wind was blowing in the direction of their homes, the vegetation in their gardens and around their homes withered and turned brown. In an attempt to demonstrate that crops were not affected by the smelter, the company established a dairy farm near Trail. The com- plaints continued, however, and on several occasions the company paid smoke easement—compensation for crop damage caused by the smelter fumes. By 1930, the damage to the vegetation in and around Trail was so bad that large areas became vir- tually barren and many residents no longer tried to grow lawns and trees in their yards.

An International Problem

The problem was not confined to Trail, however. The **prevailing winds** in the Columbia River Valley blew south into Washington state, carrying the fumes from Trail with them. As the smelter fumes drifted through the Columbia Valley, farm- ers swore they could see their crops wither, their farm animals become sick, and the paint peel from their buildings. Cominco offered to pay compensation for damages and to buy farms from those who suffered unduly, but since Washington state law prohibited foreign corporations

Emissions from the smelter at Trail spewed toxic smoke into the air in the 1920s and 1930s. Is this kind of pollution common in Canadian cities today? Explain.

from buying land, another solution had to be found.

The dispute was referred to the International Joint Commission (IJC), a body set up by Canada and the United States to deal with matters of concern to the two countries. At the same time, officials at Cominco recognized that they had to do something about the pollution. They also realized they could make money by trapping the gases and using them to manufacture fertilizer. After carrying out tests, the company built a fertilizer plant, and in 1929, it began operating the first of four sulphur recovery units. But in spite of these efforts, pollution levels remained high.

The IJC's Decision

In 1931, the IJC ruled that Cominco had to reduce its sulphur dioxide emissions as soon as possible and it ordered Canada to pay US$350 000 in compensation for all environmental damage that had occurred before the end of 1931. Although the Canadian government paid the award, the US government refused to accept it and demanded that the case be re-examined by an arbitration **tribunal**.

In 1935, the tribunal—consisting of a chairperson from Belgium and representatives from Canada and the US—was established. Both governments appointed scientists to assist the tribunal in studying the technical and environmental issues. Operating night and day, airplanes and balloons measured wind direction, velocity, and sulphur dioxide concentrations in the air. After several years of investigation, the tribunal ruled in 1941 that the smelter had been polluting Washington's environment since 1932. Canada was ordered to pay an additional US$78 000 to the United States in compensation. The tribunal also ruled that the smelter should be forced to control the levels of its sulphur dioxide emissions. To accomplish this, Cominco was ordered to maintain equipment that monitored wind velocity and direction, air turbulence, air pressure, and sulphur dioxide concentrations at the smelter. Readings from these instruments were to be used to keep sulphur dioxide emissions at or below levels established by the tribunal. If the smelter could not maintain the prescribed sulphur dioxide levels, then the tribunal could award further compensation to the United States.

The Outcome

The Trail pollution case was the first of its kind and it set a legal **precedent** for similar cases in the future. It established that both Canada and the United States accepted that cross-border disputes could be resolved by the IJC or by a jointly established arbitration process. In addition, both sides agreed that pollution caused by a commercial operation in one country that affected residents of the other country was the responsibility of the country in which the operation originated.

The results of Cominco's emission-control program were encouraging. Crop losses and vegetation damage were reduced and the plant life in Trail began to regenerate. By the 1960s there were trees on the banks of the Kootenay and Columbia rivers near Trail, and residents were once again mowing lawns and pruning trees.

◄═ MAKING CONNECTIONS ═►

1. Do you think the Canadian government should have paid for the damages caused by Cominco's smelter? Explain.

2. There is an ongoing dispute between Canada and the United States over the problem of acid rain in eastern Canada. Research the problem and compare it with the Trail smelter dispute. Explain whether or not the same solution should be applied.

KEYWORDS

Commonwealth

sulphur dioxide

prevailing winds

tribunal

precedent

In Quebec during the 1930s the government took unprecedented steps to suppress political and religious groups that were critical of the established order. How far should government be allowed to go in protecting society from subversion?

Change in Quebec

The Depression affected every realm of life, including politics. Voters across the country were unsatisfied with the way traditional parties were responding to the economic crisis. In the West, a coalition of intellectuals formed the Co-operative Commonwealth Federation (CCF). In Alberta, the new Social Credit party was elected to power. Change was on the minds of most Canadians, and Quebeckers were no exception.

The Liberal party had been in power in Quebec since 1897. For many voters this was far too long. They were disgusted by corruption in the government and impatient with its lack of new policies. In 1936, Quebeckers turned to a new party, the Union Nationale, and elected a new premier, Maurice Duplessis.

Duplessis rode to power on the promise of reform. Once in office, however, he seemed to forget about many of the pledges he had made. Instead, he passed anti-strike laws to suppress labour protests and did nothing to curb the handouts and political favours that had discredited the previous government. But perhaps the most notorious legislation of his first term was the so-called "Padlock Law."

In 1937, the Quebec National Assembly passed the Act Respecting Communistic Propaganda. The government claimed that **communists** were a threat to Quebec society. The new law gave authorities the power to enter any public or private building to search for communist material. The law did not define what was meant by "communist," leaving authorities to decide for themselves. If offending material was found, it was destroyed and the premises were padlocked by police. Owners then had to appear before a judge to prove they were innocent. Anyone printing, publishing, or distributing "communist" literature was liable to imprisonment for up to a year, without the right to appeal. It was not even necessary to produce evidence that someone actually did plan to **subvert** the government.

In effect, the Padlock Law made it illegal to read certain materials or to hold certain thoughts in Quebec. Thus Duplessis silenced radical political opposition by making it illegal. The law remained in force for the next 20 years, until the Supreme Court of Canada ruled it unconstitutional. It remains one of the most flagrant violations of civil liberties in Canadian history.

This statue of Maurice Duplessis stands in front of the legislature in Quebec City. For many years it was kept in a warehouse gathering dust because Quebeckers were embarrassed by events that took place during the Duplessis era. In 1977, a new government decided it was time to bring Duplessis out of the shadows. The statue was reinstated. Do you agree with the decision?

A Place in History

Maurice Duplessis's party lost the next election, held in 1939 following the outbreak of war. The Liberals were able to convince Quebeckers that a vote for Duplessis was a vote for conscription. However, he regained power in 1944, and remained premier until his death. He was leader of Quebec for a total of 18 years, making him the longest reigning premier in the history of the province.

Duplessis ruled rather like a dictator, earning him the nickname *le chef*. In return for large contributions to his party, he helped companies by ensuring trade unions remained weak. The most notorious incident was in 1949 when Duplessis sent in the provincial police to crush a strike of asbestos miners.

Duplessis was a conservative politician who admired and upheld traditional Quebec society. People were discouraged from questioning authority or participating in the urban, industrial economy. (In the 1950s, for example, Duplessis banned drive-in movie theatres, arguing they were a threat to morality.) Under Duplessis, business affairs in the province were left more or less to English-speaking people. Critics called this arrangement an "unholy alliance" of church, government, and anglo-

Demonstrators protested the Padlock Law in Montreal in 1937.

phone business leaders. They referred to this period as *la grande noirceur,* "the great darkness"— Quebec's Dark Ages.

On the other hand, Duplessis had his defenders. He was popular with voters, who elected his government five times. They admired his **nationalism**. Duplessis stood up for Quebec and the French language against any attempt by the federal government to interfere in provincial affairs. "I intend them to know in Ottawa that we are masters in our own house," he said, "and we wish to remain masters in our own house." *Maîtres chez nous*— "masters in our own house"— became a slogan that is still fervently proclaimed by many people in Quebec.

Duplessis also ruled in a period of great economic prosperity. He came to power as the Depression was ending, then took advantage of the good times following the Second World War. Under his leadership, the Quebec government undertook many public works— bridges, schools, highways, and power dams—of which Quebeckers were proud. Better yet, he did it without raising taxes or going into debt.

Following Duplessis's death, voters strongly reacted against his government. For years afterwards he was a much-hated figure. More recently, Quebeckers have started reassessing Duplessis's role in Quebec history. They have concluded that many of the things he accomplished were good for the province. However Duplessis is judged, there is little doubt that Quebec's longest-serving premier is also its most controversial.

▄▅▀ MAKING CONNECTIONS ▀▅▄

1. Why are laws such as the Padlock Law dangerous in a democratic society?

2. a) Do you believe there are occasions when the government should have the power to suppress the free exchange of ideas? What would those occasions be?
    b) Should people have the right to free speech even if they use it to advocate the destruction of the government? Explain your answer

KEYWORDS

communist

subvert

nationalism

THE ROWELL-SIROIS COMMISSION
Federal-Provincial Relations
FOCUSSING ON THE ISSUE

As Canadians grew more impatient with the economic situation of the 1930s, the government considered ways of tackling the problem. What obstacles did the government face? What impact did the Rowell-Sirois Commission have?

The Bennett Solution

Despite the predictions of economists that the end of the Depression was "just around the corner," by 1934 it appeared to most Canadians that the Depression was in fact growing worse. As a result, Prime Minister Bennett announced a series of programs similar to the **New Deal** initiatives of US President Franklin Roosevelt. Bennett's program included unemployment insurance; new laws on hours of work and wages; laws to control prices and marketing of agricultural products (especially wheat); laws regulating mortgage **foreclosures** and banking; and proposals to improve pensions and **social security**.

Bennett's critics, however, were quick to point out that many of his proposals fell under the jurisdiction of the provinces and therefore could not be introduced by the federal government. Mackenzie King suggested that Bennett's plan was a Tory trick to buy votes because Bennett knew that ultimately his proposals would be declared illegal by the courts.

The King Solution

King fought the 1935 election largely on the slogan that "Tory times are hard times." The voters, tired of hard times, gave the Liberals 171 of the 245 seats in the House of Commons. As the new prime minister, King had to find a way to end the Depression and bring back good times. While King supported the ideas behind Bennett's legislation in principle, he

This political cartoon depicts the three federal party leaders during the 1935 election campaign. What message is the cartoonist conveying?

refused to spend any money on programs that might be declared illegal. He decided to refer the new laws to the courts and, until a decision was rendered, he would not implement any of the programs. In 1937, the Justices of the **Privy Council** ruled that many of the initiatives of Canada's New Deal were illegal because they fell under the provincial powers over property and civil rights. Implementing the programs would require a constitutional amendment.

King believed it would be impossible to convince the provincial premiers to agree to a constitutional amendment that would transfer some of their powers to the federal government. Unable to find a solution, he appointed a **Royal Commission** to examine the economic and financial relationship between the federal government and the provinces and the distribution of legislative powers. The Commission was to conduct hearings across the country, receive submissions from interested parties, and recommend any changes that would improve the federal-provincial relationship. Critics argued that King took this approach in the hope that either the Depression would cure itself while the Commission sat or its recommendations would have such wide support that he would have no trouble implementing them.

The Commission's Report

Appointed in 1937, the Rowell-Sirois Commission (named after its successive chairpersons, N.W. Rowell and Joseph Sirois) delivered its report in 1940. The report was the most thorough investigation of federal-provincial relations and the most comprehensive survey of the Canadian economy since Confederation. Its main recommendations called for significant amendments to the **BNA Act**, including the reordering of federal and provincial legislative powers. The Commission also recommended that the federal government take over all provincial debts and all responsibility for unemployment programs. In return, the provinces should forfeit, among other things, federal **subsidies** and their right to collect certain taxes. The federal government should provide grants to enable the poorer provinces to maintain an average Canadian standard for education and social services. In addition, a procedure should be developed to allow the Canadian Parliament to amend the BNA Act.

By the time the Commission's report was submitted to Parliament, however, Canada was already involved in the Second World War. Previous judicial decisions had ruled that "peace, order, and good government" gave the federal government virtually unlimited authority to make laws during a national emergency. Acting on this **precedent**, the King government passed the laws it believed were necessary to the war effort.

At the 1940 conference called to consider the Commission's report, British Columbia, Alberta, and Ontario opposed many of the recommendations. Confronted by this opposition, the government filed the Commission's report and got on with the business of fighting the war. The economic demands of the war were already stimulating the economy. Industries from coast to coast began to convert to the production of war materials. Unemployment rates plummeted as civilians enlisted and the factories began working overtime. Of the Commission's recommendations, the King government acted on two points: the creation of a national Unemployment Insurance program in 1940 and the introduction of **Family Allowances** in 1944.

KEYWORDS

New Deal

foreclosure

social security

Privy Council

Royal Commission

BNA Act

subsidy

precedent

Family Allowance

⊷◼ MAKING CONNECTIONS ◼⊶

1. a) How did the Commission propose to solve the problems of the provinces?
   b) Would the Commission's recommendations for national standards be useful today? Explain.

PUBLIC RADIO

The Creation of the CBC

FOCUSSING ON THE ISSUE

*Since 1936 Canada has had a mixed broadcasting system
of privately and publicly owned stations. Why is the question
of who controls the mass media important?*

Private Versus Public

By 1931, radio was an increasingly popular form of entertainment. Over 30 per cent of all homes had a radio, and that number would grow to 75 per cent by the end of the decade. Local radio stations were bought by Americans, who built stations along the border and beamed their programs into Canada. Canadians began to worry about the number of programs coming from the United States.

In 1929, the Royal Commission on Radio Broadcasting—also known as the Aird Commission after its chairperson, John Aird— recommended that the federal government create a publicly owned company to operate radio in Canada. The public company would regulate the private stations, as well as operate its own stations. The Commission maintained that radio was a public service, not just a private business, and that government should intervene to make sure high-quality Canadian programs were available.

The government did not act on the Aird Report right away. Strong opposition to the idea of public broadcasting was mounted by private radio stations. In response, supporters of public radio organized the Canadian Radio League to **lobby** the government. "The question is the State or the United States," one of the league's founders said. Finally, in 1932, Prime Minister Bennett created the three-person Canadian Radio Broadcasting Commission (CRBC) to regulate the air waves in Canada.

Private radio stations funded themselves by selling advertising time during their programs. Public stations relied, at least in part, on government funding. "Advertising has hurt radio programs," argued Hector Charlesworth, the first head

"Radio, I've always contended, was intended by God especially for Newfoundland, and having done it for Newfoundland, He graciously allowed it to be used in other parts of the world. It was meant for Newfoundland. It was meant for a remote and isolated people who never met. Who never saw each other. Radio was the great unifying thing."

Joey Smallwood, former premier of Newfoundland

"Hello, Canada and hockey fans in the United States and Newfoundland." With these words, Foster Hewitt, the voice of hockey, began his regular broadcast. Hewitt was one of the first announcers in the world to do the play-by-play of a hockey game over the radio. It was 22 March 1923, and he actually called the game into a telephone connected to the radio station. He sat in a glass booth at rinkside to keep the noise of the crowd out, but the glass fogged up and he could barely see. That first game went into three overtime periods. By the time it was over Hewitt had been talking for three hours.

In 1931, Hewitt broadcast the first game from Maple Leaf Gardens in Toronto. From then on his high-pitched voice screaming "he shoots, he scores!" became familiar to hockey fans from coast to coast. When *Hockey Night in Canada* moved to television in the 1950s, Hewitt followed. He made his final NHL broadcast in 1978.

of the CRBC. "When you put your broadcasting in the hands of advertisers, you no longer depend on the good taste of the artist but upon the taste of the advertiser." However, the CRBC had no intention of eliminating private radio. Its job was to create a parallel system of public stations, both English and French, for those who wanted to listen to them. The co-existence of private and public stations has been a feature of broadcasting in Canada ever since.

In 1936, the CRBC was reorganized into the Canadian Broadcasting Corporation (CBC). The CBC received funding from the $2.50 licence fee that every private radio owner had to pay. It was soon operating a network of ten stations. As well, it provided programs for many private stations. By 1937, CBC radio was available to 76 per cent of the Canadian population.

When it was created, the CBC not only ran its own stations, it also regulated private radio. Private

owners complained it was unfair because they had to compete against a public system that also had the authority to tell them what to do. Finally, in 1958, the government created the independent Board of Broadcast Governors to regulate all stations, private and public. This board, later renamed the Canadian Radio-television and Telecommunications Commission (CRTC), still operates today.

MAKING CONNECTIONS

1. Do you think it is important for a country to have control over its own mass media? Explain your answer.

2. Read the quote from Joey Smallwood. In what way was radio "the great unifying thing"? How does Smallwood's remark apply to Canada as a whole?

KEYWORDS

lobby

THE LEAGUE OF NATIONS
The Road to Failure

FOCUSSING ON THE ISSUE

Political developments in the 1930s demonstrated that the League of Nations was ineffective. Why did the League fail?

The Early Years

The League of Nations was created in 1919 to provide **collective security** following the Great War. (See page 78.) It enjoyed some minor successes in the 1920s, settling a dispute between Finland and Sweden over the Aland Islands in 1921 and a border conflict between Greece and Bulgaria in 1925. The Great Powers, however, continued to deal with international issues out of self-interest and with little concern for collective security. In 1923, France and Belgium occupied the Ruhr Valley in Germany, while Italy invaded the Greek island of Corfu. Although the League objected to both actions, it failed to take measures to reverse them. In the 1930s, the ineffectiveness of the League became even more evident as first Japan and then Italy committed acts of aggression against other nations.

Manchuria

In 1930, Prime Minister Hamaguchi of Japan was shot and seriously wounded by a **right-wing ultranationalist**. The following year ill health forced him to resign. Hamaguchi had been a strong supporter of liberal democracy. Now, however, control of Japan was in the hands of the military. In the fall of 1931, without the support of the government, Japanese troops seized control of the Chinese province of Manchuria. This marked the beginning of the decline of Japanese democracy. Over the next five years, radical members of the armed forces, many influenced by the ideas of Hitler and Mussolini, gained increasing control over the Japanese government. Ultra-nationalist civilians enthusiastically supported them, as did many industrialists—though more reluctantly—who shared their anti-**communist** views

A series of assassinations by nationalist groups and military officers further destabilized the government. The Japanese military launched further acts of aggression against China. Once again, the League condemned Japan's **annexation** of Manchuria. In response, Japan simply withdrew from the League in 1933.

The Rome-Berlin-Tokyo Axis

To protect their forces in Manchuria, the Japanese military signed the Anti-Comintern Pact with Germany in 1936. Germany and Japan agreed to co-operate against the Comintern (the world communist movement led by the Soviet Union). With this agreement, the USSR was threatened on two fronts—by Japan in the east and Germany in the west. The following year, Italy joined the pact, creating the Rome-Berlin-Tokyo Axis.

Ethiopia

Italy's invasion of Ethiopia in 1935 demonstrated even more clearly the inability of the League of Nations to deal with aggression. Italy had first invaded Ethiopia in 1895 but had been defeated. In the 1930s, Italy's **fascist** dictator, Benito Mussolini, renewed his country's **imperialist** designs. On 3 October 1935, Italian troops, supported by tanks and bombers, launched their invasion. Four days later the League of Nations found Italy guilty of violating the League's **covenant**. Despite the appeals of the Ethiopian emperor, Haile Selassie, the League did little to reverse Italy's action. Lacking any provisions for armed intervention, the League imposed **economic sanctions** on Italy. Yet it failed to enforce the sanctions, and vital supplies like gasoline still reached Ethiopia, fuelling Italy's tanks and aircraft and securing its military conquest.

In May 1936, Mussolini proclaimed Italy's king, Victor Emmanuel III, the new emperor of Ethiopia. Haile Selassie was forced to flee the country. Germany, which had abandoned the League in 1933 after Hitler came to power, was the first country to recognize the Italian conquest. In October 1936, Hitler

142   *Canadian Issues: A Contemporary Perspective*

and Mussolini signed an agreement committing their countries to joint action in support of their common goals, which were based on aggression and expansion. Italy formally withdrew from the League of Nations in 1937. The League never recovered from this setback. It continued meeting in the late 1930s but was unable to act effectively.

Evaluating the League

The League of Nations was basically an open forum for international discussion, but it had no power or authority to accomplish its goals. From its inception it encountered problems with membership, and three of the world's powers—Germany, Russia, and the United States—did not join at first. (The US never held membership in the League.) These factors, combined with economic and political rivalries, caused the League to fail in its ultimate goals—preventing war and preserving peace. Despite this failure, the League was an important pioneering venture in international affairs. The recurrence of war only emphasized the world's need for this type of association. When the United Nations was founded in 1945, it was modelled after the structure and methods of the League.

Italian troops moved southward after capturing Ethiopian soldiers in the north.

KEYWORDS

collective security

right-wing

ultra-nationalist

communist

annexation

fascist

imperialist

covenant

economic sanctions

◄🔌 MAKING CONNECTIONS 🔌►

1. In October 1935, the Haitian delegate to the League of Nations argued that "great or small, strong or weak, near or far, white or coloured, let us never forget that someday we may be somebody's Ethiopia." Explain this argument in your own words.

2. What are the benefits to Canada of active participation in world affairs? What are the costs? Are there circumstances under which Canada should not participate in world affairs?

CANADIANS IN SPAIN
The Mackenzie-Papineau Battalion

FOCUSSING ON THE ISSUE

In 1936, the Spanish army revolted against its government, beginning a civil war that lasted three years. Why did Canadians get involved in the fighting? Why were they not recognized for their contribution?

A Noble Cause

They called it a noble cause in defence of justice and equality. Thousands of idealistic young men and women came from all over the world to fight for democracy in Spain. In return, they were called **communists** and **anarchists**, ignored by their own governments.

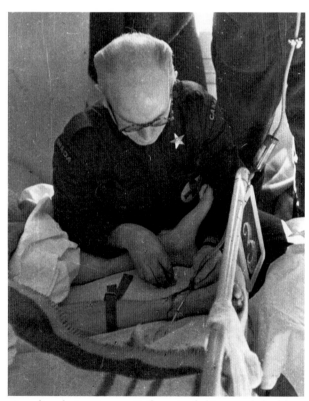

Canadian doctor Norman Bethune tended to wounded soldiers in Spain in 1936. The Canadian government kept a careful neutrality in the Spanish conflict. In what way was the government's reaction to the Spanish Civil War part of the policy of appeasement that led to the Second World War?

Today they are remembered as the first soldiers in the war to stop **fascism**.

In 1936, the Spanish elected a **left-wing** government committed to social and economic reforms. But the country was divided, and in July a group of army officers launched a rebellion to topple the government. The army, led by General Francisco Franco, had support from the dictators in Germany and Italy—Hitler and Mussolini. Without soldiers to defend itself, the Spanish government fought back by arming loyal workers and farmers. It was the beginning of a civil war.

Many countries did not want to get involved in the conflict, fearing the war in Spain might snowball into a Europe-wide conflict. Canada was among these countries. The war in Spain had aroused strong emotions in Canada. Many Canadians felt that Spain should not be allowed to fall into the hands of Franco and his soldiers, as did others around the world. But many Catholics in Canada, especially in Quebec, thought Franco's army was a **bulwark** against godless communism. Prime Minister King feared disunity in the country. He also feared getting entangled in a distant war. His official policy towards the war was **non-intervention**, and his government passed a law making it illegal for Canadians to join a foreign army.

Nonetheless, among the volunteers from around the world arriving in Spain to fight on the side of the government, there were 1250 Canadians. Many were unemployed victims of the Depression. Because of Canada's policy of non-intervention, Canadian volunteers had to leave the country secretly, sailing from the United States to Europe, then walking across the mountains into Spain. At first, Canadians in Spain fought alongside volunteers from other countries. Soon, however, they formed their own battalion. They called it the Mackenzie-Papineau Battalion, after William Lyon Mackenzie and Louis-Joseph Papineau, the two leaders of the Canadian rebellions in 1837 and 1838. The Canadians became known to everyone as the Mac-Paps.

The Mac-Paps fought fiercely in several important battles during 1937 and 1938. About half of the Canadians who volunteered in Spain—600 men—died in the fighting. But the Spanish government's side was outnumbered and outgunned. Finally, in March 1939, Franco's rebels triumphed, replacing the government with a military dictatorship that would last until 1975. Canadian volunteers limped home in defeat. Their contribution to the fight against fascism was ignored. Many of them re-enlisted when the "official" war against fascism began in 1939. Others resumed their place in civilian life. "It was the wrong war," said one of them. "No bands played for us."

BIOGRAPHY: NORMAN BETHUNE

The best-known Canadian volunteer in Spain was Norman Bethune (1890–1939), a doctor from Montreal. "It is in Spain that the real issues of our time are going to be fought out; it is there that democracy will survive or die," Bethune said. He led a medical team to the front where he saw many soldiers dying from their wounds because it took so long to get them to a hospital. Bethune designed a mobile blood transfusion unit to collect blood in the cities and carry it to the front lines where wounded soldiers could get transfusions as soon as they were needed. The unit used a Renault van equipped with a refrigerator so that the blood would not spoil. It was a revolutionary idea that saved many lives.

Bethune strongly believed in the fight against fascism. When he returned to Canada, he launched a speaking tour to mobilize public support for the Spanish volunteers. In 1938, he went to China, which Japanese troops had just invaded. "Spain and China are part of the same battle," he declared. He joined Mao Zedong's army, which was fighting the Japanese, and helped to train Chinese doctors and nurses to work at the front. During one operation he cut his hand. The infection spread and he died of blood poisoning. Mao's communist army eventually won the war and ever since, Norman Bethune has been a hero to the Chinese. "We must all learn the spirit of absolute selflessness from him," said Mao.

1. Why did Bethune believe the war in Spain was so important?

MAKING CONNECTIONS

1. Some of the Canadian volunteers who fought in Spain are still alive. They consider themselves war veterans, just like soldiers who fought in the world wars. In recent years they have been trying to obtain government recognition as veterans in order to qualify for medical and pension benefits. The Canadian government has maintained that the Spanish volunteers were not fighting for Canada. In fact, they were breaking Canadian law by going to Spain. The government's position is that they went as individuals, not as part of a Canadian army, so Canada owes them nothing.

   What do you think? Stage a debate on this issue in your class: "Canadian veterans of the war in Spain deserve all the recognition of Canadian soldiers in other foreign wars."

KEYWORDS

communist

anarchist

fascism

left-wing

bulwark

non-intervention

TROUBLE IN EUROPE
Canada at War, Again

FOCUSSING ON THE ISSUE

*During the 1930s, a crisis loomed in Europe as attempts
to contain German expansionism failed. What was Canada's attitude
to the prospect of another war?*

Prime Minister King strode through Berlin alongside Nazi officials during his 1937 visit. King was treated like a visiting celebrity. Did his visit suggest that Canada approved of Hitler's regime? King believed that it was best for leaders to meet face to face to try to settle their differences rather than isolating an unfriendly government. Do you agree?

The Policy of Appeasement

As relations between countries in Europe worsened, Prime Minister King strongly believed that he had a role to play in maintaining peace. With a background in labour negotiations, he saw himself as the great **conciliator** between Britain and Germany. King was also a **spiritualist**. Though Canadians did not know it at the time, their prime minister was convinced he was in

contact with the world of the dead. One of the messages he was receiving told him that it was his destiny to bring about peace.

King agreed with the policy of **appeasement** being followed by Britain and France. He realized how devastating another war would be, and thought that almost any price was worth paying to avoid it. Many historians now argue that the policy of appeasement was a great mistake. If the world had stood up immediately to Hitler, they say, he would

have stopped his aggression before it was too late. At the time, however, no one could have imagined just how brutal and murderous Hitler's regime would become. Furthermore, some Canadians shared the sentiments of **anti-Semitism** that were then sweeping Germany. Jews in Canada were singled out because of their different religion and because it was believed they could not assimilate to Canadian life. They became scapegoats for the hard times afflicting the country. The government responded by clamping down on the number of Jews it allowed into the country. Between 1933 and 1945, when so many Jews wanted to escape persecution in Europe, Canada accepted less than 5000.

In 1937, King visited Germany to meet with Hitler. He wanted to make sure that the German leader knew that if he started a war with Britain, Canada would not hesitate to join the war against Germany. On a more positive note, he wanted to convey a message to Hitler that Britain and the rest of the Allies were only interested in peace.

Hitler's undemocratic activities in Germany were no secret to the rest of the world. He had banned political parties and trade unions and stifled all opposition to his regime. In the name of fighting communism he put many Jews, intellectuals, and political opponents into detention camps. In 1936, he sent troops to reoccupy the Rhineland, a part of Germany that was demilitarized under the terms of the Treaty of Versailles. When King arrived in Germany in June 1937, the worst of Hitler's crimes were still to come. Nonetheless, King must have known he was dealing with a brutal dictator. As a friend wrote to the prime minister just before he left: "Don't let him [Hitler] hypnotize you....He is the head of a detestable system of force and persecution and real horrors go on in Germany today for which he is responsible." Yet King *was* hypnotized. He was very impressed by the dictator and came away from the meeting convinced that Hitler only wanted peace. Events during the next two years revealed just how wrong King had been.

Canada Declares War

On 1 September 1939, Germany invaded Poland, and Europe was once again at war. In 1914, at the outbreak of the First World War, Canada had automatically followed Britain to war as a colony in the Empire. This time things were different. The Statute of Westminster (1931) had recognized Canada as an independent country with the right to determine its own foreign policy. Canadians still felt strong ties to Britain, but these were emotional

This famous photograph shows soldiers of the British Columbia Regiment marching through Vancouver on their way to war. A youngster reaches out to say goodbye to his father as he passes.

ties, not legal ones. It did not matter what the British did. Canada would go to war only when Canadians said they wanted to do so.

As the crisis in Europe unfolded, King called Parliament into session to debate what action to take. Overwhelmingly, the decision was to join the fight against Hitler's Germany. Enthusiasm for the war was not quite as strong in Quebec, however. King tried to win Quebec support by promising, in no uncertain terms, there would be no

conscription as there had been during the First World War. On 10 September, a week after Britain's declaration, Canada formally declared war on Germany. Even though it was unlikely Canada would remain neutral, King wanted to emphasize that it was an independent, made-in-Canada decision. "We take this stand on our own," he said, "not in any colonial attitude of mind."

⊣⊏▪ MAKING CONNECTIONS ▪⊐⊢

1. How did Canada's entry into the Second World War differ from that of the First World War?

2. Would you have voted for or against Canada's entry into the war? Explain your vote.

KEYWORDS

conciliator

spiritualist

appeasement

anti-Semitism

conscription

UNIT 5:

Pegi Nichol MacLeod, Untitled (WRCN's in Dining Room) (n.d.)

Pegi Nichol MacLeod (1904-1949) was an established artist when she was invited to join the Canadian War Artists Program in 1943. MacLeod's work, in which the human figure dominated, recorded many aspects of the women's services. Her loose watercolour paintings expressed the feelings of the moment, whether they depicted women at work or at leisure.

COMING OF AGE

1941-1950

*Skills and Processes

A GLOBAL WAR
The World in 1941
FOCUSSING ON THE ISSUE

By the end of 1941, most of the world would be at war or would be affected by the Second World War. How did the war spread beyond Europe and China to become a global conflict? Why did civilian casualties far outnumber the loss of military life?

A New Kind of War

As 1941 began, fighting was occurring in China, North Africa, and parts of Europe. A year later the war would expand to include most of the world's nations. Global escalation of the war caused each participating country to commit its human and economic resources to the war effort. Technological advances, especially in aviation, expanded the battlefield to include all of an enemy's territory. Civilians would suffer horribly in the war that raged over the next four and a half years. The toll of civilian dead and wounded would far outnumber that of soldiers, sailors, and aviators.

Germany's **blitzkrieg** (lightning war) attack on Poland followed by its swift conquest of all western Europe except Britain marked the beginning of a new kind of war. New technologies introduced in the First World War, especially tanks and airplanes, had changed the pace of war. Armies in trenches no longer faced each other in battle, locked in a war of attrition. By 1941, one nation could attack

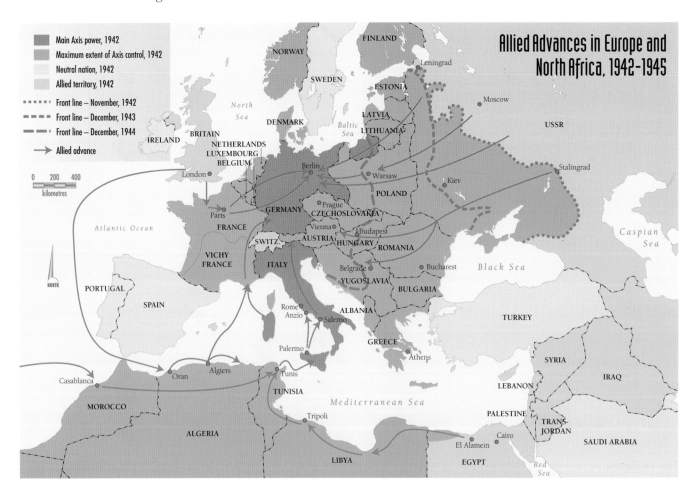

Allied Advances in Europe and North Africa, 1942-1945

Main Axis power, 1942
Maximum extent of Axis control, 1942
Neutral nation, 1942
Allied territory, 1942
Front line – November, 1942
Front line – December, 1943
Front line – December, 1944
Allied advance

another thousands of kilometres away in a matter of hours or days. Motorized forces, supported by aircraft, could overrun military defences and attack civilian and industrial targets over a broad area.

This new approach to war demanded the production of fast and effective weapons of mass destruction. Many skilled workers were required for the factories that produced weapons, munitions, vehicles, aircraft, and ships. Highly trained men and women were needed to service and maintain them. Foot soldiers still fought battles and controlled captured territories, but their importance diminished as the role of military technology expanded.

Sophisticated communications systems were needed to co-ordinate air, sea, and land units in wide-ranging and fast-moving operations over large areas. **Cryptologists** were employed to break secret codes, locate enemy targets, and control weapons systems. In research laboratories, scientists joined the war by working to create new ways to attack other countries or defend their own.

This kind of war placed a heavy burden on the resources of the warring nations. Countries needed large populations, advanced industrial capacity, and abundant supplies of food and raw materials.

Modern warfare also required vast amounts of fuel for factories and for the tanks, aircraft, and ships they produced. Participating nations had to mobilize all their human and physical resources to the war effort. Germany and Japan met most of these requirements, but lacked the natural resource base needed to sustain such a war effort. Both went to war, in part, to expand their territories into areas that could provide needed resources.

The US and the USSR Enter the War

Two nations, the United States and the Soviet Union, met all of these requirements in 1941. Neither was yet at war, but both were preparing to enter the widening conflict. Soviet leader Josef Stalin had signed a **non-aggression pact** with Hitler in 1939. Hitler, however, began planning an invasion of the Soviet Union in the fall of 1940 after failing to defeat Britain. This invasion, code-named Operation Barbarossa ("red beard"), was scheduled for the following summer. In June 1941, more than a million German soldiers, backed by thousands of tanks and aircraft, invaded the USSR. By year's end, German forces had driven the Red Army far back into the heart of Russia. In an effort to keep supplies out of enemy hands, retreating Soviet troops systemati-

cally destroyed crops and livestock in a "scorched earth" campaign. As the harsh Russian winter set in, German troops were laying siege to Leningrad and were advancing towards Moscow. But they faced two enemies—the Red Army and the vast, wintry Russian landscape thousands of kilometres from home and the resources needed to fight such a war.

On 7 December 1941, Japan launched a surprise attack on Pearl Harbor, Hawaii. The Japanese military command hoped to destroy the US Pacific fleet, especially its aircraft carriers. The attack was intended to give Japan's navy control of the Pacific in preparation for attacks on British, Dutch, and American colonies in the region. The United States responded by declaring war on Japan. In Germany, Hitler—against the advice of his generals—supported Japan by declaring war on the United States. Hitler had brought the US and USSR together as allies.

MAKING CONNECTIONS

1. How does war stimulate the development of new technology? Give examples.

2. Changes in military technology meant that civilians were now at greater risk of death or injury than military personnel. What impact would this have on the countries that were involved in the fighting and were part of the "battlefield"?

KEYWORDS

blitzkrieg

cryptologists

non-aggression pact

1942
A Year of Crisis

*In 1942, Canadian soldiers in Europe launched a disastrous raid at Dieppe.
At home, the Canadian government faced a crisis over conscription.
What role did both events play in the outcome of the war?*

Germany's First Defeat

By 1942, virtually all of Europe was in the hands of Germany and its **Axis** ally, Italy. Two years earlier, the German army had swept across the Netherlands and Belgium into France and marched right into Paris. Norway and Denmark had been conquered, and Spain was controlled by the dictator Francisco Franco. Most of southern France continued to have its own government—known as the Vichy regime because it was centred in the town of Vichy—but it was strictly under the thumb of the conquering Germans.

Only Britain remained unconquered. Hitler had tried to bomb the British into submission during 1940–1941. This was the Battle of Britain, when Hitler ordered his airforce, the *Luftwaffe*, to destroy military targets in the United Kingdom. At the end of August 1940, the Germans began attacking civilian targets as well, dropping bombs on London and other large cities, in what was known as the "Blitz." Night after the night, the sky was filled with enemy aircraft as terrified residents huddled in underground shelters. The Royal Air Force, along with many Canadian pilots, fought back until finally, in May 1941, the German air raids

ceased. The Battle of Britain lasted eight months and cost the lives of 40 553 men, women, and children. In the end, Hitler had to give up his plan to conquer the island, turning his army against the USSR instead. It was the first major German defeat in the war.

Rehearsal for Invasion

By 1942, the Allies were making plans to retake Europe. Russia was suffering under the German invasion; it wanted the Allies to attack in western Europe and perhaps force the Germans to divert some of their troops. The Americans had recently entered the war and wanted to see some action. So did Canadian soldiers, who were growing impatient in their British training camps.

The first step in the invasion of the continent was to test German defences. To accomplish this the Allies launched a series of raids across the English Channel. One of these raids was against the French resort town of Dieppe, which was in enemy hands. Canadian troops were given the job of capturing the town.

Early on the morning of 19 August, a fleet of landing craft crossed from England and began unloading Canadian soldiers onto the beach at Dieppe. Immediately,

Although the invasion at Dieppe was a disaster, the Allies learned that launching an attack from the sea on a heavily defended port was a poor strategy. This influenced the site of the Allies' D-Day attack on Normandy in 1944.

THE CONSCRIPTION DEBATE

German military successes in the early years of the war greatly alarmed many people in Canada. With Britain besieged and most of Europe in enemy hands, Canadians who still regarded themselves as "British subjects" demanded **conscription**—the forced enlistment of recruits into the armed services. During the federal election of 1940, Liberal prime minister Mackenzie King had promised "no conscription." He knew how unpopular a measure it was in Quebec, as French Canadians did not feel the same **allegiance** to Britain. King, who won the election, believed that conscription might fracture the country.

As the war progressed, however, pressure mounted on the government to introduce conscription to provide more soldiers for overseas fighting. Faced with a divided Cabinet, King chose to let the voters decide in a national **referendum**. On the ballot, the prime minister asked to be released from his election promise and given the freedom to use conscription if needed. "Not necessarily conscription, but conscription if necessary" was his new slogan.

On 27 April 1942, Canadians voted. The result revealed the country to be deeply divided. English-speaking Canadians voted overwhelmingly for conscription, while French-speaking Canadians were just as strongly opposed. The referendum gave King the power to conscript soldiers but, ever cautious, he did not use it until late in the war. In the end, 12 908 conscripts were sent overseas before the war ended in 1945, only a small percentage of the total number of Canadians who fought in the war. Nonetheless, the conscription debate managed to leave a legacy of anger and suspicion between Canada's two founding peoples.

everything began to go wrong. The plan had been to surprise the enemy and attack under cover of darkness, but the ships had been delayed and the men were forced to come ashore in daylight. They immediately encountered enemy fire from the cliffs above. Bombers were supposed to destroy the German guns from the air, but they too were delayed. Soldiers who did make it to shore were picked off as they scrambled for cover. Commanders in the boats could not see what was happening on shore, and they continued to send reinforcements onto the beach.

By noon, the raiders were in full retreat, trying to get back to the ships that would carry them to safety. Most of the soldiers did not succeed. Out of the 4963 Canadians who landed at Dieppe, 2853 were killed or captured during the raid. It was the first major battle on the Western Front for Canadian troops, and it ended in disaster. More Canadian soldiers died in those few hours at Dieppe than in any other day of the war.

MAKING CONNECTIONS

1. a) Why did so many people in Quebec oppose conscription? Would you have supported conscription? Explain.
   b) Is a referendum a good way to resolve a divisive national issue such as conscription? Explain whether you think that King's handling of the issue helped or hindered national unity.

2. Imagine you are a Canadian soldier who survived the disaster at Dieppe. Write a letter home in which you describe your experience that day.

KEYWORDS

Axis

conscription

allegiance

referendum

SKILL BUILDER
Using Historical Maps
FOCUSSING ON THE ISSUE

*Historical maps help us to understand and interpret history.
How can we use maps to study issues and events from the past?*

A Variety of Maps

When studying history, we can use a variety of maps to enhance our understanding. The types of maps include thematic, political, and **topographic** maps. Thematic maps use shading, colours, and symbols to communicate information on a given topic, such as population, trade, or natural resources. Political maps reproduce the political boundaries of provinces, states, countries, and continents, and identify major cities and towns. Topographic maps represent the physical features of an area, such as mountains, oceans, rivers, and lakes. All of these maps are effective visual tools: they quickly and directly convey information and ideas about the world.

Historical Maps

There are two types of historical maps. The first are those maps that are created during a particular historical period. They reflect how people perceived the world at that time. For example, maps of North America created during the time of exploration show much greater detail about eastern North America than about the West. The second kind of historical maps are those created in contemporary time that are meant to represent facts—events and social realities or perceptions—from historical periods. For example,

on page 20, a **cartographer** has drawn two historical maps outlining the political boundaries of Canada before and after 1905. On page 41, a single map represents the system of alliances in Europe before the First World War. Historical maps are a useful interpretive tool and allow us to trace political and social changes over time as well as the evolution of world views.

Interpreting Historical Maps

Follow these steps when interpreting historical maps:

1. *Identify the map:* Titles and legends in historical maps identify the time period, location, and focus of the map.
2. *Read the map:* What does the map illustrate? How does it illustrate it? Read the legend and the map, paying close attention to the tools the cartographer has used (shading, lines, markers).
3. *Draw conclusions:* Based on your reading of the map, draw conclusions about the historical event or features it illustrates. Explain the importance of these conclusions to the historical period being examined.

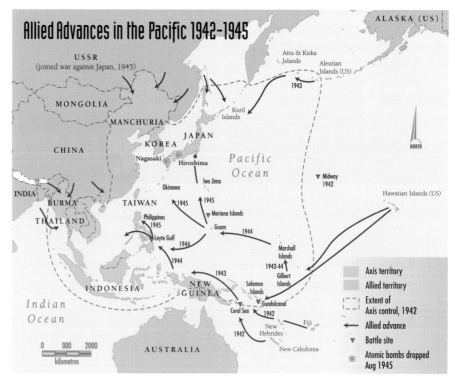

THE DIEPPE RAID

On 19 August 1942, landing craft unloaded Canadian soldiers onto the beach at Dieppe. (See pages 152-153.) This historical map summarizes the Allied raid and German defence of the French town and surrounding area by means of directional arrows and some topographic information.

1. Using cardinal directions and distance, describe the planned Allied troop movements. Then compare these with the actual movements by Allied troops. How do you account for the discrepancies?

2. Describe the general pattern of German troop movements during the Dieppe raid.

3. What geographic advantage(s) did the Germans have over the Allied troops who landed, or tried to land, on the beach north of Dieppe?

4. Military maps can be of two kinds: maps of enemy territory, to be used in attack, or maps of one's own territory, to be used in defence. To make this historical map of Dieppe into a military map, what information would you need if you were a) German? b) Canadian or British? In your answers, consider positions of batteries, roads and bridges, railway lines, military headquarters, armories, troops, power stations, strategic buildings, and the topography of the land.

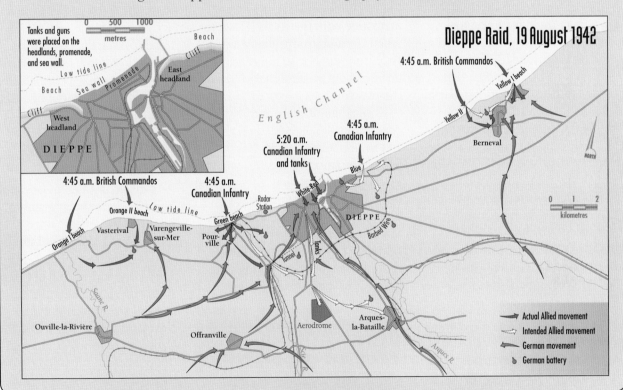

MAKING CONNECTIONS

1. Research an event from the First or Second World War in which Canadians were involved. Then, using the steps for interpreting historical maps as a guide, create your own historical map of this event. Present it to the class. How effective is your map in illustrating the historical event you selected?

KEYWORDS

topographic

cartographer

CANADIANS IN COMBAT
The Liberation of Europe
FOCUSSING ON THE ISSUE

During the Second World War, Canadian troops saw action in Italy, Hong Kong, and the Netherlands. What role did Canadian soldiers play in the liberation of Europe?

The Italian Campaign

After the raid on Dieppe in 1942, Canadian troops continued their training in Britain and waited for another chance to go into battle. Meanwhile, the tide of war was turning. The battle of El Alamein in October-November 1942 marked the beginning of the end of Germany's campaign in northern Africa. In Russia, the invading German army had to admit defeat early in 1943 following the battle of Stalingrad. The stage was set for the **Allies** to begin the reconquest of Europe.

Canadians were anxious to take a more active role in the conflict. At the insistence of Prime Minister King, two Canadian army divisions joined the assault on Italy. In July 1943, Allied soldiers streamed onto the island of Sicily. Italian troops surrendered in great numbers. Facing defeat, the government of the Italian dictator, Benito Mussolini, was overthrown. A new Italian prime minister signed an **armistice** with the Allies. However, when German troops flooded into Italy from the north, the Allies decided they would have to invade the mainland.

Canadian, British, and American soldiers landed on the soft under belly of Italy's "toe" in September and began a slow march up the peninsula. They encountered fierce fighting as they advanced. The biggest test for the Canadians came at Ortona on the coast of the Adriatic Sea east of Rome. Tanks could not manoeuvre through the narrow, twisting streets of the ancient town. Ortona had to be taken by foot soldiers moving from house to house, many of which were booby-trapped with explosives. Although casualties were high, the Germans were driven out and the town was in Canadian hands. The Italian campaign dragged on for another year before Canadian troops were called back to England to join the final campaign of the European war.

D-Day and After

On 6 June 1944—D-Day—the long-awaited Allied invasion of Europe across the English Channel began. It was code-named Operation Overlord and involved almost 1 million soldiers. British, American, and Canadian troops stormed ashore along the entire coast of the French province of Normandy. Juno Beach was the Canadian objective. Canadian troops struck at first light, pouring out of their landing craft and advancing across the sand up into the town of Caen. Once again the army suffered many casualties, but this time the enemy was routed. The Allies were back on French soil. The liberation of Europe could begin.

D-Day marked the beginning of the end for Germany, but victory was another year in coming. As they withdrew back towards their own territory, German soldiers put

Canadians in the Italian Campaign 1943-1945

THE BATTLE FOR HONG KONG, 1941

The former British colony of Hong Kong at the edge of China was a long way from the European war zone. But the Allies were also at war with Japan, and the British believed that their colony needed defending. When Canada was asked to supply the troops, a force of Canadian soldiers crossed the Pacific by ship and took up positions around Hong Kong.

When the Japanese attacked, the Canadians were sitting ducks. They were outnumbered and most of them were not yet trained. In any case, all the experts agreed that the colony was indefensible. After a fierce fight lasting less than three weeks, the Canadians surrendered on Christmas Day, 1941.

But the ordeal was far from over. Survivors were rounded up by the Japanese. They spent the rest of the war in prison camps where they suffered terrible mistreatment. In total, 555 Canadians—more than one-quarter of the entire force that had gone to Hong Kong—did not return home.

up fierce resistance. Canadians were ordered to clear the French ports along the English Channel, a job that took months of constant fighting. Then they helped liberate Belgium and the Netherlands from German control. In early May 1945, as Canadian soldiers prepared to attack the port of Wilhemshaven, the Germans finally surrendered. The war in Europe was over.

But Japan fought on. After the Battle of Hong Kong in 1941, Canadians were mainly bystanders in the war against Japan. They expected to take part in the planned invasion of Japan, but the invasion never took place. Early in August 1945, the United States dropped atomic bombs on the Japanese cities of Hiroshima and Nagasaki, killing and maiming more than 275 000 civilians. Devastated by this destruction, the Japanese surrendered, finally ending the Second World War.

During the war, more than 1 million Canadians served in the armed forces. Of these, 42 042 were killed and another 54 414 wounded. After Britain, France, and the United States, Canada contributed the most soldiers to the fight against Nazi Germany. Considering that when the war began Canada had less than 10 000 men and women in uniform, it was a remarkable achievement.

Canadian soldiers in Caen had to worry about booby-trapped buildings and German snipers hiding in the windows. Many European towns looked like this after bombardment and house-to-house fighting had reduced them to rubble.

MAKING CONNECTIONS

1. Compare and contrast the involvement of Canadian troops in the First and Second World Wars based on the following criteria: command structure, cultural participation, and military campaigns.

2. The atomic bomb that was droped on Hiroshima killed 80 000 people instantly, while another 60 000 people died from the effects of **radiation** within a year. In Nagasaki, another 40 000 people died. Do you think the use of atomic bombs could ever be justified? Explain.

KEYWORDS

Allies

armistice

radiation

BATTLE OF THE ATLANTIC
Canada's Merchant Navy
FOCUSSING ON THE ISSUE

Canada played a vital role in supplying Britain with materials to support the war effort and to feed its civilian population. Convoys of merchant ships, massed together for defence against submarines, regularly crossed the Atlantic. What role did Canada's merchant sailors play in the war? How were they treated by the government after the war?

Lifeline to Britain

During the Second World War, supplies for England and the Allied forces in Europe were carried by ship across the North Atlantic Ocean. Thousands of Canadian merchant sailors served on ships carrying food, fuel, weapons, ammunition, and other wartime supplies to English ports. These sailors faced the constant threat of attack from German submarines. Just as dangerous were the fierce winter storms that swept across the cold waters of the North Atlantic. Thousands more Canadians served on naval vessels and in aircraft that were assigned to protect the merchant ships from enemy attack.

In 1940, the Germans knew that Britain depended on supplies from Canada and the United States to survive. To prepare for the planned invasion of Britain in June, the German navy launched a campaign of submarine warfare. Germany hoped to subdue the British by starving them, using **U-boats** to cut off Britain's overseas lifelines. By the summer of 1940, Germany had submarine bases in Norway and France. The German navy had only 28 submarines but sank nearly 6 million tonnes of supplies by May 1941. Germany built many more submarines during the next two years; U-boat **wolf-packs** would pose a threat to Britain until the spring of 1943. Terrible losses were inflicted on Allied ships and merchant sailors during this period. It was not until November 1942 that Canadian and American shipyards were able to build merchant ships at a faster rate than the U-boats were sinking Allied vessels. Winston Churchill, Britain's wartime prime minister, called this campaign the Battle of the Atlantic.

Canada, aided by the United States, played a very significant role in the battle. Canadian naval vessels based in Halifax joined British ships from Newfoundland in guarding the convoys. In March 1941, the US Congress passed the Lend-Lease Act, giving President Roosevelt power to spend $7 billion to lend or lease military aid to Britain and its allies. After the act was passed, the number of convoys crossing the Atlantic increased greatly.

From November to March, bitter winter gales blowing out of the Arctic create towering waves that hammer small vessels. Sailors whose ships were torpedoed by U-boats could survive only a few minutes in the icy waters.

The convoy system was introduced in the First World War to protect merchant ships from submarine attack. An average convoy consisted of 12 to 40 supply or troop ships, protected by an escort of warships. The convoy system was very successful in this war; fewer than 500 out of nearly 100 000 ships that crossed in convoys were lost by the Allies.

MERCHANT SAILORS—THE FORGOTTEN VETERANS

More than 12 000 Canadian merchant sailors took part in wartime convoys. One in ten lost their lives—five times the death rate for the Royal Canadian Navy. Many others were injured or taken as prisoners of war. After the war, the Canadian government treated these sailors as civilian participants in the war effort, despite the fact that they had sailed into combat zones. Veterans of the wartime merchant navy were not given the same benefits as veterans of the army, navy, and air force. They were excluded from the War Veterans Allowance Act, pensionable benefits,

free university education, housing and land-grant benefits, small business financial aid, and veterans' health-care benefits.

By the late 1990s, only a handful of the Canadians who served on the North Atlantic convoys were still living. Most were in their seventies or eighties, often in ill health as a result of their wartime experiences. The government was urged to recognize them as veterans on the same footing as other men and women who served during the war.

The Convoy System

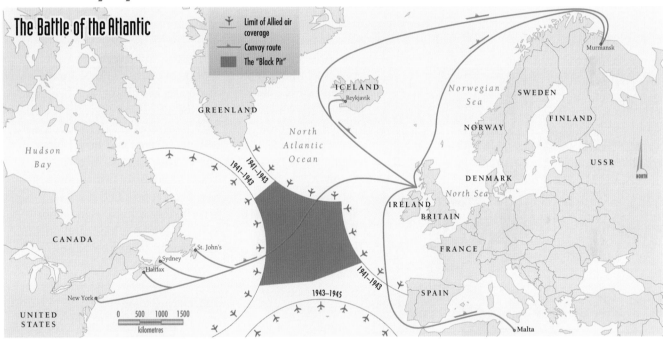

The Battle of the Atlantic

Legend:
- Limit of Allied air coverage
- Convoy route
- The "Black Pit"

The convoy system used by the Allies in 1941 was similar to that developed in the First World War, except that aircraft were now used

both to defend and attack convoys. Canadian and American anti-submarine patrol aircraft provided cover within the limits of the range

of land-based planes. Only a small area of the mid-Atlantic, known as the black pit, lay beyond the range of land-based aircraft. Canadian air crews accounted for 23 of the 788 German submarines destroyed in the Second World War.

MAKING CONNECTIONS

1. a) How important was the merchant navy to the overall war effort? Explain.
   b) Find out if the government has recognized the merchant sailors as war veterans.

KEYWORDS

U-boats

wolf-pack

SERVING THEIR COUNTRY
Canadian Women's Wartime Role
FOCUSSING ON THE ISSUE

Thousands of Canadian women became involved in the Second World War, both overseas and on the home front. Did the role of women in Canada change as a result of their contributions during wartime?

Overseas

Early in the war, women were accepted into the armed services for the first time in Canadian history. In 1941, the Canadian Army created the Canadian Women's Army Corps. During the same year, the Royal Canadian Air Force (Women's Division) was established, followed by the Women's Royal Canadian Naval Service. By 1945, over 43 000 women were serving in Canada's armed forces. Overseas, women filled non-combative positions such as radio operators, first-aid workers, nurses, and ambulance drivers. Their jobs earned them less authority and lower pay than men's jobs. Nevertheless, many Canadian women joined the armed services because they wanted to serve their country.

On the Home Front

On the home front, Canadian women were recruited or volunteered for many kinds of work. Because so many Canadian men had left to fight the war, the commitment of Canadian women was essential. In 1942, the federal government established the National Selective Service (NSS) to recruit as many women as possible for wartime work. As a result, thousands of women worked in war industries building ships, airplanes, and weapons. In rural areas women operated farms, and across the country they filled a variety of positions traditionally held by men.

The volunteer work of Canadian women was also invaluable. As in the First World War, women knitted socks and sweaters for the troops overseas, wrapped parcels for prisoners of war, and operated service clubs and canteens for military personnel. They conducted **salvage drives** and raised money for **Victory Bonds**. As many wartime advertisements reveal, it was even considered patriotic to run a thrifty household, plant victory gardens for extra food, and nurture clean, well-dressed children!

The cartoon portrays a woman stepping out of her traditional role as homemaker and morale booster. She is dressed in overalls and a bandanna, symbolic of her war work in the munitions factory or on the farm. The cartoon implies that Canadian women's roles were expanding as a result of their war efforts.

Kitchen Brigade
Behind each gallant fighting man,
Loyal we stand, the kitchen
    brigade.
Our weapon is the frying pan—
We'll see that glycerine is made.

Out of the frying pan, fat flows,
Not one drop wasted, if you
    please;
Out of the frying pan it goes
Into the fire—at our enemies.

May Richston, from National Home
Monthly, *August 1943.*

What do you think the poem is saying about women and the war effort?

Canadian women were not only encouraged to support the war effort, they were eager to do so. Because their help was so urgently needed, the federal and provincial governments provided incentives for women, such as tax exemptions and child-care facilities. In virtually every sphere of Canadian society, it appeared that women were adopting new roles and improving their social and economic status. Nevertheless, women made only temporary breakthroughs in expanding their traditional roles in Canadian society. At the end of the war, many women gave up their jobs to returning soldiers. Most of the mechanisms that the government put in place to assist women during the war, including tax breaks and child care, were quickly dismantled at war's end. The Second World War challenged the conventional attitude towards women, but in the end it did not fundamentally change that attitude.

Almost 4500 women joined the Canadian Nursing Services (shown here) during the war. Over 20 000 women joined the Canadian Women's Army Corps, over 16 000 joined the Women's Auxiliary Air Force, and over 6600 joined the Women's Royal Canadian Naval Services.

KEYWORDS

salvage drives

Victory Bonds

patriarchal

MAKING CONNECTIONS

1. Compare the images on these pages with those of Canadian women in the First World War on pages 62-63. In what ways were the roles of Canadian women similar in the two world wars? In what ways were they different? How do you account for these similarities and differences?

2. After the war, Canadian society seemed to revert to the **patriarchal** family model—the man as primary bread-winner and the woman as dependent, with specific responsibilities and ties to the home and family. Why do you think attitudes towards women's "place" did not fundamentally change as a result of the war?

JAPANESE CANADIANS
Wartime Persecution

During the Second World War, all people of Japanese background living on the coast of British Columbia were forced to leave their homes. Why were Japanese Canadians unjustly singled out?

The Relocation Begins

In February 1942, Prime Minister King made a dramatic announcement. By **order-in-council**, under the War Measures Act, all people of Japanese background living within 62 km of the coast of British Columbia would be moved away from the coast. The RCMP could search their homes without a warrant; there would be no trials or investigations. It did not matter how long people had been living in Canada, or whether or not they were citizens—and many were.

Immediately, authorities began rounding up people of Japanese background. Over the next few months about 20 000 were removed from their homes and taken to **internment camps** in the interior of BC, where they were

forced to live for the rest of the war. Others were sent to work as labourers in the Prairies and Ontario. While they were gone, the federal government took their property and sold it at auctions.

The evacuation was explained as a security precaution. The war with Japan was going badly. At the end of 1941, the Japanese had carried out a surprise air attack on the US naval base at Pearl Harbor in Hawaii. Then they overran much of East Asia. These events convinced people in BC that a Japanese invasion was certain. As it turned out, an invasion did not occur, but for many months British Columbians lived in fear that the war would reach their doorstep.

In this situation, it was argued, people of Japanese origin posed a threat. British Columbia already had a long history of discrimination against its Chinese, Japanese, and South Asian residents. The war provided an excuse for this prejudice to come bubbling to the surface again. People suspected that Japanese Canadians were more Japanese than Canadian, that they would feel loyalty to

their country of origin and become spies and **saboteurs** on its behalf. There is no evidence that this ever happened, but such was the strength of public prejudice that the government felt it had to give in to it.

As anti-Japanese feelings grew, some people began to fear outbreaks of violence and argued that the Japanese should be moved for their own safety. Since the fall of Hong Kong in December 1941, many Canadian soldiers were prisoners of war in Japanese detention camps. The government worried that if any harm came to Japanese residents in Canada, the Japanese would take revenge on the prisoners.

Apologizing for Injustice

After the war, the persecution of Japanese Canadians continued. For several years they were not allowed to return to the coast. Many were deported back to Japan or sent to live in eastern Canada. At the time, most Canadians approved the relocation of the Japanese. Today, it is recognized as one of the worst violations of human rights in the history of the country. Innocent people, most of them Canadian citizens, were forcibly uprooted and taken from their homes and sent to camps or labour jobs across the country. They lost their possessions and their livelihoods. All of this was

This internment camp near Slocan, BC, was typical of the settlements in which Japanese evacuees were forced to live.

Although the relocation of Japanese Canadians was justified as a security measure, most historians do not agree with this explanation. They point out that the government's own defence experts concluded that the Japanese posed no threat to the country. In 1981, Ann Sunahara wrote:

The documents demonstrate that each order-in-council... that affected Japanese Canadians—uprooting, confinement, dispossession, deportation and dispersal—was motivated by political considerations rooted in racist traditions accepted, and indeed encouraged, by persons within the government of the day. The documents also show that at no point in the entire seven years of their exile were Japanese Canadians ever a threat to national security.

Ann Sunahara, The Politics of Racism (Toronto: James Lorimer, 1981), p. 3.

Roy Miki, another writer on the subject, argued that the relocation was a plot to rid British Columbia of Japanese people once and for all:

The documents clearly show that certain politicians and public leaders, well known for their racist animosity towards Japanese Canadians, manipulated the potentially volatile wartime atmosphere on the west coast to have their way with these "people of Japanese race"....For racist politicians, the uprooting of Japanese Canadians from the west coast was the opportunity to confiscate and liquidate their properties—to eradicate their presence in BC.

Muriel Kitagawa, ed. by Roy Miki, This is My Own (Vancouver: Talonbooks, 1985), pp. 55-6, 62.

Other historians are less critical of the decision. They do not condone it, but they believe it happened for understandable reasons that were not racist. In a recent book, four historians—Patricia Roy, Jack Granatstein, Masako Iino, and Hiroko Takamura—argue that the government was motivated mainly by a desire to protect Canadians who were prisoners in Japan from retribution. They conclude:

The Canadian government and the Canadian people treated the Japanese Canadians...very harshly during the war. Nonetheless, the evacuees and internees, no matter what their citizenship, unquestionably were better treated than Canadian soldiers and civilians in Japanese hands.

Patricia Roy et al, Mutual Hostages (Toronto: University of Toronto Press, 1990), p. 217.

1. List Ann Sunahara's five stages of the relocation process, and explain each one.
2. Do you believe it is appropriate to equate the treatment of Japanese Canadians living in BC with the treatment of Canadian soldiers held captive in Japan? Why or why not?

done seemingly to preserve national security, which almost everyone now agrees was never at risk.

Japanese Canadians persisted in seeking compensation for all they had suffered. They also wanted the government to admit that an injustice had been done. Finally, in 1988, the government of Canada agreed. It admitted that "the treatment of Japanese Canadians during and after World War II was unjust and violated principles of human rights as they are understood today." It apologized and agreed to pay $21 000 to every evacuee who was still living, as well as other money to the Japanese-Canadian community as a whole.

MAKING CONNECTIONS

1. Historians use the same evidence, yet often come to different conclusions. Why does this happen?

KEYWORDS

order-in-council

internment camp

saboteur

THE HOME FRONT

The Civilian War Effort

By 1941, the war dominated Canada's economy, affecting factories and households across the country. How did wartime shortages affect Canadians? What role did the government play in the wartime economy?

Wartime Restrictions

In some ways, the war helped Canada's economy. It ended the Great Depression. Unemployment vanished as men and women enlisted in the armed forces and as factories hired workers to make weapons and munitions. At the same time as the war brought full employment to Canada, it also resulted in shortages of many

How might this ad encourage Canadians to support the war effort?

goods. Canadians remembered the shortages during the First World War. When war broke out again in 1939, those who could afford to rushed to the stores to stock up on items they feared might soon vanish from the shelves. The result of this panic buying and hoarding of goods was **inflation**. By 1941, the cost of living in Canada was 20 per cent higher than it had been two years earlier.

Faced with shortages and rising prices, the Canadian government began to take control of the country's economy. In December 1940, it passed a law regulating the wages of workers in war industries. This law also limited increases in the prices of a variety of goods and services, including rents, iron and steel, lumber, sugar, and milk. Still, prices continued to rise.

In the fall of 1941, the government assumed even greater economic control. Most prices and wages were frozen and rationing was introduced. Each man, woman, and child was issued a ration book, which set limits on how much coffee, tea, butter, jam, milk, or meat a person could buy. Sugar rationing coupons were introduced in 1942. Provincial liquor control boards rationed sales of alcohol. Gasoline, so vital to mechanized war, was also rationed. Faced with shortages of gasoline, oil, and rubber tires, motorists drained their engines and fuel tanks and put their cars up on blocks for the duration of the war.

Some goods were not available at all. Silk stockings vanished from shops as silk was needed to make parachutes. (Eventually, through the inventiveness of industrial chemistry, nylon stockings would replace silk.) Women's skirts got shorter as wool and cotton cloth became scarce. Defiant young men bought suits with extremely long jackets, padded shoulders, wide lapels, and baggy trousers. Their "zoot suits," as they came to be called, were symbols of the extra money they had to spend from wartime wages. Soldiers greatly resented the "zoot suiters;" fights, even riots, involving the two groups were not uncommon.

Civilians and the War Effort

Wartime shortages led to Canada's first organized recycling programs. Girl Guides, Boy Scouts, and other community groups held salvage drives. They travelled door-to-door in their neighbourhoods collecting aluminum, steel, copper, and similar materials to be turned into aircraft, tanks, and other military equipment. Families planted victory gardens, growing food for their own tables.

Canadian civilians also helped the war effort by lending the government money. The government issued Victory Bonds, much like today's Canada Savings Bonds. The bonds had two purposes: they allowed the government to borrow money to meet the extremely high cost of the war and they reduced the amount of money Canadians had to spend. Encouraging Canadians to save rather than spend was another way in which the government tried to keep price levels low in order to contain inflation.

Wartime Propaganda

The Canadian government also launched a **propaganda** program to encourage civilians to do their part in the war effort. Radio announcements, magazine and newspaper advertisements, and wall posters urged Canadians to spend wisely, participate in salvage drives, tend victory gardens, or buy Victory Bonds. Perhaps the most important of the propaganda efforts was the

National Film Board, created in 1939. The NFB turned out hundreds of documentaries and short informational films during the war. Each was designed to make Canadian civilians feel that they were part of the war effort.

One of the most influential of the NFB's creations was a series of films entitled *Canada Carries On* about men and women working in war-related industries. Other series included *The War at Sea* and *The World in Action*. Such films as *Rationing, Story of Wartime Controls*, and *The Main* explained **wage-and-price controls**, the rationing program, how to use meat wisely and economically, and other wartime measures. These films were shown across Canada in movie houses as shorts to accompany feature films and newsreels. They were also shown in schools, community halls,

Posters helped to promote the NFB's propaganda films.

and other meeting places. The National Film Board was so successful in creating propaganda films that it emerged from the war as an important Canadian institution. Since the war, the NFB has gone on to win many international awards for the quality of its work.

MAKING CONNECTIONS

1. The word *propaganda* is often considered to have negative connotations. Is it possible to create "positive" propaganda? Assess the extent to which the types of films the NFB produced might be considered positive or negative propaganda.

2. a) Compare and contrast wartime salvage drives with today's recycling activities.
   b) Salvage drives and rationing were dropped soon after the war ended. Suggest reasons why these activities were discontinued despite their environmental benefits.

KEYWORDS

inflation

propaganda

wage-and-price controls

WORLD PEACE
Canada and the United Nations
FOCUSSING ON THE ISSUE

At the end of the Second World War, the international community created the United Nations. What did Canada hope to accomplish by its involvement in the UN?

The Creation of the UN

As the Second World War drew to a close, delegates from countries around the world gathered in San Francisco to create an organization that would ensure that such a global conflict would never happen again. Everyone agreed on one thing—that the new organization had to be more effective than the League of Nations, which had turned out to be powerless to prevent the outbreak of war.

Out of the talks in San Francisco emerged the United Nations. The UN was a compromise among the most powerful nations in the world—the United States, Britain, France, China, and the Soviet Union—and other, smaller countries. The so-called great powers were reluctant to share their authority with the rest of the international community. On the other hand, smaller countries, including Canada, did not want to belong to an organization unless they had some influence in it.

The charter of the United Nations reflected this division, creating six distinct parts:

1. The General Assembly resembles a world parliament, with all member countries having one seat and one vote. Delegates debate international crises as well as the internal affairs of the UN. The Assembly has no power to enforce decisions; it can only make recommendations.
2. The Security Council is responsible for keeping world peace. It consists of five permanent members—China, Russia, the United States, Britain, and France—and ten other members that join for two-year terms. Each of the so-called Big Five has the power to veto any decision, an arrangement that has, in some circumstances, left the Security Council powerless to act.
3. The Secretariat consists of the members of the UN staff who carry out the day-to-day operations of the organization. Employees are drawn from 140 nations and are scattered throughout the world, including the headquarters in New York. One of the objectives is to create a world body of civil servants whose loyalties are to the international community. The head of the Secretariat is the Secretary General. The first UN Secretary General was Trygve Lie, a politician from Norway.
4. The Economic and Social Council consists of 54 members chosen by the Assembly. It considers economic and social issues.

THE STRUCTURE OF THE UN

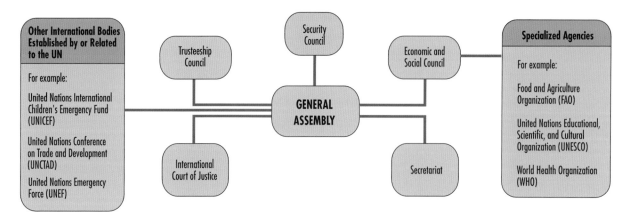

Other International Bodies Established by or Related to the UN

For example:

United Nations International Children's Emergency Fund (UNICEF)

United Nations Conference on Trade and Development (UNCTAD)

United Nations Emergency Force (UNEF)

Trusteeship Council

Security Council

Economic and Social Council

Specialized Agencies

For example:

Food and Agriculture Organization (FAO)

United Nations Educational, Scientific, and Cultural Organization (UNESCO)

World Health Organization (WHO)

GENERAL ASSEMBLY

International Court of Justice

Secretariat

5. The Trusteeship Council is responsible for administering non-self-governing territories, almost all of which are now independent countries.
6. The International Court of Justice is a world court that hears disputes between member nations.

The purposes of the United Nations are:

- to keep peace among nations
- to increase co-operation between nations
- to defend human rights
- to improve the living conditions of people everywhere in the world.

The UN plays an important role in maintaining world peace, but it is more than just an international security organization. It sponsors a wide variety of agencies that carry out legal, economic, and humanitarian work around the world. They include:

- the World Health Organization (WHO), which battles global health problems
- the United Nations International Children's Emergency Fund (UNICEF), which was originally responsible for assisting child welfare in countries devastated by the Second World War, but expanded its scope to developing countries after 1950

- the International Labour Organization (ILO), which works to improve labour conditions and living standards for the world's workers
- the United Nations Educational, Scientific, and Cultural Organization (UNESCO), which works to improve education standards and promote cultural activities.

Lester Pearson was the Canadian ambassador to the United States in 1945 when he attended the San Francisco Conference and signed the UN charter for Canada.

A Role for Canada

From the beginning, Canadians played prominent roles at the United Nations. Unlike the end of the First World War, when Canada retreated into **isolationism**, at the end of the Second World War the government agreed that international co-operation was the best recipe for world progress. A doctor from Ontario, Brock Chisholm, was the first head of the World Health Organization. A Montreal law professor, John Humphrey, helped to draw up the first International Declaration of Human Rights. The International Civil Aviation Organization, a major UN agency that establishes international standards and regulations for the world's airlines, had its headquarters in Montreal.

Canada has always seen the UN as the best means of contributing to world peace and to solving the problems of global health, poverty, pollution, and discrimination. In the past, Canadian aid to developing countries in Asia and Africa was funnelled through the UN. During the 1950s, Canada's most important contributions to international peace were as part of UN peacekeeping efforts in Korea and the Middle East. (See page 216.) As a **middle power** with limited influence, Canada has tried to use the UN as a vehicle for making a difference on the world stage.

◄□▪ MAKING CONNECTIONS ▪□►

1. How did Canadian foreign policy after the Second World War differ from foreign policy after the First World War? How do you explain this difference?

2. List three current benefits to Canada of participation in the United Nations. Explain why you think these are benefits.

KEYWORDS

veto

isolationism

middle power

SOCIAL SECURITY
The Welfare State in Canada
FOCUSSING ON THE ISSUE

The poverty, hunger, and unemployment that accompanied the Depression convinced many people that governments should provide for their citizens. The result was the creation of the welfare state. How did Canada begin to move towards the welfare state?

The Early Years

The 1919 Liberal party convention adopted a resolution calling for "an adequate system of insurance against unemployment, sickness, dependence, old age and other disability" to be established by the federal government and the governments of the provinces. Over the next 20 years, both Liberals and Conservatives made some attempts to implement these kinds of programs, but the federal government was unable to accomplish very much. The courts had ruled that the power to pass the necessary laws belonged to the provincial governments. As the Rowell-Sirois Commission had indicated, constitutional change was the best method of implementing national programs. (See page 138.) However, the federal and provincial governments could not agree on a way to amend the constitution.

Constitutional problems were not the only obstacles in the way of social programs. In 1919, many people thought the creation of welfare programs was radical and revolutionary. Many Canadians believed that pensions would remove the motive to save for their retirement. Unemployment insurance would pay workers for not working, so there would be no incentive to work. Even after the disaster of the Depression, when thousands of workers crisscrossed the country in a futile search for jobs, many Canadians still believed that the main cause of unemployment was the laziness of the workers.

The Beginning of the Welfare State

On 25 June 1940, Prime Minister King presented to the House of Commons a proposal to have the **BNA Act** amended by adding "unemployment insurance" to the list of powers specifically belonging to the federal government. The country was at war and there was full employment, so there was little debate about the proposal. The British Parliament amended the BNA Act, and the subsequent passage of the Unemployment Insurance Act created a new form of unemployment protection for Canadians. Employees and employers both paid into the plan and, if workers became unemployed, they could collect their insurance benefits.

As part of its war-effort strategy, the government had become heavily involved in regulating the lives of Canadians and the economy. Many Canadians came to believe that if the government could intervene in the name of the war effort, then it should also be able to intervene to provide a better **standard of living** for Canadians. Since it was only a matter of time before the war would be won, many Canadians were growing concerned about what the postwar world would be like. They could still remember the Depression and unemployment that had followed the First World War. They were now becoming more willing to accept the idea that society owed its members a higher degree of **social security** than had been previously acceptable.

What Kind of Security?

There was vigorous debate, however, over what social security meant. To some, it meant enough money to enable the breadwinner to provide a reasonable level of food and shelter for the family. To others, social security had a much broader meaning and included unemployment and medical insurance; old age and retirement security; and provisions for people with disabilities, families whose breadwinners had been killed in war or an accident, and families with inadequate incomes.

By 1943, the government had before it two reports urging an expansion of the social security net to include a health-care program, medical insurance, expanded pensions, and family allowances. Both

CASE STUDY

In 1994-95, the total spending of all governments in Canada was $357.6 billion dollars. Much of this money funds social services, education, and health care. In recent years, however, governments at all levels have been struggling to reduce the **deficit** and to manage the **debt**. The debt load has meant that governments have less to spend on other services. Approximately 30 per cent of total spending goes towards debt charges, compared with 10 per cent in the mid-1970s. Of the world's seven largest economies, Canada has the second-highest debt burden.

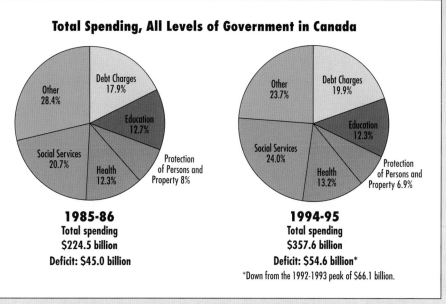

Total Spending, All Levels of Government in Canada

1985-86
Total spending
$224.5 billion
Deficit: $45.0 billion

1994-95
Total spending
$357.6 billion
Deficit: $54.6 billion*
*Down from the 1992-1993 peak of $66.1 billion.

1. a) Compare total government spending for different services in 1985-86 and 1994-95. What changes in spending can you identify?
   b) Create your own pie graph showing how you would distribute government funds. Explain your reasons.

reports emphasized that these should be nationwide programs, allowing Canadians to move freely between provinces while retaining their eligibility under the plans.

In 1944, the federal government proposed a **Family Allowance** program that provided a **sliding scale** of benefits depending on the age and number of children in a family. The cheques were to be mailed monthly to the mother in the belief that she would be more aware of the children's needs. Opponents of the plan argued that the payments would depress wages, that parents would misspend the money on alcohol or gambling, that the plan would encourage people to have large families, and that it would be too expensive to maintain. The government passed the Family Allowance Act in 1944 in spite of the opposition. The first cheques were mailed out in July 1945. With King's blessing, Canada was on the road to the "cradle to grave" security of the **welfare state**.

MAKING CONNECTIONS

1. Should social security programs be "insurance" programs where the beneficiaries contribute towards the costs? Explain.

2. Conduct a mock radio call-in program to discuss the issue of increased spending on social programs versus reducing the country's deficit.

KEYWORDS

BNA Act
standard of living
social security
Family Allowance
sliding scale
welfare state

FUNDAMENTAL CHARACTER
Postwar Immigration Policy

FOCUSSING ON THE ISSUE

At the end of the Second World War, hundreds of thousands of immigrants and refugees looked to rebuild their lives in a new land. Canada faced pressure from the United Nations to open its doors to more newcomers. The debate at home focussed on the "fundamental character" of the Canadian population and what immigrants the country should accept.

Immigration Policy

The Immigration Act of 1910 gave the federal Cabinet the power to regulate immigration and to establish the qualifications for prospective immigrants. Immigration policy was governed by two main factors: the country's economic needs and the "fundamental character" of Canadian society. Canada's immigration policy often discriminated against certain groups, in particular immigrants from Asia. Following the Second World War, the Liberal government of Mackenzie King did little to change the status quo.

The Immigration Act of 1946 defined acceptable immigrants as British subjects from Britain, Ireland, Newfoundland, Australia, New Zealand, and South Africa (with the exclusion of "non-white" subjects); US citizens; and the wife and unmarried children under 18, or the fiancé, of a legal resident of Canada. The regulations also allowed war brides to enter the country as relatives of Canadian nationals. In addition, three special

---

CASE STUDY

CANADIAN CITIZENSHIP

Until 1947, there was no such thing as a Canadian citizen. Canadians were British subjects. Immigrants from other countries were encouraged to become **naturalized** British subjects, a process that required an oath of allegiance to the Crown and three years' residency in Canada.

The Canadian Citizenship Act established Canadians as citizens of their country rather than subjects of Britain. Under the act, all those born in Canada or who had become naturalized British subjects automatically became Canadian citizens on 1 January 1947. New immigrants could gain citizenship if they had legally entered the country and had lived in Canada for four of the past six years. Candidates for citizenship were also required to have an adequate knowledge of French or English and to be of "good character."

In 1976, a new Citizenship Act was passed to reflect changes in Canadian society. Under the new act, all children born to a Canadian living outside Canada were considered Canadian citizens. (Previously, only those children born to a Canadian father living outside Canada were considered citizens. If the mother was a Canadian citizen but the father was not, the child was not considered a citizen.) The residency requirement was reduced to three of the previous four years. Citizenship candidates were also expected to have adequate knowledge of Canada and the responsibilities of Canadian citizenship.

People coming to Canada to live as permanent residents are known as **landed immigrants**. They are governed by the same laws as all residents of Canada, and they enjoy the same social benefits, such as health care, employment insurance, and education. They also pay the same taxes as Canadian citizens. However, they do not enjoy all of the privileges of Canadian citizenship. For example, only citizens can cast their votes in an election, run for public office, or hold many positions in the **civil service**. To enjoy all the rights and privileges of Canadian society, many landed immigrants choose to become Canadian citizens.

IMMIGRATION: THE GOVERNMENT'S POSITION

In May 1947, Prime Minister King delivered a speech outlining his government's position on immigration.

The policy of the government is to foster the growth of the population of Canada by the encouragement of immigration. The government will seek...to ensure the careful selection and permanent settlement of such numbers of immigrants as can advantageously be absorbed in our national economy....With regard to the selection of immigrants, much has been said about discrimination. I wish to make it quite clear that Canada is perfectly within her rights in selecting the persons whom we regard as desirable future citizens. It is not a "fundamental human right" of any alien to enter Canada. It is a privilege. It is a matter of domestic policy....There will, I am sure, be

general agreement with the view that the people of Canada do not wish, as a result of mass immigration, to make a fundamental alteration in the character of our population. Large-scale immigration from the Orient would change the fundamental composition of the Canadian population. Any considerable Oriental immigration would, moreover, be certain to give rise to social and economic problems of a character that might lead to serious difficulties in the field of international relations.

Prime Minister W. L. M. King, *Canada*, House of Commons Debates, *Vol. 3, 1947, pp. 2644–47.

1. What did King mean by "fundamental character"?
2. Do you think it is a "fundamental human right" of any alien to enter Canada? Explain.

---

categories of immigrants were created for Polish ex-servicemen then in Britain and Italy, Dutch farm workers (under a special agreement with the Dutch government), and qualified residents from Malta.

But as King's 1947 statement on immigration indicated, Canada's immigration policy remained discriminatory. While almost 380 000 immigrants came to Canada between 1945 and 1950, the admission of Asians was limited to the wife, husband, and unmarried children under the age of 21 of Canadian citizens living in Canada. The annual **quotas** for Asian immigrants were severely restricted—for example, 150 from India, 100 from

Pakistan, and 50 from Ceylon (now Sri Lanka). Not until 1962 would discrimination be eliminated from Canada's immigration policy.

War Refugees

The devastation and upheaval of the war had produced an unprecedented number of refugees. In 1945, the first task of the UN's newly created International Refugee Organization was to find new homes for the more than 1 million refugees. Many of these displaced persons were eastern Europeans who had fled west to escape the advance of the Soviet army. Most of them had no homes left to return to

after the war, or no desire to remain in their home countries now that they lay within the postwar Soviet **occupation zone**. The refugees were seeking an opportunity to start a new life far away from the ruins of Europe.

In November 1946, King introduced emergency measures that would bring some of the refugees to Canada. In March 1947, two inspection teams from the Immigration Department were dispatched to Germany to co-ordinate Canada's refugee program. Between 1947 and 1952, almost 170 000 refugees were resettled in Canada.

KEYWORDS

naturalized
landed immigrant
civil service
quota
occupation zone

◄▪◘▪ MAKING CONNECTIONS ▪◘►

1. Do you think countries such as Canada have an obligation to accept refugees, regardless of their country of origin? Explain your answer.

NEWFOUNDLAND
The Tenth Province
FOCUSSING ON THE ISSUE

Canada added a new province in 1949. Why did Newfoundland decide to join Confederation?

Debating Confederation

Residents of Newfoundland were the only Canadians who actually voted to join Confederation. On 3 June 1949, they went to the polls to vote in a **referendum** that gave them the rare opportunity to decide their own political future. Would they become independent, remain a British colony, or join Canada?

The roots of the Confederation referendum went back to the 1930s. Newfoundland was

---

PRE-CONFEDERATION PROPAGANDA

The debate over Confederation promoted **propaganda** on both sides. This excerpt from *The Confederate* made joining Confederation seem like an ideal situation for all Newfoundlanders.

Are You in This List?

To All Mothers: Confederation would mean that never again would there be a hungry child in Newfoundland. If you have children under the age of 16, you will receive every month a cash allowance for every child....

To All War Veterans: Canada treats her Veterans better than any other country in the world. She has just increased their War Pensions 25 per cent....

To All Wage-Workers: All wage-workers will be protected by Unemployment Insurance. Newfoundland, under Confederation, will be opened up and developed. Your country will be prosperous. Your condition will be better.

To All Over 65: You would have something to look forward to at the age of 70. The Old Age Pension of $30 a month for yourself, and $30 for your wife will protect you against need in your old age.

To All Railroaders: You will become employees of the biggest railway in the world, the CNR. You will have security and stability as CNR employees. Your wages and working conditions will be the same as on the CNR. Under any government you face sure and certain wage-cuts and lay-offs...

To All Building Workers: Under Confederation Newfoundland will share fully in the Canadian Government Housing Plan, under which cities and towns are financed to build houses. 1000 new homes will be built in St. John's under this plan.

To All Light Keepers: You will become employees of the Government of Canada. Your wages and working conditions will be greatly improved.

To All Postal-Telegraph Workers: You will all become employees of the Government of Canada, at higher salaries and much better working conditions.

To All Fishermen: The cost of living will come down. The cost of producing fish will come down...The Fish Prices Support Board of Canada, backed by Canada's millions, will protect the price of your fish.

To All Newfoundlanders: The cost of living will come down. The 120 000 children in our country will live better. The 10 000 Senior Citizens of our country will be protected in their old age. Newfoundland will be linked up with a strong, rich British nation. Newfoundland will go ahead with Canada.

From The Confederate, *31 May 1948.*

1. Which factors do you think would have been most persuasive? Why?

devastated by the Depression. Its economy depended on exports of natural resources—fish, wood products, and minerals. When world markets for these goods collapsed, Newfoundlanders were thrown out of work by the thousands. Meanwhile, the government was going bankrupt because it had borrowed so much money that it was unable to pay the interest on the loans. Unlike Canada, Newfoundland was still a colony of Great Britain; it had decided not to join Confederation in 1867. The British decided that they had to rescue their floundering colony. In 1934, elected government on the island was abolished. It was replaced with an appointed Commission of Government, which was given the job of running Newfoundland's affairs.

The Second World War brought an end to economic hard times. Both Canada and the United States established naval, air, and army bases in Newfoundland, providing jobs for thousands of people. At the end of the war the British realized they had to restore democracy to the island. And in the aftermath of the war, Britain no longer wanted the financial responsibility for the colony. In 1946, Newfoundlanders elected 45 delegates from all over the island to a national convention to discuss where their future lay. It was concluded that the people should decide in a referendum.

Referendum Results		
Options	First	Second
Status quo	14.3%	–
Confederation	41.1%	52.3%
Situation pre-1934	44.6%	47.7%

What was the status quo? Why was that option removed from the second referendum?

Making the Choice

The convention voted not to include Confederation with Canada as one of the options on the referendum ballot. Voters were supposed to choose between the **status quo** and a return to the situation that existed pre-1934. But Britain favoured Confederation. It wanted to be rid of the expense and responsibility of having Newfoundland as a colony, and it did not want the island falling into the American **orbit**.

Britain found an ally in Joey Smallwood. He organized a large petition demanding that Confederation be included as one of the choices on the ballot. With such a show of public support for the idea, the British were happy to agree. When Newfoundlanders voted in the referendum, they were given three options: (1) returning to self-government as it existed before 1934; (2) continuing the Commission of Government; or (3) entering into a union with Canada. If one of the choices did not gain a majority of the votes, then a second referendum on the two leading options would have to be held.

The main argument in favour of Confederation was economic. Compared to Canada, Newfoundland was impoverished. Incomes were only one-third as high, and Canada had far better support programs for poor and unemployed people. Smallwood and others believed that as part of Canada, Newfoundland would improve its prospects for international trade. Arguments against Confederation were also economic. Many islanders feared that competition from Canada would destroy local businesses. They also did not look forward to paying the high Canadian income tax. Religion also came into play; Catholics were concerned about the status of their schools in a union with Canada.

In the first referendum, the Confederation option ran second. But no choice won a majority, so on 22 July 1948, the people voted again. This time Confederation carried the day. Arrangements were finalized, and on 31 March 1949, Newfoundland became the tenth Canadian province.

◄▣ MAKING CONNECTIONS ▣►

1. Compare the factors leading to Newfoundland's union with Canada to the factors leading to Confederation in 1867. What factors were different? What factors were similar?

KEYWORDS

referendum

propaganda

status quo

orbit

THE CCF IN POWER
Socialism in Saskatchewan

Saskatchewan elected the first socialist government in North America. What was the national significance of Tommy Douglas's 17 years as premier of the province?

The CCF

On 15 June 1944, while most of the world was mesmerized by the Allied invasion of Europe, **socialism** came to North America. That was the day voters in Saskatchewan elected the Co-operative Commonwealth Federation (CCF) to power. During the campaign, the CCF did not disguise the fact that it favoured socialist policies. It presented a platform designed to increase government involvement in the economy and improve social programs.

The new premier of Saskatchewan was Tommy Douglas. A Baptist minister, Douglas turned to politics during the Depression and was elected as a Member of Parliament for the CCF. In 1944, he resigned his seat in the House of Commons to become leader of the party in Saskatchewan. Although he was small in stature, Douglas's opponents soon learned not to underestimate him. As a young man he had been a lightweight boxing champion, and he carried his combative spirit into the political ring as well.

Saskatchewan was an agricultural province, and the CCF was supported by the majority of farmers. Among the first things Douglas's government did was to pass new laws protecting farmers from losing their land because they could not afford to pay debts incurred during bad harvests. The government also made electricity more widely available in rural areas and introduced improvements to country schools. For urban workers, the government raised the minimum wage and required employers to give employees at least two weeks paid vacation a year.

As a socialist party, the CCF believed that provincial resources belonged to the people and therefore should be developed for the benefit of the public, not for the

Tommy Douglas was a witty speaker. One of his favourite opening lines was: "Canada is like an old cow. The West feeds it. Ontario and Quebec milk it. And you can well imagine what it's doing in the Maritimes." Explain how this joke reflects eastern and western Canada's attitude towards central Canada.

profits of private investors. To meet this objective, Douglas expanded the publicly owned telephone system and created the Saskatchewan Power Corporation to deliver hydroelectricity. He also introduced government automobile insurance for all drivers in the province. The CCF tried to extend government ownership into the manufacturing sector in order to diversify the economy, but a small local market and high freight rates made it difficult to establish successful manufacturers. Douglas profited from a healthy economy during his time in power. Despite all the new programs he introduced, he was able to balance the provincial budget year after year and to reduce the debt to almost nothing.

The CCF encountered some criticism, however, during the height of the Cold War when Douglas and the party were often denounced as communists. Opposition parties and much of the press criticized the Saskatchewan government for being so deeply involved in the economy. The voters, however, continued to support the CCF. Douglas himself remained premier until he resigned in 1961 to become national leader of the newly organized New Democratic Party (NDP). The CCF remained in power in Saskatchewan for another three years before it was finally defeated in an election, in part because of the struggle to introduce **Medicare**. It was the longest-serving government in the province's history.

The success of the CCF in Saskatchewan had an important impact on Canadian politics. It showed that in the wake of the Second World War, Canadians cared deeply about social programs and would support parties that shared this concern. As a result, other political parties followed the CCF model and adopted new social policies of their own.

C A S E   S T U D Y

THE FIGHT FOR MEDICARE

The policy with which Tommy Douglas's government will always be associated is Medicare. The CCF believed that everyone should have access to medical care. The first step was the introduction of public hospital insurance in Saskatchewan in 1947. For a **premium** of five dollars a year, every person in the province received hospital care when they needed it. What the premiums did not cover, the government paid for through tax revenues. The system was universal in that it included everyone, rich and poor alike.

Hospitals were only one part of the health-care system, however. People still had to pay for visits to the doctor. So in 1959, Douglas announced a complete health insurance plan that included the payment of doctors' fees. After winning re-election in 1960, he put his plan in action. Saskatchewan's doctors were bitterly opposed, however, as were private insurance companies. In July 1962, the doctors went on strike. Many left the province to set up practice elsewhere. Refusing to back down, the government brought in doctors from other places who believed in the new system. It was a bitter struggle, but after three weeks the doctors gave in and returned to work. Public health insurance was a reality in Saskatchewan.

In 1966, the federal government introduced a national health-care plan, modelled on the Saskatchewan plan, for all Canadians. As a result, Tommy Douglas is recognized today as the founder of socialized medicine in Canada.

1. a) Suggest reasons why doctors opposed Medicare when it was introduced in Saskatchewan.
   b) Suggest reasons why private insurance companies opposed Medicare.

MAKING CONNECTIONS

1. **Why do you think the CCF was more successful in Saskatchewan than in other provinces?**

KEYWORDS

socialism

Medicare

premium

GAINING INDEPENDENCE
The Supreme Court of Canada

Prior to 1949, the Supreme Court of Canada was not the highest court of appeal in the country. The decisions of the Supreme Court were subject to the final authority of the Privy Council in London, England. What became "supreme" about the Supreme Court of Canada in 1949?

The Road to Independence

The Supreme Court of Canada is the most powerful court of law in the country. It consists of nine impartial judges who have the last word in interpreting the law in legal disputes between individuals and between people and the government. In Canada, the Supreme Court is the court of last resort. However, this was not always the case. For many years, the Supreme Court of Canada existed in the shadow of the **Judicial Committee of the Privy Council** in London, England.

In the years immediately following Confederation, the federal government looked for ways to cen-

*The Supreme Court of Canada is made up of nine federally appointed judges, three of whom must be from Quebec because it is the only province with **civil law** (the other provinces follow **common law**). These judges live in Ottawa and must be impartial—that is, they must not be involved in any political activities, and must not hold any other paid position. Supreme Court judges, like all other judges in Canada, must retire at age 75. Considering their great responsibilities, what qualifications do you think judges should have?*

tralize power in Ottawa. One step towards this centralization was the creation of a Supreme Court with the power to review the decisions of lower provincial courts across the country. The **BNA Act** of 1867 had given Parliament the power to "provide for the constitution, maintenance, and organization of a General Court of Appeal for Canada." However, in the early years of Confederation, many politicians and members of the legal community opposed a Supreme Court of Canada. They argued that it would take away too much authority from provincial courts and that it would interfere with the traditional right to **appeal** to "the foot of the throne"—the Privy Council in London. Despite the opposition, however, the Supreme Court of Canada was finally created in 1875 under the Liberal government of Alexander Mackenzie.

The Court began its work amidst protests from several MPs demanding that it be abolished. For many years, the Supreme Court had a poor reputation. The judges often quarrelled among themselves, and some became involved in messy political entanglements. Many lawyers preferred the judgements of their own provincial superior or appeals courts to the rulings of Canada's Supreme Court.

But as the twentieth century progressed, the Supreme Court gradually gained respectability. As it did so, many Canadians began to question why the decisions made by the highest court in the land should be reviewed, and sometimes overruled, by judges in Britain. In addition, the Statute of Westminster in 1931 had ended Britain's right to make laws for Canada. Discontent with the Privy Council intensified in the late 1930s when the Council struck down a series of federal acts designed to help the provinces cope with the Depression. Plans to abolish the appeals process were stalled during the Second World War. But when the war ended, Canada was determined to make the Supreme Court truly supreme. In June 1949, the Liberal government of Louis St. Laurent passed the bill that finally ended appeals to the Privy Council in London.

The Impact of Independence

There was little fanfare when the Supreme Court of Canada gained its independence. Nor was the period following the termination of appeals to London one of innovation. Gradually, though, the Supreme Court of Canada began to meet the challenges of its new status. Among the cases heard by the Court after 1949 were those involving the **civil liberties** of Jehovah's Witnesses in Quebec. In *Saumur v.*

City of Quebec (1953), the Court declared a Quebec City bylaw invalid because it interfered with the distribution of pamphlets by Jehovah's Witnesses. For the first time in Canada, Supreme Court judges were being asked to determine the legal foundations for the protection of individual rights. This was a difficult task because there was no reference to individual rights in Canada's constitution. The Supreme Court's ruling on the rights of Jehovah's Witnesses ultimately led to the call for a Bill of Rights that would clearly establish the fundamental rights and freedoms of all Canadians.

The Supreme Court of Canada was originally established to review the decisions of lower provincial courts. Before 1949, it was denied a decisive voice in the development of Canadian law. When the decisions of the Supreme Court were no longer subject to the scrutiny of the Privy Council, the Court had to live up to its new role as the court of last resort in Canada. Citizens would now expect the Supreme Court to fulfil its ultimate responsibility of interpreting the law and defining and upholding the rights and freedoms of all Canadians.

KEYWORDS

Judicial Committee of the Privy Council

civil law

common law

BNA Act

appeal

civil liberties

⊲⊏▪ MAKING CONNECTIONS ▪⊐▷

1. How did having to appeal to London affect Canada, Canadians, and the Supreme Court of Canada?

2. What new responsibilities accompanied the Supreme Court's independence from London in 1949? Why was it difficult for the court to meet these new challenges? Give at least two reasons.

ABORIGINAL VETERANS
The Impact of the War
FOCUSSING ON THE ISSUE

Many Aboriginal peoples enlisted in the armed forces during the Second World War. What was the impact of the war on Canadian Aboriginal peoples?

Fighting for Canada

Under the terms of the **Indian Act** of 1876, Aboriginal peoples were not citizens of Canada; instead, they were wards of the state. As a result, they did not hold certain basic rights shared by all other Canadians, for example, the right to vote. Still, when the war broke out, many Aboriginal people volunteered to serve with Canadian forces overseas. Because they were not citizens, Aboriginal volunteers had to seek permission from the

Private Huron Brant (left), a Mohawk soldier from Deseronto, Ontario, is awarded the Military Medal by British General Bernard Montgomery in Sicily, 1943. During the invasion of Italy, Brant single-handedly attacked and captured a force of 30 enemy soldiers. The next year he was killed in northern Italy. More than 200 Aboriginal soldiers died in combat during the war.

Department of Indian Affairs to enlist for war. They were also expected to **enfranchise**, which meant that they had to give up their status as registered Indians. For Aboriginal soldiers, serving Canada meant the loss of their own identity.

More than 3000 Aboriginal soldiers fought in the Canadian forces during the Second World War. Once enlisted they did not always receive equal treatment. Both the Canadian navy and the air force only accepted recruits who were "of pure European descent." The army, on the other hand, accepted Aboriginal volunteers as equals with their non-Aboriginal peers. They received the same privileges as other Canadian soldiers and the same recognition for their efforts in combat. Aboriginal soldiers fought, and died, in all the major campaigns of the war, including Hong Kong, Dieppe, Italy, and the final liberation of Europe.

Returning Home

The experience of equality, even with the hardships of war, was not forgotten when Aboriginal soldiers returned home. For many of them, it was the first time they had felt they were a real part of Canada and equal to other Canadians. Like many non-Aboriginal soldiers, they had acquired training and skills that they hoped to put to good use in civilian life.

Once the war ended, however, the Canadian government seemed determined to return to the **status quo**. Aboriginal veterans returned to a life in which the rights and freedoms afforded to other Canadians were not extended to them. Aboriginal veterans did not receive the veteran's pension. They still were not allowed to vote or own land. They returned to impoverished reserves segregated from the mainstream of Canadian life. As one Aboriginal veteran, Clarence Silver, observed: "When I served overseas I was a Canadian. When I came home I was just an Indian."

In the long term, however, the Second World War was a catalyst for change. The experiences overseas of some Aboriginal soldiers made them determined to force changes at home. At the same time, many non-Aboriginal people began recognizing, for the first time, the second-class status of Aboriginal peoples. Had not Canadians just fought a war against racism and barbarism in Europe? Perhaps it was time to consider the shortcomings of their own dealings with Aboriginal peoples.

In 1946, the federal government established a joint committee made up of members from the House of Commons and the Senate to consider changes to the Indian Act. The committee's hearings lasted until 1948. It learned the true extent of the inequalities afflicting

Aboriginal peoples: how their incomes were a fraction of what other Canadians earned; how their schools were inferior; how their diet and living conditions on the reserves resulted in appalling health standards.

For the first time, Aboriginal spokespeople were invited to give testimony to a government committee. They came from across the country to tell their stories. "When it comes to defence of his country, his services were accepted and generously offered," Peter Kelly, a Haida from British Columbia, told the committee about the Aboriginal veteran. "Yet he is denied any voice in the affairs of the land."

As it turned out, the parliamentary committee did not bring about dramatic change for Aboriginal peoples. It listened to their concerns, then made some changes to the Indian Act. For instance, it repealed the ban, which had been in place since 1884, on the **potlatch** and other Aboriginal ceremonies. The changes did not go as far as Aboriginal leaders had hoped, but the committee did succeed in putting Aboriginal issues at the top of the public agenda, at least for a while. Aboriginal peoples had found a voice and non-Aboriginal people were hearing it with empathy. The stage was set for an Aboriginal political resurgence in the years to come.

BIOGRAPHY: TOM PRINCE

The career of Tom Prince (1915–1977) sums up the paradoxical situation of Aboriginal soldiers who were hailed as heroes in wartime, then neglected as outcasts in their own country after the war. Prince was a Saulteaux from Manitoba. During the Second World War he served in Italy and France and was a member of an elite commando unit called the Devil's Brigade. On one occasion during the Italian campaign, Prince crept behind enemy lines and established an observation post from which he used a field phone to direct artillery fire towards enemy guns. When the phone connection to his own lines was cut off, he boldly dressed up to look like an Italian peasant and walked out in plain sight of enemy soldiers to repair the line. For this act of bravery he won the Military Cross.

When the Korean War began, Prince re-enlisted and again showed remarkable bravery in front-line action. By the time the war ended in 1953, he had won a total of ten medals, making him Canada's most decorated Aboriginal soldier. However, in peacetime

Tom Prince (second from right) is shown with a group of Canadian soldiers who won medals for bravery during the Second World War.

he had difficulty finding work and suffered from the injuries received in combat. He died in poverty, forgotten by the society for which he had gone to war, but not by his fellow Aboriginals who gave him a hero's burial.

MAKING CONNECTIONS

1. Since Aboriginal peoples were not treated as equals in Canadian society, why do you think so many volunteered to fight for Canada during the war? Would their reasons have been different from those of non-Aboriginal volunteers? Explain.

2. In the aftermath of the Second World War, how did attitudes towards Aboriginal peoples change?

KEYWORDS

Indian Act

enfranchise

status quo

potlatch

CANADA-US RELATIONS
The Postwar Era
FOCUSSING ON THE ISSUE

*The Second World War brought Canada even more closely into partnership
with the United States, but it was evident that this was an unequal relationship.
What issues arose after the war as a result of Canada-US relations?*

Second Fiddle

Andrei Gromyko, the Soviet delegate to the United Nations in 1948, described Canada as "the boring second fiddle in the American orchestra." Embarrassed at being excluded by the superpowers from the peace treaty discussions during the Second World War, many Canadians felt there was truth in Gromyko's biting words. It was hard to accept, but many Canadians believed their nation was in no position to seek a more forceful independent role in the postwar world.

Canada's **geopolitical** location between the two superpowers—the US and the USSR—presented little hope of neutrality and considerable possibility that it might become the battleground for some future nuclear war. Under the circumstances, Mackenzie King and, later, his successor, Louis St. Laurent, found it prudent to seek stronger ties to the US while pursuing **collective security** through the United Nations.

Canadian diplomats did achieve some success in creating alliances in Europe. Canada played a key role in the 1949 creation of the North Atlantic Treaty Organization (NATO). For the most part, however, Canada found itself in the awkward role of a **middle power**—too small in population and military power to be a major force in world affairs, but too prosperous and economically significant to be ignored.

Under the American Umbrella

During the Second World War, Canada's army had been organized, trained, and equipped along British lines. The postwar era brought Canada militarily closer to the American sphere. After 1947, the Canadian

What do you think the cartoonist is trying to say?

military adopted US standards for weapons, equipment, tactics, and training. Nowhere was this Americanization of Canada's armed forces more evident than in air defence. In Europe, Canadian fighter aircraft serving with NATO forces were stationed at US air bases. Following the testing of atomic weapons by the USSR in 1949, the United States and Canada established a series of radar stations across Alaska and Canada's vast northern landscape. The Distant Early Warning System (DEW), along with the Mid-Canada and Pine Tree radar air defence lines, were intended to provide early warning of an attack by the Soviet Union, allowing Canadian and US fighter aircraft to intercept and destroy the invaders—over Canadian territory!

American influence over Canadian policies was clearly illustrated in 1949 following the victory of the communists, led by Mao Zedong, in the Chinese civil war. Under normal circumstances, Canada might have been expected to recognize the new Chinese government at the same time as Britain and other European powers did. However, the United States had close ties to the defeated Nationalists led by Jiang Jie Shi—forced into exile on the island of Formosa (now Taiwan)—and

refused to recognize the legitimacy of Mao's government. Canada followed the US's lead; two decades would pass before Canada would normalize diplomatic relations with the People's Republic of China.

The ideological influence of the US could be seen in smaller ways, too. In the early 1950s, the Toronto Symphony Orchestra refused to hire some refugee musicians from Europe; the reason—the American government would not allow them to enter the US because they had once been members of socialist or communist parties.

By the late 1940s, the Canadian economy had become closely intertwined with that of the US. American investors now owned or controlled much of Canada's resource and manufacturing industries. Most of the brand-name products used in daily life were the same as those used south of the forty-ninth parallel. American products, along with American media, were

American culture crossed the border into Canada in films like this one, entitled How to Marry a Millionaire.

now so much a part of Canada's cultural landscape that the cultural distinctions between the two nations were beginning to blur. These cultural influences were almost entirely one-sided, with the exception of exports of maple syrup and the National Hockey League teams in New York, Chicago, Detroit, and Boston!

MAKING CONNECTIONS

1. Should Canada have followed so closely American foreign and domestic policies regarding communism and socialism in the postwar era? Provide arguments to support your answer.

2. Relate the nuclear arms race cartoon to Canada's geopolitical position on the globe. Use a **polar projection map** from your school atlas to help you.

KEYWORDS

geopolitical

collective security

middle power

polar projection map

THE POSTWAR BOOM
Living in a Material World
FOCUSSING ON THE ISSUE

In 1945, Canada was prepared for the return of its armed forces and for the conversion of war industries into peacetime production. What role did the government play in the changeover from a wartime to a peacetime economy? How did Canadians respond to peacetime conditions?

A Stronger Economy

At the end of the Second World War, Canada had the world's third-largest navy and fourth-largest air force. The ships and planes had been produced in Canadian factories. As a result of the war, Canada's industrial economy had strengthened, which had helped to end the Depression. The jobs in the factories paid well, thanks in part to unionization and in even greater measure to the shortage of labour created by the men and women who had gone to war.

The slogan of the Liberal government as the war ended was "orderly decontrol." Soon after V-E Day, the country went to the polls. Mackenzie King and the Liberals promised a combination of **free enterprise** and government controls to prevent another depression. If re-elected, King assured the voters, his government would offer incentives to both industries and consumers to get the peacetime economy rolling. King's government won the election of 15 June 1945 with a slim **majority**, but it was enough for King to launch his "New Social Order." Returning military personnel were paid to go to university, take job training, or relocate to find work. A new National

Housing Act provided low-cost mortgages, stimulating a postwar housing boom and creating jobs in the construction industry. As factories began producing peacetime products, the Unemployment Insurance program, introduced in 1941, helped make the shift to a postwar industrial economy easier by ensuring financial assistance to workers temporarily laid off in the transition from wartime production.

The government also provided incentives to factory owners to speed up that transition. Government-built wartime factories were transferred to the private sector at a small fraction of their cost to the taxpayers. Factory and business owners were given generous tax incentives such as **depreciation allowances** to encourage them to buy new equipment and to upgrade their plants. An export insurance program, designed to reduce the risks faced by Canadian exporters, was paid for by the government to help sell Canadian goods abroad. The incentives worked. Factory output dipped briefly in 1945–1946 as firms shifted to peacetime production, then soon soared to pass wartime peaks.

Trade unions had gained the legal right to **collective bargaining** during the war. Membership in unions grew steadily after 1945, reaching 30 per cent of factory

Job counselling was among the many services provided to war veterans.

workers by 1950. Canadian workers now enjoyed greater job security, higher wages, better benefits, and longer vacations than ever before. In 1946, the average Canadian worker earned $1516 a year; two years later the figure was nearly 30 per cent higher as the average hourly wage for men reached $1.00. It would take eight more years for women to reach that level.

The Baby Boom

The Second World War had completed Canada's transformation from a rural to a mainly urban society. It also set off one of the greatest economic booms in Canadian history. People were ready to raise families in these peaceful and prosperous times. In the years immediately after the war, a single industrial

After the war, there was a shortage of housing. At one point, 16 000 veteran families were without homes. These houses were built specifically for returning war veterans.

wage could support a family, and families were indeed growing. In 1941, children under five accounted for 9 per cent of the population; by 1951, this figure had risen to 12 per cent. This population boom led to an increase in school construction and growth in

the number of teaching jobs. Canada's universities, colleges, and vocational schools grew quickly in the postwar years, their enrolments swelled by young women and men who had served in the armed forces and who now saw higher education as a road to success.

CASE STUDY

WOMEN AFTER THE WAR

The period between 1945 to 1950 is the only time during the twentieth century in which Canada's female workforce shrank. Immediately after the war ended, 48 000 women came to Canada as war brides. Also, 50 000 service women received their discharge papers from the armed forces. Another 80 000 women were laid off from industry. Any woman in a "replacement position" was forced to quit her job if the man she had replaced wanted it back. The gov-

ernment then introduced several measures to discourage women from seeking employment. It closed all the nurseries that had been opened during the war to allow women with children to work. The civil service renewed its rule barring married women from holding positions in its ranks. This rule stayed in force until 1955.

Jan Coomber and Rosemary Evans, Women Changing Canada. Copyright © Oxford University Press 1997. p. 37. *Reprinted by permission.*

◄■ MAKING CONNECTIONS ■►

1. Compare and contrast economic conditions in Canada following the First World War with conditions following the Second World War.

2. How would the emphasis on education for returning service personnel have affected postwar employment figures?

KEYWORDS

free enterprise

majority

depreciation allowance

collective bargaining

UNIT 6:

Alfred Pellan, *Floraison (Blossoming)*, (c. 1956)

In the 1930s and 1940s, Alfred Pellan (1906-1988) explored a broad range of artistic styles, from representational to abstract. His mature work emerged in the 1950s, where his interest in Surrealism and the relationship between human and animal life to the plant world resulted in paintings of intense colour and rich texture.

THE NEW SUBURBAN SOCIETY

1951-1960

*Skills and Processes

A NEW ERA
The World in 1951
FOCUSSING ON THE ISSUE

The 1950s marked the beginning of a new era in international politics, scientific technology, and popular culture. What issues and events shaped the world in the years following the end of the Second World War?

The Cold War

In the 1950s, the **Cold War** became the dominant force in international politics. It divided the world between two opposing ideologies: **totalitarian communism** and **democratic capitalism**. The capitalist nations, led by the United States, and the communist countries, led by the Soviet Union, competed for influence over, or control of, the rest of the world. Most of the countries the two sides sought to dominate were developing countries or former colonies of Western powers. Thus the developing world became the battleground for the two new superpowers.

At times the Cold War intensified as debates in the United Nations and heated diplomatic exchanges were replaced by fighting. When the decade began in 1951, the Cold War centred on Korea. (See page 188.) The conflict was the first open warfare between communist forces and pro-Western forces—the USSR and China versus the United States and its allies. The Korean War ended in 1953, only to be replaced by a long and bloody war in French Indo-China that would eventually draw the United States into combat in Vietnam.

In 1951, the United States tested its first hydrogen bomb. It was a devastating weapon of **mass destruction**, nearly 1000 times as powerful as the bombs dropped on Hiroshima and Nagasaki that had ended the Second World War just six years earlier. The Soviet Union followed with the testing of its first hydrogen bomb in 1953. A new arms race was under way as both superpowers continued to develop and test larger and more destructive nuclear devices. By the decade's end, guided missiles were beginning to replace bombers as the most effective means of launching nuclear warheads against enemy targets. The United States and the Soviet Union were now able to attack targets 10 000 km away in less than one hour.

The arms race led to a space race. If missiles could send hydrogen bombs halfway around the world, then they could also carry **nuclear payloads** into space. The USSR launched its first satellite armed with a nuclear warhead in 1958; the US soon followed. Scientists eventually began exploring the possibility of using satellites for peaceful means, such as communications and space exploration.

Scientific Advances

The 1950s also saw major advances in scientific and medical research. In 1954, several major discoveries took place in the scientific community. An American researcher, Dr. Jonas Salk, developed a vaccine that eradicated polio, a debilitating childhood disease. Two British scientists, James Watson and Francis Crick, discovered **DNA**, the basic building block of life. Medical research first identified a clear link between smoking cigarettes and lung cancer. The "Big Bang" theory of the creation of the universe was first published, using data—received through radio telescopes—from events that happened billions of years ago.

The world first became aware of the problem of air pollution in the early 1950s. It was discovered that black fog filled with soot and ash from industrial emissions caused lung problems and even deaths in London and Mexico City. A six-year study released in 1954 identified the **photochemical action** of sunlight on car-exhaust emissions as the cause of the smog that plagued Los Angeles.

Life in the Fast Lane

Speed and convenience were the hallmarks of the 1950s, and nowhere more so than in North America. Frozen dinners that could go straight from the freezer into the oven became a common grocery item in North American homes. Suburban housing communities,

SMOG IN CANADA

Smog was first identified in the 1950s. Over the years, the problem has intensified. Today smog takes a heavy toll on Canadians' health as well as the environment and the economy.

Urban dwellers and people downwind of big cities and industrial complexes breathe an airborne chemical soup of unburned fuels, household and industrial chemicals, and waste gases. There is mounting evidence that this mixture of pollutants, often described as smog, has health effects ranging from discomfort to increased illness to premature death....But smog is not just an urban problem. In Canada high amounts of ground-level ozone reach 100 km down the Fraser Valley from Vancouver. In central Canada, the pollution corridor extends from Windsor to Quebec City....In the Maritimes, the smog belt reaches from New Brunswick to western Nova Scotia....Ground-level ozone causes about $70 million worth of crop damage a year in southern Ontario, and more than $8 million in the Fraser Valley.

Michael Keating and the Canadian Global Change Program, Canada and the State of the Planet: The Social, Economic and Environmental Trends That Are Shaping Our Lives. Copyright © The Royal Society of Canada, 1997. pp. 46 and 47. Reprinted by permission of Oxford University Press Canada.

linked by expressways to urban centres, became a symbol of North American cities. Around the world, the first jet airliners made international travel commonplace.

The United States continued to dominate the world's popular culture in the 1950s. In 1951, colour-television images were broadcast for the first time. In 1952, the first automobiles featuring air-conditioning appeared on the market. Disneyland was created in California in 1955, while millions of children around the world faithfully tuned in to *The Mickey Mouse Club* on television. Rock 'n' roll hit the airwaves with the release of "Rock Around the Clock" by Bill Haley and the Comets in April 1954. Two years later, a young country singer named Elvis Presley topped the record charts with "Heartbreak Hotel." The term *teenager* was also invented in the 1950s, as was the **mass marketing** of fads and popular culture aimed exclusively at the adolescent market. (See page 200).

Much of what has happened since the 1950s has involved either the refinement or acceleration of trends already begun in that decade. For example, early in the 1950s two important engineering discoveries—the magnetic-core memory and the transistor-circuit element—rapidly found their way into new models of digital computers. In many ways, the 1950s set the pattern for the second half of the twentieth century.

KEYWORDS

Cold War

totalitarian
communism

democratic
capitalism

mass destruction

nuclear payloads

DNA

photochemical action

mass marketing

sustainable development

MAKING CONNECTIONS

1. What political, scientific, and cultural aspects of life from the 1950s are still evident in our lives today? Explain.

2. Working in groups of five, prepare a case study on the relationship between economic development in your area since the 1950s and its impact on the environment. Outline a plan for **sustainable development**.

THE KOREAN WAR
Putting the UN to the Test
FOCUSSING ON THE ISSUE

The war in Korea marked the first armed conflict of the Cold War. Why did the international community become involved in the war? Why were Canadians involved in the fighting?

Canadian artillery pounded the enemy lines in Korea, 1951.

Invasion

The first shot in the Cold War was fired at 4:00 a.m. on 25 June 1950. In North Korea, tanks and soldiers surged across the border into South Korea, starting a war that would last for three years. While the future of Korea was at stake, so too was the future of the United Nations. Would the international community allow one country to be overrun by another without lifting a finger to help, as it had done in the years leading up to the Second World War? Or would it honour the principle of **collective security** and come to the defence of South Korea?

Korea had been **annexed** by Japan in 1910. When Japan surrendered at the end of the Second World War, Korea was divided into two countries. The division was supposed to be temporary, but the two sides quickly developed very different types of government. North Korea, controlled by the Soviet Union, established a **communist** government. South Korea was an unstable democracy under the influence of the United States.

International Response

In 1950, the North tried to reunite the country under its control. At first, North Korean soldiers met with easy success as they conquered the South Korean capital of Seoul and drove the southern army towards the sea. But the world reacted strongly to this aggression.

The United Nations condemned North Korea and called for an international force to resist the invasion. The United States sent the largest number of troops, aided by 16 other nations.

By November 1950, UN-backed forces in South Korea, commanded by the American general Douglas MacArthur, had pushed the invading army back across the border at the thirty-eighth parallel. Then China joined the North Korean forces. The balance tipped once again as South Korean soldiers were driven back by a massive onslaught of Chinese forces.

The war moved back and forth along the Korean peninsula as first one side, then the other, gained the upper hand. Finally, it settled into an armed stand-off roughly along the thirty-eighth parallel. Peace talks began at Panmunjom in the summer of 1951. But it was another two years before an **armistice** was signed on 27 July 1953. The deal established a **demilitarized** zone, four kilometres wide, dividing North and South Korea. Today, Korea is still divided into two separate countries.

Canada's Role in Korea

Within days of the invasion of South Korea, Canada offered three naval destroyers to the UN force. Before the war was over, about 25 000 Canadians saw action in the

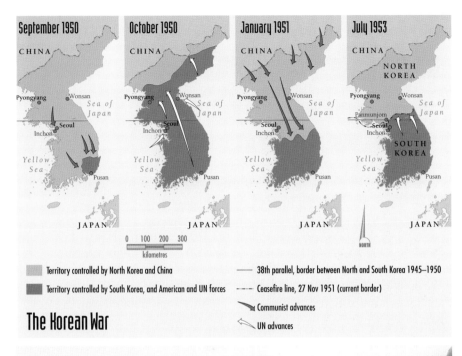

September 1950

CHINA

Pyongyang
Wonsan
Sea of Japan
Seoul
Inchon
Yellow Sea
Pusan

JAPAN

October 1950

CHINA

Pyongyang
Wonsan
Sea of Japan
Seoul
Inchon
Yellow Sea
Pusan

JAPAN

January 1951

CHINA

Pyongyang
Wonsan
Sea of Japan
Seoul
Inchon
Yellow Sea
Pusan

JAPAN

July 1953

CHINA

NORTH KOREA

Pyongyang
Wonsan
Sea of Japan
Panmunjom
Seoul
Inchon
SOUTH KOREA
Yellow Sea
Pusan

JAPAN

NORTH

0   100   200   300
kilometres

☐ Territory controlled by North Korea and China

☐ Territory controlled by South Korea, and American and UN forces

— 38th parallel, border between North and South Korea 1945–1950

---- Ceasefire line, 27 Nov 1951 (current border)

➤ Communist advances

➤ UN advances

The Korean War

During the Korean War, René Lévesque, shown here interviewing Canadian soldiers, was a young news reporter with CBC Radio. Years later, Lévesque founded the separatist Parti Québécois and served as premier of Quebec from 1976 to 1985.

┤■ MAKING CONNECTIONS ■├

1. The Korean War, which has been called the "forgotten war," was the last major war before the introduction of television. What effect do you think television has had on the way people think about war?

conflict, mainly as part of a much larger **Commonwealth** force. Despite the loss of 312 Canadian lives, one historian has called it "the most popular war Canada ever fought." Korea may have been far away, but most Canadians were convinced that they were supporting the "free world" in a fight to stop the spread of communism.

Canada's involvement in Korea transformed its foreign policy. Canada had traditionally been connected with Britain, but now the US exerted greater influence. Canadian policy makers used their position as a trusted ally to do what they could to restrain American policy. As was often the case during the Cold War, Canada found itself on the same side as the US, but not always agreeing with everything the US wanted to do.

The Korean War also sparked a dramatic increase in the size of Canada's armed forces. By 1953, defence spending was ten times higher than it had been just six years earlier. Fearful of communist expansion, Canada sent troops to Germany as part of its involvement in NATO. It was the first time that Canada stationed a permanent force outside its borders during peacetime. For Canadians, this was the long-term legacy of the war in Korea.

KEYWORDS

collective security

annex

communist

armistice

demilitarize

Commonwealth

THE BABY BOOM
The Impact on Canadian Society
FOCUSSING ON THE ISSUE

Postwar affluence and optimism in Canada were reflected in the baby boom, which began in 1946 and continued through the 1950s. How did the sharp increase in Canada's birth rate after the Second World War affect Canadian society? How will the baby boomers affect future generations?

A New Generation

Fifteen years of depression and war had left their mark on Canadian society. Hard times and uncertain futures saw Canadian marriage and birth rates drop between 1929 and 1945. Many couples postponed marriage during this period. Family life was put on hold as Canadian men and women waited for better times. The average age of Canada's population had risen steadily through the early 1940s. Years of falling birth rates had combined with deep cuts to immigration to reduce the number of children relative to the adult population. However, the postwar **baby boom** changed this ratio significantly.

Rising wages and the "baby bonus," as the **Family Allowance** was soon called, led to the baby boom. In the years immediately following the war families began growing. In 1941, children under five accounted for 9 per cent of the population; by 1951, that number had risen to 12 per cent. It peaked at 12.4 per cent in 1956, eventually falling to 11 per cent in 1966 as the baby boom drew to an end.

The Impact of the Baby Boom

While the baby boom was first experienced in hospitals across Canada as early as 1946, it would be another five years before the first baby boomers started school. Canada's school systems had to scramble to accommodate the large number of children that began passing through their doors. Between 1945 and 1961, school enrolment more than doubled as over 500 000 new students entered school each year. To accommodate the baby boomers, hundreds of new schools had to be built and thousands of new teachers had to be trained.

Industrialization and technological innovations demanded that workers have a higher level of education than previously expected. As a result, the baby boomers tended to stay in school longer than earlier generations. This, in turn, affected Canada's postsecondary institutions, increasing the demand for technical schools, colleges, and universities.

Canadian schools became more permissive and democratic as the baby boomers advanced through them. This development was the result of an influential American, John Dewey, whose "progressive" views of education had wide appeal in the 1950s. Dewey's approach emphasized learning through varied activities rather than rigid curricula. He was opposed to authoritarian methods of teaching because he believed they did not prepare students for life in a democratic society. Although Dewey opposed authoritarian methods, he did not advocate permissiveness. He was critical of education that focussed on amusing students to keep them busy and programs that concentrated on **vocational** training rather than on a broad general education.

Changing Mortality Rates

The baby boom was accompanied by significant improvements in Canada's health-care system, which enabled more people to live longer. **Infant mortality rates** had dropped sharply in the 1940s; by 1946, fewer than 1 per cent of all infants died before the age of one. By the 1950s, Canada had one of the lowest infant mortality rates in the world, a factor that contributed to the baby boom.

Canadians were starting to live longer, too. **Life expectancy** for both women and men increased by about 10 per cent; the average woman lived to 65.3 years in 1946 and 74.7 years in 1971; the average man lived to 63.1 years in 1946 and 68.5 years in 1971. These changes meant that children born during the baby boom would live longer, placing greater strains on health and pension programs.

AGEING BABY BOOMERS

Canada's population is ageing and living longer than ever before. The baby boomers are now entering their forties and fifties. Since the baby boom ended, the birth rate has declined. By the second decade of the twenty-first century, the baby boomers will begin to retire. Some of the financial costs of an ageing population will pass to a new, and much smaller, generation of middle-aged Canadians. This will have a significant impact on Canada's health-care system and pension fund.

1. What conclusions can you draw from the ageing of the baby boomers concerning the types of jobs and services that may increase in importance in the early twenty-first century? What jobs or services may decrease in importance?

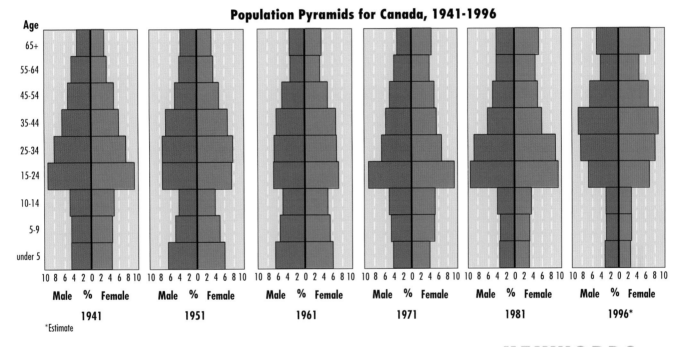

Population Pyramids for Canada, 1941-1996

*Estimate

MAHING CONNECTIONS

1. In what years did Canada's baby boomers reach child-rearing age? Examine the **population pyramids** carefully and trace the baby boomer effect in the pyramids of 1961, 1971, 1981, and 1996. When will the baby boomers born in the late 1940s and early 1950s reach retirement age?

KEYWORDS

baby boom

Family Allowance

vocational

infant mortality rate

life expectancy

population pyramid

baby boom echo

THE SUBURBS
Changing Lifestyles
FOCUSSING ON THE ISSUE

The car and the house—the symbols of affluence for Canadians in the 1950s—came together in a new feature of postwar Canadian cities, the suburbs. How did the move to the suburbs affect Canadian society and culture? What social and cultural issues arose from life in the suburbs?

Leaving the City

Before 1950, most urban Canadians lived in rented housing. While a few families owned their own homes on small city lots, only wealthy people could afford large homes surrounded by lawns and gardens. The creation of new suburban communities on the urban fringes made home ownership possible for a much larger number of Canadians.

The first suburbs had emerged in the 1920s and 1930s as electric railway lines began to fan out from major cities like Vancouver and Toronto. But the growth of the suburbs was slowed first by the Depression and then by the war. In the 1950s, however, a combination of factors led to the rapid growth in both the size and the number of suburban communities. Canada experienced rapid population growth as a result of both **natural increase** and postwar immigration from Europe. This, in turn, created a greater demand for housing, which was in short supply. The move to the suburbs was largely driven by the search for affordable housing.

Developers in the 1950s had to look beyond the urban centres to find inexpensive land for new housing projects. Land was cheaper the farther it was located from the central business district. The rapid increase in the number of automobiles and extensive road networks made it possible for urban workers to live considerable distances from their workplaces. Workers who were willing to commute to work by car could afford homes in the suburbs that would be beyond their financial reach in the city. The creation of the Central Mortgage and Housing Corporation by the federal government in 1946 also stimulated home ownership. The corporation provided mortgage assistance for returning veterans and insured mortgages that home-buyers obtained from the banks.

A Place to Call Home

More than anything else, the suburbs came to be a place for Canadians to enjoy the symbols of new-found prosperity in the 1950s. In the suburbs, an average working family could afford to buy a private home in which to raise a family, and could do so on one income. This allowed the mother to stay home with the children, something only middle- and upper-income Canadians could do in the first half of the twentieth century.

Suburbia was in many ways a mental and emotional space, not just a geographic location. The emphasis in the suburbs was on home and family. People who lived in the suburbs were able to distance themselves from their places of work and to concentrate on raising

The Toronto suburb of Don Mills was Canada's first planned "new town."

MOVING TO THE SUBURBS

Typically, the new suburban dwellers were young couples with two children. Drawn by low prices, they were also looking for a suitable place to raise a family. The following experience was typical of many families moving to the suburbs in the 1950s and 1960s:

We chose this house because of the price. It was the best we saw for the money. We drove around on Sunday afternoons looking for a place and we found this one. We wanted something out of the city—a good place to bring up children....We may have come a little far out—I would prefer a place in closer, you know; what everybody wants: a place that has the advantages of both, all the conveniences of the city and good country air besides.

S.D. Clark, "The Suburban Society," in Bumstead, The Peoples of Canada: A Post-Confederation History, (Toronto: Oxford University Press, 1992) p. 357.

their children in the "right" setting. Life in the suburbs emphasized the nuclear family. Gender roles were clearly defined, with an emphasis on the role of the man as breadwinner and the woman as child-rearer, nurturer, and manager of daily household activities. The size of suburban houses allowed each member of the family to have his or her own private space. The traditional centre of the Canadian family—the kitchen—now gave way to the recreation room as the place where the family gathered together, usually in front of the television set, or where teenagers would gather to listen to their rock 'n' roll records.

Suburban communities gradually developed their own culture that focussed on the family, the local church, community activities,

Shopping malls, like this one in Vancouver, became the symbol of the suburbs.

and the consumption of goods and services. In many ways the cultural heart of the suburbs was, and still is, the shopping mall. Instead of driving their cars downtown, people in the suburbs went to large shopping plazas, another innovation of the 1950s.

Suburbs were clearly secondary to cities in the 1950s—people lived in the suburbs but commuted to the city to work. However, the growth in suburban workplaces such as office and medical complexes, industrial parks, and retail and cultural centres in the late twentieth century has increased the economic self-sufficiency of the suburbs.

MAKING CONNECTIONS

1. Describe the changes in family life that might have occurred as the gathering place in Canadian homes shifted from the kitchen to the recreation room.

2. Suggest some reasons why teenagers living in suburbs in the 1950s might have experienced feelings of alienation, isolation, or boredom. What were some advantages for teenagers of living in suburban communities?

KEYWORDS

natural increase

WESTERN VOICES
Seeking Equal Status
FOCUSSING ON THE ISSUE

The 1950s saw a dramatic increase in the economic prosperity and self-confidence of the four western provinces. Western Canadians saw themselves as emerging from a kind of colonial status to become full and equal provinces in the federation. What role did western Canada seek in the Canadian federation?

West Versus East

In the opinion of many western Canadians, eastern Canadians unfairly divided the country into four regions: Ontario, Quebec, the Atlantic provinces, and the West, with occasional references to an indistinct area called the North. They felt that Easterners viewed western Canada as a vast expanse of uniformly treeless plain ending with the range of mountains that is British Columbia.

For reasons of history and geography, however, western Canadians have viewed the West somewhat differently. While the three Prairie provinces acknowledge their similarities in geography and climate, they see clear distinctions among themselves in their histories, economies, and societies. British Columbians believe their province differs even further, not only because of geography and climate, but because of politics. Unlike the three Prairie provinces, which were created by the federal government, British Columbia was a separate British colony that voluntarily joined the Canadian federation.

Almost since the beginning of Confederation, the western provinces have been unhappy with their relationship with the rest of Canada. In British Columbia, the federal government's failure to complete construction of the railway on time—promised as part of BC's terms of entry into Confederation—produced an early distrust of federal politicians. Ottawa's continued control over their natural resources angered many people in Alberta and Saskatchewan, and the federal government's tariff and freight-rate policies convinced many Westerners that their interests would always take second place to those of central Canadians.

In the years before the Depression, western Canadians were busy developing their societies and building their economies. They paid little attention to their political status in Canada. However, the economic hardships created by the Depression caused many Westerners to take a closer look at their place in the federation. Westerners believed the federal government and eastern bankers had shown little concern for western problems during the Depression, focussing instead on the needs of

This potash plant at Patience Lake, Saskatchewan, contributed to the province's economic prosperity in the 1950s.

central Canada. As a result, many western Canadians began to demand a greater voice in the affairs of the country.

The Boom in the West

The rapid economic growth of the postwar years brought wealth and a sense of importance to Canada's four western provinces. The booming forestry and mining industries in BC, the oil and gas industries of Alberta, the **potash** developments and bumper wheat crops in Saskatchewan, and the mining and forest developments in Manitoba brought prosperity and self-confidence to western Canadians. They believed the federal government should recognize this new importance by granting the West a greater role in national affairs.

The new self-confidence of the western premiers was first demonstrated at the 1951 dominion-provincial conference. The western premiers united in favour of a constitutional amendment that would allow the provinces greater federal participation in social programs. But the other provinces refused to accept the proposal. The western premiers returned home even more convinced that they had to find a way to alter the balance of power in Ottawa.

Western Alienation

In the 1950s, western Canadians

Bumper wheat crops contributed to economic prosperity in the West and a new self-confidence on the part of many Westerners.

increasingly began to see themselves as the victims of what they saw as eastern arrogance and indifference to Western concerns. As long as the bulk of the Canadian population lived within the Great Lakes-St. Lawrence corridor, they believed the legitimate aspirations of the West would never be realized. But an end to eastern domination seemed at hand in 1957 when the Progressive Conservatives chose John Diefenbaker from Saskatchewan as their new leader. Westerners rewarded Diefenbaker in the election that year with a virtual sweep in the West, helping to give him the largest **majority** of any Canadian prime minister. (See page 208.) Diefenbaker's government promptly returned the favour by negotiating a major wheat sale to China, which helped both Prairie farmers and the ports of BC. Other national issues soon pushed western concerns into the background, however, leaving western Canadians disenchanted once again.

KEYWORDS

potash

majority

◄█▪ MAKING CONNECTIONS ▪█►

1. In a democracy, is there a way to ensure that minority interests will be addressed? Explain.

2. Establish a mock royal commission to investigate the demands of western Canada for greater influence in federal policies. Prepare a list of your Commission's recommendations.

INDUSTRIAL LOCATION
The Kitimat Smelter
FOCUSSING ON THE ISSUE

Governments often provide incentives to attract resource industries to remote, resource-rich areas. What factors led to the construction of an aluminum smelter in a remote location of northern BC? What issues were raised by the construction of the Kitimat smelter?

An Energy-based Industry

The Second World War greatly increased the demand for aluminum. Lightweight and easily fabricated, aluminum was ideal for making everything from aircraft to soft-drink cans. The most abundant metal in the earth's crust, aluminum is only found in combination with other elements. Most of the world's aluminum comes from bauxite, a mineral that results from the chemical weathering of aluminum-rich soils under tropical conditions. Because bauxite is a compound with very tight chemical bonds, a great deal of electrical energy is needed when refining it to make aluminum. The world's largest aluminum **smelter,** at Arvida, Quebec, had operated to full capacity during the Second World War and postwar demand for aluminum was increasing.

In the 1920s, the Water Rights Branch of the British Columbia government surveyed the province's hydroelectric power potential. After the war, this study formed the basis of an elaborate program to create a series of hydroelectric power dams throughout BC. The motivation of the government was the economic development of remote, sparsely populated, but resource-rich, areas of the province. Constructing a series of hydroelectric power dams seemed an attractive solution, especially if done by the private sector.

In the late 1940s, the BC government asked the Aluminum Company of Canada (Alcan) to explore the possibility of building an aluminum smelter using the Nechako River as a hydroelectric power source. The Nechako **watershed**, located 600 km north of Vancouver and 100 km west of Prince George, is a vast network of rivers and lakes draining 14 000 km^2 of north-central British Columbia. Alcan identified a desirable location for a smelter at Kitimat. Named for the Kitimat people of the Hāisla nation, this former Hudson's Bay Company trading post was located at the head of Douglas Channel, a long, deep **fjord** just south of Prince Rupert.

Costs and Benefits

Before building the smelter, Alcan had to weigh the costs of locating so far from the bauxite mines, the markets, and a skilled labour force. Bauxite is mined in tropical regions of the world, including Jamaica, Australia, and Guyana. The cost of both the smelter and the power plant was $500 million in 1951—

Kitimat and the Nechako Watershed, BC

The Kitimat smelter never developed to its full potential due to the factors of isolation, climate, and political economics.

THE CHESLATTA CARRIER NATION AND THE KEMANO DAM

Prior to 1952, the people of the Cheslatta Carrier Nation had a largely self-sustaining lifestyle, based on the fish, game, and plant life of their traditional area. They developed extensive herds of horses, cattle, and other livestock, and cultivated clover and hay as well as vegetables for their own use. While trade with surrounding communities was extensive, contact with government was limited prior to 1952.

In 1952, the BC government granted Alcan the right to all of the water flowing into the Nechako River. Alcan planned to build a dam, create a reservoir, and then redirect the water through tunnels to giant turbines at Kemano to generate electricity for its aluminum smelter at Kitimat. To avoid shutting off the river flow entirely, Cheslatta and Murray Lakes would be used as secondary reservoirs. This would maintain enough water in the Nechako River to support its valuable fish stocks. Cheslatta Lake, however, was where the Cheslatta people lived.

In March 1952, Alcan and the BC and federal governments decided to flood Cheslatta and Murray Lakes. Six days later, the local Indian Agent convened a meeting of the Cheslatta people and advised them "to start moving now." Intense pressure was exerted on the Cheslatta people to surrender their lands. But the people insisted that certain conditions be met. The government and the company finally agreed to the following terms: graves would be moved to a place above flood levels, relocation costs would be covered, and compensation would be paid for lost buildings and other immovable property.

The Cheslatta people then trekked northward to Grassy Plains, carrying only the barest essentials. As soon as they had left, all of their buildings were burned before they could retrieve any of their belongings. Of the many graves situated on the old reserves, only four were eventually moved. When the people revisited the area several years later, they found that the discharge of water from the Nechako Reservoir had washed away the cemeteries.

The Cheslatta people, once a close-knit, stable society, were now scattered in all directions. Their ties to their traditional land had been severed, and their sense of community destroyed.

"Cheslatta/Kemano Summary and Plea," *NativeNet*: nn-web@gnosys.svle.ma.us

nearly $4 billion today. If the smelter were to be built on this site, Alcan would have the additional expense of establishing a new town—complete with educational, medical, and recreational facilities—for the workers and their families. While the costs were high, the benefits were significant and Alcan gave the project the green light. The site would provide a long-term supply of low-cost hydroelectric power; a large, flat area for building the smelter and town; and deep water access via Douglas Channel, which would allow bauxite to be shipped into Kitimat and refined aluminum to be shipped out.

In 1951, the effects of such large-scale projects on the environment and on Aboriginal lifestyles were not considered in a **cost-benefit analysis**. Neither weighed heavily in either the provincial government's desire for economic development in the region or in the company's criteria for choosing an appropriate site for the new smelter.

MAKING CONNECTIONS

1. Select an example of industrial location in conflict with the environment. Working in a group, role-play the various interest groups involved. Make sure that all **stakeholders** present their point of view. Have a three-person panel rule on the future of the project.

KEYWORDS

smelter

watershed

fjord

cost-benefit analysis

stakeholders

THE ST. LAWRENCE SEAWAY
A Transportation Breakthrough

The 1950s witnessed many impressive feats of engineering. Among these was the St. Lawrence Seaway. Why was this project so important to shipping and industry in eastern North America?

New Industrial Achievements

The 1950s was an era of spectacular industrial growth in Canada. Perhaps no other construction project in the country illustrated the magnitude of new industrial feats better than the St. Lawrence Seaway.

The St. Lawrence River had been an important transportation route since Jacques Cartier first navigated its waters in 1535. When he reached Montreal, however, Cartier was prevented from sailing further by the rushing waters of what is today known as the Lachine Rapids. For the next 400 years, all ocean-going ships were forced to stop at the rapids. Only small vessels were able to make their way to the Great Lakes using canals built to cross the treacherous waters.

For years, the Canadian and American governments discussed plans to expand the inland waterway to allow ocean vessels to travel all the way from the Atlantic Ocean to the western end of Lake Superior. The new shipping pathway would provide easy access to the massive markets in eastern Canada and the United States. However, the American government faced stiff opposition to the seaway plan by the railway companies, which feared they would lose business. In 1951, Canada decided it would tackle the massive construction project on its own. Faced with the prospect of a seaway completely under Canadian control, the

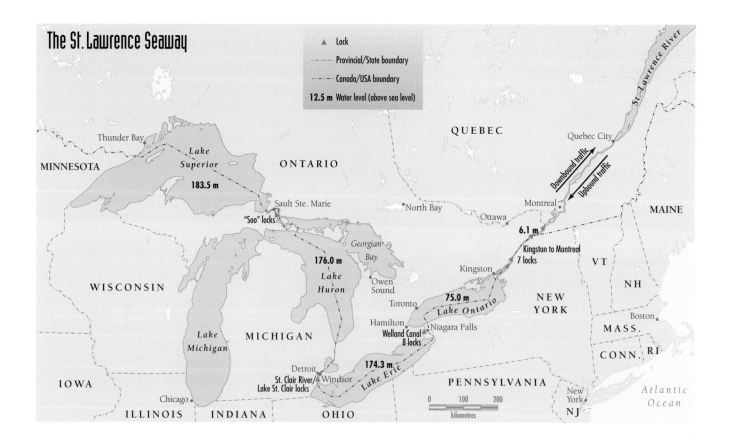

The St. Lawrence Seaway

Legend:
- ▲ Lock
- Provincial/State boundary
- Canada/USA boundary
- 12.5 m Water level (above sea level)

Fewer ships are now able to navigate the locks here at the Welland Canal.

American government decided to join in the venture.

Construction began in 1955. For the next four years, Canada and the United States collaborated on building the most advanced waterway engineering project in the world. The St. Lawrence Seaway system created seven huge locks, which enabled ocean-going vessels to cross the rapids. The project also provided the opportunity to harness the rapids for hydroelectric power. A power dam flooded large areas along the shores of the St. Lawrence in eastern Ontario. Several towns and villages had to be relocated, while over 60 km of railway track had to be rerouted. When completed, however, the project provided much-needed power for the people and industries of Ontario and New York state.

On 26 June 1957, the St. Lawrence Seaway was officially opened. Queen Elizabeth and US president Dwight Eisenhower presided over the ceremonies. Goods from around the world now had easy and direct access to the large and lucrative consumer markets of eastern North America. The seaway increased the importance of the Great Lakes ports and contributed to the prosperity of the **industrial heartland.**

The Seaway Today

The amount of cargo moving through the St. Lawrence Seaway reached its peak in the late 1970s. In 1977, 57.5 million tonnes of cargo—mostly grain, iron ore, and coal—moved through the Montreal-Lake Ontario section, while the Welland Canal section reached its

peak at 66.2 million tonnes in 1979. Since these record levels were reached, however, Seaway traffic has declined substantially. Several factors have played a role in this decline—the downsizing and restructuring of the North American steel industry, the replacement of coal-fired electricity generating stations with nuclear power plants, and the shift of grain cargo to other markets and routes. In 1994, however, there was a reversal in the downward trend. Tonnage on the Montreal-Lake Ontario section increased by 20 per cent, to 38.4 million tonnes, and on the Welland Canal section by 24.5 per cent, to 39.6 million tonnes.

Another threat to the economic viability of the St. Lawrence Seaway is the loss of its shipping fleet. Many small vessels that are able to navigate the waters of the St. Lawrence are being retired from service. The St. Lawrence Seaway Authority estimates that by the year 2000, only 42 vessels in the world will be capable of navigating the Seaway.

To ensure the Seaway's economic stability, a tentative agreement was reached in 1996 between the federal government and a group representing the Seaway's major shippers and carriers. Their objective is to establish a not-for-profit corporation to operate the Seaway. Canada is also seeking a more integrated approach to the management of the Seaway with it American partner.

MAKING CONNECTIONS

1. Using the map scale, calculate the total shipping distance from the easternmost city to the westernmost. What is the difference in the water level between these two cities?

KEYWORDS

industrial heartland

ROCK 'N' ROLL

Popular Music in Canada

In the 1950s, rock 'n' roll became a major part of popular culture for the baby-boom generation. What roll did popular music play in the lives of young Canadians?

The "King" in Canada

Elvis Presley's first film, *Love Me Tender*, opened in Toronto in 1956. His appearance, even though it was only on film, resulted in near riots. Young people lined up outside the theatre before dawn to buy tickets. Before the film began, they broke down the doors, knocking over ushers and police officers, then ripped down movie posters and scrawled "I love you, Elvis" in lipstick on his photograph in the foyer! When Elvis appeared in person at Toronto's Maple Leaf Gardens wearing his $10 000 gold lamé suit, 18 000 teenage fans screamed ecstatically as the ex-truck driver performed such hits as "Hound Dog," "Heartbreak Hotel," and

"Love Me Tender." Adults and music critics were perplexed by the popularity of this new music. Some were even outraged by the way Elvis performed on stage with an explicitly aggressive sexuality. But the kids loved it.

The Origins of Rock 'n' Roll

The primary source of rock 'n' roll was rhythm and blues, a style of music popular among African Americans. Rhythm and blues began to draw a wider audience during the late 1940s, and in 1951 an American disc jockey, Alan Freed, began to play rhythm and blues on his late-night radio show in Cleveland. He played an impor-

tant role in attracting white teenagers to the music and later claimed that he had coined the term *rock 'n' roll*. Noting the success of rhythm and blues and rock 'n' roll songs, major record producers issued "covers," which were competing, "sanitized" versions of the same songs but recorded by white artists. Covers brought new stylistic influences to rock 'n' roll, such as country-and-western and popular music. Freed refused to play white versions of rhythm and blues originals, and the interracial concerts he promoted helped break the racial barrier in pop music.

A Mass Audience

Rock 'n' roll came to Canada in the early 1950s. Teenagers danced at high-school **sock-hops** to Bill Haley's "Rock Around the Clock" in 1955. Soon everybody was listening, dancing, and "going steady" to a rock 'n' roll beat.

Rock 'n' roll was a carefully marketed phenomenon, but the teenagers of the 1950s did not seem to know or care. To them, the new music symbolized freedom from the stuffy adult values that had been shaped by the hardships of the Depression and global war. Rock 'n' roll arrived in Canada at the same time as television and postwar prosperity. Disc jockeys began to feature the new music on their radio shows. In 1957, the television show

Teenagers danced to the new craze called rock 'n' roll.

Elvis Presley was rock 'n' roll's first superstar. Born in 1935, Elvis's musical background was country-and-western. Although he did not invent rock 'n' roll, he was its first personality and became the prototype for the rock star as cultural hero. With his dynamic vocal style, long sideburns, and sex appeal, he was admired by young people around the world. His electrifying energy and provocative movements, however, were controversial, particularly among older generations.

Elvis's success began when he cut the single called "That's All Right, Mama" in 1954, which was soon followed by other hits such as "Don't Be Cruel." His concerts, television appearances, and movies attracted enormous audiences.

Even after his death at his estate, Graceland, in 1977, Presley's **personality cult** continues. Hundreds of thousands of fans still visit Graceland to pay their respects to the "King of rock 'n' roll."

American Bandstand went on air to showcase new rock 'n' roll songs and performers. (It stayed on the air for 30 years!) Teenagers in the 1950s had money to buy records and record players, as well as other consumer goods. They quickly became one of the most important segments of mass market consumerism in North America. Television and radio programming as well as advertising increasingly targeted the teenage audience.

Teen Bands

In the 1950s, many Canadian teenagers formed their own bands and vocal groups in imitation of their favourite rock 'n' roll stars. Sales of electric guitars and amplifiers boomed. The basis of rock 'n' roll was its simplicity. The common characteristics of hit songs were light-hearted lyrics, a catchy tune, and a heavy, continuous beat just right for dancing.

Four young men from Toronto formed a group called the Crew Cuts. Their hit single from 1954 contained the memorable lines "*Sh-boom, ah-boom, ya-ya-ya, ya, ya, ya, yaya. Ya, ya, ya, ya, ya, ya, ya.*" More than a million copies of this single were sold in Canada and the United States. Another Toronto group, The Diamonds, topped the charts in 1957 with two gold records, "Little Darlin'" and "The Stroll." That same year, Paul Anka, a teenager from Ottawa, dropped out of grade 10 and headed for New York. The next year, his hit single "Diana" sold 6 million copies! At the age of 16, Paul Anka had an income of $600 000 a year and was performing on five continents.

What was the appeal of rock 'n' roll for the teenagers of the 1950s? The combination of its driving beat, its direct message, and its implication of youthful rebellion reflected the feelings and concerns of young people. Rock 'n' roll was a vehicle for teenagers to express themselves against the background of the adult world.

MAKING CONNECTIONS

1. Many parents in the 1950s did not understand rock 'n' roll, nor did they approve of it. How do your parents react to the music you listen to? Why do you think they react the way they do?

KEYWORDS

sock-hop

personality cult

HOCKEY NIGHT IN CANADA
Contributing to Canadian Identity

FOCUSSING ON THE ISSUE

Hockey Night in Canada has been one of Canada's most popular television series for many years. How does hockey reflect Canada's national identity?

Canadian Television

Before 1952, the few Canadians who owned TV sets had been tuning into US programs for several years. In 1952, when the first Canadian television stations began beaming made-in-Canada shows into living rooms across the country, people responded by buying TV sets as never before. Soon the television set was as common a piece of living-room furniture as the sofa and chair. By the end of 1957, there were 3 million TV sets in Canada—about one for every five Canadians—and 44 television stations broadcasting nationwide.

Until 1962, the Canadian Broadcasting Corporation (CBC) was the only television network broadcasting in Canada. American stations were freely available, of course, but in Canada the public network was the only one on the air. From the beginning, the CBC operated two networks, one broadcasting in French, the other in English. The 1950s are sometimes called the "Golden Age" of Canadian television because many high-quality, made-in-Canada programs appeared on the air. Quiz shows, dramas, comedies, talk shows, public affairs programs—the CBC offered them all. Popular series

included *Front Page Challenge*, which aired for the first time in 1957 and ran for almost 40 years, making it the longest-running television game show in North America. On the French network, *La famille Plouffe*, a weekly drama series based on a novel by Roger Lemelin, ran for six years and was broadcast in translation on the English network as well. The Plouffe family gave many English Canadians their first glimpse into the daily life of the Québécois.

Hockey Comes to Television

Of all the programs available, none was as popular as *Hockey Night in Canada*. Even today it remains the most popular program on Canadian television. It began in 1931 as a radio broadcast from Maple Leaf Gardens, the home of the Toronto Maple Leafs of the National Hockey League (NHL). The play-by-play announcer was the legendary Foster Hewitt. (See page 141.) When *Hockey Night in Canada* made the jump to television in 1952, Hewitt went with it. In Montreal, Danny Gallivan called the games in English, while René Lecavalier handled the play-by-play in French for 36 years.

Officially, lacrosse is Canada's national game, but in reality many people embrace hockey as our national sport. "Hockey captures the essence of the Canadian experi-

In what way does television unify a society? In what way can it fragment it?

ence," one commentator, Bruce Kidd, has written. "In a land so inescapably and inhospitably cold, hockey is the dance of life, and an affirmation that despite the deathly chill of winter we are alive." Hockey is a game for winter, and so is ideally suited to a country that experiences such long ones. On frozen rinks and ponds all over the country, Canadians defy the cold by going outside and playing in it.

For many years Canadians took pride in producing the best hockey players in the world. Most of the players in the National Hockey League came from Canada, even if they played for American teams. No one disputed the fact that the NHL was the best league in the world. During the 1950s, teams from Canada dominated world hockey championships. NHL teams did not compete internationally, but small-town teams with part-time players still managed to beat the best that the rest of the world had to offer. In 1955, a team from Penticton, British Columbia, won the world championship, followed by teams from Whitby, Ontario, in 1958 and Belleville, Ontario, in 1959. Fans, too, took their hockey seriously. In 1955, when Montreal hockey superstar Maurice "The Rocket" Richard was suspended for attacking an official with his stick, fans rioted in the city's streets.

More than any other sport, hockey has been a force for unity in Canada. It is something that all Canadians, and most particularly French- and English-speaking Canadians, experience together. Fans from Vancouver to Trois-Rivières are ardent supporters of the game. In the 1950s, when the Montreal Canadiens played the Toronto Maple Leafs, the game brought anglophones and francophones together in a shared experience that no other national event could match.

Television has played an important role in making hockey a part of the national identity. Following its first broadcast in 1952, *Hockey Night in Canada* became a national institution. Every Saturday night millions of hockey fans from coast to coast huddled around their television sets to watch the game. There was probably no other occasion when so many Canadians were doing exactly the same thing at exactly the same time.

Today, in the 500-channel universe, there are many hockey games on television every day. As a result, *Hockey Night in Canada* has lost the central place it once had in the lives of so many fans. Still, hockey itself remains an important part of the Canadian identity. While only 6 of the 26 teams in the NHL are Canadian, over 65 per cent of the

Canada's National Women's Hockey Team played at the World Championships in Kitchener, Ontario, in 1997.

players are from Canada. But while Canada continues to produce great hockey stars, their dominance in the game is being challenged by players from the United States, Russia, and Europe.

Hockey continues to thrive in Canada—not only in NHL arenas. Canadian women have practised the sport for over a century. But it was not until 1987 that women's hockey gained international attention with the first Women's World Hockey Tournament. The Canadian team beat out nine other competitors to win the championship. Canada also captured the Women's World Hockey Championship in 1990 and 1992. And amateur hockey is still alive and well in Canada. In communities across the country, thousands of Canadian kids head to their local arenas each week dreaming of a future in the NHL. While only a few will achieve this goal, the dream is evidence that hockey remains an important part of the Canadian **psyche**.

MAKING CONNECTIONS

1. Discuss ways in which organized sports, such as hockey or football, reflect the values of a country.

2. Do you think hockey will continue to play such a strong role in the Canadian identity in the twenty-first century? Give reasons for your opinion.

KEYWORDS

psyche

THE PIPELINE DEBATE
Encouraging Economic Development
FOCUSSING ON THE ISSUE

The involvement of the government in the construction of a gas pipeline provoked one of the nastiest parliamentary debates in Canadian history. What is the proper role of government in encouraging economic development?

Building a Pipeline

Following the Second World War, great quantities of oil and natural gas were discovered in Alberta and Saskatchewan. These new natural resources, which were used to heat homes and fuel industries, sparked an economic boom in the West.

Pipelines were the best way to transport needed fuel to markets in eastern Canada and the United States, but they were very expensive to build. In 1955, TransCanada Pipelines, a group of Canadian and American business interests, began construction of a pipeline to carry natural gas from Alberta across the prairies and northern Ontario to Montreal. The company itself did not have enough money to pay for the line. So in May 1956, the federal Liberal government introduced a bill that would provide a loan of $80 million to cover part of the cost and would allow the company to sell surplus gas in the US.

The pipeline bill stirred up a great deal of controversy. The company needed money partly because the Liberal government was asking it to build the pipeline entirely through Canada, a more expensive route than laying some of it through the US. The government was in a hurry to pass the bill because the construction season began in June, so the company needed the money

soon if it was going to accomplish anything that year. Conservatives objected to the bill because TransCanada Pipelines was controlled by American interests and much of the gas would eventually be sold in the US—an aspect of the project that riled nationalists. The CCF argued that the entire project should be built by the government, not private interests.

Debate in the House

Once it reached the House of Commons, the debate became even more complicated. The Liberals announced on 14 May that in order to hurry the bill through Parliament, they intended to invoke **closure**, a little-used power that allows a government to cut off debate and force a vote. The opposition erupted in outrage, and for weeks the House of Commons was in an uproar. The government argued that opposition parties were obstructing an important national project. The opposition shot back that the government was violating a basic democratic principle.

The pipeline debate was one of the most disruptive in Canadian parliamentary history. MPs mocked each other and hurled insults across the House floor. Sessions lasted all night as the opposition tried to halt the government steamroller. At one

point, a Conservative MP was evicted for trying to speak when the Speaker had ruled he could not. In response, a colleague draped a flag over his empty chair and the uproar continued.

The matter finally came to a vote after a month. As expected, the government won and the bill passed. Two years later the pipeline to Montreal was completed. By that time, however, the Liberal government of Louis St. Laurent was no longer in power. The pipeline debate, and the government's use of closure, had angered Canadians, who felt the Liberals were becoming arrogant after many years in power. In the federal election of 1957, voters expressed their displeasure by ousting the Liberals.

The Larger Debate

The parliamentary debate was followed by a larger political debate involving two important questions. The first was how far the government should involve itself in helping private companies in order to encourage economic development. Industries in central Canada needed reliable supplies of fuel, and the construction of a pipeline was a huge, expensive project. The government believed that Canadians would profit from federal assistance. Government partnership with private enterprise has a long tradition

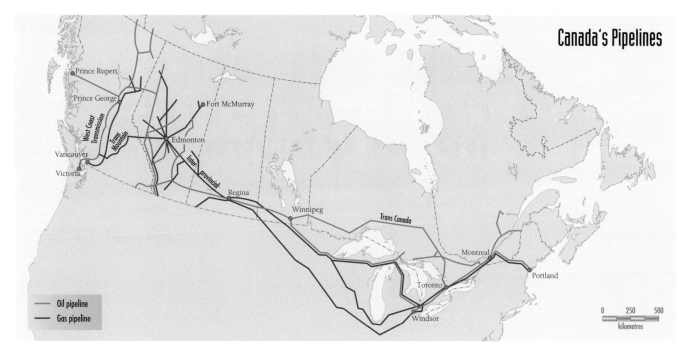

Oil pipeline

Gas pipeline

0   250   500
kilometres

in Canada. The Canadian Pacific Railway for example, was built with loans from the government.

The situation was complicated by the fact that the pipeline company was majority-owned by Americans. Many Canadians wondered why Canadian taxes should support an American project. Others questioned why tax dollars should support the project at all. If the pipeline was necessary, then the government should build it so that profits would be returned to taxpayers. This was not just the view of the socialist CCF. It was shared

by Liberal Cabinet minister Lester Pearson, who wrote in his memoirs that, in his view, "this natural gas pipeline should be built and financed not by Texas millionaires but by the government or governments of Canada with public control and ownership."

The second question the debate raised was whether the government was ever justified in cutting off democratic debate. Closure was seldom used, but in this case the government argued that it was necessary. If the debate went on, a year of construction time would be lost. The

point of closure was to stop prolonged, **partisan** debate from holding up a matter of national importance.

The opposition parties argued that nothing was more important in a democracy than free and unlimited debate. They accused the government of wanting to have its own way, no matter what anyone else thought. In the end, the opposition lost the battle but won the war. The pipeline bill passed, but it cost the Liberals their hold on power.

MAKING CONNECTIONS

1. Pipelines are the most economical method of transporting oil and gas over land. Pipelines link the oil and gas fields of western Canada with the energy-consuming markets of the east. What two factors make it unprofitable to supply Atlantic Canada with Canadian-produced oil and gas?

2. If you were a member of the federal government today, would you support the construction of a pipeline in the Canadian North? Why or why not?

KEYWORDS

closure

partisan

SKILL BUILDER
Interpreting Cartoons
FOCUSSING ON THE ISSUE

Artists have long used cartoons to make satirical or ironic comments on the events and people of their time. What skills are needed to use cartoons as sources of historical information?

Cartoons

Comic strips and editorial or political cartoons are the most common types of cartoons. Comic strips are generally made up of a series of drawings that tell a story and may be either serious or humorous. Generally, editorial cartoons consist of only one panel and deal with a single contemporary issue, event, or person. Their purpose is not simply to amuse but also to stimulate thought and discussion. Although the quantity of detail may vary considerably, cartoons are generally line drawings that make their point through the use of caricature and symbols. Editorial cartoons are seldom flattering to their subjects and offer an often ironic, occasionally nasty, view of real events and people. They are designed to make the reader think about both the event or people being portrayed and the message the cartoonist is trying to communicate.

The Cartoonist's Tools

Caricature

Although some cartoons attempt to provide a recognizable likeness of the people they are commenting on, most use caricatures. Essentially, a caricature is a quick line drawing of a person that exaggerates some feature or characteristic that is readily associated with that person. This exaggeration is often not complimentary. The characteristics may be hair style, body shape, clothing style, or facial features, and may be used alone or in combination. For example, during the Second World War, the British prime minister, Winston Churchill, was often

General James Wolfe was a British soldier who led British forces to victory against French troops in Quebec on the Plains of Abraham in 1759. One of Wolfe's officers drew this cartoon about the general's constant and detailed inspections.

The income tax department was established as a "temporary measure" in 1917. This cartoon was drawn much later as a commentary on the nature of government programs.

drawn with a round body, a round head, and a cigar.

Symbols

Cartoonists frequently use a variety of symbols when drawing cartoons. These symbols can be a simple flag or banner used to identify a country or an animal (the Canadian beaver) or human figure (Uncle Sam for the US). Occasionally, countries are represented by male or female figures in national costume or, more traditionally, by female figures dressed in Greek or Roman style.

Stereotypes

Cartoonists also use **stereotypes**, especially where the specific identity of the person is not important to the cartoon. For example, rich people may be drawn dressed in formal attire, revolutionaries with bombs in their pockets. Although it is unacceptable today, the use of racial stereotypes was common in editorial cartoons in the early twentieth century and during both world wars. Examining the use of caricatures, symbols, and stereotypes in cartoons is one of the ways we can track social attitudes over time.

Text

Most cartoons have a caption or title across the top or bottom of the cartoon, usually outside the main body. Labels are used in a variety of ways as shortcuts in identifying elements of a cartoon. The comments being made by the cartoon's characters are contained in dialogue bubbles.

MAKING CONNECTIONS

1. Study the Diefenbaker cartoon.
   a) What issue, event, situation, or idea does the cartoon deal with? (See pages 208-209.)
   b) What methods does the cartoonist use to identify the issue?
   c) Who are the people in the cartoon? What methods does the cartoonist use to identify them?

2. a) What is your reaction to the Diefenbaker cartoon? Is it thought-provoking? funny?
   b) What is the point of view of the cartoonist? Where does the cartoonist stand on the issue?
   c) What message is the cartoonist communicating?
   d) In what way(s) does the cartoon provide historical insight?

KEYWORDS

stereotype

MINORITY GOVERNMENT
The 1957 and 1958 Elections
FOCUSSING ON THE ISSUE

*After many years in power, the Liberals were defeated in the 1957 election
by the Conservatives, who formed a minority government.
What are the advantages and disadvantages of minority government?*

An Election Upset

On the morning of 11 June 1957—the day after the federal election—Canadians woke up to discover that for the first time in almost a quarter of a century the Liberal party was not in power in Ottawa. The Conservatives had pulled off a surprising upset. No one had expected it. During the campaign the Liberals seemed to be cruising to victory. *Maclean's* magazine had already gone to press predicting a Liberal win.

Several factors led to the Conservative upset, including the popularity of their new leader. John Diefenbaker was a lawyer from Prince Albert, Saskatchewan—the only person from that province ever to be elected prime minister. In the courtroom he had learned to be an effective debater and a confident public speaker. All his life he had been a crusader for the underdog. He expressed a vision of the country that inspired voters. Diefenbaker spoke of "One Canada" where all people, no matter where they came from or what their position in society, had the same rights and the same opportunities. He easily overshadowed his opponent, Louis St-Laurent, the Liberal prime minister. "Uncle Louie," as he was called, had been in power for a decade and seemed worn out compared to the dynamic "Dief the Chief."

Another factor in the Conservative victory was the fact that the Liberals had been in power for so long. Voters felt it was time for a change. The pipeline debate (see page 204) of the previous year seemed to indicate that the Liberals had become arrogant. Many people felt it was time to show them that they could not rule forever.

The Election of 1958

Still, the Conservatives won the 1957 election by a narrow margin. They formed a **minority government** and could continue in power only with the support of MPs from other parties. As it turned out, the government lasted just a few months. After passing some minor legislation, Diefenbaker dissolved the House

When Diefenbaker was elected, he became the first Conservative prime minister in 22 years.

of Commons and called another election early in 1958.

The 1958 election pitted John Diefenbaker against the new leader of the Liberal party, the respected diplomat Lester B. Pearson. It was the beginning of several years of competition between these two politicians whose personalities and policies were so different. The next decade in Canadian politics would be dominated by their rivalry.

The 1957 election has been called a "dress rehearsal" for 1958. The Conservatives ran a spirited campaign and emerged from the election with 208 seats in Parliament. It was the biggest landslide in Canadian history. No other government has ever won as great a percentage of the seats. (In 1984, the Conservatives under Brian Mulroney won 211 seats, but the number of seats in Parliament had been expanded from 265 to 282.) One reason for the Conservatives' success in 1958 was that they managed to take 50 seats in Quebec, far more than the nine they had won a year earlier. The popular, and conservative, Quebec premier Maurice Duplessis had urged his supporters to back the Diefenbaker Conservatives against the Liberals.

WHAT IS MINORITY GOVERNMENT?

Minority government occurs when no political party wins more than half the seats in the legislature. This was the situation following the 1957 federal election. The party with the most seats may form a government, but there is no guarantee that it will win every vote in the House. The governing party will try to win the support of enough members of the other parties to give it a **majority**. However, if the opposition parties unite to vote against it, the government will be defeated. When this happens, either another party is given a chance to form a government, or Parliament is dissolved and another election is called. In the case of the Diefenbaker government in 1958, the prime minister himself decided to dissolve Parliament because he was confident that in an election he would now win a majority.

A minority government is unstable because at any time the government might be defeated by a **vote of nonconfidence**. Sometimes, it gives more power to small parties with just a few seats whose support determines whether or not a government remains in power. This situation usually forces a minority government to be more responsive to the demands of the opposition than it would be if it had a majority and did not need to bargain for support.

Election Results (number of seats)

Of 265 seats	1957	1958
Conservatives	112	208
Liberals	105	49
CCF	25	8
Social Credit	19	0
Independents	4	0

1. In 1957, how many opposition votes did the Conservatives need to form a coalition majority government?

MAKING CONNECTIONS

1. Why would an opposition party choose to support a minority government?

2. Some people believe that a minority government is often more responsive to the public's interests and therefore more effective. Would you agree with this? Give examples from another minority government, either federal or provincial.

KEYWORDS

minority government

majority

vote of nonconfidence

GROUNDING THE ARROW
Canada's Defence Role
FOCUSSING ON THE ISSUE

In 1959, the most expensive military weapon developed in Canada was scrapped. How did this decision affect Canada's role in the military defence of North America?

Defending North America

The defence of North America was a crucial issue during the 1950s. The Cold War with the Soviet Union was heating up. The Soviets had developed missiles armed with nuclear weapons that were able to fly over the North Pole to destroy North American cities. Canadians realized that because of their location between two quarrelling superpowers they were likely to get caught in any crossfire.

One response to the threat was to join the United States in a defence plan for North America. In 1957, the two countries formed NORAD, the North American Air Defence Command. (In 1981, its name changed to the North American Aerospace Command.) Both the American and the Canadian air forces contributed to NORAD.

During the 1950s, the government was also involved in the development of a new military jet aircraft. The Avro Arrow was built by the A.V. Roe Company at its plant in Malton, Ontario. It was expected to be one of the most advanced war planes of its kind. Canadians took pride in the fact that the country had an aircraft industry capable of producing such a world-class machine. The project also produced thousands of jobs requiring highly skilled people.

The Arrow's development was initially approved by the Liberal government in 1953, but the Diefenbaker government that came to power in 1957 had a different opinion about the project. The plane was very expensive; at $12.5 million it was many times more costly than other fighter planes. Military tech-

The Avro Arrow was a beautiful piece of machinery, but some analysts believed it was outdated before it even took to the air. Why? How did the Arrow project become entangled in Canadian-American relations?

While Diefenbaker defended his decision regarding the Arrow, his Liberal opponent, Lester Pearson, called the decision irrational.

I realize that defence production is an important weapon in the battle against unemployment. However, I say with all the seriousness I can put at my command, that the production of obsolete weapons as a make-work program is an unjustifiable expenditure of public funds.

John Diefenbaker defending his decision to cancel the Arrow in Parliament, 23 February 1959.

There were reasons of defence and economics that could have been advanced to justify this decision but none to justify the way it was done. Suddenly, on 20 February 1959, without any effort to keep together the fine professional team of scientists and engineers which had been *assembled, Mr. Diefenbaker pronounced his government's policy. There was even an apparent vindictiveness in the decision to scrap the five completed planes and the others half completed so that no museum of science and technology would ever be able to show what we could design and produce. It was on this irrational element in the decision that we centred our attack, thus reflecting the feelings of most Canadians.*

Lester B. Pearson, Mike, The Memoirs of Lester B. Pearson, Vol. 3 (Toronto: University of Toronto Press, 1975), pp. 47–8. Reprinted by permission of University of Toronto Press Inc.

1. How did Diefenbaker defend his government's decision to scrap the Arrow project? Is this a valid reason?
2. What was the basis of Pearson's criticism of the decision?

nology was changing as guided missiles replaced crewed aircraft. No other country wanted to buy these planes. Even the Canadian military told the government that it did not want the Arrow. In addition, there was pressure from the Americans to buy US missiles.

After prolonged indecision, Diefenbaker cancelled the Arrow project. Instead, the government agreed to acquire American Bomarc missiles as part of the NORAD agreement. This decision made financial sense, but it had serious political consequences. Thousands of Canadian workers lost their jobs. Many were scientists who had to leave the country to find work, some in the US space program. Critics charged that the government had abandoned a made-in-Canada project in favour of a made-in-the-US defence policy. They claimed that the entire Canadian aircraft industry was crippled by Diefenbaker's decision.

A few years later, the prime minister stirred up another controversy when he refused to accept American nuclear warheads for the Bomarc missiles. Diefenbaker felt that arming the missiles with nuclear warheads would be a setback for global nuclear **disarmament**. He preferred to store the warheads in the United States until they were needed. But without them, the missiles were useless. Canadians naturally wondered why the government had acquired a weapon it could not use, and they began to question Diefenbaker's judgement. The issue mired the government in controversy, and it was a key factor in the poor showing of the Conservatives in the 1963 federal election.

MAKING CONNECTIONS

1. List the factors—pro and con—facing the Diefenbaker government as it tried to decide what to do about the Arrow project. Which factors were technological and which were political?

2. Over the years, many people have regretted Canada's decision to scrap the Arrow. Why might there have been cause for regret?

KEYWORDS

disarmament

FUNDAMENTAL FREEDOMS
The Canadian Bill of Rights

For the first 75 years of their country's history, Canadians saw no need to formally document their rights and freedoms. Why, in the 1950s, did some Canadians believe a legislated list of rights was necessary?

The War Measures Act

By the beginning of the Second World War Canada had become an industrialized and independent country, far different from the colony that had passed the War Measures Act in 1914. After the federal government invoked the War Measures Act in 1939, it exercised extensive control over the lives of Canadians. Laws were passed giving the federal government power to direct workers to essential jobs; control prices, rents, and wages; ration certain foods and strategic supplies; and reduce or eliminate the manufacture of non-essential goods. A Cabinet order created the Defence of Canada. These were regulations that gave the government the power to impose **censorship**, allow search without warrant, and impose other limits on individual rights and freedoms. While the war was being fought, most Canadians accepted the restrictions on their liberties as necessary for a successful war effort.

During the war, the issues of human rights and fundamental freedoms gained greater prominence through such highly publicized declarations as the Atlantic Charter and the United Nations Charter. When these were followed by the Universal Declaration on Human Rights—a document that the Canadian government signed—support for a Canadian Bill of Rights increased. By the end of the war, many Canadians had come to regard the arbitrary powers of the federal government as a real threat to their liberties. They were alarmed by the extent of the government's control and how easily it was exercised. Events such as the arbitrary imprisonment and forcible expulsion of Japanese Canadians from their homes led some Canadians to demand more concrete protection for their rights and freedoms.

Proposals

One of the first Canadian politicians to advocate a Canadian Bill of Rights was the CCF MP Alistair Stewart. In 1945, he introduced a motion in the House of Commons calling for an amendment to incorporate a Bill of Rights into Canada's constitution. Unfortunately for Stewart, his **private member's bill** did not get the support of the House and so did not come to a vote.

Another early campaigner for a Bill of Rights was Conservative MP John Diefenbaker. He had joined Stewart in his attempt to get a constitutional amendment and he continued to raise the issue at regular intervals in the following years. But it was not until he was elected leader of the Progressive Conservative party that Diefenbaker had an opportunity to bring his ideas to national attention. When he led the PCs in the 1957 and 1958 elections, passage of a federal Bill of Rights was an important campaign promise.

Canada Gets a Bill of Rights

After he won the 1958 election, Diefenbaker faced the problem of implementing his Bill of Rights promise. To make the bill as strong as possible would require amending the Constitution. However, Diefenbaker was not able to obtain the provincial consent that constitutional amendments required, so he moved instead to pass a federal law. Critics argued that such a law would be ineffective because it would be **declarative legislation**— that is, the law would list the rights and freedoms of Canadians but would not provide for enforcement. In addition, because it was an ordinary federal statute, subsequent governments could repeal it at any time by a simple majority vote.

Believing that a limited Bill of Rights was a practical solution to the problem and was better than nothing, Diefenbaker ignored the critics and moved ahead with the legislation. Although it might not be a constitutional amendment binding on all Canadians, Diefenbaker believed it would force lawmakers to give consideration to the issues of human rights when preparing legislation. He also believed that public support for the measure was such that no politician would even contemplate repealing it. He was right.

On 1 July 1960, Diefenbaker celebrated the passage of the Canadian Bill of Rights with the following statement:

I am a Canadian, a free Canadian, free to speak without fear, free to worship God in my own way, free to stand for what I think right, free to oppose what I believe wrong, free to chose those who shall govern my country. This heritage of freedom I pledge to uphold for myself and all mankind.

Diefenbaker's Bill of Rights was eventually superceded by the Charter of Rights and Freedoms in 1982. But the original Bill of Rights is still in force for federal matters and for property rights not covered in the 1982 charter.

CASE STUDY

THE CANADIAN BILL OF RIGHTS

Part I

1. *It is hereby recognized and declared that in Canada there have existed and shall continue to exist without discrimination by reason of race, national origin, colour, religion or sex, the following human rights and fundamental freedoms, namely,*

   (a) *the right of the individual to life, liberty, security of the person and enjoyment of property, and the right not to be deprived thereof except by due process of law;*

   (b) *the right of the individual to equality before the law and the protection of the law;*

   (c) *freedom of religion;*

   (d) *freedom of speech;*

   (e) *freedom of assembly and association; and*

   (f) *freedom of the press.*

2. *Every law of Canada shall, unless it is expressly declared by an Act of the Parliament of Canada that it shall operate notwithstanding the Canadian Bill of Rights, be so construed and applied as not to abrogate, abridge or infringe... any of the rights and freedoms herein recognized and declared, and in particular, no law of Canada shall be so construed or applied so as to*

   (a) *authorize or effect the arbitrary detention, imprisonment or exile of any person;*

   (b) *impose or authorize the imposition of cruel and unusual treatment or punishment;*

   (c) *deprive a person who has been arrested or detained [of his or her legal rights].*

   The four subsections that follow describe a Canadian's rights at trial.

3. This section compels the Minister of Justice to screen any proposed laws or regulations for violations of the provisions of the Bill of Rights.

MAKING CONNECTIONS

1. In your own words, explain the difference between a right and a freedom.

2. In order of their importance to you, rank the rights listed in Part I, Section 1, of the Canadian Bill of Rights. Explain the effects of these rights on your everyday life.

KEYWORDS

censorship

private member's bill

declarative legislation

A MEASURE OF EQUALITY
Aboriginal Peoples and the Vote
FOCUSSING ON THE ISSUE

For many years Aboriginal peoples in Canada did not have the right to vote in elections. How did the right to vote reflect government policy towards Aboriginal peoples in general?

A Fundamental Right

In Canada today the right to vote in elections, known as the **franchise**, is extended to everyone who has Canadian citizenship and is at least 18 years of age. We think of voting as a fundamental right that every member of a democratic society should have.

It has not always been so. Over the years, different groups in Canada have been denied the franchise for different reasons. Following Confederation, only men who owned a certain amount of property were allowed to vote. Gradually, property qualifications were discarded, and around 1900, universal male **suffrage** was estab-

lished. However, women, and men who belonged to visible minorities, were still denied the franchise. In 1918, all women were allowed to vote in federal elections for the first time, although it was 1940 before the last province, Quebec, granted women the provincial vote. (See page 107.) Meanwhile, Chinese, Japanese, and South Asian

Aboriginal peoples cast their ballots for the first time in a federal election after being granted the franchise in 1960.

Canadians, who were excluded from voting because of their racial origins, received the franchise in 1947.

The last people in Canada to receive the right to vote were Aboriginal peoples. They had been denied the vote because European Canadians believed that Aboriginal peoples had no experience in democracy and so were incapable of casting their votes intelligently. Despite the fact that Aboriginal peoples had been ruling themselves successfully for generations before the arrival of Europeans, and despite the fact that Aboriginal soldiers had fought for Canada in two world wars, government policy still did not consider them to be citizens. They were wards of the state, treated more as children than as responsible adults.

Aboriginal peoples could only acquire the right to vote through a process called **enfranchisement.** When Aboriginal peoples were enfranchised, they gave up their status under the **Indian Act** and were no longer considered to be registered Indians. They lost all the rights and privileges that went with status, and in return they became ordinary citizens of Canada and acquired, among other things, the right to vote.

Enfranchisement was a policy aimed at assimilating Aboriginal peoples into mainstream white society. Few Aboriginal peoples voluntarily agreed to enfranchisement, preferring to retain their Aboriginal identity. Sometimes it was forced upon them; for example, when an Aboriginal student attended university, he or she automatically became enfranchised. For the most part, however, Aboriginal peoples considered enfranchisement too high a price to pay for the rights of full citizenship. They saw no reason why they could not be fully Canadian and Aboriginal at the same time.

Winning the Vote

In 1948, a joint parliamentary committee that was holding hearings into the Indian Act recommended that Aboriginal peoples receive the vote in federal elections. The next year Aboriginal peoples in British Columbia became eligible to vote in provincial elections. (This happened at the same time as the franchise was restored to people of Asian background in the province.) One by one the other provinces followed suit until the last, Quebec, granted the franchise to Aboriginal peoples in 1969. Meanwhile, in 1950, Inuit received the federal vote. But despite these developments, the federal franchise was still denied to other Aboriginal groups.

In part, this was because Aboriginal peoples could not agree among themselves on whether they really wanted the vote. On the one hand, voting was a fundamental political right and meant that Aboriginal peoples had achieved a measure of equality in Canadian society. On the other hand, some Aboriginal peoples worried that the vote was another attempt to assimilate them and to eradicate Indian status. This group argued that none of the privileges that came with status should be given up in exchange for the vote. For example, Aboriginal peoples living on reserves did not have to pay certain taxes and the government was asking that this exemption be given up in return for the franchise. When the federal government finally agreed that the franchise would result in no other changes to official status, the last roadblock to full voting rights came down.

In 1960, the federal franchise was finally extended to Aboriginal peoples, the last group in Canada to be granted the vote in general elections.

MAKING CONNECTIONS

1. Why is the granting of the franchise considered an important milestone in Aboriginal history? Explain whether or not you think the franchise gave Aboriginal peoples influence over some government policies.

2. Role-play the parliamentary hearings of 1948 in which Aboriginal peoples and federal politicians discussed extending voting rights to Aboriginal peoples.

KEYWORDS

franchise

suffrage

enfranchisement

Indian Act

CANADA AS PEACEMAKER
The Suez Crisis
FOCUSSING ON THE ISSUE

Since the 1950s, one of Canada's major roles in the world has been helping to keep peace between warring nations. How did Canada become so involved in international peacekeeping?

The Suez Canal

The Suez Canal in Egypt is a key transportation corridor, 160 km in length. By allowing ships to travel through the neck of land separating the Red Sea from the Mediterranean, the canal greatly reduces the distance between Europe and Asia. For many years it was privately owned by British and French investors. Then, in July 1956, Egypt's president, Gamal Abdel Nasser, **nationalized** it. This move outraged the British and French, who worried that Nasser might interfere with the passage of crucial oil supplies for Europe. It also made Egypt's neighbour and enemy, Israel, very nervous about what further steps the Egyptians might be planning.

On 29 October 1956, Israeli forces invaded Egypt and headed for the Suez Canal. According to a secret deal worked out with Israel in advance, Britain and France issued an ultimatum ordering both Egypt and Israel to withdraw from the canal zone. Egypt refused, as the allies knew it would. In response, British and French forces joined the Israeli invasion.

The dispute quickly escalated into an international crisis. The Soviet Union threatened to come to the aid of Egypt. The Americans broke with their European allies and demanded a withdrawal of troops. Many **Commonwealth** countries sided with Egypt and condemned the invasion. The western alliance seemed threatened.

Into this web of conflicting loyalties stepped the Canadian external affairs minister, Lester Pearson. Pearson thought that the use of force against Egypt was a mistake, but Canada was not about to take a public stand against two of its oldest allies. The challenge was to find a way to convince Britain and France to withdraw from the conflict without embarassing the two nations. At the United Nations, the General Assembly passed a resolution demanding a ceasefire. The combatants refused. Meanwhile, Pearson was working behind the scenes to create a UN Emergency Force (UNEF) to intercede between the warring factions and keep the peace until a permanent settlement could be worked out. "We need action not only to end the fighting," Pearson said, "but to make the peace."

After much bargaining at the UN, Pearson's idea of an Emergency

Lester Pearson, with his wife Maryon, displays his Nobel Peace Prize in 1957.

Force was approved. The force included 1000 Canadian soldiers, as well as troops from Colombia and Scandinavia. Canada's General E.L.M. Burns was placed in command. With the arrival of the UN force, peace was restored to the region. In recognition of his contribution, Lester Pearson was awarded the Nobel Peace Prize in 1957, one of the highest honours ever given to a Canadian.

CASE STUDY

CANADIAN PEACEKEEPERS

The Suez crisis created a new role for Canada in world affairs—peacekeeping. It is a role for which Canada seemed uniquely suited. The wars in which Canada had fought had always been overseas. As a result, the armed forces were experienced at transporting soldiers long distances and keeping them equipped. Not many armies had this expertise, so Canada was a valued partner in distant peacekeeping operations.

The Canadian public supported this new role for the armed forces. It seemed to be a way to establish a place for Canada in world affairs, independent of the United States or Britain. Although it has cost millions of dollars over the years, Canadians generally have come to accept the role of peacekeeper as Canada's unique way of contributing to international stability. Peacekeepers are soldiers who intercede between warring parties, separate them, and try to keep the two sides from shooting at each other until a peaceful settlement of their differences is reached. Peacekeepers must be neutral; if they seem to favour one side over the other, they will not be trusted. Peacekeeping forces are made up of soldiers from more than one country, operating under the United Nations. They do not resolve a dispute, however; they simply buy time for diplomats to find a solution.

Since the Suez crisis, Canada has taken an active role in peacekeeping on several occasions:

- *Congo, 1960*: When the Congo (formerly Zaïre and now the Democratic Republic of the Congo) became independent from Belgium, it dissolved into warring factions. The UN sent peacekeepers to halt the civil war, including 280 Canadian soldiers and several airplanes.
- *Cyprus, 1964*: Cyprus is an island in the Mediterranean occupied by Turkish and Greek Cypriots. After years of fighting between the two sides, the UN sent in a peacekeeping force to avert a war between Greece and Turkey. Canadian soldiers remained on the island until 1993.
- *Former Yugoslavia, 1992*: As this country disintegrated into a bitter civil war, the UN sent in troops to protect civilians. A Canadian, Major General Lewis MacKenzie, was the first commander of the force, which remained in the region until 1995.

These are a few of the instances when the UN has called on Canada to contribute to a peacekeeping force. Canada has participated in more UN peacekeeping missions than any other country in the world.

MAKING CONNECTIONS

1. Under what circumstances do you think that Canada should agree to contribute soldiers to a peacekeeping operation? Explain your answer.

2. Each year the Nobel Peace Prize is awarded to someone who has made an important contribution to peace. Prepare a short report on one of the recipients of this prize. Present the background to the international crisis in which the recipient was involved, and explain how this individual contributed to a peaceful solution.

KEYWORDS

nationalize

Commonwealth

UNIT 7:

Joyce Wieland, *Time Machine Series*, 1961

Joyce Wieland (1931-1998) focussed on a wide variety of materials, media, and themes in her art. In *Time Machine Series*, she blended abstract expressionism with the feminist movement to create an image of male and female sensuality.

CHANGING TIMES

1961 - 1970

	Social	Cultural	Political	Legal	Economic	Environmental
	✔	✔	✔			
		✔	✔			✔
	✔	✔				
	✔		✔		✔	
			✔		✔	✔
	✔	✔		✔		
					✔	
	✔				✔	✔
	✔		✔			
		✔				
	✔		✔	✔	✔	
	✔				✔	
	✔	✔	✔	✔		
			✔	✔		✔
			✔			✔
	✔		✔	✔		
	✔	✔				

*Skills and Processes

CHANGING TIMES
The World in 1961
FOCUSSING ON THE ISSUE

The 1960s saw widespread questioning of long-standing traditions and institutions around the world. What forces led to the social and political changes that marked this period?

A New Era

John F. Kennedy was sworn in as president of the United States in January 1961. Millions of people watched on television as the handsome young president took the oath of office. For many, Kennedy's inauguration signalled the beginning of a new era, not only in the US but around the world. The Cold War, the Suez Crisis, and the bitter remnants of **colonialism** in Africa and Asia had led many people to doubt

the ability of an older generation of political leaders to deal with the issues facing the world. Kennedy appealed to many people who wanted change and who were willing to take up his challenge of the **New Frontier**. They were ready to tackle the issues of poverty and social injustice at home and abroad and to seek peace and understanding among the nations of the world.

There was a dark backdrop to this hopeful beginning, however. Outgoing president Dwight D.

Eisenhower warned the world of the **military-industrial complex** that he saw becoming more powerful than democratically elected governments in many parts of the world. The danger of nuclear war was a constant reality as the Cold War continued. The Berlin Wall, constructed in 1961, became a symbol of the ideological division in the world. Conflicts between the US and Cuba threatened to turn the Cold War hot, starting with the botched Bay of Pigs invasion by the

CASE STUDY

AVERTING NUCLEAR WAR

In April 1961, the US tried to overthrow Cuban leader Fidel Castro by sending an army of just under 2000 Cuban exiles and CIA agents to the Bay of Pigs on the southwest coast of Cuba. The operation was a disaster. News of the attack had leaked out in advance, and President Kennedy refused to provide air support for the US invasion. The Cuban army easily routed the invaders, and Castro's prestige and popularity in Cuba rose.

Cuba strengthened its ties with the USSR and the Soviets installed missile-launching bases on the island. In October 1962, the US threatened to blockade Cuban ports and search Soviet ships to prevent missiles from reaching the launching platforms. After six nerve-racking days, the Soviet Union relented and agreed to dismantle the launching pads. In exchange, the US promised not to invade Cuba and to remove its missiles in Turkey. The prospect of nuclear war had never seemed closer.

Range of Cuban Missile Sites if Built

Americans that same year. The following year, the world waited anxiously as the Cuban Missile Crisis brought the US and the USSR to the brink of armed conflict. In the aftermath, the two superpowers began negotiating to reduce the risk of a future nuclear **holocaust**.

Still, ideological conflicts dominated much of the world in the early 1960s. The war in Vietnam became the focus of the world's attention as the US entered the conflict. Many young Americans began to question their country's involvement. No issue would more greatly divide the American people during the decade. In many parts of the world, the American presence in Vietnam represented a new form of western **imperialism**.

The first wave of baby boomers were in high school and would soon enter universities and colleges in record numbers. No longer in school, however, were four young musicians from Liverpool, England—the Beatles—whose cheerful music and irreverent attitude marked the beginning of the "British Invasion" of the world's airwaves. In the 1960s, rock music became openly associated with drug use, especially marijuana and LSD. Music also became a vehicle for political protest, as folk singers and rock musicians questioned traditional authority. Student protests in

Prague, Czechoslovakia, led to a brief period of greater openness—the infamous Prague Spring of 1968— only to be crushed when **Soviet bloc** tanks rolled in.

A Decade of Dreams and Dashed Hopes

On 28 August 1963, American civil rights leader Martin Luther King spoke to an audience of more than 200 000 civil rights supporters gathered at the Washington Monument. His "I Have a Dream" speech expressed the hopes of African Americans and of oppressed peoples everywhere in words as moving as any in history:

I have a dream that one day this nation will rise up and live out the true meaning of its creed: 'We hold these truths to be self-evident, that all men are created equal.'...I have a dream that my four little children will one day live in a nation where they will not be judged by the colour of their skin but by the content of their character.

King's speech led to the Civil Rights Act of 1964, which prohibited discrimination in employment and in public facilities associated with interstate commerce. It also established the Equal Employment

Canadian students joined in protest against the war in Vietnam.

Opportunity Commission. For his efforts, King was awarded the Nobel Peace Prize in 1964.

Three months after King's Washington speech, on 22 November 1963, President Kennedy was assassinated in Dallas. It was a tragedy that would be repeated two more times before the decade ended. In April 1968, King, too, died from an assassin's bullet. Two months later, in June, Robert F. Kennedy, the late president's younger brother, was shot to death while making his own run for the presidency. A decade that had started with such bright promise ended in a dark cloud of gloom and broken dreams.

MAKING CONNECTIONS

1. Listen to the music of the Beatles, Bob Dylan, or other bands of the 1960s. What issues do they deal with in their songs?

2. Write your own "I have a dream" speech. Do you think that in Canada the ideals expressed in King's speech are realized? How might an Aboriginal leader respond to King's speech?

KEYWORDS

colonialism

New Frontier

military-industrial complex

holocaust

imperialism

Soviet bloc

GEOGRAPHY AND IDENTITY
The Impact on Canada
FOCUSSING ON THE ISSUE

Canada's geography has always played a role in shaping Canadian identity. How did geography shape ideas about communications in the 1960s? How did it affect the country's new flag?

Bridging the Gaps

Canadians have always felt a connection between their geography and their identity as a nation. The great size of the country, its northern climate, and its vast wilderness areas all contribute to a sense of national distinctiveness. The Group of Seven conveyed this idea in their paintings (see page 88); others have expressed it through words or music.

If Canadians have found uniqueness in their geography, they have also found a challenge there. Distance has always been a fact of life, and many projects undertaken by Canadians have been related to bridging the gaps between the different parts of the country. The transcontinental railways, for example, attempted to unite Canada from coast to coast. So did the creation of a national network of radio and television stations. Canada is a place where staying in touch takes extra effort. It was no accident that in the 1960s Canadians became the world's greatest users of telephones, both for business purposes and to talk with family and friends.

Communications

Following the same trend, during the 1960s, Canada produced the world's leading philosopher of communications, Marshall McLuhan. McLuhan, who was born in Edmonton, studied at universities in Manitoba and Cambridge, England, before settling into the University of Toronto where he taught literature for many years. Gradually, he became interested in the way that communications media influence our view of the world. For instance, McLuhan believed that centuries ago, the rise of print media (mainly books and newspapers) produced a certain way of thinking and a certain kind of society. In the twentieth century, McLuhan observed, electronic media (television, radio, and computers) were becoming more important than print. These new media communicated various types of information in new formats, and they required different understanding skills. For example, television presents information in quite a different way than newspapers do. It is faster and more visual and, unlike the calm absorption of the reader, viewers receive the messages in high-speed bursts of image, sound, and movement.

McLuhan's famous phrase "the medium is the message" suggests that the means we use to communicate are just as important as the information they convey. The fact that we now communicate instantly around the world via satellite is as important as the messages the satellite carries.

McLuhan's ideas have implications for issues of national identity and geography. New electronic technology has annihilated the concept of distance. This was another of McLuhan's insights. He foresaw that as televised signals bounced around the world, they would draw everyone into the same community of images, which he called the

(Herbert) Marshall McLuhan (1911–1980) wrote about the impact of mass communications on society in several books, including The Gutenberg Galaxy *(1962) and* Understanding Media *(1964). What do you think his popular slogans "the medium is the message" and "the global village" mean?*

global village. Slowly, cultures would blend into one another, becoming more alike as they experienced the same media and absorbed the same information. He theorized that distinctive national identities would dissolve as the distances created by geography succumbed to the instant interaction created by technology.

Canada Gets a Flag

McLuhan was also interested in the power of symbols, so he would have been fascinated when Canadians became embroiled in a debate about a new national flag in 1964. A flag is an important symbol of a country's identity. Following Confederation, Canada's flag remained the British Union Flag, commonly called the Union Jack. Over the years, attempts to change it failed. For many Canadians, the Union Jack was an important symbol of Canada's British heritage. For them, replacing it meant rejecting Britain. On the other hand, people who viewed themselves as Canadian, not British, were not comfortable being represented by a "foreign" symbol.

The New ..

The Old ..

These Also Ran..

Commonwealth?

The Union Jack was replaced with a flag showing a single red maple leaf. Do you think this is an appropriate Canadian symbol? Explain.

After leading his Liberal party to victory in the 1963 election, Prime Minister Lester Pearson unveiled his proposal for a new Canadian flag. The design, featuring a cluster of three red maple leaves on a white background with blue bars on either side, touched off six months of debate about how the new flag should look. Finally, a parliamentary committee, with members from all parties, took on the job of coming up with an acceptable design. The committee recommended a single maple leaf, with red bars instead of blue ones. The debate raged on until the government forced a vote. The design passed 163 to 78, and following agreement by the Senate, the new Canadian flag was unfurled for the first time on 15 February 1965.

The use of the maple leaf in the new flag was an indication that Canadians still found at least part of their national identity in their geography. Maple trees grow in every province and maple leaves have been used as emblems in different provincial coats of arms since 1868. Displaying the maple leaf on the flag symbolizes Canadians' identification with the land as an important source of their unique national identity.

-◖▮▮- MAKING CONNECTIONS -▮▮◗-

1. a) In the "global village" of Marshall McLuhan, cultures around the world would be more alike through exposure to the same media messages. Do you agree with McLuhan on this point? Explain.

   b) Do you think that cultures becoming more alike is a positive or negative thing? Give reasons for your answers.

2. a) Why do countries have flags? Do you agree that the maple leaf is an appropriate symbol for Canada? Explain.

   b) Design a flag that reflects your view of Canada's identity.

KEYWORDS

global village

BILINGUALISM
Two Official Languages

In 1969, the Official Languages Act made Canada a bilingual country. How widespread was bilingualism intended to be, and how was it supposed to redress the inequalities between French- and English-speaking Canadians?

A Language Crisis

In 1963, Prime Minister Lester Pearson appointed the Royal Commission on Bilingualism and Biculturalism to examine French-English relations in Canada. In its report several years later, the commission declared that a crisis was at hand. It found that Quebeckers were alienated from the rest of Canada, in large part because the French language was not considered equal to English throughout the country. It recommended, among many things, that government services in French should be expanded across the country, that steps should be taken to ensure that the federal civil service was open equally to French- and English-speaking employees, and that the teaching of French as a second language had to be improved.

When Pierre Trudeau became prime minister in 1968, he was determined to address the language issue. He believed that if French-speaking Canadians had the same access to government services and the same opportunity for government jobs as English-speaking Canadians, they would feel more like equal partners in Confederation. He felt a policy of official bilingualism could accomplish this. The Liberal government, with the support of other parties,

passed the Official Languages Act in 1969. The act gave equal status to English and French, officially making Canada a bilingual country.

The Official Languages Act raised a furore among some English-speaking Canadians who preferred to think of Canada as an English country with a French-speaking minority, and not as a country in which both language groups enjoyed equal status. These people charged that the government was trying to "ram French down their throats." They believed that French-speaking Canadians were getting special treatment in Ottawa, and they questioned why so much money was being spent on making French services available in parts of the country where few people spoke the language. These sentiments were intensified in 1977 when Quebec declared French to be the only official language in that province, suggesting there was a double standard in the country— one language in Quebec but two in the rest of Canada.

Improvements to the Official Languages Act

In 1988, the Official Languages Act was improved to include a more precise recognition of Canada's two-language character. Now, among other things, the act:

- provides for full and equal access to Parliament and to courts established by Parliament, in both official languages

Do you agree that packaging on products sold in Canada should be bilingual? Explain.

Although official bilingualism was introduced in 1969, the debate over the policy continued even in the 1990s.

It is not about providing special benefits to any group in society, or forcing Canadians to learn a second language; nor is it about making Canada bilingual from coast to coast. Rather, it is about federal institutions serving all citizens with the respect and courtesy they deserve, in the official language they feel most comfortable using, wherever there is significant demand.

From the Office of the Commissioner of Official Languages, 1993

*In practice, although not in public pronouncements, the Canadian government actively promotes enforced bilingualism in nine provinces, and tolerates enforced French-only **unilingualism** in Quebec. This is a complete change of course from the country-wide bilingualism envisioned by Pierre Trudeau when he first came to office....*

Many critics of official language policy...express frustration at the apparent willingness of the federal government to continue spreading the gospel of universal language rights for minorities outside Quebec at a time when the provincial government within that province has repeatedly shown contempt for the rights of its own minorities....

Twenty-five years after the introduction of the Official Languages Act, the continued decline of French outside Quebec and of English inside the province serves as proof that efforts to build a bilingual nation have been an exercise in futility. In retrospect, it seems it would have been easier for the Canadian government to legislatively move the Rocky Mountains to Quebec than to save the isolated French-language communities scattered in their shadow, or to stop the erosion of English communities in Quebec's Gaspé Peninsula and the Eastern Townships.

Reprinted with permission from Lament for a Notion: The Life and Death of Canada's Bilingual Dream by Scott Reid (Arsenal Pulp Press, 1993).

1. According to the Office of the Commissioner of Official Languages, Canada's language policy is not intended to make all Canadians bilingual. What is it intended to do?
2. Scott Reid calls bilingualism an "exercise in futility" because the use of French outside Quebec is declining, as is the use of English in Quebec. Do you agree that this represents a failure of bilingualism?
3. Why do opponents object to the policy of bilingualism? Do you agree with any of these objections? Explain.

- gives Canadians the right to receive federal government services in either French or English in the National Capital Region and wherever there is a significant demand
- aims to ensure equal employment and career-advancement opportunities in all federal institutions for English- and French-speaking Canadians
- commits federal institutions to hiring, under the principle of merit, English- and French-speaking Canadians in numbers that reflect their proportion in the overall Canadian population
- gives federal employees the right to work in the official language of their choice in the National Capital Region and in designated regions.

MAKING CONNECTIONS

1. Is Canada a truly bilingual country? Should it be? Explain, referring to your own experience.

KEYWORDS

unilingualism

THE QUIET REVOLUTION
Change in Quebec
FOCUSSING ON THE ISSUE

*The Quiet Revolution was a period of unprecedented change in Quebec.
How did it affect Quebec's relations with the rest of Canada?*

La Révolution tranquille

More than any other Canadian province, Quebec experienced rapid social, economic, and political change during the 1960s. So profound were these changes that they came to be called a revolution. But because they were non-violent changes, it was a *révolution tranquille*—a "quiet revolution."

The Quiet Revolution began with the election of Jean Lesage and the provincial Liberal party in 1960. The Liberals promised to bring an end to the corruption and **patronage** that had marked the previous government of Maurice Duplessis. (See page 136.) They wanted to modernize Quebec, to reduce the dominance of the Catholic Church in Quebec society, and to make the French-speaking majority *maîtres chez nous*—"masters in our own house"—a slogan they had borrowed from Duplessis.

The Quiet Revolution's main objectives required making changes in four areas:

The Economy
The Quiet Revolution sought to establish a stronger French presence in the provincial economy. Many, if not most, industries in Quebec were owned and managed by **Anglophones**. In many businesses English was the language of the workplace. The Quiet Revolution changed all that. One major initiative was the takeover of several private power companies to create Hydro-Québec, a publicly owned electricity company. Through Hydro-Québec, the government was able to influence the province's industrial development. As well, investment agencies were set up to help finance business initiatives by **Francophones**, and a French Language Office was established to promote the use of French in business.

Social Services
Quebeckers wanted to ensure that their province had the same standard of social services as the other provinces. To improve health care, new hospitals were built and a provincial hospital insurance plan was introduced. Plans for old age pensions and free dental care for children were also established. Public servants received the right to strike, and the minimum wage was increased.

Education
Education in Quebec had long been the responsibility of the Church. The new government appointed a commission to investigate the education system. It recommended the creation of a provincial department of education and the transfer of

One of the hydroelectric dams built by Hydro-Québec during the 1960s. Why did hydro power become one of the symbols of the "new" Quebec during the Quiet Revolution?

schools from religious to government control. In 1967, a province-wide network of junior colleges, known as CEGEP, was established.

More Autonomy

To bring about the changes they wanted, Lesage and the Liberals demanded more powers and more money from the federal government. Quebec and the other provinces were granted the power to levy their own extra taxes. They were also allowed to **opt out** of national social programs and devise their own provincial programs, as long as they met national standards. A new phrase, "co-operative federalism," was coined to describe these new federal-provincial arrangements. Quebec also began to establish its own diplomatic links with French-speaking countries. Since 1961, when the Quebec government signed co-operation agreements with France, the province has established delegations on three continents.

Special Status

The Quiet Revolution was a period of rapid change in Quebec, but not everyone agreed on how far change should go. Some, like Lesage and his government, wanted a more assertive Quebec within Confederation. They considered Quebec to be a unique province

In 1960, many businesses in Montreal were run by Anglophones. Quebeckers of British origin earned the highest wages, with an average annual income of $4940. From this level, the average wages of other largely Anglophone cultural groups declined in the following order: Scandinavian, Jewish, German, Polish, and Asian. French-Canadian Quebeckers, with an average annual income of $3185, were nearly at the bottom of the wage scale.

and the homeland for French-speaking people in North America. Therefore, they believed the province should have special powers in order to protect and encourage French language and culture. This came to be known as "special status." Others, like Pierre Trudeau, a law professor in Montreal, believed Quebec simply needed to exert greater influence in Ottawa by electing better qualified representatives. In 1965, Trudeau and two friends, Gérard Pelletier and Jean Marchand, known as the Three Wise Men, joined the federal Liberal government. Meanwhile,

René Lévesque, a minister in the Lesage government, chose another option. He believed that Quebec needed to separate from Canada. In 1967, he quit the Liberals to found a new party, the Parti Québécois. Its objective was the creation of an independent Quebec.

Events in Quebec had a significant influence on events in the rest of the country because they affected relations between the federal government and all the provinces. As Quebeckers debated their future they were also debating the future, of Canada. "What does Quebec want?" was a common question. Finding an answer would become a central challenge to Canadian political life for the rest of the century.

MAKING CONNECTIONS

1. What was quiet about the Quiet Revolution? What was revolutionary?

2. What does the phrase "masters in our own house" mean?

3. Describe the argument in favour of "special status" for Quebec. Explain whether or not you agree with it.

KEYWORDS

patronage

Anglophone

Francophone

opt out

DAMMING THE COLUMBIA RIVER
International Co-operation
FOCUSSING ON THE ISSUE

The Columbia River flows out of Canada into the United States. What issues, both political and environmental, arise when development occurs on a major river crossing national boundaries?

The Columbia River Treaty

The Columbia River is one of the great rivers of North America. Originating in southeastern British Columbia, it flows 2000 km through BC and across the border through Washington state before reaching the Pacific Ocean near Portland, Oregon. The Columbia has a vast **drainage basin** of 155 000 km². Today, some of the largest power dams in the world have been built on the Columbia, producing electricity for communities in Canada and the US.

Many issues arise when a river is shared by two countries, especially when one country has a greater need for water than the other. In the case of the Columbia, most of the economic activity along its banks is located in the US, but British Columbia has the ability to control the flow of the river. What if BC diverted the river and left Americans needing water? Or, what if upstream users were polluting the river? How could people living downstream obtain some control over water quality? These issues require international co-operation to properly manage the water resource.

After the Second World War, American and Canadian officials began discussing plans to modify the flow of the Columbia. In the US, the river was notorious for flooding—large areas of land that might become prime farmland if the water could be controlled were often inundated. Furthermore, the Americans needed electricity to supply the booming cities in the Pacific Northwest. They had already built hydro dams on the river, the most famous being the Grand Coulee Dam west of Spokane, one of the largest hydro projects in the world. But as their needs increased, the Americans saw advantages in damming the Columbia on both sides of the border.

The Americans found a willing partner in BC premier W.A.C. Bennett, who was looking for ways to finance his dreams of industrial development for the province. As far as Bennett was concerned, BC had control over its own resources and could do with them as it pleased. When it came to the Columbia River, however, the federal government disagreed. It argued that the issue affected international relations and therefore was a federal matter. It even went so far as to pass a law requiring federal approval for any development projects on an international river. Bennett was livid, but for the time being there was nothing he could do.

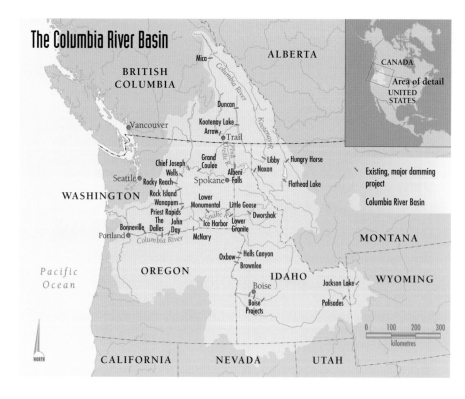

The Columbia River Basin

Meanwhile, discussions with the Americans about the Columbia continued until finally, on 17 January 1961, the two countries signed an agreement covering developments on the river for the next 60 years. Canada agreed to construct three dams in the BC portion of the drainage basin and to operate the dams in accordance with American downstream needs. In return, the US agreed to pay Canada US $64.4 million and to return to Canadian users half the electrical power generated by new facilities in the US.

At this point, the government of BC intervened. It wanted to sell its share of the electricity back to American consumers, taking cash instead of power. In August 1961, Premier Bennett **nationalized** the giant power company BC Electric, creating what eventually became BC Hydro, a provincial **Crown corporation**. He felt he needed a publicly owned power company to carry out developments on the Columbia. Then he simply refused to **ratify** the treaty until he got his own way. The federal government objected at first, then gave in to BC's demands. A renegotiated treaty was signed early in 1964 and, under its terms, the province received prepayment of US $254 million for the sale of electricity over the next 30 years. Critics later claimed that Bennett received far too little money for a precious natural resource, but at the time he felt pressured to obtain the money to construct the dams required by the treaty.

The Impact on the Environment

The Columbia River Treaty brought many economic benefits to BC, including jobs, revenue from hydroelectric power sales, and recreational opportunities on the artificial lakes created by the dams. Critics of the treaty argued that it largely benefited the US, which received power, water for irrigation, and flood control—all at a very low cost. In BC, residents of the Kootenay complained that too little of the money from the deal went to their region. (In 1994, when a new hydroelectric power agreement with the US was reached, the province announced plans to invest part of the proceeds in the economic development of this part of southern BC.)

But the most important impact of development on the Columbia River was on the environment. Hydroelectric power is often considered a "clean," environmentally friendly form of energy because it does not consume the resource on which it depends—water—and it does not produce harmful gases or chemicals. As well, hydro dams often prevent damaging floods. Nevertheless, large-scale dam construction does come with a cost to the environment.

For one thing, the vast reservoirs created upstream flood river valleys, destroying farms and forestry operations and forcing some communities to relocate. Changing the flow of a river may have serious, unintended consequences for the wildlife that depends on it. Before the first dams were built on the Columbia, for example, it was one of the world's most important salmon spawning rivers. Today, it contains and produces comparatively few salmon. As well, though improved water control and irrigation may allow for more farming along a river, this in turn leads to an increase in the water of chemicals from fertilizers and pesticides.

When they were built, the dams on the Columbia River were considered a blessing, producing economic prosperity and much-needed electricity. Today, the issue is less clear as the long-term results of the project are assessed. What is clear is that no energy source comes without a price in terms of its impact on the environment.

MAKING CONNECTIONS

1. Electricity provides about 21 per cent of all the energy used in British Columbia. This figure is close to double the percentage for Canada as a whole. How does BC's geography help to explain its heavier reliance on hydro power?

KEYWORDS

drainage basin

nationalize

Crown corporation

ratify

NEW IMMIGRATION POLICIES
Eliminating Discrimination
FOCUSSING ON THE ISSUE

As a result of growing opposition to discrimination and the new focus on human rights, Canada's immigration laws came under attack in the 1960s. What steps did the federal government take towards establishing a non-discriminatory immigration policy?

Existing Immigration Policies

In 1952, the Canadian Parliament passed the first new Immigration Act since 1910. While the act brought some improvements to the existing system, it maintained the practice of establishing and controlling immigration policy through regulations rather than **statutes**. This gave the Cabinet wide powers to change Canada's immigration regulations and therefore the country's immigration practices. The Cabinet could admit, limit, or prohibit immigrants on virtually any criteria it chose by using **orders-in-council**. It did not have to refer the politically sensitive issue of immi-gration policy to Parliament for debate.

Under the act, preferred categories of immigrants were still those from Britain, the United States, France, and other European countries. Immigrants from Asia, Africa, the Caribbean, and southern Europe remained in the prohibited or limited categories. In general, immigrants had to apply from outside the country and had to meet the criteria established by the regulations. Immigration officers had wide discretionary powers over admissions. Individual officers often interpreted the regulations differently. Many officers were accused of making arbitrary, and frequently racist, decisions. This created the public perception that the system was open to abuse.

Not surprisingly, the immigration process generated a lot of criticism. Within a year of the passage of the act, various sectors of Canadian society were calling for its revision and amendment.

A New Approach

In the past, many new immigration ministers had announced plans to amend the act or introduce a new one. But the controversial and politically sensitive nature of immigration policy made it difficult to convince the Cabinet to consider legislative changes to the act. The matter was further complicated by

ILLEGAL IMMIGRATION

C
A
S
E

S
T
U
D
Y

An ongoing problem for authorities in the 1960s was illegal immigration among Chinese immigrants from Hong Kong. Since Chinese immigration was extremely limited, those who wanted to come to Canada found ways around the regulations. A thriving, though illegal, business developed in Hong Kong involving the sale of immigration documents. These documents identified prospective immigrants as family members of Chinese people who were residents of Canada and were eligible to sponsor relatives. While immigration officials made repeated attempts to stop the practice, many Canadians who opposed the gov-ernment's immigration policies applauded the efforts of Chinese people. In 1960, faced with the impossibility of identifying and deporting the illegal immigrants, the minister of immigration announced an **amnesty** program. Under the program, those illegal immigrants who came forward and who "were of good moral character" could have their status legalized. Nearly 12 000 illegal Chinese immigrants came forward and had their status "adjusted" between 1960 and 1970. In spite of the Immigration Department's efforts, the sale of forged documents continued.

the fact that some provinces, especially Quebec, wanted greater influence and control over immigration policy. However, a major change in approach was signalled when politicians began talking about Canada as a nation of cultural diversity. This approach rejected the **melting pot** philosophy of US immigration in favour of a **cultural mosaic**, which was the beginning of Canadian **multiculturalism**.

On 19 January 1962, the minister of citizenship and immigration, Ellen Fairclough, tabled a new set of immigration regulations in Parliament. On the surface, at least, the new regulations removed racial discrimination from Canada's immigration policy. To gain admission to Canada, individual immigrants had to be able to demonstrate they would be able to establish themselves here and had enough money to support themselves until they did.

It was in the category of sponsored immigrants that discrimination continued. Canadian citizens could sponsor their relatives, provided they could demonstrate they could support their family members until they were established in Canada. Relatives that were eligible for sponsorship were those from any country in Europe and other

NATO nations; from Egypt, Lebanon, or Israel; or from any country of North, Central, or South America and adjacent islands. The new regulations ruled out the sponsorship of immigrants from other countries in Asia and Africa, except close family members. A peculiarity of the definition of "close relative" in the act—as it applied to Asians and Africans—was that, for them, it did not include brothers and sisters.

In spite of the government's promise to eliminate racial discrimination from immigration policy, the complaints continued. Since the focus of the department was to attract immigrants who had the education, training, and skills to become contributing members of the labour force, or who had the financial resources to establish their own businesses in Canada, immigration officers could still exercise their own discretion in approving applicants.

In 1967, a points system for immigrants was added to the criteria for admission. Now, immigration officers could award a number of points for such fac-

tors as education, training and experience, occupational demand, perceived adaptability of the immigrant, age, and knowledge of French or English. If the points awarded to the immigrant added up to 50 or more, the individual was eligible for admission. The government hoped that this program would make the process fairer and more objective, since the selection of applicants would not be on the grounds of cultural group or geographic region. The program was well received by both immigration officials and immigrants. From time to time, the criteria for admittance are revised to take into account changing circumstances in the world.

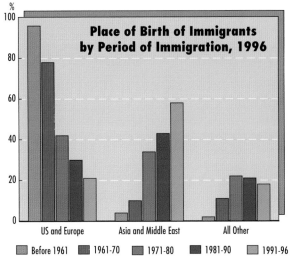

Describe the changing pattern of immigration since 1961.

KEYWORDS

statute

order-in-council

amnesty

melting pot

cultural mosaic

multiculturalism

THE AUTOPACT
Sectoral Free Trade

FOCUSSING ON THE ISSUE

In 1965, the Canadian and US governments signed an agreement that effectively created a single automobile market for the two countries. What issues did the Autopact address?

In the 1960s, North Americans were in the middle of their love affair with the automobile. No one gave much thought to conserving gasoline, and the term compact car had not been invented yet. Car designers indulged themselves with gleaming chrome, soaring tail-fins, and aerodynamic styling. Cars, the symbol of North American prosperity, just kept getting bigger and more powerful.

Two Markets

The 1950s and 1960s were boom years for Canada's automobile industry. Postwar prosperity led to skyrocketing sales. New highway construction, the migration to the suburbs, and a strong economy all combined to put more and more Canadians in the driver's seat.

In 1961, most cars bought in Canada were made in North America. Traditionally, cars imported from Europe did not sell well because they were ill-suited to Canadian driving conditions or were too expensive for most consumers. (Only Sweden's Volvo could stand the test of a Canadian winter, while Germany's Volkswagen "beetle" was the only affordable European import.) Japanese-built

cars, such as the Datsun, began to arrive in Canada in the early 1960s, but they were considered odd because they were small and boxy compared to the large North American models.

Some of the cars Canadians purchased were manufactured in Canada. Most, however, were made in the United States, then imported across the border. These American-built cars were subject to import duties that had been introduced to protect Canadian car manufacturers. But by the 1960s, the Canadian automobile industry the **tariffs** were meant to protect had vanished. Manufacturers had either been bought out by the "Big Three" American car companies—General Motors, Ford, and Chrysler—or they had fallen into bankruptcy.

Now the tariff barrier seemed only to divide Canada and the US into two separate markets, with Canadians paying higher prices for the same product.

Over the years, American companies had built plants in Canada or bought them from local manufacturers who could not compete against the Americans' larger market. They produced a variety of models for Canadian consumers, putting different trim and distinctively Canadian names onto American bodies. By the 1960s, Canadians were paying 30 per cent more than Americans for the same car, mainly because the Canadian market was only 10 per cent the size of the US market. Canadian auto plants were small, turning out a fraction of the output of their American counterparts. **Economies of scale** dictated that the fewer cars produced, the higher the cost of each car. The problem was compounded by Canadian consumers who naturally wanted just as much choice in car models as Americans, and at the same price.

Sectoral Free Trade

Lobbying by both consumers and the automobile industry in the early 1960s led to the negotiation of a **sectoral** free-trade agreement limited to the auto industry. Before the agreement was reached, the issue of removing tariff barriers was hotly

ECONOMIES OF SCALE

Economies of scale reveals a great deal about the nature of industrialization. Modern factories require heavy investment to cover the costs of land, production facilities, and machinery. These are *fixed costs* of production; they do not change regardless of the number of goods produced. Raw materials, energy, and labour, on the other hand, are *variable costs* of production; they change as the output of goods rises or falls. The price of any good includes its fixed costs, variable costs, taxes, payments on loans, and profits. As the number of items produced—the **production run**—increases, the portion of the selling price resulting from fixed costs drops, within certain limits.

For example, if a car maker has fixed costs of $50 million a year and the plant produces 100 000 cars that same year, the fixed cost per car would be $500 ($50 million ÷ 100 000). Using the same facility to produce 500 000 cars would reduce the fixed cost to $100 per car. Though variable costs might increase in this case—more labour, energy and raw materials—the cost per car would still remain lower. The increased economies of scale in the second case means either lower selling prices for consumers or increased profits for producers, or both.

1. Many car manufacturers now use robotics on their assembly lines. Find out more about robotics, then use the concept of fixed costs of production to explain why car makers use them.

debated. Canadian auto-worker unions feared that removing the tariff would lead to the closure of auto plants in Canada as American producers got free access to the Canadian market and no longer saw any advantage in producing north of the border. The Canadian government responded by negotiating a minimum Canadian-content requirement for cars imported into Canada under the agreement. This meant that a certain percentage of every car had to be made in Canada.

The Canada-US Automotive Products Agreement, known as the Autopact, was signed in 1965. As expected, the elimination of tariffs in the auto industry led to lower prices for Canadian car buyers. It also led to increased specialization in car and truck production on both sides of the border. The agreement protected the jobs of assembly-line workers in Canadian plants, though critics of the deal point out that the Canadian industry is still dominated by American owners and almost all the senior management and design jobs remain in the US. Overall, however, most economists agree that the Autopact turned out to be a good deal for the Canadian economy.

Ironically, the pact came at a time when even greater changes were about to hit the North American automobile industry. By the late 1960s, the number of cars imported from Japan was on the rise. Over the next decade, the growing popularity of Japanese cars would dramatically affect the fortunes of auto makers on both sides of the border.

MAKING CONNECTIONS

1. List the advantages and disadvantages to Canadians of the Autopact.

2. Canadian automobile production is centred almost entirely in Quebec and Ontario. Using maps of central Canada and the eastern United States, identify the geographic factors that would explain this.

KEYWORDS

tariff

economies of scale

sectoral

production run

DISTRIBUTING WEALTH
Regional Economic Disparity

Canada's geographic structure makes it a country of regions. Unfortunately, the nation's wealth is not spread equally throughout these regions. What impact has this disparity had on Canada?

Canada's Regions

With its large land area and variety of physical characteristics, Canada divides naturally into several regions. There is the collection of mountains and valleys of the Western Cordillera and the vast expanse of the Prairies that abuts the northern forests and the arctic tundra beyond. Next is the great Canadian Shield that extends to the Great Lakes-St. Lawrence region along the Canada-US border. Farther east are the rocky hills and fertile valleys of Atlantic Canada.

In a country as large as Canada there are also differences in economic prosperity from one region to another. Some provinces have slow economic growth, low wages, and high unemployment; others thrive. This **regional disparity** is the result of several factors. Climate, for example, determines the type and extent of agricultural activity in a region, while distribution of natural resources means that some provinces have an abundance of valuable minerals or energy sources while others do not. In regions a long distance from manufacturing bases, customers pay higher prices for goods because of transportation costs. Densely populated regions can offer services that may not be available to people in less populated places.

Regional Development

Because control of natural resources

is in the provincial domain, people tend to assume the natural resources belong to their province rather than to the entire country, and that they should be developed for their advantage. In the early stages of Canada's development, all areas of the country set out to develop their resources to supply their ever-growing markets. The supply of resources seemed inexhaustible. However, the exploitation of natural resources on its own is not enough to sustain economic growth. Industrial patterns have a significant impact in determining the development and continuation of regional economic disparity.

Historically, the Great Lakes-St. Lawrence lowlands have developed faster and more vigorously than any other region in Canada. Transportation routes running through broad river valleys provided relatively easy access to the region. Great numbers of people settled along the banks of the St. Lawrence and the shores of the Great Lakes. As Canada began to industrialize, large factories located where the population had concentrated. The rich mineral resources of the Canadian Shield were also within easy reach of this region, and it quickly became the wealthiest part of Canada.

By contrast, the Atlantic region, with its collection of small and isolated fishing ports, grew more slowly. Its industrial development was mainly in **primary production**.

However, as fishing, shipbuilding, and agriculture entered a long period of decline—partly because of over-fishing, new technological developments in shipbuilding, and agricultural competition from other areas of North America—the population and the economy shrank. The distance from larger markets, transportation costs, and the concentration of manufacturing in the Great Lakes-St. Lawrence lowlands meant that the industries in Atlantic Canada could no longer compete against cheaper domestic and foreign suppliers.

The situation was quite different on the Prairies and in British Columbia. These regions developed after the industrial strength of central Canada was established, so that their initial development was designed to provide central Canada with **raw materials** and markets. The construction of railways served the needs of central Canada, but the high cost of shipping goods east meant that any industries that developed in the western regions had difficulty competing with those in the Great Lakes-St. Lawrence lowlands.

Addressing Disparity

Development programs have long existed in Canada, most significantly the system of income transfers among the provinces that resulted from the Rowell-Sirois Commission in 1940. (See page

138.) In 1962, special programs to foster economic growth and development in depressed regions were established under the Area Development Agency. This was replaced by the Department of Regional Economic Expansion (DREE) in 1969. DREE's mandate was to create employment opportunities based on two categories of need. The first was "designated region"—this referred to areas with high unemployment levels but with an existing **infrastructure**. Companies that wanted to build new factories or expand existing ones were eligible for grants. In the second category, "special areas," no infrastructure was in place, nor were there any social services or other amenities. Extensive programs were set up in these areas to develop vocational training, jobs in the service and manufacturing sectors, new housing and industrial parks, and health and social services. In some provinces, the federal and provincial governments shared the responsibility of overseeing and financing both categories of programs, but in the economically depressed provinces the federal government assumed a larger share of the cost.

ATLANTIC CANADA

The Atlantic region has been dealt some severe economic blows in recent years. In addition to the economic recession experienced across Canada, there were major cutbacks in the fishing, pulp and paper, and mining industries. The collapse of the fishing industry alone resulted in over 30 000 layoffs. The Department of National Defence also closed many military facilities in the region. As a result, unemployment in Atlantic Canada in 1995 was 15 per cent, 4 per cent higher than the national average of 11 per cent.

The problem in Atlantic Canada is a lack of economic diversity. The economy is largely resource-based, with limited secondary manufacturing. As a result, when the resource industries experience difficulties, there are few employment alternatives.

The Atlantic Canada Opportunities Agency (ACOA) was established in 1987. Its objectives are to promote small- and medium-sized business ventures that create jobs and diversify the economy. Headquartered in Moncton, New Brunswick, the agency has regional offices in the provincial capitals of Nova Scotia, Prince Edward Island, and Newfoundland.

In 1995, the federal government announced another economic assistance program for Atlantic Canada. The Atlantic Groundfish Strategy (TAGS) will spend $1.9 billion over five years to restructure the Atlantic fishery. This includes the renewal of fish stocks as well as retraining programs for those people forced out of the fishing industry. The federal government will also work with the provincial governments to create more business and job opportunities in aquaculture, tourism, and information technologies.

In Newfoundland, the government has also developed a Strategic Economic Plan to help overcome its fisheries crisis. New companies locating in the province will have a tax "holiday"—that is, they will be exempt from paying provincial corporate income taxes, payroll taxes, and retail sales taxes for ten years. They will also have the opportunity to purchase Crown land (land owned by the government) at low prices.

Fraser Cartwright, Gary Birchall, and Gerry Pierce,
Contact Canada, Second Edition
(Toronto: Oxford University Press, 1996), pp. 398-399.

◄▣ MAKING CONNECTIONS ▣►

1. Should governments provide financial incentives to encourage businesses to locate in depressed regions? Explain.

2. Working in a small group, outline a strategy for economic development in Atlantic Canada. Suggest new business opportunities and explain why you think they would succeed.

KEYWORDS

regional disparity

primary production

raw materials

infrastructure

THE VIETNAM WAR
The Impact on Canada

FOCUSSING ON THE ISSUE

In the Vietnam War, American troops intervened in a civil war between North and South Vietnam. The war was politically controversial in the United States and around the world. What impact did it have on Canada?

A Giant Shadow

The war in Vietnam fell across the 1960s like a giant shadow. It divided families, set a generation of young people against its government, saw the destruction of countless lives, and forced an American president from office. The war lasted from the early 1960s until 1975. It was the longest armed conflict in American history and almost brought that country to the brink of civil revolution.

American involvement in Vietnam began in 1960 when 800 military "advisors" were sent to South Vietnam to provide support in a war against communist forces from the North. During the administration of US president John F. Kennedy, the number of American military personnel increased to 16 000. Yet the South Vietnamese army was still unsuccessful in containing the North Vietnamese forces. Lyndon Johnson, Kennedy's successor, took a hard-line approach, escalating American military involvement through bombings and the use of **chemical weapons**. Although war was never formally declared, by 1965 there were over 500 000 US troops stationed in Vietnam.

The war sparked a level of public protest that had never been seen in North America. Repelled by tele-

vision images of destruction and death in rural villages in Vietnam, thousands of people took to the streets in protest against the war. The American government's position was that US troops were in Vietnam to stop the spread of communism. But many Americans questioned why the US should tell the Vietnamese what to do in their own country, and saw their government's tactics as bullying. The war was so unpopular that it forced Johnson to decline from running for a second term of office in 1968.

After Richard Nixon was elected president, peace talks were launched with North Vietnam in Paris. First, Nixon wanted to turn back time to the early years of the conflict when US troops played only a supporting role to South Vietnamese forces. Second, he needed to establish "Peace with Honour" so that both sides could pull out without either appearing to have lost and without the US appearing to have abandoned its allies in the region. The long process of negotiation ended on 17 January 1973, when a peace agreement was reached and immediately followed by a cease-fire. American military personnel were withdrawn from Vietnam within 60 days, but fighting between North and South Vietnamese troops continued for two more years. On 30 April 1975,

South Vietnam fell to an invasion from North Vietnamese troops and the country was finally reunited.

Canada and Vietnam

For Canada, Vietnam was a diplomatic dilemma rather than a military one. The Canadian government disliked the Americans' military actions in Vietnam. Prime Minister Lester Pearson worried that the US might resort to nuclear force to win a decisive victory. There were also fears that the conflict might widen into a broader war involving all of Southeast Asia. It could even start a third world war.

It was difficult for Canada to speak out openly against such a close ally as the United States. Occasionally, Pearson would publicly call for a halt to the US bombings, but mainly the government opted for quiet diplomacy, working behind the scenes to try to soften American war policy.

There was, however, another side to Canada's position on Vietnam. While the government disagreed with American tactics, it did not disagree with their overall objectives. Thus Canada provided support to the Americans throughout the conflict. Canadian diplomats in North Vietnam, who were supposed to be neutral, gave the Americans information about the

LUNCH WITH THE PRESIDENT

On 2 April 1965, Prime Minister Lester Pearson gave a speech at Temple University in Philadelphia in which he urged the US to halt its bombing of North Vietnam. At lunch the next day, Pearson asked President Lyndon Johnson what he thought of the speech. Johnson exploded, shouting angrily that Pearson had no business coming to the US to publicly criticize its actions. For over an hour, Johnson ranted at Pearson, at one point grabbing him by the lapels of his coat. Aides were afraid the two men would come to blows.

Finally Johnson calmed down. Pearson readjusted his clothing and the two men went out to meet reporters. Both of them put on smiling faces and pretended that nothing had gone wrong. "I haven't much to say except that it has been a very pleasant couple of hours," Pearson told the press. In fact, it was a very low point in Canadian-American relations.

A famous photograph of Lyndon Johnson showed him picking up his dog by its floppy ears. This cartoon compares that incident to the meeting between Johnson and Pearson. Why was Johnson so angry at Pearson? Do you think he had cause to be?

military situation there. Canada provided military arms and supplies to the war effort and tested some of the most destructive chemical weapons used in Vietnam. While many Canadians protested the war and Canada's involvement in it in rallies and demonstrations, thousands of others volunteered to fight with the American forces. So, while Canada's support was reluctant, it was always very much in the American camp.

Canada was also affected by the arrival of tens of thousands of Americans who came to the country to avoid the war—by deserting the army or dodging the **draft**. These young men were fugitives, unable to return home without being arrested. Canada provided a safe haven. Most of these Americans remained in Canada, even after an **amnesty** in 1977 made it possible for them to return legally to the US.

The war in Vietnam contributed to a growing spirit of **nationalism** in Canada during the 1960s. Many Canadians felt morally superior to the US, which they saw as a violent society. They questioned whether Canadian foreign policy was too closely allied with the Americans. Why should Canada, they asked, be associated with a nation capable of waging such a brutal, unjust war? The impact of the war, said journalist Robert Fulford, was to make Canadians "feel our separateness from the US more than we had felt at any time since the Second World War."

MAKING CONNECTIONS

1. How would you describe the Canadian government's policy towards the war in Vietnam?

2. Why do you think so many people opposed the war in Vietnam? If you had been a teenager during this time, what would your position have been? Why?

KEYWORDS

chemical weapons

draft

amnesty

nationalism

EXPO '67
Canada's Birthday Bash

Canada turned 100 years old in 1967. How did the celebration affect the way Canadians felt about their country?

The Montreal World's Fair, Expo '67, attracted 50 million visitors to its site on the St. Lawrence River along Montreal's waterfront. The event was the highlight of Canada's Centennial celebration.

A Birthday Bash

When Canada turned 100 years old, the government decided to celebrate by throwing a year-long birthday bash. A Centennial Train, carrying displays about Canadian history and culture, toured the country. Millions of dollars were spent on special projects to commemorate the event. Communities from coast to coast joined in with their own Centennial projects, ranging from new ice rinks to libraries to statues. One prairie town even built a landing pad for alien spaceships! Bobby Gimby, a well-known trumpet player, wrote a special song called "Ca-na-da," which became the Centennial anthem.

The centrepiece of the Centennial was the world exposition called Expo '67. Fairgrounds were built on Île Ste-Hélène in the St. Lawrence River at Montreal. A second island, Île Notre-Dame, was created for the event by dumping 25 000 t of dirt into the river. Expo opened in April and ran for 183 days. It was full of amazing attractions, including architect Buckminster Fuller's geodesic dome, which housed the US pavilion; the giant La Ronde amusement park; and Habitat '67, the futuristic housing complex designed by architect Moshe Safdie. The fair included an arts festival showcasing some of the top musical and theatrical performers in the world. By the time Expo closed in October, 50 million visitors had passed through the gates and hundreds of millions of tourist dollars had been attracted to Montreal.

The fair made headlines around the world and attracted many famous people. Ed Sullivan, the most popular television host in the US at the time, came from New York to do a show from the site. Many world leaders visited Montreal that summer, including Charles de Gaulle, the president of France. He injected a sour political note into the celebrations, however, by declaring "Vive le Québec libre!" ("Long live a free Quebec") from the balcony of Montreal's city hall. His proclamation seemed to be a call to **separatism**. It was viewed not only as interfering in Canada's internal affairs, but as a slap in the face of the federal government. Prime Minister Pearson was so

While many people felt that Expo '67 created a feeling of national pride and was cause for celebration, not everyone viewed the fair so optimistically.

This was the greatest thing we have ever done as a nation and surely the modernization of Canada—of its skylines, of its styles, of its institutions—will be dated from this occasion and from this fair.

Peter C. Newman, Toronto Star, 28 April 1967.

Expo has done more for Canada's self-confidence than anything within memory..."We're on the map," a friend told me. "They know who we are in New York now."

Hugo McPherson...now head of the National Film Board, said in an interview: "We have our own 'scene' in Canada now....it's no longer fashionable, the way it used to be, for Canadians to knock everything Canadian. Perhaps Expo will be the event we'll all remember as the roadmark. I think it's going to be a vast Canadianizing force, not only in Quebec but all across the country. There's a new feeling of national gaiety and pride at Expo...."

Others go even further, demanding an alarmingly high emotional return from what is after all only a world's fair. A good one, maybe even the most enjoyable one ever. However, within it there lies merely the stuff of a future nostalgic musical, not the myth out of which

a nation is forged. Unless it is to be a Good Taste Disneyland.

Mordecai Richler, Hunting Tigers Under Glass (Toronto: McClelland & Stewart, 1968), p. 36. Reprinted by permission of the author.

*We've witnessed the corrosion of the ideal of national cohesion which made the dream of Expo so vivid. Back then it was still possible to imagine that there might be some kind of pan-provincial experience which we could call Canadian....Today, after the ravages to the national dream perpetrated by factors as wide ranging as sepa-ratism, **recession**, government cutbacks, aboriginal poli-tics, **free trade** and **multiculturalism**, it is not only more difficult to speak with any assumption of consensus about "Canadian" experience, it's almost absurd.*

Geoff Pevere and Greig Dymond, Mondo Canuck, (Toronto: Prentice Hall, 1996), p. 55.

1. Why did people believe that Expo '67 was so important for the country?
2. What did Mordecai Richler mean by a "Good Taste Disneyland"?
3. Geoff Pevere and Greig Dymond identified sev-eral factors that they think have corroded a sense of national unity in Canada. Do you agree with them? List these factors and explain the effect each has had on Canadian unity.

angry with de Gaulle that he refused to meet with him during his visit.

National Pride

Political controversy aside, Expo '67 went off without a hitch. It seemed to unleash a new feeling of national pride and confidence. Canadians from across the country who con-verged on the fair discovered that they had more in common with each other than they had previously thought. The rest of the world was impressed by Expo as well. Canadians began to realize they had created something special, and even began to think that perhaps Canada was special. There was a strong sense that Expo's success marked Canada's coming of age as a nation.

KEYWORDS

separatism

recession

free trade

multiculturalism

MAKING CONNECTIONS

1. In 2067, Canada will celebrate its 200th birthday. Write a short story describing Canada in the year 2067.

THE STATUS OF WOMEN
The Royal Commission

FOCUSSING

FOCUSSING ON THE ISSUE

The Report of the Royal Commission on the Status of Women revealed basic inequalities between men and women in Canadian society. In what ways did the commission improve the status of women in Canada?

An Unequal Society

The Royal Commission on the Status of Women was the first commission to examine the inequality, discrimination, and oppression experienced by women in Canadian society. The inquiry was inspired by the political and cultural climate of the 1960s. Canadian society was influenced by the anti-war, women's liberation, and **counterculture** movements taking place in many Western countries. **Feminist** literature, such as Simone de Beauvoir's *The Second Sex* and Betty Friedan's *The Feminine Mystique,* drew people's attention to women's issues. Social expectations about family size and personal lifestyles were also changing. The high birth rates

of the postwar years were replaced by declining rates in the 1960s. With the availability of the birth control pill, women had greater control over their own sexuality and had more reproductive choices.

In the 1960s, most Canadian women lived within the boundaries of the traditional family structure. Men were the primary wage earners while most women stayed home to raise their families. Those who worked outside the home were usually confined to "female" positions such as secretary, teacher, and nurse. Women were paid less than men even if they were doing the same work. In all aspects of life— social, political, legal, and cultural—women were treated as unequal to men.

Dissatisfaction with the **status quo** was beginning to grow. Women's groups across the country campaigned for equal rights, equal job opportunities, and an end to discrimination based on sex. The call for a federal inquiry came from the Committee for the Equality of Women (CEW), an organization formed in 1966 that represented 32 women's groups. Together with the Fédération des femmes du Québec (FFQ), and under the leadership of Laura Sabia, the CEW lobbied for a Royal Commission on the Status of Women. Prime Minister Lester Pearson's government agreed and established the commission in 1967.

Towards Equal Status

The commission was given a broad mandate "to inquire and report upon the status of women in Canada, and to recommend what steps might be taken by the federal government to ensure for women equal opportunities with men in all aspects of Canadian society." Under the leadership of Florence Bird, a feminist broadcaster and journalist from Ottawa, the commission began its investigations in the spring of 1968. It examined the issues that most affected women and held public hearings across the country. In all, 468 briefs were heard and 1000 letters were received expressing the

In 1996, Joan Grant-Cummings (centre) was elected the new president of the National Action Committee.

widespread problems experienced by Canadian women from all walks of life.

The commission's report was tabled in the House of Commons in December 1970. It contained 167 recommendations for improving the status of women in Canada, the last chapter outlining structures needed to implement the recommendations. These included an agency to continue the work of the commission and "create a favourable climate for equality of opportunity for the women of Canada." As a result, the National Action Committee on the Status of Women (NAC) was founded in 1973. Other new offices included a portfolio for the Status of Women in the federal Cabinet (1971) and an Advisory Council on the Status of Women (1973). As a result of the commission's report, several federal statutes were amended to remove sections that were discriminatory to women. The Canadian Labour Code (1971), for example, ensured women equal wages with men if they were employed "in the same industrial establishment...performing, under the same or similar working conditions, the same or similar work on jobs requiring the same or similar skill, effort, and responsibility." In 1972, sections of the Canadian Criminal Code pertaining to jury

duty were also amended; women became liable for jury duty on the same terms as men. The law now stated: "No person may be disqualified, exempted or excused from serving as a grand or petit juror in criminal proceedings on the grounds of his or her sex...."

The Royal Commission on the Status of Women was a consciousness-raising exercise for all Canadians. While it drew much-needed attention to the status of women in Canada, many of these

problems persist today. Women still face discrimination in the workplace and earn less money than men. They are more likely than men to live in poverty and suffer from physical, mental, and sexual abuse. Participation rates for women in politics continue to be proportionately low. While some gains have been made, there is much to be done before Canadian women enjoy truly equal status with men.

The Wage Gap

Average Annual Earnings[1] (Full-time, Full-year Workers)

	Women $	Men $	Earnings Ratio[2] %
1967	17 760	30 405	58.4
1972	22 267	37 222	59.8
1977	24 944	40 198	62.1
1982	25 087	39 198	64.0
1987	26 331	39 808	65.1
1992	29 032	40 383	71.9
1993	28 580	39 572	72.2
1994	28 423	40 717	69.8

[1] Expressed in constant 1994 dollars.
[2] Represents women's earnings as a percentage of those of men.
Statistics Canada, Catalogue 13-217. Used with permission of the Minister of Industry, 1998, as Minister responsible for Statistics Canada.

Using the statistics in the table above, create a bar graph showing average annual earnings of men and women for each of the years indicated. From your bar graph, identify the patterns that emerge. Suggest reasons for these patterns.

◄▣ MAKING CONNECTIONS ▣►

1. Are there any issues within your school that would benefit from a "consciousness-raising" investigation? Identify one issue, and design an investigation kit that will raise consciousness in your school. Your kit could include pamphlets, posters, articles or ads in the school newspaper, etc.

2. Divide into groups according to gender, and conduct a debate about "the equality of the sexes."

KEYWORDS

counterculture

feminism

status quo

Researchers use information from human experience and from statistics to examine social issues. How do researchers gather relevant information from appropriate sources?

Two Types of Research

Research into social issues can be divided into two main categories: qualitative and quantitative. Qualitative research seeks information that comes from human experience. The purpose of such research is to increase our understanding of a society, an economy, or a political system. It uses narrative accounts of history that describe the impact of events and social issues on people's lives. Quantitative research uses numerical **data** as the basis for its investigations. Researchers gather information about the amount of raw materials or goods produced, the value of a nation's imports or exports, the size of cities, or the number of people who voted in a particular election. These values are said to be "measures" that not only describe but also "qualify" what is happening in a nation or community. Historians often concern themselves with how these measures change over time, seeing the data as a record of a nation's growth or development. For example, on page 241, quantitative data, in the form of **statistics**, were used to measure the changing role of women in Canadian society.

Established in 1918 as the Dominion Bureau of Statistics, Statistics Canada is the country's central statistical agency. StatsCan, as it is commonly known, is a government agency that works with government departments to develop integrated social and economic statistics for Canada and the provinces. StatsCan is charged with meeting the statistical needs of all levels of government and the private sector for research, policy formulation, decision making, and general information. Economists like René Morissette analyse much of the data.

Qualitative Research

Qualitative research relies to a great extent on interviews, diaries, journals, and other personal stories. Qualitative researchers are aware that such accounts are, to some degree, biased or distorted. However, this aspect of the account is not a problem to be overcome; instead, it is part of the information to be obtained. Qualitative researchers do not attempt to distance themselves from the subjects of their studies or from the information they gather. When presenting their results, they ensure that their own biases and points of view are made clear. For example, when the Royal Commission on the Status of Women was being conducted in the late 1960s, the commissioners received hundreds of **briefs** and letters from individuals and citizen's groups about the plight of women in Canada. Many of these reports were in the form of qualitative information. Women told the commissioners about the challenges they faced as women in Canada. They were often very personal accounts that could not be quantified statistically but that nevertheless spoke of the inequality and discrimination women were then experiencing across the country. Such information was invaluable to the Royal Commission.

Employment Levels of Women Versus That of Men

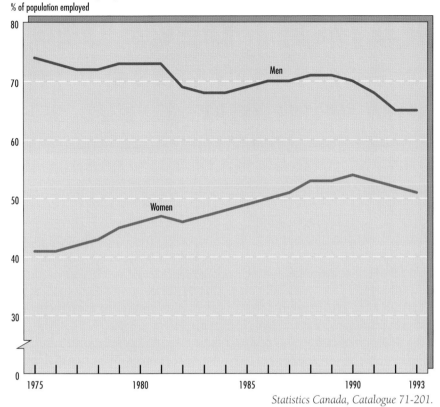

% of population employed

Statistics Canada, Catalogue 71-201.

Quantitative research is especially useful in tracking change and progress over time. Among the most pronounced social and economic changes in the Canadian labour force in the past two decades has been the increase in women's employment. This graph illustrates the levels of employment for men and women from 1975 to 1993. Describe the changes in employment levels in the graph. What factors might account for the relative drop in men's employment since 1975? What do you think accounts for the relative rise in women's employment in that same period?

Quantitative Research

Quantitative research uses numbers and mathematical methods to examine issues and report findings. Much of the data presented in social science research today appears in the form of statistics. Statistical data are gathered by economists, sociologists, political scientists, and geographers in order to find patterns of human behaviour or to predict future social and economic trends.

Statistics, placed in context, can help researchers in many ways by providing discoveries, explanations, insights, predictions, and confirmations. For the commissioners on the Royal Commission on the Status of Women, statistics became a useful measure of women's position in Canadian society. The commission's report included various statistical charts, graphs, and tables dealing with such issues as women's levels of income, employment, and education. Three decades after the report was published, we still use statistics effectively to measure the extent to which women's lives have changed or improved.

MAKING CONNECTIONS

1. a) Working in groups, explore a current social or economic issue at the local level—either school- or community-based. Divide your group in half. One half of the group should collect qualitative information about the topic by talking with the people involved and consulting available resources. The group should prepare a short report of its findings. The second half of the group should conduct a statistical survey using appropriate criteria. The group should compile its findings in the form of a chart or graph.

   b) Compare the findings from the qualitative and quantitative research. Are they similar? Different? What have you confirmed about your topic? What can you conclude? What predictions can you make? Present your findings to the class.

KEYWORDS

data

statistics

briefs

THE LIBERATION DECADE
Rejecting the Status Quo
FOCUSSING ON THE ISSUE

The decade of the 1960s was an era of significant social, political, cultural, and sexual revolution that dramatically altered Canadian society. It came to be called the "liberation" decade. How did the liberation decade change Canada?

The Counterculture

During the 1960s, baby boomers were coming of age in the new television era. Events like the Quiet Revolution in Quebec and the **civil rights movement** in the US were broadcast across the nation and caused many young Canadians to question the **status quo** in their society.

After the Cuban Missile Crisis (see page 220), many young people became angry that they had nearly become victims of events beyond their control. They began to reject the attitudes of their parents and challenged society's values and norms. Protests occurred over nuclear armament, war, American involvement in Canadian affairs,

and human rights for social groups, including Aboriginal peoples and African Canadians. Other young people rebelled by dropping out of society altogether. They quit schools and universities, left their jobs, and outwardly renounced mainstream society. Many preached global peace and love. Some set off across the country to "find themselves" and to discover meaning in their lives. Some experimented with drugs. Others went "back to the land" where they lived in communes and farmed organic produce. They were known as "hippies."

In the 1960s social revolt, young people rejected anything they considered to be part of the **establishment**—government, big business, and the values and mate-

rialism of their parents' generation. The more liberal child-rearing practices of the baby boom years (see page 190) had created a generation that expected more freedom. The civil rights and peace movements made young people aware of the failures of the existing order. Rock music reinforced these negative perceptions of the adult world. All of these new attitudes and trends reached mass audiences through the knowledge explosion created by television.

The new **counterculture** favoured bell bottoms, mini-skirts, beads, and long hair over the older generation's traditional style of dress. Many sought psychedelic experiences through the use of hallucinogens, such as LSD, mescaline, and hashish. The traditional family was rejected in favour of other arrangements, such as couples living together or groups of young people living in communes. The counterculture spawned music festivals, which reached their peak in the summer of 1969 at the Woodstock Festival in New York state. Drawn by the most famous rock musicians of the time, 450 000 young people camped in the rain for three days, enjoying music and camaraderie. The event was covered by all the major news media and became a symbol of solidarity for the sixties' generation.

The Woodstock Festival in August 1969 came to symbolize the counterculture movement.

Individual Rights

In the summer of 1960, the federal government distributed colourfully printed copies of the Canadian Bill of Rights, informing Canadians of the rights they possessed as citizens of a free and democratic society. In addition, several provincial governments passed human rights codes to prevent discrimination in housing and the workplace. As a result of these bills, Canadians became less willing to accept discrimination or to defer to authority and began insisting on their rights.

People under 30—nearly 50 per cent of the population—were most influenced by these developments. Men began to wear their hair longer; some grew beards, and most adopted more casual clothing styles. Although women's fashions had changed dramatically with the introduction of the mini-skirt and the pant suit, a combination of the youth revolution and the **feminist** movement released women from the decrees of the fashion world. Employers who fired employees for violating the company dress code were forced to reinstate their employees as a result of the Bill of Rights and the Human Rights Commission. University and high school students also demanded greater freedom in hair and clothing styles and pressured most public schools into abandoning their dress codes. Canadians were beginning to value the rights of the individual over the rights of society. "Doing your own thing" became the norm.

A Just Society

In Canada, Pierre Elliott Trudeau personified this new attitude. Elected as an MP in 1963 and appointed minister of justice in Lester Pearson's 1965 Cabinet, Trudeau introduced some controversial changes to Canadian divorce and criminal law. The grounds for divorce were expanded to include physical and mental cruelty and the new concept of marriage breakdown. Among the amendments to the criminal code was the removal of the **vagrancy** section, which allowed police to arrest anyone loitering on the streets. Since many hippies and wandering young people fit this category, there was agreement that standing on a corner with no money in your pocket did not make you a criminal. Other amendments provided for therapeutic abortions when approved by a hospital committee and removed the sections making it a crime to provide birth control information. Those sections dealing with homosexual acts between consenting adults were also removed. Trudeau's justification for these changes was that "the state has no business in the bedrooms of the nation."

In 1968, The Globe and Mail *offered this explanation of Trudeau's appeal: "It may be that what Canadians see in Mr. Trudeau is this new side to themselves, a readiness to gamble on the unknown, to move into areas not explored before."*

When Prime Minister Pearson retired in 1968, Trudeau, the charismatic, swinging bachelor, adopted a unique campaign style. He circulated among the crowds, shaking hands and kissing supporters. He advocated a "just society" that valued all Canadians. He had a particular connection with young people. Trudeaumania, a cross between political enthusiasm and rock-star frenzy, swept Trudeau into the prime minister's office and changed Canadian society.

KEYWORDS

civil rights movement

status quo

establishment

counterculture

feminist

vagrancy

⫸ MAKING CONNECTIONS ⫷

1. When large numbers of people adopt a new style— longer hair, for example—are they "doing their own thing" or following the crowd? How can you tell?

2. Much of the change during the liberation decade involved public morality. Who should dictate moral standards? Who does? Explain your answers.

THE NORTHWEST PASSAGE
Canadian Sovereignty in the Arctic
FOCUSSING ON THE ISSUE

In 1969, the oil tanker SS Manhattan *made a historic voyage through Arctic waters to determine if oil could be shipped safely through the Northwest Passage. The voyage was controversial. Do the waters of the Arctic belong to Canada, or are they international waters that should be accessible to all countries?*

Voyage of the *Manhattan*

During the past century, North Americans have looked to the Arctic as a source of oil and gas. While there are ample supplies of these fuels in the North, extreme weather and ice conditions make the drilling of wells expensive. In addition, there is the problem of how to transport the fuel to markets in the south without damaging the fragile Arctic environment.

The conventional means for transporting oil and gas over long distances is the supertanker. These monster vessels carry millions of tonnes of fuel across the world's oceans. In 1969, the Humble Oil Company of New Jersey wanted to find out if it was possible to use a specially built tanker to pioneer a route from the oil fields of Alaska through the **Northwest Passage** north of Canada. The SS *Manhattan* weighed 155 000 t. (The *Gjoa*, the first vessel to navigate the northern passage, weighed 47 t.) It had a double hull, which meant that if the outer hull was damaged by ice, its cargo would not leak into the water. For the test run, the *Manhattan* was not carrying any oil, but environmentalists and government officials were alarmed at the thought that one day it might.

The voyage of the *Manhattan* raised more than environmental concerns, however. It also raised the important political question of who owns the Arctic. The US argued that the Northwest Passage was an international strait and, as such, it was open to ships from all countries. Canada maintained that it controlled the Northwest Passage and was concerned that the Americans had not asked permission for the *Manhattan* to make the trip. For Canada, control of the Arctic waterways had other implications. If Canada did not control the waterways, would its claim to ownership of the Arctic islands be threatened as well?

Canada found a way to combine environmental concerns with political objectives. In 1970, the government passed the Arctic Waters Pollution Prevention Act. This established a **coastal zone** in which Canada asserted control over all shipping in order to protect the environment. In effect, the law claimed ownership of the area for Canada. When the *Manhattan* embarked on a second trip, it did so in the company of a Canadian icebreaker and followed Canadian safety standards.

As it turned out, the oil companies decided that supertankers were not a practical method of transporting oil from the Arctic, so the idea

The American oil tanker Manhattan *was accompanied by the Canadian icebreaker* Sir John A. Macdonald *as it made its way through the Northwest Passage.*

was shelved. Instead they built a pipeline to carry oil from Prudhoe Bay on the north coast across Alaska to the ice-free port of Valdez, from where tankers transported the oil south.

Who Owns the Arctic?

In 1985, a US Coast Guard ship, the *Polar Sea*, made a voyage through the Northwest Passage from Greenland west to Alaska. The American government informed Canada about the trip and said that Canadian officials could come onboard. While it promised to abide by the pollution act passed in 1970, the American government continued to argue that its vessel did not need Canadian permission to make the trip. As a way of asserting its claim, Canada announced that it was giving permission to the *Polar Sea* to make the journey anyway. "It is ours," Prime Minister Joe Clark said about the Arctic. "We assert **sovereignty** over it."

Eventually, tempers cooled and Canada and the United States

In 1989, the oil tanker Exxon Valdez ran aground on the coast of Alaska with a full cargo of oil onboard. It was just the sort of accident that people had feared might happen in the Canadian Arctic. Exxon spent over $1 billion on a massive clean-up operation, but the oil damaged and killed birds and sea mammals, contaminated the local fishery, and left chemical residues in the environment that will last for years to come.

worked out a compromise on the *Polar Sea* voyage. Nevertheless, on the deeper issue of who owns the Arctic, the two countries do not agree. The US remains reluctant to admit that the Northwest Passage is not an international waterway, open to anyone.

The question of who owns the Arctic waterways is compounded by the fact that Aboriginal peoples also contend that they own the North. Aboriginal land claims are being

negotiated with the federal government. (See page 346.) It may turn out that Canada's strongest claim to the Arctic in the international arena may be that its Aboriginal peoples have occupied the area since before recorded history began.

(See page 346.)

◄▣ MAKING CONNECTIONS ▣►

1. What controversies might arise from transporting oil by tanker and pipeline? Explain.

2. Why does it matter whether or not Canada has sovereignty over the Arctic waterways? Explain your answer.

KEYWORDS

Northwest Passage

coastal zone

sovereignty

GREENPEACE
Raising Public Awareness
FOCUSSING ON THE ISSUE

From its origins in Vancouver in 1970, Greenpeace has become one of the largest environmental groups in the world. How do protest groups like Greenpeace influence the political system?

A Movement Begins

It was to be a classic "David-meets-Goliath" situation. On Amchitka Island in the North Pacific, the United States was preparing to detonate a nuclear bomb as part of its testing program. Meanwhile, in Vancouver, a small group of protesters boarded a leaky old fishing boat called the *Phyllis Cormack*. They were set to sail right into the middle of the test site and dare the American government to blow them up. It was September 1970. The group called themselves Greenpeace. No one had ever heard of them, yet they were challenging the most powerful country in the world. "Our goal is a very simple, clear, and direct one," said one of the Greenpeacers, "to bring about a confrontation between the people of death and the people of life."

The confrontation never took place. The *Phyllis Cormack* had to turn back to avoid winter storms. The Americans went ahead with their test. However, Greenpeace's efforts attracted so much publicity and generated so many protests that the US announced it would cease nuclear testing in the North Pacific.

With the success of its first campaign, Greenpeace experienced dramatic growth. Donations flooded in from around the world. Soon it was no longer a small group of activists in Vancouver, but a large organization with branch offices around the globe. Greenpeace began to acquire a fleet of vessels, which it used to carry out protests against the killing of seals and whales, French nuclear testing in the South Pacific, and the dumping of **toxic waste** in the ocean. The Amchitka episode showed that

Greenpeace members were willing to risk their own lives. Their campaign to stop commercial whaling was another case in point. Protesters climbed into small rubber boats and placed themselves between the whales and the whale hunters. If the hunters wanted to kill the whales, they had to fire their harpoons through the protesters first. Thanks to tactics like this, Greenpeace managed to focus world attention on the whale hunt, leading eventually in the mid-1980s to a **moratorium** on the killing.

If Greenpeace tactics were brave, they were also clever. Members knew that their dramatic acts of protest attracted the attention of the media, and through the media the attention of the public. They calculated that by publicizing what was going on—whether it was the slaughter of seals and whales, the destruction of forests, or one of countless other issues—they would ignite public opinion and bring about change.

Not everyone approves of Greenpeace. In British Columbia, for instance, large forestry companies have accused the organization of spreading misleading information about logging. Some people think they are publicity seekers who favour confrontation over negotiation. However, there is no denying the impact that Greenpeace has had on raising the level of public con-

Greenpeace protesters in a rubber zodiac try to convince Russian whalers to give up the hunt. Suggest why photographs like this are as important to Greenpeace as the protests themselves.

cern about the environment around the world.

Interest Groups

Greenpeace is an example of a special interest group. There are many such groups involved in the political process in Canada. Unlike political parties, they work outside the electoral system to try to influence government policy. Interest groups are usually organized around a particular issue or set of issues and are not as broadly based as political parties. In the case of Greenpeace, its focus is environmental issues. Other groups confine themselves to gun control, or violence against women, or health issues, or racism, or any of the many other issues that concern Canadians.

Special interest groups use a variety of tactics to influence the public and the government. They write letters to the prime minister, to Members of Parliament, or to local politicians. They make submissions to hearings or council meetings. They write articles for the local press. They hold protests aimed at raising public awareness. They convince celebrities to support them, which attracts the attention of the media. They may even launch a court case to try to stop whatever action they oppose. These are just some of the strategies that an interest group might employ to publicize its cause.

VIEWPOINTS

CREATING CHANGE

Members of Greenpeace did not intend to stop the whale hunt or the seal hunt one animal at a time. What they wanted to do was to publicize the hunts so that people around the world would know that they were happening. They wanted to harness the power of mass communications to do their work for them. Bob Hunter, a co-founder of Greenpeace, explains:

How can any rational person convince himself that there is the ghost of a chance of having even the most minute impact on world events? The answer is simply the existence of a planet-wide mass-communications system, something that had never existed before. Its development was the most radical change to have happened since the planet was created, for at its ultimate point it gives access to the collective mind of the species that now controls the planet's fate. One person can now command the attention of the world. One group—such as Greenpeace—could do the same. In my own mind, it seemed crystal clear that awareness itself is the cure. If a mass awareness devel-

oped about the seal problem, the problem would be solved. If crazy stunts were required in order to draw the focus of the cameras that led back into millions and millions of brains, then crazy stunts were what we would do. For in the moment of drawing the mass camera's fire, vital new perceptions would pass into the minds out there that we wanted to reach. Mass media is a way of making millions bear witness at a time. If we use our brains, we can trigger a revolutionary change in the consciousness of humanity.

Robert Hunter, Warriors of the Rainbow (New York: *Holt, Rinehart & Winston,* 1979) pp. 252–3.

1. Publicity "stunts" are sometimes dismissed as trivial. Robert Hunter thinks they are vital for a protest group. Explain his reasoning.
2. What does "bearing witness" mean? Explain whether or not you agree that if the public knows about a problem, it will do something about it.

MAKING CONNECTIONS

1. Working in a group, select one environmental issue, then organize a peaceful protest campaign. Create catchy slogans and display them on placards, posters, or banners.

KEYWORDS

toxic waste

moratorium

THE OCTOBER CRISIS
Challenging Canadian Democracy

FOCUSSING ON THE ISSUE

Political violence came to Quebec and Canada in the 1960s. What prompts some people to resort to violence as the means to bring about change? Was the federal government's response of invoking the War Measures Act justified?

The FLQ first launched its terrorist campaign with bombings, like this mail box bomb in Montreal in 1963.

Terrorism Comes to Canada

The Quiet Revolution brought about deep social and economic changes in Quebec society. At the same time, during the 1960s some Quebeckers began to believe that their province should separate from the rest of the country. Most **separatists** were willing to work for change peacefully through the political system. But a tiny number of them grew impatient and chose to work for change outside the law.

Canadians were used to news reports about acts of terrorism around the world. Bombings, kidnappings, and assassinations happened with regularity, but always somewhere else, somewhere far away. But in the 1960s, terrorism came to Canada when the Front de Libération du Québec, known as the FLQ, launched a terrorist campaign in Quebec. While it consisted of only a few dozen people, the FLQ carried out a string of bombings and hold-ups, mainly in Montreal. In 1963, a bomb placed in a trash can behind an army recruiting centre exploded, killing a security officer. Later that year, bombs began appearing in mailboxes in an English-speaking district of the city. One blew up, killing an army bomb-disposal expert. In 1964, the FLQ robbed a firearms company and killed one of the executives. Members began robbing banks, stealing dynamite from construction sites, and training with terrorist groups in other countries. In 1968, the FLQ planted a bomb at the Montreal Stock Exchange that injured 27 people.

The FLQ was organized as a collection of small **cells**, each consisting of a few members. One cell did not necessarily know what the other cells were doing. This made it difficult for the authorities to break up the organization. By 1969, political violence in Quebec had reached a new high. The FLQ announced that it was going to adopt a new tactic—kidnapping politicians and important officials. Canada was poised for a serious challenge to democracy.

Kidnapped

On 5 October 1970, members of the FLQ kidnapped James Cross, the British trade commissioner, from his home. The FLQ then sent communiqués to the media; they threatened to kill Cross and demanded the release of 23 people who were in prison for terrorist acts. Politicians in Ottawa appeared willing to negotiate to give police time to locate the kidnappers and Cross. As a concession to the kidnappers, the government allowed the FLQ **manifesto** to be broadcast publicly. The manifesto argued that in Quebec the English minority held all positions of power and influence, while the French majority was disadvantaged. Though they disagreed with the FLQ's tactics, many people agreed with its analysis of the situation in Quebec.

The Quebec government announced that it would not release any prisoners. It offered instead to allow the kidnappers safe passage to another country if they released Cross. Minutes after this announcement, another FLQ cell abducted Pierre Laporte, the Quebec minister of labour, while he was playing football on his lawn with his children.

These actions caused panic to sweep the province. Government ministers sent their families into hiding out of the province. Premier Robert Bourassa and his Cabinet moved into a hotel amidst tight security. A letter was received from Laporte, pleading for his life. Meanwhile, a group of prominent Quebeckers, worried that the federal government would send in the army to deal with the crisis, issued a declaration in support of a negotiated solution. In Ottawa, Prime Minister Pierre Trudeau viewed this as a sign of weakness and his government deployed Canadian soliders in and around Quebec City, Montreal, and Ottawa to assist police.

On 16 October, the federal government announced that, because of a state of "apprehended insurrection" in Quebec, it was invoking the War Measures Act. This would give authorities the power to arrest without warrant anyone suspected of being connected to the FLQ. Over the next few days, hundreds of people were jailed. (In the end, only 20 were actually convicted of any crime.)

On 17 October, Pierre Laporte's body was discovered in the trunk of a car. Police found Cross, who was released after 59 days in captivity. In exchange for his release, five kidnappers received safe passage to Cuba. Four men—Paul Rose, his brother Jacques, Francis Simard, and Bernard Lortie—were arrested and convicted of Pierre Laporte's murder. The crisis and fear had lasted three months, ending only in January 1971 when the army withdrew from Quebec.

Was the War Measures Act Justified?

In the months and years following the October Crisis, Canadians debated whether or not the government was justified in invoking the War Measures Act and suspending **civil liberties**. In hindsight, the threat to the government of Quebec was limited. The majority of people who were arrested were released without charge. The FLQ itself numbered only a handful of people, and the police already had the authority to deal with their criminal acts. A prominent federal Cabinet minister, Gérard Pelletier, later admitted that "we used a cannon to shoot at a fly." Some Quebeckers suspected that Trudeau had used the crisis as an opportunity to smash the legal separatist movement in the province by jailing and intimidating its members.

On the other hand, public opinion supported Trudeau's decision. A poll taken at the time showed that 87 per cent of Canadians, both French- and English-speaking, supported the

Political violence was a new phenomenon in Canada. Members of the FLQ believed it was the only way to achieve their goals. The prime minister, on the other hand, was determined to squelch all terrorist tactics.

*The ruling class has social responsibility only for its own interests. It doesn't give a damn about the 90 percent of the population who have nothing to say and no decisions to make in "their" democracy. The workers have already wasted too much time waiting for the "conversion" of those who have always robbed them and scoffed at them. The workers have already been deceived too many times by all the "pure" men of traditional politics...The workers and all the clear-thinking people of Quebec must take their responsibilities in hand and stop relying on the Messiahs who are periodically thrown up by the system to fool the "ignorant." Of course it isn't easy....But determination can overcome anything at last, even the dictatorship of **capitalism** over the bodies and minds of the majority of Québécois. It is the responsibility of the workers of Quebec to learn to stand erect and to demand, to take what rightfully belongs to them. For it is abnormal, unjust, and inhuman that the economic and political power which governs the entire life of the workers should belong not to the workers themselves but to others....*

*Let us burn the papier-mâché traditions with which they have tried to build a myth around our slavery. Let us learn the pride of being men. Let us vigorously declare our independence. And with our hardy freedom, let us crush the sympathetic or contemptuous **paternalism** of the politicians, the daddy-bosses and the preachers of defeat and submission....There will be no miracles, but there will be war.*

FLQ member Pierre Vallières, "White Niggers of America," Monthly Review Press, 1970, pp. 18-20.

*I had been fighting separatist ideology for years without once considering asking the police for assistance. As long as the **secessionists** limited themselves to democratic methods to promote Quebec's withdrawal from the country, there was never any question of putting the police on their trail. But the moment they resorted to using bombs, or theft, or assassination attempts, we were no longer dealing with democratic opposition, and it became our duty to hunt them down, or at least to identify them, so that we could put an end to their criminal activities. At the time, not only were they increasing their own illegal pursuits, they were also encouraging others to do the same. The FLQ was inciting **militants** to infiltrate the Parti Québécois and other peaceful political organizations, as well as the public service and the provincial government. How successful their campaign had been we could not be sure, but we had to find out, using every means the law put at our disposal, who it was who was promoting violence....It is the duty of any democracy to protect itself against the forces of dissolution as soon as they raise their heads.*

Pierre Trudeau, Memoirs, (Toronto: McClelland & Stewart, 1993), p. 132.

1. According to Pierre Vallières, why did the FLQ adopt illegal tactics in their struggle to bring about change in Quebec?
2. According to Trudeau, in a democratic society what is the limit beyond which dissent and opposition can no longer by tolerated? Explain the distinction he makes between the FLQ and other separatist groups.

use of the War Measures Act. Trudeau was adamant that his decision was justified. In 1993, he wrote:

The emergence of the FLQ and its terrorist activities had been threatening the Quebec economy for years.

*Corporations hesitated to invest in the province, certain industries that had intended to locate factories in Quebec decided to look elsewhere. Our response to the FLQ prevented the situation from deteriorating further into **recession**, and avoided wide-scale unem-*

*ployment that would have created much social hardship, leading perhaps to **anarchy** and a general disaffection with the workings of democracy.*

Pierre Trudeau, Memoirs (Toronto: McClelland & Stewart, 1993).

Soldiers guarded a public building in Montreal during the height of the October Crisis. Why were troops sent to Quebec? How do you think Canadians reacted to such scenes taking place in their country?

MAKING CONNECTIONS

1. What did the government mean by an "apprehended insurrection"? What evidence was there that such a situation existed?

2. Do you believe there are ever circumstances in which it is appropriate for the government to suspend civil liberties? What are those circumstances? Do you think the government's actions were justified during the October Crisis? Explain.

KEYWORDS

separatist

terrorism

cell

manifesto

civil liberties

recession

anarchy

CANADIAN FOLK MUSIC
A Reflection of Changing Times

Canada has a strong folk music tradition with songs that reveal a great deal about us as a nation. What ideas were Canadian songwriters addressing in the 1960s? How did their music contribute to Canadian identity?

The Times, They Were A-Changin'

The 1960s in Canada was a decade of rapid change, marked by the quest for personal liberation and freedom from the restrictions of authority and tradition. Canadians witnessed unprecedented affluence, the women's liberation movement, mounting concern about the environment, **nationalism** (in response to Quebec's growing dissatisfaction within Confederation and to

American cultural domination), and disturbing international confrontations.

Against this backdrop of profound change, Canadian popular music flourished—particularly folk music. While it had always played a large role in Canadian music, folk music experienced a revival in the 1960s as its predominantly white musicians and audiences gathered in coffee houses and music clubs across the country. Influenced by American folk music legends like

Pete Seeger and **counterculture** prophets like Bob Dylan, Canadian folk music expressed the protests, fears, and hopes of the younger generation. Its goal was to preserve the legend and **lore** of the common people, and its themes were truth, sincerity, and authenticity. As such, it was well suited to the issues and values of the day. Folk music appealed to Canadians because it fostered national identity and expressed hope for solutions to serious problems.

BIOGRAPHY: GORDON LIGHTFOOT

Born 17 November 1938, in Orillia, Ontario, Gordon Lightfoot became one of Canada's most prolific and distinctive Canadian folk musicians. His songs often evoked the beauty of the land or the wilderness of the heart. One of Lightfoot's most enduring songs, "The Canadian Railroad Trilogy," was commissioned by the CBC in 1967 for the Centennial celebration. In the lyrics, Lightfoot demonstrates his role as a balladeer of Canadian history as he reflects on the building of the railway:

There was a time in this fair land when the railroad did not run,
When the wild majestic mountains stood alone against the sun.
Long before the white man, and long before the wheel
When the green dark forest was too silent to be real.

Gordon Lightfoot, "Canadian Railroad Trilogy," 1967 & 1969, Warner Bros. Inc.—from the album The Way I Feel, 1969
© 1996 Moose Music Inc.
Used by permission.

BIOGRAPHY: JONI MITCHELL

Joni Mitchell was born Roberta Joan Anderson on 7 November 1943, in Fort McLeod, Alberta. With her wispy voice and poetic lyrics, she came to personify the free spirit of the 1960s. An art student turned folk singer, Mitchell performed at coffee houses and music clubs in Toronto, Detroit, and New York during the mid-1960s. Her music was characterized by confessional songs about love, but she also drew from nature for her inspiration. "Woodstock," Mitchell's song about the massive music and art fair in Woodstock, New York (see page 244), has been described as a counterculture anthem of the 1960s. Another of her songs, "Big Yellow Taxi," expresses disillusionment at the cost of urban redevelopment:

. . . They took all the trees
And put them in a tree museum
And they charged the people
A dollar and a half just to see 'em
Don't it always seem to go
That you don't know what you've got
Till it's gone
They paved paradise
And put up a parking lot.

Joni Mitchell, "Big Yellow Taxi," 1970 & 1974
Siquomb Publishing Corp. (BMI)—from the
album Ladies of the Canyon.
Reprinted by permission.

Distinctly Canadian

Among the most successful Canadian folk musicians of the decade were Gordon Lightfoot and Joni Mitchell. Although their musical styles and motivations may have differed, their work is important for what it reveals about Canadian society in the decade of Expo '67, women's liberation, the Vietnam War, and the hippie movement.

Canadian folk music of the 1960s was influenced not only by the musical traditions that preceded it but also by the changing times. The music of artists like Gordon Lightfoot and Joni Mitchell in turn influenced many people who considered folk music a valuable interpreter of the times. In popular music as in other mass media, Canadians were exploring new emotions and attitudes. Folk music helped Canadians to look at themselves as they were as well to reflect on who they might become.

MAKING CONNECTIONS

1. Gordon Lightfoot has remained a resident of Canada virtually all of his life, while Joni Mitchell moved to the US early in her music career. In your view, do these facts influence the degree to which their music can be considered truly Canadian? Explain.

2. To what extent do you think music can help to form the soul of a nation? Did Canadian folk music of the 1960s help to shape the soul of the country? Explain your answer.

KEYWORDS

nationalism

counterculture

lore

UNIT 8:

Janet Mitchell, *A Day in the Street* (1978)

Janet Mitchell (1915-1998) studied at Alberta's Provincial Institute of Technology and Art and at the Banff School of Fine Art. Her work is characterized by abstract figures and bright overlapping colours.

EMERGING TRENDS

1971-1980

	Social	Cultural	Political	Legal	Economic	Environmental
SHIFTING RELATIONS The World in 1971 258			✔		✔	✔
WHO OWNS CANADA? The Foreign Ownership Debate ... 260			✔		✔	
THE FEDERAL GOVERNMENT The Legislative Branch 262			✔	✔		
PROVINCIAL GOVERNMENTS Powers and Responsibilities 264			✔	✔		
WESTERN ALIENATION Sources of Discontent 266		✔	✔		✔	✔
ARCTIC PIPELINE The Berger Commission 268		✔	✔			✔
MULTICULTURALISM Opposing Viewpoints 270		✔				
WOMEN'S RIGHTS Making Progress 272	✔		✔	✔	✔	
ABORIGINAL AFFAIRS New Directions 274		✔	✔			
ACID PRECIPITATION Cross-border Pollution 276			✔			✔
HAMILTON Creating Economic Diversity 278					✔	✔
NUCLEAR ENERGY An Ongoing Debate 280					✔	✔
THE OLYMPICS Controversy in Montreal 282	✔		✔			
POLITICS AND IMAGE The Power of the Media 284	✔	✔	✔			
SKILL BUILDER Analysing the News * 286	✔	✔	✔			
REFERENDUM Independence or Federalism? 288		✔	✔	✔		

*Skills and Processes

SHIFTING RELATIONS
The World in 1971
FOCUSSING ON THE ISSUE

In the 1970s, the Cold War began to thaw, while the politics of oil became a burning issue. What led to this shift in international relations?

The Cold War Thaws

The 1970s was marked by a shift in the pattern of international relations. Old Cold War conflicts lost some of their urgency. The war in Vietnam drew to a close. The United States and the Soviet Union settled into an era of **détente** as they began to discuss reductions in the size of their nuclear weapons arsenals. For a while the world breathed a little easier.

One of the most surprising developments in international relations was between the United States and communist China. Ever since Mao Zedong and the communists had emerged victorious from the Chinese civil war in 1949, the US had refused to recognize the People's Republic of China. Instead, the Americans regarded the nationalist government of Jiang Jie Shi, in exile on the island of Taiwan, as the legitimate government of China.

In 1971, Canada was first among Western countries to recognize Mao's regime in Beijing as the legitimate government. That same year, the People's Republic of China was admitted to the United Nations, replacing Taiwan, which had occupied China's UN seat for the past 22 years. While these events were unfolding, American secretary of state Henry Kissinger was making secret visits to Beijing in an effort to normalize relations between the US and China. His mission was aided by the fact that

relations between China and its former Cold War ally, the Soviet Union, were deteriorating. In 1973, the United States officially recognized Mao's government, and President Richard Nixon visited China. It was especially ironic that Nixon, known throughout his career as an anti-communist, was the US president who opened the door to China, one of the two communist superpowers.

The Politics of Oil

As Cold War alliances shifted and strained, a new source of international conflict emerged: oil. As the 1970s began, inflation plagued the industrialized world. Prices were on the rise, in part because of the

Vietnam War, but also because of an increase in oil prices. Oil-producing countries in the Middle East—long dominated by foreign-owned oil companies—began to take control of their resources, which were in great demand in energy-hungry North America.

Islamic oil-producing countries of the Persian Gulf region also saw petroleum as a weapon in their conflict with Israel. After Israel defeated several Arab states in the Yom Kippur War in 1973, the Arab-dominated Organization of Petroleum Exporting Countries (OPEC) retaliated by launching an oil **embargo** against the West. The drastically reduced flow of oil and the need to generate revenue forced the price of a barrel of crude oil to

The oil shortage was felt by consumers at the gas pumps, where prices in the US suddenly tripled. Because gas was in short supply, drivers sometimes had to wait for hours in long lineups to refill their tanks. Angry motorists fought over access to dwindling supplies. Highway speed limits were reduced to conserve gas. In Canada, the crisis was less severe because the government intervened to keep the price of fuel from skyrocketing.

jump from $8 in 1972 to more than $40 in 1974. This in turn led to a general increase of prices throughout the economy. The skyrocketing inflation that followed led the United States, Canada, and several European countries to introduce **wage-and-price controls** in an effort to contain it.

Consequences

The sharp rise in oil prices and the long lines at gasoline stations spurred new oil exploration. **Oil sands** development became more viable with the higher energy prices. Car makers began to manufacture smaller, more fuel-efficient cars. Better insulation in homes and buildings further reduced energy consumption. By the end of the decade, these measures had created a worldwide oil glut, and consequently, a drop in prices.

The crisis demonstrated the interdependence of the world economy and the dependence of industrial countries on fossil fuels. This encouraged new research into alternative sources of energy such as solar power. Mishaps in the oil industry also focussed attention on the fragile nature of marine **ecosystems**. Most of the world's oil is shipped in huge oil tankers. In addition, many oil deposits lie offshore beneath the ocean floor and must be extracted using huge drilling platforms. During the 1970s, several major oil spills resulted from accidents involving oil tankers or drilling platforms. This led to a growing realization that humans were seriously damaging the environment and threatening the planet's survival. This marked the emergence of the environmental movement as an international force.

EARTH DAY

Earth Day, observed internationally on 22 April, emphasizes the need to manage and protect the world's natural resources and habitats for **sustainable development**. Since its proclamation in 1970, Earth Day has become a major educational and media event in many countries. In schools, public marches, demonstrations, and academic forums, people focus their attention on the environmental problems facing our planet: the polluting of air, water, and soil; the destruction of natural habitats; the extinction of countless plant and animal species; and the depletion of our **nonrenewable resources**. Some of the solutions that Earth Day activities promote include:

- reducing consumption
- reusing or recycling manufactured materials
- conserving fuel and energy
- banning the use of chemicals and biological agents
- halting the destruction of major habitats such as rainforests and wetlands, and
- protecting endangered species.

1. a) How is Earth Day marked in your school? In your community?
   b) In your everyday activities, what are *you* doing to make the planet a better, more sustainable world?

MAKING CONNECTIONS

1. a) What reasons did the United States have for seeking friendlier relations with the People's Republic of China?
   b) How would you characterize the state of relations between China and Western countries today? What is the nature of Canada's current relationship with China?

2. List three ways in which the effects of the oil crisis of the 1970s are reflected in the world today.

KEYWORDS

détente

embargo

wage-and-price controls

oil sands

ecosystem

sustainable development

nonrenewable resources

WHO OWNS CANADA?
The Foreign Ownership Debate

FOCUSSING ON THE ISSUE

Canada has always relied on money from investors outside the country to finance its development. During the 1970s, foreign investment became a contentious political issue. In what way did it seem to threaten Canadian independence?

A Branch-plant Economy

The Canadian population has not been large enough, or wealthy enough, to pay for its own economic development. Instead, it has relied on money from foreign sources to fuel the country's growth. Early in the century, most of this foreign investment came from Britain. It was mainly British investors, for example, who financed the construction of the Canadian Pacific Railway during the 1880s. By the middle of the twentieth century, however, the trend had changed as investment from the United States now bankrolled the Canadian economy.

American investment differed from earlier foreign investment in a significant way. For the most part, British investors had simply put their money into Canadian enterprises and were content to collect profits and dividends from their investments. American investors, on the other hand, tended to buy up Canadian businesses or to establish their own **branch plants**. This meant that the actual control of a significant portion of the economy passed into foreign hands.

By 1972, 99 per cent of the petroleum and coal industries were foreign owned, as was 95 per cent of the book-publishing industry, 82 per cent of the chemical products industry, 67 per cent of the mining industry, and so on. Almost all of this foreign ownership was American. No other country in the world was experiencing such a level of foreign economic control.

Pierre Trudeau's Liberal government became alarmed as the evidence of foreign economic control mounted. Between 1968 and 1972, three government reports warned that the trend was a dangerous one. It was by no means just the Liberals who were concerned. Within the New Democratic Party, a small group of activists calling itself the Waffle condemned Canada's business class for failing to maintain control of the economy. The Waffle favoured widespread public ownership of important industries as a means of regaining control. (The Waffle proved to be too extreme for its own party, however. Ostracized by the NDP leadership, it formed its own organization for a while, then disappeared from politics.)

Meanwhile, outside the traditional political parties, a **nonpartisan** group of **economic nationalists** came together in 1971 to form the Committee for an Independent Canada. Its purpose was to lobby the government to curb foreign ownership.

The Government's Response

The federal government responded to concerns about foreign investment by taking steps to control it.

American oil companies have set up their Canadian headquarters in Calgary. Why might such a heavy concentration of American foreign ownership have been a uniquely Canadian experience?

One of the leading economic nationalists in Canada was Walter Gordon, a federal Liberal Cabinet minister and author of one of the reports that urged the government to curb foreign ownership. Gordon explained why he was concerned about American investment.

Already, in my view, we have surrendered too much ownership and control of our natural resources and our key industries to foreign owners, notably those in the United States. And history has taught us that with economic control inevitably goes political control. This is what colonialism is all about. Indeed, it is sadly ironic that in a world torn asunder by countries who are demanding and winning their independence, our free, independent, and highly developed country should be haunted by the spectre of a colonial or semi-colonial future.

Toronto Star Weekly, 1 July 1967.

1. Why did Gordon think that Canada was becoming a colony of the US? What connection is he making between economic control and political power? Do you agree?

One suggestion made by economic nationalists was that the government "buy back" control of important industries. To this end, Trudeau established the Canada Development Corporation in 1971. The CDC was supposed to buy and manage companies using money invested by the government and private Canadian investors. Two years later, Trudeau created the Foreign Investment Review Agency (FIRA) to approve foreign takeovers of Canadian companies and to screen the creation of new companies by foreign owners. Then, in 1975, the government created a new petroleum company, Petro-Canada, to compete with the large, foreign-owned oil firms.

These moves ultimately did little to stop foreign involvement in the Canadian economy, mainly because the new agencies had limited real power. The government feared that taking dramatic measures might hurt the economy. They were supported by industrial and business leaders in the country, who argued that foreign investment was crucial to create new industries—and therefore jobs—and to maintain Canada's high standard of living. By and large, the government agreed with them, and this was reflected in its policies.

By the early 1980s, following a drastic economic downturn, the issue of foreign ownership had fallen to the bottom of the national agenda. Tough times were no time to be talking about measures that might cost jobs, reduce investment, and deepen the **recession**. When he became prime minister in 1984, Brian Mulroney announced that Canada was "open for business" to investors from abroad. Foreign investment was no longer seen as a problem. Now it was a necessity.

MAKING CONNECTIONS

1. Why was direct ownership of Canadian businesses and industries considered more dangerous than indirect investment in Canadian-owned enterprises?

2. Write a paragraph agreeing or disagreeing with the proposition that Canada is an economic colony of the United States.

KEYWORDS

branch plant

non-partisan

economic nationalist

recession

THE FEDERAL GOVERNMENT
The Legislative Branch
FOCUSSING ON THE ISSUE

*Canada is a federation with a democratically elected parliamentary system
that is divided into federal and provincial levels of government.
What are the powers and responsibilities of the federal legislature in Canada?*

The Senate

The Constitution Act of 1867 gives legislative power to the Parliament of Canada, which consists of the Queen, the Senate, and the House of Commons. Members of the Senate are appointed by the governor general, who is advised by the prime minister. According to the Constitution, the Senate should have 104 members representing their provinces and territories, with 24 each from Ontario and Quebec; 10 each from Nova Scotia and New Brunswick; 4 from Prince Edward Island; 6 each from Newfoundland, the three Prairie provinces, and British Columbia; and one each from the Yukon and Northwest Territories. Senators must be at least 30 years of age, Canadian citizens, residents in the province they represent, and they must own property and have assets worth at least $4000. Since 1965, senators have been required to retire at age 75.

The Senate was intended to protect the interests of the different regions of Canada by guaranteeing them representation in the legislative branch. In addition, the qualifications for membership ($4000 was a lot of money in 1867) meant that persons of property and position would have a legislative body to balance the democratically elected House of Commons. Because the Senate cannot initiate laws that require expenditure, its legislative function is limited to reviewing and approving legislation passed by the House of Commons. This "sober second look" function of the Senate has been occasionally used to stall controversial government legislation, allowing time for popular protest to develop and sometimes forcing the government to amend or withdraw legislation.

Because the Senate has sometimes used its power to frustrate the will of the people (see page 99) and has been portrayed as a retirement home for party loyalists, it has frequently been criticized. Since the 1870s, there have been calls for the reform or **abolition** of the Senate. The Charlottetown Accord called for a reformed Senate based on equal, elected, and effective representation, with six senators from each province and one from each territory.

The House of Commons

The House of Commons is the most important part of the legislative

What message is this cartoon conveying?

ABSENTEE SENATORS

In 1990, the Senate began keeping monthly attendance records. From February 1996 to September 1997, 28 senators had an attendance rate of less than 60 per cent, with Ontario Senator Andrew Thompson's rate being the lowest at 2.2 per cent. Between 1990 and the autumn of 1997, Thompson attended the Senate 12 times, which allowed him to meet the minimum requirement to continue receiving his annual salary of $64 400 and a tax-free expense allowance of $10 100. While the Senate levies penalties for absenteeism, none of Thompson's pay was withheld because he had cited ill health as the cause of his absence. However, media reports revealed the Senator had been spending much of his time in Mexico.

In November 1997, Thompson was expelled from the Liberal caucus by Prime Minister Jean Chrétien, who stated in a letter: "Your absence from the sittings of the Senate and your record of non-participation in the work of the **caucus** over many years are totally unacceptable." In December 1997, it was announced that Thompson's salary would be withheld, and in February 1998, the Senate voted to suspend Thompson without pay. The following month, Thompson resigned.

1. Do you think the Senate should be changed, abolished, or left as it is? Explain.

branch of the government. Although almost any eligible voter can run in an election, most of the candidates for MP are members of one of Canada's political parties. Because there are usually three or more candidates in a riding, it is unusual for the winning candidate to get 50 per cent or more of the vote. Instead candidates are elected by a plurality—the individual with the most votes wins.

Members of Parliament are elected from geographical areas called constituencies, or ridings, by the votes of participating Canadian citizens 18 years of age or older. Periodically, the boundaries of ridings are redrawn and new ones are created in response to population changes. While an attempt is made to ensure **representation by population**, the geographic size of the riding is also a factor, with larger rural ridings generally having fewer voters than urban ridings.

MPs who are members of the second-largest party form the **official Opposition**. The leader of the opposition names a shadow cabinet composed of his/her members who act as opposition critics of the various government departments. Like the Cabinet ministers on the government's side, it is the critics' responsibility to speak for their party on matters affecting the government department to which they have been assigned.

MPs who are not Cabinet or shadow cabinet members are called backbenchers. Backbenchers spend much of their time providing a link between their constituents and the government and its bureaucracy. They are also active in the various parliamentary committees to which they are assigned. Because of the leader's control of the party, backbenchers have little opportunity to criticize government policy except in party caucus meetings. MPs can be critical of their leaders' policies and legislation during these secret meetings. But in the House, party solidarity demands that MPs always vote with their party.

MAKING CONNECTIONS

1. In the US Congress, members are not bound by party solidarity and are free to vote as they choose. Should Canadian MPs have the same freedom to represent their constituents' views? Explain.

KEYWORDS

abolition

caucus

representation by population

official Opposition

PROVINCIAL GOVERNMENTS
Powers and Responsibilities

Canada is divided into federal and provincial levels of government, each with assigned powers and responsibilities. What powers and responsibilities lie with the provincial governments?

PROVINCIAL GOVERNMENT

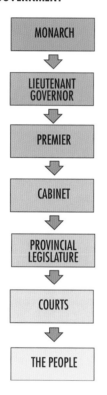

MONARCH

⇩

LIEUTENANT GOVERNOR

⇩

PREMIER

⇩

CABINET

⇩

PROVINCIAL LEGISLATURE

⇩

COURTS

⇩

THE PEOPLE

Structure

The **Constitution Act** of 1867 formally established the provincial governments and the 16 areas of provincial jurisdiction. Provincial governments are largely independent of the federal government. Each has its own executive, legislative, and judicial branches, and each has the power to levy **direct taxation**.

Like the federal government, the formal head of each province is the monarch, who is represented by a lieutenant-governor. The lieutenant-governor is appointed by the governor general on the advice of the prime minister. Like the governor general, the duties of the lieutenant-governor are largely ceremonial. They include delivering the Speech from the Throne, presiding at official functions, and signing provincial bills into law.

Forming a Government

Forming a provincial government happens much the same way as it does at the federal level. Provinces hold separate elections and have their own provincial political parties. Following an election, the leader of the party that elects the most members to the provincial legislature is formally asked to form a government by the lieutenant-governor. The leader of this party then becomes the provincial premier and chooses a number of elected members from his or her party to form a **Cabinet**. This group effectively becomes the government.

All elected representatives sit in the provincial parliament. (Their titles may vary. In British Columbia, elected representatives are called Members of the Legislative Assembly (MLAs), while in Ontario they are known as Members of Provincial Parliament (MPPs).) The party with the second-highest number of elected representatives forms the **official Opposition**. This status gives the party a greater role in legislative debates and provides public funds for the offices and staff of elected members. As in the federal Parliament, one party may not have enough seats to form a **majority** government. In such cases, a **minority** government may come to power, or two or more parties could join forces to gain a majority vote and form a **coalition** government.

Provincial Powers

The provincial government is responsible for education. The Ministry of Education establishes policies and curriculum requirements affecting all schools and students. The day-to-day operation of schools is usually under the supervision of locally elected school boards.

Health and social services are provincial responsibilities, although some aspects of heath care are shared with the federal government. While provincial policies are established by the province, daily administration of these facilities and services is often a municipal responsibility.

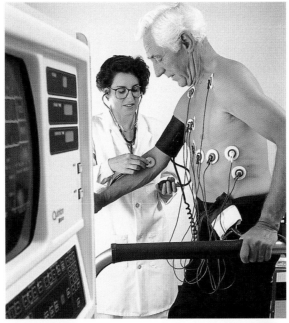

The province is responsible for provincial courts as well as some prisons. Most policing is a provincial responsibility, although police departments are usually administered by municipal governments. The provinces are also responsible for collecting provincial taxes and establishing municipal institutions.

Municipal Governments

The provinces are responsible for establishing various forms of local administration. These include city and county councils and regional governments such as the Greater Vancouver Regional District. Municipal governments establish and administer police and fire departments, libraries, local roads, water and sewage systems, garbage collection, and local zoning bylaws, building codes, permits, and licences. Members of municipal governments, such as mayors, reeves, and councillors, are elected officials. Individual citizens most directly participate in government at the municipal level.

Resource development and management fall under the province's domain. The province is responsible for establishing policies that are in the best interests of the province and its resources and for ensuring provincial regulations are followed by the private industries that utilize these resources.

MAKING CONNECTIONS

1. a) List the powers assigned to the provinces that are described here. Why do you think each of these powers was given to the provinces?
   b) Discuss, in a brief essay or in class, current issues or concerns facing *one* of the powers you have listed.

2. Who is the premier of your province? Which political party is in power? Which party is the official Opposition? Who is your provincial representative, and which party does she or he represent?

KEYWORDS

Constitution Act
direct taxation
Cabinet
official Opposition
majority
minority
coalition

WESTERN ALIENATION
Sources of Discontent

In the 1970s, western Canadians became more and more concerned about their place in Canadian society. What led to a growing sense of alienation in western Canada during this period?

Geography

The sheer physical size of Canada has always been a source of **alienation** for western Canadians. In spite of the speed of air travel, it is still a long way from Ottawa to Vancouver. In the 1970s and before, it was a trip government officials and politicians rarely made. Geography also created a country that lies across six different time zones. Because of time zones and distance, a business trip from Victoria to Toronto effectively took an entire working day. The differences in time zones also meant that after 2:00 p.m. Vancouver time, it was impossible to contact government offices in Ottawa or corporate head offices in Toronto or Montreal because they were already closed for the day. Many business deals and government communications simply had to wait until the next business day. Also because of geography, federal election results, prior to 1997, were often determined long before the polls in BC had closed, making western voters feel that their votes were meaningless.

History

In addition to geographic factors, history also played a role in western alienation. (See page 194.) Many western Canadians felt that, in spite of efforts to make their concerns known, little had changed over the years in Ottawa's attitude towards the West. Westerners resented their inability to gain a greater voice in national affairs as well as central Canada's continued control over the economy. In particular, British Columbians viewed their province as differ-ent from the other western provinces, and they wanted the federal government to acknowledge this. British Columbians believed their province, with its geographic size and economic importance, should be regarded as a separate region and should be granted a more significant role in Canadian affairs.

Culture

Cultural issues also contributed to western alienation. From its beginnings, the CBC, which was supposed to be a unifying force for Canadians, proved to be a major source of irritation in the West. When western Canadians watched the national news on television, they discovered that nothing that happened after 7:00 p.m. Toronto time (5:00 p.m. in Alberta and 4:00 p.m. in British Columbia) made it to the nightly news. To British Columbians, this left the impression that Canada closed for the day at 4:00 p.m. local time. Compounding this frustration was the fact that the majority of domestic English-language television programming was produced in Toronto. The message Westerners received was that, in the eyes of Easterners, current events in the West were unimportant and western Canada had nothing to contribute to the country's culture.

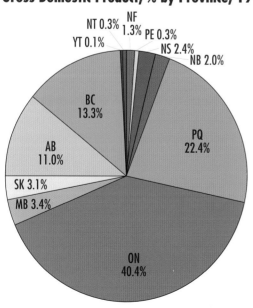

Gross Domestic Product, % by Province, 1995

NT 0.3% NF 1.3% PE 0.3%
YT 0.1% NS 2.4%
NB 2.0%
BC 13.3%
AB 11.0%
SK 3.1%
MB 3.4%
PQ 22.4%
ON 40.4%

National Unity

The federal government's preoccupation with Quebec concerns and the question of national unity was initially supported by western Canadians. But after a few years, they began to resent what they saw as the constant focus on Quebec. They began to wonder if their own problems would ever receive the national attention they deserved. Many western Canadians focussed their resentment of Ottawa's Quebec policy and the Official Languages Act. (See page 224.) Some talk-show commentators on western radio encouraged anti-bilingual feelings among their listeners. The result was a widespread perception that Ottawa, in order to win votes in Quebec, had forced **bilingualism** on a Canadian population that did not want it.

Economics

In 1973, after OPEC reduced the worldwide supply of oil and oil prices skyrocketed, western Canadians anticipated great wealth—they had vast reserves of oil that could be sold at the new world price. They were outraged

Much tension existed between the provincial governments of the West and the federal government over the pricing of oil and gas during the 1970s. Here Prime Minister Pierre Trudeau (left) and Alberta premier Peter Lougheed (right) confer at the Western Economic Opportunities Conference in 1973.

when the Trudeau government, concerned over the impact of high oil prices on the Canadian economy, froze the price of oil in Canada. The government arbitrarily decided that western oil fields were a national asset for the benefit of all Canadians. Although an export tax was placed on oil shipped to the United States, the proceeds were used to subsidize the cost of imported oil for eastern Canadians. Western alienation reached a new high when angry Westerners printed bumper stickers urging their provincial governments to turn off the oil and let Easterners "freeze in the dark."

◁═ MAKING CONNECTIONS ═▷

1. Western Canadians frequently complained that it was pointless to vote in federal elections because, by the time the polls closed in western Canada, the election had already been decided in the East. In the 1997 election, opening and closing times at the polls were more closely synchronized across the country. Do you think this kind of change will affect Westerners' perceptions of their importance in federal elections? Explain.

2. What evidence is there of alienation in the West today? Is the problem widespread, in your view? What do you think the federal government should do to address this issue? What should Westerners themselves do?

KEYWORDS

alienation

bilingualism

ARCTIC PIPELINE
The Berger Commission
FOCUSSING ON THE ISSUE

The Mackenzie Valley Pipeline Inquiry was formed to investigate issues surrounding the construction of a pipeline through the Arctic. Is modern economic development compatible with the needs of the environment and Aboriginal societies in the North?

A Travelling Commission

The oil shortage of the early 1970s demonstrated the urgent need to find new sources of fuel in North America. One source was on the north coast of Alaska, where a major gas field was under development at Prudhoe Bay. A **consortium** of Canadian and American companies proposed building a pipeline to carry the gas, and later, oil as well, from Alaska through the Mackenzie River valley in the Northwest Territories to consumers in the south. The pipeline was to be the largest construction project ever undertaken in the North. But the construction of a pipeline through the fragile Arctic environment would have a significant impact on the land, wildlife, and Aboriginal

Judge Tom Berger listens to residents of Nahanni Butte, Northwest Territories. What are the advantages of conducting a royal commission in this way?

societies along its route. Therefore, in 1974, the federal government set up a royal commission known as the Mackenzie Valley Pipeline Inquiry to investigate the environmental impact. It was led by a Vancouver judge named Tom Berger.

Berger's inquiry turned out to be one of the most unorthodox royal commissions in Canadian history. Instead of holding hearings in a southern city, as most inquiries were conducted, Berger took his inquiry on the road. Over a period

VIEWPOINTS
VOICES FROM THE BERGER INQUIRY

Berger's inquiry hearings were widely publicized and allowed southern Canadians to hear for themselves the points of view of northern residents. The inquiry had a significant impact on the understanding and attitude of other Canadians towards the North and the Aboriginal peoples who lived there.

I was hoping to raise my family until they get of age, and then they could make a good living out of that country, because there was lots of game. But now, since the pipeline came in, I am scared to go any place. I don't know where to go, because wherever I want to go, there is a seismic line, with trucks rolling back and forth on it, and planes are flying overhead and it scares the moose and the game away. Ever since they came in I couldn't make a living out of the country.

Johnny Klondike, Fort Liard, NWT, where an earlier pipeline had been built, in Northern Frontier, Northern Homeland, *(Ottawa: 1977) p. 124.*

To really bring the whole picture into focus, you can describe it as the rape of the northland to satisfy the greed and the needs of southern consumers, and when development of this nature happens, it only destroys; it does not leave any permanent jobs for people who make the North their home. The whole process does not leave very much for us to be proud of, and along with their equipment and technology, they also impose on the northern people their white culture and all its value systems.

Louise Frost, Old Crow, Yukon Territory in Northern Frontier, Northern Homeland, *p. 36.*

Now, Mr. Berger, it seems like this is the end of a lot of food for us. If they ever drill [for oil] in the Beaufort Sea, if they ever have an accident, nobody really knows how much damage it will make on the Beaufort Sea. Nobody really knows how many fish it will kill, or whales, polar bears, the little whales and the bowheads. These people that did research on the Beaufort Sea will never be able to answer these things. When will the fish and the whales come back?

Sam Raddi, Inuvik, NWT, in Northern Frontier, Northern Homeland, *p. 70.*

To the Indian people our land really is our life. Without our land we cannot—we could no longer exist as people. If our land is destroyed, we too are destroyed. If your people ever take our land you will be taking our life.

Richard Nerysoo, Fort McPherson, NWT, in Northern Frontier, Northern Homeland, *p. 94.*

We look upon the North as our last frontier. It is natural for us to think of developing it, of subduing the land and extracting its resources to fuel Canada's industry and heat our homes. Our whole inclination is to think of expanding our industrial machine to the limit of our country's frontiers....But the native people say that the North is their homeland. They have lived there for thousands of years. They claim it is their land, and they believe they have a right to say what its future ought to be.

Tom Berger, in Northern Frontier, Northern Homeland, *p. 1.*

1. Explain the differences between the concepts of *frontier* and *homeland*. Draw up a list of characteristics under each heading.
2. a) According to the testimony of these witnesses, list some of the negative effects the pipeline project would have on the North and its residents.
   b) What might be some positive effects of a project like the pipeline?

of two years he visited 35 communities in the Yukon and Northwest Territories. He held meetings in town halls and Aboriginal lodges to hear what ordinary residents of the North had to say about the pipeline and how it might affect their lives. For most Northerners, this was the first time anyone from the government had bothered to ask them what they thought about the issues that affected them.

In 1977, Berger published his report, called *Northern Frontier, Northern Homeland*. It concluded that the fragile northern environment would be seriously damaged by the pipeline construction. Berger also warned that Aboriginal societies would be significantly disrupted by a sudden influx of outsiders. His report pointed out that the North was the homeland of many Aboriginal peoples, not just a resource frontier to be exploited by southern Canadians for their own benefit. He recommended that the pipeline project be postponed for at least ten years so that Aboriginal land claims could be settled. Berger's report was accepted. In the end, no pipeline was ever built.

MAKING CONNECTIONS

1. Investigate an environmental issue in another country that has had an impact on Aboriginal societies. Consider the destruction of the tropical rainforests in Brazil or Malaysia, disappearing wetlands in Australia or parts of Africa, or massive hydroelectric projects in Malaysia or Brazil as possible topics. Research the issue and prepare a report outlining the development scheme, its impact on the Aboriginal peoples, and the outcome or status of the project today.

KEYWORDS

consortium

MULTICULTURALISM
Opposing Viewpoints
FOCUSSING ON THE ISSUE

*Canada is a multicultural country, in fact and in law.
Does multiculturalism promote or discourage social harmony?*

The Dr. Sun Yat-Sen Classical Chinese Garden in downtown Vancouver is the only full-size classical scholar's garden outside China. It was built by a team of experts from China using materials imported specially for the project. Make a list of buildings in your community that reflect the presence of people from different cultural backgrounds.

nature of Canadian society by making **multiculturalism** an official government policy.

There cannot be one cultural policy for Canadians of British and French origin, another for the original peoples and yet a third for all others. For although there are two official languages, there is no official culture, nor does any ethnic group take precedence over any other. No citizen or group of citizens is other than Canadian, and all should be treated fairly....I wish to emphasize the view of the government that a policy of multiculturalism within a bilingual framework is basically the conscious support of individual freedom of choice. We are free to be ourselves.

Pierre Trudeau, announcing his new policy of multiculturalism, 1971

The policy of multiculturalism pledged the government to pursue four basic objectives:

A Multicultural Society

For years, Canada was officially a bicultural country based on its French and British heritage. From the outset, this view of Canada failed to acknowledge the presence of Canada's first inhabitants, the Aboriginal peoples. The concept of **biculturalism** became increasingly

inaccurate as more and more immigrants arrived from other European countries and from Africa, Asia, and Latin America. In reality, Canada had become a multicultural country—that is, a place where people from many cultural backgrounds lived together. By 1971, the government of Pierre Trudeau decided it was time to recognize the diverse

- to assist cultural groups in Canada to carry on their own cultural practices and activities
- to assist cultural groups to overcome any barriers to their participation in any aspect of Canadian life
- to promote relations between all cultural groups
- to assist immigrants to learn either French or English so that they may become full participants in Canadian life.

Although cultural diversity is a fact of life in Canada, there is considerable debate over the official policy of multiculturalism. At issue is whether the government should encourage and protect it. Supporters of the policy argue that diversity is positive and something of which all Canadians should be proud. They believe that a variety of cultures enriches the social fabric. Critics charge that multiculturalism highlights the differences between people and promotes disunity. They argue that Canada cannot develop a distinct culture of its own if every cultural group holds onto its own identity.

We assume that those who bring a culture with them from elsewhere want to maintain it—and will be grateful if Canada helps them do so. On this belief we base our view of ourselves as a diverse country....

By emphasizing race, multiculturalism tries to freeze us into ethnic categories that may express only the least important qualities of an individual. In the natural course of things some citizens will choose to identify themselves with their historic culture and others will choose to move outside it. Government policy should never for a moment even hint that one choice is more desirable than the other.

Pluralism, the side-by-side existence of many forms of human association, is an essential quality of modern Canada. Official multiculturalism...was a bad idea in the beginning, and in time will probably be seen as one of the gigantic mistakes of recent public policy in Canada.

Abridged version of "Do Canadians Want Ethnic Heritage Freeze-dried?" by Robert Fulford from The Globe and Mail. *Reprinted by permission of the author.*

Multiculturalism is not about songs and dances, not about special interest groups. It is an affirmation of the right of those Canadians whose heritage is neither French nor English—40 per cent of our population—to be participants in the mainstream of Canadian life....

A third fallacy is that multiculturalism provides special privileges to special interest groups. The true issue is that true equality and fairness cannot be achieved by uniform treatment. It would not be fair if the physically disabled were treated like the able-bodied and not provided with ramps and elevators. It would be unjust if young people were treated the same as senior citizens and deprived of employment opportunities or free education.

Under the multiculturalism rubric, employment equity measures are not special privileges but tools to remove barriers and ensure fair and equal access for all.

A fourth myth is that multiculturalism should accentuate similarities and minimize difference. The fact is that similarities should be recognized and celebrated, but the whole essence is to accept and respect difference. Only when cultural difference is accepted and recognized will there be harmony in society.

Lilian To, *"Does Official Multiculturalism unite Canada?"* The Vancouver Sun, *10 April 1997, p. A15.*

1. a) Why does Robert Fulford oppose multicultural policy?

   b) Imagine you are Lilian To. Respond to Fulford's argument in a letter to the editor of his newspaper.

MAKING CONNECTIONS

1. Explain the difference between multiculturalism and official multiculturalism. What is the purpose of official multiculturalism?

2. One of the objectives of the policy of multiculturalism is to overcome discrimination against Canadians because of colour, cultural background, language, or religion. How does such a policy fight discrimination? Do you think it is successful? Explain your answer using examples from your local newspaper, then discuss these in class.

KEYWORDS

biculturalism

multiculturalism

WOMEN'S RIGHTS
Making Progress
FOCUSSING ON THE ISSUE

In the 1970s, there was a growing public awareness of the importance of women's issues. What steps were taken towards establishing equality for women in Canada during this decade?

A New Era

The report of the Royal Commission on the Status of Women in 1970 set the stage for a new era in women's rights. (See page 240.) In 1972, the National Action Committee on the Status of Women (NAC) was formed to monitor the government's response to the commission's recommendations. NAC served as an umbrella organization for a variety of women's groups. It represented not only women in general but also physically challenged women, lesbian women, and women of different races and religions.

Increasingly, the women's movement in Canada, as in many other countries, was characterized by marches and demonstrations. The lives of women were celebrated through music, art, and literature. Many Canadian women writers, such as Margaret Atwood, Margaret Lawrence, and Alice Munro, gained recognition for their work, both at home and abroad. Artists such as Mary Pratt and Joyce Wieland also gained prominence in the art world. Women rose to occupy key positions in business and industry, and more women ran for political office. The success of these trailblazing women inspired a new, young female generation to seek a lifestyle outside the traditional roles of women in Canadian society.

Timeline

1970 Report of the Royal Commission on the Status of Women published

1972 National Action Committee on the Status of Women formed

Five women—Flora MacDonald, Monique Bégin, Jeanne Sauvé, Albanie Morin, and Grace MacInnes—elected to the House of Commons

Rosemary Brown becomes first Black woman to be elected to a provincial legislature in Canada as MLA in British Columbia

1974 Reforms to Canada Pension Plan allow women who work within the home to claim part of spouse's pension contribution

Shirley Carr becomes first female vice-president of Canadian Labour Congress

Rosemary Brown makes unsuccessful bid for federal leadership of New Democratic Party

1975 Bertha Wilson becomes justice of Ontario Court of Appeal

Provinces pass laws recognizing a woman's right to claim part of a couple's assets in a divorce settlement

1976 Federal government and six provinces pass maternity-leave legislation

Flora MacDonald makes unsuccessful bid for leadership of Conservative party

Grace Hartman becomes first woman to head a national union when elected president of Canadian Union of Public Employees

1977 Federal legislation extends concept of equal pay for work of equal value to any jobs requiring comparable skills and education

The United Nations declared 1975 to be International Women's Year. The objectives of the UN declaration were to promote equality of the sexes and to ensure women's full participation in all aspects of life. In Canada, the government added its own goal: "to inform and educate the general public of the changing attitudes towards women's roles in society." While the events of 1975 were greeted with enthusiasm and optimism by many Canadians, others were doubtful that a year of high-level publicity would have any lasting impact.

International Women's Year...has finally come to its dismal end....In Canada what has been achieved in this illusive Year of the Woman—1975? Precious little, and as far as legislation is concerned, zero.

Laura Sabia, Chair, Ontario Status of Women Committee

Despite the numerous criticisms, some think the deliberations, the projects, the buttons, and the banners of

International Women's Year have done more to increase awareness about the concerns of women in the 70s....

A lot of criticism has been directed at the government about tokenism...claims that special focus on the concerns of women will end on December 31st. Let me assure you that this will not be the case in Ontario.

Bette Stephenson, Minister of Labour, Ontario

It has proven to be a year of major achievements. Within federal jurisdiction, legislative action has been taken to improve women's position through the introduction of several bills....It takes courage to put our convictions to work. That is the work left to be done. When we no longer allow the stereotypes of roles to dictate our choices and affect our perceptions and those of our children—it is then that women's equality will be achieved.

Marc Lalonde, Minister of National Health and Welfare

1. Do you think declarations like International Women's Year have any long-term impact? Explain your answer.

Closing the Wage Gap

One of the priorities of the women's movement was to close the wage gap between men and women. Women's groups believed the best strategy was to begin at the root of the problem by providing better educational opportunities for females. Initiatives in education included eliminating sexism and stereotypes in textbooks and other learning materials and encouraging female students to enroll in subjects traditionally dominated by males, such as math, science, and technology.

The next step was **affirmative action** in the workplace. Many employers introduced programs designed to create a better balance of males and females in all job categories. Although some governments supported affirmative action, many people opposed it. They argued that such plans discriminated against qualified men who were passed over for jobs and promotions in favour of women who, in some cases, might not be as qualified. By the end of the decade, women were beginning to make inroads in management and male-dominated professions. Still, many women encountered the glass ceiling—the invisible barrier that keeps women from reaching top positions.

MAKING CONNECTIONS

1. Affirmative action programs have been implemented to help both women and minorities in the workplace. Debate the pros and cons of such programs.

KEYWORDS

affirmative action

ABORIGINAL AFFAIRS
New Directions
FOCUSSING ON THE ISSUE

In 1970, the Canadian government proposed sweeping changes to its Aboriginal policy. The proposal marked the beginning of a fundamental change in relations between Aboriginal peoples and the federal government. In what ways did this relationship change?

No to the White Paper

A dramatic change took place in relations between the federal government and Aboriginal peoples in 1970. In 1969, the government had presented a **White Paper** on Aboriginal policy. The paper was based on the philosophy that Aboriginal peoples should be like all other Canadians, having complete equality and no special privileges—in other words, Aboriginal peoples should be **assimilated** into the mainstream of Canadian society.

To achieve this, the government proposed to abolish the Department of Indian Affairs, eliminate the **reserve** system, turn over responsibility for Aboriginal peoples to the provincial governments, and terminate Indian status. Yet these major changes in policy were announced after minimal consultation with the Aboriginal peoples themselves.

Aboriginal communities responded to the White Paper with one voice. The government's inten-

tions appalled Aboriginal peoples and they began making their views known. They did not want to be assimilated and they did not want to lose their special status. They felt betrayed by the government and believed it was trying to shirk its special responsibility to Aboriginal peoples as compensation for the lands that had been taken from them. They were particularly upset that their point of view had not even been considered by the government. They demanded that the

government listen to what they had to say.

In the face of vehement opposition, the government withdrew the White Paper and agreed to begin negotiations with Aboriginal peoples. The uproar surrounding the White Paper sparked a new determination on the part of Aboriginal peoples to organize and fight for their rights. Aboriginal organizations quickly became a political force to be reckoned with, growing in number and strength.

As a result of opposition to the White Paper, governments began direct negotiations with Aboriginal peoples.

One of the new political organizations formed in the wake of the White Paper controversy was the Indian Brotherhood of the Northwest Territories. In 1975, the Indian Brotherhood (which changed its name to the Dene Nation in 1978) issued a declaration that summed up the desires and demands of many Aboriginal peoples. Since the declaration, the Dene, Métis, and Inuit peoples of northern Canada have all signed agreements with the federal government giving them extensive control over their own territories and societies. (See pages 344-347.)

We the Dene of the NWT insist on the right to be regarded by ourselves and the world as a nation.

Our struggle is for the recognition of the Dene Nation by the government and people of Canada and the peoples and governments of the world.

As once Europe was the exclusive homeland of the European peoples, Africa the exclusive homeland of the African peoples, the New World, North and South America, were the exclusive homeland of Aboriginal peoples of the New World, the Amerindian and the Inuit.

Colonialism and imperialism is now dead or dying. Recent years have witnessed the birth of new nations or rebirth of old nations out of the ashes of colonialism.

As Europe is the place where you will find European countries with European governments for European peoples, now also you will find in Africa and Asia the existence of African and Asian countries with African and Asian governments for African and Asian peoples....

But in the New World, the Native Peoples have not fared so well...Nowhere in the New World have the Native Peoples won the right to self-determination and the right to recognition by the world as a distinct people and as nations.

While the Native People of Canada are a minority in their homeland, the Native People of the NWT, the Dene and Inuit, are a majority of the population of the NWT.

The Dene find themselves as part of a country. That country is Canada. But the government of Canada is not the government of the Dene. These governments were not the choice of the Dene, they were imposed on the Dene.

What we the Dene are struggling for is the recognition of the Dene Nation by the governments and peoples of the world.

And while there are realities we are forced to submit to, such as the existence of a country called Canada, we insist on the right to self-determination as a distinct people and the recognition of the Dene Nation....

Our plea to the world is to help us in our struggle to find a place in the world community where we can exercise our right to self-determination as a distinct people and as a nation.

*What we seek then is independence and **self-determination** within the country of Canada. This is what we mean when we call for a just land settlement for the Dene Nation.*

Rick Ponting and Roger Gibbins, Out of Irrelevance (Toronto: Butterworths, 1980), pp. 351ff.

1. Summarize three main points of the Dene Declaration in your own words.
2. According to the declaration, what would be the relationship between the Dene and the rest of Canada?

MAKING CONNECTIONS

1. a) Define the following terms as they apply to Aboriginal peoples in Canada: *status, non-status, Métis, Inuit, treaty, band, reserve, nation.*
   b) How do these terms establish a distinct status for Aboriginal peoples?

KEYWORDS

White Paper

assimilate

reserve

self-determination

ACID PRECIPITATION
Cross-border Pollution
FOCUSSING ON THE ISSUE

Perhaps no environmental issue made Canadians more aware of the problem of pollution than acid precipitation. Much of this pollution originated outside the country. What are the causes and the effects of acid precipitation? When pollution does not recognize borders, how can it be stopped?

Noting the Effects

In the late 1960s and early 1970s, researchers in the Canadian Shield discovered that levels of **acidity** in the region's lakes were on the rise. At the same time, they noticed that the number of fish and other lake species was declining. Trees, particularly sugar maples in Ontario and Quebec, were losing their leaves and appeared to be dying. Similar conditions were reported in Sweden.

Scientists determined that oxides of sulphur and nitrogen in the atmosphere were to blame for the damage being inflicted on lakes and forests. When **fossil fuels** (coal or petroleum) are burned in factories, power plants, and internal-combustion engines, noxious gases are created. These combine with moisture in the atmosphere to produce sulphuric and nitric acid. This residue falls back to earth in the form of **acid precipitation** (rain or snow, depending on the season),

which poisons the water and soil and harms vegetation. Acidity also acts on rocks and soil to release harmful metals such as mercury and aluminum into the water supply. Carried aloft by winds and clouds, the acidic moisture may inflict damage many kilometres away from the industrial plants that produce it.

Cleaning Up

Once the phenomenon of acid precipitation was recognized, the question was who would clean it up? Part of the problem was domestic, caused by Canadian industries and power companies. Federal and provincial governments joined forces to impose emission reductions. Smokestack industries were urged to switch to fuels that were lower in sulphur content. They installed pollution-control devices, called scrubbers, which reduced the sulphur content of gases released into the atmosphere. These measures were implemented during the 1970s and 1980s at a cost of billions of dollars, and they succeeded in dramatically reducing harmful emissions.

Most acid precipitation, however—between 75 and 80 per cent—originated in the **industrial heartland** of the United States south of the Great Lakes. This pol-

The problem of acid precipitation in northern Canada was caused in part by attempts to reduce air pollution in industrial cities in the south by building taller smokestacks to carry emissions higher into the atmosphere. Upper-level winds blew the polluted air away from the local area, only to carry it to other parts of the country, or the continent, where it caused just as much damage.

lution drifted north across the border to wreak its havoc on Canadian lakes and forests. Unable to legislate American factories, Canadian officials had to fight the problem through diplomatic channels. Canadian scientists, environmental groups, and politicians asked the US government to pass legislation limiting harmful emissions. For their part, the American industries that were involved lobbied their government to reject Canada's appeal as too costly. It was not until 1990 that the US Congress passed a Clean Air Act providing for a 40 per cent reduction of emissions by the year 2000. The following year, Canada and the United States signed a joint agreement limiting dangerous emissions.

While these measures made some progress towards reducing harmful emissions, in 1997 Prime Minister Jean Chrétien had to admit that the clean-up was not going as originally promised. Although changing the way industries are fuelled is expensive, the economic costs of environmental damage from unchecked acid precipitation

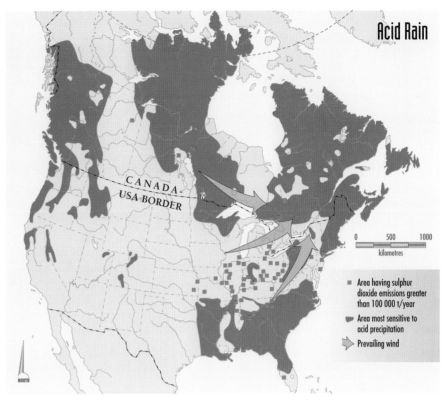

Acid Rain

would be monumental. Meanwhile, the problem on a global scale continues to worsen. Developing countries are less strict about controlling emissions. As they attempt to industrialize, they do not believe they can afford the cost of pollution controls. International co-operation seems to be the only way to address this serious environmental challenge.

Using this map, explain why certain parts of North America are more susceptible to acid precipitation than others.

- Area having sulphur dioxide emissions greater than 100 000 t/year
- Area most sensitive to acid precipitation
- Prevailing wind

0   500   1000
kilometres

MAKING CONNECTIONS

1. In your class, set up a mock conference on acid precipitation, with the goal of reducing harmful emissions. Include government, environmental, industry, and other special interest groups, and clearly establish their agendas. At the end of your conference, chart the progress you have made, identify any remaining roadblocks, and establish a timetable for achieving your goals.

2. How serious a problem is acid precipitation where you live? Contact a local environmental group or the local office of the department of the environment to obtain information. What are the sources of the acid precipitation? What steps have been taken to control or reduce it?

KEYWORDS

acidity

fossil fuels

acid precipitation

industrial heartland

HAMILTON
Creating Economic Diversity

In the 1970s, the economy of Hamilton, Ontario, suffered a serious decline. Thousands of workers lost their jobs. How did Hamilton's experience typify the deep structural changes taking place in the Canadian economy?

Steeltown

Steeltown, as the city of Hamilton west of Toronto called itself, developed as a centre of heavy industry. At the heart of the city's economy were the great blast furnaces and smokestacks of the huge iron and steel mills located along the shore of Lake Ontario. The largest was Stelco, the Steel Company of Canada, created in 1910 and the city's largest employer for much of the century. The Second World War and the postwar expansion of Canada's economy created thousands of jobs in Hamilton. By the early 1970s, about 40 000 people worked in iron and steel production, while thousands more worked in related industries making railway cars, auto parts, appliances, and construction materials.

The steel industry divided Hamilton into clearly defined social classes. Those skilled labourers who worked in the mills and factories lived in small, simple houses located near the plants, while the managers, accountants, and engineers employed by the steel companies lived further away in larger, fancier homes. Yet the two classes had one thing in common: the recognition that their well-being depended on steel. They accepted the sounds and smells of the mills, the sooty, polluted air, and the toxic

sludge in Hamilton harbour as reminders of the source of their prosperity.

In the late 1970s, however, things began to change. Like most other industrial cities in North America, Hamilton was dealt a series of economic blows. First was the impact of the OPEC oil **embargo** on the automobile industry. (See pages 258-259.) Higher petroleum prices created a demand for smaller, more fuel-efficient cars. These cars required less steel to make, and often aluminum and plastic were used as lightweight substitutes. At the same time, North Americans were becoming aware of the damaging effects of air and water pollution on both the natural environment and human health. Nowhere was the effect of industrial pollutants more evident than in the Great Lakes, part of the **industrial heartland** of North America. Governments began to demand that heavy industries reduce toxic waste and other emissions they discharged into the air and water through costly pollution-control devices.

During the worldwide recession of the early 1980s, the North American demand for steel plummeted once again. At the same time, Hamilton's steel makers faced competition from new producers. Japan had rebuilt its war-shattered

iron and steel industries, and by the 1970s, its mills were newer and more efficient than those in North America. Japanese, along with Korean and Taiwanese, manufacturers increasingly gained a greater share of the North American steel market. Hamilton's steel manufacturers were forced to reduce production, close older mills, and lay off workers. New and improved mills were opened, but they were highly automated and required fewer workers. Between 1981 and 1993, almost 20 000 Hamilton steelworkers lost their jobs. This had a devastating effect on the city's economy. The unemployment rate soared above the national average and the number of people on welfare increased sharply.

The Turnaround

Despite this disaster, in the 1990s Hamilton regained its prosperity. In 1997, the unemployment rate was two-thirds the national average, while the average **per capita** income was more than 10 per cent over the national norm. Steel continues to play a leading role in the city's economy, but the number of workers employed by the industry has dropped. What, then, accounted for the economic turnaround? In a word, **diversification**. The problems of the steel industry

For most of the twentieth century, Hamilton's economic prosperity was based on its steel industry.

showed Hamiltonians that they could not rely on a single industry to maintain their economy. All three levels of government got involved in attracting new and different industries to the area. At the same time, they offered retraining to former steelworkers and workers in related industries. Much of this training focussed on new, high-technology industries that relied on computers and automation rather than heavy equipment and assembly lines.

Today, the health-care industry is Hamilton's largest employer, providing jobs for more than 15 000 people. McMaster University's Faculty of Health Sciences is a leading innovator in health-care education and research. It attracts more than $40 million a year in research grants and creates new jobs and spin-off industries. To ensure the continued growth of **knowledge-based industries** and to maintain a diversified economy, the local government created the Greater Hamilton Technology Enterprise Centre. It offers land and facilities to technologically advanced companies wanting to open for business in Hamilton. Through these programs, Hamilton hopes to maintain economic stability and prosperity well into the twenty-first century.

MAKING CONNECTIONS

1. Explain the connection between diversification and economic stability in a community.

2. The economic transformation of Hamilton is typical of many communities in Canada. Investigate your own community. How has its economy changed in the past 25 years? Have certain industries died out and been replaced by new ones? What are the three biggest employers? Are they knowledge-based industries?

KEYWORDS

embargo

industrial heartland

per capita

diversification

knowledge-based industry

NUCLEAR ENERGY
An Ongoing Debate

In the 1970s, the use of nuclear power plants to generate electricity proliferated around the world. Why is nuclear power so controversial?

Power for the Future

By the 1970s, nuclear energy was being hailed as the power source of the future. As a way of generating electricity, nuclear plants were considered cleaner than coal-fired plants, more convenient than hydroelectricity, and more dependable than imported oil and gas. Experts predicted that nuclear power would soon provide most of the energy needs of North America.

Canada was at the forefront of the development of nuclear energy for peaceful purposes. Since the Second World War, Canada has been a leading producer of uranium, the key substance in the production of nuclear power. The first

Energy produced by a nuclear reaction generates high-pressure steam, which is used to operate the generators that produce electricity. The process does not give off the smoke and soot associated with the burning of fossil fuels. It does, however, produce dangerous waste products that no one yet knows how to get rid of.

Canadian nuclear **reactor** opened at Chalk River, Ontario, in 1945. It was only the second reactor in the world. The use of nuclear energy to produce electricity began in the 1950s, then expanded enormously in the 1970s as a result of the rapid rise in oil prices. In Canada, Ontario Hydro built several nuclear power plants, while New Brunswick and Quebec each built one.

Late in the 1970s, however, disaster struck. On 28 March 1979, at the Three Mile Island nuclear power station in Pennsylvania, USA, a reactor overheated and began leaking **radioactive** water. Authorities feared the plant would explode with the force of a nuclear bomb. The reactor was shut down

---

CASE STUDY

CANDU: CANADA'S REACTOR

In 1952, the federal government created Atomic Energy of Canada Ltd. (AECL), a **Crown corporation**, to spearhead the development of the nuclear power program. Scientists at AECL and Ontario Hydro designed a reactor they called CANDU, which stands for Canada Deuterium Uranium. Unlike other reactors, the CANDU reactor uses an inexpensive form of uranium as fuel. It also employs a substance called heavy water, a form of water that contains deuterium. **Nuclear fission** inside a reactor produces an enormous amount of heat. Heavy water is used to cool the reactor and moderate the chain reaction that results.

The first CANDU reactor appeared in 1967. It proved to be simple and safe to operate, and it is the only type of reactor in use in Canada. It was also sold widely to other countries. Korea, India, Argentina, and China have all bought CANDU reactors. CANDU reactors have the best safety record of any reactor type in the world, though their reputation took a beating in 1997 when serious problems were found with Ontario's reactors. Some critics of the CANDU program fear that countries buying a reactor may be able to use it to develop nuclear weapons, though none ever has.

Critics of nuclear power make two main arguments:

- Nuclear reactors are highly dangerous. Exposure to nuclear radiation may be fatal. If radioactive material from a reactor escapes, it could kill thousands of people and leave large areas uninhabitable. In the worst-case scenario, a total **meltdown** of a reactor would produce an explosion like a nuclear bomb.
- Reactors produce radioactive waste that remains lethal for long periods of time. Currently, this waste is stored in sealed, stainless steel cylinders, but no one has a safe way of disposing of them. Even if a safe place is found to store the waste, transporting such a dangerous substance from the reactor to the disposal site remains a problem.

Advocates of nuclear power think these fears are exaggerated. They point to these benefits:

- Nuclear energy production does not contribute to **global warming** or **acid precipitation** and it does not destroy the **ozone**. In this sense, it is "cleaner" than burning oil, natural gas, or coal to produce electricity.
- Nuclear plants are able to produce much more power with far less fuel, therefore they consume less of the world's **nonrenewable resources**.
- Although nuclear power is dangerous, so are hydroelectric dams and coal mining. The world needs electricity. If it is not produced by nuclear energy it will have to be produced by other fuels, and the dangers of these fuels are just as great if not greater.

1. Do you find the arguments for or against nuclear power more convincing? Why? Which arguments are proven, and which are speculation? Explain.

and 100 000 people were evacuated from nearby homes. In the end, the damage was contained and no one was killed or injured. But public opinion, which had been divided over nuclear power from the beginning, now turned strongly against it. There has not been a new nuclear power plant built in North America since Three Mile Island.

Public concern increased again after an explosion at a plant in Chernobyl in Ukraine in the former Soviet Union in 1986. The blast released a large quantity of radioactive material that swept across parts of Europe in a toxic cloud. Thousands of people developed fatal diseases from the fallout, which contaminated soil and vegetation over a wide area. Then, in 1997, Ontario Hydro was forced to shut down its reactors because of safety concerns. Today only a small percentage of Canada's electricity is generated by nuclear power as experts grapple with the problems of how to avoid accidents like Three Mile Island and Chernobyl and how to dispose of the highly dangerous waste.

KEYWORDS

reactor

radioactive

Crown corporation

nuclear fission

meltdown

global warming

acid precipitation

ozone

nonrenewable resources

◄▣ M A K I N G   C O N N E C T I O N S ▣►

1. Write a short essay in which you predict the future of nuclear power.

THE OLYMPICS
Controversy in Montreal

In 1976, the Olympic Games came to Canada for the first time.
What controversies surrounded the Games in Montreal?

Montreal's Challenge

After a spirited competition, Montreal beat out Los Angeles and Moscow to win the right to host the 1976 Summer Olympic Games. The real challenge, however, lay ahead in building the facilities on time and on budget. The cost of building the tracks, swimming pools, rowing courses, shooting ranges, living quarters, and other venues was set at $310 million. Montreal mayor Jean Drapeau promised that taxpayers would not have to pay a cent.

He planned to raise the money through the sale of special Olympic coins and stamps and tickets for a national lottery. But as construction of the vast Olympic Stadium and other facilities progressed, it became clear that preparations were behind schedule and over budget. Some of the buildings, including the Olympic Stadium, were not even finished on opening day!

Still, organizers managed to accommodate all the events, and the 1976 Olympics saw some spectacular performances. The most

thrilling was in gymnastics, where 14-year-old Nadia Comaneçi, from Romania, made sporting history by becoming the first gymnast to score a perfect 10 in Olympic competition. She did it not once, but seven times on her way to winning five medals and the all-round women's gymnastics championship.

For Quebeckers, the Olympics did not end when the athletes went home. In spite of Drapeau's promise, they were left with the job of paying for the games through their tax dollars. The total cost of the Montreal Olympics has been estimated at $3 billion—ten times the original budget. The Olympic Stadium, which was not finished until many years later, became a symbol of the excess and extravagance of the Games. The round stadium, now home to the Expos baseball team, became known as "The Big Owe!" The province of Quebec and the city of Montreal sank deeply into debt to pay for Drapeau's dream. The city did not finish paying for its share of the debt until 20 years after the Games. The province will not finish paying for its share until early in the twenty-first century.

Montreal's successful bid for the 1976 Summer Olympics was inspired by one person, the city's mayor, Jean Drapeau (right). Drapeau was one of the most successful politicians in Canada. Except for a three-year period, he served as mayor of Montreal from 1954 to 1986, and brought the city many of its greatest achievements—the subway system, the Place des Arts concert hall, the Montreal Expos baseball team, and Expo '67. His critics pointed out that he preferred grand gestures to providing basic needs like housing and social services.

Political Controversy

While the cost of the Olympics created controversy at home, politics created controversy on the international stage. Countries and athletes often use the Olympics to showcase their political quarrels. In 1968, in Mexico City, for instance, two American sprinters who had won medals raised their clenched fists in a Black Power salute—while their national anthem played—as a protest against racism in the US. In 1972, in Munich, Germany, terrorists infiltrated the athletes' village, killing 11 Israeli competitors.

Although the Montreal Games avoided violence, they had their share of controversy. South Africa, because of its racist **apartheid** policy, was banned from the Olympics. But African countries were angry that athletes from New Zealand were allowed to participate because the New Zealand rugby team had broken the international boycott against South Africa by going there

to play. Olympic organizers pointed out that because rugby was not an Olympic sport, they had no cause to bar the New Zealand Olympic team. Nonetheless, African countries wanted New Zealand punished. In protest, 20 nations refused to participate in Montreal. (In 1980, Canada joined many other countries in boycotting the Summer Olympic Games in Moscow in protest against the Soviet invasion of Afghanistan.)

Greg Joy, from Vancouver, surprised everyone in the 1976 games by winning a silver medal in the high jump. Despite some excellent personal results, however, Canada did not do well at its own Olympics, winning just 11 medals—5 silver and 6 bronze. The overall winner was the Soviet Union with 125 medals, followed by the United States with 94, and East Germany with 90.

OTHER NOTABLE OLYMPICS

Canada played host to the Olympic Games for a second time in 1988. This time it was the Winter Olympics and the site was Calgary. Events took place in the city and in the nearby mountains. Financially, the 1988 games were a success, primarily because the Olympics had started receiving sponsorships from private companies. As a result, the hosts were left with no outstanding debts.

Canada's most embarrassing Olympic moment came later that year at the 1988 Summer Games in Seoul, Korea. Toronto sprinter Ben Johnson won a gold medal in the 100 m race, setting a world record in the process. All of Canada celebrated, until it was revealed a few days later that

Johnson had been using **steroids**, a banned substance. He lost his medal, and his world record.

Canada had it best results ever at the Olympic Summer Games in Atlanta, Georgia, in 1996. Canadian athletes won 22 medals, including Donovan Bailey's gold medal in the men's 100 m (an Olympic and world record run) and gold medals in the men's 4 x 100 m relay and the women's double skulls in rowing. In 1998, in Nagano, Japan, Canada enjoyed its best Winter Games, winning 15 medals, and, for the first time in Olympic history, winning more medals than the United States.

CASE STUDY

MAKING CONNECTIONS

1. Do you think that the Olympic Games, or any sporting event, is a proper place to carry out political protests? Explain your answer.

2. In what ways do you think the Olympic Games benefit the host city, the host country, and their athletes?

KEYWORDS

apartheid

steroids

POLITICS AND IMAGE
The Power of the Media
FOCUSSING ON THE ISSUE

Most Canadians get their information about the world from the media.
What role do the media play in forming our perceptions of politics and politicians?

Providing Information

The news media are an important part of the political process. Without newspapers, radio, and television, it would be almost impossible for citizens to get infor-

This photograph of Conservative leader Robert Stanfield was taken during the 1974 election campaign. How does the image affect your opinion of Stanfield? Do you think it might influence your vote? Stanfield had caught the ball several times before this photograph was taken. Why do you think newspapers chose to publish a photograph of a fumble instead of a catch? Do you think this was fair?

mation about their government and their politicians. Providing this information is one of the fundamental jobs of the media.

The media are expected to report the news fairly, without **bias** or **censorship**. But, like everyone else, reporters and editors have opinions and prejudices. Inevitably, their personal views are sometimes reflected in the stories they report and the way in which they report them. Under time and space restrictions, editors must choose from a mass of information which items to report and which ones to drop. The act of choosing is in itself a form of censorship. In other words, the media not only inform the public, they also influence what the public thinks about issues, and which issues the public will think about.

Television is the most powerful news medium. People get more of their information from television than from any other source. As a result, politicians have to perform well on television to be successful. The way a politician looks and acts sometimes becomes more important than what he or she has to say about the

issues. Because complex policies cannot be easily explained in a brief television clip, critics claim that television has turned politics into a personality contest where image is more important than issues.

Trudeau and Clark

There is no question that a politician's reputation depends on how he or she is portrayed by the media. When Pierre Trudeau became leader of the Liberal party and prime minister in 1968, he was treated favourably by reporters. On the surface, Trudeau was everything Canadians did not expect their politicians to be. He drove flashy sports cars, dated beautiful women, and seemed to have new, unorthodox ideas about everything. During his first election campaign in 1968, the country was swept up in "Trudeaumania." Much of the frenzy was created by the media, which concentrated more on Trudeau's personal style than on his political policies. In time, reporters became more critical of Trudeau. But they never stopped treating him as a serious intellectual, and they continued to showcase his personal style.

Joe Clark was a different story. He became leader of the Conservative party in 1976. The next day, a major newspaper ran the headline: "Joe Who?" The media seemed to decide almost at once

The role and power of the news media is a hotly debated topic in Canada. There are a variety of charges levelled against journalists, including the following comments.

The normal journalistic reaction is not to praise but to criticize. There is a tacit understanding among journalists that to write favourably about events or people is, if not perverse, at least gutless and certain to harm one's career. Criticism, charges, and accusations produce the most jolts on television news and the biggest headlines in the papers.
    Journalist Clive Cocking in Following the Leaders, (Toronto: Doubleday, 1980).

Television has never quite been able to free itself of the constraints of its own rigid format, which dictates that all any reasonable person needs to know about anything can be told in a minute and a half. That leads to the sort of interview where the interviewer comes with a prepared list of questions, none of which is ever allowed to be answered properly, because eliciting answers is not the object of the exercise, but asking. What else plagues public affairs television is its inability to escape the influence of its life partner, entertainment, which leads to confrontation for the sake of confrontation, and lack of background because background is not readily susceptible to visual presentation.
    Journalist George Bain, in Gotcha: How the Media Distort the News, (Toronto: Key Porter, 1994), p. 246. Excerpt reprinted by permission.

I am deeply concerned about the lack of ethical background in the practice of journalism today. More importantly, I am concerned that this profession increasingly contributes to the erosion of our democratic process, with its negative reporting and its lack of balanced analysis of political events and issues. The mainstream news media, particularly in this province, are largely out of control.

They see their role as adversaries to government and politicians, yet they have no mandate from the people. They are accountable to no one but their bosses. No one ever gets to vote them out of office. They demonize politicians. They slander them. They demand a degree of openness, honesty, and tests of integrity from politicians that many among them could never pass.
    Mike Harcourt, premier of BC, 1991-96, in A Measure of Defiance by Mike Harcourt with Wayne Skene, p. 169. ©1996. Published by Douglas & McIntyre. Reproduced with permission of the publisher.

1. List four criticisms of the media made by these writers. Does the photograph of Robert Stanfield support any of these criticisms? How do you suppose a reporter would answer these charges?
2. Many critics believe that television is particularly ineffective at conveying information about public affairs. Why?

---

that Clark was a lightweight, regardless of what he said or did. They made fun of his appearance, his mannerisms, his walk, and the way he spoke. When he toured Asia, the media reported that he lost his luggage instead of reporting on his policies!

Clark managed to get elected prime minister with a minority government in 1979, defeating the charismatic Trudeau. But his government only lasted nine months before falling to the Liberals in another election. Canadians never had a chance to take Clark seriously as a leader. While there were many reasons for this, one of them was that he was never able to overcome his media image as a bumbler.

MAKING CONNECTIONS

1. Collect articles from local newspapers that mention the present prime minister or the premier of your province. How would you describe the image that is presented? Is it a biased view, in your opinion? If so, in what way?

KEYWORDS

bias

censorship

SKILL BUILDER
Analysing the News
FOCUSSING ON THE ISSUE

Canadians depend on the news media to be informed about the world. How can we analyse the news to ensure we are getting a balanced, unbiased presentation of events?

Informing the Public

An informed public is essential in a democratic society. But what is the role of the news media in creating an informed public?

A good news report should present the facts in a balanced and unbiased way. It should report both sides of the story, not just one point of view. In presenting the facts, a news report must answer six questions: who, what, when, where, why, and how? These questions should be answered in the first few sentences, whether it is a newspaper article or a television broadcast. The details of the event follow after. The amount of detail provided is determined by the length of the article or broadcast as well as the importance of the event.

Media News

Victoria   April 30, 1998

PRESIDENT OUSTED

New Leader Takes Over

Housing Prices Hit Record High

Troops Withdraw

Local Hero

Which news item on this mock front page do you think is the most important? The least important? Why?

Newspapers

Although most Canadians get their news from television, to be better informed you need to read a newspaper. Newspapers provide the details behind the television news headlines.

The way in which a newspaper is set up tells you a few things about the events it is covering. The front page is the primary selling feature. The main story is the one with the biggest headline, placed at the top of the page. Less important stories receive smaller headlines. Occasionally, one event, such as the death of Diana, Princess of Wales in August 1997, is so shocking and dramatic that it is the only headline and story on the front page.

Newspaper articles are written in an inverted pyramid style. The story places the most important information—the ending—first in order to grab the reader's attention. The details of the story follow, beginning with the most important points. Knowing how the news story is reported will help you to evaluate facts the next time you read a newspaper.

Newspapers have to rely on carefully chosen words to capture the sights and sounds of a news story. Sometimes an effective photograph can help portray an event. What newspapers do best, however, is present facts and figures. These details are the key to helping you analyse and interpret the information.

Television

Most Canadians get their news from television. Modern telecommunications technology has enabled television to broadcast news events live as they happen from just about anywhere in the world. Live coverage creates an immediacy and a sense of audience participation that newspapers cannot achieve. Television stations even interrupt regular programming to bring audiences the latest reports on major breaking news stories. Such interruptions create a sense of urgency that quickly defines the importance of the event.

Most news broadcasts, however, appear at regularly scheduled times. The stories they report are limited to an average of 60 seconds. Such time restrictions allow the story to convey the emotion and action of an event, but not the detailed facts and figures. Critics argue that such brief news clips, with their dramatic **sound bites** and contrived photo opportunities, present only superficial coverage of events. The dramatic appeal of a particular story's videotape determines its news coverage rather than the importance of the story itself.

Analysis

Newspapers and television news broadcasts may also provide ana-

TV VERBAL DUELS MAY NOT SWING TOO MANY VOTERS

Joe Clark didn't knock over his glass of water.

Pierre Trudeau didn't swear.

There were no strings visible behind Ed Broadbent's back leading to Dennis McDermott.

The Great Debate, therefore, could be called a success for all three party leaders.

But it's doubtful Sunday's nationally televised encounter will have much effect on the voters...

They already knew, without seeing them lined up for them on their TV screens, that Broadbent is to the left of Trudeau while Clark is to his right, or somewhere nearby.

They already knew that Clark is no match for Trudeau in close verbal combat, that the prime minister has a poor memory, that Broadbent has delusions of grandeur.

Still, it was nice to see all three of them together again after seven weeks on the road in search of votes. Nearly everything they've been saying since they began the campaign was included in the nearly two-hour TV show.

It would have been more entertaining, though, if the moderator, McGill University president-elect David Johnston, and the three TV newsmen from the three networks that put on the show, hadn't been there.

As soon as anyone began to show any heat, or get into real argument, they were steered to a new topic. Invariably when Clark was one of the debaters it was the Conservative leader who breathed a sigh of relief.

Clark lost

Trudeau has had to hold his own with university students. Broadbent has had to argue his way through union halls. Clark, though, appeared lost without the Speaker of the House of Commons to keep the debate in bounds.

Both Broadbent and Trudeau spent a lot of time talking about the inconsistencies of Clark's campaign promises—deficit, no deficit; PetroCan, no PetroCan; negotiation with Quebec, no negotiation with Quebec.

In vain, Clark asked the NDP leader to "try a little harder to understand" what he was saying.

Both Broadbent and the prime minister claimed to have caught the Tory leader out in new inconsistencies during the show, but Clark was able to remind viewers that Trudeau himself had changed his mind on wage and price controls in 1974.

As the prime minister—in his best university lecturing style—recited his often-repeated list of vascillations by Clark, the Tory leader stood before him like a schoolboy with a guilty grin on his face.

By the end of his television encounter with Pierre Trudeau, Joe Clark was seized with an attack of nervous guffaws. The prime minister, not very kindly, guffawed back at him....

From the Ottawa Citizen, 14 May 1979, p.1.

1. Which points expressed in this story are facts? Which are opinions? What impressions of each leader does the writer convey? Do you think this is balanced reporting? Explain.

MAKING CONNECTIONS

1. In your class, design the media coverage for a recent news event. In four groups, cover the story a) as a newspaper story, b) as a television news report, c) as a newspaper editorial, and d) as a television editorial commentary. Afterwards, discuss the degree to which each groups's coverage was balanced and reliable.

2. Watch the evening news on television. Select one important news item and make notes of the amount of detail the story provides. Find the same story reported in the newspaper and note the detail it provides. How do the two accounts compare?

lysis of key news events. Columnists and commentators provide insights beyond the reporting of facts. The news media may also offer interpretation of news events in the form of editorials. Editorials express personal opinions that are designed to get you thinking about an issue.

KEYWORDS

sound bites

REFERENDUM
Independence or Federalism?
FOCUSSING ON THE ISSUE

In 1976, Quebec voters elected, for the first time, a government committed to separation from Canada. Four years later the issue was put to a referendum. Did Quebeckers want independence, or did they want a renewed form of federalism?

René Lévesque celebrates the joy of victory (left) in 1976 and suffers the agony of defeat (right) in 1980. What are the events surrounding these photographs?

A New Political Force

During the 1970s in Quebec, the Parti Québécois (PQ) gradually gained popular support. Founded in 1968, the PQ brought together different groups with a common objective: the peaceful, democratic transition to an independent Quebec. Under the leadership of René Lévesque, the PQ emerged from its first provincial election in 1970 with almost 25 per cent of the popular vote. In the 1973 election,

over 30 per cent of Quebec voters supported the party.

Lévesque was the most popular politician in Quebec during the 1970s. He spoke passionately about Quebec in a language everybody understood. Unsure that a majority of voters supported separation, he cleverly promised that if the PQ was elected he would hold a **referendum** on the question of separation. In other words, people could vote for the PQ without necessarily voting for independence.

This strategy paid off in the provincial election of 1976. The incumbent Liberal government, under premier Robert Bourassa, was discredited by scandal and plagued by economic problems. The PQ swept to victory with 41 per cent of the popular vote and a majority of the seats in the National Assembly. But was the election of the PQ a vote for better government, or a vote for separation? Only time would tell.

Bill 101

One of the most important measures introduced by the new government was Bill 101, the so-called "Charter of the French Language." The law was passed in response to fears that French was slowly disappearing in Quebec. The birth rate among French-speaking Quebeckers was low. Many immigrants to the province were not learning French. Use of the language seemed to be declining in everyday life.

The passage of Bill 101 in 1977 made French the only official language in Quebec. It required all public services to be offered in French and most businesses to operate in French. Most children, with few exceptions, were required to attend French-language schools. Outdoor signs in languages other than French were banned. From the point of view of French-speaking Quebeckers, Bill 101 protected their language. Quebec was, after all, surrounded by English-speaking North Americans, and was constantly bombarded with English through the media. English-speaking Quebeckers, on the other hand, felt threatened by Bill 101. It prompted many of them to leave the province.

Oui or Non?

In 1980, the PQ held a referendum on the future of Quebec's relationship with the rest of Canada. The referendum did not offer a straightforward choice for or against independence. What the PQ proposed was **sovereignty-association**. Instead of independence, Quebec would form a partnership with Canada. It would continue to share certain institutions, such as a supreme court, a currency, a banking system, and free trade, as well as a permanent joint commission to deal with grievances. Otherwise, Quebec would make its own laws and collect its own taxes. This was a proposal only—the federal government never agreed to the idea.

The referendum ballot asked voters whether or not they agreed to give the Quebec government "a mandate to negotiate sovereignty-association with Canada." The result of those negotiations would then be put to another referendum. It was a step-by-step process that disappointed fervent separatists who wanted an outright declaration of independence. Non-separatists also criticized it, arguing that the PQ was trying to confuse the electorate into voting for independence without ever explicitly asking the question.

The referendum campaign was hard-fought and emotional. Lévesque rallied the "Yes" side, while Claude Ryan, the leader of the provincial Liberal party, led the "No" side. Ryan was supported by federal politicians of all parties, and most strongly by the Liberal prime minister, Pierre Trudeau. He promised that if the vote was "No" he would discuss changes to the Constitution in an effort to satisfy Quebec's grievances.

On 20 May 1980, Canadians held their breath as the ballots were counted. The result was a safe, but not overwhelming, victory for the "No" side with 60 per cent of the vote. Among French-speaking voters, however, the split was about even. For the time being at least, it looked as though the separatist challenge to Canadian unity had been rebuffed.

Still, there was much work to be done. Quebec had served notice that it was not happy with the political and constitutional **status quo**. Trudeau had promised to discuss a "renewed" federalism. The Quebec referendum was not the end of the debate. Rather, it was the beginning of a long process of negotiation that would occupy most of the next decade.

◀═⊏ MAKING CONNECTIONS ⊐▶

1. a) Define sovereignty-association in your own words. Do you think it is the same as separation?
   b) If the same question regarding sovereignty-association had been asked of Canadians outside of Quebec in 1980, what do you suppose the results would have been? Defend your view.

2. In the 1980 referendum, those who voted "No" tended to be English-speaking, newly immigrated, older, poorer, and less educated. "Yes" voters tended to be French-speaking, younger, wealthier, and better educated. Why do you think each of these groups voted the way they did?

KEYWORDS

referendum

sovereignty-association

status quo

UNIT 9:

Kenojuak Ashevak, *Birds at Sunset* (1987)

Kenojuak Ashevak (1927-) is an Inuit artist living in Cape Dorset. Her drawings, prints, and sculptures draw on her imagination and the vision of things in her own eye rather than subjective reality.

SHIFTING CURRENTS

1981-1990

*Skills and Processes

A NEW WORLD ORDER
The World in 1981
FOCUSSING ON THE ISSUE

*The 1980s began with a worldwide recession, then blossomed into several years
of frantic economic expansion. But the most important event of the decade
was the dramatic collapse of communism. What forces led to the end of the Cold War?*

Recession and Reaction

The developed world was in the middle of a deep **recession** when the 1980s began. In many countries, at least 10 per cent of the workforce was unemployed by the autumn of 1982, and the standard of living was steadily declining. Even when the world economy began to recover in 1983 and unemployment rates began to fall, tens of thousands of traditional manufacturing jobs had disappeared. New jobs, mostly in the service industry, took their place, but they paid less and were less secure.

For the wealthy and powerful, the decade became a prosperous time, personified by the yuppy (young urban professional)—a successful, rich, high-living overachiever. But not everyone could be a yuppy. The prosperity had a fragile foundation. Governments in many developed countries borrowed increasing amounts of money to deal with the social costs of the recession. In October 1987, stock markets around the world tumbled, coming very close to repeating the crash of 1929 that had plunged the world into depression. (See page 116.) This time the markets recovered, but it was a sobering experience for investors.

As the economies of developed nations reeled from recession to recovery and almost back again, voters shifted to the right. In Britain, Margaret Thatcher led the Conservative party to power in 1979, promising to end Britain's economic decline and to reduce the role of government in society. Re-elected in 1983 and 1987, Thatcher was the first British prime minister in the century to serve three consecutive terms. (She was also the first woman in that country to become prime minister.) Her government **privatized** several publicly owned industries and cut funds for social programs, including education, housing, and health care. During her time in office, unemployment rose sharply in Britain and the government's role in the economy was sharply curtailed.

Thatcher's policies were much admired by Ronald Reagan, who became president of the United States in 1981. Reagan came to office with the support of business leaders, who wanted fewer government regulations; defence contractors, who wanted more government spending on weapons; and wealthy people in general, who wanted their taxes cut. Reagan's support for traditional values won him the support of the churches, and his opposition to the Soviet Union appealed to hard-line anti-communists who believed the US should strengthen its military in order to deter commu-

nist aggression everywhere in the world. In 1983, Reagan called the USSR an "evil empire" and proposed a new anti-missile system based in outer space. He called it the Strategic Defence Initiative, but it was known popularly as "Star Wars." American voters liked Reagan's easygoing, optimistic style and re-elected him to a second term in 1984.

The Collapse of Communism

Ironically, even as Reagan rallied the American people against the "evil empire," the Soviet Union was crumbling. Mikhail Gorbachev became leader of the USSR in 1985 and was determined to reform Soviet society. He attempted to transform the inefficient Soviet system, produced by decades of Communist party rule, through the policies of **perestroika** ("restructuring") in the economy and **glasnost** ("openness") in political and cultural matters. He reduced the power of the party and expanded the role of elected legislatures. He withdrew troops from Afghanistan, where the USSR had been involved in a fruitless war since its invasion of that country in 1979. He also improved relations with China, and entered into a series of arms-control agreements with the US.

It became clear that under Gorbachev, the Soviet Union would not ruthlessly suppress anti-communist dissent among **bloc** countries as it had in the past. As a result, discontent with the communist system surfaced in many parts of Eastern Europe. In Poland, opposition to communist rule had been threatening the political status quo since 1980, when the trade union Solidarity was formed. Strikes and demonstrations erupted as the government could no longer deal effectively with the country's social and economic problems. By 1989, Solidarity had won the right to free elections, and in June of that year the labour union won 260 of 261 seats in the new parliament.

East Germans took to the streets in 1989 demanding an end to communist rule. The Soviets did not intervene, and the East German government fell. Demonstrators rushed to the Berlin Wall and began tearing it down. One by one, other bloc countries in Eastern Europe ousted their communist-led governments. It was one of the most remarkable moments in history. Communism was suddenly in retreat. The Cold War seemed to be over.

Government leaders in China, however, were determined to show that *glasnost* would not be tolerated in their country. In 1989, young demonstrators occupied Tiananmen Square in Beijing to demand greater freedom from their government. As the world watched the television news in dismay, Communist party leaders sent in the army to crush the rebellion. More than 5000 Chinese were killed, and the reform movement was quashed.

Despite Tiananmen Square, 1989 was undoubtedly a major turning point in the history of the modern world. Since the end of the Second World War, events had been dominated by ideological conflicts between communist and noncommunist countries. During the 1980s, with the collapse of communism—at least in Eastern Europe—people heralded the beginning of a "New World Order." One writer even called it "the end of history," meaning that the great struggle that had

Following its construction in 1961, the Berlin Wall came to symbolize the great ideological gulf between communist and non-communist countries. What did its destruction in 1989 symbolize?

driven events in the modern world was over. As the decade came to a close, no one could say what the new order would look like. Everyone hoped that it would bring an era of world peace and prosperity, but only time would tell.

◄█═ MAKING CONNECTIONS ═█►

1. Why did voters in the Western democracies generally elect right-wing governments during the 1980s?

2. Throughout Eastern Europe, 1989 was a remarkable year of change. Divide the class into groups and prepare reports on events that occurred in 1989 in East Germany, Romania, Czechoslovakia, Poland, and Yugoslavia. How were the events in each country similar? How were they distinctive?

KEYWORDS

recession

privatize

perestroika

glasnost

bloc

CANADA IN RECESSION
Inflation and Unemployment
FOCUSSING ON THE ISSUE

As the 1980s began, Canada entered the worst recession since the 1930s. Thousands of Canadians lost their jobs, inflation remained high, and many businesses faced bankruptcy. What events led to the recession? What were the effects of the decline?

Causes of the Recession

A series of events in the 1970s had a major impact on Canada's economy in the 1980s. The first was the **devaluation** of the Canadian dollar. Between 1945 and 1973, currencies were always defined in terms of gold or the US dollar. In 1973, however, the US government "unpegged" the American dollar from the price of gold and allowed its value to be determined by market forces. The price of gold then increased dramatically, which led to a decrease in the value of many world currencies, including the Canadian dollar. It declined steadily from par with the US dollar in 1977 to a low of 69¢ to $1 US in 1985. Consequently, it cost more for Canadians to buy imported goods, which led to **inflation**.

A second event was the oil embargo of 1973. The Organization of Petroleum Exporting Countries (OPEC) cut back its exports and raised the price of oil. (See page 258.) The price increase, combined with falling currency values, sparked an inflationary spiral for all trading nations, including Canada. Caught in the financial squeeze, workers demanded, and received, significant wage increases, which pushed inflation even higher.

The third event was the introduction of compulsory **wage-and-price controls**. (See page 259.) In the 1972 election campaign, Prime Minister Trudeau had promised to bring down inflation. However, by 1975, Trudeau had to admit he had failed as the inflation rate reached 12 per cent. He decided to adopt wage-and-price controls for a three-year period. But while controls held inflation to 7 per cent in 1976, by 1978 the rate had rebounded to 9 per cent. By the 1980s, many workers were demanding greater pay hikes to gain back the ground they felt they had lost in the 1970s.

At the same time, unemployment levels began to rise as businesses and industries tried to control costs by freezing hiring and laying off workers. The federal and provincial governments faced increasing costs as a result of inflation and expanded job creation policies, but now there were fewer taxpayers to contribute to government revenues. Governments increased the size of their **deficits** to fund programs and then borrowed the money they needed to pay for them. The result was a steadily growing federal debt.

Soaring Interest Rates

In times of high inflation, financial institutions increase their **interest rates** on the money they lend so that they match or exceed the inflation rate. Because governments in Canada always pay their bills, their loans are considered low risk, so their interest rates are the lowest available. But businesses and individuals are much higher risks because there is no guarantee of their financial stability or their ability to repay the loans. As a result, financial institutions charge them higher interest rates. For businesses this means it costs them more to provide their goods and services. These costs are passed on to consumers in the form of higher prices. This, in turn, continued to fuel the inflationary spiral. By the 1980s, the combined effect of the events of the 1970s had let to skyrocketing interest rates of over 20 per cent and a return to double-digit inflation. Business expansion and new construction slowed dramatically. Consumer spending also decreased as prices soared and jobs became less secure. The decline in construction starts and consumer spending led to a further increase in unemployment, as businesses continued to lay off workers. In the early 1980s, Canada found itself in the worst recession since the Depression of the 1930s.

The Impact of the Recession

The health of an economy is usually measured by the Gross Domestic Product (GDP). This is the value of all goods and services produced in the country over a period of time, usually one year, adjusted for inflation. Using the GDP, it is possible to compare real growth in the economy from year to year. In 1981 and 1982, Canada's GDP recorded negative growth for six consecutive quarters. It was the longest economic downturn in Canada since the Depression.

The severity of the recession was also evident in the rising unemployment rate. But the figures were deceptive. Statistics Canada changed the way it calculated the unemployment rate when it reached 11 per cent. Those people whose unemployment benefits had run out or who had given up trying to find a job were no longer counted in the unemployment rolls. So while official unemployment climbed close to 12 per cent, many researchers estimated the actual figure to be between 14 and 20 per cent.

At the same time, the number of business and personal **bankruptcies** rose dramatically. The going-out-of-business sale and the garage sale became the latest trends in merchandising. Even large corporations were affected as companies such as Dome Petroleum and Chrysler Motors were pushed to the edge of bankruptcy by falling revenues and rising costs. Faced with the potential loss of thousands more jobs, governments

provided "bail out" packages of loans and loan guarantees to many faltering businesses. In the early 1980s, Canadians learned a new word to describe the state of their economy: *stagflation*—a stagnating economy with a high inflation rate.

Economic Growth in Canada, 1978-1983

YEAR	UNEMPLOYMENT %	INCREASE IN NO. OF JOBS	PRIME RATE* %	CONSUMER PRICE INDEX
1978	8.3	3.5	9.69	8.9
1979	7.4	4.1	12.9	9.2
1980	7.5	3.0	14.25	10.2
1981	7.5	2.8	19.29	12.5
1982	11.0	-3.3	15.81	10.8
1983	11.9	0.8	11.17	5.8

*The prime rate is the interest rate financial institutions charge their best customers. Most businesses and consumers pay rates above prime.
**Consumer Price Index is the measure of the average price of goods and services purchased by a typical urban Canadian household. It is calculated by comparing current prices of goods and services with the prices of the same goods and services at an established base year.
Canada Year Book, *1988*

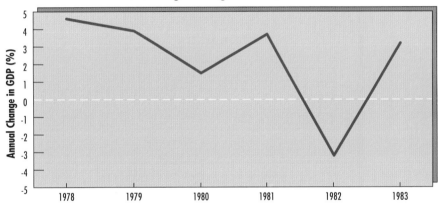

Percentage Change in GDP, 1978-1983

KEYWORDS

devaluation

inflation

wage-and-price controls

deficit

interest rate

bankruptcy

◄▩ MAKING CONNECTIONS ▩►

1. What connections can you find between the graph and the table?

2. Some economists suggest that the major cause of the recession was a loss of faith in the future, which caused people to cut spending. Suggest reasons to support this view.

CANADA'S CONSTITUTION
Patriation and Meech Lake
FOCUSSING ON THE ISSUE

The 1980 Quebec referendum showed that many people in that province were not happy with their place in Confederation. How was constitutional change expected to accommodate the desires of Quebeckers?

This proclamation, signed by Queen Elizabeth in Ottawa in 1982, declared the new Canadian constitution in effect. Why was the Queen involved in this process?

The Constitution Act

During the 1980 referendum campaign, Prime Minister Trudeau agreed that the Canadian constitution needed to be changed and he promised to do something about it: "Following a No vote, we will immediately take action to renew the constitution and we will not stop until we have done that," he declared.

Since 1867, the power to amend the Canadian constitution had rested with the British Parliament. While the Statute of Westminster in 1931 gave Canada independence in almost every respect, the power to change the Constitution had remained with Britain because Canadian politicians could not agree on an amending process. Trudeau was determined to

change this and make Canada a fully independent nation. So in 1980, he set out to **patriate** the Constitution. In September 1980, Trudeau met with the provincial premiers to come up with a plan for patriation. But the talks ended in a stalemate as both the federal and provincial governments argued to increase their powers at the expense of the other. When the talks broke down, Trudeau announced that the federal government would go ahead with its own request to the British Parliament to patriate the Constitution.

Trudeau's determination was reinforced by a Supreme Court ruling that declared it legal for the federal government to act on its own. Wanting to ensure that the provinces' interests were addressed, the premiers agreed to return to the negotiating table. In the fall of 1981, Ottawa and nine of the ten provinces reached a compromise deal. Only the Quebec premier, Réne Lévesque, remained apart, angry that the others would not give Quebec a **veto** over future constitutional changes—a veto Lévesque believed was necessary to protect his province's special place in Confederation.

The proposed constitutional changes won the approval of both the Canadian and British parliaments. On 17 April 1982, Queen Elizabeth officially signed the new Constitution Act in Ottawa. After 115 years, Canada finally had full control over its own government.

Meech Lake

The absence of Quebec's signature on the new constitution created new political controversy and uncertainty in the country. Once again, Quebec seemed to be divided from the rest of Canada. When Brian Mulroney became prime min-

ister in 1984, he was determined to bring Quebec into the constitutional family. In April 1987, he and the provincial premiers gathered at Meech Lake, north of Ottawa, to launch a new round of negotiations. Quebec's Liberal premier, Robert Bourassa, put five key demands on the table:

- the recognition of Quebec as a "distinct society"
- a veto for Quebec over all constitutional amendments
- greater power over immigration
- the right to opt out of shared-cost programs with Ottawa without financial penalty
- the right for the provinces to nominate some Supreme Court judges.

Much to the surprise of many observers, the prime ministers and the premiers were able to reach a deal. As part of the agreement, however, the federal Parliament and the legislatures of all ten provinces would have to ratify the Meech Lake Accord within three years.

The deal ran into opposition almost immediately. People began to question what "distinct society" really meant. Did it mean simply *different*, or did it mean *special*, in which case many Canadians outside Quebec were unwilling to accept the principle. There was also concern that the accord reduced the power of the federal

government to a level that some people feared threatened the unity of the country. As well, Aboriginal peoples felt that the accord ignored their concerns. In spite of the opposition, however, eight of the ten provinces ratified the agreement. But when it came to a vote in the Manitoba legislature in June 1990, a lone member, Elijah Harper, a Cree who felt that the accord did not meet the needs of Aboriginal peoples, refused to support it. Without his approval, the accord failed to pass in the Manitoba legislature. Without Manitoba's approval, the Meech Lake Accord died.

In Quebec, the defeat of Meech Lake was seen as a rejection of Quebec by the rest of the country. Many Quebeckers believed that the demands put forward by Premier Bourassa were the least Quebec could ask for, yet the deal had still been defeated. The fact that the majority of the provinces had approved the accord was forgotten in the emotional aftermath. Instead, the failure of Meech Lake served to renew the separatist movement in Quebec. Meanwhile, in the other provinces people were growing tired of talking about the constitution. They wanted to move on to other issues, such as the economy. As the decade ended, Quebec's position in Canada remained uncertain while Canadians themselves seemed more divided than ever.

MAKING CONNECTIONS

1. Prepare a timeline listing the major events in the constitutional debate from the Quebec referendum to the defeat of the Meech Lake Accord.

2. In your view, is Quebec a "distinct society"? Explain what the term means to you.

KEYWORDS

referendum

patriate

veto

THE PRIME MINISTER
Power in the Executive Branch

As the role of the prime minister has changed since the 1960s, so too has the bureaucracy surrounding the prime minister. How much power should be concentrated in the hands of the prime minister, the Privy Council Office, and the Prime Minister's Office in a democratic society?

The Prime Minister's Role

Although the Constitution gives wide powers to the governor general, this individual always acts on the advice of the prime minister, which makes the PM the most powerful person in the federal government. (See page 94.) For example, while the governor general has the power to make a wide variety of appointments, this power is in fact exercised by the PM. The PM not only considers Cabinet appointments, but also thousands of others—often called **patronage** appointments—to the **bureaucracy**, federal boards and commissions, **Crown corporations**, and other government agencies. The power to appoint and dismiss gives the PM tremendous control over the government bureaucracy.

In addition, like the other party leaders, the PM approves all candidates who run for the party in an election. Because of the expense of modern elections, few candidates can afford to run without the support of a political party. The PM's control of party nominees is a powerful weapon in maintaining party solidarity and keeping dissent to a minimum.

The Cabinet

After an election, the prime minister chooses a group of MPs to form the Cabinet. Each of these MPs takes charge of a government department, or **portfolio**. Since the PM can appoint or dismiss Cabinet ministers throughout the term, the size of the Cabinet and the assignments of the ministers may vary from time to time. Generally, the PM will attempt to appoint the Cabinet so that it fairly and accurately reflects the makeup of the country—at least one minister from each province, a number of female ministers, and where possible, ministers representing various cultural groups. Together, the PM and the Cabinet manage the affairs of the nation.

GOVERNMENT OF CANADA

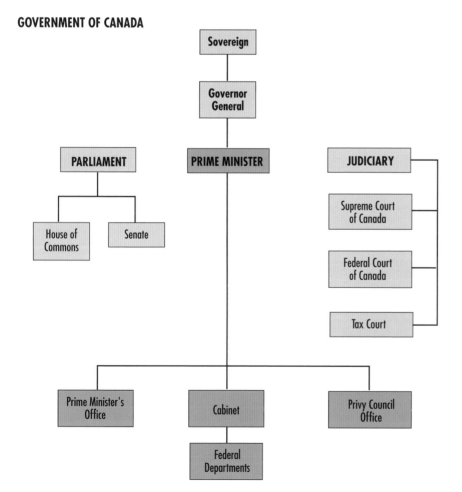

Since the 1970s, however, the Cabinet has been challenged by the growing power and importance of two offices: the Privy Council Office (PCO) and the Prime Minister's Office (PMO).

The Privy Council Office

The PCO, headed by a civil servant called the Clerk of the Privy Council, is in effect the PM's department of government. The role of the Clerk and the PCO is to serve the PM as leader of the government. The Clerk is also responsible for ensuring that all necessary information and documentation are available at Cabinet meetings. Since the Clerk and the PM work closely together setting agendas and priorities for Cabinet meetings, the Clerk has virtually unlimited access to the prime minister.

Given the heavy workload of a Canadian prime minister today, much of the responsibility for setting Cabinet agendas, resolving interdepartmental disputes among Cabinet ministers and their deputies, negotiating compromises on departmental priorities, establishing spending priorities, and similar administrative duties falls to the Clerk of the Privy Council. Because the Clerk is one of the PM's key advisors, this individual is one of the most influential and powerful non-elected government officials. Many Cabinet ministers and senior bureaucrats resent the fact that they must work through the Clerk to get to the PM, but few Cabinet ministers or their deputies are willing to challenge the Clerk's recommendations on the organization of government business.

The Prime Minister's Office

The PMO serves the prime minister as leader of a party and is largely made up of politically appointed staff. The prime minister's principal secretary is in charge of the staff administering the Prime Minister's Office. Part of the PMO's responsibility is to organize and schedule the PM's appearances at various political functions. It monitors the public's responses to government programs and policies through frequent public opinion polls, and it tries to measure the government's popularity and chances for re-election. One of the most important responsibilities of the PMO, however, is ensuring the PM has a positive public image and a good relationship with the media. The senior members of the PMO are sometimes referred to as "spin doctors" because of their efforts to put a positive "spin" on media reports concerning the PM and the government.

The main responsibility of the principal secretary is to give political advice to the prime minister. This position is usually given to an old and trusted friend of the prime minister because of the need for frankness and honesty. As a political advisor, the principal secretary also recommends people for the thousands of patronage appointments made by the PM. Thus, like the Clerk of the Privy Council, this non-elected **partisan** official is one of the most powerful people in Ottawa.

Too Much Power?

Critics of the PMO and the PCO maintain that too much power is concentrated in the hands of the two people who lead them. They argue that, in reality, the government of Canada is the prime minister, the principal secretary, and the Clerk of the Privy Council. Cabinet members are reduced to administrative clerks with little policy-making influence, while individual MPs are simply there to vote the party line when called upon to do so. Supporters of the **status quo** contend that modern government is so complex and the demands on the prime minister are so great that government would grind to a halt if the PMO and the PCO did not exist.

MAKING CONNECTIONS

1. Do you think the prime minister has too much control over the government? Explain.

2. Role-play a discussion among the PM, the Clerk of the PCO, the principal secretary to the PM, and several Cabinet ministers about a recent issue of concern to the federal government. Each person in the discussion must maintain her/his perspective throughout.

KEYWORDS

patronage

bureaucracy

Crown corporation

portfolio

partisan

status quo

RIGHTS AND FREEDOMS
A Charter for Canadians

In 1960, the Diefenbaker government passed the Canadian Bill of Rights, while several provinces passed their own human rights codes. Why, then, did Canada need a Charter of Rights and Freedoms included in the Constitution in 1982?

The Charter of Rights

Although Canada had a Bill of Rights in 1981, it applied only to areas of federal jurisdiction. If the Bill of Rights were to be **entrenched** in the Constitution, it would have to be applied to all laws at all levels of government, past, present, and future. However, an entrenched bill of rights would require a constitutional amendment and, as every prime minister from Mackenzie King to Lester Pearson had discovered, constitutional amendments were difficult to achieve in Canada.

During the 1980 Quebec **referendum** (see page 288), Prime Minister Trudeau had promised that following a "No" vote, he would

push to patriate the Constitution, thereby removing the last legal connection to Britain and making Canada truly independent. As part of his constitutional package, he promised a charter that would protect the rights of all Canadians, and especially those of French Quebeckers in the areas of language and education. Because many of the provincial premiers had joined the "No" campaign and had made promises of their own to Quebeckers, Trudeau believed that they would co-operate with his plan for **patriation**. But at the constitutional conference convened in 1981, the premiers rejected Trudeau's patriation package. (See page 296.)

The charter of rights and freedoms originally proposed by Trudeau and his justice minister, Jean Chrétien, provided for the entrenchment of the kind of democratic, civil, and legal rights that Canadians had long enjoyed. In many ways, its provisions were similar to the existing Canadian Bill of Rights. (See page 212.) The proposal was opposed by some Canadians who did not believe that entrenchment of these rights was either desirable or necessary. They believed the rights of Canadians could be ensured through the traditions of the unwritten constitution. Convention, they argued, would continue protecting civil rights while maintaining the flexibility

---

VIEWPOINTS

ENTRENCHING RIGHTS AND FREEDOMS IN THE CONSTITUTION

At the Constitutional Conference in 1968, then Justice Minister Pierre Trudeau first expressed his views about the need for a Charter of Rights and Freedoms.

I have been asked what need there is in Canada for a bill of rights.... We are not in this country innocent of book-burning or [book]-banning legislation, or deprivations by law of previously guaranteed minority-language rights, of

legal expropriation which at times appears to be more akin to confiscation, of persons arrested in the night and held incommunicado for days. We have no reason to be complacent. How many Canadians know that Canadian law permits evidence to be introduced by the police in criminal trials no matter how illegally that evidence may have been obtained?

Pierre Elliott Trudeau, Minister of Justice, at the Constitutional Conference, February 1968.

EXCERPTS FROM THE CHARTER

The Charter states in part:

Section 2. Everyone has the following fundamental freedoms: (a) freedom of conscience and religion; (b) freedom of thought, belief, opinion and expression, including freedom of the press and other media of communication; (c) freedom of peaceful assembly; and (d) freedom of association.

Sections 7-14. (These sections guarantee Canadian's legal rights such as life, liberty, and security of person; the right to a trial, and a lawyer; and protection against arbitrary imprisonment.)

Section 15. (1) Every individual is equal before and under the law and has the right to the equal protection and equal benefit of the law without discrimination,

and, in particular, without discrimination based on race, national or ethnic origin, colour, religion, sex, age or mental or physical disability.

Section 33. (1) Parliament or the legislature of a province may expressly declare in an Act of Parliament or of the legislature, as the case may be, that the Act or a provision thereof shall operate notwithstanding a provision included in section 2 or sections 7-15 of this Charter....

1. Despite the hopes of many, the notwithstanding clause (Section 33) of the Charter has been used. Research the instances of its use and explain whether you think it was necessary.

---

needed to meet the demands of a continuously changing society.

In defending his patriation proposal, which he called "the people's package," Trudeau argued that in an age of big and powerful governments, citizens needed the protection of an entrenched bill of rights. The only way to force lawmakers at all levels to protect and foster citizens' rights, he believed, was to include those rights as part of the nation's constitution. Trudeau also argued that the language and education rights guaranteed by the proposed charter would ensure that French Quebeckers would be full and equal participants in the

Canadian federation. He believed that those guarantees were necessary to block the separatist movement and keep Quebec in Confederation.

Entrenching the Charter

During the final stages of the 1981 Constitutional Conference, a compromise was reached. Nine of the ten premiers agreed to support the federal government's patriation package if a "notwithstanding clause" were added. This clause allowed legislatures to exempt some legislation from Charter provisions

under certain circumstances. Hoping that none of the legislatures would use the clause, and believing that a weakened charter was better than no charter, Trudeau accepted the compromise. When the Constitution was patriated in 1982, the Charter of Rights and Freedoms was entrenched in Canadian law.

MAKING CONNECTIONS

1. Trudeau had support in Canada to seek **unilateral** patriation of the Constitution, including a Charter without the notwithstanding clause. If you had been prime minister at the time, what would you have done? Why?

2. In small groups, discuss the following question: Should the Charter apply only to Canadian citizens or to all persons in Canada? Explain.

KEYWORDS

entrench

patriation

referendum

unilateral

CANADA'S LEGAL SYSTEM
Criminal and Civil Law

The legal system exists to protect the rights and freedoms of all individuals and to ensure that everyone is treated fairly and equally. What are the elements of Canada's legal system?

The Courts

The Canadian court system was established to interpret and apply the laws passed by the federal Parliament and the provincial legislatures. Courts, and the judges who preside over them, have a responsibility to protect Canadian society from offenders through **criminal law** and to resolve disputes between individuals or between individuals and businesses or government through **civil law**. The courts must also ensure that the provisions of the Canadian Charter of Rights and Freedoms are upheld for all citizens.

Responsibility for Canadian courts is shared between the federal and provincial governments. The federal government is responsible for the Supreme Court of Canada, the Federal Court, and the Citizenship Court, while the provinces are responsible for all other courts. The court systems vary from province to province. In general, however, more serious cases are tried before higher provincial courts, while less serious offences are heard before lower courts.

Criminal Law

Criminal law deals with offences against society, such as murder, assault, and theft. Canada's criminal law is founded on British legal prac-

THE CANADIAN COURT SYSTEM

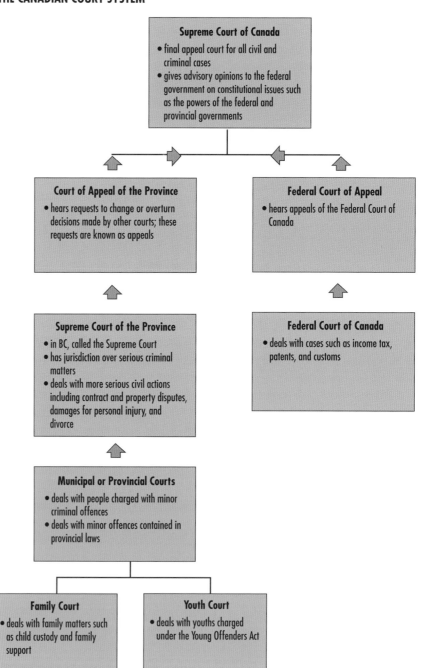

Supreme Court of Canada
- final appeal court for all civil and criminal cases
- gives advisory opinions to the federal government on constitutional issues such as the powers of the federal and provincial governments

Court of Appeal of the Province
- hears requests to change or overturn decisions made by other courts; these requests are known as appeals

Federal Court of Appeal
- hears appeals of the Federal Court of Canada

Supreme Court of the Province
- in BC, called the Supreme Court
- has jurisdiction over serious criminal matters
- deals with more serious civil actions including contract and property disputes, damages for personal injury, and divorce

Federal Court of Canada
- deals with cases such as income tax, patents, and customs

Municipal or Provincial Courts
- deals with people charged with minor criminal offences
- deals with minor offences contained in provincial laws

Family Court
- deals with family matters such as child custody and family support

Youth Court
- deals with youths charged under the Young Offenders Act

tices. It is sometimes called case law because, over a number of years, the system has been revised and expanded as a result of rulings in other trials.

Criminal offences and their penalties are set out in the Criminal Code of Canada. For an action to be considered a crime, it must meet three criteria: it must be an offence under the Criminal Code; the accused must have intended to break the law or have been aware that his or her actions were illegal; and the accused must be of **sound mind**. A person accused of a crime is considered innocent until proven guilty in a court of law.

Criminal conduct is divided into two classes. Summary offences are less serious acts that carry lower maximum penalties. These offences, which include traffic violations and disturbing the peace, are tried in a provincial court before a **magistrate**. Indictable offences are more serious crimes. They fall into three categories. The least serious indictable offences, such as theft under $1000, are tried before a magistrate or provincial court judge. For more serious crimes, such as armed robbery, the accused may choose to be tried before a magistrate, a judge, or a judge and jury. The most serious indictable offences, such as murder, are tried in provincial superior court before a judge and jury. This follows a preliminary hearing before a magistrate in which it is determined if there is enough evidence to hold the accused for trial.

Civil Law

Civil law involves matters such as property ownership, contract disputes, and family rights. In Canada, civil law is based on British common law and Quebec's Civil Code. Nine of the ten provinces follow common law. This is a system of rules based on **precedents**, judicial rulings, and customary practices. The system has evolved over hundreds of years as it has been adapted to reflect changing circumstances.

Quebec's Civil Code is also based on legal principles dating back centuries. Founded on the French legal code, the Civil Code is a comprehensive statement of rules of law. The Civil Code relies less on precedent than common law. As a result, it is modified from time to time by the Quebec National Assembly to reflect contemporary Canadian life.

The purpose of civil law is to make sure individuals honour their agreements and do not violate the rights of others. In criminal cases, it is the government or the Crown that takes the accused to court. In civil cases, one party, called the plaintiff, **sues** another party, called the defendant. The court listens to the evidence presented by both sides and then rules in favour of one side or the other. The court can award **damages** or financial compensation, but it cannot impose punishment.

CANADA'S LEGAL SYSTEM

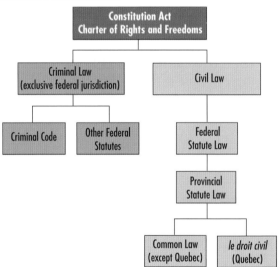

MAKING CONNECTIONS

1. Judges can only be removed from office for a criminal or serious moral offence. This is to ensure that the judiciary remains unbiased and independent of any government. Do you think this makes a judge unbiased? Do you think it is possible for anyone to be unbiased? Explain your answer.

2. Select one of the legal issues discussed in this book and trace its process through the Canadian court system.

KEYWORDS

criminal law

civil law

sound mind

magistrate

precedent

sue

damages

JUVENILE JUSTICE
The Young Offenders Act

FOCUSSING ON THE ISSUE

According to the Young Offenders Act, young people who break the law must be treated differently from adult offenders. How are young people treated when they commit crimes? What are the controversies surrounding the Young Offenders Act?

Changing Views

In the nineteenth century, children 14 and older who broke the law were tried in adult court. If found guilty, they faced the same punishment as adults. Around the turn of the century, society began to take a different view of youth crime. In Canada, this was reflected in the Juvenile Delinquents Act of 1908. Youths who broke the law were no longer treated as criminals but as misguided children in need of rehabilitation rather than punishment.

Over the years, however, many people became increasingly critical of the act because it failed to take into account the legal rights of young people. Juvenile delinquents seldom had legal representation in court. Their trials were conducted informally behind closed doors. Judges, lawyers, and probation officers who handled delinquency cases were often poorly trained, yet they had the power to decide arbitrarily the fate of the young people who came before them.

In the early 1960s, the federal government initiated efforts to replace the Juvenile Delinquents Act. But no consensus could be reached among politicians, the judiciary, law-enforcement officials, or concerned citizens about what reforms were necessary. As a result, two decades passed before new legislation was drafted.

In 1984, the Young Offenders Act was introduced to replace the Juvenile Delinquents Act. It sought to balance the just treatment of young offenders with the best interests of society. While it gave young people special protection under the law, it also made them accountable for their actions.

Terms of the Act

The Young Offenders Act defines a young person as someone aged 12 to 17. Anyone under 12 cannot be charged with an offence, while anyone over 17 is tried as an adult. In serious cases, such as murder, armed robbery, or sexual assault, a youth who is at least 14 at the time of the offence may be transferred from youth court to adult court. All young offenders have the right to a lawyer, to a fair trial, and to be free from **arbitrary detention**. Parents must be notified of all proceedings and may be ordered to attend court.

A young person convicted of a criminal offence receives a disposition, which is the equivalent of a sentence in an adult trial. Dispositions can range from an absolute discharge to secure custody. This allows a judge to consider the particular circumstances of the offender, the needs of the victim, and the protection of society. If

a judge feels a young offender needs some limits imposed upon his or her freedom, he or she may order **probation** for up to two years. The most serious disposition is a **custody order**, which is seen as a last resort. It is issued only when a youth is considered a danger to society, when other forms of disposition have failed, or when the crime was extremely violent. Custody can either be open custody in foster or group homes, or secure custody in wilderness camps or detention facilities. The maximum period a young offender may be kept in a custody facility is three years for most offences, and ten years for first-degree murder (if tried in adult court).

When a young person is charged with a crime but acquitted, or when the charge is dismissed, all records are destroyed. If the youth is found guilty, the records are kept for five years in the case of a **summary offence** and for five additional years after the disposition is completed in the case of an **indictable offence**. Furthermore, in reporting an offence and the subsequent trial, the media are not allowed to reveal the name of the accused person. Destroying records and protecting the identity of the accused ensure that young offenders are given a fresh start.

304   *Canadian Issues: A Contemporary Perspective*

IS THE YOUNG OFFENDERS ACT EFFECTIVE?

Under the Young Offenders Act, young people face the consequences of their actions but not the same consequences as adults. Many people support the act, but others feel that it is too lenient towards young people. Whether or not the Young Offenders Act is in step with the times is a matter of heated public debate.

David Nameth recalls how his mom nervously drove blocks out of her way one evening to avoid a group of youths standing on the street near her home. She didn't realize the ominous-looking "gang" was nothing more than her 18-year-old son and a bunch of his friends.…"That really showed me how afraid people are of teenagers because of young offenders," Nameth says of his mother's reaction…"We've just got a bad reputation because of a few that choose to do crime," adds classmate Lindsay Williamson, 17."

Sandra Cordon, "Teenagers Say Law too Easy on Youth," Vancouver Sun, 14 April 1997, p. A4. Reprinted with permission of The Canadian Press.

Dr. Michael Way…a consultant with Alberta Justice, guessed that the teen [convicted of a violent attack on a Brinks guard] had more than an 80 per cent chance of being rehabilitated in the youth system but only a 10 per cent chance in a federal penitentiary.…Mr. Black [the victim]…had returned to work.…[He]comments, "It looks like you have to die before someone gets transferred [to adult court]…the justice system, by focusing on reha-

bilitation, often ignores the rights of victims, the protection of the public, and the delivery of justice. Furthermore, the ability of the penal system, youth and adult, to rehabilitate is suspect."

Abridgement of "Soft Landing for a Faceless Thug: A Calgary Judge Refuses to Send a Murderous Youth to Adult Court," by Les Sillars in Alberta Report, vol. 11 (10), 25 March 1996. Reprinted by permission of Alberta Report.

Priscilla de Villiers, president of Caveat (Canadians Against Violence Everywhere Advocating its Termination) [says]…there has been a "frightful" increase in violent predations by 11- and 12-year-old children. [She] is incensed that many federal politicians refuse to acknowledge the problem. "It's a mistake to say people are overreacting.…Nor is public concern about youth crime merely hysteria based on media over-reporting.…If there seem to be more violent crimes now, the impression is real."

Abridged version of "Younger and Much More Brutal: Crime Trends Point to an Explosion in Adolescent Criminality," British Columbia Report, vol. 7 (43), 24 June 1996, pp. 18–21. Reprinted courtesy of British Columbia Report.

1. What is the attitude towards young people or the Young Offenders Act in each of these viewpoints? Which of these viewpoints do you agree with most strongly? Disagree with most strongly? Explain your answers.

MAKING CONNECTIONS

1. In your opinion, what are the fundamental differences between children and adults? Should Canada's laws reflect these differences? Give reasons for your answer.

2. Research amendments made to the Young Offenders Act since 1984. Discover the reasons for each amendment. Are there any current amendments being proposed to the act?

KEYWORDS

arbitrary detention

probation

custody order

summary offence

indictable offence

SKILL BUILDER
Written Presentations
FOCUSSING ON THE ISSUE

Among the most essential skills of a social scientist is the ability to make effective written presentations. In writing about issues, how do you decide on focus and structure? What skills are involved in writing clearly, succinctly, and logically?

Written Presentations

There are various forms of written presentations, ranging from personal accounts or imaginary stories to formal reports or essays. A written presentation on a particular issue that takes the form of a subjective or personal viewpoint—a play, dramatic dialogue, diary, or memoir—can be very effective and instructive, as long as it includes enough factual detail. A written presentation of a more formal nature—a report, essay, or editorial—follows a more rigid format, but is a valuable skill to develop in analysing and interpreting important issues.

In order to create an accurate, thought-provoking written presentation about an issue—no matter what the format—you must consider several important factors. First, begin with an issue and develop a focus for that issue. For example, in an essay on the controversial Young Offenders Act, your focus might be: "Should youth be treated differently from adults under the law?" Then, do some research to learn more about your issue and, perhaps, to adjust the focus of your work. On the issue of young offenders, you might decide to take a historical view of the issue. In doing so, you would adjust your focus to compare how young people in Canada have been treated under the law in the past with how they are treated today, and to explain the reasons for the difference in treatment.

Next, consider your audience. Who will read your work or be influenced by your point of view— a convicted young offender? A probation officer? A parent? Or a mock judicial inquiry into juvenile justice? Choose an appropriate format and length for your presentation.

The following outline explains the steps to follow in preparing a written presentation.

Focussing on the issue
- What are the questions you would like to ask about the issue? Prepare a list.

Developing a plan
- What is the time frame in which you must complete your presentation? Draw up a schedule.
- How are you going to organize the information that you research? Consider using flow diagrams/charts, organizers, graphs, tallying/ranking lists, and timelines.
- Are there any secondary issues that should be explored? Add these to your focus questions.

Finding sources, researching information, and recording notes
- Refer to several types of sources such as databases, information/vertical files (for recent articles, pamphlets), audiovisual materials, CD-ROM databases, Internet websites, indexes, almanacs.
- Sort through the material, setting aside useful information and discarding the rest. Make precise notes about each source you use: author/editor; title; publication information (place, publisher, year of publication); page numbers where the information appears.
- Research the sources for ideas and make notes. Write a **synopsis** of the information.

Assessing your research
- Determine what information is based on fact and what is based on opinion.
- Decide if the information is pertinent to your topic and if it is clear.
- Review your focus questions. Check that your information answers all of them; if necessary revise your focus questions or your plan.
- If you need further information, refer back to your original sources or research different sources.

Reaching conclusions
- What **inferences** can you make from your information? What opinions can you draw and on what evidence are they based?

Communicating your findings
- Using the results of your research and the conclusions you have reached, write some general

FORMATS FOR WRITTEN PRESENTATIONS

The Research Essay

An essay differs from a report: a report presents facts to describe or explain; an essay presents facts to support a particular point of view or argument. Writing a research essay can be fun because it gives you the opportunity to argue and persuade others that your ideas have merit. It is also a useful skill to develop because in any occupation or career you will be called upon to process information, make decisions, and present your ideas.

Steps

1. *Thesis:* A thesis describes what you will prove in your essay, summing up your main argument. You should be able to express your thesis in one sentence.
2. *Outline:* Prepare an outline to organize the information you have collected. Group main ideas into paragraphs that each have an objective and arrange them in logical sequence. Make sure you have evidence (sub-points) to support the main idea of each paragraph.
3. *Writing:* Follow your outline, presenting your ideas clearly. Always keep your thesis in mind, and make sure all your ideas and sub-points support it.
4. *Conclusion:* Review your main arguments and how they prove your thesis.
5. *Review:* Set your essay aside for a few days. Then reread it with fresh eyes. Is your thesis clear? Do your arguments clearly support it? Are your arguments proven by facts? Is your essay persuasive? Is it grammatically correct? Make any revisions you feel will improve your essay.

A Play

A play, though quite different from an essay, can be quite effective in expressing your point of view on an issue. Writing a play allows you to argue and persuade others in creative ways—through the use of drama, dialogue, and characters.

Steps

1. *Elements:* Decide on setting, characters, plot, mood, theme, and the main dilemma in the play. Provide a bold, thought-provoking, or cliff-hanger ending.
2. *Facts:* Gather factual information through researching the issue. Consider which side of the issue you want to emphasize. Who will be your sympathetic characters? Who or what will be the antagonist(s)?
3. *Performance:* Decide upon the audience, the format (live performance or taped), and the length of your play. To keep your audience's attention, it is better to write two or three main scenes than several short, choppy ones.
4. *Show and Tell:* Make sure your play informs the audience; it must reveal the facts and various viewpoints about the issue. You must not only *show* the audience the issue through dramatic action and dialogue, you must *tell* them about the issue. Avoid the assumption that they already know about the issue; spell it out for them.

MAKING CONNECTIONS

1. Prepare a written presentation—essay or play—on one of the following topics relating to the Young Offenders Act. Be sure to include a list of research sources with your written presentation.
   - Public disclosure of young offenders
   - Violence among the young: is it on the rise?
   - Does the YOA create young offenders?
   - Separate justice: should youth be treated differently from adults under the law?

statements about the issue. Decide how your findings can be put to their best use. Consider how much time you have and the audience you are addressing. Here are some suggested written formats for expressing your findings: an essay; an editorial; a play or a poem; or a memoir or diary.

KEYWORDS

synopsis

inference

SPACE EXPLORATION
Canada's Contribution
FOCUSSING ON THE ISSUE

What has Canada contributed to and gained from space exploration?
How is it beneficial and is it worth the cost?

Blasting into Space

The space race was launched in October 1957 when the Soviet Union sent the *Sputnik* satellite into space, where it circled the earth for several months. Space exploration began in 1961 when Russian **cosmonaut** Yuri Gagarin orbited the earth once and touched down safely a short time later. The Americans were close behind and vowed to land a person on the moon before the end of the decade. This ambitious goal was achieved in July 1969, when two US astronauts, Neil Armstrong and Buzz Aldrin, landed on the moon in their small landing vehicle. "That's one small step for a man, one giant leap for mankind," said Armstrong as he became the first human to step onto the moon's barren surface.

Following a series of successful lunar landings, the American space program turned to another ambitious endeavour—the development of the space shuttle. The shuttle is a reusable spacecraft that blasts off like a rocket, but returns to earth like an airplane. The first shuttle, *Columbia*, was launched in 1981. From then on shuttle flights were a regular occurrence. Each one extended the length of time its crew remained in space, and each collected more and more knowledge about the world beyond the earth's atmosphere.

In January 1986, however, tragedy struck when the shuttle *Challenger* exploded just 73 seconds after blast-off, killing its entire seven-member crew. The shuttle program was suspended temporarily while the vehicle was redesigned. Shuttle flights resumed in 1988.

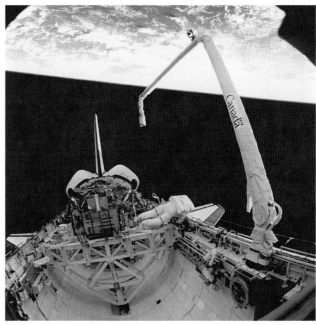

The Shuttle Remote Manipulator System, known as Canadarm, was Canada's first contribution to the US shuttle program.

Marc Garneau, Canada's first astronaut, took his flight on the space shuttle Challenger *in October 1984.*

Canadarm

Canada's first major contribution to the space program was Canadarm, developed by scientists at SPAR Aerospace Ltd. in Toronto. Canadarm has been part of the shuttle program since its inception. It is a long, remote-controlled arm mounted on the shuttle, intended to manipulate heavy objects in space. Canadarm is able to lift satellites out of the shuttle's cargo hold and set them in orbit. It can also retrieve damaged satellites and deftly carry out repairs to the shuttle in space.

Canadian Astronauts

The first Canadian in space was Marc Garneau, an electrical engineer from Quebec City. Garneau was one of six Canadians chosen from 4300 applicants for the country's first astronaut training program. He blasted off in the shuttle *Challenger* in October 1984 and spent eight days circling the earth while carrying out experiments in space science. Canadian to the core, in his baggage he carried the first hockey puck into space!

Canadian scientists are currently working on technology for the orbiting space station that the US plans to build in the twenty-first century. Canadian astronauts will be part of the station's crew.

VIEWPOINTS
AN ENVIRONMENTAL ETHIC

Dr. Roberta Bondar, a neurologist and medical researcher from Sault Ste. Marie, Ontario, was the first Canadian woman in space. Like Garneau, she was a member of the first "class" of Canadians in the US space program. Her flight was onboard the shuttle *Discovery* in January 1992. Bondar's adventure in space made her especially aware of the fragility of the earth's environment and the need to preserve its great diversity.

After observing the planet for eight days from space, I have a deeper interest and respect for the forces that shape our world. Each particle of soil, each plant and animal is special. I also marvel at the creativity and ingenuity of our own species, but at the same time, I wonder why we all cannot see that we create our future every day, and that our local actions affect the global community, today as well as for generations to come. From the distance of space flight, it's easy to believe that we can live in harmony with one another and the environment. It's important, though, that we all share this view, not just the few Earthlings who fly in space. Young people in particular need good role models so that they understand the importance of an environmental ethic. We must not thrust upon children the responsibility of saving the environment. We are all involved.

*In our schools, respect for other individuals and other cultures should be taught hand-in-hand with respect and caring for our **ecosystem**. The strong sense of bonding that develops when individuals work together as a team also occurs in the depths of space, in a thin piece of metal hurtling at more than twenty-five times the speed of sound. In space, where there were no other life-forms aside from my fellow crew members, I felt the strength of those we had left behind on the planet. As part of an intricate and complex life system, we should not have any difficulty in conceiving that other people, and other life-forms, are as important to us as we are to ourselves.*

Excerpt printed with permission from Touching the Earth by Roberta Bondar (Toronto: KeyPorter Books, 1994), pp. 87–88

1. Roberta Bondar speaks of an "environmental ethic." What does this term mean to you?
2. How do you think Bondar's flight affected her thinking about the world?

MAKING CONNECTIONS

1. Canada's space program costs hundreds of millions of dollars every year. Do you think this is money well spent?

KEYWORDS

cosmonaut

ecosystem

EXPO '86

Vancouver Celebrates

Vancouver welcomed the world in 1986. What is the impact of large-scale events such as a World's Fair or the Olympics on their host communities?

A Centennial Celebration

In 1986, the city of Vancouver was 100 years old. It celebrated the centennial with a huge fair called Expo '86. The world was invited to join in the celebration, and 41 countries built pavilions at the Expo site, which stretched along the shore of False Creek in the middle of downtown Vancouver. Once home to sawmills, lumber yards, and other industries, the fairgrounds became a bustling sea of theatres, restaurants, plazas, pavilions, and rides.

Expo '86 opened on 2 May with the Prince and Princess of Wales presiding at the ceremony. When it ended six months later, more than 20 million visitors had passed through the gates. The official theme of the fair was the future of transportation and communication. But Expo was also about tourism and economic development. Large events like international expositions pump millions of dollars into the economy. Visitors spend money on food, hotels, and entertainment. If they have a good time, they spread the word to friends and relatives, who may fuel the tourist industry in the future. Building the site creates construction jobs for years prior to the event. In Vancouver, the Skytrain rapid transit service, the Convention Centre, and BC Place were all built in conjunction with Expo. More jobs are created for those who plan the attractions and work at the site. Expo '86 also had a political agenda. The provincial government was heading into an election. Attracting the exposition to Vancouver was a positive accomplishment that the government hoped would get them votes.

After the fair closed, the government sold the Expo site to a Hong Kong billionaire, Li Ka-Shing. It was the largest real estate deal in Canadian history—84 ha of prime land for $320 million. Many people felt that the government had sold the land too cheaply and too quickly. Within a short time the value of the land skyrocketed and Li Ka-Shing made millions of dollars. Most of the Expo buildings were torn down and the False Creek site, once the industrial heart of the city, was redeveloped with high-rise apartments, condominiums, offices, and parkland. Expo '86 turned out to be the catalyst for the transformation of much of downtown Vancouver.

Expo '86 ended with a deficit of $300 million. Some felt this didn't matter when compared to the amount of money the fair brought into the city. Others argued the money would have been better spent on social programs.

Supporters of Expo '86 pointed to the economic benefits and international prestige the event would bring to the city and the province. Critics argued that Expo was taking place at a time when the province was experiencing cutbacks in education and social services and questioned the government's financial priorities.

Expo will be a turning point in BC's history. It will provide massive and welcome economic relief . . . When Expo closes, you will see a surge of construction on the site far bigger than the fair itself and it will confirm Vancouver's reputation as one of Canada's most dynamic cities.

Bill Bennett, premier of British Columbia, 1975–1986

British Columbia now has a profile it never had before. We've been on every television network, magazines and newspapers around the world. So now we have a recognition factor that just did not exist before.

Claude Richmond, House Leader, Social Credit government

We were celebrating the centennial of a great city, largely unknown, about to achieve its proper destiny on the Pacific. We were celebrating an unheralded ability to host the world in style. We were celebrating the achievements of humanity in an oasis of amicable competition. We were celebrating history, and hope.

Patrick Reid, commissioner-general, Expo '86

Expo is really a giant urban redevelopment project, an expenditure of more than one billion dollars to spur public and private land development. Without Expo there would have been no Skytrain, no BC Place Stadium, no Canada Harbour Place, no evictions of hundreds of long-time residents in the Downtown Eastside, no rezoning of the lands to the east and west of the Expo site, no new Cambie Bridge, and fewer redevelopment pressures on other surrounding communities. Because of Expo Vancouver will never be the same.

*Yet it is not a new Vancouver that anyone in the city was asked about. There were no public meetings to establish people's aspirations and goals for their city. There was no planning process to come up with the best expenditures of public funds to achieve those goals. Most astonishing, there were no impact studies to assess how Vancouver's neighbourhoods would be affected. Instead, there were **unilateral** decisions made in secret by the Social Credit government...*

Excerpt from The Expo Story ed. by Robert Anderson and Eleanor Wachtel (Madeira Park, BC: Harbour Publishing), 1986, p.65. Reprinted by permission of Harbour Publishing.

There was a clear need for the First Nations to have a presence on the site, a house to the world. Otherwise it was just White Nations inviting other nations. A pavilion of that nature would have allowed us to tell our story, the story of the First People, that we're real people, not second class. False Creek is Indian territory to us.

Squamish Chief Joe Matthias on the lack of a pavilion for Aboriginal peoples at Expo

1. List some of the benefits of Expo '86 to the city of Vancouver. How did all citizens of the province share these benefits, or did they?
2. What was Robert Anderson and Eleanor Wachtel's complaint about the fair? Why did they think that more people should have been consulted before the fair was allowed to go ahead?
3. Draw up a proposal for a pavilion that would have shown Aboriginal peoples' contribution to Vancouver.

MAKING CONNECTIONS

1. Compare Expo '86 with Expo '67. (See page 238.) In what ways were they similar? In what ways were they different?

KEYWORDS

unilateral

THE ABORTION DEBATE
Pro-life Versus Pro-choice
FOCUSSING ON THE ISSUE

In 1988, the Supreme Court of Canada ruled that abortion was no longer a criminal offence. The ruling sparked a great debate: Should a woman have the right to choose whether or not to continue with a pregnancy? Or should the rights of the unborn take precedence?

Legal Developments

For much of the twentieth century, abortion—the termination of pregnancy, especially if deliberately induced—was classified as a criminal offence in Canada. Following the Second World War, pressure to legalize abortion on certain grounds intensified. This pressure was the result of greater support for women's rights, growing concern for the consequences of unwanted children, and high death rates associated with illegal abortions. In 1969, Canada's abortion laws were liberalized, but overall abortion remained a criminal offence. Abortion was legal only if it was performed by a doctor in an **accredited** hospital after a therapeutic abortion committee certified that the continuation of the pregnancy would endanger the mother's life or health.

The abortion amendments were seen by some Canadians as progressive. To others, however, the new law was seriously flawed. The law was not applied equally across the country because some hospitals refused to establish therapeutic abortion committees. Because the law did not define "life" or "health," those hospitals that had committees had to establish their own guidelines. The law also failed to specify the age or degree of development of the **fetus**, making it unclear up to what stage of pregnancy a woman could abort.

Throughout the 1970s and 1980s, amendments were challenged by both pro-life and pro-choice activists. Pro-life activists opposed abortion under any circumstances. Pro-choice activists argued that the law continued to place restrictions on a woman's right to self-determination. Dr. Henry Morgentaler was the most outspoken and defiant critic of the law. He operated several free-standing abortion clinics in Quebec, Ontario, and Manitoba. The clinics were the sites of many clashes between pro-life and pro-choice activists.

Eventually, the issue of abortion made its way to the Supreme Court of Canada. In 1988, the court ruled that abortion was not a criminal offence, declaring that the 1969 law was in conflict with Section 7 of the Charter of Rights and Freedoms, which guarantees a woman's right to security of person. The ruling, in effect, made abortion in Canada virtually available on demand.

Demonstrators on both sides of the abortion debate frequently gathered outside Morgentaler's abortion clinics.

The Supreme Court ruling did not end the abortion debate. The issue is still one of the most controversial topics in Canada. Pro-life supporters base their arguments on moral or religious principles, and the rights of the unborn. They argue that life begins at conception, and that the rights of the unborn outweigh those of the mother. Pro-choice advocates argue that it is within a woman's right of self-determination to choose whether or not to continue with a pregnancy. They maintain that abortion is a moral issue that should be decided by individuals, not the state.

What has happened to our belief in rights, that in the name of a lesser right, the primary one, the right to life, can be denied to members of our own species? Not only is the woman's own right to life affirmed but it includes her right to freedom and privacy, and well-being, and all sorts of other good things. Yet she herself, her own unique unrepeatable self, was once growing in her mother's womb. What magic occurred with the passage of time that gives her all these rights, and denies the fetus any?

George Grant and Sheila Grant, "Aboriginal Rights," in Technology and Justice (Toronto: House of Anansi, 1986). Reprinted by permission of Stoddart Publishing Co. Ltd.

The pro-life movement began in the 1960s. Several ordinary people gathered together to share concerns that Canada was moving towards accepting abortion—the destruction of an innocent human life. Realizing abortion was the beginning of a process that would devalue human life, pro-life people rallied together.

Today, over 30 years later, the pro-life movement has grown to thousands of people educating others about attacks on human life.…Pro-life people are committed, working towards a society in which all human life is valued and protected.

Michelle Blanchette, Executive Director, Alliance for Life Canada

[The decision to have an abortion] is one that will have profound psychological, economic and social consequences for the pregnant woman.…It is a decision that deeply reflects the way the woman thinks about herself and her relationship to others and to society at large. It is not just a medical decision; it is a profound social and ethical one as well. Her response to it will be the response of the whole person.…It is probably impossible for a man to respond, even imaginatively, to such a dilemma not just because it is outside the realm of his personal experience (although this is, of course, the case) but because he can relate to it only by objectifying it, thereby eliminating the subjective elements of the female psyche which are at the heart of the dilemma.

Madame Justice Bertha Wilson in Shelagh Day and Stan Persky, eds., The Supreme Court of Canada Decision On Abortion (Vancouver: New Star Books, 1988), p. 133.

I know what motherhood means. I know one can't make a decision to be a mother casually. It's a decision that profoundly, to the core of your existence, changes who you are in the world. That experience should never, ever be imposed upon a woman.

Joy Thompson, pro-choice activist with the British Columbia Coalition for Abortion Clinics, in Deborah Jones, "Guns and Money: The New Abortion Wars," Chatelaine, May 1996.

1. Conduct a debate in your class on the following resolution: Abortion is a moral issue to be decided by individuals, not by the state.

MAKING CONNECTIONS

1. To what extent is abortion still an issue today? Collect a variety of viewpoints about abortion in Canada from newspapers and magazines. Decide what positions the writers hold and how they justify their positions. Report your findings in the form of a bulletin board, presentation to the class, or documentary film.

2. Compare and contrast pro-life and pro-choice activism in Canada with activism in at least two other countries.

KEYWORDS

accredited

fetus

IMMIGRANTS AND REFUGEES
A Shift in Policy
FOCUSSING ON THE ISSUE

A change in Canada's immigration policy in 1978 opened the doors to immigrants from countries other than Britain, the United States, and Europe. Where did the majority of immigrants come from in the 1980s? What is Canada's policy towards refugees?

Elected to the BC legislature in 1972, Rosemary Brown was the first black woman elected to political office in Canada. Born in Jamaica, she came to Canada in 1950. Many newcomers to Canada, like Rosemary Brown, have made a difference in their adopted communities. Brainstorm a list of prominent new Canadians in your community and their contributions.

An Attractive Destination

Because of its wealth and political stability, Canada is an attractive destination for people in other countries seeking new lives. Each year, thousands of immigrants come to Canada. They bring with them talents, skills, and resources that make a valuable contribution to Canada's economic prosperity and cultural diversity.

There are always more people applying to immigrate to Canada than the country is able to accept. As a result, in the late 1970s the government set up immigration guidelines based on three broad policy objectives:

- humanitarian considerations to unite families and provide a safe haven for those who are persecuted
- economic considerations to provide skilled labour for the Canadian workforce and to encourage economic growth and investment
- **demographic** considerations to maintain steady population growth.

The number of immigrants Canada accepts each year varies according to conditions. In the early 1980s, Canada was experiencing a serious **recession**. Businesses were failing and unemployment was high. Under such adverse circumstances, the country could not absorb a high number of newcomers. Public pressure to reduce unemployment led the government to decrease the annual immigration **quota**. In 1985, only 84 300 immigrants entered Canada. As the economy improved, the annual level of immigration increased. By 1993, it had peaked at over 292 000.

The countries of origin of new Canadians have also changed over the years. During the 1960s, most newcomers came from Britain, the United States, and European countries. As economic conditions in their own countries improved, however, Europeans were less likely to seek new lives in Canada. Instead, by the 1980s, the majority of immigrants came from Asia, the Caribbean, and Latin America in search of greater prosperity and political stability. A significant number of immigrants came from Hong Kong, where the future was uncertain as Britain prepared to return the colony to the People's Republic of China on 1 July 1997.

Another reason for this change was a shift in Canadian policy. The government no longer gave preference to people from specific countries. Instead, it established criteria that all applicants had to meet, regardless of their country of origin. The Immigration Act of 1978 recognized three classes of immigrants:

- *Family class*: people sponsored by members of their immediate family who are already permanent residents of Canada
- *Refugee class*: people who are persecuted in their own countries
- *Economic class*: people applying to come to Canada on their own initiative, admitted on the basis of their skills, the financial resources they are willing to invest, and the needs of the Canadian labour market.

Immigration is necessary for Canada. The current population is not reproducing itself, so newcomers are needed to keep the population growing. Immigrants also stimulate the economy. They work hard, create jobs, pay taxes, and purchase the goods and services that keep our economy healthy. The question is, how many immigrants should Canada accept? During the 1980s the number was comparatively low, but in the 1990s Canada accepted between 210 000 and 250 000 newcomers annually. Critics of this level of immigration fear the country cannot absorb this many people without creating serious social problems, especially in the major cities where most newcomers settle.

Providing Safe Haven

Refugees are people with a reasonable fear of being persecuted in their home countries because of their religion, political views, race, nationality, or social standing. Since the 1950s, Canada has provided a safe haven for people escaping war and persecution in such countries as Hungary, Vietnam, Chile, Somalia, Cambodia, and Croatia.

During the 1980s, the number of refugees worldwide skyrocketed to 12 million as political turmoil and cultural persecution spread throughout the world's trouble spots. As the number of refugees rose, Canada offered shelter to a growing number of displaced people, many of whom arrived in the country with nothing more than the clothes on their backs. In 1986, Canada was honoured by the United Nations for its willingness to accept so many of the world's refugees. In fact, Canada accepts the greatest number of refugees per capita of any country in the world.

Unfortunately, some of these so-called refugees are not really refugees at all. Some are people who do not qualify as immigrants or who do not want to wait to go through normal immigration channels. In response, the government has periodically introduced new regulations designed to screen out false claimants from legitimate immigrants and refugees. Every claimant must appear before a refugee board, which evaluates the case. There is concern, however, on the part of refugee activists and groups such as Amnesty International that restrictions are making it difficult for genuine refugees to find safe haven in Canada.

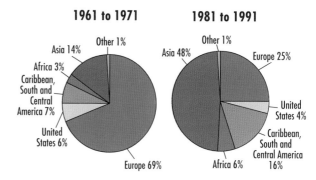

Recent Immigrants More Likely to Come from Asia

1961 to 1971

Other 1%
Asia 14%
Africa 3%
Caribbean, South and Central America 7%
United States 6%
Europe 69%

1981 to 1991

Other 1%
Asia 48%
Europe 25%
United States 4%
Caribbean, South and Central America 16%
Africa 6%

MAKING CONNECTIONS

1. Imagine you are a member of a government committee charged with establishing a new immigration policy. What criteria would you use to select who would be allowed to immigrate to Canada? Explain your reasons.

2. Some people advocate an open-door immigration policy that accepts all immigrants and refugees, with the exception of criminals and others who may strain the country's social programs. Write a newspaper editorial either supporting this point of view, or explaining why Canada needs to set limits on the number of immigrants it accepts.

KEYWORDS

demography

recession

quota

VIOLENCE AGAINST WOMEN
The Montreal Massacre
FOCUSSING ON THE ISSUE

Each year on the anniversary of the Montreal Massacre, candlelight ceremonies are held across Canada and many people wear white ribbons to protest violence against women. Why has violence against women been tolerated for so long? What can be done to end the violence?

A Tragic Event

In the early evening of 6 December 1989, about 20 students were attending class at École Polytechnique, the University of Montreal's engineering school, when a man carrying a semi-automatic rifle entered the classroom. He ordered the male students to leave the room, then opened fire on the female students, shouting that they were all **feminists**. When he left the room, six women lay dead or dying, while the others lay still on the floor pretending to be dead so that he would stop shoot-ing. He continued to walk calmly through the building, shooting any woman he encountered. When he finally ended his rampage, 27 women were wounded, and 14 eventually died. The killer, 25-year-old Marc Lepine, then shot himself, dying instantly.

Later, police found a suicide note and a letter in which Lepine had identified his other intended victims—women he described as feminists. Having been rejected when he applied for admission to the engineering school, he blamed feminists for ruining his life. Little was known about the man, a loner with few close friends, until this tragedy. In its aftermath people expressed their horror and distress, and tried to answer the question—why?

Profile of a Murderer

Although he was drawn to guns and ammunition, Lepine had no previous criminal record. His father was a violent man who repeatedly battered Marc and his mother. Having endured his father's many beatings, Lepine gradually learned to look upon aggression as a way of dealing with his problems. His application to join the Canadian Forces was rejected; he enrolled in a variety of postsecondary institutions but never graduated from any of their programs. Lepine then found himself unemployed. When he could no longer face his predicament, he turned to a familiar solution—violence.

Society's Attitudes

In 1991, largely as a result of the Montreal Massacre, the federal government appointed a panel to study the problem of violence against women. Reports drawn up by this and other panels invariably point out

Female students comforted one another outside the École Polytechnique in the aftermath of the tragedy.

STATISTICS ON VIOLENCE AGAINST WOMEN

- Fifty-one per cent of Canadian women have experienced at least one incident of physical or sexual violence (as defined by the Criminal Code of Canada) since the age of 16. Twenty-five per cent of all women have experienced physical or sexual violence at the hands of a marital or common-law partner.

  Statistics Canada, 1993

- A Canadian Union of Public Employees survey reported that 61.2 per cent of female respondents had experienced at least one incident of actual or threatened violence on the job. Fifty-two per cent reported three or more incidents, and 20 per cent reported receiving death threats. *Toronto Star, 18 November 1993*

- In 1991, one half of all murdered women were shot to death. Every six days in Canada, a woman is shot to death by a man with a handgun, rifle, or shotgun. Seventy-two per cent of these guns were legally owned and 50 per cent of victims were killed in the home.

  Canadian Centre for Justice Statistics, 1994

- Sons learn violence from violent fathers. For 39 per cent of women in abusive marriages, children were present to witness the assault. In 52 per cent of those assaults, the women feared for their lives. Women who reported having a violent father-in-law were three times as likely as women with non-abusive fathers-in-law to be assaulted by their partners.

  Statistics Canada, 1993

- Only 14 per cent of all violent incidents were reported to the police. Assaults not involving marital partners were more likely to result in a charge than were assaults by spouses. Victims in 22 per cent of violent incidents told no one about the experience. *Statistics Canada, 1993*

- Acquaintances or relatives were responsible for 72 per cent of the violent attacks committed against women, compared with 37 per cent of violent attacks committed against men.

  Status of Women in Canada, 1993

that Lepine's behaviour was the ultimate act of violence against women in a society that has commonly tolerated this type of violence. For many women in Canada, acts of aggression against them are part of the regular pattern of their lives.

Violence against women is exhibited in many forms of behaviour, including **sexual harassment** and assault, intimidation, battering, and murder. Women encounter violence in their homes, communities, and workplaces. Abusers are found in every segment of Canadian society. Children are often present during incidents of **domestic violence** and are physically assaulted themselves. It is impossible to measure the cost of violence—the physical pain, the anguish, and the loss of human lives. The financial cost of violence against women in Canada is thought to exceed $4 billion each year. The provincial and federal governments acknowledge that behavioural change is necessary to put an end to this violence. Their long-term goals are to bring about a change in societal attitudes resulting in zero tolerance towards all forms of violence against women and children.

MAKING CONNECTIONS

1. In small groups, list the violent images you've seen in the past week. Identify the sources of these images. Which sources depict violence most frequently? Why do you think this is so? What kind of behaviour do you think violent imagery encourages? Explain.

KEYWORDS

feminist

subordinate

sexual harassment

domestic violence

CULTURAL REVIVAL
The Resurgence of Aboriginal Art
FOCUSSING ON THE ISSUE

By the 1980s, a revival in all aspects of Aboriginal culture was in full swing.
What role did the arts play in this resurgence?

Spirit of Haida Gwaii *is a huge sculpture cast in bronze by Haida artist Bill Reid. It shows a large canoe overflowing with figures from Haida legend, including a bear, a raven, Mouse Woman, Dogfish Woman, an eagle, a beaver, and a frog. How does this sculpture symbolize Canada?*

Artistic Revival

In 1980, a new sculpture was unveiled at the Museum of Anthropology at the University of British Columbia. Called *The Raven and the First Men*, the sculpture is carved from yellow cedar and stands over 2 m tall. *The Raven and the First Men* is the work of the late renowned artist Bill Reid. Reid was a member of the Haida First Nation, the original inhabitants of the Queen Charlotte Islands (or

Haida Gwaii, as the people themselves call these islands) off the northwest coast of BC. The sculpture depicts a huge raven standing on top of a clam shell, out of which the first people are emerging. It is meant to symbolize the creation of the world, but it could also symbolize the rebirth of Aboriginal culture as a strong presence in Canadian life.

Art played an important role in Aboriginal society before European contact. Every object was hand-made and decorated with designs

depicting family history or representing the spiritual world of the people. Artistic expression reached its peak on the BC coast where the Aboriginal peoples had an elaborate social structure and ceremonial life, all of which was reflected in the production of masks, canoes, totem poles, jewellery, woven baskets and clothing, and many other objects.

The arrival of the Europeans brought many hardships for Aboriginal peoples. Diseases to which they had no immunity reduced the population dramatically. Much of the land was occupied by the newcomers, while Aboriginal peoples were shunted off to small reserves where they found it difficult to hunt and fish for food in the traditional manner. Outsiders came to the villages and carried away many Aboriginal spiritual and cultural objects for display in distant museums. Governments outlawed Aboriginal ceremonies and attempted to force the people to **assimilate** into mainstream society. This involved sending Aboriginal children to residential schools away from their families. (See page 76.)

Under these circumstances, traditional artistic practices among the Aboriginal peoples went into decline. Many of the ceremonial objects that artists had once produced were no longer used; neither were the skills required to make them. Amid all this turmoil, however, a few

Aboriginal artists struggled to keep their traditions alive.

Starting in the 1950s, the trend began to reverse itself. The flame of art that so nearly died out was revived. Aboriginal peoples reasserted a pride in their cultures. One of the leaders of this resurgence was Bill Reid. Reid was working as a radio broadcaster in Toronto when he developed an interest in jewellery making. His style drew on his Haida background. He moved back to Vancouver and became a full-time carver-designer, making totem poles, masks, and large-scale sculptures such as *The Raven and the First Men*, as well as jewellery. Reid died in 1998.

Learning by Example

Young Aboriginal artists often train as **apprentices** to older, more experienced artists. The young artist learns the qualities of the materials and how to use the proper tools. Because so much of Aboriginal art has a spiritual theme, the apprentice also studies the spiritual beliefs of the people. Apprentices today blend the old with the new. They learn techniques handed down from the distant past and combine them with modern techniques and tools to produce art that is both traditional and modern.

Summer Camp Scene by Pitseolak Ashoona. A growing number of Aboriginal artists, such as Pitseolak Ashoona, Jessie Oonark, and Daphne Odjig, have gained international recognition.

Bill Reid took on apprentices, one of whom was Robert Davidson, also a Haida, who became a fine artist in his own right. Totem poles and masks carved by Davidson have been purchased by collectors around the world. In 1984, when Pope John Paul II visited Vancouver, he was presented with a **ceremonial talking stick** carved by Davidson.

Like Reid, Davidson is one of the artists credited with gaining international recognition for Northwest Coast Aboriginal art. He also expressed the importance of art as a spiritual force for Aboriginal peoples:

We Haida were surrounded by art. Art was one with the culture. Art was our only written language. It documented our progress as a people, it documented the histories of the families. Throughout our history, it has been the art that has kept our spirit alive.

Robert Davidson, in Ian M. Thom, ed., Eagle of the Dawn, (*Vancouver Art Gallery*, 1993), p. 8.

MAKING CONNECTIONS

1. Compare the role of the artist in Aboriginal and non-Aboriginal society. How would you describe the differences?

2. Produce your own "gallery" of Aboriginal art. Collect illustrations of paintings, sculptures, and carvings by Aboriginal artists. Describe each piece in your own words. How it was made, and what message you think the artist intended to convey?

KEYWORDS

assimilate

apprentice

ceremonial talking stick

THE FREE TRADE AGREEMENT
A Divided Response
FOCUSSING ON THE ISSUE

Supporters of the Canada-US Free Trade Agreement hailed it as a major step towards Canadian economic prosperity, while opponents saw it is as the beginning of the end of Canadian sovereignty. Why did the agreement generate such a divided reaction?

Economic Dependence

During the 1970s, many Canadians were concerned about Canada's economic dependence on the United States. Between 75 and 80 per cent of Canada's exports went to the US market and more than 70 per cent of Canada's imports came from the US. American corporations owned or controlled most of Canada's energy industry and dominated many other sectors of the Canadian economy. As a result, the federal government passed a number of laws limiting and controlling foreign investment in Canada, including the Foreign Investment Review Agency (FIRA) in 1971 and the National Energy Program (NEP) in 1980. Canada also pursued trade relations with countries in Asia and Central and South America. The NEP and FIRA were opposed by US

Brian Mulroney and Ronald Reagan at the "Shamrock Summit" in 1985. In 1983, when he was campaigning for the Conservative leadership, Mulroney quoted Sir John A. Macdonald's comment about a proposed economic union with the US: "It might be that the lion and the lamb would lie down together, but the lamb would be inside the lion." Mulroney then went on to reject free trade, saying "Don't talk to me about free trade. We'd be swamped. We have in many ways a branch plant economy in certain important sectors. All that would happen with that kind of concept would be the boys cranking up their plants through the United States in bad times and shutting their entire branch plants in Canada. It's bad enough as it is." Why do you think Mulroney rejected free trade in 1983 but then launched free trade negotiations in 1985?

businesses and investors, who also objected to Canada's trade relations with communist countries such as Cuba and China. Some members of the US Congress, angry about their country's **trade deficit** with Canada, urged their government to adopt stricter protectionist trade policies. By the 1980s, trade relations between Canada and the United States were becoming increasingly strained.

In the 1984 federal election campaign, Conservative leader Brian Mulroney promised to improve relations, particularly economic ones, with the United States. When he was elected prime minister, he moved quickly to carry out this promise, dismantling the NEP and weakening the FIRA. In March 1985, US president Ronald Reagan and Mulroney met in Quebec City at the Shamrock Summit, as it was called, where they discovered they shared many of the same views. The two leaders agreed to support negotiations that would improve the trade relationship between their respective countries.

At the First Ministers Conference in August 1985, all the premiers except the Ontario leader asked that the federal government begin immediate free-trade negotiations. Public opinion polls showed that Canadians supported the idea by a margin of three to one. In May 1986, formal negotiations began in Ottawa.

Reaching a deal would not be easy, however. The talks dragged on until October 1987. Most of the discussions were carried out in secret, which caused many Canadians to be concerned about just what was being negotiated. Opponents of free trade claimed that Canadian industries would be unable to compete with larger American companies and would close down. They feared that thousands of jobs would be lost as Canadian **branch plants** closed as the American parent companies simply increased production at the main plant or as businesses relocated to the US. Amidst the controversy, public support for free trade gradually began to slip away. Trade unions, churches, women's groups, nationalists, pensioners, and many ordinary citizens hoped a deal would never be reached. But support remained strong in the business community, with the Canadian Chamber of Commerce, the Canadian Consumers Association, and most of the provincial premiers, except those of Manitoba, Ontario, and Prince Edward Island, in favour of a free trade agreement.

Reaching a Deal

In January 1988, Canada and the US reached an agreement-in-principle. Some of the highlights of the Free Trade Agreement included:

- *Elimination of tariffs*: Starting on 1 January 1989, the US and Canada would abolish tariffs on goods and services and would be allowed free access to each other's markets.

- *Dispute-settlement mechanism*: Trade problems between the two countries would be reviewed by a panel of five members, with at least two members from each country.

- *Energy*: Canada could not impose limits on sales of energy resources to the US unless there was a shortfall; in that case, Americans could purchase a proportional amount of existing supplies.

- *Agriculture*: Over a ten-year period, all tariffs on agricultural goods and processed foods would end.

- *Investment*: Regulations on American investment in Canada would be relaxed. However, the Canadian government could investigate and authorize takeovers in cultural industries, such as publishing.

The Free Trade Agreement became the central issue in the 1988 federal election. The Conservatives were the only party that supported it. When opinion polls showed that the Conservatives might lose, supporters of free trade joined forces with the Tories in an advertising campaign designed to sell the deal. They succeeded, and Mulroney and the Conservatives won the election. The Free Trade Agreement was quickly approved and it became law on 1 January 1989. It had been one of the hottest and most **partisan** political debates in recent Canadian history.

◄▢ MAKING CONNECTIONS ▢►

1. Brainstorm a list of the advantages and disadvantages of free trade.

2. Conduct a panel discussion about free trade.

KEYWORDS

trade deficit

branch plant

partisan

UNIT 10:

Paterson Ewen, *Decadent Crescent Moon* (1990)

Paterson Ewen (1925-) began to experiment with materials other than canvas in the 1970s. Images painted on gouged plywood offered greater artistic satisfaction. *Decadent Crescent Moon* combines acrylic and metallic paint on galvanized steel and gouged plywood to create an energized image of the natural element it illustrates.

*Skills and Processes

AFTER THE FALL
The World in 1991
FOCUSSING ON THE ISSUE

At the end of the twentieth century, the world entered a new, post-Cold War era. What forces were fragmenting the world into warring factions? What forces tended to unite the international community?

The World Watched

Hundreds of millions of television viewers around the world watched the fall of the Berlin Wall in 1989. Images of a bloodless revolution—young people climbing the hated wall with hammers and champagne bottles in hand—suggested that a new era of peace and freedom was beginning. In 1991, communism continued to collapse as the Soviet Union disintegrated. In December, the USSR voted itself out of existence and Mikhail Gorbachev resigned as president. It had not been his intention to destroy communism, only to reform it; but the forces he unleashed could not be controlled. The once-mighty union fragmented into several smaller countries, each one politically unstable and economically fragile. Only China, North Korea, and Cuba, where hard-line communist regimes remained in power, resisted the tide of political liberalization.

Regional tensions continued in the Middle East, Asia, and Africa. On a global scale, the United States emerged from the Cold War as the most powerful nation in the world. When Iraq invaded Kuwait in 1991, the US had a chance to show the impressive armed force it could deploy. The issue in the Gulf War was not ideology, but oil. The Americans were more dependent on imported fossil fuels than ever

The end of the Cold War was supposed to usher in a period of peace and security. Yet it turned out that the new world order looked a lot like the old one. The dust had hardly settled on the crumbling Berlin Wall when American troops were at war in Iraq, opposing Saddam Hussein's strongly anti-Western regime. How did the Gulf War differ from earlier, Cold War conflicts?

before, and the Iraqi invasion threatened the security of US supplies. Once the Americans launched an all-out attack, the war soon ended. Iraq was no match for the armed might of the world's last superpower.

New World Disorder

As the Gulf War demonstrated, the end of the Cold War did not usher in the hoped-for era of peace and security. New conflicts came to dominate the world stage. Images of ethnic, tribal, and religious wars, many in former communist countries, appeared almost daily on the television news. Tensions ran high in the long-running civil war

between Protestants and Catholics in Northern Ireland. Conflicts broke out in former European colonies in Africa, where artificial boundaries drawn by outsiders united fierce tribal enemies together in the same countries. The most horrendous of these wars occurred in Rwanda, spreading to neighbouring Burundi, Uganda, and Zaïre (now Democratic Republic of the Congo). Stories of men, women, and children hacked to death with machetes shocked people around the world. There was little discussion, however, of the **imperialism** that had created conditions where such violence might erupt. The fact that arms-makers and governments in developed countries sold the weapons that made it possible was also overlooked.

Ironically, while political conflict continued to divide countries, cultural groups, and religious communities, the world was actually drawing together economically. **Transnational corporations**, many of them richer than some countries, operated all over the world wherever wages, labour codes, production costs, and environmental laws most favoured them. Long-established industrial towns in Europe and North America saw factories close and traditional manufacturing jobs vanish as companies relocated in Mexico, Brazil, or Southeast Asia to keep costs low and profits high. This process, called the **globalization** of the world economy, was making boundaries between countries less significant.

Speeding the process along was a worldwide trend to reduce trade barriers. Nowhere was free trade more evident than in Western Europe, where the European Community (now, the **European Union**) began the process towards becoming a single, integrated economy in 1994. Its most influential member was the newly united Germany. By the end of the century, many formerly communist Central and Eastern European countries

What pressures are placed on the environment as a result of rapid population growth and increasing resource consumption?

were hoping to join the European Community.

As the fear of nuclear war receded in the 1990s, the fear of environmental destruction increased. Depletion of the ozone layer in the atmosphere, global warming, deforestation, and desertification were just some of the issues facing the world. There were many others. The earth's **carrying capacity** was increasingly taxed and the world's population was three times what it had been at the beginning of the century. In developed countries such as Canada and the United States, many people continued to expect increasingly higher standards of living, regardless of the **drawing**

down of **nonrenewable resources**. Populations grew steadily during the 1990s, particularly in the least developed countries of Africa, central and south Asia, and Latin America. By 1998, the world population had reached 6 billion people. Climate change, overpopulation, and habitat destruction threatened the future for all countries. It was recognized that the world had become a single entity and that the solutions to these problems would require international co-operation on a global scale.

KEYWORDS

◄⟶ MAKING CONNECTIONS ⟶

1. With reference to the international situation, explain whether or not you think the world is a safer place to live in now than it was in 1958. How might your answer differ if you lived in South Africa, China, or Eastern Europe?

THE DEFICIT DEBATE
The Defeat of the Conservatives

In the 1990s, Canadians worried more than ever about their government having enough money to pay for its programs and services. What was the solution to the growing public debt?

Debt and Deficit

At the beginning of the 1990s, Canadians believed they were facing a crisis in public finance. Each year the government was borrowing an extra $40 billion just to pay its expenses. This figure, known as the **deficit**, represents the difference between the amount of money the government raises in taxes and fees each year and the amount of money it spends on programs and services. Each year's deficit is added to the total debt, which in 1997 was approaching $600 billion. The amount was even higher when the debts of the provincial governments were included.

The debt and the deficit are considered bad for the economy because the government has to pay **interest** charges on the money it borrows. The more money borrowed, the higher the interest payments and the more public money has to be spent just paying for the debt. Much of this interest is paid to Canadian financial institutions that lend money to the government. But much of it leaves the country in the form of interest payments to foreign lenders, which is a loss to the Canadian economy.

The Fall of the Tories

Many Canadians blamed the economic situation on the Conservative government led by Brian Mulroney, who had been prime minister since 1984 and had failed to curtail the deficit. Mulroney was very unpopular for a number of reasons, and as he approached an election in 1993 his advisors told him to retire or face certain defeat. Rather than end his career on a losing note, Mulroney retired.

The Conservatives chose Kim Campbell to succeed Mulroney as leader of the party and prime minister. Not only was Campbell the first woman to hold the country's top job, she was also the first British Columbian. (John Turner, a former Liberal prime minister, represented a Vancouver riding in Parliament, but he had lived most of his life in eastern Canada.) Campbell seemed a perfect choice. Canadians seemed ready, perhaps even eager, to have a woman as prime minister. Relatively new to federal politics, Campbell offered a fresh face. At the same time, she had Cabinet experience, having served as minister of justice and minister of defence. Riding a wave of popular support for their new leader, the Conservatives called an election for 25 October 1993.

During the election campaign everything changed dramatically. Once the novelty of a new leader wore off, Canadians remembered Brian Mulroney. Many people wondered why they should reward his party with re-election just because it had switched leaders. In addition, Campbell and her advisors ran a poor campaign. At one point, asked about planned changes to social programs, Campbell seemed to answer that an election campaign was no time to talk about serious issues. That response lost her much support.

On election day, the results were astonishing. The Liberals won 176 seats, Reform took 52, the Bloc Québécois, 54, and the NDP, 9. The Conservatives were left with only 2 seats. It was no surprise that the Conservatives lost, but no one expected them to lose so badly. In no other election had a party fallen so far, from 169 seats in 1988 to 2 seats in 1993. Kim Campbell lost her own seat and retired from politics. It was the worst election debacle in Canadian history.

Was the 1993 election a one-time setback for the Conservatives, or were they finished as a successful national party? That was the question many people asked themselves after the election. It was answered, at least in part, when the country again went to the polls in 1997. With a new leader, Jean Charest, and a new platform, the Conservatives won 20 seats in the new Parliament and close to 20 per cent of the popular vote. Apparently, many voters believe the party still has a place in Canadian politics.

The candidates (from left, Jean Chrétien, Kim Campbell, Lucien Bouchard, Audrey McLaughlin, and Preston Manning) awaited the start of a televised debate in the 1993 federal election.

Deficit Fighting

All political parties agreed that it was necessary to reduce the deficit, and the new Liberal government, led by Jean Chrétien, set out to do so. By 1998, the deficit was eliminated, and the federal government presented a balanced budget for the first time in almost three decades. (The country's debt, however, remained to be paid.)

How can a government eliminate such a huge deficit? One method is to increase taxes. By collecting more money from taxpayers, the government has to borrow less money to pay for its programs. Raising taxes is politically unpopular, however, so the Liberals avoided this option. Instead, they reduced spending so that the government required less money to operate. Public servants were laid off; government services were reduced; spending on health care and education was cut; and the budgets of **Crown corporations**, such as the CBC, were slashed.

Not everyone thought the deficit was the result of government overspending, however. Some people blamed it on the high level of unemployment, which hovered close to 10 per cent throughout the 1990s. They argued that the government should have adopted policies that would get people back to work rather than cut spending. More people working would mean more tax revenues for the government, which could have been used to cut the deficit. The public, however, seemed to accept the government's efforts to reduce the deficit. In the 1997 federal election, the Liberals were returned to power, although with a smaller majority than they had received in 1993.

MAKING CONNECTIONS

1. a) Do you think the fact that Kim Campbell was a woman helped or hindered her election chances?
    b) Why do you think so few women have been elected to government when half the electorate is female?

2. Kim Campbell was the first person from BC to lead a national political party and to become prime minister. What are the obstacles for politicians from BC to achieving leadership positions?

3. From the news and from your own experience, identify three changes in government services that were caused by cutbacks in spending.

KEYWORDS

deficit

interest

Crown corporations

SPOUSAL VIOLENCE

The Case of Lyn Lavallee

FOCUSSING ON THE ISSUE

In 1986, Lyn Lavallee admitted to killing her spouse, yet a jury found her not guilty of murder. The verdict was upheld by the Supreme Court of Canada in 1990. Why was Lavallee acquitted? What are the implications of this case?

The Facts

The accused, 22-year-old Lyn Lavallee, had been living in Winnipeg, Manitoba, in a **common-law** relationship with Kevin Rust since she was 18. Their relationship had been characterized by frequent violent arguments, and Rust had repeatedly battered Lavallee. On the night of 30 August 1986, the couple held a loud party at their house. In the early hours of 31 August, after most of the guests had left, Lavallee and Rust had an argument in an upstairs bedroom that was used by Lavallee. Rust was killed by a single shot to the back of the head from a .303 calibre rifle fired by Lavallee as Rust was leaving the room.

Lyn Lavallee was charged with murder. Her defence was that she had acted in self-defence. She did not testify at trial. At the defence counsel's request, Dr. Fred Shane, a psychiatrist with extensive professional experience in treating battered wives, prepared a psychiatric assessment of the accused. His professional opinion was that Lavallee had been "terrorized by Rust to the point of feeling trapped, vulnerable, worthless, and unable to escape the relationship despite the violence." Dr. Shane believed that the continuing pattern of abuse endangered her life, and that the shooting was a

Violence
against
women –
It's a
crime

Ministry of
the Solicitor General

Governments have launched advertising campaigns aimed at reducing violence against women. Do you think ads like this are effective? Explain.

final desperate act by a woman who believed she would be killed that night. During his testimony, the psychiatrist referred to certain facts and incidents that were not before the court as admissible evidence, including what Lavallee had told him.

The jury acquitted Lyn Lavallee, but the verdict was overturned by

the Manitoba Court of Appeal on the grounds that the trial judge's **charge to the jury** had been insufficient regarding the admissibility of expert evidence. Lavallee appealed this decision. The case was brought before the Supreme Court of Canada, which in a decision on 3 May 1990 restored the original verdict.

Dr. Fred Shane provided expert testimony about the effects of the abusive relationship on Lavallee.

She had stayed in this relationship, I think, because of the strange, almost unbelievable…relationship that sometimes develops between people who develop this very disturbed…quality of a relationship…the spouse gets beaten so badly—so badly—that he or she loses the motivation to react and becomes helpless and becomes powerless… the person who beats or assaults, who batters, often… makes up and begs forgiveness….The spouse feels that she again can do the spouse a favour and it can make her feel needed and boost her self-esteem for a while….

I think she felt…in the final tragic moment that her life was on the line, that unless she defended herself, unless she reacted in a violent way that she would die. I mean he made it very explicit to her…that she had…to defend herself against his violence.

Dr. Fred Shane, testimony at trial, Manitoba Queen's Bench, [1990] 4 W. W. R, pp. 7, 26, 27

In restoring the original verdict and acquitting Lyn Lavallee, the Supreme Court of Canada made the following rulings:

On the Admissibility of Expert Evidence

*Expert evidence on the psychological effect of battering on wives and common law partners must…be both relevant and necessary in the context of the present case. How can the mental state of the **appellant** be appreciated without it? The average member of the public (or of the jury) can be forgiven for asking: Why would a woman put up with this kind of treatment?…How could she love a partner who beat her to the point of requiring hospitalization? We would expect the woman to pack her bags and go. Where is her self-respect?…Such is the reaction of the average person confronted with the so-called "**battered-wife syndrome**." We need help to understand it and help is available from trained professionals.*

On the Question of Self-Defence

If it strains credulity to imagine what the "ordinary man" would do in the position of a battered spouse, it is probably because men do not typically find themselves in that situation.

Section 34(2)(a) requires that an accused who intentionally causes death or grievous bodily harm in repelling an assault is justified if he or she does so "under reasonable apprehension of death or grievous bodily harm." In the present case, the assault precipitating the appellant's alleged defensive act was Rust's threat to kill her when everyone else had gone.

The issue is not…what an outsider would have reasonably perceived but what the accused reasonably perceived, given her situation and her experience.

Wilson J. in R. v. Lavallee [1990]

MAKING CONNECTIONS

1. In what other circumstances might a plea of self-defence be justifiable in a murder case? How do these circumstances compare with those of Lyn Lavallee and Kevin Rust?

2. Reconstruct the events of the Lavallee case in the form of a mock trial using the information about the case from the expert's testimony and the Supreme Court rulings.

KEYWORDS

common-law

charge to the jury

appellant

battered-wife syndrome

GUN CONTROL
An Ongoing Debate

FOCUSSING ON THE ISSUE

Concerned by what they perceive as an increase in gun-related crime and violence, the majority of Canadians have demanded stricter gun control. Do guns have a place in modern Canadian society?

Public Concern

Canadians were shocked and outraged in December 1989 when Marc Lepine used a military assault rifle to kill 14 young women at the University of Montreal. (See page 316.) Canadians had watched TV news reports of young children carrying guns to school in the US and angry California motorists shooting others on highways. The term "drive-by shooting" made its way into common usage in the US as armed individuals drove along streets shooting at random. The Montreal murders added to the belief that crime and violence were also escalating in Canada. This led to a widespread demand for stricter gun-control regulations.

Before 1989

In the 1970s, the federal government passed the Criminal Law Amendment Act, which amended the sections of the **Criminal Code** relating to firearms. These amendments established a new system for obtaining firearms. Individuals wanting to purchase a firearm first

---

VIEWPOINTS

DEBATING GUN CONTROL

Some people view guns as symbols of violence and crime that are unnecessary in a modern society such as Canada. Other people see guns as symbols of independence and self-reliance that they believe are essential to the preservation of a democratic society.

Anti-Gun Control

Few social policy issues in this country generate the emotional energy, diversity of opinion, and level of public misinformation as the one on "gun control."

Government officials introduce "tough gun laws"…and are perplexed by the legislation's subsequent inability to reduce the levels of violent crime and firearm-related violence.

Canadians know that the crime situation in the United States has deteriorated. It's described on television every night. In actual fact, however, Canadians know very little about crime, firearms, and firearm laws south of the border, and we understand even less the interaction of guns within our own society.

The Canadian government has never identified any correlation between a certain level of restriction and the

*amount of crime controlled, or undertaken even the most rudimentary **cost-benefit analysis** of the effect their gun legislation has on the social fabric of this country.*

*Is there a "powerful pro-gun **lobby**" in Canada? There are no major firearm manufacturers in this country, only importers, yet the CGC [Coalition for Gun Control] constantly repeats an erroneous claim that the shooting organizations in Canada have "at least a dozen paid lobbyists" working on behalf of pro-gun groups. The official government Lobby Registry lists only four who could be considered attached to firearm interests, and only two representing major recreational shooting organizations. The list also includes the professional lobbyist representing the Coalition for Gun Control.*

One of the Coalition's tactics, adopted from the prohibitionist US lobby group "Handgun Control Incorporated," is to attempt to convince members of the public that firearms use in Canada represents a serious "public health" issue, easily remedied by confiscating, without compensation, legally owned firearms and other related property from responsible Canadians.

Observations on a One-Way Street: The Canadian Firearm Control Debate, *Ontario Handgun Association, 1994.*

Pro-Gun Control

While gun control is not the cure-all for violence in Canadian society, the available evidence shows that gun control saves lives.

December 6, 1989....Marc Lepine, armed with a legally owned military assault weapon and 30-round magazines, walked into l'École Polytechnique in Montreal and shot 27 people, killing 14 women.

Compared to the United States, Canada's gun laws are strict. However, countries such as Britain, Australia and Japan have much stricter laws, and predictably, lower rates of gun-related deaths and violence....

Of the 1324 gun-related deaths in 1990, 180 were homicides, 66 accidental shootings, 1054 suicides, and 22 were by other forms.

Despite popular misconceptions, homicides and assaults in Canada are not typically committed by strangers....Firearms are used in over 30 per cent of homicides in Canada and in almost 50 per cent of the murders of women by their husbands.

Since improvements introduced in 1978, the trend has been an overall reduction in firearms-related crime. This supports arguments that an increase in gun control is accompanied by a reduction in violent crime.

Women account for one-third of all victims of murders committed with guns; they account for under 5 per cent of the users.

From a pamphlet written by the Coalition for Gun Control, reprinted in Observations on a One-Way Street: The Canadian Firearm Control Debate, *Ontario Handgun Association, 1994.*

1. What persuasive techniques, such as emotional appeals, expert opinions, irrelevant arguments, and faulty reasoning, do the authors of each of these viewpoints use? Give examples.

had to acquire a Firearms Acquisition Certificate (FAC) from their local police department. Before a certificate would be issued, however, the police would perform a background check of the applicant.

The Criminal Code categorized firearms under three headings: *prohibited weapons*—mainly automatic weapons, which were unlawful to possess; *restricted weapons*—handguns and similar weapons that required a valid FAC and a registration certificate from the RCMP; and *other firearms*—hunting rifles, target weapons, etc., which required a valid FAC.

Among other changes, the Criminal Law Amendment Act also established criteria for transporting firearms, created new criminal offences in relation to firearms use, and increased the penalties for a variety of weapons offences.

After 1989

In 1991, Parliament passed a new firearms law in response to the murders in Montreal. The new law extended the definition of "prohibited weapon" to include a number of semi-automatic firearms, placed a number of other firearms in the restricted category, and prohibited high-capacity **magazines**. Applicants for FACs would now have to prove they had safe storage for their weapons and that they had taken an approved firearms training course. The application for an FAC was more detailed and the required police checks more rigorous. While many gun owners complained about the changes, the majority of Canadians supported the new regulations.

In 1995, the government introduced Bill C-68. This proved to be the most contentious gun control legislation ever presented to Parliament. The new law required all gun owners to register their weapons; penalties would be imposed on those who failed to do so. Police were given new powers to search for and seize weapons. Opponents of these new gun-control provisions mounted a massive protest campaign that culminated in a demonstration on Parliament Hill. Protesters vowed to disobey the law and not register their firearms. But the government passed the legislation, and it was proclaimed law on 6 December 1995—the sixth anniversary of the Montreal Massacre.

MAKING CONNECTIONS

1. Compare the requirements for owning and operating a car and the requirements for owning and operating a gun. On that basis, do you think gun control regulations are reasonable? Explain.

KEYWORDS

Criminal Code

cost-benefit analysis

lobby

magazines

SKILL BUILDER
Sampling Public Opinion
FOCUSSING ON THE ISSUE

*Surveying public opinion is an important social science tool that enables us
to determine which issues and events are important in our society.
How should we conduct a public opinion survey? How should we analyse the results?*

Conducting Surveys

Conducting public opinion surveys is an excellent way to discover what Canadians think about issues, governments, and public figures. Surveys are used in a variety of ways to gauge the public's mood. Governments use opinion polls to monitor their public support, which helps them determine when the time is favourable to call an election. Independent pollsters survey voters during and between election campaigns to discover trends that may be emerging. Businesses survey the marketplace to discover what products and services consumers want and need.

Public opinion surveys can be conducted on a nationwide scale. They can reveal how people feel and think about controversial issues, such as abortion or gun control. They can also be conducted on a small scale to determine how local residents feel about an issue that affects their community, such as a landfill site being located in their neighbourhood or the expansion of the public transit system.

Although polls reflect public opinion, they have their limitations. They are not 100 per cent reliable because they reflect only what people feel at a given time; feelings can change rapidly as new information becomes available or as other events

unfold. Also, some of the people surveyed may not express their true opinions. Therefore, in any public opinion survey, a **margin for error** must be taken into account. To maintain a low margin for error, pollsters try to get a large sample for their surveys. The larger the number of people surveyed, the more accurate the results are likely to be. Most official polls are usually accurate to within four percentage points either way.

Developing a Survey

In conducting a survey, you must first decide what information you want to learn. For example, you may want to find out how the people in your community feel about gun control. Once you have focussed on the issue, the next step is to decide on your target audience and the size of your survey group. If you were to poll public opinion about gun control, for example, you would want to survey a wide range of people in your community because this is an issue that affects everyone. But if you want to find out how people feel about a new school policy, you would restrict your target audience to teachers, students, and parents, because these are the people who are directly affected by it.

Once the parameters of your survey are established, you can prepare your questionnaire. Make sure the questions you ask are:

- written clearly and precisely, in simple language so as to avoid misinterpretation
- arranged in logical sequence
- worded in an unbiased way that will not offend anyone
- designed to provide the information you are seeking without "leading" the respondents to any particular answer.

In addition, the questions in your survey should be closed—that is, they should give the survey participants simple answers and ask them to choose one. For example, a question on a gun-control survey might be "Do you think Canada should have stricter gun-control laws?" Participants would then check off Yes ❏ , No ❏ , or No Opinion ❏ . Closed questions are easier to analyse and will make your survey more accurate. If the majority of the people you survey respond with "No Opinion," then you know that the question is not an important issue.

Once you have written your survey, test it out on other students and ask for their feedback. For example, are the questions clearly worded and easily understood? Are they too long? Is the survey too

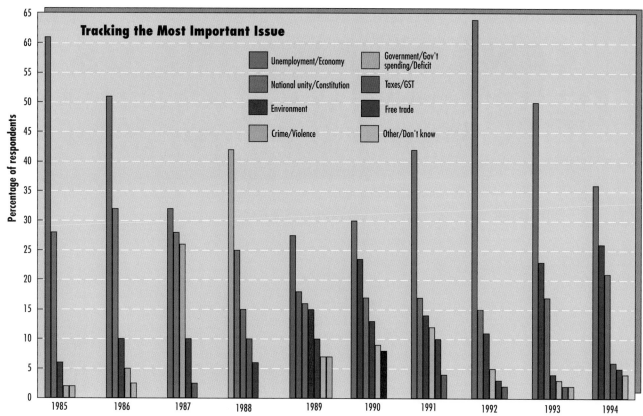

Tracking the Most Important Issue

Legend:
- Unemployment/Economy
- National unity/Constitution
- Environment
- Crime/Violence
- Government/Gov't spending/Deficit
- Taxes/GST
- Free trade
- Other/Don't know

Percentage of respondents (y-axis, 0 to 65)

Years: 1985, 1986, 1987, 1988, 1989, 1990, 1991, 1992, 1993, 1994

From Maclean's, *2 January, 1995, p. 21.*

long? Is it long enough? Once you are satisfied with your survey, prepare the final draft. It should be neatly typed and designed, with clear instructions for the respondents.

Conducting a Survey

Conduct your survey among your target audience. Tabulate the results, and prepare your findings in a report. Your report should identify the purpose of the survey, the size of your sample group, and a copy of the questionnaire. Use graphs and tables to display your findings. Write a conclusion of your survey results.

MAKING CONNECTIONS

1. In Canada, *Maclean's* magazine publishes an annual survey on how Canadians feel about the most important issues facing the country. The results since 1985 are shown in the graph above. Which issue has been rated most important most often since 1985? Why do you think this is so? What relationship exists between this key issue and another issue, such as the environment? Can you explain why?

2. Update this poll by surveying your school and community to find out what they consider to be the most important issues in Canada today. Add any other issues that are of concern. Graph the results. How do they compare with the data collected in the *Maclean's* survey?

KEYWORDS

margin for error

CANADA AND THE US
Resisting Cultural Integration
FOCUSSING ON THE ISSUE

*Free trade between Canada and the United States has increased the economic integration
between the two countries. Is free trade leading to cultural integration as well?
What is the role of symbols in representing national identity?*

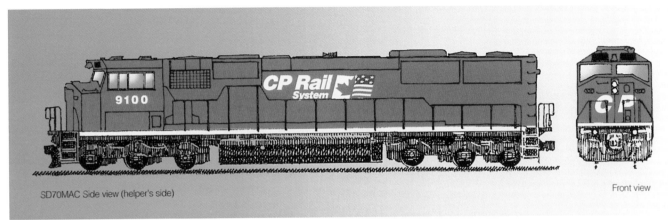

SD70MAC Side view (helper's side)

9100

CP Rail System

CP

Front view

The new Canadian Pacific promotional mark was introduced in 1993. Why do you think the company felt this was an appropriate symbol? Why did some Canadians feel betrayed by the change?

Maintaining a Canadian Identity

Since the Free Trade Agreement between Canada and the United States in 1988 (see page 320), the economies of the two countries have become more interconnected. Indeed, the point of free trade, which now includes Mexico, is to create one large North American economy. Many Canadians wonder if it is possible to become so connected to the US economically and still maintain Canada's identity as a separate country. This became a key issue at the heart of Canada-US relations at the end of the twentieth century.

Two incidents illustrated the importance of the issue of Canadian identity. The first occurred in November 1993 when Canadian Pacific Railway presented a new promotional mark, which was to be displayed on the sides of its trains. The symbol included elements of the Maple Leaf and the Stars and Stripes. The CPR explained that it had included this US symbol to reflect the fact that so much of its business took place in and with the United States.

The announcement sparked some outrage from people who thought that the CPR, a historic Canadian company, should not emblazon its trains with the American flag. Over the years, the railway had become a symbol of Canadian unity and identity. It was generally believed that, by creating a coast-to-coast transportation network, the railway had made possible the existence of Canada as a distinct country from the United States. To some people, the new CPR promotional mark represented the Americanization of one of Canada's national treasures.

The second incident occurred in 1995. The Royal Canadian Mounted Police, Canada's historic police force, announced that it was selling the rights to market its image to the American-owned Disney Corporation. Many products use the image of the red-coated Mountie, from postcards to souvenirs to cuddly toys. Under the new arrangement, Disney paid for the right to have exclusive control of who was allowed to use the image for commercial purposes.

For the RCMP, the decision made good economic sense. The agreement promised to raise a lot of money for the force. What shocked many Canadians was the fact that an American company was chosen

THE GULF WAR

Since the Second World War, Canada has become recognized as the peacekeeper in the international community. Canadian soldiers are often called upon to help keep the peace in war-torn countries, and the blue helmet of the peacekeeper is an important Canadian symbol. The symbol of Canada as peacekeeper was also brought into question in the 1990s through our relations with the US and our involvement in the Gulf War.

The Gulf War was a brief conflict between the United States—backed by the United Nations—and the Middle Eastern country of Iraq. The confrontation began in August 1990 when Iraq's leader, Saddam Hussein, ordered his army to invade Kuwait, an oil-rich neighbour. It was a clear act of aggression and the UN responded quickly, imposing **economic sanctions** on Iraq and demanding its withdrawal from Kuwait. Only **humanitarian aid** would enter Iraq until the country agreed to withdraw.

Hussein refused to budge. On 16 January 1991, the day after a UN deadline expired, the United States, supported by a coalition of forces from 28 countries, launched air strikes against Iraq. The bombs and missiles inflicted terrible damage. Still, Hussein refused to withdraw. On 23 February, coalition ground troops attacked, expelling Iraqi forces from Kuwait. Within five days Iraq had surrendered.

Canada sent naval destroyers, fighter planes, and medical personnel to the Gulf War as part of the UN coalition. It was the first time Canadian troops had participated in combat since the Korean War in the 1950s. Some people opposed Canada's involvement, believing that Canadian troops should not be fighting for what were basically American interests. There was concern that the symbol of Canada as peacekeeper was now somewhat tarnished. However, opposition to the war was not widespread. Most Canadians believed that as an ally of the US and a supporter of the UN, Canada belonged on the battlefield.

to represent a distinctly Canadian institution. It seemed that another national symbol was being taken over by American interests. Moreover, Disney was associated with cartoon characters and lavish theme parks. The business arrangement seemed to trivialize the RCMP by putting a national police force on the same level as Mickey Mouse, turning an important aspect of Canadian history into an amusement for tourists.

Both incidents illustrated a clash of values between economics and national identity. Canadian Pacific and the RCMP had sound business reasons for making their respective decisions. On the other hand, both organizations played such important roles in Canadian history that they had become symbolic of the country and the things Canadians value. So it seemed like a betrayal when they became involved and identified with American interests.

MAKING CONNECTIONS

1. a) In what way is the railway a symbol of Canadian national identity? What is the function of symbols, such as the railway, in the way people think about their country?

   b) Brainstorm a list of symbols that seem to represent Canada and explain the significance of each.

2. Canadians have always been exposed to American culture through television, magazines, and movies. At the same time, Canadians have always resisted American influences by protecting and stimulating Canadian culture. Do you think that American influence gained strength in the 1990s? Explain your answer with examples.

KEYWORDS

economic sanctions

humanitarian aid

SOMALIA
Crisis in the Canadian Forces
FOCUSSING ON THE ISSUE

Canadians were proud of the accomplishments of their armed forces during the first half of the century. They were equally proud of the troops Canada consistently committed to peacekeeping efforts. What caused the crisis of confidence in the Canadian Armed Forces?

The Somalia Mission

In 1992, the Canadian government agreed to send forces to assist in a US-led multinational peace-enforcement mission in Somalia. The African country was being torn apart by clan warfare and ravaged by famine. In December, the first members of Canada's respected Airborne Regiment began arriving in the Somali village of Belet Huen.

By March 1994, media reports began circulating about the Canadian soldiers. Investigations eventually revealed that soldiers had wounded one looter near the Canadian camp and killed another. Canadian soldiers also captured Shidane Arone, a 16-year-old Somali, in their camp and beat him to death. They took photographs of themselves with their bloody victim which, along with videotapes of soldiers from the Airborne Regiment engaged in gross and sadistic **hazing rituals**, were eventually discovered and made public. To make matters worse, it appeared that not only did the officers in charge tolerate the actions of their **subordinates**, at times they seemed to encourage them.

Two members of the Airborne Regiment were charged with murder in the death of Arone, were found guilty of manslaughter, and were sentenced to five years in jail. Several other members of the regiment,

including some officers, were charged with various offences and disciplined accordingly. In response to the public and political outcry, the government disbanded the disgraced Airborne Regiment in March 1995.

The issue did not go away, however. A reporter who requested information from the Department of Defence discovered that documents were being altered before release. The Freedom of Information Act entitles any Canadian to request and examine government documents—within certain limitations— in an effort to make the government and the bureaucracy accountable for their actions. Tampering with these documents in any way is illegal. Reports of an attempted cover-up forced the government of Jean Chrétien to establish an independent commission to investigate what was now being called the Somalia Affair.

The Somalia Inquiry

The Somalia Commission's task was to investigate not only the incidents in Somalia but also the administration of the Canadian Forces. Several witnesses testified at the inquiry that documents on Somalia had gone missing or had been shredded. Certain senior officers were alleged to have lied to the inquiry's commissioners or to have deliberately destroyed

documents or ordered others to do so. At one point, Canada's entire military operations shut down for a day while personnel searched military offices for documents about Somalia that had survived the shredders.

After more than two years of contentious hearings at a cost of millions of dollars, the government ordered the commissioners to wrap up their hearings and submit their report. This was the first time a Canadian government terminated an independent public inquiry. Many observers speculated that the government feared what else the inquiry might discover about military, bureaucratic, and political authorities, and how these revelations might affect the up-coming election. Charging that they had been deprived of the opportunity to complete their inquiry, the commissioners nevertheless delivered their report, entitled "Dishonoured Legacy," to the government. The

Chief of Defence Staff General Jean Boyle (right) testifies at the Somalia Inquiry.

report condemned the military high command, and accused leaders of attempting a cover-up, lying in their testimony, laying blame on subordinates, and allowing a collapse of military discipline in the Airborne Regiment. It also stated that military personnel were inadequately prepared both for the mission and for the conditions in Somalia. Responding to the report, defence minister Art Eggleton stated that corrective measures were being taken to ensure a similar disaster could not occur in the future.

Nonetheless, Somalia left a stain on Canada's military. Questions remained about the state of leadership and management at the heart of Canada's Armed Forces. And the image Canadians had of themselves as a peaceful, non-violent country that acted as peacekeepers for the world was forever altered.

VIEWPOINTS
THE SOMALIA INQUIRY

The decision to shut down the Somalia Inquiry was a controversial one. One of the commissioners, Peter Desbarats, condemned the government's actions. The government, however, put a more positive spin on the commission's findings.

A Commissioner's Diary
Many people are interpreting this [the termination of the inquiry] as the ultimate victory of the civilian and military bureaucrats at the head of our defence establishment....If this is true, the end of our inquiry will also mark the end of an opportunity for Canada to introduce real changes in our top-heavy defence establishment. The senior brass and bureaucrats will have protected their own....The lower ranks will have borne the brunt of punishment. Soldiers who believed in our ability to expose wrongdoing at the very highest levels and to clean house at National Defence Headquarters have been betrayed and, in the cases of some who have voluntarily testified before us, left vulnerable to retribution.

Peter Desbarats, Somalia Cover-Up: A Commissioner's Journal. *Used by permission, McClelland and Stewart, Inc. The Canadian Publishers.*

The Government's Response
To ensure accountability in the implementation of reforms, I have asked Canadians, from wide ranging backgrounds, to be part of a Monitoring Committee on Change in the Canadian Forces and the Department of National Defence. The Committee will report directly to me and prepare semi-annual reports that I will release to the public. I believe the establishment of the Monitoring Committee along with the many other initiatives described in our response will ensure the openness, transparency and accountability of the Canadian Forces and the Department of National Defence....

As we move forward, we must not forget that Canada's military is made up of women and men who volunteer to serve their country.

"A Commitment to Change: Report on the Recommendations of the Somalia Commission (Ottawa: Public Works and Government Services Canada, October 1997). Used by permission of the Minister of Public Works and Government Services Canada, 1998.

1. Debate the following resolution: The government was right in terminating the Somalia Inquiry early.
2. How would the involvement of members of the Canadian public in the Monitoring Committee improve accountability within the Canadian Forces? Do you think that organizations like the Canadian Forces are capable of policing themselves? Explain.

MAKING CONNECTIONS

1. In your view, how can we ensure that incidents such as the Somalia Affair do not happen again?

2. Do you think the Somalia Affair has permanently tarnished Canada's international reputation as a peacekeeper? Explain.

KEYWORDS

hazing ritual

subordinate

A NEW ECONOMIC REVOLUTION
The Impact of Technology
FOCUSSING ON THE ISSUE

Along with the rest of the world, Canada is going through a post-industrial revolution. What impact is this having on the economy and people's ability to find employment?

Many postsecondary institutions prepare students for the post-industrial economy. These students at Sheridan College are studying computer animation. How does this field represent the post-industrial economy?

The Post-industrial Economy

At the dawn of the twenty-first century, Canada has been undergoing another revolution. The industrial economy that dominated the twentieth century has been replaced by what experts call the **post-industrial economy**. In this new era, more and more jobs are performed through **automation** and fewer and fewer by people. In today's factories, instead of workers making products themselves, they supervise machines that make products. Many more people work in service industries—that is, businesses that provide services and information rather than manufactured products. Computer programmers, medical researchers, engineers, and technicians have become the common jobs in the post-industrial economy.

Three trends characterize the post-industrial economy:

The best-paying jobs are highly skilled and require training and education. New technology has been emerging at a rapid pace. With it comes a need for workers to be more highly skilled. Many unskilled jobs have been exported to other countries where people work for less money. While the Canadian economy creates new jobs, most are only for people with the specific skills and education required to

The Industrial Revolution

Towards the end of the nineteenth century, Canada went through an **Industrial Revolution**. It was a revolution because of the speed at which industrial change took place. Steam-powered technology was applied to work processes in a factory setting, replacing muscle power and water wheels as the "engines" of industry. Workers no longer practised their trades in small workshops. Instead, products were assembled in large plants by workers doing repetitive tasks using heavy machinery. These innovations changed the way in which goods were produced and sparked a period of incredible economic growth.

THE CANADIAN WORKFORCE

- The economy needs to produce about 200 000 additional jobs each year to employ all the new people entering the workforce.
- In October 1997, there were 1 409 000 unemployed Canadians—9.1 per cent of the workforce
- Between 1990 and 1996, computer technology wiped out 220 000 traditional clerical jobs. At the same time, many thousands of jobs were created in computer programming and technology.
- In 1977, 12.5 per cent of all jobs in Canada were part-time. In 1997, that figure was 20 per cent.

- In 1998, 31 per cent of all part-time workers want full-time jobs but cannot find them.
- While unemployment remained at 9 per cent or higher in the late 1990s, many Western mining companies claimed they could not find enough workers for the oil patches.

1. Suggest three policies that the government might introduce to help unemployed people get back to work.

perform them. In today's world, inexperienced and unskilled workers discover that it is increasingly difficult to find jobs.

There is a growing disparity in the wages paid to skilled and unskilled workers. Skilled jobs requiring more education generally pay higher wages. Meanwhile, the gap is widening between the wages of unskilled and skilled workers. Furthermore, when the economy suffers a **recession**, unskilled workers are usually the first to be laid off and the last to be rehired.

For most of the twentieth century, the incomes of average Canadians rose steadily. That trend has changed, however. Since 1989, the average income after taxes has fallen 5 per cent. However, not all Canadians are earning less. Many skilled workers in the new high-

technology industries have enjoyed a rising **standard of living**. Nevertheless, Canadian workers as a whole are worse off today than they were a few years ago.

The post-industrial economy is less able to provide jobs for everyone. In the 1990s, unemployment rates in Canada have hovered around 10 per cent. This is high in a country where 7 per cent is considered full employment. Today, in many traditional industries, a number of unskilled or low-skilled jobs have been relocated to other countries or have been replaced by labour-saving automated devices. As a result of these changes, some economists worry that Canada is developing a two-tier economy. At one end are the "haves"—skilled, educated workers with lots of employment opportunities in reasonably

well-paying jobs. At the other end are the "have-nots"—unskilled workers with shrinking opportunities, eking out a living from poorly paid full- or part-time jobs.

Are these changes in wages and work opportunities a permanent part of the post-industrial economy? Or do they simply reflect a transition period as the economy adjusts to rapid technological change? And can **knowledge-based industries** provide enough jobs to keep Canadians working and to maintain a prosperous economy? These are some of the most important economic questions Canadians are asking.

MAKING CONNECTIONS

1. Some parts of the country experience greater unemployment than others. What factors might account for these differences? Do you think the post-industrial economy will add to this disparity? Explain.

KEYWORDS

Industrial Revolution

post-industrial economy

automation

recession

standard of living

knowledge-based industry

PICTURE GALLERY
Life at the End of the Century
FOCUSSING ON THE ISSUE

Canada and the world changed dramatically over the course of the twentieth century. What do these pictures reveal about Canada today? How do they compare with the picture gallery in Unit 1?

*Canada Day celebrations in Toronto highlight the **multiculturalism** of Canada's urban centres. How has multiculturalism changed Canadian society in the twentieth century? What predictions can you make about Canadian multiculturalism in the twenth-first century?*

New Canadians take the oath of citizenship in a ceremony in Montreal. What does this photograph suggest about the origin of new immigrants to Canada in the 1990s? Compare these origins to those in other decades of this century.

Female students today have greater educational opportunities than ever before. Do you think that women have attained true equality in Canadian society?

This 16-year-old girl, living on the streets of Victoria, is pregnant, but cannot afford the bus fare to return home to her mother in Brandon, Manitoba. What do you think should be done to ensure that all young people in Canada have the same opportunities?

These Aboriginal children live in an impoverished reservation in northern Manitoba. What does this photograph suggest about the success of Canada's Aboriginal policies in the twentieth century? What do you suppose will characterize the Aboriginal policies of the future?

Canada's postal workers solicited public support during the postal strike in November 1997. What role do unions play in the Canadian labour force today?

Many Canadians, particularly young people, are concerned about the environment. How does this attitude reflect the changing values of Canadians? Will you become more, or less, concerned about the environment during your lifetime?

A Toronto doctor distributes medical supplies in Democratic Republic of Congo (formerly Zaïre) for the volunteer agency Médecins San Frontières/Doctors Without Borders Canada. To what degree do you think Canadians are encouraged to become responsible global citizens? In what ways can Canadians become more responsible global citizens?

◁▢ MAHING CONNECTIONS ▢▷

1. Identify the social, political, cultural, economic, and environmental values that are represented in this photo gallery.

2. Look back to the photo gallery on page 8, and compare and contrast the images there with the images here. Which gallery presents a greater number of contrasts? Why do you suppose this is?

3. a) Throughout this book, you have been compiling your own photo gallery. Organize your collection and display it in your classroom to illustrate how life in Canada has evolved in the twentieth century.
   b) Among the photo galleries displayed in your classroom, which images are most common? Which photos do you find most compelling, and why? What images of life are not represented in the photo galleries displayed? Why not?

KEYWORDS

multicultural

ABORIGINAL SELF-GOVERNMENT
Recognizing Aboriginal Rights

Self-government emerged in the 1980s as a major objective of Aboriginal peoples across Canada. What does self-government mean? How is it being implemented in Canada?

Self-government

Self-government is the right of Aboriginal peoples to govern themselves in their own communities. For a century, the federal Department of Indian Affairs, working through the Indian Act, made almost all decisions affecting the daily lives of Aboriginal peoples. Then, the right to self-government was endorsed in 1983 by a committee of the federal Parliament, which said that Aboriginal societies "form a distinct order of government in Canada." (The right to self-government was later included in the Charlottetown Accord.) Self-government meant that decisions would now be made by Aboriginal peoples themselves. The process of giving Aboriginal peoples control over their own affairs is already well established. In many parts of the country, bands have taken over their own health care, education, policing, and other services.

There are different forms of self-government, depending on the circumstances in different parts of the country. In 1986, the Sechelt First Nation in British Columbia became the first band in Canada to achieve a form of self-government. The Sechelt Government Indian District has powers similar to those of a municipality. The Sechelt Act created the Sechelt Band as a legal entity, having the capacity, rights,

powers, and privileges of a natural person. According to the act, the band may enter into contracts or agreements; acquire and sell property; and expend, invest, and borrow money. The band is also responsible for programs, services, and economic development that affect its membership.

In northern Canada, where Aboriginal peoples form the majority, another form of self-government is being applied as of 1 April 1999. The new territory of Nunavut (meaning "our land" in the Inuit language) is completely controlled by the Inuit, with the territorial government exercising many of the powers of a province.

Nunavut evolved through a long period of negotiation and consultation. In 1971, Inuit residents of the North formed an organization called the Inuit Brotherhood, subsequently renamed the Inuit Tapirisat, to speak with a united voice on their behalf. A few years later, the Inuit Tapirisat proposed the creation of Nunavut as a separate territory where the Inuit, because they are the majority, would have control of their government. In a **referendum**, the residents of the Northwest Territories agreed to divide the Territories; a constitutional forum was created to discuss how to do so. A major issue was that some of the Inuit people, the Inuvialuit, lived in the western

Arctic, outside the proposed area of Nunavut. Where would they belong? In the end, the Inuvialuit decided to remain in part of what was left of the Northwest Territories, also called Denendeh (an Athapascan word meaning "land of the people").

As part of the agreement to form Nunavut, the Inuit also received direct ownership of 352 000 km² of land—about 18 per cent of Nunavut's land—and $1.15 billion in exchange for giving up their claims of ownership of the rest of the territory.

Nunavut includes the eastern portion of the Northwest Territories that lies roughly north of the tree line. It covers 2.2 million km² and has 26 000 residents, 85 per cent of whom are Inuit. The capital is Iqaluit, a village on Baffin Island. Nunavut is one of three northern territories, along with Yukon and the Northwest Territories

ABORIGINAL PEOPLES IN AUSTRALIA

While the plight of Aboriginal peoples throughout the world varies, there are many similarities. When immigrants began arriving from other lands, Aboriginal peoples' lives were permanently changed. Their forms of government, their family life, and their affinity for the land suffered as a result of the newcomers. While all Aboriginal peoples today hope for political, economic, and social justice, the Aboriginal peoples in North America have probably been more successful than those in other parts of the world in making people aware of injustices.

Activism among Aboriginal groups in Australia has been on the rise since the 1960s, when they began to dispute old laws and standards and to seek the full rights of Australian citizens. The Department of Aboriginal Affairs was established in the early 1970s to oversee policies on self-determination for Aboriginal peoples and to investigate issues such as land rights, educa-tion, and health. The Australian government then increased its spending on Aboriginal health and welfare. A **Royal Commission** on Aboriginal land rights recommended that Aboriginal reserve lands be returned to them and that Aboriginal peoples be eligible for financial support in using their land as they please. In 1992, in a decision on an Aboriginal land claim, the High Court of Australia overturned the long-standing notion that prior to European settlement, Australia belonged to no one, thus it could be legally taken over. This decision not only opened the way for Aboriginal peoples to make claims on Crown land if they could establish an enduring link, but also officially recognized the fact that Aboriginal peoples had been unfairly dispossessed of their lands.

Adapted from Don Scott and Lindsay Dann, Australia in the Twentieth Century *(Melbourne: Oxford University Press, 1995), p. 177; and Mina Shafer,* Visions of Australia: Exploring Our History *(Melbourne: Oxford University Press, 1996), p. 38, by permission of Oxford University Press.*

Debating Self-government

Self-government is a complex issue. There is considerable debate about the degree and types of power that Aboriginal governing bodies should have. There are hundreds of Aboriginal bands in Canada, each with its own population, location, and economic opportunities. A form of government suitable for one may not be suitable for another.

Who should control and receive the benefits of taxation on the reserves? Who should make decisions about contentious issues such as gambling? How should Aboriginal governments share in decision-making beyond the boundaries of the reserves? For instance, if there is an Aboriginal legal system, what happens if a reserve resident breaks the law outside the reserve, or if someone from outside the reserve commits a crime on Aboriginal territory? And what about the large numbers of Aboriginal people who do not live on reserves? How will they participate in self-government? These and many other issues will be resolved as Aboriginal peoples move towards the full realization of self-government.

The fundamental significance of self-government is that Aboriginal peoples will control their own affairs. Aboriginal peoples are not *asking* for self-government; they believe they have always had the right to govern themselves. What they *are* asking is for other Canadians to recognize that fact.

◄▣— MAKING CONNECTIONS —▣►

1. How does Aboriginal self-government differ from the idea of Quebec separation?

2. Invite representatives from two or three Aboriginal bands in your area to visit your class and discuss what self-government means to them. Does it matter that there may be more than one form of self-government?

KEYWORDS

self-government

referendum

Royal Commission

CLAIMING THE LAND
Treaty-making in British Columbia
FOCUSSING ON THE ISSUE

*Relations between Aboriginal and non-Aboriginal peoples in British Columbia
are being transformed through a process of treaty-making. Why are treaties necessary?
How will they benefit Aboriginal peoples?*

A Claim to the Land

In 1992, British Columbia began a period of **treaty**-making with Aboriginal peoples that will last well into the twenty-first century. In much of the rest of Canada, treaties between Aboriginal groups and the federal government were signed long ago. The government recognized that the original inhabitants had a claim to the land because of their long occupation and use of it. Between 1850 and 1921, huge tracts of Ontario, the West, and the North were included in treaties in which the rights of Aboriginal peoples were clarified.

Treaties were nothing new to the Aboriginal peoples. They had been negotiating agreements among themselves long before the arrival of Europeans. They used treaties to formalize arrangements over who was going to use the land and for what purpose. To the Aboriginal peoples, this was also the meaning of the early treaties they signed with Europeans. They were not abandoning the land; they were simply agreeing to the ways in which both sides would use it. The Canadian government, however, had a different view of the treaties. It thought of them as land sales that effectively ended any further Aboriginal claims to the land. These differing views ultimately led

to misunderstandings and eventually conflict.

Historically, the situation in British Columbia has been different than the rest of Canada. In BC, a few treaties were signed with Aboriginal peoples on Vancouver Island in the 1850s. Then, with one exception, treaty-making stopped. (The exception was a small corner of northeastern BC that was included in Treaty Number 8, an agreement negotiated in 1899 that mainly dealt with Alberta and the Northwest Territories.)

Aboriginal peoples were forced off the land to settle in small reserves. But like their counterparts who signed the early treaties in the rest of Canada, they never agreed to give up their territories. The provincial government, on the other hand, simply refused to accept that Aboriginal peoples had any claim to the land. Over the years, Aboriginal groups appealed to the province to acknowledge their title and to make treaties with them, but to no avail. It was only after several court cases ruled that Aboriginal land claims did exist that the provincial government agreed to negotiate.

The first treaty was an agreement between the province, the federal government, and the Nisga'a people. The Nisga'a inhabit the Nass River area in northern BC. For 100 years they asserted their claim

to this territory. Then, in 1976, the federal government agreed to open negotiations. British Columbia joined the talks in 1990. Six years later, an historic agreement-in-principle was signed giving the Nisga'a $190 million, more than 2000 km² of land, a guaranteed share of the Nass River salmon run, and a degree of self-government. The settlement established a huge precedent for Aboriginal land claims.

The Treaty Process

While the Nisga'a agreement was being negotiated, the provincial government announced some ground rules for treaty-making with other Aboriginal groups. No one owning property in the province would be asked to give it up because of a treaty, nor would taxpayers be asked to pay more than the provincial economy could bear. For their part, Aboriginal peoples were not asking that they be given back all the land they used before the arrival of Europeans. What they asked for is more land for their communities and a share of the resources produced from their territories in order to attain economic self-sufficiency.

The treaty-making process is being guided by the BC Treaty Commission, a five-person panel charged with keeping the negotiations on track. Such matters as land and resource ownership, local government, economic development, and education are among the issues on the negotiating table. Along with the federal and provincial governments and the Aboriginal community, the public at large is represented in the process by a special advisory committee.

The question of Aboriginal land claims gained new legitimacy in December 1997. The Supreme Court of Canada ruled that Aboriginal peoples have title to their land and that their oral histories, on which they base these claims, are as valid as written European history. The Court stated that governments have "a moral, if not legal, duty" to negotiate land claims. It was a landmark decision.

Not all Aboriginal groups in BC want to be involved in treaty negotiations, however. Some consider themselves to be sovereign nations and do not accept the jurisdiction of the provincial government. Others feel that the federal government has sole responsibility for Aboriginal peoples so there is little point in negotiating with the province. Still, most BC Aboriginal groups have decided to participate. It is expected that it will take at least 20 years before the treaty-making process is complete. While the issues involved are complex, in the end, they will result in a new relationship between Aboriginal peoples and other British Columbians.

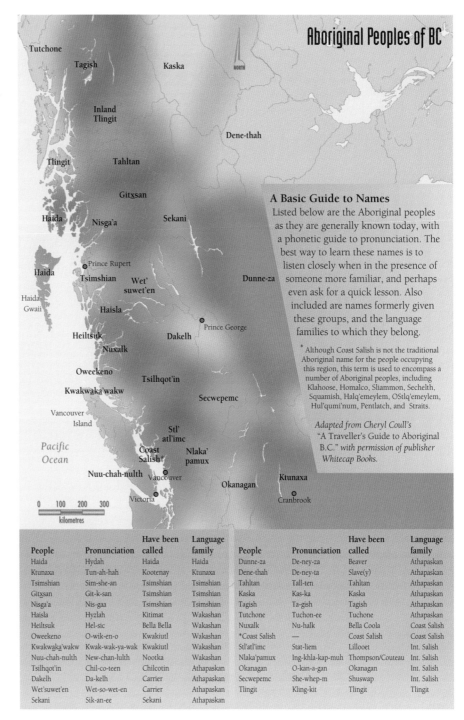

Aboriginal Peoples of BC

A Basic Guide to Names

Listed below are the Aboriginal peoples as they are generally known today, with a phonetic guide to pronunciation. The best way to learn these names is to listen closely when in the presence of someone more familiar, and perhaps even ask for a quick lesson. Also included are names formerly given these groups, and the language families to which they belong.

* Although Coast Salish is not the traditional Aboriginal name for the people occupying this region, this term is used to encompass a number of Aboriginal peoples, including Klahoose, Homalco, Sliammon, Sechelt, Squamish, Halq'emeylem, OStlq'emeylem, Hul'qumi'num, Pentlatch, and Straits.

Adapted from Cheryl Coull's "A Traveller's Guide to Aboriginal B.C." with permission of publisher Whitecap Books.

People	Pronunciation	Have been called	Language family	People	Pronunciation	Have been called	Language family
Haida	Hydah	Haida	Haida	Dunne-za	De-ney-za	Beaver	Athapaskan
Ktunaxa	Tun-ah-hah	Kootenay	Ktunaxa	Dene-tha	De-ney-ta	Slave(y)	Athapaskan
Tsimshian	Sim-she-an	Tsimshian	Tsimshian	Tahltan	Tall-ten	Tahltan	Athapaskan
Gitxsan	Git-k-san	Tsimshian	Tsimshian	Kaska	Kas-ka	Kaska	Athapaskan
Nisga'a	Nis-gaa	Tsimshian	Tsimshian	Tagish	Ta-gish	Tagish	Athapaskan
Haisla	Hyzlah	Kitimat	Wakashan	Tutchone	Tuchon-ee	Tuchone	Athapaskan
Heiltsuk	Hel-sic	Bella Bella	Wakashan	Nuxalk	Nu-halk	Bella Coola	Coast Salish
Oweekeno	O-wik-en-o	Kwakiutl	Wakashan	*Coast Salish	—	Coast Salish	Coast Salish
Kwakwaka'wakw	Kwak-wak-ya-wak	Kwakiutl	Wakashan	Stl'atl'imc	Stat-liem	Lillooet	Int. Salish
Nuu-chah-nulth	New-chan-lulth	Nootka	Wakashan	Nlaka'pamux	Ing-khla-kap-muh	Thompson/Couteau	Int. Salish
Tsilhqot'in	Chil-co-teen	Chilcotin	Athapaskan	Okanagan	O-kan-a-gan	Okanagan	Int. Salish
Dakelh	Da-kelh	Carrier	Athapaskan	Secwepemc	She-whep-m	Shuswap	Int. Salish
Wet'suwet'en	Wet-so-wet-en	Carrier	Athapaskan	Tlingit	Kling-kit	Tlingit	Tlingit
Sekani	Sik-an-ee	Sekani	Athapaskan				

MAKING CONNECTIONS

1. From the point of view of an Aboriginal person, write a paragraph explaining why the treaty-making process is important for your people. Then respond with another paragraph in a non-Aboriginal voice expressing your opinion about the treaties.

KEYWORDS

treaty

SALMON WARS
Crisis in the Fishing Industry
FOCUSSING ON THE ISSUE

*Salmon is the most important catch in the Pacific Coast fishery.
What events led to a crisis in the salmon fishery in 1997?*

Talks Break Down

In 1985, Canada and the United States signed the Pacific Salmon Treaty, which regulated the salmon catch for fishers in British Columbia, Washington state, and Alaska. But the treaty was never really considered acceptable by either country, and both sides had their own interpretations of the key issues. Talks aimed at clarifying the treaty and establishing quotas on the salmon catch had failed each year since 1994. With no quotas in place, fleets from both countries were trying to maximize their catches.

West Coast Salmon Fishery, Catch by Species, 1993-1996				
	British Columbia		Alaska/Washington	
	Number (millions)	Value	Number (millions)	Value
Coho	7.8	$54.4	29.3	$131.3
Sockeye	39.9	$367.4	14.3	$134.7

From Maclean's, "Salmon Stakes," 21 July 1997. Reprinted by permission.

The situation reached a crisis point in July 1997. For the first time in several years, fishers from Washington broke an informal agreement and intercepted a portion of the salmon run returning to BC. The dispute erupted after renewed talks on the Pacific Salmon Treaty broke down in June. The impasse centred on two related issues—how much sockeye salmon bound for the Fraser River the Americans should be allowed to catch and how much coho salmon, which spawn in US waters, Canadians should be allowed to harvest. While sockeye stocks were not endangered, the number of coho had been steadily declining. To compensate, the United States wanted a reduction in the Canadian coho **quota** and greater access for themselves to the sockeye catch.

The salmon wars ignited a political battle of wills. BC premier Glen Clark had threatened to cancel a lease granted to the US navy at Nanoose Bay on Vancouver Island unless American boats stopped overfishing. His decision angered not only politicians in Washington, DC, but in Ottawa as well. The Canadian government feared that if Clark acted, the US might retaliate with a trade war. Many BC politicians, however, felt that the federal

Canadian fishing boats block the passage of the US ferry Malaspina. *Do you think the Canadian fishers should have resorted to such action? Explain your answer.*

government was more concerned with appeasing the Americans than with supporting the rights of the BC fishing industry. While the politicians engaged in verbal battles, fishers on both sides announced plans to aggressively intercept and catch more fish than usual bound for each other's country.

In late July, the tension reached new heights as militant members of the BC fishing community held an Alaska ferry captive for three days. The *Malaspina* was blockaded by 200 Canadian fishing boats, effectively holding 385 passengers on board as hostages. In response, the US Senate voted 81 to 19 in favour of a **resolution** calling for US president Bill Clinton to send in the navy to protect Alaskan ferries.

Foreign affairs minister Lloyd Axworthy was dispatched to Washington, DC, to mend fences. However, the two sides failed to reach an agreement. The only progress made was the appointment of two negotiators to look for new ways to restart talks over the Pacific Salmon Treaty.

Resolving the salmon dispute is not easy, in part because of the complexity of the salmon industry itself. The salmon run is not a single event. In fact, it does not even involve a single species. There are five types of Pacific salmon, each with its own migratory schedule and patterns. The crisscrossing of international boundaries further complicates the rules and their interpretation. Both sides want to protect their own fishing interests. **Ecologists**, however, fear that the commercial fisheries in both countries threaten the survival of all salmon, regardless of their origin.

CASE STUDY

HABITAT UNDER ATTACK

Like all wildlife, salmon are vulnerable to the effects of human activity. The salmon's unique life cycle means that it lives in a variety of **habitats**. Salmon begin life in the spawning beds of freshwater rivers. After their first year, they migrate to ocean saltwaters. There, many mature fish are harvested in the offshore fishery. Eventually, the remaining adult fish return to their birthplace stream. Some are caught along the migration routes near the mouths of the rivers. The rest make their way upstream, where they reproduce before they die.

Canada's greatest salmon resource is the Fraser River (see page 52), which accounts for 25 per cent of the province's salmon catch. The mouth of the river where freshwater and saltwater mix is a vital part of the salmon habitat. Today, however, this **estuary** is threatened; over 2 million people live near it, and a variety of industries operate alongside it. Logging, landfills, and industrial and agricultural pollution have all seriously damaged the salmon habitat.

MAKING CONNECTIONS

1. In class, set up negotiating talks aimed at settling the salmon dispute between Canada and the United States. Make sure the interest groups on both sides are represented. For Canada, this should include BC fishing representatives as well as federal and provincial officials. For the United States, both Alaska and Washington should be represented along with the federal government. Try to negotiate an agreement, then outline the terms of the treaty.

2. Find out what progress, if any, has been made in the salmon dispute since the crisis in 1997.

KEYWORDS

quota

resolution

ecologist

habitat

estuary

WELCOME TO CYBERSPACE
Living in the Information Age

Communications technology—computers, portable telephones, fax machines, and television—has created an information revolution. How has technology changed our world? How has it affected our right to privacy?

The Information Revolution

The last quarter of the twentieth century saw an information revolution, a change as dramatic as the Industrial Revolution was in an earlier era. Following the invention of the transistor in 1948, a series of innovations in the field of electronics dramatically reduced the size of radio, telephone, television, and computer equipment and increased the speed at which data, sound, and visual images could be transmitted by an astounding rate. Half a decade later, communications technology has advanced to the point where almost all information is now digitized into tiny bits of energy that can be transmitted across great distances almost instantly. This is *cyberspace*, a term coined by Vancouver science-fiction writer William Gibson to describe the new universe of electronic communications.

The information revolution has affected all aspects of Canadian life.

Canadians now commonly use fax machines, computer networks, and other **on-line** services at school, at work, and at home. Web sites on the Internet allow people to access information from around the world. It is possible for a student in Nanaimo to communicate instantly with another student almost anywhere in the world through e-mail. Even politicians use cyberspace to deliver their messages to voters, and some even encourage voters to send their own messages back in a possible preview of interactive democracy in the future.

Technology has also changed the way Canadians do business. From large corporations to home offices, businesses rely on computers to store information, monitor sales, and record transactions. Today more documents are kept as electronic files in computers than as paper files in filing cabinets.

Electronic communication has revolutionized our society. Automated banking machines at banks and outlets and direct debit machines at retail stores make banking and shopping faster and more convenient. Cellular telephones enable people on the go to be accessible. The ability of scientists and researchers to collect, process, and transmit information electronically via satellite has greatly expanded human knowledge.

Describe the ways in which information technology plays a part in your life.

But what are the costs of this information revolution? There are concerns about the amount of personal information on ordinary citizens that is being stored in computer data banks. Just how secure is this information? "Hackers" routinely gain access to secret military and government files via their home computers. Can they do the same thing to obtain credit card information, bank account numbers, and other private information? And if so, how might they be able to use it to illegally gain access to someone else's money?

Aside from criminal misuse, there are other questions about the nature and quality of information stored in government, business, and medical files. Could inaccurate data or inappropriate use of data affect a person's credit rating, insurance coverage, or even personal freedom? In a relatively new and rapidly changing world, many questions have been raised, but as yet, few have been answered.

Access to Information

Federal and provincial governments are trying to address these concerns through access-to-information laws and regulations. In most provinces and at the federal level, Canadians have a right to find out what information about themselves is in the records kept by government agen-cies, schools, hospitals, and the justice system. But it is more difficult to monitor and control information kept by businesses, clubs, and social organizations. Often these groups sell their mailing lists or other client data to other businesses and organizations. Buyers use the data to contact potential customers by mail or telephone to try to sell them their products or to solicit their support. In Canada, consumers can request that businesses not sell information about themselves in this way.

Electronic communications may also threaten privacy within businesses themselves. In recent years, many workers have discovered that their messages on the company e-mail systems are being read by their supervisors. In some cases, these messages have revealed employees' unfavourable opinions about the company or their supervisors, resulting in the dismissal of the workers. Court decisions have upheld employers' rights to monitor the company's communications and to act when they feel it is in the company's best interest. Many people feel this is an invasion of employee privacy. Others argue that monitoring electronic communication is necessary because e-mail has been used to send threatening or harassing messages from one employee to another. The debate will likely intensify as society becomes more deeply entrenched in the information age.

Censorship

Modern electronic communication systems have created an unlimited flow of all kinds of text and visual information. A flood of messages flows across the border into Canadian households via satellite television and the Internet. Some of these messages are shocking and offensive. There are web sites on the Internet providing racist hate literature, child pornography, and scenes of violence and degradation. Anyone hooked up to the Internet has access to this information. Electronic technology can do many things, but it cannot determine the age of the user. Many Canadians are concerned that their children can gain access to these web sites. They also object to the fact that these web sites can openly promote socially unacceptable attitudes and behaviour.

The issue of **censorship** of electronic media is controversial, even to prevent the use of the media for degrading or hateful purposes, such as disseminating pornagraphy or hate literature. Opponents of censorship argue that it is a question of free speech and freedom of expression and that individuals should decide for themselves what they choose to read, see, or hear. Those who advocate censorship say that the preservation of community standards and the protection of children is more important than the individual's right to free choice.

MAKING CONNECTIONS

1. Write a newspaper editorial advocating the censorship of the new electronic media to protect children from violent and pornographic images. Propose ways that this might be done.

2. Conduct a search of the Internet for opinions about issues of privacy and censorship. Collect these views and discuss them in class.

KEYWORDS

on-line

censorship

VANCOUVER
A Multilingual City
FOCUSSING ON THE ISSUE

Rapid immigration has changed the face of Vancouver.
What effect has it had on the use of English in the city?

English now a minority language in Vancouver

Language spoken at home
Vancouver public school students
By language - 1995

Vietnamese 5%
Punjabi 4%
Other 15%
English 44%
Chinese 32%

A Changing City

On 2 November 1996, the *Vancouver Sun* displayed the headline above across its front page. The accompanying article began:

If you feel like you're in the minority if you speak English in the city of Vancouver, you're right.

A majority of people living within the city limits now speak a language other than English at home....

It happened...some time in the past five years....The last time [Statistics Canada] crunched the numbers after

the 1991 census, English was still the predominant language inside civic boundaries. Of a total of 471 844 heads counted, 318 585 reported they spoke English at home, compared to 125 805 speaking Chinese languages, 72 330 Punjabi-speakers, and a few thousand speaking 138 other tongues.

But the past five years has seen an unprecedented influx of Asian immigrants moving into Vancouver, coupled with a mass movement of English-speakers selling their high-priced Vancouver city homes and cashing in by moving to the suburbs....

The result: just 43.96 per cent of the children in Vancouver schools report English as the language they speak at home, according to a study by the Vancouver school board.

And that number, says city social planner Baldwin Wong, translates into an accurate account of the linguistic realities of city homes, meaning that more than 56 per cent of the population of the city speaks a language other than English at home....

Later on the article pointed out that the trend may not be a permanent one.

Younger immigrants will soon learn English in school and blend into the social fabric to succeed academically and financially, [David Schweitzer, a sociologist] said. Older immigrants find it harder to learn new languages, and...grandparents are unlikely ever to learn either of Canada's official languages and will speak the language of their homeland the rest of their lives.

"If it takes a generation [for English to return as the dominant tongue] that shouldn't be terribly disturbing," Schweitzer said.

"English now a minority language in Vancouver," Rick Ouston, The Vancouver Sun.

Do you think there is a language trend in your community? Explain.

Growth of a City

The population of Greater Vancouver grew enormously during the 1990s. Much of this growth was the result of immigration. In 1996, immigrants accounted for 35 per cent of Vancouver's population, giving it the country's second-largest immigrant population after Toronto. Because of western Canada's location on the **Pacific Rim**, 80 per cent of the newcomers it attracts are from Asia and the Middle East. Many of these immigrants do not speak English when they first arrive. As a result, today Vancouver is a **multilingual** city with people from many different cultural backgrounds speaking many different languages.

Newcomers to Canada continue to use their own language because it is familiar to them. However, to fully participate in Canadian society, it is necessary to speak one of Canada's official languages, English

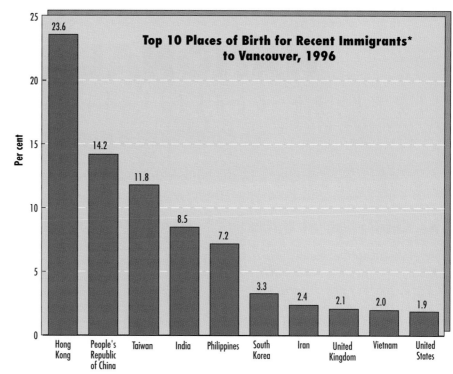

Top 10 Places of Birth for Recent Immigrants* to Vancouver, 1996

Per cent

- Hong Kong: 23.6
- People's Republic of China: 14.2
- Taiwan: 11.8
- India: 8.5
- Philippines: 7.2
- South Korea: 3.3
- Iran: 2.4
- United Kingdom: 2.1
- Vietnam: 2.0
- United States: 1.9

*Recent immigrants are those who immigrated between 1991 and the first four months of 1996. *From Statistics Canada.*

or French. In British Columbia, English is the common language. While younger immigrants tend to learn their new language quickly, older generations may have less opportunity to learn English. To help all immigrants learn their new language, there are classes called English as a Second Language (ESL). The purpose of ESL is to provide immigrants with English language skills so that they can carry on their education in English. By the mid-1990s, more than half of all Vancouver students were enrolled in ESL classes.

MAKING CONNECTIONS

1. a) What is the message of the newspaper article? Do you think that the headline accurately reflects what the article says? Does the article give the impression that the use of languages other than English is a good thing? A bad thing? Can you identify any instances of **bias**?

    b) A press council is an independent panel that hears complaints from the public about news media reports. Establish a three-person press council in your class. Have a group of students prepare a brief to the council complaining about the headline and article from the *Sun.* Have another group of students prepare a brief defending the newspaper. Members of the council will then hand down a decision based on the two presentations.

2. How many languages are represented in your classroom? Make a pie chart showing the percentage of the class represented by each language.

KEYWORDS

Pacific Rim

multilingual

bias

NATIONAL UNITY
Seeking Constitutional Solutions

*Quebec's place in the Constitution has presented the greatest challenge
to national unity in the 1990s. How have Canadians responded to this challenge?*

The Challenge of Unity

One of the main themes of Canadian politics has always been the challenge of unity: how to satisfy the needs and aspirations of different parts of the country without weakening the central government so much that the federation unravels. Every generation of Canadians seems to think it is dealing with this challenge for the first time. In fact, the challenge has been around since Confederation.

Four days before the 1995 Quebec referendum, 100 000 Canadians from all across the country travelled to Montreal to stage a monster rally to persuade Quebeckers to remain within Canada. Do you think dramatic gestures like this one have any impact on the way people feel about the country?

During the 1990s, the challenge emerged once again as the federal and provincial governments tried to find a formula for bringing Quebec into the Constitution. At the beginning of the decade, the Meech Lake Accord had failed. (See page 296.) That failure sparked a flurry of political activity. In Quebec, a new political party, the Bloc Québécois, was created to fight for Quebec independence in the federal Parliament. In the 1993 election, the Bloc won enough seats to become the **official Opposition** in Ottawa. Meanwhile, Quebec premier Robert Bourassa set up a public commission. It presented a report calling for greater powers for Quebec as the price of remaining in Confederation. On the national scene, the federal government established its own commission, the Citizens' Forum on Canada's Future, to hear the public's views.

All this activity culminated in another meeting of federal and provincial leaders in Charlottetown, PEI. The negotiations produced a new constitutional agreement. Among the important elements of the Charlottetown Accord were a clause recognizing Quebec as a distinct society, an elected Senate with equal representation from every province, and the **inherent** right to **self-government** by Aboriginal peoples.

The Charlottetown Accord, signed on 28 August 1992, won a wide measure of acceptance among political leaders. Ultimately, however, it was the people who would decide. Prime Minister Brian Mulroney announced that a national **referendum** would ask Canadians to answer *Yes* or *No* to the question: "Do you agree that the Constitution of Canada should be renewed on the basis of the agreement reached on August 28, 1992?" The agreement included many issues, and in the days leading up to the vote, support for the accord dwindled. In the end, Canadians voted an overwhelming *No.*

However, the issue did not go away with the defeat of the Charlottetown Accord. Quebec decided to hold another referendum asking provincial voters if they wanted the government to begin to negotiate Quebec **sovereignty**. On 30 October 1995, the *No* side won the referendum, but it was by the narrowest of margins—51 per cent to 49 per cent. What was particularly disturbing was that the majority of French-speaking Quebeckers voted *Yes.*

Far from settling the issue of Quebec separation, the referendum made it more uncertain. The only thing anyone could say for sure was that Quebec's place in Canada would stay at the top of the political agenda for years to come. Indeed, at the First Ministers Conference in September 1997, known as the Calgary Summit, nine provincial premiers endorsed the draft of yet another constitutional amendment. It expressed the recognition of Quebec's "unique character" while reaffirming that all Canadians and all provinces are equal in status. And so the unity debate continued.

VIEWPOINTS

THREE VISIONS OF CANADA

The relationship between French and English Canada and Quebec's place in Confederation sparks a variety of opinions.

Much of Canadians' fragile self-esteem rests on the condition that Quebeckers must or should "love" us. Part of our progress toward political maturity must lie in accepting that they neither do nor should "love" Canada, and in admitting to ourselves that we do not—and cannot— "love" them. Patriotism, like individual human bonds, can only proceed from intimate knowledge. The experience of nations generally is that people cannot know each other across a language barrier....

There are signs...that the large English-Canadian public is also coming to accept this difficult truth. In my view this is a benediction: it means we can finally get on with the job of building the English-Canadian nation.

This does not necessarily mean that Quebec will go the full route to independence. The presence of the United States has always been a good reason for English and French Canadians to seek mutual support, and remains so. But the Quebecois have never felt a sense of belonging to the entity called "Canada"; and it is unlikely they ever will. The only useful relationship between the two peoples would seem to be a contractual one, based on mutual need and benefit.

From Impossible Nation *by Ray Conlogue, (Stratford, ON: The Mercury Press, 1996). Reprinted by permission of the Mercury Press.*

The Canadian federation's essential problem has always been that Francophone Quebecois identify Quebec as

their nation and Canada as their state, while English-speaking Canadians identify Canada both as their nation and as their state. So long as Quebec believed that it needed the rest of Canada for its own survival, this asymmetry did not prove fatal. Since 1960, however, Quebec has used its powers within the federal system to become a state within a state and to develop its own economy. Quebec has never needed Canada as a nation. Now it is asking itself whether it even needs it as a state.

Excerpt from Blood and Belonging *by Michael Ignatieff. Copyright © Michael Ignatieff, 1993. Reprinted by permission of Penguin Books Canada Ltd.*

But when will you English Canadians get it through your thick collective skull that we want to live in a French society, inside and outside, at work and at play, in church and in school. Is this so difficult to understand? Do you get some kind of secret satisfaction from forcing us to repeat this simple fact time after time?

Daniel Latouche, Letters to a Québécois Friend *(Montreal: McGill-Queens University Press, 1990), p.89.*

1. Ray Conlogue suggests that people who do not speak the same language can never really know one another. Do you agree? Why or why not?
2. What is the difference between the terms *nation* and *state* as Michael Ignatieff uses them? Is your Canada a nation, a state, or both?
3. Many Quebeckers believe that "wanting to live in a French society," as Daniel Latouche puts it, requires political independence. Do you agree? Explain your answer.

MAKING CONNECTIONS

1. **Discuss the political situation in Quebec today. What significant events have taken place since the 1995 referendum? Is Quebec sovereignty as big a threat to Canadian unity today as it was then? Explain.**

KEYWORDS

official Opposition

inherent self-government

referendum

sovereignty

UNIT 11 :

Emily Carr, *Vanquished* (1930)

Emily Carr (1871-1945) developed a spiritual relationship with nature, particularly with the forest landscape of British Columbia. In her writing, she likened loggers to nature's executioners, and she expressed these same feelings on her canvases. Carr's spirit of environmentalism made her a pioneer in today's modern environmental movement.

CANADA IN THE WORLD COMMUNITY

	Social	Cultural	Political	Legal	Economic	Environmental
GLOBAL INTERDEPENDENCE Canada and the World 358		✔	✔		✔	✔
FOREIGN AID Canada's Contribution 362			✔		✔	✔
GENDER EQUITY Towards a Fairer World 364	✔	✔			✔	
HUMAN RESOURCES Population Growth 366	✔	✔				✔
ECONOMIC DEVELOPMENT The Quality of Life 368	✔	✔			✔	✔
THE URBAN REVOLUTION A Universal Phenomenon 370	✔					✔
SKILL BUILDER Analysing Thematic Maps 372						✔
THE GLOBAL ENVIRONMENT An Overview 374	✔			✔	✔	✔
AIR RESOURCES Damaging the Atmosphere 378						✔
LAND RESOURCES Temperate Rainforest Deforestation.. 380			✔			✔
WATER RESOURCES Surpluses and Shortages 382			✔			✔
LOOKING INTO THE FUTURE Challenges in the 21st Century 384	✔	✔	✔	✔	✔	✔

*Skills and Processes

The world has become increasingly interconnected and interdependent.
What is the nature of international relations today? What is the nature of Canada's
international ties, and how do we benefit from them?

End of an Era

For approximately 45 years following the end of the Second World War, the **Cold War** dominated the world stage. Political spheres of influence were divided into east and west, with the United States and its Western allies on one side and the Soviet Union and the **bloc** countries of Eastern Europe on the other. While both sides vied for influence in the developing world, many developing countries maintained a policy of **nonalignment**. The end of the Cold War in the late 1980s, however, created an opportunity to redefine global relationships. Today, the global focus has shifted from East-West to North-South.

The Global South

Over 75 per cent of the world's people live in developing countries. While these countries are diverse and each is unique, they share some fundamental traits: generally, they are economically weak, the majority of their people are poor, and they have little power in the global arena.

In 1992, 128 developing countries gathered at a conference in Jakarta, Indonesia, to establish their place in an era of globalization. The conference called for the re-evaluation and restructuring of relations between North and South, and a new name for the developing world was adopted—the Global South.

The conference marked the collective emergence of the Global South as an international political force. The Global South identified its economic and political grievances against the developed countries of the North and called for a greater voice in the United Nations. It is demanding the right to establish its own priorities and set its own agenda.

Canada has consistently championed the cause of the South since the 1970s. Along with the Netherlands, the Scandinavian countries, and increasingly, Australia, Canada has urged its peers to listen to the concerns of the South. Canada has also exhibited leadership on several vital issues, including development co-operation, **apartheid**, human rights, and the empowerment of women.

There are approximately 110 million landmines already laid in 69 countries, most of them developing nations. Each week, landmines kill an estimated 500 innocent civilians, many of them children, and maim thousands more. In 1996, Canada led an international campaign to ban landmines. In December 1997, representatives of over 120 countries gathered in Ottawa to officially sign the agreement, including Jody Williams, who won the Nobel Prize for her campaign to eliminate landmines.

Shridath Ramphal, the Secretary General of the Commonwealth from 1975 to 1990, noted that "the world would be much the poorer without the quality of internationalism that has been peculiarly Canada's."

Security and freedom from threats of violence are important elements of human development in the new global community.

*Troubles travel. We have escaped a global conflict for half a century, but no country is a fortress today. We cannot pull up a drawbridge against terrorists or drug traffickers. Climate change and **pandemics** will respect no borders. Even when the trouble is distant in a geographic sense, it can haunt and affect us. How many Canadians 10 years ago knew where Somalia was, or had ever met a Somali?*

Clyde Sanger, "Overview: The Glass As (More Than) Half Full," in The Canadian Development Report 1996-97 (Ottawa: The North-South Institute, 1996), p. 5.

1. As a class, discuss ways in which violence in one country or region can have an impact in other parts of the world, including Canada.

International Ties

Canada maintains ties with many countries around the world and for many reasons. Our **multicultural** heritage creates a variety of cultural links. The quest for international peace and security fosters strategic links. And our need to trade in natural resources, manufactured goods, information, and technology forges economic links.

Cultural Links

Canada's cultural ties fall into two categories: formal and informal. Our informal connections are created by the immigrants from countries around the world who now call Canada home. Our formal ties are made with organizations having members who share a common heritage. The most significant formal links for Canada are the Commonwealth and la Francophonie.

Originally, membership in the Commonwealth was based on the **colonialism** of the British Empire. Today, it has shed its political ties to become a cultural bond uniting 51 independent countries representing over 1.4 billion people. Its most important objective is to promote

racial harmony and understanding among its diverse membership.

Not all members of the Commonwealth share the same **quality of life**, however. Developed countries like Canada and Australia have a better quality of life than developing countries in Africa or Asia. Part of the Commonwealth's mandate is to create more educational opportunities, improve health care, and provide greater economic opportunities for member countries in the developing world.

Founded in 1960, la Francophonie is a co-operative association of countries in which French is an official language or is widely spoken. The organization unites 46 countries; almost half a million people share a common French heritage. Like the Commonwealth, many members of la Francophonie are developing countries. Through health, educational, agricultural, and other scientific and social programs, developed countries like Canada and France offer assistance

Members of the Commonwealth

Antigua and Barbuda	Kenya	Seychelles
Australia	Kiribati	Sierra Leone
Bahamas	Lesotho	Singapore
Bangladesh	Malawi	Solomon Islands
Barbados	Malaysia	South Africa
Belize	Maldives	Sri Lanka
Botswana	Malta	Swaziland
Britain	Mauritius	Tanzania
Brunei	Namibia	Tonga
Canada	Nauru	Trinidad and Tobago
Cyprus	New Zealand	Tuvalu
Dominica	Nigeria	Uganda
The Gambia	Pakistan	Vanuatu
Ghana	Papua New Guinea	Western Samoa
Grenada	St. Kitts and Nevis	Zambia
Guyana	St. Lucia	Zimbabwe
India	St. Vincent and The	
Jamaica	Grenadines	

Members of la Francophonie

Belgium	Dominica	Morocco
Benin	Egypt	New Brunswick
Bulgaria	Equatorial Guinea	Niger
Burkina Faso	France	Quebec
Burundi	Gabon	Romania
Cambodia	Guinea	Rwanda
Cameroon	Guinea-Bissau	St. Lucia
Canada	Haiti	Senegal
Cape Verde	Laos	The Seychelles
Central African	Lebanon	Switzerland
Republic	Luxembourg	Togo
Chad	Madagascar	Tunisia
Comoros	Mali	Vanuatu
Congo	Mauritania	Vietnam
Côte-d'Ivoire	Mauritius	Zaïre
Djibouti	Monaco	

to developing countries to achieve a better quality of life.

In addition to Canada's membership in la Francophonie, both Quebec and New Brunswick have official status as "participating governments" because of their large French-speaking populations. They are able to cast votes on issues of development and co-operation, but on political issues, only Canada has voting rights.

Strategic Links

After the Second World War, Canada formed many strategic alliances. The most important of these have been its memberships in the United Nations and the North Atlantic Treaty Organization.

Canada was one of the 50 founding members of the United Nations at the San Francisco Conference in 1945. The main objective of the UN is to maintain international peace and security. Since 1947, Canada has played a leading role on the world stage as a peacekeeper, with over 100 000 military personnel having served in over 40 peacekeeping operations. (See page 216.)

The creation of the North Atlantic Treaty Organization

(NATO) in 1949 was a direct result of the newly emerging Cold War between the United States and its allies and the Soviet Union and the bloc countries of Eastern Europe. The alliance is a common defence pact in which members consider an armed attack against one as an attack against all.

During the Cold War, Canada contributed troops and military equipment to NATO operations in Europe. But after the collapse of the Soviet empire in 1991, Canada gradually removed its troops as the need for military security in Europe diminished and public criticism increased. In this new political order, NATO must redefine its role. Following the internal conflict in the former Yugoslavia, which ended in 1995, NATO troops have played the role of peacekeepers. NATO is also undergoing another transformation as countries of the former Soviet bloc—the same countries NATO was created to defend against—seek membership in the **collective security** of the alliance.

Economic Links

In the last two decades of the twentieth century, the world witnessed a trend towards freer trade between

nations. In the new **global economy**, Canada has forged new economic links and strengthened long-standing ones.

The United States has long been Canada's dominant trading partner. Today the two countries share the largest two-way trade in the world. In 1989, this relationship was recognized in the Free Trade Agreement, which called for the elimination of tariffs between the trading partners by 1998. (See page 320.) In 1994, the agreement was extended to include Mexico in the North American Free Trade Agreement (NAFTA).

The linking of Canada, the United States, and Mexico creates the largest free trade zone in the world in terms of population and geography. With over 360 million consumers, the three countries have a combined **Gross Domestic Product** (GDP) of over $7 trillion. Under the terms of NAFTA, most tariffs among the three countries will be eliminated by 2003.

NAFTA offers Canadian industries access to the huge markets of the United States and Mexico. It is the only free trade zone in the world with advanced businesses and technology, an abundant supply of food and natural resources, and an expanding labour pool. These are considered the key ingredients for economic growth and prosperity in the twenty-first century.

In 1994, the Summit of the Americas created the promise of even broader trade horizons as 34 countries, including Canada, agreed to establish a free trade zone encompassing the entire Western Hemisphere by 2005. In 1998, Canada and Chile were taking the first step towards a Free Trade Agreement of the Americas between these two countries.

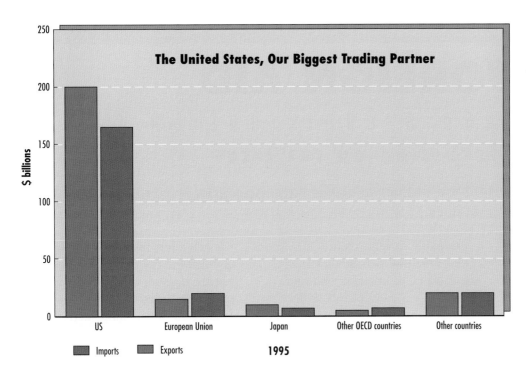

The United States, Our Biggest Trading Partner

$ billions

250

200

150

100

50

0

US   European Union   Japan   Other OECD countries   Other countries

■ Imports   ■ Exports   **1995**

In addition to its close trading relationship with the United States and Mexico, Canada has a variety of other economic links. Canada is a member of the World Trade Organization (WTO), formerly known as the General Agreement on Tariffs and Trade (GATT). The WTO promotes trade in goods and services across international boundaries. The G-7 is an organization of the seven major industrial democracies—Canada, the United States, Italy, Britain, Japan, Germany, and France—and the **European Union** (EU). Members of the G-7 meet annually to discuss mutual economic and political concerns. The Organization for Economic Co-operation and Development (OECD) promotes economic and social policies among its 27 members. In 1998, the OECD was negotiating a Multilateral Agreement on Investment (MAI) designed to make it easier for investors to move assets across international borders. A Canadian, Don Johnston, is the Secretary-General of the OECD until his term expires in 2001.

Canada also has strong trade ties with Japan and Britain, which are our second- and third-largest trading partners respectively. Since the late 1980s, trade with the newly industrialized economies of the **Pacific Rim** has boomed. Canada is one of 18 members of the Asia-Pacific Economic Co-operation (APEC) group. Canada has joined in a commitment to create a Pacific Rim free trade zone for developed members by 2010, with an extension to all members by 2020.

MAKING CONNECTIONS

1. In your opinion, what role—enforcer, observer, developer, or peacekeeper—should Canada take in shaping global events in the twenty-first century?

2. On an outline map of the world, shade in the countries that have cultural, strategic, and economic links with Canada. Use appropriate shading, especially where the links overlap. What conclusions can you draw about the general pattern that emerges?

3. What are the benefits to Canada of a) cultural, b) strategic, and c) economic links with other countries? What are the disadvantages?

KEYWORDS

Cold War

bloc

nonalignment

apartheid

multicultural

colonialism

quality of life

collective security

global economy

Gross Domestic Product

European Union

Pacific Rim

FOREIGN AID
Canada's Contribution

One of the strongest connections between Canada and developing countries is international aid. How does Canada fund aid programs? Should conditions be attached to Canada's international assistance?

Government Aid

Each year, the Canadian government, through the Official Development Assistance Program, sets aside billions of dollars for short-term **humanitarian aid** and long-term development strategies. The Canadian International Development Agency (CIDA) is the government organization responsible for administering these federal aid programs. When natural disasters, such as earthquakes, hurricanes, and floods, strike, CIDA contributes money, supplies, and human resources to help relieve the hardships. To create long-term **sus-tainable development**, CIDA sponsors medical personnel, farmers, teachers, technicians, and other advisors to help people in developing countries find permanent solutions to their problems.

Types of Aid

Canadian aid is distributed in three ways. Multilateral aid is the funding provided to international organizations such as the World Health Organization and programs operated under the auspices of the United Nations. Bilateral aid is the aid that is negotiated between Canada and a specific country.

Canada offers bilateral aid to many countries in the developing world, but the amount of aid is determined on a country-by-country basis. Some government aid is tied aid. This means that there are certain conditions placed on receiving the funds. Usually, the money must be spent on Canadian goods or services. Tied aid is often criticized as being self-serving on the part of the donor country and too restrictive for the recipient country. In 1995, 56 per cent of Canada's bilateral aid and 19 per cent of its multilateral aid was tied to purchases of Canadian goods and services.

CIDA also donates money to **non-governmental organizations** (NGOs). These agencies raise millions of dollars annually for aid programs through private donations. CIDA then donates money on a matching basis—that is, it may equal, double, or even triple the amount received through private fundraising. There are over 240 NGOs in Canada, among them Oxfam, World Vision, and the Red Cross. In 1996, Canadian NGOs raised over $300 million for foreign assistance programs.

Human Rights

As monitoring organizations like Amnesty International focus the public's attention on **human rights** violations around the world, there

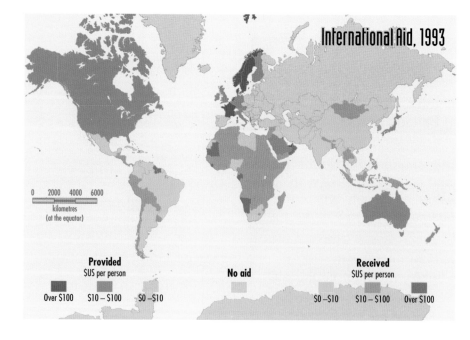

International Aid, 1993

0 2000 4000 6000
kilometres
(at the equator)

Provided
$US per person

Over $100 $10 – $100 $0 – $10

No aid

Received
$US per person

$0 – $10 $10 – $100   Over $100

has been a growing demand that foreign aid be linked to a country's record of protecting its citizens' civil, social, and political rights. Canada was one of the first countries to embrace this philosophy. In 1990, the Canadian government announced its intention not to provide economic aid to those countries that fail to uphold democracy and human rights. That same year, Canada reduced its aid to Sri Lanka as a result of that country's human rights violations in the armed conflict between the Sinhalese majority and the Tamil minority. The aid it continued to provide was redirected into conflict resolution. In 1991, Canada suspended new aid projects in Indonesia to protest against a massacre in a town in East Timor. In addition, Canada's aid activities have taken on new forms of intervention. More funds are now allocated to democratic development, human rights organizations, legal aid groups, and women's organizations. Still, Canada continues to have normal relations with some countries that violate human rights. In China, for example, Canada protested the massacre in Tiananmen Square in 1989 and cancelled aid programs. But in 1991, relations had returned to normal without any evidence that China's human rights record had improved.

Canadian foreign aid is involved in this massive dam project in China. Proponents of the dam say it will provide hydroelectric power, prevent flooding, and aid in navigation. Opponents argue that it will not directly benefit the people in the area; instead, 1.6 to 1.9 million people will have to be relocated. In return for Canadian aid, China has awarded large contracts to Canadian engineering firms.

Small businesses like this family-run agricultural operation provide jobs for more people than large, automated factories. Small businesses are better able to meet the needs of the local population using local resources. This type of development ensures that profits remain within the community instead of being channelled to some corporate head office.

◀▭ MAKING CONNECTIONS ▭▶

1. Do you think foreign aid should be tied to a country's human rights record? Give reasons for your answer.

2. Working with a partner, contact CIDA or an NGO for information about a development project currently underway in a country of your choice. Prepare a visual and written presentation about this project that can be displayed in class.

KEYWORDS

humanitarian aid

sustainable development

non-governmental organization

human rights

GENDER EQUITY
Towards a Fairer World
FOCUSSING ON THE ISSUE

Inequity between women and men is the most widespread form of discrimination in the world today. What progress has been made towards gender equity? What remains to be done to create a fairer world?

Towards Equity

One of the key issues in creating a fairer world in the twenty-first century is **gender equity**. Gender discrimination is firmly entrenched in a society's cultural beliefs and traditional values. Inequalities between women and men exist in all countries, and there is no society in which women truly enjoy all of the same rights as men.

Gender roles do not have to remain fixed, however. Since International Women's Year in 1975, the lives of women in many countries have improved. More women graduate from university, support themselves in the labour force, and are represented in government than at any time in history.

Gender and Development

In 1975, governments and development agencies began to embrace the concepts of opportunity, security, and human rights for women. A new approach to women's issues, known as Women in Development (WID), attempted to involve women in economic development through their participation in local craft industries. After a decade, however, criticism of this approach was growing. In 1985, a new approach, called Gender and Development (GAD), began to evolve. GAD stressed the need to first understand, and then challenge, the existing relationships of power between men and women in society.

Activism in the 1990s

At the Earth Summit in Rio de Janeiro, Brazil, in 1992, women established themselves as stewards for the protection and preservation of the environment. Through grassroots activism, women are acting as a major force for change in environmental policies at the international, national, and local levels.

In 1993, women's groups exposed gender discrimination as a violation of human rights at the UN Conference on Human Rights in Vienna, Austria. They argued that governments had failed in their responsibilities by allowing discrimination against women.

In Beijing, China, in 1995, 35 000 women from around the world gathered at the Fourth World Conference on Women. The conference identified connections between gender inequity and other global problems, including poverty, war, environmental degradation, and debt. Representatives of 189 governments endorsed the *Platform of Action* to promote the status of women to the benefit of society as a whole. It established priorities glob-

Discrimination lies in the values placed on the roles and responsibilities of women; traditionally, a low value has been placed on women's responsibilities. As a result, daycare workers—most of whom are women—earn less than janitors—most of whom are men.

ally, regionally, and locally in several key areas, including poverty, health, education, human rights, violence against women, the media, and the environment.

There is also a growing demand to place value on women's unpaid work, such as childcare and home-making. According to the United Nations Development Program, the value of women's unpaid work is $11 trillion annually. Recognizing the financial worth of women's work would more accurately reflect the importance of women's traditional contributions to society.

What benefits do you think conferences like the one in Beijing have for any movement?

Where Canada Stands

Canada has been a leader in efforts to promote gender equity. In its work, the Canadian International Development Agency emphasizes equality and the empowerment of women. CIDA funds initiatives developed by women's groups in the South as well as projects that integrate women and men. **Non-governmental organizations** also promote gender equity. One of the leaders is the March International Centre, which exclusively funds women's projects in the South.

Canada has also used its membership in organizations like the United Nations, la Francophonie, and the Commonwealth to promote women's rights. The UN Declaration on the Elimination of Violence Against Women in December 1993 was a Canadian initiative. The federal government also established the International Centre for Human Rights and Democratic Development, which works closely with governments and women's groups to eliminate violence against women. The centre also promotes the creation of rehabilitation services for victims of gender-based violence and more accurate reporting of violations of women's human rights.

Still, while Canada is at the forefront of the movement for gender equity, there is much more that Canada—and all countries—must do. The emphasis so far has been primarily on *gender analysis*—that is, establishing the differences between women and men. To move forward, the emphasis must turn to *gender action*—taking the necessary steps to ensure social change. This will require the political will of both men and women in government, business, and the community to change attitudes and behaviour.

Is Equity Possible?

To achieve gender equity, women's groups need to work together to overcome barriers and win political support through **coalitions** with individuals in key positions in both government and business. Women's groups also need to show that inequity carries a high price, especially in the case of violence against women, and that equality benefits the entire community. More gender specialists are required to evaluate both foreign and domestic policies and practices for their impact on the status of women. To create a fairer world in the twenty-first century, women must have the same choices as men.

KEYWORDS

gender equity

non-governmental organization

coalition

MAKING CONNECTIONS

1. a) Role-play a scene at work, school, home, or socially in which there is discrimination against women. Then re-enact the scene *without* discrimination. Discuss the contrasts of the two scenes.
   b) Make a list of recommendations for non-discriminatory behaviour in your school or community.

2. Suggest ways in which women locally, nationally, and internationally can achieve gender equity.

HUMAN RESOURCES
Population Growth
FOCUSSING ON THE ISSUE

In 1997, the earth's population surpassed 6 billion. What are the components of population growth?

Rapid Acceleration

The world's population first began to accelerate rapidly about 200 years ago. Then, there were 1 billion people living on the planet. Today, there are more than 6 billion, and each year the world's population increases by 80 million people (almost three times Canada's population). According to the United Nations, the world's population will reach 7 billion by 2010 and 8 billion around 2020. It is expected that 90 per cent of this growth will occur in developing countries, where over 80 per cent of the world's people already live.

Components of Growth

World population growth is influenced by two factors: fertility and mortality. The **fertility rate** is the average number of live births each year for every woman of childbearing age (usually between 15 and 45). These rates vary from country to country. They are the result of a variety of factors, including the level of economic development, the quality of health care, and social and cultural traditions. Canada's fertility rate is low at 1.7 births per woman, while in Malawi in Africa the rate is 7.7—the highest in the world.

One factor that contributes to fertility rates is the **infant mortality rate**—the number of infants who die before reaching the age of one.

In a country such as Malawi, where 93 of every 1000 babies die before their first birthday, parents have many children to ensure that some of their offspring survive. In Canada, the infant mortality rate is 6.8 per 1000 births.

Population Pyramids

All countries have distinct population structures. These vary according to the percentage of people in each age group and the distribution between males and females.

Population structure can be illustrated in a population pyramid. This is a back-to-back bar graph that shows the percentage of the total population in five-year age groups beginning with 0 to 4 years at the bottom and ending with the oldest group at the top. Usually, males are represented on the left side of the graph and females on the right.

The shape of the pyramid is determined by the **crude birth rate**. A high crude birth rate translates into a relatively high number of children and creates a broad pyramid base. If a country has a low crude birth rate and a large number of older people, the upper sections of the pyramid are wider.

The age structure of a population is important in understanding similarities and differences in economic development among countries. The key factor is the **dependency load**—that is, the percentage of people who are either too young or too old to support themselves. A high dependency rate places a greater financial burden on those who work. People under 15 and over 65 are generally classified as dependants. In many developing countries, especially in Africa and Asia, more than 40 per cent of the population is under 15, while in

Population Pyramids for a High Growth and a Low Growth Country

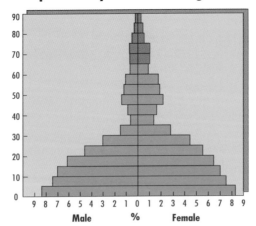
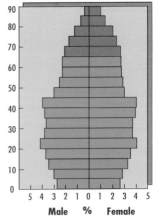

Describe the population growth patterns in each of these pyramids. How do they compare?

developed countries in North America and Europe, the rate is less than 20. The situation is reversed in the over 65 age group. In developed countries, over 15 per cent of the population falls into this category, while the rate is only 5 per cent in developing nations.

Countries with a large percentage of children are usually in the early stages of the **demographic transition**. These countries are financially strained to provide services such as schools, daycare facilities, and hospitals and to find jobs for older children once they leave school. Countries with a higher percentage of older people need government to provide retirement income and increased health care.

In countries such as Canada and the United States, over 25 per cent of government spending is in services for the older population. Countries with a large percentage of older people also have higher **crude death rates** than countries with younger populations.

The Demographic Transition

*There are four stages to the demographic transition. In stage 1, high birth and death rates means there is no long-term **natural increase**. In stage 2, high birth rates and declining death rates produce high rates of population growth. In stage 3, both birth rates and death rates decline and the rate of natural increase begins to slow down. In stage 4, low birth and death rates produce no long-term natural increase.*

Population by Age and Sex

Age Group	HAITI, 1993 Male (%)	Female (%)	CANADA, 1993 Male (%)	Female (%)
0-4	7.6	7.5	3.6	3.4
5-9	6.7	6.6	3.6	3.4
10-14	5.9	5.9	3.5	3.3
15-19	5.2	5.1	3.4	3.3
20-24	4.6	4.6	3.5	3.4
25-29	3.8	4.0	3.8	3.7
30-34	3.3	3.5	4.4	4.4
35-39	2.6	2.9	4.3	4.3
40-44	2.2	2.5	3.9	3.9
45-49	1.8	2.0	3.5	3.5
50-54	1.5	1.7	2.7	2.7
55-59	1.2	1.4	2.2	2.3
60-64	1.0	1.1	2.0	2.1
65-69	0.7	0.9	1.8	2.0
70-74	0.5	0.6	1.4	1.9
75-79	0.3	0.4	0.9	1.4
80+	—	—	0.9	1.7

━◻▪ MAKING CONNECTIONS ▪◻━

1. Using the data for Canada and for Haiti, plot a population pyramid for each country. What differences are there in the number of males and females in each age group? At what stage of the demographic transition is Canada? At what stage is Haiti?

2. Canada's fertility rate is 1.7 births. To maintain our current population, however, the fertility rate must be 2.1. Some experts predict Canada's population could decline to 18 000 000 by the year 2050 if this trend continues. What impact would a shrinking population have on employment, goods and services, transportation, and education?

KEYWORDS

fertility rate

infant mortality rate

crude birth rate

dependency load

demographic transition

crude death rate

natural increase

ECONOMIC DEVELOPMENT

The Quality of Life

FOCUSSING ON THE ISSUE

The quality of life reflects the economic, social, political, and environmental standards of a country. What indicators determine the quality of life? How does Canada's quality of life compare with that of other countries?

Quality of Life

There is a great deal of **economic disparity** among the nations of the world. Not all countries enjoy the same **standard of living** or **quality of life**. Standard of living refers to the quantity and quality of the products and services available to people. Quality of life includes not only the material standard of living but also social, political, and environmental factors.

Economic development is the process by which the condition of people's lives is improved through knowledge and technology. Economic development does not have a beginning or an end. It is a continuous process of constant improvements in people's health, education, and prosperity.

In broad terms, high- and middle-income countries are called the developed world, while low-income countries are called the developing world. However, only those countries at the extreme ends of the economic spectrum can truly be this simply classified. Most countries fall somewhere in between very wealthy and very poor. There are even different levels of economic development and opportunity within countries. A city like São Paulo, Brazil, for example, is as modern as any city in Canada, yet much of Brazil experiences

The Human Development Index, 1996

Rank (top 10)	Country	Rank (bottom 10)	Country
1	Canada	165	Angola
2	United States	166	Burundi
3	Japan	167	Mozambique
4	Netherlands	168	Ethiopia
5	Norway	169	Afghanistan
6	Finland	170	Burkina Faso
7	France	171	Mali
8	Iceland	172	Somalia
9	Sweden	173	Sierra Leone
10	Spain	174	Niger

From United Nations Development Program, Human Development Report. Copyright © 1996 by the United Nations Development Program. Used by permission of Oxford University Press, Inc.

The Human Development Index (HDI) measures the quality of life by ranking countries in three important areas: a long and healthy life, knowledge, and a decent standard of living. Three indicators—life expectancy, education, and purchasing power—are used to measure these areas. Where does Canada rank?

Human Development Index Indicators

Region	Life Expectancy Total/Male/Female (in Years)	Secondary School Enrollment Male/Female (%)	Per Capita GNP ($US)
Africa	55/53/56	36/30	660
America	76/73/79	99/98	25 220
Latin America/ Caribbean	69/66/72	unavailable	3 290
Asia	65/64/67	57/45	2 150
Europe	73/68/77	89/94	12 310
Oceania	73/71/76	70/71	13 770

1996 World Population Data Sheet, © 1996, Population Reference Bureau (Washington, DC).

Using these HDI indicators, rank regional quality of life from highest to lowest.

POVERTY AND THE ENVIRONMENT

More than one-fifth of humanity lives in absolute poverty—a condition characterized by malnutrition, illiteracy, disease, short life expectancy, and high infant mortality. About the same number of people live on the margins, with just the minimal necessities of life.

During the past five decades, world income measured as per capita GDP has increased sevenfold, but this gain has been spread very unequally, and the inequality is growing. In the past decade, 15 nations with 1.5 billion people, mostly in East Asia, had a surge in economic growth. During the same period, there was an economic decline or stagnation in 100 countries. In Haiti, Liberia, Nicaragua, Rwanda, Sudan, Ghana, and Venezuela, per capita income is less than it was in 1960. The UN Development Program estimates that about 1.6 billion people live on no more than $1 a day, and this number is growing by nearly 25 million a year. Even in the wealthiest nations, there are great differences between rich and poor. In Canada, the top 20 per cent of income earners make seven times more than [the] lowest 20 per cent. The top 10 per cent make nearly 25 per cent of the country's total income.

Although Canada does not know the deep and widespread poverty that affects some parts of the world, the impact of global poverty can be felt even here. Poverty degrades the people who suffer it, and it leads to environmental degradation. Poor countries use inefficient equipment that wastes energy and produces high levels of pollution. Poor people often cut down too many trees because they cannot afford other fuels for cooking and heating. Hunger drives them to over-farm the soils and to let their animals graze the land too intensively. Poor regions tend to have the

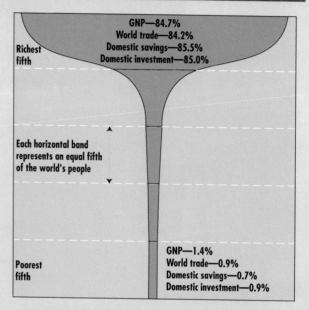

Richest fifth
GNP—84.7%
World trade—84.2%
Domestic savings—85.5%
Domestic investment—85.0%

Each horizontal band represents an equal fifth of the world's people

Poorest fifth
GNP—1.4%
World trade—0.9%
Domestic savings—0.7%
Domestic investment—0.9%

highest birth rates, which increases the number of people who need to live off the environment. The results include more calls for foreign aid, more environmental refugees seeking to move to other nations, including Canada, and a steady depletion of environmental resources, including the world's tropical forests.

From Canada and the State of the Planet: The Social, Economic, and Environmental Trends That Are Shaping Our Lives by Michael Keating and the Canadian Global Change Program. Copyright © The Royal Society of Canada, 1997. Reprinted by permission of Oxford University Press Canada.

1. Imagine going without the necessities of life for a day, a week, a month, or a year. Describe your life to the rest of the class through pictures, song, dramatic monologue, or a combination of formats.

extreme poverty. Similarly, the distribution of wealth is uneven within wealthy countries and regions. Some communities in the Canadian North, for example, have more in common with a developing country than they do with cities like Vancouver and Toronto. Even in Canadian cities, **subcultures** of poverty exist with street kids and homeless people.

MAKING CONNECTIONS

1. Develop your own criteria for your personal quality of life—now, 5 years from now, 10 years from now, 25 years from now. Compare your criteria with other students. What are the three most common criteria?

KEYWORDS

economic disparity

standard of living

quality of life

subculture

THE URBAN REVOLUTION
A Universal Phenomenon
FOCUSSING ON THE ISSUE

The urban revolution is the greatest mass migration in history.
What factors have led to urbanization? What are the effects of urbanization?

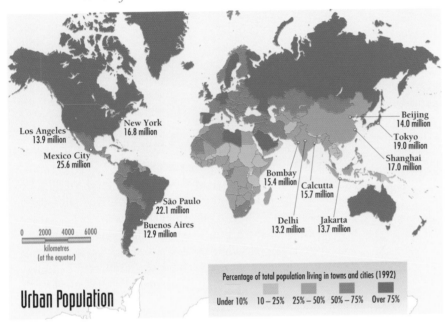

Los Angeles
13.9 million

New York
16.8 million

Mexico City
25.6 million

São Paulo
22.1 million

Buenos Aires
12.9 million

Bombay
15.4 million

Calcutta
15.7 million

Delhi
13.2 million

Jakarta
13.7 million

Beijing
14.0 million

Tokyo
19.0 million

Shanghai
17.0 million

0 2000 4000 6000
kilometres
(at the equator)

Urban Population

Percentage of total population living in towns and cities (1992)

Under 10%   10 – 25%   25% – 50%   50% – 75%   Over 75%

Urban Growth

Since the middle of the twentieth century, the world has become increasingly urban. Two hundred years ago, only 5 per cent of people lived in cities and towns. London, with a population of just 1 million, was the world's largest city. At the beginning of the twentieth century, the number of people living in urban centres had risen to 14 per cent. During the twentieth century, however, this figure skyrocketed to 45 per cent. The United Nations predicts that over half of the world's people will live in cities and towns by 2005, and that by 2025 the figure will be 65 per cent.

Part of the shift towards **urbanization** is the creation of megacities. These are cities with populations greater than 8 million. In 1950, only two cities, London and New York, were considered megacities. By 1995, however, there were 22 megacities—16 of which were in the developing world where urbanization has taken place at a rapid pace since the middle of the twentieth century. By 2015, experts predict there will be over 30 megacities. Another 500 cities will have populations exceeding 1 million.

Developed Countries

Urban migration is not a new phenomenon. It started as a result of the Industrial Revolution, which began in Britain over two centuries ago and spread to Europe and North America in the nineteenth century. New industrial technology transformed manufacturing and created a wealthier society. New machinery enabled farmers to increase their production and feed the rapidly growing population. With fewer people needed to produce food, many rural residents went to the cities to work in the new factories.

In addition to creating jobs, the shift to an urban society brought about a significant increase in services, such as retailing, finance, and communications. Today, the majority of people living in industrialized cities work in the service sector.

While urban life has improved in many ways in the developed countries, the problems of urbanization have also increased. A growing number of people live below the **poverty line**. There is a shortage of low-income housing, and homelessness is becoming more widespread. Traffic congestion brings cities to a standstill at peak hours of the day. Excessive consumerism is depleting natural resources and contributing to the overall deterioration of the quality of air, water, and soil.

In cities in developed countries, the *pattern* of urban growth has had a greater impact on the environment than the *amount* of growth.

Urban sprawl has destroyed wildlife habitats. For these cities to be sustainable in the twenty-first century, experts say we need to use urban space more efficiently by zoning high-density "urban villages" and requiring infilling of urban land before allowing new subdivisions. We also need to reduce our consumption of resources, limit our production of waste, and become more aware of and sensitive to the complex interrelationships between the environment and socioeconomic development.

Where Canadians Live			
Year	% Urban	% Rural	% Rural Living on Farms
1901	37	63	N/A
1931	53	47	67
1961	76	30	38
1995	80	20	10

Statistics Canada

Cities and their inhabitants occupy only 2 per cent of the earth's surface, but consume 75 per cent of the world's natural resources and generate the same amount of the world's waste.

Urban Land Use

Residential
Commercial
Industrial
Institutional and
    Public Buildings
Transportation
Open Space and
    Recreational

These colour codes are the ones most commonly used on land-use maps.

Developing Countries

The process of urbanization did not begin in the developing countries until the middle of the twentieth century. Two trends led to urban growth in developing countries: the rate of **natural increase** and rural-urban migration. The United Nations estimates 60 per cent of urban growth is the result of natural increase. While urban birth rates are lower than rural rates, death rates are lower still. This is because urban centres usually have better health-care facilities and other social services, which contribute to lower **infant mortality rates** and increased **life expectancy**.

Migration from rural areas to cities is usually the result of high rates of population growth. Many rural people do not own or have access to land and therefore they are unable to provide for them-selves or their families. As a result, they are "pushed" off the land into the cities, where they hope to find work. The expansion of large and highly commercial farms also displaces rural labourers who must join the rank of migrants heading to the cities. Sometimes the environment may force people off the land and into the cities. Overuse of soil can destroy farmland through soil exhaustion. Natural disasters such as floods and droughts can also render the land useless. Thus many factors can contribute to the rapid rate of urbanization in developing countries.

Once they arrive in the urban centres, many migrants are forced to live on marginal lands that ring the cities. The rate of growth threatens to break down already strained **infrastructures**. The result is that many people are forced to live in squalid housing environments without clean water, adequate sanita-tion, or electricity. The impact on the people is devastating. So is the impact on the environment. Raw sewage and other waste pollute the water and soil. Eliminating these problems is beyond the current financial capabilities of these governments. In the long run, developing countries will have to experience economic growth, social reform, and slower population growth to resolve the problems of rapid urbanization.

KEYWORDS

urbanization
poverty line
urban sprawl
natural increase
infant mortality rate
life expectancy
infrastructure

MAKING CONNECTIONS

1. Create a land-use map of your local area. Identify and explain any environmental issues that have resulted from local land-use practices. Find out what plans your local council has to solve these environmental problems.

SKILL BUILDER
Analysing Thematic Maps
FOCUSSING ON THE ISSUE

Maps are important sources of information. What are the basic elements of maps? How do we read and analyse thematic maps?

Map Basics

Maps present information about the world or a specific country or place. They may also show information about specific topics, such as population, climate, the environment, or the effects of human activity. These thematic maps usually use colours and symbols to show information.

All maps require four key elements: a title, a directional symbol, a scale, and a legend. The title should state what information the map is conveying. A directional symbol indicates in which direction north is. It is important to know where north is in order to establish all other directions. The scale represents the distance and size on the map in terms of actual distance and size. Small-scale maps show only generalized features, while large-scale maps show more details.

Scales enable us to measure distances between places. There are three types of scales. Statement scales indicate that a particular unit of measure represents an actual distance. For example, the statement scale 1 cm:1 km means that 1 cm on the map represents 1 km of actual distance. Representation fraction scales are written as $\frac{1}{50\,000}$, or more commonly as 1:50 000. There is no specific unit of measurement so any unit of measurement can be applied—in this case, for example, 1 cm on the map represents

50 000 cm of actual distance. Line scales are simply straight lines subdivided into units. For example, the line scale ⊢0—1—2⊣ KILOMETRES means that the length of this line represents 2 km of actual distance.

A legend is essential if we are to read and understand a map. A legend identifies the meaning of the different colours and symbols on a map. Different colours usually represent different subjects while different shades of the same colour usually represent different percentages or amounts of the same subject. Symbols are used to represent information, such as the locations of natural resources or cities.

Latitude and Longitude

Imaginary lines running east-west and north-south are used to identify location and direction on the earth's surface. These lines are numbered in degrees (0°). The horizontal lines that run from east to west are called parallels of latitude, so-called because they run parallel north and south from the Equator, which is numbered 0°. There are 90 parallels between the Equator and the North Pole at 90°N and another 90 parallels between the Equator and the South Pole at 90°S. The two halves above and below the Equator are known as the Northern and Southern Hemispheres.

The vertical lines that run from north to south are called meridians

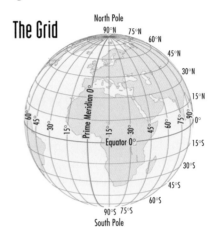

The Grid

of longitude. The meridians extend from the North Pole to the South Pole. The starting point, or 0°, is called the Prime Meridian, which runs through an observatory at Greenwich, England. The lines of longitude extend by degrees east and west from this point until they meet exactly halfway around the world at 180° at the **International Date Line**. The two halves east and west of the Prime Meridian are known as the Eastern and Western Hemispheres.

Together, these imaginary lines form the earth's **grid.** This grid enables us to locate places on maps and to determine direction. Physical maps and topographic maps usually include lines of latitude and longitude.

Reading Thematic Maps

You will find several thematic maps in this unit. These maps show infor-

CASE STUDY

Computer and aerospace technology has enabled us to get new perspectives of the earth from a unique vantage point—satellites that orbit the earth. Computers on board the satellite gather information about the earth using **multispectral scanners**. The information is relayed to earth, where the computer codes are converted into images and displayed on a monitor or reproduced on paper. The process of creating these satellite images is called **remote sensing**.

Satellite images can be used to improve our quality of life and to safeguard the environment for the future. Some of the applications for satellite images include:

- ice reconnaissance on shipping routes
- monitoring of areas of productive fish stocks
- monitoring of the loss of rainforests, wetlands, and other natural habitats as well as the loss of farmland due to urban sprawl
- identification of geological structures that could contain new oil, gas, and mineral deposits

This satellite image of Clayoquot Sound shows various stages of forest growth. Old growth forests are dark green; new growth is light green. Clear-cuts are visible as the purple to black shades.

- monitoring of oil spills
- observation of the spread and effects of acid precipitation
- monitoring of drought patterns and soil erosion.

mation about specific topics—international aid on page 362, world urban population on page 370, ecological hot spots and world population on page 376, global warming on page 378, temperate rainforests on page 380, and water surpluses and shortages on page 382.

Before you can read a thematic map, you must first be sure what the map is showing. The title, of course, provides a summary, but you need to study the legend to learn the specifics. You should practise reading the map by identifying the various features it represents. Once you understand the map, draw conclusions about the information it presents by looking for relationships.

MAKING CONNECTIONS

1. a) For each thematic map in this unit, identify i) the title; ii) the scale; and iii) the information in the legend.
   b) Choose one thematic map and analyse and describe the patterns and information it presents.

2. Create your own thematic map of a current global issue. Gather relevant information, simplify it as necessary, and map it.

KEYWORDS

International Date Line

grid

multispectral scanners

remote sensing

THE GLOBAL ENVIRONMENT
An Overview
FOCUSSING ON THE ISSUE

The health of the planet is being threatened by the environmental consequences of human activity. How can sustainable development protect and preserve the planet for the future?

Global Concerns

For much of human history, people did not consider the impact their activities had on the natural world. Today, however, we know that our actions directly affect the environment. The earth is a single, fragile unit upon which we all depend for our survival. As the world's population continues to grow, we have to be concerned about the ability of the planet to support and sustain life in all its forms.

The threats to the environment are global. They are found in both developed and developing countries. In developed countries, the high rate of consumption of natural resources is at the heart of human activity and its environmental consequences. In the developing world, the demand for natural resources to meet the basic needs of a rapidly growing population is largely responsible for pressures on the environment.

Sustainable Development

Global environmental issues fall into four categories: air, water, land, and life. Atmospheric concerns include **acid precipitation**, **global warming**, and **ozone depletion**. Threats to water resources include the abuse of rivers and oceans for waste and sewage disposal, groundwater contamination, and overfishing. On land, human activity has resulted in soil erosion, desertification, and deforestation. All of these environmental problems threaten the earth's living species—plant, animal, and human. Indeed, many species are already extinct, while countless more are endangered or threatened.

In June 1992, representatives of 179 governments gathered at the Earth Summit in Rio de Janeiro to devise a worldwide plan for environmental responsibility into the twenty-first century. The summit produced a comprehensive and wide-ranging set of measures for creating socially, economically, and environmentally **sustainable development**.

According to environmentalists, efforts for achieving sustainable development must occur on four levels. At a planetary level, the

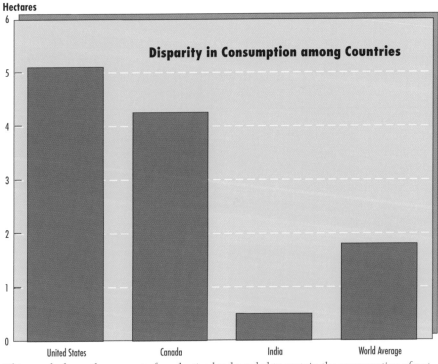

Disparity in Consumption among Countries

Hectares (y-axis: 0, 1, 2, 3, 4, 5, 6)

United States · Canada · India · World Average

This graph shows the amount of productive land needed to sustain the consumption of natural resources by people in the United States, Canada, and India, and the world average. Canadians require more than 4 ha of the earth's productive land per person to sustain our level of consumption and to absorb our waste. Americans average more than 5 ha. In India, the average person needs less than half a hectare. If everyone in the world lived like North Americans, we would need two more planets to sustain the world's population.

VIEWPOINTS

MAJOR CHARACTERISTICS OF COMPETING WESTERN WORLD VIEWS

Some environmentalists believe that the dominant social world view will have to give way to a new environmental world view if sustainable development is to be achieved.

	Dominant Social World View	New Environmental World View
Humankind and nature	Domination of nature	Harmony with nature
	Natural environment valued as a resource	Natural environment intrinsically valued
Growth and technology	Continual economic growth	Sustainable development
	Market forces	Public interest
	Supply orientation	Demand orientation
	Confidence in science and technology	Limits to science
Quality of life	Centralized	Decentralized
	Large-scale	Small-scale
	Authoritative (experts influential)	Participative (citizen involvement)
	Increased material consumption	Decreased material consumption
Limits to the biosphere	Unlimited resources	Limits to resource extraction
	Nonrenewable resources	Renewable resources
	No limits to growth	Limits to growth

1. Compare and contrast these two world views. Do you agree that a new environmental world view is essential in the twenty-first century? Explain your answer.

Adapted from R.C. Kuhn, "Canadian Energy Futures: Policy Scenarios and Public Preferences," Canadian Geographer 36, no. 4 (1992), p. 352. Reprinted by permission of the Canadian Association of Geographers.

health of the planet must be preserved because the human race depends on the earth's life-sustaining processes for its own survival. On a global level, the gap between developing and developed nations is the greatest threat to sustainable development. There must be a partnership among nations to ensure all basic human needs are met. On a regional level, we must focus on such issues as the preservation of natural resources and the disposal of waste. We must establish a partnership between the environment and society through community involvement in environmental management. Finally, on a local level, the diversity of the environment around us must be protected

and preserved. All citizens must learn to care for and respect the environment and to act responsibly towards it.

While sustainable development must be practised in all countries, not all countries should practise sustainable development in the same way. Each country is unique, with its own set of environmental concerns. In Canada, achieving sustainable development will require fundamental changes in government policies, business attitudes, and social values. Responsibility for environmental and resource management in Canada is divided between the federal government and the provinces. They will need to set politics aside for the benefit

of the generations that will follow. Business and industry must not only consider the benefits of development in the present, but must weigh the environmental consequences over the long term.

Of course, sustainable development is not just the concern of government and industry. To be responsible environmental citizens, all Canadians need to question and re-evaluate the attitudes and values of our consumer society. Young Canadians are much more aware of the impact people have on the environment than the generations that have preceded them. In the twenty-first century, this generation will be the leaders of the movement to protect and preserve the environment.

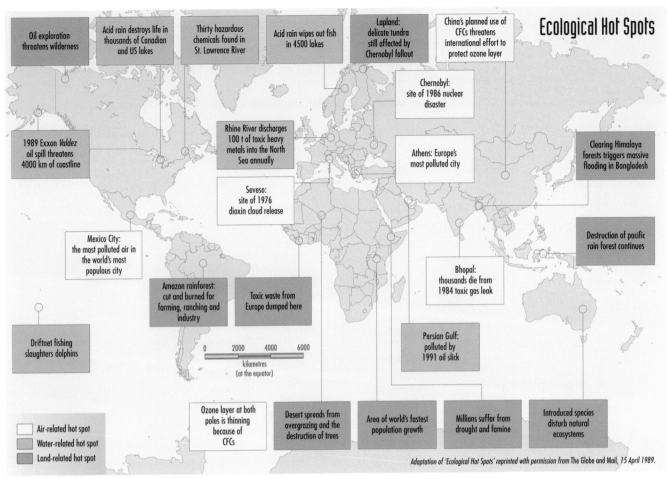

Adaptation of "Ecological hot spots" reprinted with permission from The Globe and Mail, 15 April 1989.

The map shows the world's ecological hot spots. What patterns can you identify? What geographic regions appear to be the most seriously threatened? How does this map compare with the world map of population density? What conclusions can you draw from this?

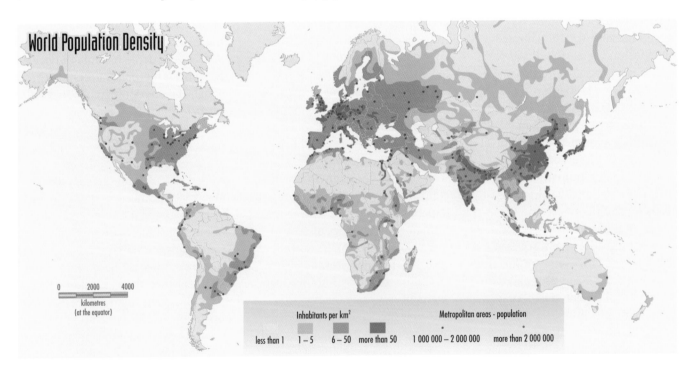

ENVIRONMENTAL PROTECTION IN CANADA

CASE STUDY

In 1988, the Canadian government passed the Canadian Environmental Protection Act (CEPA). It was the most comprehensive environmental act in Canadian history and it gave the federal government broad powers to control toxic chemicals and protect the environment.

CEPA takes an ecosystem approach to the environment. It considers the management and protection of our air, water, soil, and wildlife resources to be an integrated process—harm to one resource ultimately harms another. The act is especially concerned with the effects of toxic waste, which is one of the greatest threats facing Canada and many industrialized countries. Among CEPA's powers are:

- controlling the trade of toxic substances that damage the atmosphere
- establishing the level of risk associated with various toxic substances
- ensuring industries control the use of toxic substances and apply strict safety standards
- setting standards for the use of toxic substances.

Administered jointly by Environment Canada and Health and Welfare Canada, CEPA has the power to impose severe fines and penalties for offences. Fines range from $200 000 to $1 million, and polluters can be fined consecutively for each day the infraction continues. Jail terms range from six months to five years, giving CEPA considerable power over industries that pollute the environment and the company executives who allow it. CEPA also requires the federal government to report regularly to the Canadian public on the state of the environment. The first report was issued in 1986, followed by reports in 1992 and 1996.

Since 1990, new environmental initiatives have been launched by the Canadian government. In 1992, the Federal Environmental Stewardship was established to co-ordinate good environmental practices among government agencies. This was followed by the creation of the Commissioner for the Environment and Sustainable Development in 1995, a position created to assess the progress towards creating "greener government."

1. Do you think the Canadian Environmental Protection Act goes far enough to safeguard the environment against industrial polluters? Explain.

MAKING CONNECTIONS

1. a) In groups, list and rank the top ten global environmental concerns. Justify your rankings.
   b) Using the ten issues you identified, prepare a questionnaire to be distributed to 50 people in your school and community. Have each person respond to the seriousness of each issue on a scale of 1 to 5, with 1 being the least serious and 5 being the most serious. Tabulate the results, then list the issues in order of importance, beginning with the most serious. How does this compare with the rankings your group listed?

2. A bumper sticker expressing concern for the global environment reads "Think Globally, Act Locally." Draw up a list of local initiatives you could begin or join to help solve the global environmental crisis. For each initiative, identify potential "road blocks" and strategies for overcoming them.

KEYWORDS

acid precipitation

global warming

ozone depletion

ecosystem

sustainable development

AIR RESOURCES
Damaging the Atmosphere

The quest for economic development has inflicted considerable damage on the earth's atmosphere. What is the impact of atmospheric pollution?

Global Warming

Economic development comes with a price tag. Within the past two decades, the impact of unrestrained growth upon the environment has become increasingly evident. We have been forced to recognize the damage our way of life has caused and we have begun to take steps to clean up the environment. One of the biggest challenges facing the world is **global warming**.

The earth absorbs the sun's energy and re-emits it as heat. Gases in the earth's atmosphere then trap this heat, keeping the temperature on earth at a level that sustains animal and plant life. This is called the **greenhouse effect**. The gases that allow for it include carbon dioxide (CO_2), methane (N_2O), ozone, and chlorofluorocarbons (CFCs).

The level of these atmospheric gases, however, has been increasing, which has caused the earth's average temperature to also increase—in the past century, it has risen by half a degree, and by the middle of the twenty-first century, it is expected to rise by 4.5°C. This trend, referred to as global warming, is caused by human industrial activity. The production of greenhouse gases has been steadily

mounting. Since the Industrial Revolution, the level of carbon dioxide in the atmosphere has increased by 25 per cent.

The continued burning of fossil fuels and the burning and deforestation of rainforests generate higher levels of carbon dioxide, and landfill waste and agricultural production contribute to methane emissions. Though the use of CFCs has declined since the 1970s when their use in aerosol cans was reduced, they, and other greenhouse gases, keep being released into our atmosphere at an alarming pace.

One of the most significant impacts of global warming would

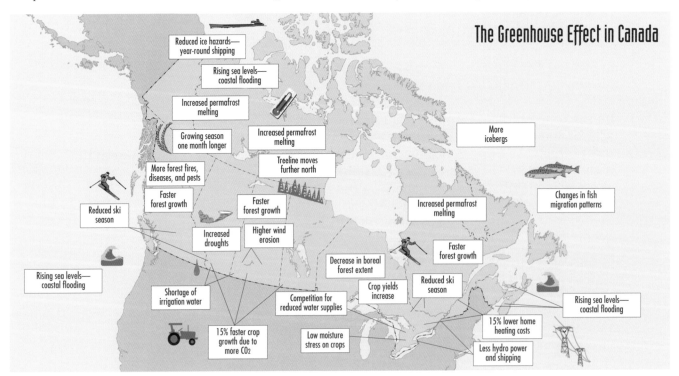

The Greenhouse Effect in Canada

Reduced ice hazards— year-round shipping

Rising sea levels— coastal flooding

Increased permafrost melting

Growing season one month longer

Increased permafrost melting

More icebergs

More forest fires, diseases, and pests

Treeline moves further north

Faster forest growth

Faster forest growth

Changes in fish migration patterns

Reduced ski season

Increased permafrost melting

Increased droughts

Higher wind erosion

Decrease in boreal forest extent

Faster forest growth

Rising sea levels— coastal flooding

Shortage of irrigation water

Competition for reduced water supplies

Crop yields increase

Reduced ski season

Rising sea levels— coastal flooding

15% faster crop growth due to more CO2

Low moisture stress on crops

15% lower home heating costs

Less hydro power and shipping

be a rise in sea levels around the world, caused by melting ice in the Arctic and Antarctic, warming ocean waters, and decreasing atmospheric pressure. Many of the world's major cities are located at sea level, as are some of the most productive lands. In fact, it has been estimated that 33 per cent of the world's croplands might be inundated with sea water in the next 50 years if the warming trend continues, and millions of people would be flooded out of their homes.

Warming trends would also affect climate conditions, ultimately disrupting the balance of many forms of life. For example, drier conditions, rising carbon dioxide levels, and warmer climates would alter the growth patterns and general well-being of plants. The United Nations Environment Program states that deserts and grasslands worldwide would expand while forest cover would decrease. There would be an increase in forest fires and river flow patterns would be altered, which would make some existing hydroelectric plants useless.

Governments are beginning to take action to reduce the problem of global warming. At an environment conference in Kyoto, Japan, in December 1997, 159 countries endorsed a plan to reduce greenhouse gas emissions from the burning of fossil fuels. The world's 38 most developed countries set an overall reduction target for themselves of 5.2 per cent by 2012. This included an 8 per cent cut in the European Union and a 6 per cent cut in Canada. While the deal was cloaked in controversy, it signalled a change in attitude for the twenty-first century.

Ozone Depletion

A second serious challenge to the environment is **ozone depletion**. Ozone is a pale blue gas that is present in a thin layer in the **stratosphere** high above the earth's surface. It is formed when oxygen in the atmosphere reacts with sunlight. The ozone layer forms a protective shield around the earth. It filters out **ultraviolet radiation** from the sun, which is dangerous to living things.

Scientists have discovered that the ozone layer is getting thinner. As a result, more radiation is reaching the earth's surface than is safe for living things. Causes for some of this thinning occur naturally, like volcanic eruptions, but the primary cause of ozone depletion is human industrial activity and the gases it produces. These gases rise into the stratosphere, where they destroy the ozone.

A major source of one of the ozone-destroying gases—CFCs—is aerosol spray cans, which is why they are now banned in North America. Another culprit is the refrigerator, which uses large quantities of this gas. This is not a problem as long as the refrigerator is working, but when it is old and discarded the dangerous gas may be released.

Thinning of the ozone layer has already caused an increase in the number of cases of skin cancer, which can be caused by harmful radiation. The increase of ultraviolet rays may also be harming plant life. In the world's oceans, fish depend on algae, which are very sensitive to light. If these small organisms are destroyed as a result of increased radiation, it will upset the ocean's entire food chain, including the fish on which much of the world's population depends for food.

In time, ozone holes may be replenished if destructive products are eliminated. Countries have started taking steps to control the output of ozone-depleting gases. International agreements like the Montreal Protocol in 1987 promise to reduce the amount of ozone-depleting chemicals released into the atmosphere by 50 per cent by 1999. Unfortunately, both the United States and Canada have already admitted they will not meet this deadline.

Much of the worst air pollution has been caused by the industrial world. Important changes have been made to reverse the damage that has been done to the environment. At the same time, people living in poorer countries seek their fair share of the world's wealth. They want to follow in the path of the industrialized countries, and sometimes feel that pollution control is a luxury they cannot afford. If the world is going to remain a livable place, we are going to have to find a way to share the resources without destroying the environment.

KEYWORDS

global warming
greenhouse effect
ozone depletion
stratosphere
ultraviolet radiation

◄-◘-▣ MAKING CONNECTIONS ▣►

1. **List some of the changes to the environment that might result from warmer temperatures. What might be the consequences of these changes?**

LAND RESOURCES
Temperate Rainforest Deforestation
FOCUSSING ON THE ISSUE

Deforestation threatens many of the world's forests. What are the effects of deforestation? What are some of the issues surrounding deforestation in Canada?

Deforestation

About 10 000 years ago, before the beginning of agriculture, trees covered about 50 per cent of the earth's land surface. Today that figure has dropped to only 27 per cent. Forests provide habitats for thousands of plant and animal species. Many of these have yet to be discovered, but they could hold the key to future scientific and medical breakthroughs. In addition, forests provide recreational sites, timber, fuelwood, and raw materials for manufacturing.

Deforestation is one of the most serious threats to the world's forests. It has occurred on a global scale only in the last few decades. Today it continues at a rate of 170 000 km^2 a year—about 466 km^2 each day. While much of the world's attention focusses on tropical rainforest destruction, deforestation also threatens temperate forests, including those in Canada. Although **reforestation** of temperate forests is increasing in many countries, including Canada, the quality of these forests is inferior to that of natural forests. Cultivated forests do not support the same high level of **biodiversity** as ecologically complex natural forests do.

Forests in BC

Many Canadians believe that our forests have much more than a purely economic value. They believe that forests should be protected and preserved for what they contribute to the environment **aesthetically** and ecologically. In the last two decades, the forests of Clayoquot Sound and the Carmanah Valley in BC have been two of the hot spots in the debate over the fate of **old-growth forests**.

Massive trees like the Douglas Fir dominate old-growth forests on the Pacific Coast. Reaching heights of 100 m, these giant trees make the BC forests highly productive. British Columbia accounts for almost 50 per cent of the wood cut in Canada while possessing only 21

Those who oppose clearcutting advocate selective cutting, which removes only part of the harvestable timber in a forest in any year. The forestry industry argues that selective cutting is not financially viable and that clearcut forests regenerate naturally over time.

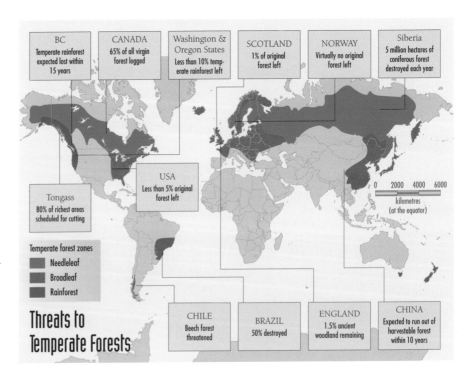

BC
Temperate rainforest expected lost within 15 years

CANADA
65% of all virgin forest logged

Washington & Oregon States
Less than 10% temperate rainforest left

SCOTLAND
1% of original forest left

NORWAY
Virtually no original forest left

Siberia
5 million hectares of coniferous forest destroyed each year

USA
Less than 5% original forest left

Tongass
80% of richest areas scheduled for cutting

0 2000 4000 6000
kilometres
(at the equator)

Temperate forest zones
Needleleaf
Broadleaf
Rainforest

Threats to Temperate Forests

CHILE
Beech forest threatened

BRAZIL
50% destroyed

ENGLAND
1.5% ancient woodland remaining

CHINA
Expected to run out of harvestable forest within 10 years

Clayoquot Sound on the west coast of Vancouver Island is one of the largest old-growth temperate forests remaining in the world today. Many of the massive trees are especially old and provide a forest habitat for an abundant and diverse range of plant and animal species.

In the early 1980s, Clayoquot Sound became the centre of controversy as various groups debated the future of these old-growth forests. The land-use conflict had a variety of **stakeholders.** The forest industry wanted liberal logging rights. Labour groups favoured more logging because it provided jobs in Port Alberni. Likewise, the government of Port Alberni supported a strong forestry industry. Aboriginal peoples opposed logging as Clayoquot Sound was a revered place and was at the heart of unsettled land claims. Conservationists opposed the logging of old-growth forests because of its impact on the environment and because they believed such ancient forms of nature should be preserved. The tourism industry wanted the forests preserved for their aesthetic appeal.

Over the years, attempts to resolve the conflict through a committee of stakeholders had failed.

This led the provincial government to settle the dispute on its own. It called for one-third of the area to be protected while the rest was opened for logging. The decision failed to satisfy Aboriginal peoples, environmental groups, and tourism interests. Large-scale protests led to the arrest of over 800 citizens and attracted international attention. In response, the government established a scientific committee to investigate and recommend logging practices. In July 1995, the province announced that it would implement all of the committee's 120-plus recommendations, including an end to conventional clearcutting methods in Clayoquot Sound. The government also gave Aboriginal peoples the right to consider all logging plans in the region until their land claims are settled.

The Forest Practices Code, implemented in 1994, created strict standards for sustainable forestry. Forest companies opposed parts of the code, particularly the **stumpage fees**, which they argued would have a devastating financial impact. Environmentalists argued that the measures did not go far enough to ensure that BC's old-growth forests would survive. This debate will continue well into the twenty-first century.

per cent of the country's commercial forests.

These old-growth forests have survived longer than those in central and eastern Canada because

European settlement did not occur on the Pacific Coast until much later. In the 1920s, however, logging began to emerge as a significant resource industry in British

Columbia. Since then, **clearcutting** has left parts of the once-lush forest landscape a barren shell.

MAKING CONNECTIONS

1. Look at the satellite image of clearcutting on page 373 and the photo of a forestry operation in Clayoquot Sound. What effects do you think clearcutting has on the environment?

2. The confrontations between environmentalists and the forest industry over old-growth forests have received international attention. As a class, divide into two groups representing both interest groups. Research the issues and arguments for your group, then role-play a lively discussion between the two sides.

KEYWORDS

deforestation

reforestation

biodiversity

aesthetic

old-growth forest

clearcutting

stakeholder

stumpage fee

WATER RESOURCES
Surpluses and Shortages
FOCUSSING ON THE ISSUE

The availability of freshwater is a critical issue for many countries.
Why do some countries face water shortages? What are some possible solutions?

Patterns and Usage

Water is the most important commodity on earth. All forms of life need it to survive. There are over 1.4 billion cubic kilometres of water around the globe. But 97 per cent of this is the saltwater of the vast oceans. Only 3 per cent is **freshwater**, and most of it is in the form of groundwater or ice.

The freshwater that is available for human consumption is unevenly distributed around the world. Some countries, like Canada, are water rich; others, like Egypt, are water poor. While Canada has no major water shortages, some parts of the country experience water scarcity, particularly the Prairies. Scientists fear that the water supply there could be further threatened in the twenty-first century by **global warming**. The retreat of large icefields in the Rockies—upon which many major rivers depend for their water supply—could affect the continued water flow. A water shortage would not only affect people but natural ecosystems as well.

Irrigation accounts for more than 80 per cent of water consumption around the world. But the pattern of water use varies from country to country. Egypt, for example, devotes 98 per cent of its water to irrigation; Canada uses only 10 per cent for this purpose. Much of the water channelled into irrigation comes from rivers, which means the water supply is greatly reduced for the users downstream.

The other freshwater crisis is in groundwater. One in four Canadians depends on groundwater for domestic water supplies. In many regions, these groundwater supplies are declining as a result of over-pumping. In densely populated southern Ontario, for example, many municipalities draw their water supply from underground **aquifers**. As the population continues to grow, however, so does the demand for water. But the water in these aquifers was deposited at the end of the last ice age about 10 000 years ago. It is a finite supply. When it runs out, expensive **aqueducts** may have to be built to transport water from northern lakes to southern markets. Contamination from agricultural and industrial chemicals and overflow from poorly maintained septic tanks also threaten groundwater supplies. This contamination is worsened by the fact that groundwater—unlike rivers, which flow quickly—moves slowly. Contamination can remain in groundwater for hundreds of years.

Shortages

On a global scale, water shortages threaten the economic development of many countries. Shortages could limit food production and industrial development. They could even lead to disputes or armed conflicts among some nations. While there

World Water Surplus and Deficit

Surplus mm/year		Deficit* mm/year	
0 – 1000	Over 1000	0 – 1000	Over 1000

0   2000   4000   6000
kilometres
(at the equator)

* *Amount by which evapotranspiration exceeds annual precipitation From M. Falkenmark, "Do We Need Hydrological Research?" in Swedish, Forskning och Framsteg, No. 5, 1974.*

CANADIAN WATER EXPORTS

Climate change will affect the water supplies of the United States. Many studies predict that water levels in the Great Lakes could drop as the climate warms. This is because evaporation would increase because of the higher temperatures. Droughts would become more common in the Corn Belt—that area stretching from Ontario, Michigan, Ohio, Indiana, and Illinois west to Iowa and Minnesota. Climates would also become drier in the wheat-growing areas of the Great Plains that stretch from Saskatchewan to Kansas. Rivers in the southwestern United States, from Colorado and New Mexico west to California, would have lower runoff flows. This would result in more problems in a region that already suffers from serious water shortages. Lower river flows would mean less irrigation water for farmers in Arizona and California—water that is used to grow a wide variety of fruits and vegetables that are imported to Canada in the winter.

These changes would increase the pressure for Canada to export some of its surplus water to the United States. Many Canadians are opposed to such exports, however. They feel that Canada should be cautious about preserving such a precious resource. Once we begin to sell water, it would be difficult to reverse the decision, even if we experienced our own water shortages. Others see an opportunity to turn our excess water into a valuable export. Canada could earn money for surplus water that is currently unused. Furthermore, the United States would pay for the building of canals and pipelines to move the water south. Some of these facilities could bring water to the Prairies and southern Ontario. This would offset the possible effects of the drier climate created by global warming.

Fraser Cartwright, Gary Birchall and Gerry Pierce, Contact Canada, 2nd edition. Copyright © Oxford University Press Canada 1996. Reprinted by permission.

1. List the arguments for and against exporting Canadian water to the United States. Do you think we should export our water resources? Give reasons for your answer.

---

are more than 300 shared river basins around the world, only 30 of these have shared-water agreements. Experts believe that a crisis could be averted through more efficient water distribution systems and reduced waste through conservation. International disputes could be avoided if countries that share mutual water resources negotiate agreements on their fair use.

To have a reasonable quality of life we need about 80 L of water per person each day. Canadians' average daily use is 360 L, making us second only to the United States in water consumption per capita.

Use of Water (by sector, selected countries)

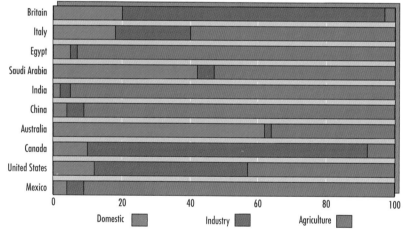

Domestic ▢ Industry ▢ Agriculture ▢

◄═ MAKING CONNECTIONS ═►

1. a) List all the ways in which you and your family use water every day. Is any of this water use wasteful? Explain.
   b) List the ways in which Canadian society as a whole uses water, then prioritize the list. Do you think Canadians should try to reduce their level of water consumption? If so, in what ways? If not, explain why.

KEYWORDS

freshwater

global warming

aquifer

aqueduct

LOOKING INTO THE FUTURE
Challenges in the 21ˢᵗ Century
FOCUSSING ON THE ISSUE

The future holds many challenges for Canada and the world. How do we prepare for the future? What issues must Canadians address in the twenty-first century?

What will life be like in the future?

Predicting the Unpredictable

We are all concerned about the future. It is, after all, where we will be spending the rest of our lives! People who actually think about and predict the future are called futurists. They perform an important function by preparing us for the changes that lie just around the corner. By studying current trends, futurists project forward in time to estimate where these trends will lead us in the years to come and what impact they will have.

But this is only part of what futurists do. It is not enough to assume that tomorrow will be the same as today, only more so. Great changes often occur that no one could ever expect or predict. In the 1940s, no one could have predicted the invention of the personal computer and the creation of a new communications era. In the 1950s, no one expected women would establish themselves in the work-place in such large numbers and the changes this would lead to for the economy and for the family. In 1981, a world that had been in the grip of the **Cold War** for an entire generation could not foresee that within the decade that war would be over as the mighty Soviet Union and its communist empire collapsed. Yet all these things happened and shaped how we live today. It is the job of the futurist to prepare us for such unexpected events.

Alvin Toffler, an American futurist, coined the phrase "future shock" to describe the chaos created by rapid, unpredictable change. Rapid change usually brings about a period of turmoil and instability as people and countries adjust to the unexpected. As change takes place more and more rapidly, future shock intensifies and the importance of the futurist increases. The more clearly we can see what lies ahead, the less painful the transition from today to tomorrow.

Future Challenges

It is time to become futurists ourselves. What are some of the challenges facing Canada in the century ahead?

Social
Canada has created a unique social fabric. In a country with such dynamic regional, cultural, and eth-

nic diversity, the challenge for the future will be to maintain social harmony and stability within such a diverse society.

Cultural

What it means to be a Canadian is always changing. It used to be that the cultural mainstream was British or French. Most people came from one of these backgrounds. Today, Canada is a **multicultural** society that welcomes newcomers from around the world. At the same time, American culture is flooding the world with US products, images, and ideas. Some people worry that a unique Canadian identity is being lost. The challenge for the future is to remain open to outside ideas while maintaining our Canadian values.

Political

Since the 1960s, Canadian governments have tried to satisfy the desire of many people in Quebec to have more control over their culture and economy. At the same time, other provinces have been unhappy with their place in Confederation. The challenge for the future is to maintain national unity while finding a distribution of powers that satisfies the needs of all the provinces.

Legal

In a changing world, new legal issues come to the forefront while old issues may have to be re-evaluated. The information revolution has raised questions about privacy and censorship. Other issues, such as juvenile justice or abortion, continue to spark ongoing debate. The challenge for the future is to ensure that Canada remains a just society.

Economic

The shift to a **knowledge-based economy** has cost many people their jobs and their security. Traditional industries, such as fishing and logging, appear to be in crisis. At the same time, high-technology industries are creating jobs in the new information era. The challenge for the future is to ensure that all Canadians are able to participate in this new economy. Another challenge will be to produce innovative technology that will enable us to continue to provide for a growing population while causing little or no environmental damage.

Environmental

Global population growth is threatening to overwhelm the ability of the world to sustain itself. Even in Canada, which does not have an overly large population compared to its vast size, some cities are becoming crowded and, some people fear, unlivable. Pollution from industry and automobiles is poisoning the air. Housing developments are gobbling up all the green space, while sewage and toxic chemicals are ruining the water. **Global warming** and **ozone depletion** threaten everyone's way of life. The challenge for the future is to achieve a level of **sustainable development** whereby we replenish the resources we use and conserve the resources we cannot replace.

All of these challenges present problems, but they are problems with solutions. Working together to find and implement those solutions is the greatest challenge of all.

MAKING CONNECTIONS

1. Make three predictions about how your world will change in the next 50 years. What steps should we be taking to prepare for these changes?

2. a) As a class, brainstorm a list of important social, cultural, political, legal, economic, and environmental issues facing Canada.
   b) Select one issue. Research the topic and present a short presentation on why this issue is important for Canada.

KEYWORDS

Cold War

multicultural

knowledge-based economy

global warming

ozone depletion

sustainable development

Glossary

abolition the elimination of something

abstinence the voluntary avoidance of indulging in certain foods or pleasures

accredited recognized as meeting an official standard

acid precipitation rain or snow with a pH level of less than 5.6

acidity the level of acid existing in a material

aesthetic concern with physical beauty or its appreciation

affirmative action a program or policy designed to help a group of people who have been discriminated against in some way

agrarian having to do with the land and its use

algae a large group of simple plants that live in aquatic habitats or moist regions

alienation to feel detached or estranged from the majority

allegiance loyalty to a person or country

alliance an agreement or treaty between two or more countries to protect one another in case of attack

Allies in WWI, the countries that fought against Germany and Austria; in WWII, the countries that fought against Germany, Italy, and Japan

amnesty a general pardon for a past offence

anarchist a person who believes that society should have no government, laws, police, or other authority

Anglo-conformity following the culture of Anglophone society

Anglophone a person whose principal language is English

annex (annexation) to join or add to something, as to take over a country

anti-Semitism hostility towards, or prejudice against, Jews

apartheid a racial policy introduced in South Africa in 1948 classifying residents into two separate and distinct classes, white and non-white

appeal to ask that a case be reconsidered by a higher court

appeasement the policy of satisfying or giving in to demands

appellant one who appeals a legal ruling

apprentice a person who learns a trade or craft by working at it under skilled supervision

aqueduct a structure, often built like a bridge, that carries water over a valley or low ground

aquifer a water-bearing layer of rock

arbitrary detention to be detained or jailed by the decision of a judge

armistice a formal agreement among warring countries to cease hostilities

artifacts objects made by humans that are collected and preserved through archeology

artillery mounted guns and cannons

assembly line a row of workers or machines along which work passes until a final product is made

assimilate (assimilation) to absorb people into a larger social group

attrition the gradual process of wearing down or eliminating something

automation a method of manufacturing that uses built-in controls in machines

autonomy (autocratic) ruling without checks or limitations

Axis in WWII, Germany, Italy, Japan, and their allies

baby boom the marked increase in the birth rate that began after WWII and continued until the mid-1960s

baby boom echo the influx of children born in the 1980s and 1990s to adult baby boomers

bankruptcy the condition of being unable to pay one's debts

battered-wife syndrome a legal defence that may be used by woman who kills an abusive spouse

bias a preference that makes it difficult or impossible to judge fairly

bicameral a law-making body that consists of two houses

bicultural (biculturalism) a policy that favours the existence of two distinct cultures

bilingualism having knowledge of two languages

biodiversity the existence of a wide variety of species of plants, animals, and micro-organisms in a natural habitat

blitzkrieg a violent offensive military action designed to crush the enemy quickly

bloc See *Soviet bloc*

BNA Act the British North America Act, 1867, Canada's original constitution, renamed the Constitution Act, 1867, in 1982

bohemian an artist or write who lives in a free or unconventional way

Bolshevism (Bolshevik) the radical wing of the Russian Social Democratic party that seized power in November 1917

branch plant a business that is owned and controlled by a company with its headquarters elsewhere

brief a formal statement of opinion

bulwark a safeguard or defence against a person or thing

bureaucracy the officials who administer the government

business cycle the process by which an economy fluctuates up and down causing booms and depressions

by-election an election held in one riding to fill a vacant seat in the House of Commons or a provincial legislature

Cabinet the executive committee of the government formed by members of the majority party in a legislature

capitalism (capitalist) an economic system based on private investment and profit-making

carrying capacity the maximum potential number of inhabitants that can be supported in a given area

cartographer a person skilled in making maps and charts

casualty a member of the Armed Forces who is wounded or killed in battle

caucus a meeting of the MPs of a party to discuss policies and strategies

cause something that produces an effect

cell a small revolutionary political movement

censorship the act of requiring written or visual material to conform to a prescribed standard

ceremonial talking stick a symbolic tool used in traditional Aboriginal ceremonies

charge to the jury an order from a judge to a jury

chemical weapons deadly gases and other chemicals used in combat

civil law the body of law that regulates private rights and that is applied in civil courts

civil liberties the right of an individual to do or say what she/he pleases as long as it does not harm another or break the law

civil rights movement in the US, the struggle by African-Americans to obtain equal rights

civil service the administrative body and its employees that performs the day-to-day work of the government

clearcutting a method of timber harvesting in which the trees in a given area are completely cleared

closure in a legislature, the means of concluding a debate and getting an immediate vote

coalition a formal arrangement by which political parties work together for a period of time or to meet a specific objective

coastal zone an area along a country's coast in which that country asserts control

coercion the use of force to control something

coincidence the chance occurrence of two things happening together

Cold War the period between 1945 and 1991 characterized by political tension between the United States and the Soviet Union and the threat of war this created

collective bargaining labour negotiations between workers as a group and their employers

collective security a group of countries acting co-operatively to ensure peace and stability

colonialism the practice of one nation ruling or seeking to rule over other nations as colonies

command economy an economic system that is completely controlled by the state

common law the body of law based on the customs and usage of the ancient unwritten laws of England

common-law of or having to do with common law, as in marriage

Commonwealth an association of states that were once part of the British Empire

communism (communist) an economic system based on public ownership of all property and on workers being paid according to their abilities and needs

conciliation (conciliator) to gain good will or favour through friendly acts

conscientious objector a person whose beliefs do not allow him/her to engage in combat during war

conscription compulsory military service

consolidated school the forerunner of the modern school system, first established in the early twentieth century

consortium a group or association formed by agreement

constitution a system of fundamental principles by which a country is ruled

Constitution Act Canada's written constitution, patriated in 1982; see also the *British North America Act*

constitutional monarchy a monarchy in which the sovereign has only the duties granted to him/her by the country's constitution

consumer confidence the public's faith in the economy as exhibited by personal spending

convoy a ship or fleet accompanied by a protective escort

cosmonaut a Russian astronaut

cost-benefit analysis an evaluation in which the costs of a certain action are weighed against the benefits of that action

counterculture a movement that rejects the traditional values of society in favour of an alternative lifestyle

covenant a formal agreement or pact

credibility the quality of being reliable or trustworthy

Criminal Code the behaviours considered to be criminal in Canadian society and the appropriate punishments for these behaviours

criminal law law concerned with the punishment of offenders

Crown corporation an agency or company of the federal or provincial government

crucify to put to death by nailing or binding the hands and feet to a cross

crude birth rate the number of live births per 1000 population in a given year

crude death rate the number of deaths per 1000 population in a given year

cryptologist a person who deciphers secret codes

cultural mosaic a society in which ethnic groups maintain their cultural heritage

custody order a legal ruling to confine or detain someone

damages money paid to make up for harm done to a person or property

data facts or concepts presented in a form suitable for processing and drawing conclusions

declarative legislation a federal law passed by the government but not entrenched in the Constitution

deficit the amount by which a sum of money falls short

deflation a reduction in the level of economic activity

deforestation the clearing of forests by cutting and/or burning

demilitarize to free from military control

democratic capitalism a political and economic system based on private ownership and corporate profit in a democratic society

democratic socialism a political philosophy committed to socialist policies such as public ownership through democratic elections

demographic transition a hypothetical model that illustrates the stages of demographic development

demography the statistical and mathematical study of human populations

dependency load the percentage of a population that is under the age of 15 and over the age of 65

depreciation allowance taking into account the lowering of the value of something

depression in economics, a period of low output and investment with high unemployment

détente the easing of political tensions between countries

devaluation the lowering of a currency against other currencies so that exports become cheaper and imports become more expensive

dictatorship a government in which absolute authority rests with one person

direct taxation the levying of a tax directly on the person who must pay it

disarmament the act of reducing or eliminating military arsenals

diversification the process of having variety

DNA (deoxyribonucleic acid) molecules that contain the genetic information for each living being

dogfight close combat between two or more aircraft

domestic violence physical abuse in which one partner harms the other

dower rights a widow's right to share in her husband's estate

draft a system for selecting people for compulsory military service

drainage basin the area of land drained by a river and its tributaries

drawing down the diminishing or reduction of something

dreadnought a large, powerful battleship equipped with heavy armour and large guns

dryland farm a farm in an arid area, usually without irrigation

Dust Bowl the area of the Great Plains of North America that experienced extensive wind erosion in the 1930s

ecologist a person who studies plants and animals in relation to each other and their habitats

economic disparity the differences in economic standards among countries or regions

economic imperialism the control or domination of a country's economy through investment or exploitation by another country

economic nationalist one who believes that foreign investment in a country should be controlled

economic sanctions economic restrictions imposed by a nation(s) against another nation to force it to comply with international law

economies of scale in economics, when the cost of an increase in production is more than compensated for by the greater volume of output

ecosystem a community of plants and animals within a particular physical environment

effect something that is produced by a cause

egalitarian the belief in social equality

El Niño the occasional warm water current off the coasts of Chile, Ecuador, and Peru that replaces the normal cold water current

embargo the prohibition by a government of trade with another country

enemy alien a person living in a country that is at war with her/his homeland

enfranchise (enfranchisement) to grant the right to vote

entente an understanding or agreement between countries

entrench to firmly establish

epidemic the rapid spread of disease so that it affects many people

establishment the people who have the greatest social and political influence in a country

estuary the area of a river mouth affected by sea tides

European Union the economic association of European nations previously known as the European Community

fallacy a mistaken belief or a mistake in reasoning

Family Allowance an allowance paid by the federal government to parents or guardians for children under the age of 18

fascist a member of an extreme right-wing political party

feminism (feminist movement) a movement that favours increased rights for women

fertility rate the number of births in a year per 1000 women of reproductive age, generally between 15 and 45

fetus human offspring in the womb from about nine weeks after conception

fjord a long, narrow, and deep arm of the sea created as a result of the "drowning" of a glaciated valley

foreclosure to take away one's right to redeem something

forgery the act of creating a false document

fossil fuels coal, oil, and other hydrocarbons deposited in a previous geological age

Francophone a person whose principal language is French

free enterprise an economic system in which businesses operate for profit with minimum interference from government

free trade international trade free from protective tariffs

free-market a market in which prices are determined by unrestricted competition

freshwater non-salt water

Galician a Slavic immigrant to western Canada, especially a Ukrainian

gastrointestinal of or having to do with the stomach and intestines

gender equity equality between males and females

general strike a mass work stoppage by workers from many businesses and government that has wide-ranging effects on a community or economy

geological survey the gathering of data relating to the earth's rock structure

geopolitical the study of government and its policies as these are affected by physical geography

glasnost a policy of openness and increased freedom in social and cultural matters introduced in the Soviet Union in 1986

global economy the trend towards lower trade barriers and increasing economic links between countries

global village the whole world considered as a single village linked together by telecommunications

global warming the potential increase in temperature of the earth's surface caused by the greenhouse effect

globalization the expansion of economic activities throughout the world

gold standard a system under which a country's currency is exchangeable for a fixed weight of gold on demand

greenhouse effect the raising of atmospheric temperature by the trapping of heat by carbon dioxide, methane, and other gases

grid reference lines on maps, usually at right angles, used to locate places

Gross Domestic Product a measure of the total domestic output of a country, including exports but not imports

Gross National Product the total market value of a country's goods and services

habitat the natural environment in which an organism lives successfully

haymarket historically, a market for selling farm produce

hazing ritual something a person is forced to do as part of an initiation

head tax a tax imposed by the federal government on immigrants entering Canada

holocaust large-scale destruction, usually by fire

homestead a parcel of public land granted to a settler by the federal government

human rights the freedom granted to all people that protects them from unlawful arrest, torture, or execution

humanitarian aid financial assistance that benefits human beings

hypothesis in a research study, an assumed statement to be proven

immunization a medical procedure designed to protect people from disease

imperialism (imperialist) the policy by which one country extends its authority to other parts of the world through the acquisition of colonies

impressionist an artist who presents a subjective, often emotional, impression of nature using bright colours and spontaneous brush strokes

income security financial aid provided by the government to supplement income

independent a person elected to a legislature who does not belong to any political party

Indian Act the act introduced by the Canadian government in 1876 that set out the rules that controlled Aboriginal communities

indictable offence a serious criminal offence, such as armed robbery or murder

individualism a theory that individual freedom is as important as the interests of the greater whole

industrial heartland in North America, the central part of Canada and the northeastern portion of the United States in which the majority of industrial activity is concentrated

Industrial Revolution the social and economic changes that began in Europe in the eighteenth century, characterized by a shift away from agriculture and craft shops to mechanized factories

infant mortality rate the number of infants per 1000 births who die before the age of one

inference something that a reader or listener finds out by what she/he reads, sees, or hears

inflation in economics, an increase in the general level of prices

infrastructure the framework of communications networks, health facilities, administration, and power supply needed for economic development

inherent self-government See *Self-government*

interest rate the rate charged for the use of borrowed money

International Date Line the division line at 180° longitude as one day ends and the next begins

internment (internment camp) the act of being confined within a country or place

interurban between cities or towns

intervention the act of interfering by one nation in the affairs of another

isolationism (isolationist) remaining separate or apart from the affairs of other nations

jingoist a person who favours an aggressive foreign policy that could lead to war

Judicial Committee of the Privy Council the superior court of the Privy Council

knowledge-based industry a modern industry founded in the new information age

laissez-faire economy the absence of government regulation in the economy

landed immigrant a person admitted to live in Canada as a potential citizen

left wing in politics, parties that favour socialist policies

legacy something that is handed down from one's ancestors

life expectancy the average lifespan of a population

lobby a person or group that tries to influence legislators

lore stories about a particular subject

magazine a holder for gun cartridges to be fed into the gun chamber

magistrate a government official appointed to hear cases in a lower court

majority government a government created when one political party wins more

seats than the combined total of the other parties

malnutrition a condition in which there is a deficiency of proteins, minerals, or vitamins in a diet

manifesto a public declaration of a person's or group's intentions or objectives

margin for error in opinion polls, the possibility of the results being inaccurate, usually within four percentage points either way

mass communication the means of communicating or transmitting information to the population as a whole

mass destruction in war, the ability to destroy vast areas and kill many thousands of people with a single weapon

mass marketing the promoting of a product so that it appeals to the general population

mass media the various means of modern communication

mass production the making of goods in large numbers using a standard process

mass society the increasingly urban, industrial society that first emerged at the beginning of the twentieth century

means test a measure of a person's financial status to determine eligibility for financial benefits

Medicare a government-sponsored health-insurance plan that includes hospital costs, doctors' fees, and other medical expenses

meltdown a serious nuclear accident in which the reactor's cooling system fails and part of the metal core reaches the point of melting

melting pot a theory that society benefits when people's ethnic identities are broken down over generations

mercy flight an aircraft sent to transport an ill or injured person to hospital, especially in the North

middle power a country without the military might to be a superpower but with enough economic power and political stability to have some influence in world affairs

militarist a person who believes in a powerful military organization

military-industrial complex the potential misplacement of power that might result from the union of the military establishment and the arms industry as a result of the Cold War

minority government an elected government in which the governing political party does not old a majority of the seats in the legislature

mobility the ability to move quickly or easily

modernism of or pertaining to the present time

monopoly the control of a market or service without competition

moratorium a temporary pause in the action surrounding an issue

motion of censure in a legislature, official criticism or condemnation

multiculturalism a policy supporting the existence of a variety of distinct cultural groups in one society

multilingual having the knowledge of or ability to speak several languages

multispectral scanner a device on board a satellite that scans the earth's surface recording variations in surface colour as computer codes

munitions material and equipment used in war

nationalism (nationalist) a sense of national consciousness that fosters loyalty to the country

nationalize to take over something on behalf of the state in which the property lies

naturalize to grant the rights of citizenship to a person from another country

New Deal the social and economic programs introduced by US president Franklin Roosevelt in 1933 to combat the Depression

New Frontier the term used to describe the vision of freedom and social justice of US president John F. Kennedy

nomadic the movement of people from place to place to be near food or water or to find pasture

non-aggression pact an agreement among nations not to attack another nation

nonalignment the policy of a country not being associated with any other country

nonconfidence vote See *vote of nonconfidence*

non-governmental organization service agencies and non-profit organizations that provide aid to other countries

non-intervention a policy of not becoming involved in the affairs of another nation

non-partisan not supporting any single political party

nonrenewable resources a finite natural material that cannot be replaced

Northwest Passage a route for ships from the Atlantic to the Pacific via the Arctic

nuclear fission a nuclear reaction in which an atomic nucleus such as uranium splits and releases large quantities of energy

nuclear payload nuclear cargo carried into space via satellite

occupation zone an area or territory that is occupied by a foreign country

official Opposition the principal political party opposed to the party in office

oil sands porous oil-filled sand or sandstone at or just below the earth's surface

old-growth forest a forest of ancient trees that has never been harvested

on-line a system that allows a computer to work interactively with its users

opt out the decision of a provincial government not to participate in a federal program

orbit the range of a country's influence over other countries

order-in-council a regulation of the federal or provincial government

ozone a layer of oxygen stretching from 15 to 50 km above the earth's surface that shields the earth from ultraviolet radiation

ozone depletion the loss of ozone from the ozone layer caused by CFCs and other chemicals

Pacific Rim those countries that border the Pacific Ocean

pagan a person who practices no religion

paradox a statement that may be true but seems to say two different things

parliamentary democracy a democratic government with a law-making body which, in Canada, consists of the Senate and the House of Commons

parliamentary representation a democratic government in which the people are represented in a parliamentary legislature

partisan someone who expresses strong support for a person, party, or cause, often based on emotion rather than reason

patriarchal having to do with the father of a family

patriate (patriation) to bring government under the direct control of the people

patriotism loyal support for one's country

patronage jobs or favours given to people in return for political support

per capita for each person

perestroika the policy of restructuring economics and government in the Soviet Union in the 1980s

personal narrative an account of events by the person who experienced them

personality cult the extreme adulation of an individual

photochemical action an action caused by light or ultraviolet radiation

piecework work paid for based on the amount done rather than the time it takes to produce it

platform a political party's plan of action or statement of principles

polar projection map a type of map used to study the polar regions

pontoon a low, flat-bottomed boat

population pyramid back-to-back bar graphs set on a vertical axis that show the age/sex breakdown of a country's population

portfolio the position and duties of a Cabinet minister

post-industrial economy the current economic era in which machines have replaced many factory workers and more businesses focus on services and information rather than manufacturing

potash any of several potassium salts mined and processed for use in agriculture and industry

potlatch a celebration, commonly practised among Aboriginal peoples of the West Coast, at which the host presents gifts to the guests

poverty line the measure of the lowest income considered necessary to cover a family's basic needs

precedent a case that serves as an example for a later case

premium an amount of money paid for a contract of insurance

prevailing winds the most frequent wind direction at a given location

primary production industrial activity involving the use of primary resources

primary source the original account of

an issue or event, or a document that gives reliable first-hand evidence

prisoner of war a person taken captive by an enemy country

private member's bill a bill brought before the legislature by a backbencher

privatize the changing of a business from public to private ownership

Privy Council the body of government advisors appointed by the monarch or the monarch's representative

probation the system of letting convicted people go free under the supervision of a probation officer

production run the amount of an item that is produced at a given time

profiteering making an unfair profit by taking advantage of public necessity

prohibition a law against making or selling alcohol

proletariat those classes in society that possess no property and must survive through the sale of their labour

propaganda the art of controlling public opinion

protectionism (protectionist) the imposition of tariffs or import quotas to discourage foreign competition with domestic products

psyche the human soul or spirit

pull factor a positive factor that attracts people to move to a certain location

push factor a negative factor that causes people to move away from a certain location

quality of life the standard of living and non-material things that people have

quarantine to isolate from others to prevent the spread of disease

quota the quantity that is allowed

radiation radioactive rays that harm or destroy living things

radical advocating fundamental changes in the social or economic structure

radioactive giving off radiant energy as a result of the breaking up of atoms

rainshadow an area of relatively low rainfall on the lee side of mountains

rate of natural increase See *natural increase*

ratify to formally approve an act

raw materials the unprocessed substances used in manufacturing

reactor the mechanism that produces energy by nuclear fission

realism an art form that presents things in their true nature, without glossing over what is painful or undesirable

recall the removal of a public official from office by a vote of the people

recession in economics, a decline in business activity lasting more than a few months

reciprocity a mutual exchange of trading privileges between two countries

recruitment to enlist people to join the Armed Forces

referendum submitting an issue to the direct vote of the people

reforestation the planting of trees in an area of cleared forest

regional disparity the economic differences among regions in a country

relief money supplied through government funding to meet the necessities of life

remote sensing the process of creating satellite images

reparations compensation demanded from a defeated enemy for destruction of territory during war

representation by population a system of government in which the number of elected representatives in a given region reflects the region's population

reserve a residential area allocated for Status Indians

residual powers those powers not specifically assigned to one jurisdiction

resolution the formal expression of opinion by a group

right wing in politics, parties that favour more conservative or reactionary policies

Royal Commission an investigation into an issue or event on behalf of the federal or provincial government that recommends appropriate action

saboteur a person who deliberately damages or destroys something in order to hinder or hurt

salvage drive a campaign to save discarded goods for reuse

secondary source an account of an issue or event based on hearsay or evidence that can no longer be verified

sectoral a distinct part of the economy

self-determination the decision of the people of a nation to choose their form of government without outside interference

self-government government of a group by its own members

separatism (separatist) in Quebec, a person who favours the separation of the province from the rest of Canada

sexual harassment to make inappropriate advances towards or to annoy a member of the opposite sex

Slavic of or pertaining to peoples of Eastern Europe who speak a Slavic language, such as Russian, Czechoslovakian, or Bulgarian

sliding scale a scale or standard that is adjusted to fit certain conditions or situations

smelter a plant in which ore is melted to obtain metal

social dividend a regular sum of money paid to citizens in order that they can purchase goods and stimulate the economy

social security state assistance to those lacking economic security, in the form of pensions, employment insurance, etc.

socialism (socialist) a political and economic system in which the means of production are owned and controlled by a central authority

sock-hop a dance for teens in the 1950s

sound bites in broadcasting, brief excerpts of talk or sound that enhance the visual material

sound mind the ability to understand and appreciate the nature of an action or behaviour

sovereignty an independent state

sovereignty-association a policy proposed by Quebec separatists under which Quebec would become an independent state but would continue to have some associations with Canada, such as a common currency and free trade

Soviet bloc the countries allied with or controlled by the Soviet Union from 1945 to 1991

spawn in fish, to produce eggs

spiritualist a person who believes that the dead communicate with the living

stakeholders people or institutions that are affected by an issue

standard of living the quantity and quality of goods and services that people are able to purchase or attain

statistics numerical data compiled and classified systematically

status quo the existing state of affairs

status symbol a material possession that is supposed to signify a certain social rank

statute a law enacted by a legislature

stereotype an oversimplified mental picture that assigns certain characteristics to a particular group

steroids performance-enhancing drugs taken by some athletes

stock market speculation the practice of buying stocks and then selling them for quick profit

stockbroker a person who buys and sells financial securities for customers

stratosphere the layer of the atmosphere 10 to 50 km above the earth's surface

stumpage fee a government-imposed fee forest companies must pay for the trees they fell

subculture a distinguishable group of people within a larger culture

subordinate secondary in position or authority

subsidy a financial grant, often made by government

subsistence economy a society with little or no cash in which people use only the natural resources they need

suburb a district just outside of or near a city or town

subvert to undermine or overthrow something

sue to start a lawsuit against someone

suffragette a woman who demonstrated for the right to vote

suffragist a person who favours giving the vote to more people, particularly women

sulphur dioxide a heavy, colourless gas with a sharp odour

summary offence a criminal offence that is less serious than an indicatable offence and that usually carries a maximum penalty of a $500 fine or six months' imprisonment

sustainable development economic development that manages the environment and its resources in a way that allows future generations to benefit from them

sweatshop a place in which people labour for long hours for extremely low wages under poor working conditions

synopsis a brief statement expressing a general view of a subject

synthesize to combine all parts to create a whole

tariff a tax imposed on imports to reduce competition with domestic products

tariff barrier a restrictive tax or tariff designed to restrict the flow of certain products into a country

tectonic the processes that act to shape the earth's crust

terrorism a method of political opposition that relies on violent tactics

title the legal right to the possession of property

topographic a map that indicates the natural features of the earth's surface as well as human features

totalitarian a form of government that exerts strict control over society and the economy and that does not permit opposition

totalitarian communism a communist regime in which government powers rest with one individual

toxic waste poisonous refuse resulting from industrial chemicals and processes

trade deficit when a country buys more from a trading partner than it sells to it

transnational corporation a corporation that operates in many countries

treaty an agreement between nations

tribunal an authority that renders judgements

truck system a system in which employees living in a company-built town are required to purchase their supplies at the company store at company-controlled prices

tsar a former emperor of Russia

U-boat a German submarine

ultra-nationalist a person whose nationalist feelings are extreme

ultraviolet radiation electromagnetic waves coming from the sun that can be harmful to plant and animal life if not filtered by the ozone layer

unconstitutional something that does not comply with the constitution

unicameral a law-making body that consists of only one house

unilateral having to do with one side only

unilingualism the state of having the knowledge or use of only one language

universal male suffrage the extension of the right to vote to all men

urban development the growth and development of a community of 1000 people or more

urban sprawl the spread of urban communities into the surrounding rural area

urbanization the process by which an area is transformed from rural to urban

vacuum of power a political situation in which no one authority is clearly established or in control

vagrancy the criminal offence of wandering idly from place to place without suitable means of support

value judgement an assessment of something based on a person's personal beliefs or values

veto the right or power to reject or refuse to consent to something

Victorian era the period of Queen Victoria's reign in England from the mid- to late-nineteenth century

Victory Bonds bonds issued by the Canadian government during WWI and WWII to raise funds for the war effort

vocational of or having to do with an occupation or trade

vote of nonconfidence a vote showing that the majority do not support a particular policy of the government

wage-and-price controls government restrictions placed on wages paid to workers and prices charged for products

war guilt the blame assigned for creating conditions that led to war

watershed the boundary between two river systems

web diagram a chart that illustrates the connections between a key activity and other activities that are connected to it

welfare state a state in which the government provides for the welfare if its citizens through pensions, employment insurance, medical care, etc.

weltpolitik the policy of imperialism practised by the German kaiser Wilhelm II at the beginning of the twentieth century

wheat rust a disease that destroys wheat crops

White Paper a government report

wolf-pack an attacking group of submarines

Index

Railways, 13, 14-15
Reagan, Ronald, 292-93, 321
Recession, 118, 119, 261, 292, 294-95. *See also* Depression
Reciprocity, 46
Referendum
1980 Quebec sovereignty, 288-89
1995 Quebec sovereignty, 354
Charlottetown Accord, 354
conscription, 153
on division of Northwest Territories, 344
Newfoundland, 172-93
Refugees, 171, 315
Regionalism
economic disparity, 234-35
the West, 194-95
western alienation, 194, 266-67
Reid, Bill, 318-19
Relief, direct, 122
Representation by population, 263
Residual powers, 97
Resources, 234
air, 378-79
land, 380-81
water, 382-83
Rome-Berlin-Tokyo Axis, 142
Roosevelt, Franklin D., 116, 119, 127, 158
Rose, Jacques, 251
Rose, Paul, 251
Ross, Sinclair, 130-31
Rowell-Sirois Commission, 138-39, 168, 235
Royal Canadian Mounted Police, 334-35
Royal Commission
on bilingualism and biculturalism, 224
on federal-provincial relations, 138-39, 168, 235
on price spreads, 126
on radio broadcasting, 87, 140
on the status of women, 240-41
Rule of law, 96
Russia, 7
alliance with France, 41
civil war, 71
and Eastern Question, 42-43
and League of Nations, 79
and Paris Peace Conference, 78
revolution, 70-71
Russo-Japanese War, 7

Sabia, Laura, 240, 273
St-Laurent, Louis, 177, 180, 205
St Lawrence Seaway, 198-99
Salmon, 52-53, 348-49
Saskatchewan
CCF government, 174-75
creation of province, 20-21
farmers movement, 111
regional grievances, 194-95
Sauvé, Jeanne, 272
Schlieffen Plan, 59
Schools, schooling, 21, 27, 50, 77, 183, 190. *See also* Education

Scott, Duncan Campbell, 16, 108, 109
Sechelt First Nation, 344
Second World War
Canada forces, 152-53, 156-57
D-Day, 156
Eastern Front, 152
German U-boats, 158
modern warfare, 150-51
North Africa, 156
Pearl Harbor, attack on, 151
Western Front, 152
Secretariat, UN, 166
Security Council, UN, 166
Senate, 262, 354
Sexual harassment, 317
"Shamrock Summit," 320, 321
Sifton, Clifford, 21, 22
Sikhs, Sikhism, 54-55
Smallwood, Joey, 173
Smog, 186, 187
Social Credit, 132-33
Socialism, 7
democratic, 133
Social programs, 98-99, 139, 168-69, 175, 182, 190-91
Social reform
child welfare, 27-28
prohibition, 28-29
public health, 51
women's issues, 240-41
Social security, 168-68. *See also* Social programs
Solidarity movement, 293
Somalia Inquiry, 336-37
South Africa, 44-45, 93
South Asians, 54-55, 214
Sovereignty-association, 289
Soviet Union, 113
arms race, 186
Bolshevik Revolution, 70-71
collapse of communism, 293
Depression, 117
Second World War, 151
space race, 308
Suez Crisis, 216
Space exploration, 308-9
Spanish Civil War, 144-45
SS Manhattan, 246
Standard of living, 168, 339
Statute of Westminster, 93, 96, 147
Stevens Commission, 126-27
Stock market crash, 104-5
Suburbs, 34, 186-87, 192-93
Suez Crisis, 216-17
Suffrage movement, 7, 68-69
Supreme Court of Canada, 106, 176-77, 312
Sustainable development, 259, 374-75, 385

Taiwan, 181, 258
Tariffs, 105, 110, 116
Taxation, direct, 264
Television, 187, 202, 284
Three Mile Island, 280
Tiananmen Square massacre, 293,

363
Toffler, Alvin, 384
Toronto, 13, 48, 50
Toronto Maple Leafs, 203
Totalitarianism, 112-13, 117
TransCanada Pipelines, 204-5
Transnational corporations, 325
Transportation
Great Lakes shipping, 198-99
interurban, 34, 82
railways, 13, 14-15
Triple Alliance, 41
Triple Entente, 41
Trudeau, Pierre, 224, 227, 245, 251-52, 260, 270, 284, 287,296-97, 300-1

U-boats, German, 158
Ultraviolet radiation, 379
Ultra vires, principle of, 97
Unemployment, 116-17, 118, 294, 327, 339
Unemployment insurance, 139, 168, 182
Union government, 67
Union Nationale, 136-37
United Farmers of Alberta, 111
United Nations
Canada's role in, 167, 360
creation of, 166-67
and Korean War, 188-89
United Nations Education, Scientific, and Cultural Organization (UNESCO), 167
United Nations International Children's Emergency Fund(UNICEF), 167
United States, 7
and Canadian sovereignty, 246-47
and Columbia River Treaty, 228-29
cross-border pollution, 134-35, 276-77
Depression, 116
economic growth, 40
isolationism, 79
and Pacific Salmon Treaty, 348-49
and Paris Peace Conference, 78
under Reagan, 292-93
Second World War, 151
space program, 308
Universal Declaration on Human Rights, 212
Urbanization
growth of cities, 34-35
social problem, 50
urban migration, 48-49, 370-71

Vancouver, 48
1907 riot, 24-25
Expo '86, 310-11
growth of, 35
multilingual population, 352-53
roads, 100
Vancouver Island, coal mining, 36-37
Varley, Fred, 88

Versailles, Treaty of, 78, 79
Veterans
aboriginal, 178-79
merchant navy, 159
Vietnam War, 267-37

Wage-and-price controls, 164, 294
War Measures Act, 62-63, 212, 251-52
Wartime Elections Act, 67
Water resources, 382-83
Welfare state, 168-69
West, Canadian
regional disparity, 234
settlement of, 22. *See also* Regionalism

Whale hunt, moratorium, 248
Wheat, 13, 128-29
Wieland, Joyce, 272
Wilson, Bertha, 272, 313
Wilson, Cairine, 107
Winnipeg, 13, 48, 50
Winnipeg General Strike, 74-75
Women
and abortion laws, 312
assertion of independence, 82-83
feminist movement, 272-73
gender equity, 364-65
hockey, 203
operators' strike, 5
postwar workforce participation, 183
protection of rights, 27
right to vote, 7, 68-69
Royal Commission on, 240-41
Senate appointments, 106-7
teachers, 27, 49
unpaid work, 365
urban migration, 49
violence against, 316-17
and wage gap, 273
war brides, 183
war effort, 62
wartime role of, 160-61
Women's Christian Temperance Union (WCTU), 28-29, 68
Women's Social and Political Union, 7
Woodsworth, J.S., 75, 98
Workers
coal miners, 36-37
living conditions, 49-50
neighbourhoods, 34
privacy of, 351
skilled, 339
unskilled, 339
World Conference on Women, Fourth, 364-65
World Health Organization (WHO), 167
World Trade Organization (WTO), 361

Young Offenders Act, 304-5
Young Women's Christian Association (YWCA), 68